THE MONGOLS AND THE WEST, 1221–1410

The Medieval World

Series editor: Julia Smith, University of St Andrews

THE MONGOLS AND THE WEST, 1221–1410

PETER JACKSON

Harlow, England • London • New York • Boston • San Francisco • Toronto
Sydney • Tokyo • Singapore • Hong Kong • Seoul • Taipei • New Delhi
Cape Town • Madrid • Mexico City • Amsterdam • Munich • Paris • Milan

PEARSON EDUCATION LIMITED

Edinburgh Gate
Harlow CM20 2JE
United Kingdom
Tel: +44 (0)1279 623623
Fax: +44 (0)1279 431059
Website: www.pearsoned.co.uk

First edition published in Great Britain in 2005

© Pearson Education Limited 2005

The right of Peter Jackson to be identified as author of this work has been asserted by him
in accordance with the Copyright, Designs and Patents Act 1988.

ISBN 0 582 368960

British Library Cataloguing in Publication Data
A CIP catalogue record for this book can be obtained from the British Library

Library of Congress Cataloging in Publication Data
Jackson, Peter.
The Mongols and the west, 1221–1410 / Peter Jackson.
p. cm. — (The medieval world)
Includes bibliographical references and index.
ISBN 0–582–36896–0
1. Mongols—History. I. Title. II. Series.

DS19.J32 2005
951'.025—dc22

2004059429

10 9 8 7 6 5 4 3 2 1
09 08 07 06 05

Set in 10.5/13pt Galliard by 35
Printed and bound in Malaysia

The Publisher's policy is to use paper manufactured from sustainable forests.

For Rebecca

CONTENTS

CONTENTS

SERIES EDITOR'S PREFACE

In this timely book, Peter Jackson introduces us to the last great pulse of nomads from the inner Asian steppe to encounter the utterly different world of sedentary, urbanized European peoples. The military context of this story is a long front along the eastern fringe of late medieval Christendom, from Poland to the Crusader strongholds on the Syrian coast. Its cultural context is one of prejudice and curiosity stretching from Scotland to Japan, for this narrative of military encounters and diplomatic manoeuvring is set against a backdrop of fears of the unknown, rumours – frequently apocalyptic – and the details of everyday life which characterize one culture rather than another. In a fascinating exploration of the interactions between the Mongols and the Latin West, Professor Jackson invites the reader to follow Mongol armies west to Germany and to travel east to China with Christian missionaries, diplomats and traders, stopping at courts and camps at all points in between. This latest addition to the Longmans Medieval World series is thus a sustained reflection on what makes one culture, or civilization, different from another, and reminds us that the history of the European Middle Ages has a world historical context.

In the chapters which follow, we meet many famous men, real and imagined, who have excited the European imagination: Chinggis Khan, Temür (Tamerlane), Marco Polo and Christopher Columbus; Prester John, 'Sir John Mandeville', Gog and Magog. With skilful analysis, sensitive scholarship and wry humour, Jackson locates their actions – or stories about their actions – in a world characterized by the immense difficulty of long distance travel. It is a world of challenges: those facing nomads as they sought pasturage for their horses in the Syrian desert, the linguistic difficulties to be surmounted by Italian friars trying to preach Christianity to speakers of Turkish and Mongolian, the efforts of scholars in quiet European libraries trying to make sense of the limited information and mass of hearsay about the world beyond their direct experience. This is a story of the adjustments of reality to imagination – and of imagination to reality – on a vast geographical canvas, a story Peter Jackson tells with immense learning and deep humanity. I welcome it for that very reason.

Julia M.H. Smith

PREFACE

Three fortunate circumstances are responsible for the fact that this book has not taken rather longer to appear in print. The first is the enthusiastic response in 1997 of Andrew MacLennan, at that time History editor for Longman, to the information that I was contemplating a book on the Mongols and the Latin West. Andrew's support at an early stage was instrumental in persuading me to undertake to write the book. I am also grateful to his successor, Heather MacCallum, for her sustained interest in the manuscript and for seeing the finished product into the first stages of publication.

Secondly, the Institute for Advanced Study at the Hebrew University of Jerusalem offered me a Visiting Fellowship for six months in 2000, when I participated in a workshop on 'Turco-Mongolian Nomads and their relations with China and Iran', jointly chaired by Dr (now Professor) Reuven Amitai and Dr Michal Biran. The opportunity to work alongside colleagues in my own and closely related fields was invaluable, and my wife and I both still recall with warm appreciation the hospitable welcome we received in a Jerusalem that was then a happier place than it has become in more recent years.

The third fortunate circumstance was the award of a Leverhulme Major Research Fellowship for the period from October 2000 to September 2003, which provided my department with full-time replacement teaching and was accompanied by a substantial sum for research travel. Nobody who has worked within a UK university over the past twenty years can have any illusions about the difficulty of reading, thinking and writing without being exempt from teaching and administration over a sustained period. It is a pleasure to be able to express my gratitude to the Leverhulme Trust in this preface.

I have also accumulated many other debts. Thanks are due to the inter-library loans section of Keele University Library for obtaining for me numerous books and articles over the years. I am also grateful for the assistance of the staff of Cambridge University Library and of the Seeley Historical Library, Cambridge; the British Library, and the Libraries of the Institute of Historical Research and of the Warburg Institute, in London; the National Archives (formerly the Public Record Office), Kew; the Bodleian Library; the John Rylands University Library of Manchester;

the Sydney Jones Library, University of Liverpool; the Bibliothèque Nationale and the Archives Nationales, Paris; the Bibliotheek te Rijksuniversiteit Leiden; Innsbruck Universitätsbibliothek; Universitätsbibliothek Graz; Magyar Országos Levéltár (Hungarian National Archives) and Országos Széchényi Könyvtár (Széchényi National Library), Budapest; and Wrocław University Library. In addition, I greatly appreciated the promptness and courtesy of Dr Rudolf Lindpointner, of the Oberösterreichische Landesbibliothek (formerly Studentbibliothek), Linz, in sending me a digitized image of the ms. 446, fo. 267vb (the report of the Russian 'archbishop' Peter); of Herr Jens Altena, of the Niedersächsische Staats- und Universitätsbibliothek Göttingen, in supplying me with a printout of ms. 4 Hist. 61, pp. 276–301 (Carpini's *Ystoria Mongalorum*); and of Herr Hans Stein, of the Forschungs- und Landesbibliothek Gotha, for providing a printout of ms. Orient. A1559 (the first section of al-Jazarī's *Ḥawādith al-zamān*). I should also like to acknowledge here the kind permission of the Master and Fellows of Corpus Christi College, Cambridge to reproduce an illustration from ms. 16 (Matthew Paris, *Chronica Majora*) in the Parker Library. For the production of the maps I am indebted to my colleague, Andrew Lawrence, in the Keele University Digital Imaging/Illustration Services.

I have benefited greatly from the opportunity to try out parts of this book at seminars and conferences. Professor David Cannadine, then Director of the Institute for Historical Research, invited me to read what proved to be a remote forebear of chapter 6 as a plenary lecture at the 68th Anglo-American Conference of Historians, where the theme was 'Race and Ethnicity', in June 1999. Subsequently I was given the chance to experiment with the material now in chapter 10, both in Jerusalem in March 2000 and at the Conference on 'Conversion: a Medieval and Early Modern Experience', at the University of Minnesota in Minneapolis, in May 2001. An early draft of chapter 12 was read as an inaugural lecture at Keele University in January 2002, and I profited a great deal from the questions and comments of my colleagues. I am grateful, lastly, to Professor Jonathan Riley-Smith for inviting me to deliver a version of chapter 8 to the Seminar on the History of the Crusades and the Latin East in Cambridge in November 2002.

A number of other historians have helped me in various ways. Professor Peter Hoppenbrouwers, of the Rijksuniversiteit Leiden, kindly sent me a number of references to the Mongols in medieval sources from the Netherlands, which would otherwise certainly have escaped my notice. Professor Nicola Di Cosmo, of the Institute for Advanced Study at Princeton, generously provided me with the texts of two as yet unpublished conference papers. In addition, Reuven Amitai, Michal Biran,

Ann Fielding and Noreen Giffney each supplied me with valuable references. I received help from various experts on medieval Hungarian history, a field into which I was venturing for the first time: Dr Nora Berend, of St Catherine's College, Cambridge; Dr Nagy Balázs, of the Central European University, Budapest; and Dr Zsoldos Attila, of the Historical Institute in Budapest.

Three scholars have been good enough to read some or all of the book. Professor Tina Endicott read early drafts of chapters 1 and 2, and Dr Anthony Luttrell a draft of chapter 9. Professor David Morgan read a penultimate draft of the whole book on behalf of the press. I am grateful to all three for offering suggestions and for saving me from a number of errors. Naturally, I alone merit the obloquy directed at any faults that have survived their criticism. The role of intelligent lay critic was filled admirably by my father-in-law, Tom Oswald, who read and commented on chapters 1 and 2, and by my wife, who read the entire manuscript. Without her untiring support, indeed, this book would not have been written. I dedicate it to her with love and gratitude.

Peter Jackson
Keele
June 2004

ABBREVIATIONS

AAS	*Asian and African Studies* (Haifa)
AE	Odoricus Raynaldus *et al.*, eds, *Annales ecclesiastici*, 34 vols (Lucca, 1738–59)
AEMA	*Archivum Eurasiae Medii Aevi*
AF	Asiatische Forschungen
AFH	*Archivum Franciscanum Historicum*
AFP	*Archivum Fratrum Praedicatorum*
AHR	*American Historical Review*
AK	*Archiv für Kulturgeschichte*
AKO	Imre Szentpétery and Iván Borsa, eds, *Az Árpád-házi királyok okleveleinek kritikai jegyzéke. Regesta regum stirpis Arpadianae critico-diplomatica*, 2 vols in 5 parts (Budapest, 1923–87)
AM	Henry Richards Luard, ed., *Annales monastici*, RS, 5 vols (London, 1864–9)
AN	Archives Nationales, Paris
AO	Imre Nagy and Gyula Tasnadi Nagy, eds, *Anjoukori okmánytár. Codex diplomaticus Hungaricus Andegavensis*, 6 vols (Budapest, 1878–1920)
AOASH	*Acta Orientalia Academiae Scientiarum Hungaricae*
AOL	*Archives de l'Orient Latin*
AP	Αρχειον Ποντου
AQ	Ausgewählte Quellen zur deutschen Geschichte des Mittelalters
AS	*Asiatische Studien*
ASI	*Archivio Storico Italiano*
ASL	*Atti della Società Ligure di Storia Patria*
ASV, Reg. Vat.	Archivio Segreto Vaticano, Registrum Vaticanum (microfilms in the Seeley Historical Library, Cambridge)
AUO	Gusztáv Wenzel, ed., *Árpádkori új okmánytár. Codex diplomaticus Arpadianus continuatus*, 12 vols (Pest, 1860–74)
BBTS	Girolamo Golubovich, ed., *Biblioteca bio-bibliografica della Terra Santa e dell'Oriente*

	francescano, 5 vols (Quaracchi-Firenze, 1906–27)
BEC	*Bibliothèque de l'École des Chartes*
BEO	*Bulletin d'Études Orientales de l'Institut Français de Damas*
BF	*Byzantinische Forschungen*
BGQM	Beiträge zur Geschichte und Quellenkunde des Mittelalters
BHR	*Bulgarian Historical Review*
BJRL	*Bulletin of the John Rylands Library of the University of Manchester*
BL	British Library
BN	Bibliothèque Nationale, Paris
BSO[A]S	*Bulletin of the School of Oriental [and African] Studies*
CAJ	*Central Asiatic Journal*
CCCM	Corpus Christianorum. Continuatio Medievalis
CDH	György Fejér, ed., *Codex diplomaticus Hungariae ecclesiasticus ac civilis*, 11 vols in 40 parts (Buda, 1829–44)
CDRB	Gustav Friedrich *et al.*, eds, *Codex diplomaticus et epistolaris regni Bohemiae*, 5 vols in 8 parts so far (Prague, 1907–93)
CEHE, II	M.M. Postan and Edward Miller, eds, *The Cambridge Economic History of Europe*, II. *Trade and Industry in the Middle Ages*, 2nd edn (Cambridge, 1987)
CGOH	J. Delaville le Roulx, ed., *Cartulaire général de l'Ordre des Hospitaliers de S. Jean de Jérusalem (1100–1310)*, 4 vols (Paris, 1894–1906)
CHC, VI	Herbert Franke and Denis Twitchett, eds, *The Cambridge History of China*, VI. *Alien Regimes and Border States, 907–1368* (Cambridge, 1994)
CHI	*The Cambridge History of Iran*
V	J.A. Boyle, ed., *The Saljuq and Mongol Periods* (Cambridge, 1968)
VI	Peter Jackson and Laurence Lockhart, eds, *The Timurid and Safavid Periods* (Cambridge, 1986)
CHR	*Catholic Historical Review*
CICO	Pontificia Commissio ad Redigendum Codicem Iuris Canonici Orientalis, Fontes. 3rd series:

III	Aloysius L. Tăutu, ed., *Acta Honorii III (1216–1227) et Gregorii IX (1227–1241)* (Vatican City, 1950)
IV:1	Theodosius T. Haluščynskyj and Meletius M. Wojnar, eds, *Acta Innocentii PP. IV (1243–1254)* (Vatican City, 1962)
IV:2	Theodosius T. Haluščynskyj and Meletius M. Wojnar, eds, *Acta Alexandri PP. IV (1254–1261)* (Vatican City, 1966)
V:1	Aloysius L. Tăutu, ed., *Acta Urbani IV, Clementis IV, Gregorii X (1261–1276)* (Vatican City, 1953)
V:2	Ferdinand M. Delorme and Aloysius L. Tăutu, eds, *Acta Romanorum pontificum ab Innocentio V ad Benedictum XI (1276–1304)* (Vatican City, 1954)
VII:1	Aloysius L. Tăutu, ed., *Acta Clementis V (1305–1314)* (Vatican City, 1955)
VII:2	Aloysius L. Tăutu, ed., *Acta Ioannis XXII (1317–1334)* (Vatican City, 1952)
VIII	Aloysius L. Tăutu, ed., *Acta Benedicti XII (1334–1342)* (Vatican City, 1958)
IX	Aloysius L. Tăutu, ed., *Acta Clementis PP. VI (1342–1352)* (Vatican City, 1960)
X	Aloysius L. Tăutu, ed., *Acta Innocentii PP. VI (1352–1362)* (Vatican City, 1961)
XI	Aloysius L. Tăutu, ed., *Acta Urbani PP. V (1362–1370)* (Vatican City, 1964)
XII	Aloysius L. Tăutu, ed., *Acta Gregorii P.P. XI (1370–1378)* (Vatican City, 1966)
XIII:1	Aloysius L. Tăutu, ed., *Acta Urbani P.P. VI (1378–1389), Bonifacii P.P. IX (1389–1404), Innocentii P.P. VII (1404–1406) et Gregorii P.P. XII (1406–1415)* (Vatican City, 1970)
CM	Matthew Paris, *Chronica majora*
CMRS	*Cahiers du Monde Russe et Soviétique*
CRAIBL	*Académie des Inscriptions et Belles-Lettres. Comptes-rendus des séances*
CS	Camden Society
CSCO	Corpus Scriptorum Christianorum Orientalium
CSFS	Collana Storica di Fonti e Studi
CSSH	*Comparative Studies in Society and History*
CTT	Crusade Texts in Translation

DA	*Deutsches Archiv für Erforschung des Mittelalters*
DAV	F. Thiriet, ed., *Délibérations des assemblées vénitiennes concernant la Romanie*, I. *1160–1363*, DREP 8 (Paris and The Hague, 1966); II. *1364–1463*, DREP 11 (Paris and The Hague, 1971)
DHGE	*Dictionnaire d'Histoire et de Géographie Ecclésiastiques*
DIR	Eudoxiu de Hurmuzaki, Nic. Densusianu *et al.*, eds, *Documente privitóre la istoria Românilor*, 19 vols in 36 (Bucarest and Cernăuți, 1887–1938)
DM	Marco Polo, *Le divisament dou monde*, ed. Gabriella Ronchi (Milan, 1982)
DREP	Documents et recherches sur l'économie des pays byzantins, islamiques et slaves et leurs relations commerciales au Moyen-Âge
DRHC	Documents relatifs à l'histoire des croisades publiés par l'Académie des Inscriptions et Belles-Lettres
DVL	Georg Martin Thomas, ed., *Diplomatarium Veneto-Levantinum sive acta et diplomata res Venetas Graecas atque Levantis illustrantia*, I. *a.1300–1350* (Venice, 1880); II. *a.1351–1454*, ed. Riccardo Predelli (Venice, 1899)
EAH	*East Asian History*
EB	*Études Balkaniques*
EHR	*English Historical Review*
EM[S]	*Études Mongoles [et Sibériennes]*
Enc.Ir.	E. Yarshater, ed., *Encyclopaedia Iranica* (New York etc., 1980–)
Enc.Isl.[2]	Ch. Pellat *et al.*, eds, *The Encyclopaedia of Islam*, new edn (Leiden, 1954–)
EO	Zsigmond Jakó, ed., *Erdélyi okmánytár (Codex diplomaticus Transsyylvaniae). Oklevelek, levelek, és más írásos emlékek Erdély történetéhez*, I. *1023–1300* (Budapest, 1997)
FIS	Freiburger Islamstudien
FRAS[1]	Fontes rerum Austriacarum, erste Abtheilung. Scriptores
FRAS[2]	Fontes rerum Austriacarum, zweite Abtheilung. Diplomataria et Acta
FRB	Josef Emler, ed., *Fontes rerum Bohemicarum. Prameny dějin českých*, 7 vols published of 8 (Prague, 1873–1922)

GMS	Gibb Memorial Series
HDFS	J.L.A. Huillard-Bréholles, ed., *Historia diplomatica Friderici Secundi*, 6 vols in 11 parts (Paris, 1852–61)
HJAS	*Harvard Journal of Asiatic Studies*
HO	Imre Nagy, Arnold Ipolyi and Dezsö Vághely, eds, *Hazai okmánytár. Codex diplomaticus patrius Hungaricus*, 8 vols (Győr and Budapest, 1865–91)
HS¹	Works issued by the Hakluyt Society, first series
HS²	Works issued by the Hakluyt Society, second series
HUS	*Harvard Ukrainian Studies*
HZ	*Historische Zeitschrift*
IJMES	*International Journal of Middle East Studies*
IUB	Innsbruck Universitätsbibliothek
IUUAS	Indiana University Uralic and Altaic Series
JA	*Journal Asiatique*
JAH	*Journal of Asian History*
JAOS	*Journal of the American Oriental Society*
JEH	*Journal of Ecclesiastical History*
JEMH	*Journal of Early Modern History*
JESHO	*Journal of the Economic and Social History of the Orient*
JMH	*Journal of Mediaeval History*
JRAS	*Journal of the Royal Asiatic Society*
JS	*Journal des Savants*
JSAI	*Jerusalem Studies in Arabic and Islam*
JTS	*Journal of Turkish Studies* [*Türklük Bilgisi Araştırmaları*]
JWH	*Journal of World History*
LTC	Alexandre Teulet *et al.*, eds, *Layettes du Trésor des Chartes*, 5 vols (Paris, 1863–1909)
MA	*Le Moyen Age*
MAH	*Mélanges d'Archéologie et d'Histoire de l'École Française de Rome*
MAIBL	*Mémoires de l'Académie* [*Royale*] *des Inscriptions et Belles-Lettres*
MES	Ferdinandus Knauz and Ludovicus Crescens Dedek, eds, *Monumenta ecclesiae Strigoniensis*, I–III (Esztergom, 1874–1924); Gabriel Dreska *et al.*, eds, *Monumenta ecclesiae Strigoniensis*, IV (Esztergom and Budapest, 1999)
MGH	Monumenta Germaniae Historica

MGHEp.	C. Rodenberg, ed., *MGH Epistolae saeculi XIII e regestis pontificum Romanorum selectae*, 3 vols (Berlin, 1883–94)
MGHLeg.	L. Weiland, ed., *MGH Legum sectio IV. Constitutiones et acta publica imperatorum et regum*, 11 vols to date (Hanover, 1893–1992)
MGHQu.	MGH Quellen zur Geistesgeschichte des Mittelalters
MGHS	G.H. Pertz *et al.*, eds, *MGH Scriptores*, 38 vols to date (Hanover etc., 1826–2000)
MHR	*Mediterranean Historical Review*
MHSM	*Monumenta spectantia historiam Slavorum meridionalium*
MIOG	*Mitteilungen des Instituts für Österreichische Geschichtsforschung*
MMAH	Monumenta medii aevi historica res gestas Poloniae illustrantia
MN	*Il Mar Nero* (Rome)
MOL	Magyar Országos Levéltár (Hungarian National Archives, Budapest)
DF	Diplomáciai fényképgyűjtémeny
DL	Diplomáciai levéltár
Mongolensturm	H. Göckenjan and J.R. Sweeney, eds, *Der Mongolensturm. Berichte von Augenzeugen und Zeitgenossen 1235–1250*
MP	Marco Polo, *Le divisament dou monde*, composite trans. (with edn of 'Z' text) by A.C. Moule and Paul Pelliot, *Marco Polo. The description of the world*
MPH	August Bielowski *et al.*, eds, *Monumenta Poloniae Historica* (*Pomniki dziejowe polski*), 6 vols (Lwów, 1864–93)
MPH²	Tadeusz Kowalski *et al.*, eds, *Monumenta Poloniae Historica* (*Pomniki dziejowe polski*), new series (Cracow and Warsaw, 1946–)
MPV	Jan Ptaśnik, ed., *Monumenta Poloniae Vaticana*
MS	*Mongolian Studies*
NA	*Neues Archiv der Gesellschaft für ältere deutsche Geschichtskunde*
NCMH	*The New Cambridge Medieval History* (Cambridge, 1997–)
NZM	*Neue Zeitschrift für Missionswissenschaft*
OE	*Oriens Extremus*
OKS	*Ostkirchliche Studien*

OM	Roger Bacon, *Opus maius*
OOLB	Oberösterreichische Landesbibliothek, Linz (formerly Linz Studienbibliothek)
OSP	*Oxford Slavonic Papers*
PC	John of Plano Carpini, *Ystoria Mongalorum*
PFEH	*Papers on Far Eastern History*
PPTS	Palestine Pilgrims' Text Society
PRO	Public Record Office (since 2003: National Archives), Kew
PSRL	*Polnoe Sobranie Russkikh Letopisei*
PUB	R. Philippi *et al.*, eds, *Preußisches Urkundenbuch*, 6 vols so far (Königsberg and Marburg, 1882–1986)
QFIAB	*Quellen und Forschungen aus italienischen Archiven und Bibliotheken*
RDSV	F. Thiriet, ed., *Régestes des délibérations du Sénat de Venise concernant la Romanie*, 3 vols, DREP 1, 2 and 4 (Paris and The Hague, 1958–61)
REB	*Revue des Études Byzantines*
Reg. Alex. IV	C. Bourel de la Roncière *et al.*, eds, *Les registres d'Alexandre IV*, 4 vols (Paris, 1902–53)
Reg. Clem. IV	Édouard Jordan, ed., *Les registres de Clément IV*, 2 vols (Paris, 1893–1945)
Reg. Clem. V	Monks of the Order of St Benedict, eds, *Regestum Clementis papae V*, 8 vols (Rome, 1885–92)
Reg. Greg. IX	Lucien Auvray, ed., *Les registres de Grégoire IX*, 4 vols (Paris, 1896–1955)
Reg. Hon. IV	Maurice Prou, ed., *Les registres de Honorius IV* (Paris, 1888)
Reg. Inno IV	Élie Berger, ed., *Les registres d'Innocent IV*, 4 vols (Paris, 1884–1921)
Reg. Nic.IV	Ernest Langlois, ed., *Les registres de Nicolas IV* (Paris, 1886–93)
Reg. Urbain IV	Jean Guiraud and Léon Dorez, eds, *Les registres d'Urbain IV*, 4 vols (Paris, 1899–1958)
REI	*Revue des Études Islamiques*
RESEE	*Revue des Études Sud-Est Européennes*
RH	*Revue Historique*
RHC	*Recueil des Historiens des Croisades*
DA	*Documents Arméniens*, 2 vols (Paris, 1869–1906)
Occ.	*Historiens Occidentaux*, 2 vols (Paris, 1840–59)

RHGF	G. Bouquet, ed., *Recueil des Historiens des Gaules et de la France*, new edn, 24 vols (Paris, 1869–1904)
RHR	*Revue de l'Histoire des Religions*
RHSEE	*Revue Historique du Sud-Est Européen*
RIS	L.A. Muratori, ed., *Rerum Italicarum Scriptores*, 25 vols (Milan, 1723–51)
RIS²	L.A. Muratori, ed., *Rerum Italicarum Scriptores*, new edn by C.A. Garufi *et al.* (Bologna, 1934–)
RO	*Rocznik Orientalistyczny*
ROC	*Revue de l'Orient Chrétien*
ROL	*Revue de l'Orient Latin*
RRH	*Revue Roumaine d'Histoire*
RS	Rolls Series
RV	Roger of Várad, 'Epistola'
Rymer	T. Rymer, ed., *Foedera, conventiones, litterae et cuiuscumque generis acta publica* (Amsterdam, 1739–45)
SCH	Studies in Church History
SEER	*Slavonic and East European Review*
SF	A. Van den Wyngaert, ed., *Sinica Franciscana*, I
SH	'Secret History of the Mongols'
SI	*Studia Islamica*
SMIZO	V.G. Frhr. von Tizengauzen, ed., *Sbornik materialov otnosiashchikhsia k istorii Zolotoi Ordy*
SO	Károly Szabó, ed., *Székely oklevéltár*, 8 vols (Kolozsvár, 1872–98)
SOF	*Südost-Forschungen*
SRG	MGH Scriptores Rerum Germanicarum in usum scholarum
SRG²	MGH Scriptores Rerum Germanicarum in usum scholarum, new series
SRH	Imre Szentpétery, ed., *Scriptores rerum Hungaricarum tempore ducum regumque stirpis Arpadianae gestarum*, 2 vols (Budapest, 1937–8; repr. 1999)
SRP	Theodor Hirsch *et al.*, eds, *Scriptores rerum Prussicarum. Die Geschichtsquellen der preussischen Vorzeit bis zum Untergange der Ordensherrschaft*, 5 vols (Leipzig, 1861–74)
SSQ	Simon of Saint-Quentin, *Historia Tartarorum*
SV	*Studi Veneziani*
TP	*T'oung Pao*

ABBREVIATIONS

TR	'Tartar Relation'
TRHS	*Transactions of the Royal Historical Society*
TS	Thomas of Spalato, *Historia Salonitanorum pontificum atque Spalatensium*
TSCIA	Toronto Studies on Central and Inner Asia
UAJ	*Ural-Altaische Jahrbücher*
UBB	Hans Wagner and Irmtraut Lindeck-Pozza, eds, *Urkundenbuch des Burgenlandes und der angrenzenden Gebiete der Komitate Wieselburg, Ödenburg und Eisenburg*, 4 vols (Graz, Köln and Vienna, 1955–85)
UBGD	Franz Zimmermann and Karl Werner, eds, *Urkundenbuch zur Geschichte der Deutschen in Siebenbürgen*, 4 vols (Hermannstadt/Sibiu, 1892–1937)
UBGS	G.D. Teutsch and Fr. Firnhaber, eds, *Urkundenbuch zur Geschichte Siebenbürgens* (vol. I only published), FRAS[2] 15 (Vienna, 1857)
VB	Vincent of Beauvais, *Speculum historiale*
VMH	Augustin Theiner, ed., *Vetera monumenta historica Hungariam sacram illustrantia*, 2 vols (Rome, 1859–61)
VMP	Augustin Theiner, ed., *Vetera monumenta Poloniae et Lithuaniae gentiumque finitimarum historiam illustrantia*, 4 vols (Rome, 1860–4)
VSWG	*Vierteljahrschrift für Sozial- und Wirtschaftsgeschichte*
Wahlstatt	U. Schmilewski, ed., *Wahlstatt 1241: Beiträge zur Mongolenschlacht bei Liegnitz und zu ihre Nachwirkungen*
WR	William of Rubruck, *Itinerarium*
ZDMG	*Zeitschrift der Deutschen Morgenländischen Gesellschaft*
ZRGG	*Zeitschrift für Religions- und Geistesgeschichte*
ZS	*Zentralasiatische Studien*

NOTE ON TRANSLITERATION

For the spelling of Mongol and Turkish proper names, I have followed the UNESCO system adopted in J.A. Boyle, *The Successors of Genghis Khan* (London and New York, 1971), and for Arabic and Persian proper names the conventions used in *The Encyclopaedia of Islam*, 2nd edn (Leiden, 1954–), except that J replaces Dj and Q replaces Ḳ. For Chinese, I have used the Wade-Giles system, rather than Pin-yin.

The uncertain reconstruction of a proper name is preceded by an asterisk. Persian and Arabic manuscript readings are given in small capitals: the long vowels are represented by A, Y and W; Č stands for Ch, and Š for Sh.

NOTE ON PROPER NAMES

Consistency here would have had ludicrous results. To a large extent, personal names have been given the form appropriate to the country concerned: thus Hungarian 'István' rather than 'Stephen' and Spanish 'Jaime' for 'James'. But some Western European names have been spelled as in English in the case of persons familiar to medievalists (e.g. Philip, for French monarchs) or in the case of commonly-cited sources (e.g. William of Rubruck, John of Montecorvino).

Where place-names (particularly in the one-time Habsburg Empire) have a chequered history, I have in each case given the form used in the relevant source, with contemporary alternatives and the modern name in brackets. Thus, at p. 69: Hermannstadt, the German name referred to by Thomas of Spalato and Roger of Várad, followed in brackets by the Hungarian form, Nagyszében, and the modern Rumanian name, Sibiu.

NOTE ON REFERENCES

Primary sources are generally referred to by book (small roman numerals) and chapter or paragraph (arabic numerals), as well as by the page number of the printed edition: thus William of Rubruck, xv, 3, p. 201. On rare occasions, where a text is subdivided into book, chapter *and* paragraph, it has been necessary to supply a threefold enumeration, beginning with a large roman numeral and a colon, e.g. Marino Sanudo, *Liber secretorum fidelium crucis*, I:xiii, 3.

LIST OF MAPS

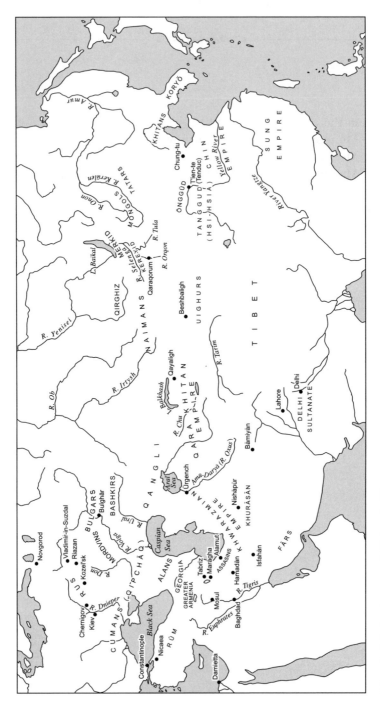

Map 1 Asia in the era of Chinggis Khan

Map 2 The Mongol invasion of Eastern Europe, 1241–2

Map 3 The Mongols and the Near East

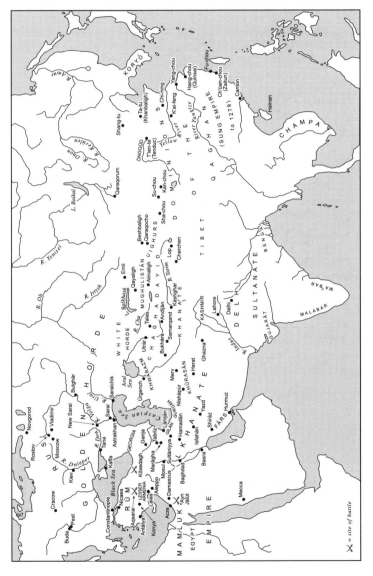

Map 4 The Mongol world after 1260 (showing Latin missionary and commercial outposts)

Map 5 Eastern Europe and the Golden Horde

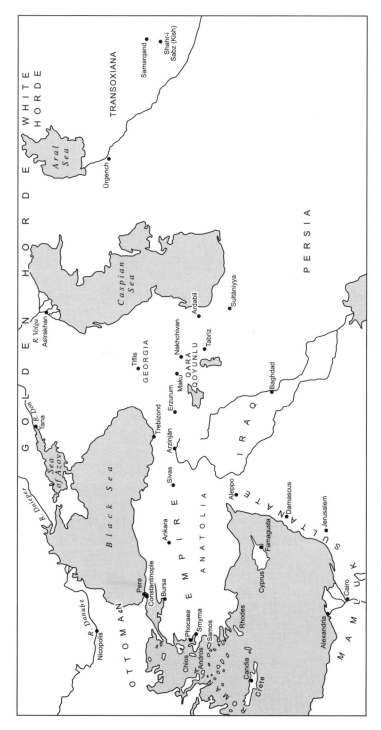

Map 6 Temür's campaigns in western Asia

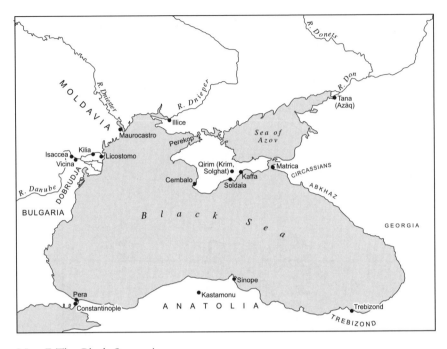

Map 7 The Black Sea region

INTRODUCTION

In the thirteenth century, a dynamic and expansive Catholic (or Latin) Christendom, which had been free of major attack from its steppe frontier for over two hundred years, was confronted by a new and alien power in the shape of the vast empire of the advancing Mongols. The Mongols – or 'Tartars', as they were known in the West – posed a grave threat to the states of Christian Europe, which was manifested most vividly in their devastation of Poland, Moravia and Hungary in 1241–2. That threat remained even after their empire splintered into a number of rival khanates in 1261–2 (notably the Golden Horde, based in the steppes to the north of the Black Sea and the Caspian, and the Ilkhanate in Persia and Iraq). Yet by this juncture their presence appeared to offer new and unprecedented opportunities. One related to the West's faltering crusading efforts, as the Mongol Ilkhans of Persia made repeated overtures to Western rulers for concerted operations against the Muslim Mamlūk empire in Egypt and Syria. Another centred on the dissemination of the Gospel, since it was now possible for Catholic missionaries to traverse great swathes of territory that had hitherto been under Muslim rule and therefore closed to Christian proselytism. And commercial opportunities, too, beckoned, as the subjection of a great many peoples first to a single government and then to just a handful of major polities created more stable conditions for trade and travel. As a consequence of the advent of the Mongols, therefore, it is commonly believed that the West's field of vision expanded remarkably.

Although the past twenty years have seen a rash of publications on the Mongol empire,[1] no comprehensive, book-length study of relations between the Mongols and Western Christendom has hitherto appeared in English. Igor de Rachewiltz's *Papal Envoys to the Great Khans* covers only diplomatic and missionary contacts.[2] The thought-provoking book of Antti Ruotsala focuses on a relatively brief period framed by the early contacts with the Mongols (1245–55).[3] Such reticence on the part of Anglophone writers hardly stems from any lack of interest in the subject. Possibly some blame attaches to the well-known problem of linguistic expertise that confronts any serious scholarship on the Mongols: as David Morgan points out in what is now the standard work, the available sources are in Mongolian, Chinese, Persian, Arabic, Turkish, Japanese,

Russian, Armenian, Georgian, Latin – and still the list is incomplete.[4] Yet the number of languages required for the study of Mongol–Western relations is in fact naturally lower than it is for tackling the history of the empire at large.

Fortunately, there is an extensive literature in other Western European languages. The work of Giovanni Soranzo, though still useful, is already over seventy years old, predating the publication of several vital documents.[5] More noteworthy are three fine books in German – the pioneering study by Gian Andri Bezzola, which appeared thirty years ago,[6] and the two rather more recent works by Axel Klopprogge[7] and Felicitas Schmieder.[8] Bezzola and Klopprogge focus on the image of the Mongols in Latin Christendom and confine their attention to the thirteenth century. Schmieder's work is far more ambitious in terms of both scope and chronological coverage, though Klopprogge's book regrettably appeared at too late a stage for her to use and she also gives relatively little space to the Mongol menace in Eastern Europe after 1242. All three authors, moreover, entered upon their task as historians of medieval Europe and utilized almost exclusively sources produced within the West.

A great many valuable studies of various aspects of the subject have of course appeared in article form, beginning as far back as the work of Abel-Rémusat in the 1820s on the diplomatic contacts between the Ilkhans and Latin monarchs.[9] In recent decades, this literature has been dominated by the researches of Robert Sabatino Lopez and Michel Balard on Western commercial activity in the Mongol dominions[10] and of Denis Sinor and Jean Richard on diplomacy;[11] and Richard's characteristically thorough examination of the Latin mission to Asia[12] remains unsurpassed. It will be obvious in the following pages how much I have benefited from the labours of these and other scholars.

This book is designed both to provide a synthesis of previous scholarship on relations between the Mongols and the Catholic world and to go beyond it by offering new approaches and conclusions, sometimes based on my own earlier work on the Mongols. Most of the sources produced by Western writers are of course in Latin, beginning with the majority of the annals that record Mongol attacks. So too are the detailed reports of the European envoys and missionaries who visited the Mongol world, notably the Franciscan Friars Carpini (1245–7) and Rubruck (1253–5), which furnish a particularly rich corpus of material. A significant minority of sources also exist in Old French and a few in Italian; the book associated with the most famous Latin visitor to the Mongols, Marco Polo, was originally written in an Italianate form of French.

I have also made wide use of sources composed by non-Europeans. Apropos of the linguistic difficulties referred to above, I have to confess at this juncture that the sources I cite which emanate from within the Mongol empire will be primarily in Persian; I have access only to the tiny fraction of the Chinese material that exists in translation. Strangely enough, a knowledge of Mongolian did not prove necessary for writing this book. Just one Mongolian narrative source has survived from the imperial era, namely the so-called 'Secret History of the Mongols', which in its original form dates from c.1228; a section added some years later furnishes a few lines on the campaign in Eastern Europe. Of the letters to Western rulers, and other relevant documents issued by the chanceries of the Mongol Great Khan (*qaghan*) or of regional khans, the overwhelming majority have reached us only in Latin translation; a notable exception is the ultimatum brought back by Pope Innocent IV's envoy Carpini (1247), which appears to have been drafted originally in Persian. I have also utilized Arabic authors writing in the Near East, much of which came under the rule of the Egyptian Mamlūk Sultans after 1260, having only briefly formed part of the Mongol dominions. They furnish us with a different perspective on the Mongol presence in this region.

One of my aims has been to examine the course of military confrontation and diplomatic relations between the Mongols and the West from the time when Latin Christians first heard of the campaigns of Chinggis Khan in far-off Central Asia in 1221. The first two chapters set the scene by outlining, respectively, the situation of the Latin West on the eve of the Mongol attacks and the creation of the Mongol empire by Chinggis Khan and his immediate successor. Chapter 3 is devoted specifically to the Mongol invasion of Hungary and Poland in 1241–2 and the near simultaneous incursion into northern Syria in 1244. Chapter 8 resumes the survey of mainly hostile contacts with the Golden Horde in Eastern Europe after 1242. Chapter 7 examines the more cordial, though abortive, diplomatic relations between the Ilkhans on the one hand and the papacy and Western monarchs on the other; this theme is taken up again in chapter 9, with a study of the West's dealings with the Turco-Mongol conqueror from Central Asia, Temür ('Tamerlane'). I have chosen to bring the coverage down to 1410 because the battle of Tannenberg in that year symbolized the decline of the Golden Horde to the status of just one among a number of rival powers in Eastern Europe. In the Near East, Temür's death only a few years previously, in 1405, marked the passing of the last 'Tartar' sovereign who was widely regarded in the West as a potential, or even real, ally against the Muslim powers, the Mamlūks and the Ottomans.

These chapters construct the chronological and geopolitical frame-work of Mongol–Western relations. Other chapters deal with specific themes that transcend such boundaries. Chapter 10 examines the efforts of Latin missionaries – overwhelmingly members of the newly-founded orders of friars, the Franciscans and the Dominicans – to convert the Mongols and their nomadic subjects to Christianity. Chapter 11 out-lines the development and decline of Western trading links with the Mongol world. At its apogee this commercial activity extended as far as the ports of southern China; but its nodal point was always the Black Sea region. And two chapters, lastly, are devoted to images: chapter 6, to the Latin images of the Mongols themselves in the three decades or so following the attacks on Hungary and Poland in 1241-2; and chapter 12, to the impact that contact with the Mongols had on the West's notions about the world beyond Islam. Far greater attention is neces-sarily given here to Western perspectives; to gain an understanding of the Mongols' view of Western Europe is virtually impossible, given the dearth of source material. For the Mongols, the subjugation and exploitation of China was of paramount interest, and campaigns in dis-tant Europe barely figure in the sources composed in the Far East. Even those subjects of the Mongols in Persia who wrote the history of the empire say relatively little even about the invasion of 1241-2, and nothing at all about the subsequent dealings of their Ilkhanid masters with the European infidel. Our picture of the Mongols' ideas about Westerners is consequently refracted through the lens of Western vis-itors to the Mongol dominions.

Where the sources written by the Mongols' subjects can be of assist-ance is in what they tell us about the Mongols themselves, their aims and their thought-world. This applies especially to the diplomatic negoti-ations between Mongol Persia and the West and to the efforts of the Catholic Church to convert the Mongols to Christianity. In trying to elicit why Ilkhanid–Western contacts bore no fruit, I have sought to analyse the Ilkhans' purposes in wooing the West, insofar as we gain some insight into their policies from a reading of their court historians; and I have linked these purposes up with the Western reservations and suspicions that were the legacy of earlier Mongol expansionism. The failure of Ilkhanid–Western negotiations, and the reasons for it, are of particular importance in view of the widespread belief in the past that they might well have succeeded and that, had they done so, the history of the Near East would have followed a very different course.

Something similar could be said of the Catholic missions to the Mon-gol world. Here too there has been a tendency to magnify the chances of success and hence what was at stake. 'It was a noble prospect', wrote

Sir Richard Southern of the hopes raised when an ambassador from the Ilkhan attended Mass in St Peter's; 'and one which, if only a fraction of it had come true, would radically have altered the history of the world.'[13] His judgement was widely shared, not least by historians of the crusades, and has retained much of its allure to this day. In this book I endeavour to explain the meagre harvest of the mission by reference not just to the distances involved, or to the small number of missionaries, or to linguistic problems, but also to the universe the Mongols themselves inhabited, and in particular their preoccupations in matters of religion, Nature and magic.

It will be obvious that this book does not set out to purvey some grand model. I am instinctively wary of formulaic approaches that risk imposing patterns on – and hence, in my judgement, doing violence to – the sources. This is not to say that what I have written has been determined exclusively by the often fragmentary information which has survived from the thirteenth–fifteenth centuries. It has been necessary to look beyond the sources for explanations – even if only tentative ones that will no doubt have to be superseded by the work of other scholars in the future. Nor does it mean that I accept uncritically whatever our sources tell us. While no disciple of Postmodernism, I have tried to stand outside the source material and to remember that historians can never hope to retrieve 'what actually happened' – though that does not, in my view, absolve them of the responsibility of trying to get as close as possible to it.

Yet the reader will look in vain, for instance, for some great confrontation between 'nomadic' and 'sedentary' societies. In the following pages, the word 'nomads' is sometimes employed where the context permits it; but I have avoided casting the phenomena I am dealing with in terms of an age-old clash of the steppe and the sown. One good reason for this apparent dereliction of duty has already been mentioned. Our literary sources, even from the Mongol side, are overwhelmingly the work of sedentary observers; the thought-processes of the nomadic pastoralist reach us, if at all, at second-hand. Another, and equally decisive, reason is that by the time they came into contact with the Latin West, the Mongol regimes themselves were touched by sedentary culture in several respects. They had recruited representatives of the various settled societies that were in the process of yielding – or had yielded – to their rule, as ministers, as generals, as chancery scribes or as envoys. Visitors from the Latin world certainly met nomads in large numbers on their journeys across Asia, and some of them have left us extremely vivid impressions of these encounters; yet the Mongol khanate with which Latin Europeans negotiated, or traded, or fought, was not some 'pure' nomadic polity but a hybrid.

I have tried, lastly, to eschew two approaches which I regard as hazardous. The first (despite the above reference to the Mongols' universe) is an unqualified focus on 'mentalités'. In recent years, a number of historians, writing in quite different contexts, have thrown into sharp relief the pitfalls that attend this kind of conceptualization;[14] and their caveats need to be borne in mind when dealing with the reactions of medieval European Christians to a newly-revealed Asiatic world. I have tried, for example, in chapter 6 to show that the West's preconceptions about the Mongols may have been reinforced by ideas current among its Muslim neighbours and even within Mongol circles; and in chapter 12 I have sought to bear in mind that what European travellers saw and reported was not conditioned simply by the mental baggage they had brought with them from home, but was determined also by the tales they picked up in Asia.

The second danger I seek to sidestep is the temptation that arises from overdosing on hindsight – the assumption, in other words, that we today can automatically see more clearly than contemporaries did. That assumption may be justified: historians' access to sources sometimes affords them an eyrie more commanding than any vantage-point available to the people they study. In the study of contacts between the two distinct cultures which are covered in this book, there has sometimes been a tendency to explain things by entering a verdict of mutual incomprehension. In some measure this is certainly appropriate here – in the case, for instance, of Western missionary endeavours. My own view is that the friars failed to grasp a number of important characteristics of steppe society and hence interpreted them as signs of particular sympathy for, or commitment to, the Christian faith. But the field of diplomacy presents a rather different picture. Although several scholars have criticized the Catholic world for its failure to perceive what the Mongols of Persia offered, I shall argue that the majority of Western observers were lukewarm about an alliance precisely because they recognized Ilkhanid ambitions for what they were. In this context the Latin reaction demonstrates that incomprehension was neither total nor unavoidable.

Notes

1. See Peter Jackson, 'The state of research: the Mongol world-empire, 1986–1999', *JMH* 26 (2000), pp. 189–210.
2. I. de Rachewiltz, *Papal Envoys to the Great Khans* (London and Stanford, CA, 1971).
3. Antti Ruotsala, *Europeans and Mongols in the Middle of the Thirteenth Century: Encountering the Other* (Helsinki, 2001).
4. David Morgan, *The Mongols* (Oxford, 1986), p. 5.

5. Giovanni Soranzo, *Il papato, l'Europa cristiana e i Tartari. Un secolo di penetrazione occidentale in Asia* (Milan, 1930).
6. Gian Andri Bezzola, *Die Mongolen in abendländischer Sicht (1220–1270). Ein Beitrag zur Frage der Völkerbegegnungen* (Berne and Munich, 1974).
7. Axel Klopprogge, *Ursprung und Ausprägung des abendländischen Mongolenbildes im 13. Jahrhundert: ein Versuch zur Ideengeschichte des Mittelalters*, AF 122 (Wiesbaden, 1993).
8. Felicitas Schmieder, *Europa und die Fremden. Die Mongolen im Urteil des Abendlandes vom 13. bis in das 15. Jahrhundert*, BGQM 16 (Sigmaringen, 1994).
9. Abel-Rémusat, 'Mémoires sur les relations politiques des princes chrétiens, et particulièrement des rois de France, avec les empereurs mongols', *MAIBL* 6 (1822), pp. 396–469, and 7 (1824), pp. 335–438.
10. See the papers collected in Robert Sabatino Lopez, *Su e giù per la storia di Genova* (Genova, 1975), and some of those in Michel Balard, *La mer Noire et la Romanie génoise (XIIIe–XVe siècles)* (London, 1989).
11. See especially Denis Sinor, 'The Mongols and Western Europe', in Harry W. Hazard, ed., *A History of the Crusades* (general ed. K.M. Setton), III. *The Fourteenth and Fifteenth Centuries* (Madison, WI, 1975), chap. 15, and repr. in Sinor, *Inner Asia and its Contacts with Medieval Europe* (London, 1977); and the five volumes of collected papers of Jean Richard: *Orient et Occident au moyen âge: contacts et relations (XIIe–XVe s.)* (London, 1976); *Les relations entre l'Orient et l'Occident au Moyen Age. Études et documents* (London, 1977); *Croisés, missionnaires et voyageurs. Les perspectives orientales du monde latin médiéval* (London, 1983); *Croisades et états latins d'Orient* (Aldershot, 1992); and *Francs et Orientaux dans le monde des croisades* (Aldershot, 2003).
12. Jean Richard, *La papauté et les missions d'Orient au moyen âge (XIIIᵉ–XVᵉ siècles)*, Collection de l'École Française de Rome 33 (Rome, 1977).
13. R.W. Southern, *Western Views of Islam in the Middle Ages* (Cambridge, MA, 1962), p. 65.
14. See Susan Reynolds, 'Social mentalities and the case of medieval scepticism', *TRHS*, 6th series, 1 (1991), pp. 21–41; David Nirenberg, *Communities of Violence. Persecution of Minorities in the Middle Ages* (Princeton, NJ, 1996), pp. 3–7; and Peter Burke, *Varieties of Cultural History* (Oxford, 1997), pp. 162–82.

chapter 1

LATIN CHRISTENDOM AND ITS NEIGHBOURS IN THE EARLY THIRTEENTH CENTURY

The unity and growth of Latin Christendom

During the eleventh and twelfth centuries Latin Christendom – the area that employed the Latin rite and looked to Rome for ecclesiastical and spiritual leadership – had grown phenomenally.[1] Around 900 it had comprised little more than the Carolingian empire (present-day France, Germany and northern Italy) and the British Isles, and had been under frequent attack by non-Christian peoples from the surrounding territories, Vikings, Muslims and Hungarians. But by 1100 this defensive phase had given way to one of pronounced expansion. The slow reduction of Muslim territory in Spain was now under way. From the former Carolingian dominions, Norman knights had wrested Sicily from the Muslims, while monks and secular clerics carried the Christian faith into the territories of their Scandinavian, Slavic and Hungarian neighbours. Instrumental in the success of Latin Christians' campaigns of conquest were the heavily-armed and mailed horseman – the knight (*miles*) – and the crossbow (*arbalista*); physically symbolic of their newly-implanted domination was the castle. The twelfth century was also an era of economic growth. Internal colonization of waste land was matched by external, as knights and settlers, both burghers and agriculturists, pushed forward into new lands beyond the frontiers of Christian rule, transporting with them to regions as far afield as the Iberian peninsula and the Baltic the legal and tenurial institutions to which they were accustomed at home. Enterprising Western merchants, notably those of Venice, Genoa and Pisa, devised new techniques of credit and investment to support commercial ventures that took them to the furthest shores of the Mediterranean.

The most spectacular instance of Latin expansion was the movement now known as the First Crusade, by which a motley force of 'Franks' – knights from France, the western borderlands of Germany, and Norman-ruled southern Italy – wrested from Muslim hands in 1098–9 a narrow strip of the Syrian–Palestinian coastline, including the Holy City of Jerusalem, and established a small and vulnerable network of Latin states. These newly-founded polities – the kingdom of Jerusalem, the principality of Antioch, and the counties of Edessa and Tripoli – became an integral part of the Latin world, and their fate a matter of vital concern to Christians throughout Western Europe. During the twelfth and thirteenth centuries, the assertion of Western dominance over the Mediterranean sea-lanes by Venetians, Pisans and Genoese – and to a lesser extent by the men of other ports like Marseilles and Barcelona – served to underpin the survival of these distant Latin outposts in Syria and Palestine.[2]

What gave some structural unity to the extensive tract that comprised Latin Christendom was above all the Latin Church, presided over by the pope. Between the Gregorian Reform of the late eleventh century and the pontificate of Innocent III (1198–1216), the prestige and influence of the papacy grew enormously. Widespread and mounting support within the ranks of the laity combined with the allegiance of the clergy, the labours of three generations of canon lawyers, and increasingly frequent recourse to letters, legates and councils, to turn papal authority into a reality that impinged alike on the ambitions of kings and on the lives of ordinary Christians. Already in the first half of the twelfth century the papal Curia was on the way to becoming the supreme juridical body in Latin Christendom. It was the nascent Reformed Papacy that had reaped the credit for the stupendous triumph of the First Crusade, launched by Pope Urban II in 1095; just over a hundred years later (1199) Innocent III registered his authority over the Church by introducing, in support of the crusade, universal taxation of ecclesiastical revenues.

An especial boost to the power of the papacy and the cohesion of Latin Christendom was the rise, around the beginning of the twelfth century, of international religious orders which looked to Rome for guidance and direction. The Cistercian monks, founded in 1098, and the Premonstratensian canons, who emerged in c.1115, were active in the settlement and exploitation of new lands in Eastern Europe; from their ranks, too, came many of the bishops who presided over the newly-founded dioceses. The military orders, of whom the earliest to emerge were the Knights Templar and the Hospitallers of St John, were warrior monks, whose primary duty was the protection and care of Christians and the defence of Christian territory. They were intimately associated with the crusading movement, and their headquarters were in the Holy Land; but gifts and bequests furnished them with property and income in virtually every part of the Latin world. The later twelfth century witnessed the appearance of other military orders, notably the Teutonic Knights (1198), who in 1226 were granted a foothold in Poland in return for defending the country against the heathen Prussians. In the early thirteenth century the mendicant orders, or friars, were founded by St Francis (d. 1226) and St Dominic (d. 1221), with the support of Innocent III. The Franciscans and Dominicans, whose members were dedicated to poverty and preaching, were well placed to spread the Gospel not merely within Latin Christendom but beyond its frontiers; in 1219, during the Fifth Crusade, St Francis in person attempted to expound the Christian message to the Egyptian Sultan. Friars are also found at a relatively early date acting as agents of the papacy, and from 1234 were employed as crusade preachers. It was no accident that in 1245 the first papal emissaries to the pagan Mongols would be chosen from their ranks.

Enemies and coreligionists

Confronting expansionist Latin Christendom were two types of opponent. In northern Europe the pagan territories into which Western knights and peasants advanced belonged to polytheists – Slavs ('Wends') or Baltic races like the Prussians, Livonians and Estonians. The rhetoric and (such as it was) the machinery of crusade were extended to these theatres during the twelfth century. The Baltic Crusade began in earnest in 1199; and from the late 1230s the German *Drang nach Osten* in the Baltic was spearheaded by the Teutonic Knights. In these regions the enemy was characterized by looser forms of political organization and by a lower level of economic and technological development. By the early thirteenth century the balance was shifting, as native princes copied the methods and borrowed the weaponry of their Latin opponents.[3] Frequently they secured their future by accepting baptism for themselves and their subjects and ranging themselves alongside their erstwhile opponents in the work of crusade and evangelism. Their admission to the family of Latin Christian rulers was accompanied by the adoption of Latin as the language of faith and government. Their policies came to mirror those practised in Christian states of longer standing, like Hungary, whose kings were enhancing their military power and potential revenues by encouraging the immigration of substantial numbers of French knights and clerics and French and German artisans.[4]

In the south, in the Mediterranean region, Latin Christians faced an adversary of an altogether different calibre. This was the world of Islam, a faith still more uncompromising in its monotheism than was

Christianity. The days of government by a universal Caliphate were long past, and its former territories, stretching from Morocco to northern India, were divided among a plethora of rulers of different dynasties and races – Arabs, Berbers, Persians, Kurds and Turks. Some of these states attained a considerable size, like the empire of the Seljük Turks, which embraced Persia, Iraq and Anatolia (Rūm) for a few decades prior to its disintegration in the early twelfth century; the branch of the dynasty that ruled Anatolia was still an important power in the early thirteenth. The fiction of a single Islamic polity was maintained. The majority of Muslim princes acknowledged the 'Abbasid Caliph at Baghdad as the source of their authority, seeking from him diplomas that granted them the status of his lieutenants and naming him, in return, on the coinage and in the public Friday prayers. The long-established exception to this, of course, was the Shī'a. But in fact there had been no major Shī'ī polity since 1171. Even the leaders of the Ismā'īlī Shī'īs who held out in the mountainous regions of northern Persia and of Syria, the so-called Assassins, abandoned their religious claims early in the thirteenth century, adopted 'Orthodox' (Sunnī) Islam and entered into friendly relations with the 'Abbasids (although this was widely taken to be an example of the Ismā'īlī practice of *taqiyya*, 'dissimulation').[5] On the other hand, a significant cleavage loomed early in the thirteenth century, with the growth of tension between the caliph and the powerful rulers of Khwārazm (the Khwārazmshāhs), who had overthrown the last Seljük Sultan of Persia in 1194; and in c.1216 the quarrel peaked when the Khwārazmshāh 'Alā' al-Dīn Muḥammad proclaimed the deposition of the 'Abbasids, setting up a rival caliph and mounting an abortive expedition against Baghdad.[6]

Yet for all this the Islamic world (*Dār al-Islām*), unlike the northern European pagans, was still characterized by a unity which more or less paralleled that of Latin Christendom. It possessed a cultural cohesion which was reinforced by the annual pilgrimage to Mecca, bringing together Muslims from territories as diverse as Morocco, Anatolia and present-day Afghanistan. It also boasted a higher standard of economic development. No city in Western Europe could as yet compete with Cairo, Damascus, Aleppo or Baghdad in wealth; even places like Acre and Tyre, in Latin-held Palestine, which were worth considerable sums to their rulers on account of the great volume of trade that passed through them,[7] were not comparable. Access to such wealth enabled the Muslims to inflict major reverses on the Latin cause in the Near East, as demonstrated in the overthrow of the county of Edessa in 1144 or in the decisive defeat of the Frankish army at Hattin in 1187 by Saladin (Ṣalāḥ al-Dīn Yūsuf), which was followed by the loss of Jerusalem.

Although the Third Crusade had secured a new lease of life for the beleaguered Latin states of Jerusalem, Antioch and Tripoli by 1192, its achievements did not include the recovery of the Holy City; and relations with Saladin's dynasty, the Ayyubids of Egypt and Syria, were henceforward marked by a series of truces. The most notorious of these truces was that made in 1229 – in the course of a crusade which apparently did not strike a single blow against the Muslims – between the Emperor Frederick II and the Egyptian Sultan al-Kāmil. By the terms of this agreement, the city of Jerusalem (for a mere fifteen years, as it transpired) largely passed back into Frankish hands.

There was one further point of contrast between the Muslims and the pagans of northern Europe. The Muslims, who possessed their own revealed religion and sacred scriptures, proved far more impervious to Christian missionary endeavours than did the Latins' weaker opponents in the Baltic. Muslim slaves in Latin Syria and Palestine, prisoners of war with little hope of repatriation to their own communities, might seek baptism; not so Muslim princes. From time to time rumours would spread of the imminent conversion of some Muslim ruler, perhaps one born of a Christian mother. The outcome was always disappointing, as in 1234, when the Seljük Sultan of Rūm corresponded on the subject with the Pope in the hope of Latin military assistance against his Ayyubid neighbours, or in 1239–40, when the alleged willingness of the Ayyubid prince of Ḥamā to embrace the rival faith occasioned great excitement in the ranks of a crusading army but proved to be merely a ploy directed against his kinsmen.[8] Yet the Catholic hierarchy did not abandon the hope that baptism might turn enemies into allies.

To the Muslims, successive attacks by European crusaders and the stubborn resistance of the Latin settlements on the Syro-Palestinian coast represented little more than a localized malaise alongside reverses on Islam's eastern frontier from the third decade of the twelfth century to the middle of the thirteenth. During the 1120s, a semi-nomadic people of (probably) Mongolian stock, the Khitan, in flight from northern China, established an empire in Central Asia. The new power, known as the Qara-('Black') Khitan, asserted its paramountcy over several Muslim princes, and when in 1141 the Great Seljük Sultan Sanjar moved to the aid of his coreligionists he suffered a crushing defeat in Transoxiana. This was the first occasion on which a significant proportion of the *Dār al-Islām* (that is, discounting Sicily and parts of Spain) had passed back under the dominion of the infidel. In time the Qara-Khitan would come to seem like the harbinger of much more formidable eastern conquerors, the Mongols, who subjugated Islamic Central Asia, Persia, Iraq and Anatolia in a series of invasions from the 1220s onwards.

For Latin Christians, on the other hand, the Muslims, prior to the 1240s, were the most dangerous enemy that they had to face. Admittedly, relations between Frankish knights and Muslim lords in Syria were on occasions cordial. Muslim warriors like the Turks might command a grudging admiration; stories circulated that endowed Saladin with the characteristics of a Frankish knight.[9] Following his crusade, the Emperor Frederick maintained friendly relations with Cairo right down to his death, addressing to the scholars at the Sultan's court questions on mathematics and scientific subjects. But generally speaking there was little understanding of the faith of Islam – indeed its nature was greatly distorted – and no real awareness of sectarian differences among Muslims before the thirteenth century.[10] What mattered above all was that pagans were wrong and Christians were right, as the 'Song of Roland' put it,[11] and in the last analysis the most appropriate medium of dialogue was the sword. Islam's territories might be wealthier than the lands of Christendom; its culture, steeped in the learning of Classical Antiquity, might seem superior. Yet there could be no doubt of the debased nature of the Muslims, who insulted Christ by polluting the Holy Places and persecuting His people.[12] There was a growing conviction, moreover, that the final demise of Islam – and with it the Last Things – were close at hand. This is often associated with the labyrinthine Biblical exegesis of the Calabrian hermit Joachim of Fiore (d. 1202), which may have had no impact on wider currents of thought until the second half of the thirteenth century. But even Pope Innocent III, who did not view Joachim's speculations with favour, appears to have endorsed the belief that Islam would collapse within a matter of decades, a conviction shared also within eastern Christian churches.[13] And when Gregory IX issued the first bull authorizing the missionary friars to preach to pagan nations in 1235, he chose to begin with the evocative phrase *Cum hora undecima* ('Since the eleventh hour . . .').[14]

During the eleventh century the very term *Christianitas*, which had originally denoted the Christian faith, was acquiring a new territorial significance, as 'Christendom' came to mean the lands occupied by Christians and the society they comprised.[15] But its content increasingly hinged on the use of the Latin rite and the recognition of the primacy of Rome; there was less and less room for variant (or, as they would have been seen, deviant) practices, and in the peripheral regions of the Catholic world immigrant clerics refashioned indigenous Christian usage to bring it into line with the metropolitan tradition. With Christians outside Latin territory who belonged to traditions altogether different from their own, the relations of Western Christians were somewhat diverse. Those with the Greek Orthodox hierarchy were the most problematic of all. Despite the so-called 'schism' of 1054, the Greeks and the Latins, as distinct from the separated churches of the east, still constituted, juridically speaking, a single entity. It is therefore more accurate to speak of Latin and Greek 'forms' and 'usages' than of different churches; but, as within Western Europe, the Latin hierarchy was increasingly disposed to be impatient of such variation. Moreover, crusading activities in the Near East had served to embitter relations between Greek and Latin. In Antioch, a formerly Byzantine city that should have been restored to the emperor in 1098, the Greek patriarch was replaced by a Westerner: thereafter a succession of Greek patriarchs promulgated their claims in exile at Constantinople. On the Latin side, resentment and jealousy of the magnificence of Constantinople and suspicion of a multi-faceted imperial foreign policy combined with differences in language, creed, liturgy and practice to nurture the view of the Greeks as 'false' Christians, decadent, treacherous and less than wholehearted in their devotion to the war on Christ's behalf.

As the power of the Byzantine empire atrophied from the late twelfth century onwards, Western rulers began to encroach upon its territories. In 1191, during the Third Crusade, Richard I of England wrested Cyprus from a rebel Greek governor. The island became a Latin possession, and remained so until its conquest by the Ottomans in 1571; from 1197 its Frankish ruler wore a crown which had been conferred on him by the Western Emperor. In 1204 the Fourth Crusade, diverted from its official goal, went on to sack Constantinople itself, and most of Byzantine Greece in turn passed into the hands of Latin lords and knights. Those territories not appropriated by Venice, which had played a prominent role in the crusade, recognized the nominal suzerainty of a Latin emperor at Constantinople; the region became known to the Latins as 'Romania'. Only a rump of the once great Byzantine polity – the despotate of Epirus in the west and the empires of Nicaea and Trebizond in Anatolia – held out under Greek rulers. In time it became apparent that Nicaea was more than a match for the feeble Latin empire, though the Nicaean Emperor did not recover Constantinople until 1261. Well before that, the popes had begun to negotiate with the Nicaean government for the recognition of papal primacy.

In time, the Latins likewise encroached upon other lands that belonged to the Greek Orthodox world. In 1217 the ruler of Serbia accepted the Latin rite and Roman primacy in return for coronation by a papal legate. Just prior to the Fourth Crusade, the Vlach ruler of Bulgaria, a kingdom which had received its Christianity from Constantinople some centuries earlier, had made the same exchange.[16] But he subsequently repudiated the union and allied with Nicaea, so that from 1238 the papacy tried to induce the Hungarian king Béla IV to lead a crusade against him.[17] It is hard to gauge the impact of the fall of Byzantium upon the Orthodox Rus′; the account of the Fourth Crusade in the Novgorod Chronicle is remarkably free of polemic.[18] But during the early thirteenth century Western expansionism was bringing the Rus′ into conflict with the Latins on their own account. To the south, the Hungarian kingdom intervened in the disputes among rival candidates for the principality of Galicia (Halych);[19] in the Baltic, aggression by Swedes, Danes and Germans provoked the opposition of the rulers of Novgorod. Competition for fisheries, furs, the products of the forest, and the tribute of Finnish tribes exacerbated a growing consciousness of the same differences in rite and practice that we noticed in Latin–Byzantine relations. Russian strongpoints were seized, like Iur′ev, which under German occupation became Dorpat (1224).[20] Rus′ resistance to the Western advance in territories of mutual interest would in time provoke the wrath of Pope Gregory IX and the authorization of a crusade against them in 1237. Even prior to this the papacy had manifested a concern to bring the Rus′ into the Catholic fold. When they were suddenly attacked and defeated by a new power in the southern steppes in 1223, Pope Honorius III appears to have hoped that the reverse would dispose them to welcome closer links with Rome (see below, p. 61).

The Greek Orthodox, of course, were only one Christian group among many in the eastern Mediterranean. Latin-ruled Syria and Palestine contained not only an Orthodox population but also large numbers of Jacobite (Monophysite) Christians. Although the situation of these eastern Christians was clearly preferable to that of the Muslim majority of the subject population, they were still in some sense second-class citizens. The Franks' occupation of Jerusalem had also brought them into closer contact than hitherto with Christians of other churches who made the pilgrimage to the Holy City, such as the Egyptian Copts and the Ethiopians. More importantly, it had introduced them to the far-flung world of Nestorian Christianity, which was centred on Iraq and had put down roots in Central Asia, present-day Mongolia and China in the eighth century; though the West did not really become aware of the Nestorian world and its geographical extent until the time of the Fifth Crusade (1218–21).[21]

Down to the early thirteenth century, however, the Latin hierarchy was generally content to leave to eastern Christians the task of converting their pagan neighbours. And there were breakthroughs in relations with these separated churches. The Maronite Christians of the Lebanon entered into union with Rome in 1182, and in 1198 the prince of Lesser Armenia (Cilicia), a region that had close relations with Frankish

Antioch, accepted a crown from the pope and brought his people, theoretically at least, into the Roman obedience.[22] Some Christian groups, like the Georgians and Armenians, had not been subject to Muslim government, and here a shared tradition of warfare undoubtedly helped to foster respect on the part of the Latins. Mutual esteem increased, perhaps, with distance. It was natural that the Syrian Franks should entertain harmonious relations with the remote kingdom of Georgia, which during the twelfth century was engaged in its own conspicuously successful struggle with Muslim powers in Armenia and Azerbaijan, and that popes discussed with successive Georgian monarchs their participation in the war in Syria. In 1220 Jacques de Vitry, bishop of Acre, who was with the army of the Fifth Crusade in the Nile delta, pinned greater hope on Georgian intervention than on reinforcements from the West.[23]

To judge at least from their historical writing, the Monophysites of the Coptic Church in Egypt felt no marked affinity with the Franks who tried to conquer their country and liberate them from Muslim rule, either in the Fifth Crusade (1218–21) or in the Seventh (1249–50), headed by Louis IX of France (St Louis).[24] But as regards other eastern Christians the prospects seemed more promising. In 1237 Philip, Dominican prior of the Holy Land, reported enthusiastically to Pope Gregory IX that the Jacobite patriarch and the head of the Nestorian communities, the catholicus, were ready to repudiate past errors and acknowledge papal primacy. Both prelates had in fact made only personal professions of faith; there was no question of entering corporately into union with Rome. For Philip, however, only the Greeks now remained obstinately outside the Catholic fold.[25]

The steppe frontier

To the south of the Russian forest zone lay the Pontic and Caspian steppes. Most of Latin Christendom had no direct contact with the nomadic herdsmen who occupied this region. This was the corridor through which, during several centuries past, a succession of races had pushed westwards into the heart of Europe. They included the Huns, who had briefly menaced the Western Roman Empire in the fifth century; the Avars, whose empire had been destroyed by Charlemagne in the 790s; and the Hungarians who, after terrorizing southern Germany and northern Italy in the tenth century, had at length settled down and become a part of Latin Christendom. Since the collapse of the Turkish empire in Central Asia in the first half of the eighth century, the majority of the nomadic populations (and certainly the ruling elements) among the peoples of the western steppe appear to have been of Turkish stock.[26]

Some, like the remote Volga Bulgars (that is, of Bulghār, not far from the later city of Kazan), were largely sedentarized and had adopted Islam.

For all the terror and disruption they inspired, the peoples of the Pontic steppe were generally fugitives who had been driven westwards by some stronger nomadic power; though the chain reactions which set on foot widespread migrations across the breadth of Eurasia over the centuries are processes almost entirely hidden from us. One such movement, which is believed to have involved a series of massive migrations, brought into the Pontic region in the 1050s the nomadic confederacy known to the Byzantines as the Cumans (Κουμανοι), to the Hungarians as the Kún, to the Muslims as the Qipchāq, to the Rus' as the Polovtsy, and to the Germans as the Valwen or Falones. The newcomers clashed repeatedly with their Hungarian neighbours as well as with the Rus'; in 1213 the Hungarian king András II briefly entrusted a sizeable area of territory to the Teutonic Order so that they might defend his kingdom.

The Cumans were not a united force. Their political organization was a loose one, and different elements allied with one group of Rus' princes against another; Qipchāq/Cuman chiefs and their followers served the twelfth-century Georgian kings as mercenaries; and in 1203 Philip of Swabia, one of the candidates in the struggle for the German crown, employed a body of Cumans.[27] There were even signs that they might succumb to the efforts of Christian missionaries, as when Hungarian Dominican friars in 1228 succeeded in bringing to the font a number of Cuman leaders and Pope Gregory IX created the missionary diocese of 'Cumania'.[28] In the 1230s Dominican missionaries ventured still further afield, in an attempt to make contact with the inhabitants of 'Greater Hungary' (*Magna Hungaria*). Nowadays tentatively identified with Bashkiria (in the Ural region), this – it was believed – was the home of the pagan descendants of that section of the Hungarian people which had remained behind in the east when their brethren crossed the Carpathians in the ninth century.[29]

Although barbarous and unclean races were to be found even within Western Europe, where by the twelfth century the Frankish aristocracy and clergy were coming to regard even Christian Celtic and Slavic peoples as exponents of an inferior culture,[30] the steppe and forest beyond Christendom's eastern frontiers – 'Scythia', to use its Classical designation – represented still more obviously alien terrain, the home of barbarism. Western observers were struck by the near-total absence of agriculture and various even less attractive characteristics. In the mid-twelfth century Bishop Otto of Freising had commented on the fact that these regions were untouched by ploughshare or mattock.[31] 'They live like beasts', the Dominicans reported in c.1236 of the people of Greater Hungary; 'they do not cultivate the land, they eat the flesh of mares, wolves and the like, and they drink mare's milk and blood'.[32] Otto of Freising had claimed that the Cumans, like their predecessors the Pechenegs, ate raw flesh, including that of unclean animals.[33] Such features, like the cannibalism imputed to other, fictitious peoples, constitute a literary *topos* with a pedigree stretching back to the Classical world.[34] Other customs that also drew the attention of observers in the Christian West – the burial of live slaves with Cuman chiefs, and oath-taking over a dog cut in two – represented practices that had been current among Inner Asian nomads for centuries.[35] What was not known at this juncture was that the Cuman confederacy and 'Greater Hungary' alike were about to be violently suppressed by a new and immeasurably stronger steppe power whose centre lay almost three thousand miles to the east.

Western Christendom and the wider world

Of the tracts that lay beyond 'Cumania', the Rus' and the Islamic Near East, Latin Christians entertained only the haziest and most inaccurate ideas.[36] To the north-east, the horizon lay around the 'marshes of Maeotis' (the name given to the Sea of Azov) and the 'Riphaean mountains', which were mentioned by Pliny and by Isidore and were believed to divide Europe from Asia.[37] 'India' was a blanket term for the entire land-mass, including Ethiopia, that lay beyond Egypt and Mesopotamia. China, known indirectly to the Romans as the land of a silk-producing people, the 'Seres', had receded from view; it was now a dim memory perpetuated by Western encyclopaedists. A work by Frederick II's astrologer Michael Scot (d. c.1235) admittedly contains an isolated reference to 'Sin' (< Chin), probably gleaned from an Arabic source; but generally the emperor's court was conservative in its geographical ideas.[38]

The West's knowledge of distant parts was derived from two sources: the Bible and the lore of Classical Antiquity. From the canonical Scriptures medieval Christians had acquired a composite picture that incorporated the postdiluvian division of the earth among the sons of Noah (Genesis, ix, 19, and x); the wanderings of Abraham's son Ishmael, an archer whose hand would be against every man, and God's promise to make his descendants into a great nation (*ibid.*, xvi, 10–12, xvii, 20, and xxi, 18); the centrality of Jerusalem (Ezekiel, v, 5, cf. xxxviii, 12; Psalm lxxiii, 12); the eastward deportation of certain tribes of Israel (the 'Ten Lost Tribes') by the Assyrians (II [IV] Kings, xvii, 6, and xviii, 11); and the story of the Three Magi of the Nativity (Matthew, ii, 1–12;

subsequently metamorphosed into kings).[39] That the Apostles had fulfilled Christ's commission to preach the Gospel throughout the world (Acts, i, 8; cf. also Matthew, xxvii, 19–20) was corroborated by the Apocryphal books of the New Testament, which claimed, in particular, that St Thomas had evangelized 'India'. The Scriptures also offered glimpses of a future that involved the obscure but innumerable Gog and Magog, a nation of horsemen (Ezekiel, xxxviii, 1–3, 14–16, cf. xxxix, 1–13), whose advent would usher in the Last Things (Revelation, xx, 7–8).

Most of the geographical writing produced by the ancient world had been lost; nor did geography loom large among the Arabic texts translated into Latin during what is known as the Twelfth-century Renaissance. Of Ptolemy's works, the *Geographia*, already well-known to Muslim scholars, was not rediscovered by the West until 1406 (a Latin translation was completed in 1410); only his astronomical–cosmological work, the *Almagest*, lay to hand by the thirteenth century. This may be symptomatic of a greater interest in astronomy than in geography: the heavenly bodies were seen as exerting a strong influence on the course of earthly events.[40]

Especially striking is the failure to translate – or even, apparently, to notice – the one Arabic geographical work which emanated from within Latin-held territory and might therefore be expected to have bridged a cultural gap. The *Kitāb Rūjār* of al-Idrīsī (*c*.1150), produced at the court of the Norman King Roger II of Sicily, would – on any estimate – have amplified and extended the knowledge of the world's geography available to Western Christians. Yet there is no evidence that anybody read it until the early fourteenth century, when al-Idrīsī's influence can possibly be discerned in the map attached to Marino Sanudo's *Secreta fidelium crucis* (1321).[41] The reason for such neglect may well be that geography was regarded merely as the handmaiden of sacred truth, as illustrating the history found in the Bible; it is no accident that a good many medieval European maps were designed originally as altarpieces.[42] Since the Qur'ān was believed to be devoid of truth, a familiarity with Arabic geography was hardly necessary or desirable.

To the knowledge that emanated from the pagan Classical world, then, the medieval Latin West had access only through mediocre compilations like Pliny's *Natural History*, which was greatly in vogue throughout the Middle Ages, the third-century encyclopaedia of Solinus, and – worse still – the burgeoning congeries of fiction now known as the Alexander Romance.[43] What these works had in common was that the information they contained represented fantasy rather than the fruit of direct observation. In this fashion Latin Christians learned of tracts inhabited by fabulous beasts and monstrous races: the Cynocephali (a dog-headed race) and Panotii (a race endowed with enormous ears) immortalized in the twelfth-century tympanum at Vézelay; the Blemmyae (a people without heads, whose faces were located in their chests); the Monopods; and so on.[44] Sometimes a substratum of genuine historical fact underlay the myth, as in the case of stories about Amazons, which probably derived from the presence of female warriors in ancient steppe societies.[45] Within this category of alien peoples we must include also those races whose inhuman practices put them beyond the pale, like the Anthropophagi or cannibals. The apocryphal account of the campaigns of Alexander the Great, dating probably from the third century AD, not only included these and other fabulous nations, but claimed also that the Macedonian conqueror had enclosed behind an impenetrable barrier certain barbarous and unclean races, to prevent them overrunning and contaminating the civilized lands.[46]

We might expect that the early Church would frown upon learning borrowed from the pagan world, but there were Christian ecclesiastics, beginning with patristic writers like Jerome, who took such knowledge on board and sought to harmonize it with the history and geography that were to be gleaned from the Bible. Although he appears to have been agnostic on the existence of monstrous races, Augustine of Hippo (d. 430), destined to become one of the most influential writers for the Middle Ages, thought that they demonstrated the power of God.[47] The *Etymologiae* of Isidore, bishop of Seville (d. 636), which also came to wield considerable authority, incorporated details from Solinus about the fabulous races and marvels of the East. It should be stressed, therefore, that for some centuries to come in the Latin world the monstrous peoples were a part of reality: eighth- and ninth-century churchmen seem to have anticipated meeting Cynocephali in the course of mission to the Baltic and beyond, and were concerned to establish whether or not they were human and hence capable of being saved.[48]

The monsters hallowed by a venerable tradition were not the East's only inhabitants. The most recent addition to the storehouse of Western European knowledge was the legend associated with the name of Prester John. In view of their geographical isolation and the inadequacy of Western efforts to aid them, it was natural that the Latin population of Palestine and Syria should be on the alert for the appearance of Christian allies in the East. At some point prior to the 1140s rumours began to spread of the existence of a Christian king called John, who was also an ordained priest. The original basis of such reports defies speculation; but by 1146, when Otto of Freising received from a Latin Syrian bishop the fullest information to date concerning Prester John, garbled reports of the Qara-Khitan victory over the Seljük Sultan Sanjar

had caused him to be located beyond Persia, in Central Asia. The Qara-
Khitan were Buddhists, but the Latin world, unaware of the existence
of Buddhism, assumed that the victors were in fact Christians under
the rule of Prester John.[49] This was, in any case, a time of optimism
concerning the status of Christianity in the world. Peter the Venerable,
abbot of Cluny, writing in 1143–4, thought that although a limited part
of the *oecumene* was ruled by Muslims, there were already no regions
without Christian inhabitants; and for Jacques de Vitry, Christians
who lived under Muslim regimes greatly outnumbered the Muslim
populations.[50]

King John's failure to advance further west and reinforce his fellow
Christians in Syria did not cause the Latin world to lose sight of him.
The celebrated 'Letter of Prester John', a Latin forgery which circulated
within Catholic Europe from the 1160s,[51] and was in turn copied, embellished and translated into several vernacular languages over the next
two or three centuries, drew on a great many legendary elements then
current in the West. Among the numerous peoples supposedly subject
to Prester John were not only the fabulous races derived from Pliny and
Solinus but also Gog and Magog. The letter has been seen as having a
primarily didactic and moralistic tone and purpose and as encapsulating
Western visions of the ideal polity.[52] However that may be, it did more
than anything else to ensconce this mythical prince in the popular imagination. In 1217 Jacques de Vitry expressed the hope that 'the numerous Christian monarchs who dwell in the East as far as the territory of
Prester John' would aid the crusaders by attacking the Muslims.[53] Consequently, when in 1221 the crusading leaders heard fresh rumours of
operations against the eastern Muslims by an allegedly Christian army,
they too were easily persuaded to link them with Prester John.

To geographical vagueness was added certainty about the future course
of events. In the seventh century an anonymous (probably Syrian) writer
claiming to be St Methodius of Patara drew upon the prophetic material
in the Bible to weave a circumstantial account of the final era of history.
In his *Sermo* or *Revelations* he foresaw the successive irruptions of the
Ishmaelites, whose domination of the world would last for forty-
nine years and who would threaten Rome, and of Alexander's unclean
peoples, whose defeat would immediately precede the coming of Antichrist.[54] For Pseudo-Methodius the Ishmaelites were represented both
by the Midianites whom Gideon had overthrown (Judges, vi, 24) and
by the Arab Muslim invaders of his own day. He called the wilderness
from which they had emerged 'Ethrib',[55] i.e. Yathrib, the former name
of the Arabian city of Medina, the refuge of the Prophet Muḥammad
and the seat of the first Caliphs. The Arabs themselves came to trace

their descent from Ishmael, and the Muslims would often figure as Ishmaelites in Western European sources.[56] But the fact that the prophecy had thus largely been fulfilled was not always appreciated in a later age. Pseudo-Methodius, whose work was soon translated into Latin, was further popularized in the twelfth century by Peter Comestor, who included a summary of the *Sermo* in his own compendium of sacred history, the *Historia scholastica*, and turned the unclean races into the Ten Lost Tribes.[57] For others, however, they came to be equated with Gog and Magog.[58] By the thirteenth century the idea that world history had entered its final phase before the coming of Antichrist was widely accepted, and Pseudo-Methodian prophecy – either directly or through the medium of Peter Comestor – wielded among Western Christians an authority second only to that of Scripture itself and of the Church Fathers: more than 200 Latin manuscripts of the work have come down to us from the Middle Ages.[59]

Discord within the West

By 1240, then, Latin Christendom stretched from the Atlantic to the Bosphorus and the River Bug and from the Arctic Circle to southern Palestine. Within the past fifty years it had come to include parts of the eastern Baltic littoral, Lesser Armenia, Cyprus, Constantinople and much of mainland Greece, and (if only temporarily) Bulgaria, and was making inroads among the nomads of the Pontic steppe. Despite local setbacks in the Baltic, and disappointments or even major crises in the Near East, the West was expansive and aggressive: more optimistic than before about the reunion of the churches, and confident in the knowledge that its military enterprises were ultimately sanctioned by God. Defeat could be written off time and again as the inevitable, and even desirable, consequence of sin (*peccatis exigentibus*) whereby God tested His faithful; remarkably few in the West questioned the tradition of sacred violence which had become firmly established by 1200.[60] The defence of the Holy Land – viewed as Christ's own patrimony – appeared the solemn duty of the kings, nobles and knights of the West.[61] The eight decades following the Third Crusade (1191–2) witnessed more frequent major expeditions in aid of Syria and Palestine, and closer links between them and Western Europe, than had most of the twelfth century. Innocent III was the first pope to require a report on political conditions in the Near East from the Latin patriarch of Jerusalem.[62]

Early in the thirteenth century, it became permissible to commute a vow made to fight in the Holy Land, or another theatre, for the purpose of participating in a crusade elsewhere, as the institutions of crusading were extended beyond the Muslims or Baltic pagans, to enemies even within the Christian fold. [63] Thus the violent suppression of the Cathar heretics in southern France was being advocated at the Third Lateran Council in 1179, though without any practical consequences until 1208, when Pope Innocent III proclaimed the Albigensian Crusade. Although the Fourth Crusade was not actually launched against the Greeks, its outcome meant that they rapidly became a logical and legitimate target of future crusading activity. Popes Honorius III and Gregory IX, faced with Nicaean irredentism, authorized expeditions to prop up the ailing Latin regime at Constantinople, though this did not prevent the loss of the city in 1261.

Holy violence against Christian rulers within Western Europe who oppressed the Church or obstructed papal policy (the 'political crusade', to use the common but unsatisfactory term), is usually associated with the kingdom of Sicily, which had been held as a papal fief since its seizure from the Muslims; and the association grew stronger once the acquisition of the Sicilian crown in 1194 by the Hohenstaufen dynasty, which ruled the Holy Roman Empire, threatened the papacy with en-circlement. There were also disputes over territory in central Italy, and papal-imperial rivalry was given additional edge by the emperor's univer-salist claims. The Emperor Frederick II, who had added to the German and Sicilian crowns that of Jerusalem (through marriage) in 1225, came to appear a formidable menace to the well-being of the papacy and of the Church at large. Having been excommunicated by Gregory IX in 1239, he marched on Rome in the following year, but was obliged to withdraw when the pope fortified the resistance of its populace by parading round the city the sacred relics of Saints Peter and Paul. This was the beginning of the crusade against Frederick, which lasted, with intervals, for the rest of his life. When Gregory convened a council to depose him, the Emperor in May 1241 simply intercepted the ships that carried French and Italian prelates on their way to the council and threw them into prison, where many underwent great hardship.[64] Frederick was again excommunicated and deposed by Pope Innocent IV at the First Council of Lyons in 1245, and his German opponents elected in succession two anti-kings, Henry Raspe (d. 1247), landgrave of Thuringia, and Count William of Holland. When Frederick died in 1250, Sicily was the only one of his territories over which he enjoyed undisputed control.

A consequence of the broadening of the crusading institution was the existence of simultaneous campaigns against quite different enemies on a number of fronts. At the end of 1240, for instance, four distinct cru-sades were in operation (not counting the Spanish theatre, which tended to attract international participation only rarely, or southern France, where a single Cathar stronghold still held out). In the Holy Land, the English prince Richard of Cornwall had just assumed the command of English and French crusaders; a major expedition had left France for 'Romania' in 1239;[65] on the Rus' frontier, the Swedes, Danes and Teutonic Knights were each engaged in a local conflict with Novgorod (though it is debatable whether any of them were responding to the pope's summons);[66] and in central Europe the pope had recently launched the crusade against the Emperor, for which in February 1241 he authorized the commutation of vows in Hungary.[67]

Whatever the ideological origins of, and justification for, crusades against Christian rulers within Latin Europe, they probably attracted a greater degree of criticism from contemporaries, although this is open to dispute. One of the grounds on which they were condemned was that they deflected much-needed military assistance from the hard-pressed Latin states in Palestine and Syria. Victory over Louis IX's crusade in 1250 precipitated a *coup d'état* in Egypt, displacing its Ayyubid rulers in favour of a series of sultans chosen from among the ranks of their Turkish military slave (*mamlūk*) élite. The new regime came to display a greater vigour and a stronger determination to expel the Franks from Syria and Palestine than had its predecessors.[68] From the early 1260s onwards, the Franks were called upon to withstand, with minimal aid from overseas, a series of hammer-blows by the Mamlūk Sultans, who destroyed the principality of Antioch (1268) and the county of Tripoli (1289) and in 1291 took Acre and obliterated the last vestiges of the kingdom of Jerusalem. And indeed it is undeniable that these very same years witnessed substantial crusading efforts against Christian powers in the western Mediterranean. In 1266 the pope sanctioned an expedition headed by Louis IX's brother, Charles of Anjou, which overthrew the Hohenstaufen king of Sicily, Frederick II's illegitimate son Manfred, and installed an Angevin government; and when Sicily rose against Charles (1282) and the king of Aragon championed the rebels' cause, the papacy launched the 'War of the Vespers' against the Aragonese from 1283 onwards.[69]

One further objection could have been levelled at holy wars against Christian lay powers: that they promised to heighten and perpetuate disunity within the West at precisely the moment when it confronted a greater menace than at any time since the Hunnish advance in the fifth century. Describing the events of 1241, an anonymous chronicler in Trier, on the western fringes of Frederick II's dominions, commented on the Emperor's concern to prevent the papal bull of excommunication from being disseminated throughout Germany. Frederick had issued instructions to his officers there to make every effort to intercept papal messengers. Whether these efforts were successful we never learn, because the chronicler's attention is suddenly and dramatically distracted by events further east. 'And behold', he continues, 'the Almighty sent messengers, but with a quite different message.'[70]

Notes

1. For an excellent treatment of the expansion of 'Frankish' culture, see Robert Bartlett, *The Making of Europe. Conquest, Colonization and Cultural Change 950–1350* (Harmondsworth, 1993), especially chaps 1, 3 and 10. On Christianization, see Richard Fletcher, *The Conversion of Europe from Paganism to Christianity 371–1386 AD* (London, 1997), chaps 12–15.
2. John H. Pryor, *Geography, Technology and War. Studies in the Maritime History of the Mediterranean, 649–1571* (Cambridge, 1988), chaps 5–6.
3. See Sven Ekdahl, 'Horses and crossbows: two important warfare advantages of the Teutonic Order in Prussia', in Helen Nicholson, ed., *The Military Orders,* II. *Welfare and Warfare* (Aldershot, 1998), pp. 119–51; Bartlett, *Making of Europe*, chap. 3 *passim*.
4. E. Fügedi, 'Das mittelalterliche Königreich Ungarn als Gastland', in Walter Schlesinger, ed., *Die deutsche Ostsiedlung als Problem der europäischen Geschichte: Reichenau-Vorträge, 1970–72*, Vorträge und Forschungen 18 (Sigmaringen, 1975), pp. 471–507, and repr. in Fügedi, *Kings, Bishops, Nobles and Burghers in Medieval Hungary*, ed. János M. Bak (London, 1986).
5. M.G.S. Hodgson, 'The Ismāʿīlī state', in *CHI*, V, pp. 468–72.
6. W. Barthold, *Turkestan Down to the Mongol Invasion*, 3rd edn, ed. C.E. Bosworth with additional chapter tr. T. Minorsky, GMS, new series, 5 (London, 1968), pp. 373–5. C.E. Bosworth, 'The political and dynastic history of the Iranian world (AD 1000–1217)', in *CHI*, V, pp. 183–4.
7. Jonathan Riley-Smith, 'Government in Latin Syria and the commercial privileges of foreign merchants', in Derek Baker, ed., *Relations between East and West in the Middle Ages* (Edinburgh, 1973), pp. 109–32 (here pp. 109–10). Peter Edbury, 'The crusader states', in *NCMH*, V, p. 596.
8. Rūm: Karl-Ernst Lupprian, ed., *Die Beziehungen der Päpste zu islamischen und mongolischen Herrschern im 13. Jahrhundert anhand ihres Briefwechsels*, Studi e Testi 291 (Vatican City, 1981), pp. 36–8. Ḥamā: Peter Jackson, 'The crusades of 1239–1241 and their aftermath', *BSOAS* 50 (1987), pp. 32–60 (here pp. 40–1).
9. Bernard Hamilton, 'Knowing the enemy: Western understanding of Islam at the time of the crusades', *JRAS*, 3rd series, 7 (1997), pp. 373–87 (here pp. 382–6).
10. Marie-Thérèse d'Alverny, 'La connaissance de l'Islam au temps de saint Louis', in L. Carolus-Barré, ed., *Septième centenaire de la mort de saint Louis. Actes des colloques de Royaumont et de Paris (21–27 mai 1970)* (Paris, 1976), pp. 235–46. Jennifer Bray, 'The Mohammetan and idolatry', in W.J. Sheils, ed., *Persecution and toleration*, SCH 21 (Oxford, 1984), 89–98. Aryeh Graboïs, 'Islam and Muslims as seen by Christian pilgrims in Palestine in the thirteenth century', *AAS* 20 (1986), pp. 309–27. Jean Flori, 'La caricature de l'Islam dans l'Occident

médiéval: origine et signification de quelques stéréotypes concernant l'Islam', *Aevum* 66 (1992), pp. 245–56.

11. Cited in Denys Hay, *Europe: The Emergence of an Idea* (Edinburgh, 1957), p. 26.

12. Penny J. Cole, '"O God, the heathen have come into your inheritance" (Ps. 78.1): the theme of religious pollution in crusade documents, 1095–1188', in Maya Shatzmiller, ed., *Crusaders and Muslims in Twelfth-Century Syria* (Leiden, 1993), pp. 84–111.

13. Jean Richard, *The Crusades c.1071–c.1291*, tr. Jean Birrell (Cambridge, 1999), pp. 295, 303–4. For Joachim's views, see Benjamin Z. Kedar, *Crusade and Mission. European Approaches Towards the Muslims* (Princeton, NJ, 1984), pp. 112–16; other prophecies about the fate of Islam, ibid., p. 136.

14. James D. Ryan, 'Conversion or the Crown of martyrdom: conflicting goals for fourteenth-century missionaries in Central Asia?', in Richard F. Gyug, ed., *Medieval Cultures in Contact* (Fordham, NY, 2003), pp. 19–38 (here pp. 23–4).

15. See, e.g., Hay, *Europe*, pp. 27–36.

16. Jane Sayers, *Innocent III: Leader of Europe, 1198–1216* (London, 1994), pp. 86–7.

17. *VMH*, I, pp. 160–1 (nos. 283, 284). See Christoph T. Maier, *Preaching the Crusades. Mendicant Friars and the Cross in the Thirteenth Century* (Cambridge, 1994), pp. 37–8; T. Senga, 'Ungarisch-bulgarische Beziehungen nach dem Mongolensturm', *Slavica* 24 (1990), pp. 77–90 (here pp. 78–9); Hristo Dimitrov, 'Über die bulgarisch-ungarischen Beziehungen (1218–1255)', *BHR* 25:2–3 (1997), pp. 3–27 (here pp. 14–16).

18. Donald E. Queller and Thomas F. Madden, *The Fourth Crusade. The Conquest of Constantinople*, 2nd edn (Philadelphia, 1997), p. 311.

19. Simon Franklin and Jonathan Shepard, *The Emergence of Rus 750–1200* (London, 1996), p. 367. Márta Font, 'Ungarische Vornehmen in der Halitsch im 13. Jahrhundert', *Specimina Nova Dissertationum ex Instituto Historico Universitatis Quinqueecclesiensis de Iano Pannonio Nominatae* 6:1 (1990 [1992]), pp. 165–74. Eadem, 'Ungarn, Polen und Galizien-Wolhynien im ersten Drittel des 13. Jh.', *Studia Slavica Hungarica* 38 (1993), pp. 27–39 (here pp. 36–7).

20. Eric Christiansen, *The Northern Crusades*, 2nd edn (Harmondsworth, 1997), pp. 132–3.

21. For a good introduction to the eastern churches, see Bernard Hamilton, *The Christian World of the Middle Ages* (Stroud, 2003), chap. 5; on relations with the Latin Church, Richard, *La papauté*, pp. 4–12. The standard work is Anna-Dorothee von den Brincken, *Die „Nationes Christianorum Orientalium" im Verständnis der lateinischen Historiographie von der Mitte des 12. bis in die zweite Hälfte des 14. Jahrhunderts*, Kölner Historische Abhandlungen 22 (Köln, 1973).

22. Bernard Hamilton, *The Latin Church in the Crusader States*, I. *The Secular Church* (London, 1980), pp. 332–47. T.S.R. Boase, 'The history of the kingdom', in Boase, ed., *The Cilician Kingdom of Armenia* (Edinburgh, 1978), pp. 17–19. Richard, *La papauté*, pp. 48–51.

23. Jacques de Vitry, 'Historia Orientalis', in J. Bongars, ed., *Gesta Dei per Francos*, 2 vols in 3 (Hannover, 1611; repr. Toronto, 1972), I:2, pp. 1141–2; for his view of the Georgians, see his 'Historia Hierosolomitana', ibid., p. 1095.

24. Françoise Micheau, 'Croisades et croisés vus par les historiens arabes chrétiens d'Égypte', in Raoul Curiel and Rika Gyselen, eds, *Itinéraires d'Orient. Hommages à Claude Cahen*, Res Orientales 6 (Bures-sur-Yvette, 1994), pp. 169–85.
25. For this letter, which is preserved by two contemporaries, the Cistercian Aubry of Trois-Fontaines and the Benedictine Matthew Paris, see CICO, III, pp. 306–7 (no. 227a).
26. See generally Peter B. Golden, 'The peoples of the south Russian steppes', in Denis Sinor, ed., *The Cambridge History of Early Inner Asia* (Cambridge, 1990), pp. 270–84.
27. Peter B. Golden, 'The Qıpčaqs of medieval Eurasia: an example of stateless adaptation in the steppes', in Gary Seaman and Daniel Marks, eds, *Rulers from the Steppe. State Formation on the Eurasian Periphery* (Los Angeles, 1991), pp. 132–57, and repr. in Golden, *Nomads and Their Neighbours in the Russian Steppe. Turks, Khazars and Qipchaqs* (Aldershot, 2003). Idem, 'Nomads and their sedentary neighbors in pre-Činggisid Eurasia', *AEMA* 7 (1987–91), pp. 41–81 (here pp. 60–73, 79–81). Eduard Winkelmann, *Philipp von Schwaben und Otto IV. von Braunschweig*, 2 vols (Leipzig, 1873–8), I, p. 288. Nora Berend, *At the Gate of Christendom: Jews, Muslims and 'Pagans' in Medieval Hungary, c.1000–c.1300* (Cambridge, 2001), pp. 68–70.
28. V.T. Pashuto, 'Polovetskoe episkopstvo', in W. Steinitz *et al.*, eds, *Ost und West in der Geschichte des Denkens und der kulturellen Beziehungen. Festschrift für Eduard Winter zum 70. Geburtstag*, Quellen und Studien zur Geschichte Osteuropas 15 (Berlin, 1966), pp. 33–40. Richard, *La papauté*, pp. 23–6. Berend, *At the Gate*, pp. 213–17.
29. For these missions, see Mary Dienes, 'Eastern missions of the Hungarian Dominicans in the first half of the thirteenth century', *Isis* 27 (1937), pp. 225–41; Denis Sinor, 'Un voyageur du treizième siècle: le Dominicain Julien de Hongrie', *BSOAS* 14 (1952), pp. 589–602, repr. in Sinor, *Inner Asia*.
30. W.R. Jones, 'The image of the barbarian in medieval Europe', *CSSH* 13 (1971), pp. 376–407. Robert Bartlett, *Gerald of Wales 1146–1223* (Oxford, 1982), chap. 6, 'The face of the barbarian'. Anngret Simms, 'Core and periphery in medieval Europe: the Irish experience in a wider context', in William J. Smyth and Kevin Whelan, eds, *Common Ground. Essays on the Historical Geography of Ireland presented to T. Jones Hughes* (Cork, 1988), pp. 22–40.
31. *Ottonis et Rahewini Gesta Friderici Imperatoris*, ed. G. Waitz, SRG (Hannover, 1884), p. 40, and tr. C.C. Mierow, *The Deeds of Frederick Barbarossa* (New York, 1953), p. 66.
32. Richardus, 'De facto Ungarie Magne', in Heinrich Dörrie, ed., 'Drei Texte zur Geschichte der Ungarn und Mongolen. Die Missionsreisen des fr. Iulianus O.P. ins Ural-Gebiet (1234/5) und nach Rußland (1237) und der Bericht des Erzbischofs Peter über die Tartaren', *Nachrichten der Akademie der Wissenschaften in Göttingen, phil.-hist. Klasse* (1956), no. 6, pp. 125–202 (here p. 157).
33. 'Ottonis episcopi Frisingensis chronicon', *MGHS*, XX, pp. 233–4; tr. C.C. Mierow, *The Two Cities* (New York, 1928), p. 371.
34. T.E.J. Wiedemann, 'Between men and beasts: barbarians in Ammianus Marcellinus', in I. Moxon *et al.*, eds, *Past Perspectives: Studies in Greek and Roman Historical Writing* (Cambridge, 1986), pp. 189–201. László Vajda,

'Ruchlose und heidnische Dinge', in Erhard F. Schiefer, ed., *Explanationes et Tractationes Fenno-Ugricae in Honorem Hans Fromm Sexagenarii A.D. VII Kal. Jun. Anno MCMLXXIX Oblatae* (Munich, 1979), pp. 373–404.

35. Aubry of Trois-Fontaines, 'Cronica', *MGHS*, XXIII, p. 950. Denis Sinor, 'Taking an oath over a dog cut in two', in Géza Bethlenfalvy et al., eds, *Altaic Religious Beliefs and Practices. Proceedings of the 33rd Meeting of the Permanent International Altaistic Conference, Budapest June 24–29, 1990* (Budapest, 1992), pp. 301–7, and repr. in Sinor, *Studies in Medieval Inner Asia* (Aldershot, 1997).

36. The best introduction to the twelfth-century West's view of the outside world is J.R.S. Phillips, *The Medieval Expansion of Europe*, 2nd edn (Oxford, 1998), pp. 3–23; see also his 'The outer world of the European Middle Ages', in Stuart B. Schwarz, ed., *Implicit Understandings. Observing, Reporting and Reflecting on the Encounters between Europeans and Other Peoples in the Early Modern Era* (Cambridge, 1994), pp. 23–63.

37. Pentti Aalto and Tuomo Pekkanen, *Latin Sources on North-Eastern Eurasia*, 2 vols, AF 44 and 57 (Wiesbaden, 1975–80), II, pp. 15–24 (Maeotis), 52–8 (*Montes Riphaei*), give references from Antiquity. Ivar Hallberg, *L'extrême orient dans la littérature et la cartographie de l'Occident des XIIIᵉ, XIVᵉ et XVᵉ siècles. Étude sur l'histoire de la géographie* (Göteborg, 1907), pp. 325–6, 434–5, includes also medieval citations.

38. For a good introduction, see Folker E. Reichert, *Begegnungen mit China. Die Entdeckung Ostasiens im Mittelalter*, BGQM 15 (Sigmaringen, 1992), pp. 65–8. On Michael Scot, see idem, 'Geographie und Weltbild am Hofe Friedrichs II.', *DA* 51 (1995), pp. 433–91 (here pp. 452, 472–3); on Frederick's court, ibid., pp. 479–81.

39. For the development of these two legends, see respectively Tudor Parfitt, *The Lost Tribes of Israel. The History of a Myth* (London, 2002), chap. 1, and Richard C. Trexler, *The Journey of the Magi. Meanings in History of a Christian Story* (Princeton, NJ, 1997).

40. A point well made by J.K. Hyde, 'Ethnographers in search of an audience', in his *Literacy and Its Uses. Studies on Late Medieval Italy*, ed. Daniel Waley (Manchester, 1993), pp. 162–216 (here pp. 165–6).

41. T. Lewicki, 'Marino Sanudos Mappa Mundi und die Weltkarte von Idrisi', *RO* 38 (1976), pp. 169–98.

42. Anna-Dorothee von den Brincken, 'Mappa mundi und Chronographia. Studien zur *imago mundi* des abendländischen Mittelalters', *DA* 24 (1968), pp. 118–86 (here pp. 122–3). Eadem, '„... Ut describeretur universus orbis". Zur Universalkartographie des Mittelalters', in Albert Zimmermann and Rudolf Hoffmann, eds, *Methoden in Wissenschaft und Kunst des Mittelalters*, Miscellanea Mediaevalia 7 (Berlin, 1970), pp. 249–78.

43. Marjorie Chibnall, 'Pliny's Natural History and the Middle Ages', in T.A. Dorey, ed., *Greek and Latin Studies. Classical Literature and its Influence: Empire and Aftermath. Silver Latin II* (London, 1975), pp. 57–78. George Cary, *The Medieval Alexander* (Oxford, 1956).

44. Rudolf Wittkower, 'Marvels of the East', *Journal of the Warburg and Courtauld Institutes* 5 (1942), pp. 159–97, repr. in his *Allegory and the Migration of Symbols* (London, 1977), pp. 45–74. John Block Friedman, *The Monstrous Races*

in Medieval Art and Thought (Cambridge, MA, 1981). Valerie I.J. Flint, 'Monsters and the Antipodes in the early Middle Ages and Enlightenment', *Viator* 15 (1984), pp. 65–80, repr. in her *Ideas in the Medieval West: Texts and Their Contexts* (London, 1988). Rudolf Simek, *Heaven and Earth in the Middle Ages*, tr. Angela Hall (Woodbridge, 1996), chap. 7.

45. Jeannine Davis-Kimball, 'Warrior women of the Eurasian steppes', *Archaeology* 50:1 (1997), pp. 45–8. K.F. Smirnov, 'Une "Amazone" du IVe siècle avant n.e. sur le territoire du Don', *Dialogues d'Histoire Ancienne* 8 (1982), pp. 121–41.

46. Andrew Runni Anderson, *Alexander's Gate, Gog and Magog, and the Inclosed Nations* (Cambridge, MA, 1932).

47. Cited in Mary B. Campbell, *The Witness and the Other World. Exotic European Travel Writing, 400–1600* (Ithaca, NY, and London, 1988), p. 77.

48. Ian Wood, *The Missionary Life. Saints and the Evangelisation of Europe, 400–1050* (Harlow, 2001), pp. 134, 251–3.

49. C.F. Beckingham, 'The achievements of Prester John', in Charles F. Beckingham and Bernard Hamilton, eds, *Prester John, the Mongols and the Ten Lost Tribes* (Aldershot, 1996), pp. 1–22 (here pp. 2–6).

50. Peter the Venerable, *Adversus Iudeorum inveteratam duritiem*, ed. Yvonne Friedman, CCCM 58 (Turnhout, 1985), p. 109; Dominique Iogna-Prat, *Order and Exclusion. Cluny and Christendom Face Heresy, Judaism, and Islam (1000–1150)*, tr. Graham Robert Edwards (Ithaca, NY, 2002), p. 299. Jacques de Vitry, *Epistolae*, ed. R.B.C. Huygens, *Lettres de Jacques de Vitry (1160/70–1240) évêque de Saint-Jean-d'Acre* (Leiden, 1960), p. 95.

51. For a persuasive hypothesis, see Bernard Hamilton, 'Prester John and the Three Kings of Cologne', in H. Mayr-Harting and R.I. Moore, eds, *Studies in Medieval History Presented to R.H.C. Davis* (London and Ronceverte, 1985), pp. 177–91, and repr. in Beckingham and Hamilton, *Prester John*, pp. 171–85.

52. Leonardo Olschki, 'Der Brief des Presbyters Johannes', *HZ* 144 (1931), pp. 1–14. Martin Gosman, 'Le Royaume de Prêtre Jean: l'interprétation d'un bonheur', in Danielle Buschinger, ed., *L'idée de bonheur au Moyen Age. Actes du colloque d'Amiens de mars 1984*, Göppinger Arbeiten zur Germanistik 414 (Göppingen, 1990), pp. 213–23. Hilário Franco, Jr, 'La construction d'une utopie: l'Empire de Prêtre Jean', *JMH* 23 (1997), pp. 211–25. For the provenance of the various elements, see Ulrich Knefelkamp, 'Der Priesterkönig Johannes und sein Reich – Legende oder Realität?', *JMH* 14 (1988), pp. 337–55.

53. Jacques de Vitry, *Epistolae*, p. 95; for the date of this letter, see ibid., pp. 52–3. For an earlier reference to Christian kingdoms 'beyond the Medes and Persians', clearly influenced by the 'Letter of Prester John', see Bernard Hamilton, 'Continental drift: Prester John's progress through the Indies', in Beckingham and Hamilton, *Prester John*, pp. 237–69 (here p. 240).

54. E. Sackur, *Sibyllinische Texte und Forschungen. Pseudomethodius, Adso und die Tiburtinische Sibylle* (Halle, 1898), new edn by Raoul Manselli (Turin, 1976), pp. 66–75, 80–93.

55. Ibid., pp. 68, 80, 84.

56. See Rudi Paret, 'Ismāʿīl', *Enc.Isl.*²

57. Anderson, *Alexander's Gate*, pp. 65–70.

58. Raoul Manselli, 'I popoli immaginari: Gog e Magog', in *Popoli e paesi nella cultura altomedievale, 23–29 aprile 1981*, II (Spoleto, 1983), pp. 487–522. But note the *caveat* in Scott D. Westrem, 'Against Gog and Magog', in Sylvia Tomasch and Sealy Gilles, eds, *Text and Territory: Geographical Imagination in the European Middle Ages* (Philadelphia, 1998), pp. 54–75, against over-generalizations regarding the role (if any) envisaged for Gog and Magog.

59. Beryl Smalley, *The Study of the Bible in the Middle Ages*, 3rd edn (Oxford, 1983), pp. 178–9. Kedar, *Crusade and Mission*, pp. 29–30. There is a good *aperçu* in Klopprogge, *Ursprung*, chap. 3. Mss.: Hannes Möhring, *Der Weltkaiser der Endzeit. Entstehung, Wandel und Wirkung einer tausendjährigen Weissagung*, Mittelalter-Forschungen 3 (Stuttgart, 2000), pp. 321–2 and n.1.

60. Keith Haines, 'Attitudes and impediments to pacifism in medieval Europe', *JMH* 7 (1981), pp. 369–88.

61. J.S.C. Riley-Smith, 'Peace never established: the case of the kingdom of Jerusalem', *TRHS*, 5th series, 28 (1978), pp. 87–102 (here pp. 89–96).

62. Richard, *Crusades*, p. 296.

63. For the extension of the crusade against enemies other than the Muslims, see Jonathan Riley-Smith, *What Were the Crusades?*, 3rd edn (Basingstoke, 2002), esp. pp. 4–5, 16–22; on commutation, Maureen Purcell, *Papal Crusading Policy: The Chief Instruments of Papal Crusading Policy and Crusade to the Holy Land from the Final Loss of Jerusalem to the Fall of Acre, 1244–1291*, Studies in the History of Christian Thought 11 (Leiden, 1975), pp. 99–114.

64. See David Abulafia, *Frederick II. A Medieval Emperor* (London, 1988), pp. 346–7.

65. Richard Spence, 'Gregory IX's attempted expeditions to the Latin empire of Constantinople: the crusade for the union of the Latin and Greek Churches', *JMH* 5 (1979), pp. 163–76. See also Maier, *Preaching the Crusades*, p. 38.

66. Christiansen, *Northern Crusades*, pp. 133–4. But cf. Evgeniya L. Nazarova, 'The crusades against Votians and Izhorians in the thirteenth century', in Alan V. Murray, ed., *Crusade and Conversion on the Baltic Frontier 1150–1500* (Aldershot, 2001), pp. 177–95 (here pp. 182–7).

67. Abulafia, *Frederick II*, pp. 315–20, 340–407. *VMH*, I, p. 178 (no. 327) = *MGHEp.*, I, pp. 706–7 (no. 801).

68. Robert Irwin, *The Middle East in the Middle Ages. The Early Mamluk Sultanate 1250–1382* (London, 1986), chaps 1–4.

69. Jonathan Riley-Smith, *The Crusades: A Short History* (London, 1987), pp. 168–73.

70. 'Gestorum Treverorum continuatio quarta', *MGHS*, XXIV, p. 403: *et ecce inmisit Omnipotens nuncios aliquos, at alia nuntiantes.*

chapter 2

A WORLD-EMPIRE IN THE MAKING

Inner Asian nomadism

Before outlining the process whereby the Mongols, under Temüjin (Chinggis Khan; d. 1227), created the largest continuous land empire in world history, it will be as well to consider some general features of Inner Asian nomadic societies. The Pontic steppes (together with their extension beyond the Carpathians into the Hungarian Alföld) formed the westernmost part of the great belt of prairie that stretches eastward as far as Manchuria. These were the lands of nomadic pastoralists – herders of oxen, goats, camels and especially sheep and horses. The nomads' livestock furnished a good deal of what they needed to survive: meat and milk products (including both horse-meat and *qumis*, the alcoholic beverage derived from fermented mare's milk),[1] wool (which was also used to make felt for covering tents) and hides. But the notion that these products conferred self-sufficiency (other than in emergency conditions) is a false one. Pastoral nomadism is now viewed as a continuum with, at one end, transhumant societies who are almost sedentarized and at the other a 'pure' form of nomadism in which the society's needs are supplied exclusively by its livestock. This 'pure' form is a hypothetical construct and has never existed. In practice, Inner Asian nomadic societies required from their sedentary neighbours grain and other agricultural products, manufactures, notably weapons and other metal goods, and luxury items; they needed the products of the forest-dwelling peoples to the north, such as fish and furs. The economy of a tribal society might be mixed. Membership was based on shared political and economic interest, rather than on strict ethnic affiliation or genealogical kinship.[2] Thus the tribe might contain both pastoralists and forest peoples; or the pastoralists might participate in regular, organized hunts to supplement their food stores; or some of the tribe, at the margins or in oasis regions, would engage in agricultural activity; and the tribal territory might contain colonies of metal-workers, who were often craftsmen taken prisoner in battle or raids.

Pastoral nomadism as a way of life has certain characteristics that lend themselves readily to the successful conduct of war.[3] Life in the saddle and exposure to extremes of climate bred a proverbial hardiness and resilience. The complex logistical problems entailed in movement between seasonal pastures provided the entire male population with a valuable military training and discipline, to which the exigencies of the annual winter hunt further contributed. It was a training that began very early, since children were taught to ride and to use the bow from around the age of three. The nomads' skill with the composite bow – a weapon that itself played an important role in their military achievements – was notorious, and access to considerable numbers of horses permitted the creation of a formidably mobile force of mounted archers. Unfortunately, one resource in short supply was the capacity to leave written records, with the result that our view of the nomads is in large measure refracted through the lens of their sedentary neighbours, for whom nomadic greed and brutishness were a byword.[4] The impact of the sedentary culture upon these tribal societies varied considerably: the Chinese distinguished the 'cooked' barbarians close to their frontiers, who were more susceptible to 'civilizing' Chinese influences, from the 'uncooked', whose territories lay further away.[5]

Since the beginning of recorded history, China had been subject to periodic attack by the pastoral nomadic peoples beyond its northern frontiers. On the nomads' side, the aim was to secure those things which they could not obtain by means of trade; the purpose behind their attacks was not necessarily the conquest and occupation of part of the territory of their sedentary neighbours, but to extort the commodities they required, either as tribute or through trade relations. From the vantage-point of successive Chinese governments, nomadic tribal leaders were merely an outlying part of the *oecumene* of which China was the centre, and their subordinate status could be expressed in the conferment of honorific titles. Trade with the herdsmen, for instance in the products of animal husbandry, had to masquerade as the offer of tribute to the emperor; and, since the Chinese were less dependent upon the nomads' goods economically than were the nomads upon theirs, the closure of frontier markets and the severance of trade relations could be deployed as a diplomatic weapon.[6]

The steppe nomads possessed imperial traditions of their own.[7] From time to time various clans would coalesce to form a super-tribal power under the rule of a charismatic royal clan which occupied a recognized sacral area and claimed a mandate from Heaven (*Tenggeri*) to rule the steppe world; the emperor (*qaghan*) possessed a special charisma and enjoyed the good fortune that was evidence of Heaven's choice. In the Orqon inscriptions, the seventh- and eighth-century qaghans of the Turks articulated such hegemonic claims, as did the rulers of the Turkish peoples who inherited their mantle, namely the qaghans of the Khazars, in the western half of the Turkish empire (seventh–tenth centuries), and those of the Uighurs, in the eastern half (744–840). Both the Turks and the Uighurs controlled a sacred centre, the *Ötügen-yish* in the Orqon valley, which seems to have enjoyed a special status in the eyes of the peoples of the eastern steppe.[8] But no further *translatio imperii* followed the overthrow of the Uighur empire at the hands of the Turkish Qirghiz. The victorious ruler did not take the title of qaghan; fugitive Uighur dynasts founded principalities elsewhere, notably in the oasis towns of the Tarim basin, where they rapidly sedentarized and adopted an agrarian economy.

Imperial pretensions did not automatically involve designs upon Chinese territory. The eighth-century Turks had clearly deemed it inadvisable to occupy the lands of the Middle Kingdom.[9] But on occasions, a nomadic power did conquer territory from the sedentary Chinese. In the tenth century the Khitan created an empire that included parts of northern China, from which they expelled the native Sung dynasty, and took the Chinese dynastic name of Liao (907–1125). Their tribal name, through its Arabic and Persian form, *Khitā*, became synonymous with northern China and, as *Chata/Catai* ('Cathay'), would come eventually in Latin Europe to denote China as a whole.[10] Steppe nomads themselves, the Khitan defeated the Qirghiz and brought under their sway several other pastoralist tribes, extending their network of garrisons deep into what is now Mongolia, in a marked departure from the policies of past Chinese regimes. The Khitan occupied the site of the old Uighur capital at Qara Balghasun, but made no use of it, which suggests that their claims to hegemony rested on a different basis.[11]

In the 1120s the Khitan were overthrown by the Jurchen, a Tungusic people from the Manchurian plains. A body of Khitan refugees fled westwards and, as we saw (p. 12), created a new empire in Central Asia, known as the Qara ('Black')-Khitan or 'Western Liao'. Its sovereigns, who bore the style of *Gür-khan* ('world-ruler'), ruled over both nomadic and sedentary elements; they may also have extended their authority over some of the tribes of what is now western Mongolia.[12] The Jurchen, who as the Chin dynasty (1123–1234) took over the Khitan territories in northern China, concentrated on the war with the Sung and advanced even further to the south. They withdrew the steppe garrisons and reverted to the traditional Chinese imperial policy of 'divide-and-rule'. The nomadic tribes who had been subject to the Khitan were left much more to their own devices until the rise of the Mongols under Chinggis Khan.[13]

Various theories have been advanced to account for the periodic emergence of steppe confederacies. The problem is that the great majority of them – the notion, for instance, that climatic changes produce either lusher pastures, and hence an increase in the nomadic population, or desiccation, and hence migrations in search of superior grazing grounds – are not susceptible of proof.[14] Professor Barfield, however, has pointed to the close link between the political development of the nomadic pastoralists and the proximity of powerful sedentary neighbours. It was believed at one time that more aggressive polities arose in the steppe at a time of Chinese weakness. But the preference for peaceful extortion over war – what Barfield calls the 'outer frontier policy' of the nomads – implies, rather, a correlation between Chinese strength and steppe pastoralist aggression. The nomads sought to prop up a weak Chinese regime, and resorted to war with China only when a stable and resilient government there prevented them from securing what they needed by any other means.[15]

Chinggis Khan and the Mongols

The Mongols are apparently first mentioned among the 'barbarian' peoples beyond the northern frontier of China in texts of the T'ang era (618–907).[16] They were subsequently subject to the Khitan-Liao empire, but with the advent of the Chin they ceased to lie within the Chinese imperial orbit. Apart from sporadic references in contemporary Chinese records, we possess a number of sources for the history of the Mongols down to the rise of Chinggis Khan in the late twelfth century. The earliest is the *Mongghol'un niucha tobcha'an* (known as the 'Secret History of the Mongols'), an epic narrative commencing with a mythical account of the formation of the Mongol people; the nearest thing we have to an original text is written in the Mongolian language but in Chinese transcription. The original version ended with Chinggis Khan's death and apparently dated from 1228, but interpolations were made later, presumably when an account of the reign of his son and successor Ögödei (1229–1241) was added.[17] It was probably early in the reign of Chinggis Khan's grandson, the qaghan Qubilai (1260–1294), that an unknown author compiled the *Altan debter* ('Golden Book') from records of councils and imperial decrees kept in the treasury. This second Mongolian source has not survived, but was apparently used both by the author of the *Sheng-wu ch'in-cheng lu* shortly afterwards and by a Jewish convert to Islam, Rashīd al-Dīn Faḍl-Allāh al-Hamadānī (d. 1318), the physician and polymath who rose to be vizier to the Mongol ruler of Iran and whose encyclopaedic *Jāmiʿ al-tawārīkh* ('Collection of chronicles'), in Persian, was completed in 1303/4.[18] In addition, the compilers of the *Yüan shih*, the official history of the Mongol Yüan regime in China produced under the Ming dynasty soon after the Mongols' expulsion in 1368, utilized the 'veritable records' of the Yüan era. The occasional detail, lastly, can be gleaned from the reports of visitors to the Mongol world from Latin Europe in the middle decades of the thirteenth century: the Franciscan John of Plano Carpini, who visited the court of the qaghan Güyüg (1246–8) as a papal emissary, the Dominican Simon of Saint-Quentin, who around the same time accompanied another papal embassy to the Caucasus region, and the Franciscan William of Rubruck, who travelled in the Mongol empire in a private capacity, as a missionary, in 1253–5.

It should be noted that none of these works dates from the era of Chinggis Khan himself. But the author of the 'Secret History' may have been one of his most prominent followers, his adopted son Shigi Qutuqu,[19] and the work undoubtedly has the advantage that – for all the problems attached to it – it furnishes us directly with a Mongol standpoint. Rashīd al-Dīn, for his part, did not merely consult Mongol materials now lost, but also derived a good deal of oral information from Bolad Chingsang (*Chʾeng-hsiang*, 'minister'; d. 1313), who in 1287 had accompanied an embassy from the qaghan Qubilai in China and had remained in Persia.[20] The *Jāmiʿ al-tawārīkh* also drew on an earlier Persian work by a Muslim author, the *Taʾrīkh-i jahān-gushā* ('History of the world-conqueror'), which ʿAlāʾ al-Dīn Aṭā Malik Juwaynī completed around 1260 and which includes some brief remarks about the Mongols prior to the rise of Chinggis Khan. Juwaynī, a Persian bureaucrat in the Mongols' service, based some of his material on the oral testimony of Mongol officials whom he met in the course of a visit to the qaghan's headquarters in 1252–3.[21] His work in turn was used by the Jacobite Christian prelate, Gregorius Abu l-Faraj, better known as Bar Hebraeus (d. 1286), who furnishes us with precious information of his own.

In the twelfth century, the Mongols, inhabiting the valleys of the Onon and Kerülen rivers, were by no means the most prominent among the tribes of the east Asian steppe. More powerful were the Naiman, whose pastures lay along the upper Irtysh and on the northern slopes of the Altai range and who may have been of Turkish stock (although their name is Mongolian);[22] indeed, Western European visitors in the 1240s thought that the Mongols had formerly been tributary to the Naiman.[23]

The principal rivals of the Naiman were the Kereyid (Kerait), on the Orqon and Tula rivers, who were probably Mongolian, but whose ruling class may have been largely Turkish.[24] At least as strong as the Mongols were the Merkid, a forest people in the regions south of Lake Baikal, along the lower Selenga, and the Tatars, who nomadized close to the Külün Nor and the Buyur Nor. The Tatars may have played a more prominent role in Inner Asian affairs earlier, in the eighth and ninth centuries, so that both for the Chinese and for Islamic writers further west their name had, it seems, become synonymous with non-Turkish peoples in general, and the Mongols, emerging from the eastern steppe, would naturally be known as Tatars.[25]

The political sophistication of these tribes varied. The Naiman were in contact with the culture of the semi-sedentary Uighurs to the south, from whom they may have borrowed a written alphabet and rudimentary administrative techniques like a chancery, and with the Qara-Khitan empire, whose influence is harder to determine. Both the Naiman and the Kereyid represented more or less stable and cohesive entities under a ruling dynasty of khans, whereas the level of social integration of the Mongols was still that of the clan (*obogh*).[26]

It is a moot point how far we can trust the account given in the 'Secret History' of the immediate ancestors of Temüjin, the future Chinggis Khan. Internal evidence, backed by the report of an envoy from Sung China in 1221, suggests that his father may have been of relatively humble stock.[27] It has been further proposed that the title of qaghan, with its imperial overtones, applied in the 'Secret History' to twelfth-century Mongol leaders like the conqueror's great-grandfather is anachronistic and is designed to promote the legitimacy of Chinggis Khan's newly-founded imperial dynasty. The fragmentary data in Jurchen-Chin sources that speak of a 'great Mongol state' in the 1150s represent, in fact, a distortion by sedentary authors who were unable to conceive of a concentration of military power in terms other than the familiar metaphors of statehood. Such amalgamations of clans as occurred in this early period were temporary affairs, designed purely to maximize success in warfare and the booty that would accrue from it, and did not outlast the campaign: they did not prefigure the Mongol empire of the thirteenth century.[28] In fact, the manner in which many of our thirteenth-century sources allude to the weakness and poverty of the Mongols prior to the rise of Chinggis Khan suggests that their political fragmentation in the twelfth century was a prominent element in their folk memory.[29]

There can be no doubt that the 'Secret History' is much more reliable when it opens a window onto a world dominated by blood-feuds[30] and constantly shifting alliances, in which Chin diplomacy was ever ready to intervene. Temüjin's father Yesügei stole his bride from the Merkid, who retaliated belatedly by abducting Temüjin's wife Börte. Yesügei, whose forebears had been confronted by an alliance between the Tatars and the Chin government, was poisoned by the Tatars, and his son would later wreak a bloody revenge on them by slaughtering all the tribe's adult males. At his father's death, the young Temüjin and his mother and brothers, who represented the Borjigid clan, were deserted by the other Mongol clans, headed by the Tayichi'ud; and the family endured many years of hardship before Temüjin was able to reconstitute Yesügei's following. This he did with the aid of Yesügei's old ally and blood-brother (*anda*), Toghril, khan of the Kereyid, whose friendship and military cooperation were instrumental in his rise to power in the steppe. The two men profited from Chin disillusionment with the Tatar alliance, and overthrew the Tatars in a joint campaign with Chin forces (1202). In recognition, the Chin gave Temüjin a lesser military rank and Toghril the Chinese honorific title of *wang* ('prince'), which was corrupted in the steppe world so that he became known as Ong Khan.

But the relationship between Temüjin and his benefactor grew strained, and in 1203 Temüjin overthrew the Kereyid ruler, who was killed while fleeing through Naiman territory. His forces augmented by those of the Kereyid, the victor next turned on the Naiman, gravely weakened by the feuds between the two sons of its late khan. The Naiman khanate too was destroyed (1204), and only a remnant, headed by Küchlüg, the son of one of the brothers, escaped westwards to take refuge, eventually, in Qara-Khitan territory. Temüjin had already crushed the Merkid. At an assembly (*quriltai*) of princes, princesses and military commanders in 1206, he was proclaimed ruler of the nomadic peoples, under the title Chinggis Khan. It was not until *c.*1218, however, at the time of his great westward expedition, that he selected as his base camp Qaraqorum, a locality close to the Orqon and hence in the region traditionally viewed as the sacred centre of their *imperium* by the Turks and Uighurs; the Franciscan missionary William of Rubruck, who travelled through the empire in 1253–5, when it had grown into a town of sorts, says that the Mongols regarded it as 'royal'.[31]

At this time China was divided among three powers. While the native Sung were still entrenched south of the Yellow River and the Jurchen-Chin dominated the north, the Tanggud, a people regarded by the Chinese as of Tibetan origin, had established in the Kan-su corridor a kingdom known as Hsi-Hsia. Chinggis Khan first gained allies in the strategic intermediate zone along the northern frontier of the Chin empire, notably the semi-sedentary Turkish Önggüd people and those

Khitan who lived under Chin rule,[32] and reduced the Tanggud kingdom to tributary status. In 1211 he embarked on a protracted war with the Chin empire; its former capital, Chung-tu (close to modern Beijing), fell to the Mongols in 1215. Although far greater success ultimately attended the Mongols' operations in China than those of their steppe predecessors such as the Khitan, the reduction of the entire country took a long time. The Chin state was not finally overthrown until 1234, during the reign of Chinggis Khan's son and successor, Ögödei. More than another generation elapsed before the Mongols eliminated the Sung empire in the south (1279). Not long prior to this, the qaghan Qubilai had adopted for his regime the Chinese dynastic style of Yüan (1271) and thus reigned as both Mongol sovereign and Chinese Emperor.

Mongol operations in the west

As early as *c.*1208 Chinggis Khan's attention was being drawn towards Central Asia. By this time, the Qara-Khitan empire was moribund. In the west, its Muslim subordinates repudiated its authority. Chief among them was 'Alā' al-Dīn Muḥammad ibn Tekish, the shah of Khwārazm on the lower Amū-daryā (River Oxus), who seized the opportunity to extend his rule over Transoxiana and Persia. The Mongol victories, moreover, had encouraged the Gür-khan's eastern clients to seek Chinggis Khan's protection, notably the ruler (*iduq-qut*) of the Uighurs of Beshbaligh, who became the first monarch of a more-or-less sedentary state to submit to the Mongols of his own free will (1209). The stability of the Qara-Khitan empire was further undermined by the influx of Naiman and Merkid fugitives in sizeable numbers under the leadership of Chinggis Khan's old enemy Küchlüg, who first married the Gür-khan's daughter and then supplanted him (1211); subsequently, he engaged in hostilities with the Khwārazmshāh. His accession to the throne of the still by no means negligible Qara-Khitan polity alerted the Mongols to a potential threat, and Chinggis Khan sent forces which hunted him down and killed him somewhere in the Pamirs (1218).[33]

Although a Mongol division had, as early as 1209–10, clashed with the forces of the Khwārazmshāh Muḥammad, harmonious relations were briefly established. Chinggis Khan evinced a desire to be on friendly terms, pointing to the trade that was to their mutual benefit; and indeed Küchlüg's activities were a matter of concern to both rulers. But the steady advance of the Mongols made the Khwārazmshāh apprehensive of his new eastern neighbour. He authorized the massacre of a group of merchants, who were acting as Mongol envoys but were suspected of being spies, and brought down upon his head a seven-year campaign

(1218–25), headed by Chinggis Khan in person. The Khwarazmian state was demolished; its principal cities were sacked and left in ruins, and Muḥammad himself died as an abject fugitive on an island in the Caspian Sea (1221). For a time the conqueror lingered in present-day Afghanistan, supervising operations against the shah's son Jalāl al-Dīn, who fled to India.

During Chinggis Khan's final years, Mongol forces were engaged in the reduction of the steppe and forest peoples further to the west. The task was rendered especially necessary, in the case of the Cumans/Qipchāq and the related groups belonging to the Qangli, by their close links with the Khwarazmian state and the shelter afforded to Merkid fugitives.[34] One important detachment active here was commanded by Chinggis Khan's eldest son Jochi. Another was headed by the *noyans* (generals) Jebe (or Yeme) and Sübe'etei, who, in pursuit of the Khwārazmshāh (of whose demise the Mongols were as yet unaware), pushed through northern Persia and northward through the Caucasus before rejoining Chinggis Khan by way of the Pontic steppe as he headed back towards Mongolia. In the course of this expedition, the Mongols ravaged Georgia, defeated the Alans in the Caucasus, and overwhelmed a Cuman/Qipchāq army and its allies among the Rus' princes on the River Kalka (1223); during their homeward journey, however, they themselves suffered a reverse at the hands of the Volga Bulgars.[35]

Chinggis Khan's last campaign was against the Tanggud kingdom, where he died in 1227, just before his generals dealt it the *coup de grâce*. The Mongol empire now stretched from Manchuria to the Caspian and from the Siberian forests to the Hindu Kush. At an early date, Chinggis Khan had apportioned the nomadic peoples among his kinsfolk, who also had their own specified pasturelands – the complex termed in Mongolian *ulus*. The larger of these units went to his four sons by Börte, his chief wife: Jochi, Chaghadai, Ögödei and Tolui. Jochi, who received the westernmost territory, predeceased his father, and his *ulus* was shared out among his numerous sons: of these, Batu effectively founded the Mongol power in the Pontic and Caspian steppes, known to historians as the 'Golden Horde'.[36]

In keeping with the conqueror's own desire, his third son, Ögödei (1229–41), was elected as his successor. While the new qaghan concentrated on the continued war in China, he did not neglect other fronts. Following his enthronement, fresh Mongol forces moved westwards. The noyan Chormaghun headed an expedition to annihilate the remnants of the Khwarazmians in western Persia; their shah, Jalāl al-Dīn, fled and was killed in the mountains of Kurdistan in 1231. Chormaghun proceeded to subjugate Christian Georgia and Greater Armenia (1236–9). Likewise in 1229, a campaign had been launched through the steppe, against not only the Cumans/Qipchāq and Qangli but the Bulgars, the Mordvins, the Bashkirs, and other forest peoples in the Volga–Ural region. Resistance proved tenacious and little progress was made,[37] but it is likely that the imperial government was concerned merely to maintain a military presence on this front for the time being. Lattimore's thesis – that Chinggis Khan sought to eliminate all potential opposition in the steppe prior to embarking on the conquest of China[38] – runs counter to the evidence. Envoys from Sung China who visited Ögödei's court in 1237 thought that Chinggis Khan had deliberately postponed further campaigns against the Qipchāq until the Jurchen-Chin should have been overthrown.[39] It appears that his successor adhered to this policy.

Thus it was not until 1236 that Ögödei despatched a large army – headed in effect by the veteran noyan Sübe'etei but under the nominal command of Batu – to complete the subjugation of the western steppes. Other princely commanders included not only Batu's brothers but the qaghan's own sons Güyüg and Qadan; Büri and Baidar, the sons of his second brother Chaghadai; and Möngke and Böchek, the sons of his youngest brother Tolui. Bulghār was sacked (1237), and the Bashkirs reduced to submission. By the end of 1239 Cuman/Qipchāq resistance was virtually over, and hordes of fugitives poured westwards into Hungary or south into the Latin empire of Romania. The Mongols had also renewed the attack on the north Caucasus region,[40] and mounted a devastating assault on Rus', defeating and killing the Grand Prince Iury II on the River Sit' (1238) and sacking, among other cities, Riazan' (1237), Vladimir-in-Suzdal' (1238) and Chernigov (1239). The spring thaws spared Novgorod from attack, but there is some slight evidence that the Mongols advanced into Karelia, on the fringes of the Baltic region.[41] Kiev, the ecclesiastical centre and metropolitan city of Rus', fell in December 1240, and Batu's forces wintered in the principality of Galicia-Volynia, while Mikhail of Chernigov and Daniil Romanovich of Galicia, who had contested both these principalities and Kiev for some years, fled to Poland.[42] The Mongols were now poised to enter the territory of Latin Christendom.

The Mongol military and administrative machine

Already, when Chinggis Khan's armies burst into the sedentary worlds of northern China and Transoxiana, the 'great Mongol people' (*yeke Mongghol ulus*) comprised not only Mongols but also other peoples of the eastern steppe, notably Tatars, Kereyid, Naiman and Önggüd. Its sway extended, too, over semi-sedentary societies like the Uighurs; and the western campaign would bring back significant numbers of slaves of both sexes, to serve as artisans and concubines.[43] By 1241 peoples of Mongolian type were almost certainly outnumbered by the Turkish nomads who during Ögödei's reign had been rolled up in the Mongol war machine. The conquerors became known in both the Islamic world and Europe as 'Tatars' – possibly, as we have seen (p. 36), a general designation further west for steppe peoples who were not Turks. Politically, the term embraced even client sedentary rulers and their subjects. 'You are now a Tatar like us', the Galician chronicle makes Batu tell Prince Daniil Romanovich when offering him *qumis* in 1246; 'drink our drink'.[44]

Although the Mongol empire had rapidly evolved into more than just a confederacy of steppe- and forest-dwelling peoples, it was governed very much as a large tribal federation. Thus all the peoples it comprised, whether pastoralist or sedentary, were subject to the customary law (*josun/yosun*) of the steppe; all were expected in addition to obey each and every regulation (*jasa/jasagh/yasa*) issued by Chinggis Khan. These *ad hoc* regulations included the conqueror's injunction that his descendants should not favour one religion above any other; but they were largely concerned, it seems, with military matters and the annual hunt.[45] In accordance with steppe tradition, the empire was regarded as the joint possession of the imperial dynasty as a whole. With the reduction of sedentary territories, Mongol princes and princesses received groups of enslaved craftsmen, revenues from particular cities, and sometimes even physical possession of such urban centres.[46] By the end of Ögödei's reign, what Professor Paul Buell has called 'joint satellite administrations', comprising representatives of the qaghan and the princes of the various branches of the imperial dynasty, had been set up for conquered sedentary regions like northern China, Transoxiana and Khurāsān, which lay outside the steppe territories assigned as princely *ulus*.[47]

Chinggis Khan's extraordinary career of conquest, and the ability of his successors to extend his empire still further, rested on a number of foundations. In some measure, Mongol strength sprang from precisely the circumstances that, as we have seen, underlay the vigour of earlier steppe powers. Every adult male was a warrior. Both Juwaynī and the Latin missionary William of Rubruck recognized this – the first when he exclaims that the Mongol forces are 'a peasantry after the fashion of an army . . . [and] an army in the guise of a peasantry', the latter when he contemplates what European peasants might accomplish were they to embrace the Mongols' lifestyle.[48] This might suggest that the Mongols achieved their conquests through sheer strength of numbers. But in fact the population of Mongolia in Chinggis Khan's day has been estimated at around 700,000, on the basis of the total of 129,000 given by Rashīd al-Dīn for the Mongol troops at Chinggis Khan's death. The figure does not include the auxiliaries required from princes who had submitted or (apart from some 20,000 Khitan and Jurchen troops) foreign contingents brought over by defectors.[49] Yet it needs to be borne in mind that Chinggis Khan's military resources were, even at this stage, stretched over a vast area from northern Persia to northern China and absorbed in simultaneous campaigns against major powers like the Chin and the Tanggud. We know, moreover, that the Mongols were adept at spreading an inflated idea of their own strength with a view to intimidating their antagonists.[50] The question whether Mongol forces were numerically superior to those of their enemies must remain unresolved. Their weaponry has certainly been underestimated; the evidence suggests that they soon borrowed both incendiary devices and gunpowder from the Chinese, but not to such an extent as to give them a decided edge over their sedentary opponents (see p. 71 below).[51] In fact, what was decisive in the Mongols' conquests, it seems, was not numbers but the composition of their armies and the impact they made on the enemy.

Most significant as mainstays in the development of the imperial structure were the emergence of the guard (*keshig*) and the partial dismantling of the tribal structure of the steppe. The *keshig* not only protected Chinggis Khan's person and performed the numerous duties associated with the imperial household; it also functioned as a training corps for those given command in the military at large (and hence, at this early stage, employed in governing the empire). As regards military organization, although observers like Juwaynī would comment on the effectiveness of the decimal system of command, in which the pivotal unit was the thousand (*mingghan*), that system did not in fact represent an innovation, having long been a feature of the armies of steppe confederacies and latterly of both the Khitan and the Jurchen.[52] Similarly, the rigorous discipline enforced within the Mongol army, which made a profound impression on contemporary observers, is unlikely to have surpassed the discipline prevalent in the ranks of the Jurchen-Chin;[53] though it does seem that the Mongols' military operations were accompanied by extremely careful strategic planning and involved adhesion to the most rigid timetable.[54] What made the Mongol military machine more cohesive was that the tribes which had mounted the most strenuous opposition, like the Tatars, the Merkid, the Kereyid and the Naiman, were systematically broken up and divided among new military units. Peoples who had submitted more or less readily were left intact; but even they were usually placed under officers from other tribes. Military commanders, personally selected by the qaghan, owed their appointments to ability and not to their status in the tribal hierarchy. By these means, the steppe nomads were welded into a single 'Mongol' people; allegiance to the imperial dynasty did not simply transcend but superseded the old tribal and clan affiliations, and in large measure neutralized the centrifugal tendencies that had led to the disintegration of previous steppe powers.[55]

The cohesiveness of the Mongol military stood in sharp contrast with the disunity of their enemies, which Chinggis Khan and his successors took care to exploit. The political fragmentation of early thirteenth-century Rus' under the prolific Riurikid dynasty is notorious.[56] But division also characterized the two most formidable polities confronting the Mongols. Jurchen rule was deeply resented by the Khitan still living in the northern borderlands of China, large numbers of whom joined the Mongols or coordinated their own operations against the Chin with those of Mongol commanders. Subsequently, even native Chinese and Jurchen officers and troops defected to the invaders.[57] In western Asia, the Khwārazmshāh's bitter quarrel with the 'Abbasid Caliph (not to mention his lack of success against his infidel neighbour Küchlüg) impaired his capacity to pose as an exponent of orthodoxy and the *jihād*, while the unreliability of significant elements in his recently accumulated dominions undermined his preparations for resistance.[58] By contrast, the religious pluralism that characterized Chinggis Khan's empire (see pp. 41, 45) also served the Mongols well, so that the Gür-khan's Muslim subjects in eastern Turkestan, who had been persecuted by Küchlüg, welcomed them as liberators.[59]

As an act of vengeance for the murder of Mongol envoys, Chinggis Khan's campaign against the Khwarazmian empire was attended by considerable destruction. Rejection of the appeal to accept Mongol rule, moreover, could result in a wholesale massacre. This was especially true where fortified cities were concerned, and where Mongol losses had been heavy or included persons of importance. Two examples will suffice. When Bāmiyān (in present-day Afghanistan) was taken (1221), every living thing was slaughtered because Chinggis Khan's favourite grandson had been killed during the siege. At Kozel'sk, in the Chernigov region of Rus', the fact that three sons of Mongol generals had fallen in the course of the investment prompted a general massacre (1238).[60] The nomadic Mongols did not understand urban culture, and one purpose behind such tactics, of course, may have been to discourage resistance on the part of other towns.[61] Even so, stories such as that retailed by the Muslim chronicler Jūzjānī, about great quantities of human bones and fat strewn on the ground not far from the Chin capital, Chung-tu, have perhaps led historians in the past to exaggerate the extent to which terror was deployed.[62]

The nascent Mongol administration bore the stamp of a number of influences. It has been proposed that Chinggis Khan borrowed a good deal from the Kereyid, of whose khan he had been a protégé during a formative period.[63] But more important for the future development of the empire was the recruitment of officials belonging to semi-sedentary peoples like the Uighurs.[64] It was an Uighur previously in the service of the khan of the Naiman who introduced Chinggis Khan to the Uighur script and, on his instructions, adapted it for the use of written Mongolian. By 1206, a rudimentary secretariat was emerging in the entourage of the Mongol ruler. The role of 'cooked barbarians' from the frontier zone between Mongolia and China, like the Khitan and the Önggüd, should also not be discounted. The influence of the officials of the defunct Qara-Khitan regime who entered the conquerors' service can perhaps be discerned in the Mongol institution of the *jam/yam* (or postal relay-system), in the use of the tablet of authority (*paiza*), and in the office of *darugha[chi]* or *basqaq* (the commissioner in charge of a conquered city, or the 'resident' appointed to the court of a subordinate ruler in order to oversee his activities and supervise the mustering of resources on the Mongols' behalf).[65] We know of two Muslim Turks who waited on Chinggis Khan and undertook, according to the 'Secret History', to initiate the Mongols into 'the laws and customs of cities', by which is possibly meant urban and commercial taxation,[66] and merchants from Inner Asia, for whom the Mongols furnished capital and protection, are known to have played a prominent role in the evolution of the Mongol polity.[67] A system of registration of the nomadic population for taxation purposes, already in existence by 1206, was extended to cover the Mongols' sedentary subjects during Ögödei's reign, beginning with a census of north China in 1236.[68]

The Mongols and religion

The indigenous cultic practices of the Mongols belonged in the category generally (but misleadingly) characterized as shamanism.[69] The role of the shaman (Turkish *qam*; Mongol *böge*) was to mediate between the community and the forces to which life was subject, in order to ensure prosperity or secure guidance. This entailed communication with the world of spirits, invisible powers which dwelt in the forests and particularly in mountains. On this more will be said later (see chapter 10). Although the 'Secret History' provides no evidence for a cult of the sky-god (*Tenggeri*, 'heaven') or any of the other gods whom the

Mongols shared with other peoples of the steppe,[70] there are nevertheless grounds for believing that during the early decades of the conquest era Tenggeri was beginning to take on the characteristics of a supreme and omnipotent deity (allowing, of course, for distortion on the part of outside observers steeped in monotheistic culture).[71]

The Mongols' expansion brought them into contact with Muslims, Buddhists and – in smaller numbers – Manichaeans; but they would undoubtedly have encountered Christianity even prior to their emergence from their homeland. Since at least the eighth century, Nestorian Christianity had been present in the eastern steppe, and Christians are found among the Tatars in the eleventh.[72] Juwaynī believed that the majority of the Naiman were Christians, and even though Bar Hebraeus was probably wrong to identify with the khan of the Kereyid a Turkish ruler converted as early as 1007, Toghril-Ong Khan's immediate ancestors bore names that are unmistakably Christian; the faith had likewise made progress among the Önggüd.[73]

The steppe tradition was one of sycretism and inclusiveness in matters of religion. The early Qara-Khitan sovereigns had treated Muslims with favour and shown reverence towards Muslim learned men ('ulamā).[74] It was Chinggis Khan's decree that his representatives and troops tolerate the practice of all religious faiths (insofar as these did not clash with the customary law of the steppe).[75] But the 'religious class' within each confessional group benefited still further, since the respect accorded to shamans extended to holy men within other religious cultures. The understanding was that they would pray for the imperial dynasty. Rubruck would observe that the qaghan Möngke wanted everyone to pray on his behalf (below, p. 271). In 1222 Chinggis Khan granted immunity from taxation and from forced labour to Taoists of the Ch'üan-chen sect, whose leader waited upon him at his invitation during the campaign in western Asia. The fact that the conqueror was interested in the secret of prolonging life in the strictly biological sense[76] should alert us to the possibilities for misunderstanding on the part of those for whom eternal life had a quite different meaning.

The ideology of world-rulership

Like earlier steppe powers, the Mongols embraced an ideology of universal dominion whereby their sovereigns ruled in the strength of their good fortune and by virtue of a mandate from Heaven (Tenggeri). Most probably Chinggis Khan derived his concept of empire from the Mongols' nomadic precursors like the eighth-century Turks and via the Uighurs: the initial formulae of Mongol diplomatic documents were in

Turkish.[77] The difference, however, was that for the Mongols the mandate came to be valid for the whole world and not just the nomadic tribes of the steppe.[78] All nations were *de jure* subject to them, and anyone who opposed them was thereby a rebel (*bulgha*). In fact, the Turkish word employed for 'peace' was that used also to express subjection (*il/el*): there could be no peace with the Mongols in the absence of submission.[79] The part that Chinese imperial ideas played in this is uncertain, though it should be noted that the Turks and later powers like the Khitan had themselves borrowed ideas from China.[80]

We should guard against the assumption that world-conquest was the Mongols' goal at the very outset, which is implicit, for instance, in Lattimore's thesis (above, p. 40). The 'Secret History' mentions Heaven's mandate to Temüjin only once, and even then puts it into the mouth of the shaman Kököchü (Teb-Tenggeri), and the context is rule over the Mongol *ulus*, i.e. (at that time) the steppe nomads; nothing is said here of world-rulership.[81] It has been proposed that the Mongols came to believe in a mandate of world-dominion only when they found that this was the task in which they were engaged, as no power appeared to be capable of withstanding them.[82] Although Juwaynī (writing *c*.1260) gives the gist of the Mongols' ultimatum to the city of Nīshāpūr in eastern Persia in 1220, in which they claimed to rule the whole world,[83] the earliest direct evidence for the belief in such a programme dates, in fact, from the 1240s. By that juncture it is clear that the Mongols not only believed in a divine mandate to conquer the world but associated this mission with an edict of Chinggis Khan himself;[84] but how accurate this tradition was, we cannot be sure. Although in his first diplomatic overtures to the Khwārazmshāh he allegedly addressed him as 'son', this implies merely that he himself was the senior prince.[85] It is conceivable, of course, that Chinggis Khan aimed initially at nothing more than the subjugation of the steppe nomadic tribes – 'the people of the felt-walled tents', as the 'Secret History' puts it when recounting his enthronement in 1206.[86] This task was not completed by the time he died; but his aspirations may have changed following the Khwarazmian campaign,[87] and his successor, equally, may have conceived of the task in broader terms.[88] Authors like Juwaynī would then have read back into Chinggis Khan's own lifetime concepts that had taken hold only in the intervening period.[89] For what it is worth, an observer in Latin Europe writing as early as 1237 formed the impression that the conqueror had begun to dream of world-conquest in the wake of the rapid collapse of the Khwarazmian empire.[90] The transition, which probably took several years, must have been hastened by the flight of nomadic groups into the lands of sedentary or semi-sedentary peoples, as for instance of Küchlüg into the Qara-Khitan empire and (more particularly) of the Cuman/Qipchāq into Rus' and later into Hungary.

Whatever the case, the ideology of world-dominion found un-equivocal expression in the ultimatums that the Mongols were sending to the Latin West by the mid-1240s. In these documents, which in the Mongol view were quite simply 'Orders of God', the recipient was informed of his place in the Mongol world-empire, was ordered to recognize it by submitting in person and making his resources and troops available to the conquerors, and was warned that persistence in 'rebellion' carried consequences which were no less menacing for being left unspecified.[91] Take, for instance, the most celebrated of these ulti-matums, the letter of the qaghan Güyüg to Innocent IV, brought back by the papal envoy Carpini in 1247:

> In the power of God, all lands, from the rising of the sun to its setting, have been made subject to us. . . . You in person, at the head of the kinglets, should in a body, with one accord, come and do obeisance to us. This is what we make known to you. If you act contrary to it, what do we know? God knows.[92]

Mongol diplomatic subterfuge

Nevertheless, this uncompromising stance could be modified in certain circumstances. In the first place, client princes or private individuals such as merchants sometimes misrepresented the character of Mongol overlordship to an independent ruler in order to persuade him to sub-mit, inflate their own standing with the Mongols and gain rewards: in this way the merchant Shams al-Dīn 'Umar Qazwīnī, bringing an ultimatum to the Seljük Sultan of Rūm, had made light of Mongol requirements and had prevailed upon him to send back a subservient message in 1237.[93] Secondly, and more importantly, the Mongols them-selves, as Carpini would observe, adopted a less harsh tone towards states which lay on the far borders of countries that had not yet yielded, in order that these distant powers might not join the fight against them.[94] More than this, the Mongols were capable of outright duplicity. Chinggis Khan's own rise to power in the steppe had shown the desirab-ility, on occasions, of allying with one people against another, in order to turn against the erstwhile ally later. In completing the reduction of the Chin, Ögödei accepted the help of their Sung enemies, only to clash with them in the following year (1235). During their westward expansion, the Mongols proved adept at splitting a heterogeneous opposition, as in 1222, when Jebe and Sübe'etei, after defeating the Alans in the Caucasus, moved against the Cumans/Qipchāq, whom they had induced to desert the Alans on the grounds of a common nomadic heritage. They essayed a similar tactic, though unsuccesfully, in order to detach the Rus' from their Cuman allies prior to the engagement on the Kalka in 1223.[95]

In particular, it seems, the Mongols exploited the religious susceptibilities of the peoples who lay in the path of their advance, so as to take them at a disadvantage. When reports of the assault on the Khwarazmian empire reached the ears of the leaders of the Fifth Crusade in Egypt (1221), the Mongols were seen – like the Qara-Khitan eighty years previously – as a Christian army on its way to help its coreligionists. Their ruler was known as 'King David' (a title which has yet to be explained), and the crusade leaders forwarded to Western Europe a lengthy, if somewhat romantic, account of his career and conquests, the *Relatio de Davide rege*. He planned to take Jerusalem, and on encountering Christian prisoners among the defeated Muslim troops he released them and sent them to the Mediterranean coast. The Nestorian origin of this tale is clear from the fact that the Catholicus, Yahballaha II ('Iaphelech'), allegedly acted as the Caliph's agent in inciting David to attack the Khwārazmshāh – an improbable role, but one which echoes contemporary Muslim notions that the Caliph had instigated the Mongol invasion of western Asia.[96] In fact, however, the reports that reached the crusaders did not merely represent a distorted perspective on Chinggis Khan's own campaigns, but embodied a pastiche of elements drawn from a number of distinct conflicts during the opening decades of the thirteenth century. They were based in part on the hostilities between the fugitive Naiman (and one-time Christian) prince, Küchlüg, and the Muslim Khwārazmshāh in the preceding few years, and drew in addition upon a series of events in the eastern marches of the Islamic world reaching as far back as 1204.[97] The bishop of Acre, Jacques de Vitry, readily identified David as the son or grandson of the long-awaited Prester John and was active in exploiting the good news in order to boost crusader morale.[98] The impact was reinforced by prophecies current in the crusading army, regarding the simultaneous arrival of Christian monarchs from East and West and the downfall of Islam.[99] The crusaders were sufficiently emboldened to reject the Egyptian Sultan's peace terms and to press ahead with a hazardous offensive up the Nile. As a result, they were defeated and obliged to withdraw from the country.[100] The Fifth Crusade had achieved nothing; nor had the expected Christian allies materialized.

Although these first reports reflected Nestorian – and then Latin – wishful thinking, evidence from other parts of the Christian world suggests that such delusions were fuelled by the Mongols' own tactics in the course of the campaigns of Jebe and Sübe'etei in 1221–3. The Georgian Constable Ivané complained to Pope Honorius III that the Mongols had tricked his people by having a cross carried at the head of their army.[101] According to the Armenian historian Kirakos Ganjakec'i, rumours had preceded them to the effect that they were 'magi' who possessed a portable tent-church and a miracle-working cross and had come to avenge the injuries suffered by Christians at the hands of the Muslims. Thus deceived, the population made no preparations for defence, while one priest and his flock even went to meet the invaders with crosses, only to be massacred.[102] There is a striking echo of this in the description of the Mongols' capture in 1223 of the small town of Novgorod-Sviatopolch, on the western bank of the Dnieper, as transmitted by the Galician chronicle. Here we read that 'the people were not aware of their treachery and came out to meet them with crosses in their hands, but the Tatars slaughtered all of them'.[103] Although nothing is said directly here of the Mongols' carrying a cross or pretending to be Christians, the episode implies that they had employed the same ruse as in Georgia. It must have been tactics of this kind which gave rise to the belief that the divisions of King David's army were each preceded by a cross.[104] The Mongols' intelligence had not failed them. They had presumably learned from the local Muslims that the Georgian army, when on campaign, was in the habit of carrying a cross aloft;[105] they would also have been informed of the reverence in which the cross was held among the Caucasian Alans, to the extent that anyone bearing a cross tied to a spear could allegedly travel in security even among pagans.[106] The question whether the Mongols were at this stage deliberately setting out to dupe the Christian powers among their enemies must perhaps remain open. But the result was, as the Georgian Queen Rusudan put it, that 'we took no precautions against them because we believed them to be Christians'.[107] Similar accusations of duplicity would be levelled at the Mongols during the invasion of Hungary and Poland in 1241.[108] It is important that we do not lose sight of these alternative, less direct, modes of Mongol diplomacy and warfare.

Notes

1. John Masson Smith, Jr, 'Mongol campaign rations: milk, marmots, and blood?', in Pierre Oberling, ed., *Turks, Hungarians and Kipchaks. A Festschrift in Honor of Tibor Halasi-Kun* (Cambridge, MA, 1984 = *JTS* 8), pp. 223–8.

2. Rudi Paul Lindner, 'What was a nomadic tribe?', *CSSH* 24 (1982), pp. 689–711 (here pp. 702–3).

3. See Denis Sinor, 'The Inner Asian warriors', *JAOS* 101 (1981), pp. 133–44, repr. in his *Studies*.

4. Idem, 'The greed of the northern barbarian', in Larry V. Clark and Paul Alexander Draghi, eds, *Aspects of Altaic Civilization II. Proceedings of the XVIII PIAC, Bloomington, June 29–July 5, 1975*, IUUAS 134 (Bloomington, IN, 1978), pp. 171–82, and repr. in Sinor, *Studies*. As unpublished work by Naomi Standen on the 'Five Dynasties' era (907–60) in northern China demonstrates, the nomads had no monopoly of raiding: sedentary powers raided the nomads and each other.

5. See Magnus Fiskesjö, 'On the "raw" and the "cooked" barbarians of Imperial China', *Inner Asia* 1 (1999), pp. 139–68 (though none of his examples is taken from Mongolia).

6. Sechin Jagchid, 'Patterns of trade and conflict between China and the nomads of Mongolia', *ZS* 11 (1977), pp. 177–204, repr. in his *Essays in Mongolian Studies* (Provo, UT, 1988), pp. 3–20; idem, 'The historical interaction between the nomadic people in Mongolia and the sedentary Chinese', in Seaman and Marks, *Rulers from the Steppe*, pp. 63–91. The standard work is now Sechin Jagchid and Van Jay Symons, *Peace, War and Trade along the Great Wall. Nomadic-Chinese Interaction Through Two Millennia* (Bloomington, IN, 1989).

7. For what follows, see P.B. Golden, 'Imperial ideology and the sources of political unity amongst the pre-Činggisid nomads of western Eurasia', *AEMA* 2 (1982), pp. 37–76, repr. in his *Nomads and Their Neighbours*; Thomas T. Allsen, 'Spiritual geography and political legitimacy in the eastern steppe', in Henri J.M. Claessen and Jarich G. Oosten, eds, *Ideology and the Formation of Early States* (Leiden, 1996), pp. 116–35.

8. Larry W. Moses, 'A theoretical approach to the process of Inner Asian confederation', *EM* 5 (1974), pp. 113–22 (here pp. 115–17). Allsen, 'Spiritual geography', pp. 124–5, 127.

9. Thomas J. Barfield, *The Perilous Frontier. Nomadic Empires and China* (Oxford, 1989), p. 148.

10. Paul Pelliot, *Notes on Marco Polo*, 3 vols with continuous pagination (Paris, 1959–73), I, pp. 216–29.

11. Keith Scott, 'Khitan settlements in northern Mongolia: new light on the social and cultural history of the pre-Chingisid era', *Canada Mongolia Review* 1 (1975), pp. 5–28 (here pp. 8–10). Barfield, pp. 170–1. Sechin Jagchid, 'The Kitans and their cities', *CAJ* 25 (1981), pp. 70–88, repr. in his *Essays*, pp. 21–33.

12. The best survey is Michal Biran, 'China, Nomads and Islam: the Qara-Khitan Dynasty (1128–1218)', unpublished Ph.D. thesis, Hebrew University of Jerusalem, 2000; see also Biran, '"Like a mighty wall": the armies of the Qara Khitai', *JSAI* 25 (2001), pp. 44–91; C.E. Bosworth, 'Ḳarā Khiṭāy', *Enc. Isl.*[2].

13. Morgan, *Mongols*, pp. 47–8.

14. Owen Lattimore, 'The geographical factor in Mongol history', in his *Studies in Frontier History. Collected Papers 1929–58* (London, 1962), pp. 241–58 (here pp. 242–4). See further Gareth Jenkins, 'A note on climatic cycles and the rise of Chinggis Khan', *CAJ* 18 (1974), pp. 217–26.

15. Barfield, esp. pp. 49–51, 91–4, 150–1.

16. Louis Hambis, 'L'histoire des Mongols avant Gengis-khan d'après les sources chinoises et mongoles, et la documentation conservée par Rašīdu-d-'dīn', *CAJ* 14 (1970), pp. 125–33 (at p. 126).

17. Igor de Rachewiltz, 'Some remarks on the dating of the *Secret History of the Mongols*', *Monumenta Serica* 24 (1965), pp. 185–206. Gerhard Doerfer, 'Zur Datierung der Geheimen Geschichte der Mongolen', *ZDMG* 113 (1963), pp. 87–111.

18. For the relationship between these works, see Paul Pelliot and Louis Hambis, *Histoire des campagnes de Gengis Khan. Cheng-wou ts'in-tcheng lou* (Leiden, 1951, vol. I only published), pp. xi–xv; William Hung, 'The transmission of the book known as *The Secret History of the Mongols*', *HJAS* 14 (1951), pp. 433–92 (here p. 478).

19. Paul Ratchnevsky, 'Šigi-Qutuqu, ein mongolischer Gefolgsmann im 12.–13. Jahrhundert', *CAJ* 10 (1965), pp. 87–120 (here pp. 114–20); more briefly in his 'Šigi Qutuqu', in Igor de Rachewiltz *et al.*, eds, *In the Service of the Khan. Eminent Personalities of the Early Mongol-Yüan Period*, AF 121 (Wiesbaden, 1993), pp. 75–94 (here pp. 90–3).

20. Thomas T. Allsen, 'Biography of a cultural broker. Bolad Ch'eng-Hsiang in China and Iran', in Julian Raby and Teresa Fitzherbert, eds, *The Court of the Il-khans 1290–1340*, Oxford Studies in Islamic Art 12 (Oxford, 1996), pp. 7–22.

21. J.A. Boyle, introduction to his translation, *The History of the World-Conqueror*, 2 vols with continuous pagination (Manchester, 1958; repr. in one volume, 1997), I, pp. xxx–xxxii, xxxix. See also Boyle, 'Juvaynī and Rashīd al-Dīn as sources on the history of the Mongols', in Bernard Lewis and P.M. Holt, eds, *Historians of the Middle East* (London, 1962), pp. 133–7; although we do not have to believe, with Boyle, that Juwaynī used SH.

22. See S. Murayama, 'Sind die Naiman Türken oder Mongolen?', *CAJ* 4 (1959), pp. 188–98.

23. PC, v, 4, p. 253 (tr. Dawson, p. 19). Benedict Polonus, 'Relatio', §8, in *SF*, p. 139 (tr. Dawson, p. 81).

24. D.M. Dunlop, 'The Keraits of eastern Asia', *BSOAS* 11 (1943–6), pp. 276–89.

25. S.G. Kljaštornyj, 'Das Reich der Tataren in der Zeit vor Činggis Khan', *CAJ* 36 (1992), pp. 72–83. Omeljan Pritsak, 'Two migratory movements in the Eurasian steppe in the 9th–11th centuries', in *Proceedings of the 26th International Congress of Orientalists, New Delhi, 4–10th January, 1964*, II (New Delhi, 1968), pp. 157–63 (here p. 159), and repr. in his *Studies in Medieval Eurasian History* (London, 1981).

26. Thomas Allsen, 'The rise of the Mongolian empire and the Mongol conquest of North China', in *CHC*, VI, pp. 321–4.

27. J. Holmgren, 'Observations on marriage and inheritances [*sic*] practices in early Mongol and Yüan society, with particular reference to the Levirate', *JAH* 20 (1986), pp. 127–92 (here pp. 132–5). Peter Olbricht and Elisabeth Pinks, eds, *Meng-Ta pei-lu und Hei-Ta shih-lüeh. Chinesische Gesandtenberichte über die frühen Mongolen 1221 und 1237*, AF 56 (Wiesbaden, 1980), p. 3.

28. Jean-Philippe Geley, 'L'ethnonyme mongol à l'époque pré-Činggisqanide (XIIe s.). Étude d'ethnologie politique du nomadisme', *EM* 10 (1979), pp. 59–89 (here pp. 65–83).

29. Juwaynī, *Ta'rīkh-i jahān-gushā*, ed. Mīrzā Muḥammad Qazwīnī, 3 vols, GMS 16 (Leiden and London, 1912–37), I, pp. 15–16, 26 (tr. Boyle, *History of the World-Conqueror*, I, pp. 21–3, 36). WR, xvii, 4–5, pp. 207–8 (tr. Jackson and Morgan, p. 124). There are echoes in SH, §254, tr. Igor de Rachewiltz, *The Secret History of the Mongols: A Mongolian Epic Chronicle of the Thirteenth Century*, 2 vols with continuous pagination (Leiden, 2004), I, p. 183; and in Jūzjānī, *Ṭabaqāt-i Nāṣirī* (1260), ed. 'Abd al-Ḥaiy Ḥabībī, 2nd edn, 2 vols (Kabul, 1342–3 H. solar/1963–4), II, p. 99, and tr. H.G. Raverty, *Ṭabakāt-i-Nāṣirī. A General History of the Muhammadan Dynasties of Asia*, Bibliotheca Indica, 2 vols with continuous pagination (London, 1873–81), II, pp. 937–42. See generally Klopprogge, *Ursprung*, pp. 213–14; and for further references, Thomas T. Allsen, *Commodity and Exchange in the Mongol Empire. A Cultural History of Islamic Textiles* (Cambridge, 1997), pp. 12–13.
30. Larry V. Clark, 'The theme of revenge in the *Secret History of the Mongols*', in Clark and Draghi, *Aspects of Altaic Civilization II*, pp. 33–57.
31. WR, xvii, 6, p. 208 (tr. Jackson and Morgan, p. 125); and on Qaraqorum, see Paul Pelliot, 'Note sur Karakorum', *JA* 206 (1925), pp. 374–5, and his *Notes on Marco Polo*, I, pp. 165–9. Cf. also Allsen, 'Rise of the Mongolian empire', pp. 347–8, and 'Spiritual geography', pp. 125–7.
32. Paul D. Buell, 'The role of the Sino-Mongolian frontier zone in the rise of Cinggis Qan', in Henry G. Schwarz, ed., *Studies on Mongolia: Proceedings of the First North American Conference on Mongolian Studies*, Studies on East Asia 13 (Bellingham, Washington, SE, 1979), pp. 63–76.
33. For a revised chronology of these and the events described below, see Paul D. Buell, 'Early Mongol expansion in western Siberia and Turkestan (1207–1219): a reconstruction', *CAJ* 36 (1992), pp. 1–32.
34. For what follows, see Th.T. Allsen, 'Prelude to the western campaigns: Mongol military operations in the Volga–Ural region, 1217–1237', *AEMA* 3 (1983), pp. 5–24 (here pp. 10–13); István Zimonyi, 'The Volga Bulghars between wind and water (1220–1236)', *AOASH* 46 (1992–3), pp. 347–55 (here pp. 351–4).
35. John Fennell, *The Crisis of Medieval Russia 1200–1304* (London, 1983), pp. 64–8. For the Bulgars, see István Zimonyi, 'The first Mongol raid against the Volga-Bulgars', in Gunnar Jarring and Staffan Rosén, eds, *Altaistic Studies. Papers at the 25th Meeting of the Permanent International Altaistic Conference at Uppsala June 7–11 1982* (Stockholm, [1984]), pp. 197–204 (here pp. 197–9).
36. For a fuller discussion, see Peter Jackson, 'From *ulus* to khanate: the making of the Mongol states, c.1220–c.1290', in Reuven Amitai-Preiss and David O. Morgan, eds, *The Mongol Empire and Its Legacy*, Islamic History and Civilization: Studies and Texts 24 (Leiden, 1999), pp. 12–38; also below, pp. 114, 125.
37. Allsen, 'Prelude', pp. 14–18.
38. Owen Lattimore, 'The geography of Chingis Khan', *Geographical Journal* 129 (1963), pp. 1–7.
39. Olbricht and Pinks, p. 209. Cf. also A.M. Khazanov, *Nomads and the Outside World*, tr. Julia Crookenden, 2nd edn (Madison, WI, 1994), p. 236, n.1.

40. Thomas T. Allsen, 'Mongols and North Caucasia', *AEMA* 7 (1987–91), pp. 5–40 (here pp. 17–25).
41. Pentti Aalto, 'Swells of the Mongol-storm around the Baltic', *AOASH* 36 (1982), pp. 5–15.
42. For a detailed survey, see Martin Dimnik, *The Dynasty of Chernigov, 1146–1246* (Cambridge, 2003), pp. 331–58 *passim*.
43. Thomas T. Allsen, 'Ever closer encounters: the appropriation of culture and the apportionment of peoples in the Mongol empire', *JEMH* 1 (1997), pp. 2–23 (here pp. 2–11).
44. *PSRL*, II. *Ipatievskaia letopis'*, 2nd edn (St Petersburg, 1908), col. 807; cf. trans. by George A. Perfecky, *The Hypatian Codex, Part II: The Galician-Volynian Chronicle*, Harvard Series in Ukrainian Studies 16:2 (Munich, 1974), p. 58.
45. D.O. Morgan, 'The "Great *Yāsā* of Chingiz Khān" and Mongol law in the Īlkhānate', *BSOAS* 49 (1986), pp. 163–76 (here pp. 166–8). I. de Rachewiltz, 'Some reflections on Činggis Qan's *jasaɣ*', *EAH* 6 (1993), pp. 91–104.
46. Jackson, 'From *ulus* to khanate', pp. 17–23.
47. Paul D. Buell, 'Kalmyk Tanggaci people: thoughts on the mechanics and impact of Mongol expansion', *MS* 6 (1979), pp. 41–59. The concept of 'joint satellite administrations' was first elaborated in his 'Sino-Khitan administration in Mongol Bukhara', *JAH* 13 (1979), pp. 121–51 (here pp. 141–7).
48. Juwaynī, I, p. 22 (tr. Boyle, I, p. 30). WR, epilogue, 4, p. 331 (tr. Jackson and Morgan, p. 278).
49. Rashīd al-Dīn, *Jāmiʿ al-tawārīkh*, ed. Muḥammad Rawshan and Muṣṭafā Mūsawī, 4 vols with continuous pagination (Tehran, 1373 H. solar/1994), I, p. 592, and tr. Wheeler M. Thackston, *Jamiʿuʾt-tawarikh. Compendium of Chronicles*, 3 vols with continuous pagination (Cambridge, MA, 1998–9), I, p. 272. Ch'i-ch'ing Hsiao, *The Military Establishment of the Yuan Dynasty*, Harvard East Asian Monographs 77 (Cambridge, MA, 1978), n.65 at p. 132. For the population estimate, see N.Ts. Munkuev, 'Zametki o drevnikh mongolakh', in S.L. Tikhvinskii, ed., *Tataro-Mongoly v Azii i Evrope. Sbornik statei*, 2nd edn (Moscow, 1977), pp. 377–408 (here p. 394).
50. PC, vi, 14, pp. 281–2 (tr. Dawson, p. 36).
51. Thomas T. Allsen, 'The circulation of military technology in the Mongolian empire', in Nicola Di Cosmo, ed., *Warfare in Inner Asian History (500–1800)* (Leiden, 2002), pp. 265–93. For armour and other weaponry, see Witold Świętosławski, *Arms and Armour of the Nomads of the Great Steppe in the Times of the Mongol Expansion (12th–14th Centuries)* (Łodź, 1999).
52. Hansgerd Göckenjan, 'Zur Stammesstruktur und Heeresorganisation altaischer Völker. Das Dezimalsystem', in Klaus-Detlev Grothusen and Klaus Zernack, eds, *Europa Slavica – Europa Orientalis. Festschrift für Herbert Ludat zum 70. Geburtstag* (Berlin, 1980), pp. 51–86.
53. Paul Ratchnevsky, *Genghis Khan. His Life and Legacy*, tr. Thomas N. Haining (Oxford, 1991), p. 171.
54. Denis Sinor, 'On Mongol strategy', in Ch'en Chieh-hsien, ed., *Proceedings of the Fourth East Asian Altaistic Conference* (Tainan, Taiwan, 1975), pp. 238–49, and repr. in Sinor, *Inner Asia*.

55. Morgan, *Mongols*, pp. 89–90. İsenbike Togan, *Flexibility and Limitation in Steppe Formations. The Kerait Khanate and Chinggis Khan* (Leiden, 1998), chap. 4, 'The new universal order'. P.B. Golden, '"I will give the people unto thee": the Činggisid conquests and their aftermath in the Turkic world', *JRAS*, 3rd series, 10 (2000), pp. 21–41 (here pp. 22–4).
56. J.L.I. Fennell, 'Russia on the eve of the Tatar invasion', *OSP*, n.s., 14 (1981), pp. 1–13. But cf. the salutary comments of Franklin and Shepard, *Emergence of Rus*, pp. 367–8.
57. Igor de Rachewiltz, 'Personnel and personalities in North China in the early Mongol period', *JESHO* 9 (1966), pp. 86–144.
58. See Morgan, *Mongols*, pp. 52–3; Ratchnevsky, *Genghis Khan*, pp. 123–5, 129–30, 173; Jürgen Paul, 'L'invasion mongole comme "révélateur" de la société iranienne', in Denise Aigle, ed., *L'Iran face à la domination mongole*, Bibliothèque Iranienne 45 (Tehran, 1997), pp. 37–53 (here p. 41, n.16); Golden, '"I will give the people"', p. 29.
59. David Morgan, 'Prester John and the Mongols', in Beckingham and Hamilton, *Prester John*, pp. 159–70 (here p. 161).
60. Kozel'sk: Dimnik, *Dynasty of Chernigov*, pp. 345–6. Bāmiyān: Ratchnevsky, *Genghis Khan*, p. 164.
61. John Masson Smith, Jr, 'Demographic considerations in Mongol siege warfare', *Archivum Ottomanicum* 13 (1993–4), pp. 329–34.
62. Jūzjānī, II, p. 102 (tr. Raverty, II, p. 965). Cf. the comments of Ratchnevsky, *Genghis Khan*, p. 160.
63. Togan, *Flexibility*, esp. chaps. 3–4.
64. For what follows, see De Rachewiltz, 'Personnel', pp. 99–100, 111–12; Morgan, *Mongols*, pp. 108–9; idem, 'Who ran the Mongol empire?', *JRAS* (1982), pp. 124–36 (here pp. 128–30, 132–3); Buell, 'Sino-Khitan administration'; Allsen, 'Rise of the Mongolian empire', pp. 373–5.
65. The duties of these two offices varied: see Elizabeth Endicott-West, *Mongolian Rule in China. Local Administration in the Yuan Dynasty* (Cambridge, MA, 1989), esp. pp. 25–9, 34–5. She regards the Qara-Khitan antecedents of the *darughachi* as unproven: ibid., pp. 35 and 151, n.55.
66. SH, §263, tr. De Rachewiltz, I, p. 194.
67. Thomas T. Allsen, 'Mongolian princes and their merchant partners, 1200–1260', *Asia Major*, 3rd series, 2:2 (1989), pp. 83–126. See also pp. 290–1 below.
68. Thomas T. Allsen, 'Mongol census taking in Rus', 1245–1275', *HUS* 5:1 (1981), pp. 32–53 (here pp. 33–6).
69. For objections and modifications to this usage, see Devin DeWeese, *Islamization and Native Religion in the Golden Horde. Baba Tükles and Conversion to Islam in Historical and Epic Tradition* (University Park, PA, 1994), pp. 32–9; Caroline Humphrey, 'Shamanic practices and the state in Northern Asia: views from the centre and periphery', in Nicholas Thomas and Caroline Humphrey, eds, *Shamanism, History and the State* (Ann Arbor, MI, 1994), pp. 191–228 (here pp. 191–208).
70. Marie-Lise Beffa, 'Le concept de *tänggäri*, «ciel», dans l'*Histoire secrète des Mongols*', *EMS* 24 (1993), pp. 215–36 (here pp. 223–6).

71. Anatoly M. Khazanov, 'Muhammad and Jenghiz Khan compared: the religious factor in world empire building', *CSSH* 35 (1993), pp. 461–79 (here pp. 465–6). See also Beffa, pp. 226–7.
72. Louis Hambis, 'Deux noms chrétiens chez les Tatar au XIe siècle', *JA* 241 (1953), pp. 473–5.
73. Juwaynī, I, p. 48 (tr. Boyle, I, p. 64). Paul Pelliot, 'Chrétiens d'Asie centrale et d'extrême-orient', *TP* 15 (1914), pp. 623–44 (here pp. 627–35). For Bar Hebraeus's interpolation, see Erica C.D. Hunter, 'The conversion of the Kerait to Christianity in A.D. 1007', *ZS* 22 (1989), pp. 142–63.
74. Biran, ' "Like a mighty wall" ', pp. 77–9.
75. Juwaynī, I, pp. 18–19 (tr. Boyle, I, p. 26). For a good overview of Chinggis Khan's 'religious policy', see Ratchnevsky, *Genghis Khan*, pp. 197–8.
76. Tao-chung Yao, 'Ch'iu Ch'u-chi and Chinggis Khan', *HJAS* 46 (1986), pp. 201–19. Morgan, *Mongols*, p. 71.
77. Paul Pelliot, 'Les Mongols et la papauté', *ROC* 23, 24, 28 (1922–3, 1924, 1931–2) [references are to the pagination of the separatum], pp. 22–3. Khazanov, *Nomads*, pp. 238–9, doubts that Chinggis Khan knew much about the earlier qaghanates; but cf. the comments of Allsen, 'Rise of the Mongolian empire', pp. 347–8, and 'Spiritual geography', pp. 125–7; Ratchnevsky, *Genghis Khan*, p. 160.
78. Khazanov, 'Muhammad and Jenghiz Khan', p. 465.
79. Igor de Rachewiltz, 'Some remarks on the ideological foundations of Chingis Khan's empire', *PFEH* 7 (1973), pp. 21–36. Klaus Sagaster, 'Herrschaftsideologie und Friedensgedanke bei den Mongolen', *CAJ* 17 (1973), pp. 223–42. On *il* and *bulgha*, see Pelliot, 'Les Mongols et la papauté', pp. 26, 126–7; Antoine Mostaert and Francis Woodman Cleaves, 'Trois documents mongols des archives secrètes vaticanes', *HJAS* 15 (1952), pp. 419–506 (here pp. 485, 492–3).
80. De Rachewiltz, 'Some remarks on the ideological foundations', pp. 32–6. Golden, 'Imperial ideology', p. 48.
81. SH, §244, tr. De Rachewiltz, I, p. 168. Beffa, pp. 222–3.
82. David O. Morgan, 'The Mongols and the eastern Mediterranean', in Benjamin Arbel *et al.*, eds, *Latins and Greeks in the Eastern Mediterranean after 1204* (London, 1989 = *MHR* 4:1), pp. 198–211 (here p. 200); cf. also Buell, 'Kalmyk Tanggaci people', p. 41. The first element in Chinggis Khan's own title (at one time believed to mean 'world-ruler'), is now seen as signifying 'fierce' or 'hard' and is consequently immaterial in this context: Igor de Rachewiltz, 'The title Činggis Qan/Qaγan re-examined', in Walther Heissig and Klaus Sagaster, eds, *Gedanke und Wirkung. Festschrift zum 90. Geburtstag von Nikolaus Poppe*, AF 108 (Wiesbaden, 1989), pp. 281–98.
83. Juwaynī, I, p. 114 (tr. Boyle, I, p. 145).
84. PC, v, 18, vii, 2, and viii, 2, pp. 264, 284–5, 293 (tr. Dawson, pp. 25, 38, 43).
85. Morgan, *Mongols*, p. 68.
86. SH, §§202, 203, tr. De Rachewiltz, I, pp. 133, 135.
87. Allsen, 'Mongolian princes', p. 123.
88. The view of Barfield, p. 198.

89. Cf. some of the evidence gathered in John Masson Smith, Jr, 'The Mongols and world-conquest', *Mongolica* 5 (1994), pp. 206–14; also Peter Jackson, 'World-conquest and local accommodation: threat and blandishment in Mongol diplomacy', forthcoming in *History and Historiography of Post-Mongol Central Asia and the Middle East. Studies in Honor of Professor John E. Woods* (Chicago, 2005).

90. Julian, 'Epistula de vita Tartarorum', in Dörrie, p. 172 (tr. in *Mongolensturm*, pp. 103–4). Cf. also the vaguer statement (probably based on Julian) in TS, p. 169 (tr. in *Mongolensturm*, p. 251).

91. Eric Voegelin, 'The Mongol orders of submission to European powers, 1245–1255', *Byzantion* 15 (1940–1), pp. 378–413. Jean Richard, 'Ultimatums mongols et lettres apocryphes: l'Occident et les motifs de guerre des Tartares', *CAJ* 17 (1973), pp. 212–22 (here pp. 216–17), repr. in Richard, *Orient et Occident*.

92. From the Persian original, edited by Pelliot, 'Les Mongols et la papauté', pp. 15–16, French tr. p. 21 (slightly modified); cf. also the English trans. in De Rachewiltz, *Papal Envoys*, p. 214. The rendering in Dawson, *Mongol Mission*, pp. 85–6, is somewhat free.

93. Ibn Bībī, *al-Awāmir al-ʿalāʾiyya fī l-umūr al-ʿalāʾiyya* (*c*.1283), ed. A.S. Erzi, Türk Tarih Kurumu Yayınlarından, I. seri, 4a (Ankara, 1956), pp. 454–6; abridged version, *Mukhtaṣar-i Saljūq-nāma*, ed. Th. Houtsma, *Histoire des Seldjoucides d'Asie Mineure* (Leiden, 1902), pp. 202–5, and tr. Herbert W. Duda, *Die Seltschukengeschichte des Ibn Bibi* (Copenhagen, 1959), pp. 194–6. Shams al-Dīn had arrived in 633 H./1236. For other examples, involving the king of Lesser Armenia and a client ruler in the Indian borderlands, see respectively Reuven Amitai-Preiss, 'An exchange of letters in Arabic between Abaγa Īlkhān and Sultan Baybars (A.H. 667/A.D. 1268–69)', *CAJ* 38 (1994), pp. 11–33 (here pp. 12–13), and Peter Jackson, *The Delhi Sultanate: A Political and Military History* (Cambridge, 1999), p. 114.

94. PC, vii, 8, pp. 288–9 (tr. Dawson, p. 41).

95. Allsen, 'Mongols and North Caucasia', p. 13, citing Ibn al-Athīr, *al-Kāmil fī l-taʾrīkh*, 12 vols (Beirut, 1385–6 H./1965–6), XII, pp. 385–6. *The Chronicle of Novgorod 1016–1471*, tr. Robert Michell and Nevill Forbes, CS, 3rd series, 25 (London, 1914), p. 65. Fennell, *Crisis*, p. 65.

96. Jacques de Vitry, *Epistolae*, pp. 144–5, 147. For the charge against the Caliph, see Ibn al-Athīr, XII, p. 440; Juwaynī, II, p. 120 (tr. Boyle, I, p. 390); Barthold, *Turkestan Down to the Mongol Invasion*, p. 400. On Yahballaha, see Jean Maurice Fiey, *Chrétiens syriaques sous les Abbassides surtout à Bagdad (749–1258)*, CSCO Subsidia 59 (Louvain, 1980), pp. 262–3.

97. Jean Richard, 'L'Extrême-Orient légendaire au Moyen-Age: Roi David et Prêtre Jean', *Annales d'Éthiopie* 2 (1955–7), pp. 225–42 (here pp. 233–5), repr. in Richard, *Orient et Occident*. Klopprogge, *Ursprung*, pp. 115–23. But cf. also Peter Jackson, 'Prester John *redivivus*: a review article', *JRAS*, 3rd series, 7 (1997), pp. 425–32 (here pp. 428–30).

98. Martin Gosman, 'La légende du Prêtre Jean et la propagande auprès des croisés devant Damiette (1218–1221)', in Danielle Buschinger, ed., *La croisade: réalités et fictions. Actes du colloque d'Amiens 18–22 mars 1987*, Göppinger

Arbeiten zur Germanistik 503 (Göppingen, 1989), pp. 133–42. Denis Sinor, 'Le Mongol vu par l'Occident', in *1274 année charnière: mutations et continuités (Lyon–Paris 1974)*, Colloques internationaux du C.N.R.S. 558 (Paris, 1977), pp. 55–72 (here p. 56), and repr. in Sinor, *Studies*. Klopprogge, *Ursprung*, pp. 140–3.

99. Paul Pelliot, 'Mélanges sur l'époque des croisades', *MAIBL* 44 (1951), pp. 1–97 (here pp. 73–97, the section repr. as 'Two passages from *La prophétie de Hannan, fils d'Isaac*', in Beckingham and Hamilton, *Prester John*, pp. 113–37).

100. See generally James M. Powell, *Anatomy of a Crusade 1213–1221* (Philadelphia, 1986), pp. 178–91.

101. *MGHEp.*, I, p. 179 (no. 252): *Tartari, cruce precedente eos, intraverunt terram nostram et sic sub specie Christiane religionis deceperunt nos....* Hansgerd Göckenjan, 'Frühe Nachrichten über Zentralasien und die Seidenstraßen in der "Relatio de Davide Rege"', *UAJ*, n.F., 8 (1988), pp. 99–124 (here pp. 113–14), sees here only the wishful thinking of eastern Christians. But cf. Pierre-Vincent Claverie, 'L'apparition des Mongols sur la scène politique occidentale (1220–1223)', *MA* 105 (1999), pp. 601–13 (here pp. 608–10).

102. Kirakos Ganjakec'i, *Patmut'iwn Hayoc'*, tr. Robert Bedrosian, *Kirakos Ganjakets'i's History of the Armenians* (New York, 1986), p. 166. This or some similar incident (though *in partibus ultramarinis*) is reported in Aubry of Trois-Fontaines, 'Cronica', pp. 943–4.

103. *PSRL*, II, col. 745 (tr. Perfecky, p. 30).

104. Friedrich Zarncke, 'Der Priester Johannes' [part 2], *Abhandlungen der Phil.-Hist. Klasse der Königlich Sächsischen Gesellschaft der Wissenschaften* 8 (1883), pp. 1–186 (here p. 59); see also Bezzola, p. 51. Richard of San Germano, 'Chronica', *RIS²*, VII:2, pp. 110–11.

105. Jean Richard, 'The *Relatio de Davide* as a source for Mongol history and the legend of Prester John', in Beckingham and Hamilton, *Prester John*, pp. 139–58 (here p. 145): his ultimate source is Bar Hebraeus. For other examples, see M.-F. Brosset, *Histoire de la Géorgie, Ire partie. Histoire ancienne, jusqu'en 1469 de J.-C.* (St Petersburg, 1849–50), pp. 440, 442, 459.

106. Richardus, 'De facto Ungarie Magne', p. 154.

107. *MGHEp.*, I, p. 179 (no. 251): *non cavebamus ab ipsis quia credebamus eos Christianos esse.*

108. Richard, 'Ultimatums mongols', p. 215 and n.12.

chapter 3

THE MONGOL INVASIONS
OF 1241-4

There can be little doubt that Europe ranked low in the order of Mongol priorities alongside China; though possibly this impression rests largely on the fact that our sole extant Mongol source, the 'Secret History', devotes merely a few vague lines to Batu's great westward campaign of 1236–42 and confuses it with earlier operations by Sübe'etei.[1] Unfortunately, no contemporary sources have come down to us from the Golden Horde – the power Batu founded in the Pontic and Caspian steppe – that might have recorded the expedition.[2] But we are not entirely without a more detailed Mongol account of these events. Juwaynī, whose informants were presumably Mongols he met during his journey to Mongolia in 1252–3, provides a short section on the campaign against the 'Keler and Bashgird', i.e. the Hungarians;[3] and Rashīd al-Dīn, who at one point reproduces Juwaynī's data, also later inserts material gleaned from a different (but surely Mongol) source.[4] Overall, however, we are dependent on authors from within the Latin world. The most important are the Croatian cleric Thomas, archdeacon of Spalato (Split), whose work was begun between 1245 and 1251 (though not completed until 1266), and Roger of Torre Maggiore, a canon of Várad (Grosswardein; Nagyvárad; now Oradea in Rumania), who wrote in 1243–4.[5] But valuable information also emanates from annalists writing in Germany and Poland, and from contemporary letters written in Eastern Europe during the crisis by the Mongols' victims or in the West by those to whom they appealed for help. Many of these are known only from texts incorporated in the *Chronica majora* of the English Benedictine Matthew Paris, a problematic source in view of the author's tendency to insert material of his own fashioning and of his desire to glorify the Western Emperor Frederick II and denigrate the Pope.[6] A few additional details can be gleaned from the reports produced in 1247–8 as a result of the papal embassies to the Mongols (see below, chapter 4), notably the 'Tartar Relation'.

The first rumours

We saw how the first reports of Chinggis Khan's campaigns of conquest had reached Latin Christendom via the Fifth Crusade in Egypt in 1221, and how the Mongols had been mistaken for the Christian army of 'King David', a notion given wide currency by the letters of the papal legate Pelagius and of Pope Honorius III.[7] Even as early as 1223, however, the newcomers had been portrayed in rather different colours. In that year the Georgian queen, Rusudan, and her Constable, Ivané, had written to Honorius apologizing for their failure to send reinforcements to the Fifth Crusade on the grounds that Georgia had been suddenly ravaged by a strange and barbarous people from the east,[8] and the king of Hungary reported an attack by these barbarians on his Rus' and Cuman neighbours.[9] The Tours annalist saw fit to insert in his chronicle that King David was accompanied by savage races who were devouring the Muslims, a detail that seems to have been interpolated into the Prester John letter (see p. 21) around this date.[10] Although King David's attack upon the Georgians and Rus' could be excused by dismissing the victims as 'bad' Christians or (in the Georgian case) by pointing to their recent alliance with Muslim powers,[11] an alternative explanation did suggest itself. There were those – wrote the Cistercian annalist Aubry of Trois-Fontaines, a monastery in close contact with its brethren in Hungary – who alleged that the newcomers were neither Christians nor pagans (by which term he meant Muslims).[12]

The Mongols were to threaten the Latin world on two fronts: in Eastern Europe and in Syria-Palestine. A full twenty years would elapse before they burst upon Poland and Hungary, and a further few years before they confronted the Franks in northern Syria. During this interval rumours of their renewed advance had been filtering through to the West – according to Thomas of Spalato, for several years.[13] Some of the material is clearly fabulous, like an apocryphal letter from the patriarch of Jerusalem to the Pope (perhaps dating from the 1230s), in which the newcomers (unnamed) are allegedly led by a pseudo-prophet masquerading as Jesus Christ and carrying a book which claims to fulfil the New Testament.[14] The manner in which Philip, the Dominican prior in the Holy Land, in a letter of 1237 to the Pope (see above, p. 16), refers almost in passing to the Mongols' devastation in Persia and the Caucasus suggests that the Curia was now familiar with their activity in Asia.[15] The name 'Tartar' was already being applied to the Mongols in Western writings, even prior to their advance into Europe and the assimilation of their common designation 'Tatar' to Tartarus, the Hell of Classical Antiquity: the first Western author to use it was Quilichinus of Spoleto (1236).[16]

The late 1230s, in particular, brought a flurry of fresh news about the Mongol advance. According to a Scottish chronicler, reports of the Mongol campaigns first reached his country in 1238.[17] Similarly in 1238, if Matthew Paris can be trusted, an embassy from Muslim princes in the Near East (including those of the 'Old Man of the Mountain', the head of the Syrian Ismā'īlī Assassins) arrived in France and England to appeal for assistance against the Mongols. Under the same year Matthew records a glut in the supply of herrings at Yarmouth owing to the failure of traders from the eastern Baltic to leave their ports in view of the Mongol threat.[18] And at some point in 1239 the Pope received an appeal for help from the Georgian queen Rusudan, whose territories had again been invaded by the Mongols; he replied that the distance was too great and that the West had first to deal with the Muslim enemy in Spain and the Near East.[19] By this juncture Aubry of Trois-Fontaines was trying to account for the increasingly sinister news from Asia on the basis that the barbarous peoples originally incorporated in Prester John's armies had risen in revolt and killed him.[20]

Fuller and more 'realistic' information on the Mongols was also reaching Western Europe as a result of the evangelistic zeal of the Hungarian church. The majority of the Hungarian Dominicans who attempted to make contact with the inhabitants of Greater Hungary in the 1230s (p. 17) perished, either from hardship or at the hands of the pagan Mordvins; but in 1237 the Dominican Julian penetrated as far as the fringes of the Ural region, only to discover that the people of Greater Hungary had just been subjugated by the oncoming Mongols.[21] At Suzdal', in the course of his return journey, he found two Mongol envoys who had been intercepted and detained by the Rus' and who carried an ultimatum from Batu in the qaghan's name demanding the submission of King Béla IV of Hungary. Béla was charged with disposing of previous Mongol embassies and with giving shelter to the fugitive Cumans:

> I, the Qa'an [Chayn], the representative [nuntius] of the Heavenly King, [the one] to whom He has given power over the earth, to raise up those who submit to me and to cast down those who resist – I wonder why, O king of Hungary, when I have now sent envoys to you on thirty [sic] occasions, you have sent none of them back to me; nor do you send me in return your own envoys or letter. I am aware that you are a wealthy and powerful monarch, that you have under you many soldiers, and that you have the sole rule over a great kingdom. Hence it is difficult for you to submit to me of your own volition; and yet it would be better for you, and healthier, were you to submit willingly. I have learned, moreover, that you keep the Cumans, my slaves, under your protection; and so I order that you do not keep them with you

any longer and do not have me as an enemy on their account. For it is easier for them to escape than for you, since they are without houses and move about in their tents, and so may perhaps be able to escape. But as for you, who dwell in houses and have fortresses and cities – how will you evade my grasp?[22]

From rumours gleaned during his travels, and more particularly from contact with Prince Iury of Suzdal', who assured him of the Mongols' determination to conquer Hungary,[23] Julian was left in no doubt of the menace confronting Eastern Europe. He duly laid considerable emphasis upon it in the report he drafted to the papal legate in Hungary on his return, the first Latin account to describe the Mongols with any accuracy. This report (including the text of the Mongol ultimatum) was passed on to the Hungarian king's uncle, Berthold of Andechs, patriarch of Aquileia, who must have transmitted it to Pope Gregory IX.[24] Even if a claim by Aubry of Trois-Fontaines that the Emperor Frederick II, too, received an ultimatum around this time is suspect,[25] the West was evidently forewarned of the Mongol advance.

It seems equally certain, however, that the warnings were largely discounted. There was, of course, no real awareness of the extent of Mongol power, but an additional circumstance that may have fostered a mood of insouciance was the marked growth in numbers of those who acknowledged Roman primacy during the past two decades. The accommodating stance of the Jacobite Church in 1237 was symptomatic. In Eastern Europe the conversion of some Cuman chiefs, as we saw (p. 17), had made possible the creation in 1228 of the new episcopal see of 'Cumania'. And when 40,000 Cuman warriors and their families, fleeing before the Mongols, were granted asylum in Hungary in 1239, one condition was the baptism of their khan, Köten;[26] King Béla duly added 'king of Cumania' to his sonorous titles. It may well be that some thought the Mongol advance was already proving to the West's advantage. Further north, the chronicler Henry of Livonia hints that the Mongol victory on the Kalka had encouraged various Rus' princes to enter into negotiations with the papal legate in Livonia; and Pope Honorius III, writing to them about the conditions for ecclesiastical union, played upon their recent tribulations.[27] In the Near East, Mongol attacks were weakening the Muslims. Describing the Assassin embassy of 1238, Matthew Paris makes the bishop of Winchester, Peter des Roches, express the hope that the Mongols and Muslims would destroy one another, so that the universal church might be founded on their ruins.[28]

The Emperor subsequently accused Béla IV of negligence in the face of the Mongol menace.[29] This was not altogether justified. The king had apparently forged an alliance with the Bulgarians as well as the Cumans in order to resist the invaders,[30] though he had failed to set in motion fortification works along the Polish and Russian frontiers until the very beginning of 1241.[31] In all likelihood, the Emperor's criticism relates specifically to the murder of Mongol envoys. In any event, the same charge of carelessness could be levelled at Frederick. When a Mongol ultimatum supposedly offered him a ceremonial rank at the qaghan's court, he is said to have joked that his interests qualified him for the post of falconer; at the height of the invasion, he was to confess that, despite frequent reports over a considerable period, he himself had imagined the threat to be far off.[32] Even if Béla himself can in some degree be exonerated, however, his subjects may not. Our two principal sources for Hungarian affairs at this juncture, Roger of Várad and Thomas of Spalato, furnish valuable images of the problems facing the government. Both tell us that the very frequency of unfulfilled rumours about the Mongols in the years leading up to 1241 had led to complacency; that the Hungarians were enervated by a long period of peace and reposed excessive confidence in their military strength, the latter charge to be echoed by the Emperor Frederick.[33] More pernicious were the strained relations between Béla and the Hungarian nobility, owing to the king's actions against certain nobles at the onset of his reign, his resumption to the Crown of baronial landholdings, his inaccessibility and his perceived dependence upon foreign elements in the administration and the military. In this context, the welcome Béla extended to the Cumans provoked further disaffection which would more than neutralize the addition they made to his resources.[34] As a result of these tensions, news of which reached the French court, a diet that Béla convened to discuss defence measures against the Mongols was unable to agree on any decisions.[35] There were rumours in the Islamic world that the king had secured his barons' cooperation against the Mongols only by dint of concessions relating to their lands.[36]

Even prior to marching against the Mongols, the Hungarians destroyed their one chance of fighting alongside allies who were familiar with steppe cavalry warfare, when suspicions that Köten was in league with the enemy came to a head and he was lynched by an angry mob. Such suspicions were possibly fuelled by the fact that the Cumans included what might be termed proto-Mongolian elements,[37] and that Batu's armies were known to include Cumans who had been rolled up into the Mongol military at an earlier date and, according to Roger of Várad, were among the prisoners used as 'cannon-fodder' in siege warfare.[38] There was consequently a widespread belief not only that the Cumans had allied with the Mongols in order to avenge previous injuries at the hands of the Hungarians, but that the invaders themselves were Cumans;[39] and some contemporary Western annalists, possibly relying on Hungarian informants, confuse the two peoples and blame the Cumans for the devastation perpetrated by the Mongols.[40] This impression can only have been reinforced by the reaction of Köten's followers, who took flight, avenging him as they went by ravaging that part of Hungary which lay west of the Danube.[41]

The Mongol invasion of Latin Europe in 1241-2

In Volynia early in 1241 the Mongol armies divided. Hungary was the principal target. But Poland, albeit fragmented into several feuding duchies, constituted a danger, since King Béla might receive military aid from his relatives among the Polish dukes, notably his son-in-law Bolesław V ('the Chaste') of Cracow and Sandomir, and his cousin Henry II ('the Pious') of Lower Silesia; and so divisions under Batu's brother Orda and Chaghadai's son Baidar were deputed to conduct a campaign into Poland.[42] The Mongol operations here began a few weeks earlier than the assault on Hungary, with an attack on the town of Sandomir on 13 February 1241; the invaders retired on meeting with resistance. On 18 March, however, Baidar's forces defeated the army of Bolesław V, who took refuge in Hungary until dislodged from there also by the advancing Mongols. Baidar next moved west into the Oder valley, forcing the dukes of Upper Silesia to withdraw before him. On 9 April the Mongols met an army under Henry of Lower Silesia in the vicinity of Liegnitz (Legnica). The duke, unable to wait for the assistance of his kinsman King Václav (Wenceslas) of Bohemia, and assisted only by Duke Mieszko of Oppeln (Opole), the Bohemian margrave Boleslas and some Templars,[43] was overwhelmed and killed, and his head carried around on a lance for several days to inspire terror in the population. Mongol detachments attacked parts of Meissen and Lausitz,[44] but perhaps in view of the proximity of King Václav, who at the time of the battle of Liegnitz was only a day's journey away, they then turned south and passed through Moravia to rejoin Batu in Hungary. En route they sacked several Moravian towns and raided those parts of Austria situated on the left bank of the Danube, including Korneuburg.[45]

The arrival of Orda and Baidar added one more to the total of four Mongol armies that had converged on Hungary. Here the deliberations of King Béla and his barons at Ofen (Buda) had been interrupted on 10 March by the first news that the enemy had broken through the fortified passes in the Carpathians.[46] Batu and Sübe'etei advanced through the Verecke pass, the so-called *Porta Rusciae*, while Qadan and Büri came through the Borgó pass (28 March); two other divisions, led respectively by Böchek and a noyan whom Roger of Várad calls 'Bogutai' (Baghatur?) entered the country from the south-east. Hurriedly mustering an army, the king took up his position at Pest and awaited the contingents of his nobles while the Mongols harassed the mobilization process. At least one clash between the royal army and the invaders is known to have occurred in the plain of Rákos (near Pest).[47] On 6 April 1241 Béla led his army as far as the plain of Móhi, adjoining the Sajó river, where the Mongol army (now united apart from the division that had ravaged Poland) was drawn up on the opposite bank, though in such a way as not to be entirely visible to the Hungarians.[48] The Hungarians' failure to mount adequate guard over the bridge, together with the arrival of a part of Batu's army which had crossed the river upstream, meant that Béla's troops were surrounded. In the battle that ensued (10 April), an earlier decision to fortify their encampment with a laager of wagons proved disastrous, since it impeded their movements when subjected to a hail of Mongol arrows. Allowing selected groups – including Béla and his brother Kálmán – to break through their ranks, the Mongols then mounted a ruthless pursuit; many of the fleeing Hungarians perished because heavy rainfall had turned the neighbouring terrain into a morass. Among the dead were the archbishops of Esztergom (Gran) and Kalocsa and the bishops of Raab (Győr), Nitra and Transylvania.[49] Kálmán, halting briefly at Pest to order the citizens to look to themselves, died of his wounds soon after reaching Croatia. Béla made for the Austrian frontier, where he was for a short time the guest of Duke Frederick II before heading south into Slavonia.

The Mongols employed the spring and summer in plundering and enslaving Béla's hapless subjects. They discovered the royal seal on the body of his chancellor, and used it to issue bogus decrees ordering the population not to flee but to remain in their homes. The task of overrunning the kingdom was eased by the fact that Hungary, as a German chronicler observed, 'had almost no city protected by walls or strong fortresses'.[50] The Hungarians, as Béla would later admit, were unused to fortresses;[51] in the overwhelming majority of cases the walls were made of earth – 'mud-pies', as they have been labelled – and the few stone castles were concentrated in the west, on the Austrian border.[52] In the early months, the Mongols' unwelcome attentions were restricted to those regions of the Hungarian kingdom east of the Danube. But on Christmas Day 1241 the great river froze, and they were able to cross to the western bank. While Batu and Sübe'etei moved on the royal residences of Esztergom (a particular target, according to Roger, on account of its wealth)[53] and Stuhlweissenburg (Alba Regia), Qadan hurried in pursuit of the king. Béla, then in the Zagreb region, fled towards the Dalmatian coast, finally securing a refuge in the island town of Trogur (Trau). After an unsuccessful attempt on Spalato, Qadan appeared before Trogur and made vain efforts to obtain the king's surrender by the inhabitants. Towards the end of March 1242, he retired through Bosnia and Serbia. The Mongols burned Cattaro (Kotor) and plundered the towns of Drivasto and Svač (Suagium), where they left behind, in Thomas of Spalato's elegant phrase, 'nobody to piss against a wall'; then they rejoined Batu's main army in Bulgaria as it moved back east into the Pontic steppe.[54] An indigenous source confirms that the Mongols invaded the Bulgarian kingdom, and a garbled passage in Rashīd al-Dīn might indicate that they sacked its capital, Trnovo; but a reported check at the hands of the Bulgarian king is probably unfounded, though the rumour even reached Bar Hebraeus in Iraq.[55] If we can trust the single allusion in an Austrian chronicle, the Mongols also attacked the Latin Emperor Baldwin II of Romania (Constantinople), in all probability because like Béla he had given asylum in 1239 to a group of Cumans.[56]

The response further west

Had the Mongols pressed on westwards beyond Hungary and Poland, it is unlikely that they would have encountered coordinated opposition. Contemporary annalists report panic as far afield as the Netherlands and Spain.[57] No help reached King Béla from his neighbours. When he sought refuge on the Austrian border, Duke Frederick II at first welcomed him, but then lured him to a nearby castle and obliged him to relinquish a large sum of money which Béla had previously borrowed. To meet this demand, the unhappy monarch was obliged to pawn to the duke three Hungarian counties. Not content with occupying the territory in question, Austrian troops began to plunder the adjacent regions of Hungary, though they were soon expelled by Béla's subjects.[58] Nor was assistance forthcoming from Hungary's other neighbour and rival, Venice: the chronicler Andrea Dandalo observes smugly that the Venetians refrained from harming the king in his hour of tribulation.[59]

Immediately following his return from Austria, Béla despatched the bishop of Vác to the papal and imperial courts with an urgent request for assistance.[60] Already informed of the crisis by other princes, Pope Gregory IX on 16 June 1241 took Béla and his brother Kálmán under the protection of the Holy See and promised them and all those who took the cross for the defence of Hungary the same indulgence as that enjoyed by crusaders to the Holy Land.[61] He not only authorized the bishop of Vác to promote the crusade in Hungary and neighbouring kingdoms but also wrote to a number of German and Austrian prelates ordering them to preach the crusade for the defence of Bohemia and Germany.[62] In allowing the Norwegian king early in July to commute a vow to crusade in the Holy Land for an expedition against neighbouring pagans, he may have had the Mongols in mind.[63] He ordered clergy to give shelter to the Hungarian king and his subjects should they seek refuge from the Mongols.[64] But as early as 1 July he warned Béla that help was unlikely until the Emperor Frederick made peace with the Church in a spirit of penitence.[65] This is hardly surprising. To blame Gregory for his reluctance to settle his differences with Frederick is to ignore the Emperor's action in intercepting and imprisoning the prelates on their way to the council in May 1241 (see p. 23) and its effect upon the old pope.[66]

When no military assistance was forthcoming, Béla sent another embassy to Rome, but the party was drowned in the Adriatic. In any case Gregory had died in August, and his successor Celestine IV, elected in October, survived a mere three weeks; thereafter the papal chair was vacant until June 1243. Béla issued a third plea on 19 January 1242, but the only response was a consolatory letter from the Cardinals, of which the king would complain to Pope Alexander IV in 1259, when Hungary was again menaced by a Mongol invasion.[67] He was not alone in his resentment. In February 1242 leaders of the secular clergy and religious orders in Hungary, together with representatives of the lay nobility and the towns, had written yet a fourth urgent appeal to Rome, in which they decried the lack of support from their mother Church.[68]

In fact, a crusade against the Mongols was under way well before Pope Gregory's summons. In April 1241 the German prelates had promulgated crusading decrees in a series of councils, fasting and penitential processions had been instituted, and the German king, Frederick's son Conrad IV, had proclaimed a *Landfrieden* throughout Germany.[69] Friars, including many who had fled westwards from Hungary and Poland, were active in preaching and in encouraging those who could not bear arms to redeem their vows for a money payment. Conrad had appointed a date of 1 July for the crusading army to assemble at Nuremberg, and in the middle of that month was at Weiden, some fifty or more miles to the east, so that it is clear the crusade actually set out. Why it proceeded no further is uncertain, but the most likely reason is the news that the Mongols had retreated from the Bohemian and German borders and were now concentrated in Hungary, east of the Danube;[70] this enabled one annalist to conclude that they had been intimidated into withdrawal by the German crusade.[71] Shortly afterwards, in September 1241, leading German magnates who had been instrumental in promoting the crusade rebelled against Conrad and his father, and Germany drifted into civil war which lasted for over a decade. The large sums collected for the crusade were largely used to finance the opposition to the Hohenstaufen cause. At any rate, the evidence suggests that the aims of the crusade did not extend to the liberation of Hungary.

It is unlikely, in fact, that any German prince encountered the Mongols. In his concern to magnify the Emperor's role as defender of Christendom against the pagan, Matthew Paris claims that he liberated Hungary,[72] and recounts various other improbable triumphs for which Frederick might ultimately take the credit. One was a victory by Conrad and his half-brother Enzio near an otherwise unknown river named the 'Delpheos' (the Dnieper?).[73] Another is mentioned in a letter (the text of which is found only in the *Chronica majora*) from a certain Ivo of Narbonne, who speaks of the relief of Wiener-Neustadt by a force under the king of Bohemia, the patriarch of Aquileia, the dukes of Austria and Carinthia and the margrave of Baden.[74] If any of the victories over the Mongols which are reported by the annalists are authentic, they would have been minor affairs, won over only small raiding parties. Such, we must assume, was the victory of Duke Otto of Bavaria, which is mentioned in more than one source.[75] Significantly, Duke Frederick, when writing of the Mongol force which attacked Austria in the spring of 1241, gives figures of only 300 and 700 for their casualties and sets his own dead at a mere 100.[76] But the idea that the Mongols had suffered a major check was remarkably widespread. Rumours of a set-back in Germany reached both the Near East and Armenia,[77] and around the turn of the century two crusading treatises would refer to their defeat on the Danube at the hands of the duke of Austria.[78]

Nor did Béla IV receive any assistance from the Emperor Frederick. En route to the papal court, the bishop of Vác had conveyed to the Emperor the Hungarian king's offer to become Frederick's vassal in return for military aid.[79] Béla's uncle, Patriarch Berthold of Aquileia, by now something of an expert on Mongol affairs, is also known to have visited the Emperor in February–May 1242 in connection with the Mongol threat.[80] But although Frederick issued urgent appeals to the German princes and to his fellow monarchs to take up arms against the Mongols,[81] he also seems to have been intent on deriving the maximum advantage from the situation in his conflict with the pope. He stressed his inability to move until peace was made between them; warned of the encouragement the Mongols would derive from the strife within Christendom;[82] complained that a crusade had been unleashed against him that should have been sent against the Muslims and the Mongols; spoke of his readiness to move north of the Alps to take over the leadership of the crusade; and expressed his hopes, after Gregory's death, that he would be able to work with a new pope in order to repel the invaders.[83] Otherwise Béla had to rest content with a letter advising him to cooperate with Conrad's army until the Emperor appeared.[84]

The accusation that Frederick forbade the crusade to move because the Hungarian king neglected to wait upon him in person[85] is surely nothing more than anti-Hohenstaufen propaganda. In a similar vein the Emperor himself was accused of having summoned the Mongols, and imperial envoys were said to have been sighted in their ranks[86] – charges that are less outlandish than they at first appear, given that in previous decades Christian princes in Central and Eastern Europe, including Frederick's uncle Philip of Swabia, had made use of the Cumans in their conflicts (above, p. 17). But there was no denying Frederick's failure to assist King Béla. Thomas of Spalato – contemptuous, no doubt, of the Emperor's inadequate response – believed that Frederick was intent on flight rather than resistance.[87] In 1245 Pope Innocent IV would release Béla from his oath of fealty on the grounds that neither Frederick nor Conrad had given him any help.[88]

The material impact of the invasion

Undoubtedly Poland and Moravia suffered less at the Mongols' hands in 1241 than did Hungary. It has been claimed, reasonably, that the devastation in Silesia was confined to the narrow strip of territory through which the Mongol army passed on its way to meet Duke Henry and subsequently during its withdrawal into Moravia.[89] The suburbs of Breslau (Wrocław) were destroyed, but the Mongols abandoned the siege of the citadel, a deliverance later ascribed to a miracle on the part of St Czesław.[90] We know that the abbeys of Mogila and Heinrichau, in the Breslau diocese, were burned;[91] the town of Troppau (Opava) was for the most part wasted.[92] In Moravia, despite a sanguine report that the fortified places escaped the devastation, the towns of Littau, Freudenthal and Gewiczko were destroyed, while Brünn (Brno), Olmütz (Olomouc) and Uničov suffered damaging sieges.[93] Many fugitives are said to have arrived in Thuringia and Meissen.[94]

Under the year 1241 a German chronicler remarked that the kingdom of Hungary had been destroyed after lasting for 350 years.[95] The verdict was premature. In Hungary, admittedly, the visitation had been more protracted; this was the only Latin kingdom to undergo a Mongol occupation. Yet here too the scale of the devastation was proportionate to the length of the Mongols' stay, so that the country east of the Danube, where the invaders pitched their tents for some months, came off worse. Transylvania is said to have been completely laid waste.[96] But in the regions to the west, the Mongols again ravaged only the territory lying in the path of their troops; Qadan was reluctant to be detained by siege operations in view of the need to overtake King Béla.[97] It should also be borne in mind that not all the destruction here was the work of the Mongols: following Köten's murder the fleeing Cumans had devastated these western provinces and sacked the larger towns such as Frankavilla (Nagyolaszi; now Mandjelos in Croatia) and St Martin (Szentmárton, now Martinci in Srem, Croatia).[98] A reading of the accounts of both Thomas and Roger shows that the towns destroyed by the Mongols for the most part lay east of the Danube: Pest, Vác (Waitzen), Eger, Várad, Csanád, Gyulafehérvár (Alba Julia), Hermann-stadt (later Nagyszében; now Sibiu in Rumania), Rodana (Ó-Radna) and Bistritz (Nösen; now Beszterce). To the west, where they were unable to take Stuhlweissenburg, however, only Esztergom was sacked; and here they failed to capture the citadel, where many of the popula-tion had taken shelter.[99]

In each of the towns that did fall, the slaughter was considerable, even allowing for the hyperbole in our sources. Entering Gyulafehérvár not long after the Mongols had left, Roger may, as he claims, have found nothing but bones and severed heads.[100] But his statement that only fifteen souls survived in Esztergom carries less conviction.[101] Nor can we believe Thomas of Spalato and the anonymous author of a note on the invasion of Hungary appended to the Freisach annals, when they assert that the dead in Pest and Hermannstadt respectively exceeded 100,000. The relatively sober figures of 4,000 or more at Rodana and 6,040 at Bistritz provided by the latter writer are more persuasive.[102]

Yet the lesson was a stark one; all these places had fallen for lack of adequate defences. Following his return from the Dalmatian coast, King Béla would make strenuous efforts to revive the economy of his kingdom and to improve its defences by the construction and licensing of stone castles.[103] In the late 1240s he again recruited Cuman bands into his service, thereby creating what would prove to be an intractable problem for his successors.[104] He is also found granting the Knights Hospitallers the territory of Severin (Zeurin) and 'the whole of Cumania', so that they might assume defensive responsibilities against the Mon-gols and other enemies; though in the event he had to station some of the Hospitallers in newly-built fortresses along the Danube.[105] Over the next fifteen years the king would try, in addition, to build a defensive wall around Hungary by forging marriage links with neighbouring dynasties.[106]

Those inhabitants of the captured towns who were of value to the Mongols – craftsmen, some priests, comely women and girls – were usually spared, to be carried off as slaves. Although documentary evidence shows that some Hungarian captives at least returned to their homeland, if only many years later,[107] they were doubtless a minority. In 1253–4 the Franciscan William of Rubruck encountered not only Hungarian clerics in Batu's encampment and many Hungarian slaves elsewhere, but foreigners domiciled in Hungary who had been captured and transported as far as Mongolia: a woman from Metz, a Parisian goldsmith, the son of an Englishman, and a nephew of a bishop in Normandy. The chief purpose of his mission had been to seek out German slaves who had been removed from Transylvania by prince Büri and were known to be employed in mining silver and manufacturing weapons in Central Asia.[108] In Hungary there appears to have been large-scale displacement of population. The account of Roger of Várad, who was himself for a time a prisoner of the Mongols but escaped during Batu's eastward withdrawal, reveals numerous fugitives in the countryside.[109] The Mongols' departure was followed by a widespread famine and heavy mortality among the peasants, who had been unable to sow crops or reap a harvest during the visitation; two observers viewed this as at least as grim an affliction as the invasion itself.[110] Reports of depopulation and lack of cultivation over the next few decades are naturally met with in Transylvania, as at Gyulafehérvár, where a new bishop in 1246 found 'few or no inhabitants'.[111] But the same phenomenon recurs further west also, and even west of the Danube. Two districts dependent on the fortress of Nógrád were said to be empty and uncultivated in 1249; the lands of the bishop of Veszprém around the town of Beren had been devoid of people and cultivation for fifteen years in 1256; and the district of Inse, in Wieselburg, was still deserted in 1268.[112] Abandoned villages, ruined churches and monasteries were a mute reminder of the long-term effects of the Mongol campaign; much agricultural land may have reverted to pasturage. Yet it is far from clear to what extent changes in settlement patterns, for instance, can be ascribed to the Mongol invasion.[113] And in any case the immediate economic dislocation should not be overstated. Béla mustered the resources not only to mount a punitive campaign against Duke Frederick of Austria immediately on his return from Dalmatia, but also to engage in wars with other neighbours during the next few years.[114]

Mongol military superiority

The flower of Hungarian knighthood, and perhaps of Polish knighthood too, had suffered a crushing defeat at the hands of an army of nomad cavalry from the steppe. How this should have transpired was a matter of perplexity to contemporaries in the West. The abundant rumours concerning the identity of the attackers and their role in history will be analyzed later (chap. 6); here we are concerned only with contemporary attempts to explain Mongol victories. For all the chroniclers' references to countless invaders, and comparisons with locusts, it was not necessarily a matter of numbers. Thomas of Spalato heard subsequently that Béla's was the larger of the two armies at the Sajó river; according to Juwaynī, the Mongols were outnumbered two to one.[115] The Mongols gave the impression of being more numerous than they actually were, both by their tactic of dispersal while ravaging the countryside and by their dense arrow-fire during battle, which the sources liken to hail or snow. Their mobility was well known: King Václav heard that they covered forty miles a day in their withdrawal from the Bohemian frontier,[116] and rapid troop movements helped to foster the impression that their army was vast, extending, in one estimate, over an area twenty days' journey by fifteen.[117] Our Western sources stress that extensive herds of horses were at the Mongols' disposal, although the precise number of spare mounts available to each warrior varies.[118] Both men and horses were distinguished for their frugal diet and hardiness. Mongol discipline, and the concomitant ability of commanders to manoeuvre large units even during an engagement, contrasted sharply with the highly individualistic mode of warfare practised by Western knights.

As regards weaponry, the Mongols might appear to have had the edge in archery. Their arrows penetrated every type of armour, claimed Thomas,[119] whereas their own armour, made from strips of hard-boiled leather, could withstand the arrows of their enemies.[120] But one weapon they did not possess was the crossbow, of which, the papal envoy Carpini would later claim, they stood in great fear.[121] It is noteworthy that Béla wanted the pope to secure him the assistance of Venetian crossbowmen (*balistarii*), that Duke Frederick of Austria urged Conrad to bring them, and that these artificers loom large in a brief list of instructions which the Emperor sent to Germany with a view to countering the Mongol menace.[122] Within a few years the author of the 'Tartar Relation' would offer his own distinctive proposals for the deployment of crossbows – the West's weapon *par excellence* – in battle against the Mongols.[123]

The reasons for the Mongol withdrawal

The notion that there was nothing to stop the Mongols reaching the Atlantic, and that their withdrawal in the spring of 1242 spared Western Europe the rather unpleasant experience of Hungary, is not confined to modern writers. At least one of the letters reproduced by Matthew

Paris warned that none of the Western powers was capable of with-standing them,[124] especially in view of the divisions that racked the Latin world.[125] The Mongols' sudden retreat from Hungary, which certainly baffled contemporaries, has consequently been more difficult to explain than their first appearance.[126] Carpini heard that the withdrawal had been prompted by news of the death (11 December 1241) of the qaghan Ögödei, poisoned by his sister, the aunt of the future qaghan Güyüg.[127] There does appear to be some historical basis to this, since Rashīd al-Dīn tells us that Chinggis Khan's daughter Altalun was later executed by Güyüg's supporters on some charge (of which she was in fact innocent);[128] though Carpini may have confused Altalun and the Kereyid princess Ibaqa, who had been accused of poisoning Ögödei.[129] As Professor Sinor has pointed out, however, the qaghan's death would only suffice to explain the Mongol withdrawal had Batu proceeded to travel all the way to the Mongolian homeland to participate in the election of a successor.[130] There were undoubtedly also other circumstances at work, including logistical problems. The Dalmatian coastlands were ill-adapted to Mongol cavalry operations; and Thomas of Spalato expressly mentions that Qadan took with him only a fraction of his contingent in view of the fact that the region afforded so little grass early in March.[131] The primary reason for the retreat, in Sinor's view (which has been adopted by other authors), was that the Mongol cavalry had exhausted the available pasturage and that the Hungarian plain was inadequate to support them further; they accordingly made for the more spacious grasslands of the Pontic steppe, where Batu pitched his tents along the Volga and shortly founded the town of Sarai, destined to be the principal residence of the Golden Horde khans. On this argument, the Mongols would have encountered the same difficulties in Central Europe as had earlier steppe invaders like the fifth-century Huns.[132]

Yet it is important also to note that by the time of the advance into Poland and Hungary the Mongol high command was deeply divided and that not all the original contingents were present. Batu had quarrelled with his cousins Güyüg and Büri, and of these the former, at least, had retired with his forces to Mongolia, where Ögödei had furiously sent him back to be disciplined by Batu. He had not yet arrived when the news of his father's death reached him, and he took no part in the operations in Latin Europe.[133] Batu's withdrawal eastwards was designed to enable him to keep a watchful eye on developments in Mongolia should his enemy Güyüg be elected qaghan.[134] For what it is worth, Güyüg's absence surfaces in the Rus' chronicle tradition, and the discord within the Mongol high command in Europe at this juncture is mentioned as the reason for the withdrawal in a Western source, albeit one dating from the early fourteenth century.[135]

Historians have also pointed to the losses the Mongols had sustained in the course of the campaigns in Eastern Europe. The problem with this line of argument is that it can all too easily become the vehicle of modern nationalistic fervour: thus we read of the Mongols being so badly mauled by the Rus' that they were unable to sustain a longer campaign further west[136] or of them harbouring a healthy respect for German military strength and hence deciding to postpone their encounter with it.[137] The evidence does suggest, nevertheless, that the invaders' losses had been serious: one commander had been killed in the attack on Sandomir, and a prince of the blood had allegedly fallen in Hungary.[138] The Mongols were also confronted in their rear with continued unrest among the Cumans, which had to be suppressed by Batu's brother Shingqur.[139] Our Latin sources must admittedly be deployed with caution. The claims of Carpini that the Mongols would have beaten a retreat had the Hungarians resisted manfully, and of the author of the 'Tartar Relation' that they were on the point of flight when the Poles turned tail at Liegnitz,[140] belong, as we shall see (p. 92), to a deliberate effort to inspire Western resistance in the event of a future invasion. Yet they are echoed in sources emanating from within the Mongol empire. Juwaynī, the 'Secret History' and Sübe'etei's biography in the *Yüan shih* show that the Hungarians and their neighbours were viewed as redoubtable opponents.[141] Such perceptions may well be linked with the reluctance of the shamans, as we learn from Rubruck, to allow the Mongols to attack Hungary again for several years to come.[142] The advance into Europe was a serious undertaking on the Mongol side.

There is, of course, one final possibility: that Batu's objectives were more limited than we have supposed. The rumours retailed in Latin sources, and current since c.1236, that the Mongols' goal at this stage was Rome or Germany (i.e. the Roman empire) very probably spring from Western assumptions that the invaders were the peoples referred to in apocalyptic literature (below, p. 144). Béla certainly assured King Conrad that the Mongols planned to invade Germany at the onset of winter 1241-2,[143] but this could have been merely a desperate ploy to secure the German king's assistance. The coins which the Mongols supposedly minted in Hungary can no longer be adduced as evidence for their long-term aims, since they are now known to bear pseudo-Arabic and Hebrew legends and to date mainly from the twelfth century.[144] The Mongols did appoint, from among the subject population, representatives (*canesii*) whose task was to extort what the conquerors needed;[145] but this does not necessarily prove that they planned a permanent occupation. We should remember that the programme of world-conquest could not be realized in a single expedition. Doubtless the purpose of this particular campaign of 1241-2 was simply to chastise Béla by devastating his kingdom (and, if possible, by capturing and killing the king), and the Mongols left because they had completed the task to the best of their ability. The merit of this – the most persuasive – hypothesis is that the retreat then requires no further explanation.[146]

The Mongols in the Near East 1242-4

One consequence of the Mongol advance into the western steppe was the flight of numerous Cumans into the Crimea and across the Black Sea, where they were enslaved: many were bought as *mamlūks* by the Egyptian Sultan.[147] But Mongol forces were also operating in the Near East. Around the time that Batu's forces began to move back eastwards into the Pontic steppe, the Mongol noyan Baichu, who had succeeded to Chormaghun's command in north-western Persia in 1241, embarked upon fresh operations against the Seljük Sultanate of Rūm.[148] Erzurum fell in 1242, and on 26 June 1243 Baichu inflicted a crushing defeat at Kösedagh on the Sultan Kaykhusraw II, who forthwith became tributary to the Mongols. While Baichu's main force occupied Sivas and sacked Kayseri, a Mongol squadron under Yasa'ur advanced in 1244 into Syria, demanding the submission of the Ayyubid rulers of Aleppo, Damascus, Ḥimṣ and Ḥamā, who bought the invaders off with the payment of tribute. Matthew Paris reports the receipt of an ultimatum by the Frankish prince of Antioch, Bohemond V, who was ordered to dismantle his fortifications, hand over his gold and silver, and surrender to the Mongols three thousand young women; he defiantly refused. It was fortunate that Yasa'ur withdrew shortly afterwards.[149] As in the European campaign, the explanation might be ecological, since two Near Eastern authors mention the damage done to the hooves of the Mongols' horses in the summer heats.[150]

Two years later King Het'um of Lesser Armenia, who had reflected profoundly upon the deliverance afforded by the Mongols from his neighbours and enemies in Rūm, sent his brother, the Constable Smbat (Sempad) to Güyüg's court to offer his submission. But otherwise this campaign had little immediate impact on the Latin world. At the time Baichu's operations were more noteworthy, perhaps, for their indirect consequences. Since c.1230 a large body of Khwarazmian horsemen had been active in the Jazīra, serving whichever of the Muslim princes offered the highest pay, including at one time the Ayyubid al-Ṣāliḥ Ayyūb, prince of Ḥiṣn Kayfā. The advent of the Mongols, with whom they doubtless had no desire to cross swords ever again, impelled them to accept an invitation from Ayyūb, now sultan of Egypt, to assist him against his Frankish enemies in Palestine and their allies among his Ayyubid relatives. In the summer of 1244 the Khwarazmians swept down through Syria, sacking Jerusalem and slaughtering its Christian population (11 August). Then they effected a junction with the Egyptian army, and on 17 October the combined forces inflicted a crushing defeat on Ayyūb's enemies at La Forbie (al-Ḥarbiyya), near Gaza. Within two years the Khwarazmians had changed masters and had been annihilated by Ayyūb's forces.[151] But La Forbie was a body-blow from which Latin Syria would never recover.

The Mongol invasions of Eastern Europe and Syria had both an immediate impact on the West and longer-term consequences. In the short term, they caused havoc in Hungary and Poland and induced terror and bewilderment further afield. They pushed large numbers of fugitives into Latin Christian territory, whether Cumans into Hungary and Greece or Khwarazmians into Palestine. They incidentally, and unintentionally, led to a growth in the military resources of the Egyptian Sultan. Whereas the Khwarazmian menace was eliminated relatively quickly, the Cuman presence in Hungary would take several decades to assimilate; the rise of the mamluk institution in Egypt would have profound consequences for the future of the crusader states. These problems confronted a Catholic world that was already in conflict with various schismatic or pagan neighbours, and which was further racked by the dispute between Empire and papacy. It fell to the newly-elected Pope Innocent IV (1243–54) to deal with them.

Notes

1. SH, §§262, 274, tr. De Rachewiltz, I, pp. 194, 205–6 (and see notes at II, pp. 958–9).
2. Charles J. Halperin, 'The missing Golden Horde chronicles and historiography in the Mongol Empire', *MS* 23 (2000), pp. 1–15.
3. Juwaynī, I, pp. 225–6 (tr. Boyle, I, pp. 270–1). For the term 'Keler', a metathetic form of 'Kerel' (from Hungarian *király*, 'king', but extended to apply to the people themselves), see the exhaustive investigation in Paul Pelliot, *Notes sur l'histoire de la Horde d'Or* (Paris, 1950), pp. 115–62.
4. Rashīd al-Dīn, I, pp. 665–8, 677–9; tr. J.A. Boyle, *The Successors of Genghis Khan* (London and New York, 1971), pp. 56–7, 69–72 (tr. Thackston, II, pp. 325–6, 331–2).
5. On these two authors, see James Ross Sweeney, 'Thomas of Spalato and the Mongols: a thirteenth-century Dalmatian view of Mongol customs', *Florilegium*

4 (1982), pp. 156–83; Franz Babinger, 'Maestro Ruggiero delle Puglie, relatore pre-Poliano sui Tatari', in *Nel VII centenario della nascità di Marco Polo* (Venezia, 1955), pp. 53–61; *Mongolensturm*, pp. 129–38, 227–35.

6. Richard Vaughan, *Matthew Paris* (Cambridge, 1958). See also Karl Rudolf, 'Die Tartaren 1241/1242. Nachrichten und Wiedergabe: Korrespondenz und Historiographie', *Römische Historische Mitteilungen* 19 (1977), pp. 79–107 (here pp. 92–6); Hans-Eberhard Hilpert, *Kaiser- und Papstbriefe in den Chronica Majora des Matthaeus Paris*, Veröffentlichungen des Deutschen Historischen Instituts London 9 (Stuttgart, 1981); for the Mongol material, J.J. Saunders, 'Matthew Paris and the Mongols', in T.A. Sandquist and M.R. Powicke, eds, *Essays in Medieval History Presented to Bertie Wilkinson* (Toronto, 1969), pp. 116–32.

7. Aubry of Trois-Fontaines, 'Cronica', p. 911. 'Annales prioratus de Dunstaplia', *AM*, III, pp. 66–7, 69–74. Fr. Zarncke, 'Zur Sage vom Priester Johannes', *NA* 2 (1877), pp. 611–15 (here pp. 612–13). Peter Linehan, 'Documento español sobre la Quinta Cruzada', *Hispania Sacra* 20 (1967), pp. 177–82. Ralph of Coggeshall, *Chronicon Anglicanum*, ed. Joseph Stevenson, RS (London, 1875), p. 190.

8. *MGHEp.*, I, pp. 178–9 (nos. 251, 252).

9. Richard of San Germano, 'Chronica', p. 110; and see Denis Sinor, 'Les relations entre les Mongols et l'Europe jusqu'à la mort d'Arghoun et de Béla IV', *Journal of World History* 3:1 (Neuchâtel, 1956), pp. 39–62 (here p. 40), repr. in his *Inner Asia*. Aubry of Trois-Fontaines, 'Cronica', p. 911.

10. 'Ex Chronico Turonensi auctore anonymo S. Martini Turon. canonico', *RHGF*, XVIII, pp. 300–1. Friedrich Zarncke, 'Der Priester Johannes' [part 1], *Abhandlungen der Phil.-Hist. Klasse der Königlich Sächsischen Gesellschaft der Wissenschaften* 7 (1876), pp. 827–1030 (here pp. 892–3, 911). Klopprogge, *Ursprung*, pp. 141–2.

11. Jacques de Vitry, *Epistolae*, p. 147. Zarncke, 'Zur Sage', p. 614. Bezzola, p. 24 and n.50. Klopprogge, *Ursprung*, p. 113, n.37.

12. Aubry of Trois-Fontaines, 'Cronica', p. 911.

13. TS, p. 133.

14. The edition in Claverie, 'L'apparition', pp. 612–13, supersedes that of Richard in *BEC* 119 (1961), pp. 243–5, but it is still necessary to compare the readings in the fuller version sent by Cardinal Hugo of S. Sabina to the bishop of Constance: see Robert Davidsohn, 'Ein Briefkodex des dreizehnten und ein Urkundenbuch des fünfzehnten Jahrhunderts', *QFIAB* 19 (1927), pp. 373–88 (here pp. 383–4). Richard's dating is to be preferred (Klopprogge, *Ursprung*, p. 154 and n.6); Claverie assumes that the text is a genuine letter from the patriarch, dated June 1221. The letter is possibly echoed in the statement by the Rus' cleric Peter (below, p. 87) that the Mongols claimed to be led by St John the Baptist: Dörrie, p. 192.

15. CICO, III, p. 306 (no. 227a): *quas terras Tartari pro magna parte vastaverunt.*

16. Klopprogge, *Ursprung*, pp. 155–9, arguing against C.W. Connell, 'Western views of the origin of the "Tartars": an example of the influence of myth in the second half of the thirteenth century', *Journal of Medieval and Renaissance Studies* 3 (1973), pp. 115–37 (here pp. 117–18). Bezzola, p. 31 and n.77,

points out that the term had been used by the Georgian Constable in 1223. Quilichinus: Schmieder, *Europa*, p. 259 and n.327; Reichert, 'Geographie', pp. 475–6.

17. *The Chronicle of Melrose, from the Cottonian Manuscript, Faustina B.IX in the British Museum*, facsimile edn by Alan Orr Anderson and Marjorie Ogilvie Anderson (London, 1936), p. 86.

18. *CM*, III, pp. 488–9. For the authenticity of the Ismā'īlī embassy, see Philip Grierson, 'Muslim coins in thirteenth-century England', in Dickran J. Kouymjian, ed., *Near Eastern Numismatics, Iconography, Epigraphy and History. Studies in Honor of George C. Miles* (Beirut, 1974), pp. 387–91; A.H. Morton, 'Ghurid gold en route to England?', *Iran* 16 (1978), pp. 167–70.

19. CICO, III, pp. 338–9 (no. 261, 13 Jan. 1240 = *Reg. Greg. IX*, no. 5022); pp. 339–40, for the Georgian offer of ecclesiastical union.

20. Aubry of Trois-Fontaines, 'Cronica', p. 942.

21. Dörrie, pp. 166, 181 (tr. in *Mongolensturm*, pp. 101, 109).

22. Ibid., p. 179 (tr. in *Mongolensturm*, pp. 107–8).

23. Ibid., pp. 177–8 (tr. in *Mongolensturm*, p. 107).

24. See P. Paschini, 'Berthold d'Andechs, patriarche d'Aquilée', *DHGE*, VIII, coll. 965–6; Sinor, 'Un voyageur du treizième siècle', pp. 600–1.

25. Aubry of Trois-Fontaines, 'Cronica', p. 943. See Reichert, 'Geographie', p. 475.

26. RV, p. 553 (tr. in *Mongolensturm*, p. 141).

27. James J. Zatko, 'The Union of Suzdal, 1222–1252', *JEH* 8 (1957), pp. 33–52 (here pp. 34–5). Henry of Livonia, *Chronicon*, xxvi, 1, 2nd edn, ed. Leonid Arbusow and Albert Bauer, *Heinrichs Livländische Chronik*, SRG (Hannover, 1955), p. 187, and tr. James A. Brundage, *The Chronicle of Henry of Livonia* (Madison, WI, 1961), p. 205.

28. *CM*, III, p. 489.

29. Ibid., IV, p. 113 = *HDFS*, V, pp. 1149–50.

30. Dimitrov, 'Über die bulgarisch-ungarischen Beziehungen', pp. 16–19.

31. RV, p. 560 (tr. in *Mongolensturm*, pp. 149–50). TS, pp. 145–6 (tr. in *Mongolensturm*, pp. 237–8). Gustav Strakosch-Grassmann, *Der Einfall der Mongolen in Mitteleuropa in den Jahren 1241 und 1242* (Innsbruck, 1893), pp. 12–13; and cf. ibid. p. 91.

32. Aubry of Trois-Fontaines, 'Cronica', p. 943 (but cf. p. 61 and n.25 above). *HDFS*, V, pp. 1139–40.

33. RV, p. 560 (tr. in *Mongolensturm*, p. 150). TS, pp. 140–3 (tr. in *Mongolensturm*, p. 237); cf. also ibid. p. 122: *quasi pro ludo reputabatur a multis. CM*, IV, p. 113 = *HDFS*, V, p. 1150.

34. RV, pp. 554–6 (tr. in *Mongolensturm*, pp. 142–5). 'Continuatio Sancrucensis secunda', *MGHS*, IX, p. 640, asserts that Béla allowed in the Cumans without the assent of his barons. For the king's relations with his nobles, see Pál Engel, *The Realm of Saint Stephen. A History of Medieval Hungary, 895–1526*, tr. Tamás Pálosfalvi (London, 2001), p. 98.

35. TS, pp. 148–51 (tr. in *Mongolensturm*, p. 238). Guillaume de Nangis (early 14th cent.), 'Gesta Ludovici sanctae memoriae regis Franciae', *RHGF*, XX, p. 342.

36. al-Qazwīnī, *Āthār al-bilād* (1275/6), ed. F. Wüstenfeld, *Zakarija ben Muham-med bin Mahmud el-Cazwini's Cosmographie, zweiter Teil: Die Denkmäler der Länder* (Göttingen, 1848), pp. 411–12.
37. Allsen, 'Prelude', pp. 7–8. Golden, '"I will give the people"', p. 33; also idem, 'Cumanica IV: the tribes of the Cuman-Qıpčaqs', *AEMA* 9 (1995–7), pp. 99–122 (here pp. 102–5), repr. in his *Nomads and Their Neighbours*.
38. Dominican 'R.' and Franciscan 'J.', in *CM*, VI, p. 82. TS, pp. 136–7, 170 (tr. in *Mongolensturm*, pp. 236, 252). RV, pp. 581, 582 (tr. in *Mongolensturm*, pp. 176, 178, 179).
39. Cumans joining the Mongols: ibid., pp. 560–1 (tr. in *Mongolensturm*, p. 150); 'Gestorum Treverorum continuatio quarta', p. 404; 'Annales S. Pantaleonis Coloniensis', *MGHS*, XXII, p. 535, *CM*, IV, p. 120. 'De invasione Tartarorum fragmentum', *MGHS*, XXIX, p. 599, may contain an echo of the Cumans' alleged perfidy in defecting to the Mongols. See also John of Garlande, *De triumphis ecclesiae libri octo* (*c*.1252), ed. Thomas Wright (London, 1856), p. 112; on this author, see Wright's introduction, pp. v–xii, and Louis J. Paetow, 'The crusading ardor of John of Garland', in Paetow, ed., *The Crusades and Other Historical Essays Presented to Dana C. Munro by His Former Students* (New York, 1928, repr. 1968), pp. 207–22. Cumans as the invaders: RV, p. 566 (tr. in *Mongolensturm*, p. 157); Constantin Höfler, ed., *Albert von Beham und Regesten Pabst Innocenz IV.* (Stuttgart, 1847), p. 30.
40. 'Continuatio Sancrucensis secunda', p. 640. 'Annales Mellicenses. Continuatio Lambacensis', *MGHS*, IX, p. 559. 'Chronicon S. Medardi Suessionensis', in Luc d'Achéry, ed., *Spicilegium sive collectio veterum aliquot scriptorum qui in Galliae bibliothecis delituerant*, new edn by Étienne Baluze *et al.*, 3 vols (Paris, 1723), II, p. 491.
41. RV, pp. 567–8 (tr. in *Mongolensturm*, pp. 158–9). Rudolf, 'Die Tartaren', pp. 100–5, proposes that the Mongol thrust towards Wiener-Neustadt reported by Ivo of Narbonne (below) was the work of Cuman bands.
42. The idea that the Mongols entered Poland from Prussia is based on a scribal error in the sole source to mention it, namely a letter of the Emperor Frederick (*CM*, IV, p. 115 = *HDFS*, V, pp. 1150–1): Joseph Becker, 'Zum Mon-goleneinfall von 1241', *Zeitschrift des Vereins für Geschichte Schlesiens* 66 (1932), pp. 34–57 (here p. 42 and n.5). For the campaign in Poland, see Hansgerd Göckenjan, 'Der Westfeldzug (1236–1242) aus mongolischer Sicht', in *Wahlstatt*, pp. 35–75 (here pp. 44–5).
43. Apart from the few Teutonic Knights based in Silesia, the Order took no part in the battle, in which the Master, Poppo of Osternau, was once wrongly believed to have been killed: Tomasz Jasiński, 'Zur Frage der Teilnahme des Deutschen Ordens an der Schlacht von Wahlstatt', in *Wahlstatt*, pp. 117–27.
44. 'Annales S. Pantaleonis', p. 535. Cf. also *HDFS*, V, p. 1147: *fines Boemie et Saxonie aggrediuntur.*
45. *HDFS*, V, p. 1216. Frederick II of Austria to Henry, bishop of Constance, 23 June 1241, in IUB ms. 187, fo. 7r. 'Annales Admuntenses. Continuatio Garstensis', *MGHS*, IX, p. 597 ('Niunburg'); and see Strakosch-Grassmann, pp. 143, 189.

46. For the campaign culminating in the battle on the Sajó river, see Göckenjan, 'Der Westfeldzug', pp. 46–59, and Strakosch-Grassmann, pp. 68–101; for Mongol operations in Transylvania, ibid., pp. 91–8, 153–8. Jean W. Sedlar, *East Central Europe in the Middle Ages, 1000–1500* (Washington, SE, 1994), pp. 210–21, provides a good overall survey.
47. MOL, DL 61178 (= *HO*, I, pp. 22–3, no. 17).
48. TS, p. 159 (tr. in *Mongolensturm*, p. 240).
49. RV, p. 572 (tr. in *Mongolensturm*, pp. 164–5), gives the full list. TS, p. 163 (tr. in *Mongolensturm*, p. 244), names the first three; cf. also MOL, DL 72302 (22 April 1244 = *CDH*, IV:1, p. 335; *AUO*, VII, p. 163, no. 107; *HO*, IV, p. 28, no. 12). 'Annales Frisacenses', *MGHS*, XXIV, p. 65 note (from BN ms. Suppl. lat. 1675, formerly at Echternach).
50. 'Annales S. Pantaleonis', p. 535.
51. *VMH*, I, p. 231 (no. 440) = *DIR*, I:1, p. 261 (no. 199). Both editors allocate the letter to 1254: it has now been convincingly redated to 1247 by Toru Senga, 'IV Béla külpolitikája és IV Ince pápához intézett "tátár" levele', *Századok* 121 (1987), pp. 583–612, which supersedes earlier literature.
52. Erik Fügedi, *Castle and Society in Medieval Hungary (1000–1437)*, Studia Historica Academiae Scientiarum Hungaricae 187 (Budapest, 1986), pp. 45–8; the citation (from Gy. Pauler) is at p. 47. See also Strakosch-Grassmann, pp. 30–1, 35.
53. RV, p. 583 (tr. in *Mongolensturm*, p. 180).
54. TS, pp. 174–7 (tr. in *Mongolensturm*, pp. 257–60). RV, p. 584 (tr. in *Mongolensturm*, p. 181).
55. Philippe Mouskès, *Chronique rimée*, ed. Baron F.A.F.T. de Reiffenberg, 2 vols (Brussels, 1836–8), II, p. 681 (vv. 30960–2); cf. Strakosch-Grassmann, p. 169. Bar Hebraeus, *Makhtebhânûth zabhnê*, tr. E.A. Wallis Budge, *The Chronography of Gregory Abu'l-Faraj. . . . Commonly Known as Bar Hebraeus*, 2 vols (Oxford and London, 1932), I (trans.), p. 398; idem, *Mukhtaṣar ta'rīkh al-duwal*, ed. Anṭūn Ṣāliḥānī (Beirut, 1890; repr. 1403 H./1983), pp. 234–5. For Bulgaria, see Peter Schreiner, 'Die Tataren und Bulgarien. Bemerkungen zu einer Notiz im Vaticanus Reginensis gr. 18', *EB* (1985), no. 4, pp. 25–9; Aurel Decei, 'L'invasion des Tatars en 1241/1242 dans nos régions selon la *Djāmiʿ ot-Tevārīkh* de Fäzl ol-lāh Räšīd od-dīn', *RRH* 12 (1973), pp. 101–21 (here pp. 120–1). Thomas of Cantimpré, *Vita piae Ludgardis* (1247/8), in J. Bolland, ed., *Acta Sanctorum. Junii III* (Antwerp, 1701), *Die decima sexta*, p. 257, believed that the Mongols had 'destroyed' Bulgaria, among other countries. Ricoldo of Montecroce, *Liber peregrinationis*, mentions the conquest of 'the Vlachs', i.e. Bulgaria, in a passage omitted from the printed text but found in Berlin ms. lat. 466: Emilio Panella, O.P., 'Ricerche su Riccoldo da Monte di Croce', *AFP* 58 (1988), pp. 5–85 (here p. 70: *et blaccos*).
56. 'Continuatio Sancrucensis secunda', p. 641, mentioning two battles, in the first of which Baldwin was victorious: possibly the Cumans were the attackers on this occasion. Cf. Jean Richard, 'À propos de la mission de Baudouin de Hainaut: l'empire latin de Constantinople et les Mongols', *JS* (1992), pp. 115–21 (here pp. 117–18), repr. in his *Francs et Orientaux*.

57. 'Annales S. Pantaleonis', p. 535. 'Balduini Ninovensis Chronicon', *MGHS*, XXV, p. 543. Cf. also 'Continuatio Sancrucensis secunda', p. 640.
58. Strakosch-Grassmann, pp. 102–4.
59. Andrea Dandolo, 'Chronica per extensum descripta', *RIS²*, XII:1, p. 299.
60. RV, p. 575 (tr. in *Mongolensturm*, p. 169). Béla's letter is in *VMH*, I, p. 182 (no. 335).
61. Béla: ibid., I, p. 183 (no. 337) = *MGHEp.*, I, p. 722 (no. 821). Kálmán: *AUO*, VII, pp. 121–2 (no. 79). Cf. also Gregory to the bishop of Vác, in *VMH*, I, p. 184 (no. 338).
62. ASV, Reg. Vat. 20, fo. 82r (= *Reg. Greg. IX*, no. 6059). *MGHEp.*, I, p. 723 (no. 822); for other recipients, see *Reg. Greg. IX*, nos. 6073–5.
63. ASV, Reg. Vat. 20, fo. 90v = Chr. C.A. Lange and Carl R. Unger, eds, *Diplomatarium Norvegicum*, I (Christiania, 1849), pp. 19–20 (nos. 24, 24c).
64. *VMH*, I, p. 184 (no. 339).
65. Ibid., p. 185 (no. 342).
66. Hans Martin Schaller, 'Das letzte Rundschreiben Gregors IX. gegen Friedrich II.', in *Festschrift Percy Ernst Schramm zu seinem siebzigsten Geburtstag von Schülern und Freunden zugeeignet*, 2 vols (Wiesbaden, 1964), I, pp. 309–21, and repr. in Schaller, *Stauferzeit. Ausgewählte Aufsätze* (Hannover, 1993), pp. 369–85.
67. *HDFS*, VI, pp. 902–4. CICO, IV:2, p. 83 (no. 42) = *VMH*, I, p. 239 (no. 454). For the Cardinals' letter, see W. Wattenbach, 'Zum Mongolensturm', *Forschungen zur Deutschen Geschichte* 12 (1872), pp. 643–8 (here pp. 643–5).
68. Fedor Schneider, 'Ein Schreiben der Ungarn an die Kurie aus der letzten Zeit des Tatareneinfalles (2. Februar 1242)', *MIOG* 36 (1915), pp. 661–70 (here p. 670). The envoys, i.e. Salomon, canon of Stuhlweissenburg and provost of St Nicholas, and some Franciscans, carried briefer letters from Uros, abbot of St Martin in Pannonia (Pannonhalma): MOL, DF 290697 (3 Feb. 1242) and 290698 (originals in Siena now lost).
69. For what follows, see generally Peter Jackson, 'The crusade against the Mongols (1241)', *JEH* 42 (1991), pp. 1–18 (esp. pp. 6–10), Hungarian trans. as 'Keresztes hadjárat a Mongolok ellen (1241)', in Balázs Nagy, ed., *Tatárjárás* (Budapest, 2003), pp. 348–61 (here pp. 349–51); Maier, *Preaching the Crusades*, pp. 59–60. Fasting and processions: Henry Raspe, in *CM*, IV, p. 110, and VI, p. 78; Václav I of Bohemia, in J.F. Böhmer, 'Briefe über den Anmarsch der Mongolen gegen Deutschland im Jahr 1241', in K.Ed. Förstemann, ed., *Neue Mittheilungen aus dem Gebiet historisch-antiquarischer Forschungen*, IV:2 (Halle, 1839), pp. 105–17 (here p. 111); Henry, bishop of Constance, in *HDFS*, V, p. 1211; 'Annales Wormatienses', *MGHS*, XVII, p. 46. These measures had been called for by the Franciscan Jordan: *CM*, VI, p. 84.
70. 'Annales Wormatienses', p. 47: *supervenerunt ... alia nova, quod Tartari ad alias partes secessissent.*
71. 'Annales Sancti Trudperti', *MGHS*, XVII, p. 294; hence, probably, 'Annales Zwifaltenses. Annales maiores', *MGHS*, X, p. 59.
72. *CM*, IV, p. 298.
73. Ibid., IV, p. 131. See Rudolf, 'Die Tartaren', pp. 100–5; Hilpert, pp. 153–64.

74. *CM*, IV, pp. 272–3. Strakosch-Grassmann, p. 146, saw this as more probable than other details in the letter.
75. 'Annales monasterii de Theokesberia', *AM*, I, p. 118. Philippe Mouskès, *Chronique rimée*, II, p. 681 (vv. 30963–5). Strakosch-Grassmann, pp. 135, 147, viewed the report as unfounded. On such 'victories', see also the comments of Sinor, 'Les relations', p. 45.
76. *HDFS*, V, p. 1216. IUB ms. 187, fo. 7r.
77. *Siyar al-abā' al-baṭārika*, ed. and tr. O.H.E. Khs-Burmester and A. Khater, *History of the Patriarchs of the Egyptian Church*, IV:2 (Paris, 1974), text pp. 144–5, tr. p. 294 (*ad annum* 1243). *Histoire chronologique par Mkhithar d'Aïrivank, XIIIᵉ s.*, tr. M. Brosset (St Petersburg, 1869), p. 106; also in A.G. Galstian, ed., *Armianskie istochniki o mongolakh* (Moscow, 1962), p. 90 (with no year). Cf. also Ibn Saʿīd al-Maghribī (late 13th cent.), *Kitāb al-jughrāfiyya*, ed. Ismāʿīl al-ʿArabī (Beirut, 1970), pp. 182–3 (reporting a Mongol defeat by the Hungarians and Germans near the town of *Sibinīqū, i.e. Šibenik, on the northern shores of the Gulf of Venice).
78. Ch. Kohler, 'Deux projets de croisade en Terre-Sainte composés à la fin du XIIIᵉ siècle et au début du XIVᵉ siècle', *ROL* 10 (1903–4), pp. 406–57 (here p. 447, mentioning the Bohemian king also). Hayton of Gorigos, 'La flor des estoires de la terre d'Orient' (1307), iii, 14 and 23, *RHCDA*, II, French text pp. 162, 173 (Latin text pp. 295, 304), adding that Batu was drowned; hence Marino Sanudo, *Liber secretorum fidelium crucis*, III:xiii, 5, in J. Bongars, ed., *Gesta Dei per Francos*, I:1 (Hannover, 1611, repr. Toronto, 1972), p. 236. Sanudo would also allude to this in a letter of 1330: Friedrich Kunstmann, 'Studien über Marino Sanudo den Aelteren, mit einem Abhange seiner ungedruckten Briefe', *Abhandlungen der historischen Klasse der königlich bayerischen Akademie der Wissenschaften* 7 (1853–5), pp. 695–819 (here pp. 780–1).
79. *HDFS*, V, p. 1142. Richard of San Germano, 'Chronica', p. 210. 'Annales S. Pantaleonis', p. 535. 'Richeri Gesta Senoniensis ecclesiae', *MGHS*, XXV, p. 310. *CM*, IV, p. 298.
80. Richard of San Germano, 'Chronica', p. 213: *pro facto Tartarorum*; also p. 214, and above, p. 61 and n.24.
81. *HDFS*, V, pp. 1151–3 (= *CM*, IV, pp. 115–18), 1167. Richard of San Germano, 'Chronica', p. 210. 'Annales S. Pantaleonis', p. 535.
82. *HDFS*, V, pp. 1142, 1151–2 (= *CM*, IV, pp. 116–17), and VI, pp. 4–5.
83. Ibid., V, pp. 1141–2, 1144–5, 1152 (= *CM*, IV, p. 116), 1166, and VI, p. 5.
84. Ibid., V, pp. 1145–6. For Frederick's attitude, see Bezzola, pp. 78–81.
85. 'Continuatio Sancrucensis secunda', pp. 640–1.
86. Höfler, p. 28. *CM*, IV, p. 298 (for a rumour in 1247 that Frederick might be driven to call upon Mongol assistance, see IV, p. 635). Philippe Mouskès, *Chronique rimée*, II, p. 681 (vv. 30967–70). 'Richeri Gesta', p. 310. 'Continuatio Sancrucensis secunda', p. 640, blamed the Mongol attack on Hungarian nobles who had murdered King Béla's mother (in 1213) and had been exiled.
87. *TS*, p. 171 (tr. in *Mongolensturm*, p. 253).
88. *MGHEp.*, II, pp. 98–9 (no. 131) = *HDFS*, VI, pp. 345–6 = *VMH*, I, pp. 199–200 (no. 369).

89. Ulrich Schmilewski, 'Schlesien im 13. Jahrhundert vor und nach der Schlacht bei Wahlstatt', in *Wahlstatt*, pp. 9–34 (here p. 25).

90. Bolesław Szcześniak, 'Hagiographical documentation of the Mongol invasions of Poland in the thirteenth century. Part I. The Preaching Friars', *Memoirs of the Research Department of the Toyo Bunko* 17 (1958), pp. 167–95 (here pp. 176–85). RV, p. 564 (tr. in *Mongolensturm*, p. 153), thought that Breslau had been completely destroyed.

91. J.M. Canivez, ed., *Statuta capitulorum generalium Ordinis Cisterciensis ab anno 1116 ad annum 1786*, II (Louvain, 1934), p. 237.

92. Winfried Irgang, ed., *Schlesisches Urkundenbuch*, II. *1231–1250* (Vienna etc., 1978), p. 191 (no. 324).

93. C.J. Erben, ed., *Regesta diplomatica nec non epistolaria Bohemiae et Moraviae*, I. *Annorum 600–1253* (Prague, 1855), pp. 510, 545–7, 572, 589 (nos. 1070, 1166, 1170, 1172, 1239, 1272). Cf. 'Annales S. Pantaleonis', p. 535: *preter castra et loca munita*.

94. 'Sifridi de Balnhusin Compendium historiarum' (down to 1304), *MGHS*, XXV, p. 704.

95. 'Hermanni Altahensis annales', *MGHS*, XVII, p. 394.

96. 'De invasione Tartarorum', p. 599.

97. TS, p. 174 (tr. in *Mongolensturm*, p. 255). RV, p. 586 (tr. in *Mongolensturm*, p. 183).

98. Ibid., p. 568 (tr. in *Mongolensturm*, p. 159).

99. Ibid., p. 585 (tr. in *Mongolensturm*, pp. 182–3). TS, p. 172 (tr. in *Mongolensturm*, p. 254). MOL, DF 258195 (= *CDH*, IV:1, p. 273); DL 255 (= *CDH*, IV:1, p. 274; *UBB*, I, p. 206, no. 290).

100. RV, p. 587 (tr. in *Mongolensturm*, p. 185).

101. Ibid., p. 585 (tr. in *Mongolensturm*, p. 182; see ibid., p. 222, n.222). For the slaughter in Esztergom, see MOL, DL 383 (late copy of document dated 28 June 1254 = *CDH*, IV:2, p. 215). But clearly a significant number of citizens survived: DF 248311 and DF 248313 (= *CDH*, IV:2, pp. 37–8, 375 respectively).

102. TS, p. 167 (tr. in *Mongolensturm*, p. 248). 'Annales Frisacenses', p. 65 note; cf. the abridged version of this text in BN ms. lat. 9666, ed. G. Kisch, 'Aus der Echternacher Klosterbibliothek', *Korrespondenzblatt des Vereins für siebenbürgische Landeskunde* 27:2 (Feb. 1904), pp. 17–20 (here p. 18). The figure of 100 dead at Hermannstadt, given in 'Annales Erphordenses', *MGHS*, XVI, p. 34, is probably an error for 100,000 (hence also 'Cronica S. Petri Erfordensis moderna', *MGHS*, XXX, p. 395).

103. Fügedi, *Castle and Society*, chap. 3.

104. Denis Sinor, 'John of Plano Carpini's return from the Mongols: new light from a Luxemburg manuscript', *JRAS* (1957), pp. 193–206 (here pp. 203, 205), repr. in Sinor, *Inner Asia*. See also *VMH*, I, p. 231 (no. 440) = *DIR*, I:1, p. 261 (no. 199); and for the date, n.51 above. For the distribution of Cuman settlement, see A. Pálóczi-Horváth, 'L'immigration et l'établissement des Comans en Hongrie', *AOASH* 29 (1975), pp. 313–33; and on the longer-term problems, Berend, *At the Gate*, pp. 134–40, 142–8.

105. *VMH*, I, pp. 208–11 (no. 393: confirmation by Innocent IV, 19 July 1250, of Béla's grant dated 2 June 1247) = *UBGD*, I, pp. 73–6 (no. 82) = *CGOH*, II, pp. 656–9 (no. 2445) = *DIR*, I:1, pp. 249–53 (no. 193); also in György Györffy, 'Adatok a románok XIII. századi történetéhez és a román allam kezdeteihez (I. rész.)', *Történelmi Szemle* 7 (1964), pp. 1–25 (here pp. 4–5, no. 6); Anthony Luttrell, 'The Hospitallers in Hungary before 1418: problems and sources', in Zsolt Hunyadi and József Laszlovszky, eds, *The Crusades and the Military Orders. Expanding the Frontiers of Medieval Latin Christianity* (Budapest, 2001), pp. 269–81 (here pp. 271–2).
106. Gábor Klaniczay, *Holy Rulers and Blessed Princesses. Dynastic Cults in Medieval Central Europe*, tr. Éva Pálmai (Cambridge, 2000), p. 277.
107. MOL, DL 270 (11 Oct. 1244 = *CDH*, IV:1, pp. 342–3); DL 16087 (*anno* 1255, transcribed in a document of 1426 = *CDH*, IV:2, pp. 300–1); and DL 40090 (26 June 1257, transcribed in a document of 1335 = *AKO*, I, p. 354, no. 1153).
108. Hungarians and others: Gregory G. Guzman, 'European clerical envoys to the Mongols: reports of Western merchants in Eastern Europe and Central Asia, 1231–1255', *JMH* 22 (1996), pp. 53–67 (here p. 63); Leonardo Olschki, *Guillaume Boucher: A French Artist at the Court of the Khans* (Baltimore, 1946; repr. New York, 1969). German miners: WR, xxiii, 2–3, and xxxiii, 1, pp. 224–5, 289 (tr. Jackson and Morgan, pp. 144, 146, 226).
109. See generally James Ross Sweeney, '"Spurred on by the fear of death": refugees and displaced populations during the Mongol invasion of Hungary', in Michael Gervers and Wayne Schlepp, eds, *Nomadic Diplomacy, Destruction and Religion from the Pacific to the Adriatic*, TSCIA 1 (Toronto, 1994), pp. 34–62; and his 'Identifying the medieval refugee: Hungarians in flight during the Mongol invasion', in Ladislaus Jöb *et al.*, eds, *Forms of Identity: Definitions and Changes* (Szeged, 1994), pp. 63–76 (I owe this latter reference to Noreen Giffney).
110. TS, p. 178 (tr. in *Mongolensturm*, p. 261). 'Continuatio Sancrucensis secunda', p. 641. See also 'Annales Sancti Rudberti Salisburgenses', *MGHS*, IX, p. 788; VB, xxxi, 149 (= SSQ, p. 78); hence, probably, Martin of Troppau, 'Chronicon pontificum et imperatorum', *MGHS*, XXII, p. 472, and 'Chronici ab Ottone Frisingensi conscripti continuatio auctore, uti videtur, Ottone S. Blasii monacho', *MGHS*, XX, p. 335. For an example, see MOL, DL 58390 (= *CDH*, IV:2, pp. 362–3).
111. MOL, DF 277178 (6 May 1246, confirmation dated 1263 = *CDH*, IV:1, pp. 414–15; *UBGS*, p. 66, no. 63; *UBGD*, I, p. 72, no. 81; *DIR*, I:1, p. 230, no. 178). The district of *Iheyke, in the county of Szábolcs, was still allegedly deserted in 1291: DL 95050 (= *CDH*, VI:1, pp. 126, 128).
112. Nógrád: MOL, DF 248300 (*anno* 1239 in error for 1249, transcribed in a document of 1323 = *CDH*, IV:2, p. 53; *MES*, I, p. 381, no. 490). Beren: DL 3633 (= *CDH*, IV:2, p. 403). Inse: *UBB*, I, p. 346 (no. 515).
113. Engel, *Realm of Saint Stephen*, pp. 101–3. But for settlement patterns, see Péter Szabó, 'Pilis: changing settlements in a Hungarian forest in the Middle Ages', *Annual of Medieval Studies at CEU* (1997–8), pp. 283–93 (here

pp. 292–3); József Laszlovszky, 'Field systems in medieval Hungary', in Balázs Nagy and Marcell Sebők, eds, . . . *The Man of Many Devices Who Wandered Full Many Ways . . . Festschrift in Honor of János M. Bak* (Budapest, 1999), pp. 432–44 (here pp. 436, 439).
114. Senga, 'Ungarisch-bulgarische Beziehungen', p. 79. Berend, *At the Gate*, p. 37. The campaign against Austria is referred to in MOL, DL 260 (= *CDH*, IV:1, p. 289), DL 434 (= *CDH*, IV:2, p. 389; *AUO*, II, p. 270, no. 179), DL 92 (= *CDH*, IV:2, p. 391), and DL 86766 (= *CDH*, VII:5, p. 274); see also *CDH*, IV:1, p. 295 = *AUO*, VII, p. 135, no. 89.
115. TS, p. 169 (tr. in *Mongolensturm*, p. 251). Juwaynī, I, pp. 225–6 (tr. Boyle, I, p. 270).
116. Irgang, *Schlesisches Urkundenbuch*, II, p. 131 (no. 212).
117. Henry Raspe, landgrave of Thuringia, to Henry II, duke of Brabant, in *CM*, VI, p. 77. See also Ponce of Albon, Templar preceptor in Francia, to Louis IX, in 'Ex Historiae regum Franciae continuatione Parisiensi', *MGHS*, XXVI, p. 605.
118. J. Richard, 'Les causes des victoires mongoles d'après les historiens occidentaux du XIIIe siècle', *CAJ* 23 (1979), pp. 104–17 (here p. 112), repr. in Richard, *Croisés.*
119. TS, p. 166 (tr. in *Mongolensturm*, p. 248). See also 'Carmina de regno Ungariae destructo per Tartaros', *MGHS*, XXIX, p. 602.
120. Richard, 'Les causes', pp. 109–10. For Mongol armour, see Świętosławski, pp. 21–41; for bows and arrows, ibid., pp. 58–66.
121. PC, viii, 7, p. 296 (tr. Dawson, p. 46).
122. *HDFS*, V, pp. 1215–16, 1217, and VI, p. 904. Becker, pp. 53–4. See also Béla's later request for 1,000 *balistarii* from Pope Alexander IV, 1259: CICO, IV:2, p. 87 (no. 42) = *VMH*, I, p. 241 (no. 454).
123. TR, §61, pp. 36–7. Marian Plezia, 'Das taktische Kapitel der neuentdeckten „Historia Tartarorum"', *Philologus* 115 (1971), pp. 234–9 (here pp. 237–8).
124. Dominican 'R.' and Franciscan 'J.', in *CM*, VI, p. 82.
125. Jordan, Franciscan vice-minister in Bohemia, ibid., VI, p. 81. For subsequent anxiety that the Mongols might profit from the divisions within Christendom, see below, pp. 198, 206.
126. For a useful survey of the literature, see Greg S. Rogers, 'An examination of historians' explanations for the Mongol withdrawal from East Central Europe', *East European Quarterly* 30 (1996), pp. 3–26. Bewilderment: 'Annales Scheftlarienses maiores', *MGHS*, XVII, p. 341; cf. also 'Richeri Gesta', p. 310.
127. PC, ix, 36, p. 322 (tr. Dawson, p. 65, with 'mistress', based on the faulty reading *amica* for *amita*); cf. also viii, 5, p. 295 (tr. Dawson, p. 45), and the unique fragment ed. Sinor as 'John of Plano Carpini's return', p. 203.
128. Rashīd al-Dīn, I, p. 735 (tr. Boyle, *Successors*, p. 121; tr. Thackston, II, p. 361). Not named here, she is described as his favourite daughter and the wife of Cha'ur Sechen (see also Thackston trans., I, pp. 147–8).
129. Ibid., I, p. 673 (tr. Boyle, *Successors*, pp. 65–6; tr. Thackston, II, p. 330). See the discussion in Paul Pelliot, *Recherches sur les Chrétiens d'Asie centrale et d'Extrême-Orient*, ed. with additional notes by Jean Dauvillier (Paris, 1973), pp. 66–7.

130. For what follows, see Denis Sinor, 'Horse and pasture in Inner Asian history', *OE* 19 (1972), pp. 171–84 (here pp. 181–2), repr. in Sinor, *Inner Asia*; also idem, 'The Mongols in the West', *JAH* 33 (1999), pp. 1–44 (here pp. 18–20); Morgan, *Mongols*, pp. 140–1.

131. TS, p. 175 (tr. in *Mongolensturm*, p. 258).

132. Rudi Paul Lindner, 'Nomadism, horses and Huns', *Past and Present* 92 (1981), pp. 3–19.

133. See Peter Jackson, 'The dissolution of the Mongol empire', *CAJ* 22 (1978), pp. 186–244 (here pp. 198–9 and n.48); Göckenjan, 'Der Westfeldzug', pp. 42–3.

134. Göckenjan, 'Der Westfeldzug', pp. 59–60.

135. *PSRL*, II, col. 785 (tr. Perfecky, p. 48). Ptolomy of Lucca (d. 1326–7), 'Historia ecclesiastica', *RIS*, XI, col. 1137: *Deo disponente, orta est discordia inter eos, et sic retrocedunt*; see also his *Annales*, ed. Bernhard Schmeidler, *Die Annalen des Tholomeus von Lucca in doppelter Fassung*, SRG² 8 (Berlin, 1930), p. 117: *tandem discordia inter eos orta retrocedunt*.

136. See, e.g., V.T. Pashuto, 'Mongol'skii pokhod v glub' Evropy', in Tikhvinskii, *Tataro-Mongoly*, pp. 210–27 (esp. pp. 212–15).

137. Strakosch-Grassmann, pp. 147–8; see also ibid. p. 52. But cf. his more plausible hypothesis, cited below.

138. TR, §§28, 29, p. 20. The only princely casualty mentioned in sources from the Mongol empire is Kölgen, a son of Chinggis Khan who had been killed outside the Rus' city of Kolomna in 1237: Rashīd al-Dīn, I, p. 668 (tr. Boyle, *Successors*, p. 59; tr. Thackston, II, p. 327).

139. Ibid., I, pp. 678–9 (tr. Boyle, *Successors*, p. 71; tr. Thackston, II, p. 332). See Allsen, 'Mongols and North Caucasia', pp. 25–6; Göckenjan, 'Der Westfeldzug', p. 60; also Pashuto, 'Mongol'skii pokhod', pp. 213–14, on a revolt in Bulghār.

140. PC, v, 28, pp. 271–2 (tr. Dawson, p. 30). TR, §28, p. 20.

141. Juwaynī, I, pp. 225–6 (tr. Boyle, I, pp. 270–1). *Yüan shih*, chap. 121, tr. in Pelliot, *Notes sur l'histoire de la Horde d'Or*, pp. 131–2. Cf. also SH, §270, tr. De Rachewiltz, I, p. 202.

142. WR, xxxv, 2, p. 301 (tr. Jackson and Morgan, p. 241).

143. Böhmer, 'Briefe', pp. 113–14 (no. 4). Cf. also Dominican 'R.' and Franciscan 'J.', in *CM*, VI, p. 82, for similar rumours.

144. Nora Berend, 'Imitation coins and frontier societies: the case of medieval Hungary', *AEMA* 10 (1998–9), pp. 5–14. For the older view, see, e.g., Bertold Spuler, *Die Goldene Horde: Die Mongolen in Rußland 1223–1502*, 2nd edn (Wiesbaden, 1965), p. 21; Göckenjan, 'Der Westfeldzug', p. 55.

145. RV, p. 581 (tr. in *Mongolensturm*, pp. 176–7).

146. Strakosch-Grassmann, p. 147. Jean Richard, 'Les Mongols et l'Occident: deux siècles de contacts', in *1274 année charnière*, pp. 85–96 (here pp. 86–7), repr. in Richard, *Croisés*. Z.J. Kosztolnyik, *Hungary in the Thirteenth Century* (New York, 1996), p. 182. Peter Jackson, 'The Mongols and Europe', in *NCMH*, V, p. 707.

147. Irwin, *Middle East*, pp. 17–18.

148. On this campaign, see Claude Cahen, *The Formation of Turkey. The Seljukid Sultanate of Rūm: Eleventh to Fourteenth Century*, tr. P.M. Holt (London, 2001), pp. 70-1.

149. Robert, patriarch of Jerusalem, to Innocent IV, 21 Sept. 1244, in *Chronicle of Melrose*, p. 92. *CM*, IV, pp. 389-90. Jackson, 'Crusades of 1239-1241', p. 57.

150. Bar Hebraeus, tr. Budge, *Chronography*, p. 409; idem, *Mukhtaṣar*, p. 255. Claude Cahen, 'Les mémoires de Saʿd al-dīn ibn Ḥamawiya Djuwaynī', in his *Les peuples musulmans dans l'histoire médiévale* (Damascus, 1977), p. 469; Arabic text in al-Dhahabī (d. 1348), *Taʾrīkh al-Islām 641-650*, ed. ʿUmar ʿAbd al-Salām Tadmurī (Beirut, 1419 H./1998), p. 13.

151. See, on these events, R. Stephen Humphreys, *From Saladin to the Mongols: the Ayyubids of Damascus, 1193-1260* (Albany, NY, 1977), pp. 272-8, 284-7.

chapter 4

A REMEDY AGAINST THE
TARTARS

The papal embassies

B y the election of Pope Innocent IV in June 1243, the Curia had
at its disposal some limited information about the invaders, beginning, no doubt, with the report which the Dominican Julian had
addressed to the papal legate in Hungary and which had been registered
in the *Liber censuum*; in addition, copies of two of Béla IV's letters from
1241–2 were among the documents transported from Italy to Lyons
when Innocent took refuge there from the Emperor in December 1244.[1]
And Roger of Várad, who had been in Rome in 1243, may have attended the First Council of Lyons in 1245.[2] The Curia further benefited
from the presence of a refugee ecclesiastic from Rus' named Peter, who
arrived at Lyons at the end of 1244 or early in 1245.[3] Peter, who was to
be interrogated about the Mongols at the Council in June but who
must surely have had a previous audience with pope and cardinals,
assured his interlocutors that the Mongols received embassies favourably
(*benigne*) and did not mistreat them.[4] The pope was encouraged by this
news, which had not been available at the time of the invasion, to send
ambassadors to the grim new power that had arisen on Latin Christendom's eastern frontiers. The agenda for the First Council of Lyons
included not just 'a remedy against the Tartars' but also perennial problems such as: Church reform; the deposition of the Emperor Frederick;
negotiations with the Greek Emperor of Nicaea, John III Ducas Vatatzes,
for ecclesiastical union; and the parlous situation of the Holy Land. It is
a measure of the importance Innocent attached to the Mongol threat,
however, that he did not wait for the opening of the Council but in
March or April 1245 despatched no less than three embassies to the
Mongols, consisting of members of the Mendicant Orders.

The most celebrated of these embassies was headed by John of Plano
Carpini (Pian di Carpine), a former Franciscan provincial minister in

Saxony (1232–9) and currently a papal penitentiary.[5] Joined at Breslau by the Polish Franciscan Benedict, Carpini's party took the route through Eastern Europe to Batu's headquarters on the Volga. While some of their colleagues remained with Batu, Carpini and Benedict were sent on to Mongolia, arriving just in time to witness Güyüg's enthronement in August 1246. The other two missions headed for the Mongol armies in the Near East. For this task the pope seems initially to have designated another Franciscan, the Portuguese Laurence, accompanied by two English Franciscans; but he then changed his mind and despatched Laurence as legate to the Latin territories in Syria and Cyprus.[6] Contact with the Mongols in the Near East was entrusted instead to two groups of Dominicans, led respectively by the Lombard Ascelin, who waited upon the noyan Baichu at Sisian in Greater Armenia in the summer of 1247, and by Andrew of Longjumeau, who probably visited Tabrīz. The pope appears to have entrusted each embassy with two letters, addressed to the Mongol 'king' and his people as a whole. In *Cum non solum* (13 March 1245) Innocent remonstrated with the Mongols, appealed to them to desist from attacking Christians and other nations, and enquired as to their future intentions; *Dei patris immensa* (5 March 1245) contained an exposition of the Christian faith and urged the Mongols to accept baptism.[7] From the summary given by Carpini, we can be sure that he carried both letters; doubtless Ascelin did also.[8]

The data concerning the Carpini embassy that have come down to us are markedly fuller than the material on the Dominican missions. In view of the distance they had travelled and the fact that they had visited the Mongol sovereign's own court, the Franciscans' return seems to have caused the greatest stir.[9] Even as they made their way back through Eastern Europe, Germany and Champagne in the early autumn of 1247, Carpini tells us, he and his colleagues were obliged to hand over the unfinished draft of their report to eager inquirers, so that interim versions were being disseminated.[10] In addition, around the end of July a Franciscan calling himself 'C. de Bridia', who may have been one of the anonymous colleagues left behind in Batu's territory, had produced the work known as the 'Tartar Relation', on the basis of information supplied by Benedict.[11] A ninth and final chapter, comprising a narrative of the journey, was added to the main report after Carpini's return to Western Europe, and revisions were made elsewhere in the text. Donald Ostrowski has proposed that these changes were not made by Carpini himself.[12] Possibly they were the work of Benedict, who in October 1247 dictated his own brief account of the party's experiences to a cleric at Cologne.[13] The account of Ascelin's embassy, written up by one of its members, Simon of Saint-Quentin, is no longer extant in its original form, but lengthy excerpts are preserved in the *Speculum historiale* of the Dominican Vincent of Beauvais (*c*.1253), who also had access to the first redaction of Carpini's *Ystoria*.[14] Only a brief abstract of Andrew's report has survived in Matthew Paris's *Chronica majora*, and we would know hardly anything about his mission were it not for the survival of letters relating to his diplomatic activities in the Near East (below, pp. 93–4).

As a *démarche* aimed at placing relations with the Mongols on a fresh footing, it cannot be claimed that the embassies were a success. Ascelin greatly offended his hosts at the outset by stating that the pope, whom Christians regarded as superior to any other man, had never heard of the qaghan, Batu or Baichu.[15] Consequently, the party did not receive unduly indulgent treatment. Because of their intransigence in the face of the requirements of Mongol protocol, they were denied an audience with Baichu and were kept waiting for a reply for some weeks, while the Mongol general allegedly issued orders for their execution on no less than three occasions before being dissuaded by his entourage. Even when they had been given permission to leave, their departure was further held up in view of the impending arrival of Arghun Aqa, the qaghan's plenipotentiary and civil governor of Persia.[16] When they finally left Baichu's encampment late in July 1247, the friars were accompanied by two Mongol envoys, Aybeg and Sargis (the latter – to judge from his name, 'Sergius' – an eastern Christian), and carried an ultimatum from the Mongol general ordering Innocent to appear before the qaghan in person, together with a copy of a letter from Güyüg delivered to Baichu by Arghun Aqa, which insisted on the publication of Heaven's edict requiring the submission of all peoples.[17] Innocent's reply to Baichu, dated 22 November 1248, merely warned him of the consequences of persisting in error.[18]

Carpini brought back for the pope an ultimatum from Güyüg, which has already been quoted (p. 47). The qaghan claimed not to understand the plea that he be baptized as a Christian or the rebuke for having attacked the Hungarians and other peoples. How did the pope, calling himself a Christian, know whom God forgave and on whom He bestowed mercy? As for the Hungarians, they had disobeyed the Order of God, killing Mongol messengers and envoys. Without God's power, the Mongols could not have achieved all their victories and conquests. The entire world, from where the sun rose to where it set, had been conferred on them; the pope was therefore instructed to come in person, with the 'kings', to make his submission.[19]

The phrasing of the letter demonstrates that Güyüg had not just been perplexed by the request concerning baptism and the reproaches for

Mongol massacres in Eastern Europe, but had misconstrued the whole character and purpose of the embassy. At the first Mongol camp the party reached, Carpini had stated that the pope wished 'all Christians to be friends of the Tartars and to have peace with them' and desired, moreover, that 'the Tartars be great before God in Heaven'.[20] And in *Cum non solum* Innocent himself spoke of his desire for 'all to live in the unity of peace' and asked the Mongols to engage in 'fruitful discourse . . . especially on those matters that pertain to peace'.[21] Now in the Mongols' vocabulary, as we have seen (p. 46), the terms for 'peace' and for 'subjection' were identical: the Turkish word *il[i]* did duty for both. The mere despatch of an embassy seemed tantamount to surrender. 'Why have you come', Rubruck was asked in amazement some years later, 'since you did not come to make peace?'[22] It is no surprise to find the Mongols now treating Carpini's arrival as a token of papal submission, so that Batu felt obliged to forward the envoys to the new qaghan. 'Having taken counsel about making peace with us', began Güyüg's reply to the pope, 'you have sent us a plea of submission';[23] and Innocent's personal appearance was required if he was 'sincere'. It seems the qaghan was affronted that the embassy had brought no gifts; immediately following his enthronement, the friars' rations were reduced.[24] Nevertheless, in Mongol eyes Innocent had, through the Carpini mission, taken the first step towards recognizing his place in the Mongol world-empire.

This impression would have been reinforced by Carpini's own conduct. He showed himself ready to adapt to practices such as passing between two fires, genuflecting three times before entering a commander's tent, and addressing Mongol leaders on bended knee;[25] the friars apparently even bowed their heads before an effigy of Chinggis Khan.[26] Ascelin, who was concerned to make no gesture that might dishearten other nations or cheer Christendom's enemies, flatly refused to perform these acts of obeisance; he also made it clear to the Mongols that the pope was not subject to them.[27] Carpini's stay at the various Mongol encampments was therefore free of the altercations that characterized Ascelin's mission. His compliance extended further. It is usually assumed that he was the only ambassador who was under orders to proceed to the Mongols' headquarters,[28] but we have no direct evidence for this. In any case, when required by Baichu to deliver his message to the qaghan in person, Ascelin refused on the grounds that his instructions were to hand the papal letters to the first Mongol army he met; eventually Baichu acquiesced.[29] By contrast, when Carpini was sent on from Batu's encampment he raised no objection.[30]

In addition to the purely diplomatic function, Carpini at least was instructed to observe and examine everything prior to reporting back to the pope.[31] His task was clearly to gather intelligence – to spy. The first eight chapters of his report constitute a systematic dossier of information on the Mongol enemy, arranged in answer to specific questions that are virtually identical with those put to the Rus' cleric Peter. Significantly, chapter 8 deals with the question of how to wage war against the Mongols. It is of course impossible to tell whether Simon of Saint-Quentin's report was equally methodical, since the material may well have been reordered by Vincent of Beauvais; but here too we find chapters devoted to the Mongols' diet, dress, weaponry, techniques of siege warfare, and so on.

Carpini's long journey afforded him a much clearer view of the vast extent of the Mongol empire. He mentions the presence at Güyüg's enthronement of the Rus' Grand Prince, Iaroslav Vsevolodovich, 'chiefs' from China and Korea, two sons of the king of Georgia, more than ten Muslim sultans, and over four thousand envoys, including those of the 'Abbasid Caliph;[32] Benedict says that an embassy from the Egyptian Sultan accompanied the party for the first fortnight of the return journey.[33] Carpini's report also furnishes a long list of those nations who had acknowledged Mongol sovereignty, including the Khitai (Chinese), Georgians, Armenians, Persians, Cumans, the people of Great Bulgaria (Bulghār) and the Ruthenians (Rus').[34] Apart from yielding at least one poignant reminder of the recent assault on Europe, in the form of Batu's very fine linen tents that had at one time belonged to the Hungarian king,[35] the mission also acquired the intelligence that Güyüg planned a fresh invasion, which would involve two separate armies attacking Poland and Hungary, and that these forces had already set out.[36] The qaghan himself allegedly stated that he wanted to send an army into Livonia and Prussia.[37] Carpini subsequently told the Franciscan Salimbene de Adam that the Mongols planned to conquer Italy.[38]

Regarding the nature of Mongol overlordship the papal envoys were in no doubt. Carpini remarked on the intolerable and unheard-of servitude that they imposed upon the subject peoples.[39] He described at length the miserable condition of the skilled craftsmen whom the Mongols enslaved, while Simon of Saint-Quentin stressed the burdensome nature of Mongol exactions.[40] The conquerors' intention was to bring the whole world into subjection, and they would accordingly make peace with no people that had not yielded to them.[41] In particular, they sought to wipe off the face of the earth all princes, nobles and knights and those of gentle birth.[42] They could not be trusted, and any initial appearance of mildness or mercy was merely pretence; at first, Carpini twice assured his readers, the Mongols spoke smooth words, but later they would sting like a scorpion.[43] In meeting the threat a coordinated effort was essential, for the Mongols were practised at picking off one kingdom at a time and using its people to subjugate their neighbours.[44]

Yet for all their emphasis on the menace posed by the Mongols, Carpini and Simon do draw attention to vulnerabilities. The enemy were weaker both numerically and physically than the Latins.[45] In their forces were to be found other nations in significant numbers, who would willingly mutiny at the approach of a Western army.[46] Carpini lists the many peoples, moreover, who had repulsed the Mongols and were still holding out.[47] The Mongols showed greater courage in fighting those who were in flight,[48] and their victories owed less to strength than to guile.[49] In fact, they feared the Franks more than any other race in the world.[50] A prophecy was allegedly current among them that they were due to rule for a further eighteen years before they were defeated.[51] All this is pressed into service as evidence that it is not only desirable but possible for the West to withstand the next invasion. In much the same way Rubruck, a few years later, would claim that the Mongols were less formidable than the Huns because the latter had advanced much further, into France, and had received tribute even from Egypt[52] – regardless of the fact that the centre of gravity of the Mongol empire lay hundreds of miles east of that of the Huns. There can be little doubt that the friars were seeking to stiffen the resistance of their fellow Latins.[53]

A buffer against the Mongol menace

Why did the pope send three missions, and in particular two to the Near East? He was certainly exercised by the plight of the Holy Land, which had been attacked by the Khwarazmians and briefly menaced by Yasa'ur's campaign in the summer of 1244 (see above, p. 74). This finds an echo in the belief of the English Franciscan, Adam Marsh, that Innocent was sending envoys 'to the nations who . . . have laid waste the Holy Land, namely the Khwarazmians, and to the Tartars and the Saracens'.[54] And certainly the patriarch of Antioch was in Europe by March 1245 to seek aid for the Holy Land.[55] But again it was probably above all the Rus' cleric Peter who had been instrumental in the pope's decision, for he had spoken of three Mongol armies, operating respectively against the Egyptians (*Babilonii*), the Turks (i.e. the Seljüks of Rūm) and the Christians of Eastern Europe (though the three armies are said, inaccurately, to be converging on Syria).[56] In fact, these three directions coincide with the routes taken by the papal embassies, since Andrew's itinerary is known to have included Syria and Palestine,[57] while Ascelin's mission took two years to reach the Mongols and Simon of Saint-Quentin's report includes a wealth of detail about the Rūm Sultanate which can only have become accessible as a result of a prolonged stay among the Seljüks.[58]

This in itself indicates that the embassies had other aims besides making diplomatic contact with the Mongols, and it may be that Innocent IV did not attach any greater importance to contact with the Mongols than to dealings with other peoples. Carpini tells us how he had decided to visit the Mongols first;[59] in other words, the choice was left to the ambassador. He describes himself as envoy of the Apostolic See to 'the other nations of the East' as well as to the Mongols;[60] and indeed Innocent IV's chaplain and biographer, Niccolò di Calvi, not only mentions that envoys were sent to the sultans of Egypt and Rūm, but treats Carpini's mission as just one among a whole series of legations to 'barbarous nations of divers territories', designed to bring about their adhesion to the Catholic faith.[61] This is a reference to the simultaneous despatch of parties of friars with the letter *Cum simus super* (late March 1245), which affirmed the primacy of the Roman Church, marshalled scriptural quotation in its support, and urged the recipients to return to ecclesiastical unity; it was addressed to the prelates of, among others, the Bulgarians, Vlachs, Serbs, Alans, Georgians, Nubians, Nestorians 'and other Christians of the East'.[62] In pursuit of his vision of a Christian world reunited under papal leadership, Innocent also engaged in renewed efforts to secure recognition of Roman primacy by the Greeks.[63]

Now the diplomatic missions to the Mongols were also part of this wider papal initiative. It will be as well to begin with Andrew. He is known to have made contact with Ayyubid princes,[64] and a visit to the camp of the Egyptian general Fakhr al-Dīn Ibn al-Shaykh, near Karak in southern Palestine, elicited a letter to Innocent in which the Egyptian Sultan al-Ṣāliḥ Ayyūb was absolved of responsibility for the Khwarazmian sack of Jerusalem.[65] Western European annalists give some prominence, relatively speaking, to the despatch of a mission in 1245 to Ayyūb, by which the pope (thought one writer) aimed to detach the Sultan from the Emperor Frederick.[66] Ayyūb's reply, expressing his determination to make no peace with the West without consulting the Emperor, bears a date corresponding to June 1245;[67] hence, if Andrew was the intermediary here (and we cannot be certain), Cairo had been his first destination. But Andrew also met with the Jacobite ecclesiastical hierarchy in Iraq, and with the Nestorian 'visitor' to the Near East, Simeon Rabban-ata; he too must therefore have carried *Cum simus super*. The purpose of his mission was apparently to explore the possibility that the Mongol threat might throw Muslim rulers into the arms of the Roman Church, and that by a parallel process the separated churches might be induced to seek Western protection by acknowledging papal primacy. In the latter sphere he enjoyed some limited success. In 1247 the Jacobite patriarch, Ignatius II, brought his church officially into union with Rome, though a significant section refused to follow his lead. On behalf of the Nestorian hierarchy, Simeon Rabban-ata forwarded a profession of faith from the catholicus and entrusted Andrew with a cordial letter to the pope in which Roman primacy was freely recognized.[68]

In other respects, however, Andrew's achievement was disappointing. The Ayyubid princes failed to swallow the bait. Al-Manṣūr Ibrāhīm of Ḥimṣ, clearly aware of the thinking behind the papal overtures, assured Innocent that the Mongols posed no threat to the Islamic world and would soon be defeated by his overlord, the Egyptian Sultan.[69] So too Innocent probably found Simeon's profession of obedience more gratifying than his plea for the pope to be reconciled with the Emperor Frederick[70] (although a separate letter to the Emperor urged him in turn to seek the forgiveness of the Holy See). What also became manifest from the correspondence with the eastern churches was that their leaders sought more favourable treatment for non-Latin Christians living under Frankish rule in Syria and Palestine. Both Ignatius and Simeon asked the pope to intervene in these territories and to prevent their confrères being treated as second-class citizens; and Simeon made the same request of the Emperor Frederick.[71] Such a change of policy on the part of the Latins would have brought them into line with the Mongols' stance towards their own subject populations. In the winter of 1248–9 a letter from the Mongol general Eljigidei (see below) to the French king, who had by then reached Cyprus, asked him to see to it that Greek, Armenian and Nestorian Christians enjoyed equal status with Latins. This, together with the responses of Ignatius and Simeon which Andrew brought back in 1247, indicates that 'separated' Christians now under Mongol protection in the Near East were beginning to exploit a stronger position in their dealings with the West.[72]

Carpini's party likewise had more than one commission. En route to Batu, they met at Cracow Vasil'ko, the brother of Daniil Romanovich, prince of Galicia and Volynia (the regions commonly, if not altogether illuminatingly, termed 'Ruthenia'), who was seeking the assistance of neighbouring Polish princes against the Mongols, and accompanied him back to Daniil's court. Daniil himself was away at Batu's encampment, but Vasil'ko convened an assembly of bishops to whom the friars read out a papal letter urging them to 'return to the unity of Mother Church', i.e. evidently *Cum simus super*.[73] In view of Daniil's absence, no response was forthcoming; but during the return journey in 1247 the friars halted at his court a second time. After further discussions with their bishops, the two princes assured Carpini of their desire 'to have the Lord Pope as their special lord and father and the Holy Roman Church as their lady and mistress'. They had previously despatched an abbot to Innocent, and now sent with the Franciscans another envoy and a letter for the pope.[74] Innocent had responded to the earlier legation, on 3 May 1246, by taking Daniil and his dominions under the protection of St Peter.[75]

At Güyüg's headquarters the Franciscans, as we saw, met the Rus' Grand Prince, Iaroslav, whom Batu had invested with Vladimir-in-Suzdal' in 1243 and had sent on to the qaghan. Iaroslav too was negotiating with the Curia. In a letter of 3 May 1246, carried by Archbishop Albert of Prussia and Livonia as papal legate, Innocent expressed his joy that the Grand Prince was ready to acknowledge the primacy of Rome.[76] Another papal letter, to his son Alexander (Nevskii), prince of Novgorod, and dated January 1248, asserts that Iaroslav had made an express profession of obedience to the Roman Church, and cites Carpini as the source of the information.[77] Carpini says nothing of discussions with the Grand Prince in his *Ystoria*, mentioning only his sudden death in Güyüg's encampment: from the fact that the body rapidly turned a striking shade of blue, it was suspected that he had been poisoned by the qaghan's mother, the regent Töregene.[78] Possibly Iaroslav's profession amounted merely to a deathbed conversion or his statement was misrepresented by the interpreter. It has been suggested that Iaroslav was poisoned precisely because of his flirtation with the pope and the West.[79] Alexander certainly displayed a marked hesitation to obey Güyüg's command to travel to Mongolia to receive the qaghan's patent for his inheritance.[80] He had, moreover, accepted union with Rome by September 1248, since Innocent then wrote to him to express his pleasure at the news, which had been transmitted by Archbishop Albert. The prince had also undertaken to raise the Latin church in his city of Pskov to cathedral status.[81]

In seeking to capitalize on the readiness of Rus' princes to recognize the primacy of Rome in return for military assistance against the Mongols, Innocent aimed at erecting a bloc of buffer-states between the Latin heartlands and the Mongol world. Late in January 1248 he asked both Daniil and Alexander, should they hear news of an impending Mongol attack, to send word to the Teutonic Knights, in Prussia and Livonia respectively, so that they in turn might inform the pope and the West thus be spared a repetition of the unexpected onslaught of 1241.[82] Daniil had already made good a promise to provide Béla IV's envoys with intelligence following his return from the Mongols in *c*.1243.[83] The pope also intended to incorporate within this anti-Mongol power-bloc the pagan peoples of Eastern Europe. The Peace of Christburg

(1249), which regulated relations between the Teutonic Knights and their pagan subjects in Prussia, may well have been designed to free their hands for conflict with the Mongols.[84] And by 1251 Innocent was in touch with the pagan Lithuanian prince Mindaugas, who in that year was baptized, in exchange for the crown conveyed to him by a Catholic bishop in 1253, and who subsequently built a cathedral in Vilnius. The Lithuanians promised to be useful allies in the face of Mongol expansion; Carpini attests to their raids deep into the old principality of Kiev.[85] Mindaugas, who in embracing Christianity had been concerned primarily to fortify his position against a neophyte rival and to detach the Teutonic Knights from the ranks of his enemies, also hoped to secure papal sanction for any conquests he might make at the expense of pagan or schismatic (i.e. Orthodox) rulers.[86]

Ultimately these negotiations bore no fruit. Within a short time of the arrival of Innocent's letter of 1248, Alexander rejected the union; his brother Andrei of Suzdal', who adhered to a pro-Latin policy, fled into exile in Sweden.[87] By 1257 Daniil too was no longer mindful of his rapprochement with Rome. When the Mongols attacked Poland in 1259, they would be accompanied by contingents from Galicia and Volynia under Lev and Roman, Daniil's sons, and Vasil'ko, his brother.[88] One circumstance that may have weighed with these Rus' princes, beyond the pope's inability to render them practical military assistance, was the additional political clout conferred on them by becoming Mongol clients. The Galician chronicler believed that Béla IV grew afraid of Daniil following the latter's return from a visit to the Mongols in 1246;[89] whether this was true or not, Daniil himself may have believed it. Zatko proposed that Alexander defected because, fresh from a visit to Güyüg's headquarters at some time early in 1248, he had perceived at first hand the extent of Mongol power and inevitably made the comparison with Western military strength; but it is as likely that what swayed him was his promotion by the qaghan to be grand prince of Kiev.[90] For his part, Mindaugas apostatized two years prior to his murder in 1263, and the Christianization of Lithuania – a hazardous and ambivalent process in Innocent IV's time – remained a dead letter until the definitive conversion of its Grand Duke in the last decades of the fourteenth century. One result of the contacts with Daniil, at least, was that his descendants – in contrast with other Rus' princes – maintained close links with their Latin neighbours.[91]

Innocent IV's plan to erect a barrier between Western Europe and the Mongols had failed. The idea had developed naturally out of papal perceptions of the situation preceding the Mongol invasion of 1241-2 (above, p. 61); it may even have assumed priority for Innocent over the avowed purposes of his letters *Cum non solum* and *Dei patris immensa*. If he had little hope in 1245 of bringing the Mongols to accept Christianity, he could and did expect the Catholic Church to reap some benefit from the predicament in which eastern Christians – and perhaps, too, the Muslims and Eastern European pagans – found themselves. This is not to say that the pope aimed to enter into an understanding with the Mongols against the West's other enemies. The erroneous notion that he sought an alliance against the Islamic world is found in the secondary literature; and Matthew Paris, it is true, heard a scurrilous rumour that during the visit of Baichu's envoys to Lyons in 1248 Innocent tried to incite the Mongols against Frederick II's son-in-law, the Nicaean Emperor John III Vatatzes.[92] Tales of this kind, in all probability, parallel the equally baseless charges that the Mongols had been summoned by Frederick (above, p. 68). There is no evidence that the pope saw them in a providential light, as allies. Ironically, however, by the time his plans to resist them lay in shreds, more encouraging reports were emerging from the Mongol empire regarding the possibility of the Mongols' own conversion.

Christianity in the Mongol empire

By the mid-thirteenth century the Latin West had been alerted to the presence of Christians not only among the peoples subject to Mongol rule but even within the ranks of the Mongol imperial dynasty. Some of these reports were simply based on false identification. At Güyüg's encampment, Carpini had heard garbled reports about the Chinese Buddhists to the east. Pagans who were said to possess an Old and a New Testament, buildings like churches, and even their own saints, they allegedly worshipped one god, honoured Jesus Christ, loved Christians, and believed in eternal life; they lacked only baptism.[93] But the populations of Central and Eastern Asia did include Christians – Jacobites, Nestorians, Greek Orthodox and Armenians.[94] Of these, the Nestorians were the most widespread and had a longer acquaintance with the new masters of Asia than had any of the other churches. In addition, they often had especial reason to value the termination of Muslim rule. In much the same way, the severe reverses inflicted on the Muslims in Central Asia by earlier pagan powers from the steppe had given rise to considerable elation among the Nestorian communities and (in however distorted a form) had nurtured the myth of Prester John.[95]

The Christians of Güyüg's entourage told Carpini that the qaghan was about to become a Christian, on the grounds that he maintained Christian clerics and kept a portable chapel in front of his pavilion, in contrast with other Mongol princes.[96] The tone in which the Franciscan records this is studiedly neutral, and he says no more about the Nestorians' position within Güyüg's empire, perhaps because he looked askance at them as schismatics. He alluded to the Mongols' toleration of the various religious communities within their empire, though in his later recension he adds the rider that it would be jettisoned once the conquerors' dominion was secure.[97] Andrew of Longjumeau and Simon of Saint-Quentin, on the other hand, observed merely that such latitude was conditional upon obedience to the qaghan.[98] Andrew was the first to draw the West's attention to the activities of the Nestorian Simeon Rabban-ata, who appears to have been responsible for Christian affairs in south-west Asia and obtained the Mongols' permission to oversee the reconstruction of Christian churches; though Simon of Saint-Quentin formed a decidedly less favourable impression of the man. Andrew also brought back the earliest report that Güyüg's mother was a Christian – a daughter, allegedly, of Prester John.[99]

More sanguine expectations were aroused by the Armenian constable, Smbat, in the course of his embassy to Güyüg's court on behalf of his brother King Het'um. Smbat, who as a member of the royal dynasty of Lesser Armenia was closely connected with the Latin East, wrote from Samarqand in 1248 to his two sisters and their husbands, the king of Cyprus and the lord of Jaffa, a letter which they presented to Louis IX on his arrival in Cyprus with the Seventh Crusade, and which was considered sufficiently important to be forwarded to Innocent IV by his legate on the crusade, Eudes de Châteauroux, cardinal bishop of Tusculum. Laying considerable emphasis on the presence of large numbers of Christians in the empire and on the way in which the Three Magi were honoured, Smbat, like Carpini, mentioned the chapels situated in front of the qaghan's court; but he went further, alleging that the qaghan himself 'and all his people' had become Christians. Güyüg's grandfather (Chinggis Khan), moreover, had enfranchised the Christians and forbidden anyone to do them any injury. A Christian king in 'India' had become the Mongols' client and with their help had inflicted a crushing defeat on his Muslim enemies. Smbat had learned of Carpini's mission to Güyüg, and transmitted a somewhat anodyne version of the ultimatum given to the Franciscan, in which Innocent IV was told that God knew whether the qaghan was a Christian or not, and if the pope wished to know he should come and find out for himself.[100]

At around the same time as he was shown Smbat's letter, King Louis was visited by envoys from the Mongol noyan Eljigidei, whom Güyüg had sent to Persia in 1247. This general, whose ostensible purpose was to seek more equitable treatment for eastern Christians living under

Latin rule, expressed cordial wishes for the success of the crusade and assured Louis that he had been sent to oversee the protection of Christians, who under Mongol rule were exempt from taxation and forced labour. How accurate this was, and what Eljigidei's aims were, will be considered later (pp. 174, 181). For the moment we should notice that his envoys – both Christians from the Mosul region – claimed not only that Eljigidei was a Christian but also that Güyüg, at the instance of his Christian mother (again called a daughter of Prester John), had been baptized at Epiphany by a Christian bishop.[101] The news, taken all the more seriously since it appeared to be confirmed by the tenor of Smbat's letter,[102] caused a considerable stir in Western Europe. Matthew Paris duly registered it in his *Chronica majora*; he included also a copy of the French translation of Eljigidei's letter which Louis had sent to his mother, Queen Blanche, in France and which she had forwarded to the English king, Henry III.[103] Adam Marsh wrote that news of the Mongols' conversion was spreading across the world.[104]

Louis and the papal legate interrogated Eljigidei's envoys, and the king was sufficiently encouraged by their replies to send them back in January 1249 with an embassy of his own, headed by Andrew of Longjumeau. Regarding this embassy we have only meagre information, most of it in the form of a garbled account by Louis's biographer Joinville, writing some decades later. The party must have met Eljigidei somewhere in Persia: since Güyüg was now dead, the general forwarded them to his widow, the regent Oghul Qaimish, who received them near Emil. They rejoined the French king at Caesarea in 1251, bringing with them the regent's letter, in which Louis's gifts were acknowledged and he was ordered to send similar 'tribute' every year in future. Joinville assures us that Louis greatly regretted having entered into contact with the Mongols.[105] As a result, when in 1253 the Franciscan William of Rubruck left the crusading army for the Mongol world in a missionary capacity, but bearing a letter from Louis, the king insisted that he should not allow himself to be taken for another French ambassador.[106]

One reason for Rubruck's journey was that further rumours had reached the Holy Land, this time regarding the Christian convictions of Batu's son Sartaq, whose pasturelands lay west of the Volga. Yet the letter Rubruck carried from the French king served to obscure his purpose. Louis asked permission for him to stay in the empire, but also felicitated Sartaq on his conversion and urged him to be a friend to all Christians. Even before they reached Constantinople, the party were rumoured to be official envoys. The mere existence of the letter gave the Mongols the impression that Louis was taking steps to submit to them; and Rubruck subsequently suspected Armenian translators of giving a tendentious rendering of the king's amicable message and turning it into a proposal for an alliance. For this reason Sartaq forwarded the two Franciscans to his father Batu, and Batu in turn sent them across almost the entire breadth of Asia to the court of the new qaghan, Möngke. There they were told that Louis's letter had been mislaid. Möngke seems to have accepted that the friars were not ambassadors, but after a few months sent Rubruck back as his own representative, with a letter requiring the French king's submission and expressly disowning the words of Eljigidei's envoys.[107]

Rubruck was disappointed in Sartaq. On leaving his encampment, the friars were told by Sartaq's chief secretary, *Quyaq ('Coiac'): 'Do not say that our master is a Christian. He is not a Christian; he is a Mongol.'[108] Rubruck was consequently in some doubt whether the prince was a Christian, and suspected him of holding Christians in derision. His territory merely happened to lie athwart the route between Batu's headquarters and a number of Christian peoples; and Muslim envoys, if they brought more valuable gifts, were sent on more expeditiously.[109] Yet Kirakos Ganjakec'i says that the Christians deeply mourned Sartaq's death.[110] And Sartaq's Christian faith is attested not merely by Christian Syriac and Armenian writers but even by Muslim contemporaries who can have had no interest in distorting the truth.[111]

*Quyaq's warning furnishes the key to the Mongols' attitudes. Rubruck deduced that they regarded 'Christian' as the name of a people (i.e. as a synonym for 'Franks') and wished only to be called Mongols.[112] There may have been some truth in this, though categorical evidence is lacking. The essential point to be grasped, however, is that Mongol princes and commanders were Mongols first and foremost; religious allegiances took second place to the task of conquering and governing the empire. Generally, in accordance with a *yasa* of Chinggis Khan, Mongol rulers were concerned to preside evenhandedly over the various religious communities within the empire. 'Holy men' representing every confessional group – rather than all Christians, as Eljigidei claimed – enjoyed freedom from personal taxation (though subject to imposts on any economic activity in which they engaged) and from military service and other kinds of compulsory labour.[113] Kirakos admits that even Sartaq granted these privileges to mosques and their personnel.[114] Juwaynī depicts Güyüg as a dyed-in-the-wool Christian who hated Muslims because he had been reared in the faith by the Christian minister, Qadaq; and he is followed by Bar Hebraeus, who says that the qaghan was 'a true Christian' and that in his reign 'the status of many followers of Christ was exalted'.[115] Yet other testimony suggests that Güyüg was, rather, anti-Muslim and that he was attached to Buddhist lamas;[116] Armenian sources, so impressed by Sartaq's Christian sympathies, are silent about Güyüg's. A similar ambivalence surrounds the qaghan Möngke and his mother Sorqaqtani (d. 1252). Sorqaqtani's Christian faith was well known, and she was buried in a Christian church in Kan-su. Yet Juwaynī, while admitting this, makes great play of her benefactions to Islamic colleges (*madrasas*) and her gifts to needy Muslims.[117] Of Möngke he says that he reserved his greatest acts of generosity for Muslims; Jūzjānī even believed that on his enthronement the qaghan recited the Islamic profession of faith (*shahāda*) at the request of his cousin Berke.[118] And still more conflicting evidence is furnished by a Buddhist source, which puts into Möngke's mouth the pronouncement that the other religions of the world stood in the same relation to Buddhism as did the fingers to the palm of the hand; while the *Yüan shih* indicates that he persevered in the shamanistic path of his forebears.[119]

The result, if not necessarily the intention, of the imperial religious policy was to 'divide and rule', as the different confessional elements jostled for favour and influence at the sovereign's court.[120] Rubruck, describing their participation in the ceremonies at Möngke's headquarters, commented scornfully on their delusions about the qaghan's spiritual allegiance: 'He believes in none of them . . . ; and yet they all follow his court as flies do honey, and he makes them all gifts and all of them believe that they are on intimate terms with him and forecast his good fortune.'[121] He was sceptical regarding the Christian faith of Güyüg, Möngke and Sartaq alike, and blamed these rumours, like the legend of Prester John, on the Nestorians' addiction to hyperbole.[122]

In the eyes of eastern Christians, even the founder of the Mongol empire acquired a providential role. The Dominicans whom Louis IX despatched to the Mongols in 1249 heard a tale concerning Chinggis Khan, which through them came to the notice of Thomas of Cantimpré and, subsequently, of Joinville. The kernel of the story was apparently that a Mongol prince, lost in the wilderness, had encountered a magnificent king on a golden throne who announced himself to be the Lord of Heaven and Earth and had a 'knight' escort the prince safely back to his people. The two versions differ. That of Thomas has a more Christian slant than Joinville's account; Joinville's magnificent king orders the prince to tell Chinggis Khan that he is giving him power to conquer the world, of which Thomas makes no mention; in Thomas's version the knight rides a white horse.

These are obviously distortions of a story current within Mongol society, about the transmission of Heaven's mandate to Chinggis Khan through Teb-Tenggeri. The shaman had subsequently grown arrogant and had threatened to cause a rift between Chinggis Khan and his brothers, with the result that it had been necessary to eliminate him. His pivotal role is merely hinted at in the 'Secret History'; but it is mentioned *c.*1260 by Juwaynī (from whom it was later borrowed by Bar Hebraeus),[123] and in 1262 the Mongol prince Hülegü would refer to it in a letter to Louis IX (see below, p. 182). According to Rashīd al-Dīn (*c.*1303–4), the common folk had believed that Teb-Tenggeri in his trances used to ascend to Heaven on a white horse, and only a few years later the expatriate Armenian prince Hayton writes of a 'knight' on a white horse conferring Heaven's mandate on Chinggis Khan.[124] Clearly the French envoys in 1249 had met Nestorians who were endeavouring to reclothe Mongol legend in Christian garb. The fact that the theme of the lost prince surfaces in Bar Hebraeus's account of the much earlier Christianization of the Kereyid[125] shows how older elements were already attaching themselves to the chimera of Mongol conversion. According to Bar Hebraeus, again, Hülegü told the Jacobite Patriarch that Chinggis Khan had been visited by Christians, who had taught him their religion and just laws.[126]

It was natural that eastern Christians should be over-optimistic regarding the susceptibility of their Mongol rulers to conversion. The majority of them had lived under Islamic rule for centuries; and the advent of the Mongols brought an amelioration of their condition, in the form of equality with Muslims and other religious communities, the promotion of Christians to administrative office, and the opportunity to preach their faith in public.[127] The perspective of the Latins, for whom acceptance of Mongol sovereignty represented precisely the enslavement from which eastern Christians had been delivered, was inevitably very different. The gulf between the eastern and western churches is nicely encapsulated in Rubruck's conversation with the Armenian monk Sargis (Sergius) at Möngke's headquarters. Sargis had assured Möngke that if he became a Christian the whole world would enter into subjection to him and that the Franks and the pope would do his bidding, and advised Rubruck to say the same thing. The Franciscan was horrified, and refused to say anything more than that the West would regard a Christian Mongol qaghan as a friend and brother.[128]

In the summer of 1254 Sartaq's chaplain, John, brought news of his master's baptism to Innocent IV, although in Sicily Conrad IV's officials had allegedly confiscated the prince's letter asking for the means of instruction in Christian ritual and practice, along with John's other effects, and he had been able to proceed only after Conrad's death in May. The pope responded late in August, urging Sartaq to make a public proclamation of his new-found faith.[129] Sartaq, who succeeded his father Batu as ruler of the Golden Horde in 1255/6, soon died in suspicious circumstances, however, and after the brief reign of his young son Ulaghchi the succession passed to Batu's brother Berke, a convert to Islam.[130] Even before the news of Sartaq's baptism, King Louis (inspired by the recent findings of his envoy Andrew of Longjumeau and not, perhaps, as disheartened by the outcome of the embassy as Joinville suggests) had proposed that members of the Mendicant Orders be promoted to vacant sees in the Caliph's territory, to cater for the needs of new converts, since it was reported that several Mongols were themselves baptized and would embrace the Christian faith fully if only preaching were set on foot. Innocent entrusted the matter to Eudes de Châteauroux.[131] But nothing came of this. Despite a sense that Mongol leaders were being won for Christianity, the creation of a network of Catholic sees in Mongol Asia was still a long way off (see chapter 10).

The crusade

By 1253, when Rubruck began his journey through the Mongol empire, its limits extended well into Europe and the Near East.[132] The Bulgarian kingdom, he tells us, paid the Mongols tribute; in all probability it had done so since the invasion of 1242.[133] He believed, mistakenly, that the Georgians were still independent, although we know that they too had been tributary to the conquerors for several years and that Güyüg had divided the kingdom between two rival claimants who had appealed to him.[134] Lesser Armenia had been tributary since 1246.[135] So too the once-mighty Seljük Sultanate of Rūm and the Greek Empire of Trebizond were subject to the Mongols. But the other Greek state in Anatolia, the Empire of Nicaea, had still not yielded: the Emperor John Vatatzes had sent envoys to the qaghan but was playing for time.[136] From Constantinople his rival, the Latin Emperor Baldwin II, is known to have opened diplomatic contact with the Mongols by c.1251.[137] Although Baichu himself was engaged in half-hearted attempts to browbeat the 'Abbasid Caliph into submission and the early 1250s did not witness any major campaigns in the Near East, Syria lay within the penumbra of the Mongol empire. In 1246 the Ayyubid Sultan of Aleppo despatched his cousin to Mongolia to attend Güyüg's enthronement, and Carpini believed that the Mongols were currently taking possession of his territory.[138] His Dominican colleagues visiting the Near East in 1247 claimed that the limits of Mongol domination now lay two days' journey south of Antioch,[139] and Matthew Paris includes Bohemond V of Antioch among those who, around 1246, became tributary to the Mongols.[140] Further south, the Franks of the kingdom of Jerusalem appear to have been anticipating an attack since 1244, for a charter issued there in 1248 is the first to make provision for the conquest of the kingdom by 'other infidels' apart from the Muslims.[141]

Innocent IV's readiness to make diplomatic overtures to the Mongols had not led him to abandon the crusade against them. From the very beginning of his pontificate, he had continued to foster armed resistance. When the Hungarians heard fresh rumours of Mongol activity in the neighbouring territories and turned to him for help, he ordered the patriarch of Aquileia to preach the cross in Germany and to promise all those who took the vow to fight in Hungary the same rewards as for the Holy Land.[142] As a result of the deliberations at the Council of Lyons, he wrote to all Christians urging them to inspect ways of access into their territories and to fortify them with ditches, walls and other structures; the pope undertook to make a financial contribution towards the work both from his own coffers and from the rest of Christendom.[143] But other concerns had not been eclipsed. Even as he authorized crusade preaching in August 1243, Innocent was prepared to commute the vow of the Norwegian duke Knut (for an expedition to the Holy Land) to participation in the crusade against the Mongols in Hungary only if they returned within twelve months; otherwise Knut was to redeem his vow with the sum of money he would have spent on a campaign in Palestine.[144] By 1245–6 the wars against the Emperor Frederick II and the Greeks appear to have outweighed all other priorities. Innocent's agents were then active even in Poland, which still smarted from the Mongol incursion of five years before, and endeavouring to recruit crusaders both against Frederick and in defence of Constantinople.[145] When, responding in 1247 to rumours of an impending Mongol attack on Hungary, the pope asked Béla IV to forward any fresh reports without delay, he promised for his own part to waste no time in sending to Hungary's assistance those who had taken the cross for Syria or Romania 'or anywhere else'.[146] His failure to mention explicitly crusaders in the war against the Hohenstaufen seems significant. Béla was evidently dissatisfied with the papal response: in a letter that should probably be dated to this same year, he expressed his amazement that Innocent was allowing Louis IX's crusade to leave for the Near East at a time when the Mongols menaced the very heart of Europe.[147]

The alarm continued to sound at intervals in the 1250s. Innocent was arranging for the crusade to be preached against the Mongols in the spring of 1253, in Bohemia, Moravia, Serbia (Sorbia?) and Pomerania, and in May 1254, in Estonia, Livonia and Prussia.[148] In June 1258 Pope Alexander IV authorized further crusade preaching by the Mendicant Orders against the Mongols throughout Germany, Bohemia, Moravia and Poland.[149] And from the Near East reports were increasingly ominous.

As Rubruck learned, the qaghan's brother Hülegü was moving west at the head of a great army, with the aim, firstly, of annihilating the Assassins and then of attacking Baghdad and John Vatatzes.[150] Following the prince's arrival in Iran, Baichu headed a fresh campaign against the Anatolian Seljüks (1256). The backwash of this fresh surge of military activity reached as far south as the kingdom of Jerusalem where, according to Matthew Paris, the government at Acre received a Mongol ultimatum in 1257.[151] In that year the patriarch of Jerusalem Jacques Pantaléon, expressed his fears of an imminent Mongol invasion to Alexander IV; while the preceptor of the Temple in the kingdom warned of an assault on Palestine in the following spring.[152] As it grew clear that there was no 'remedy against the Tartars', all the indications were that they were planning, at long last, to follow up the campaigns of 1241–4 in strength.

Notes

1. Felicitas Schmieder, 'Der Einfall der Mongolen nach Polen und Schlesien – Schreckensmeldungen, Hilferufe und die Reaktionen des Westens', in *Wahlstatt*, pp. 77–86 (here p. 85, n.61). Giulio Battelli, 'I transunti di Lione del 1245', *MIOG* 62 (1954), pp. 336–64 (here pp. 351, 364).
2. *Mongolensturm*, pp. 129–30.
3. A variant version of his report calls him archbishop of 'Belgrab': see Ruotsala, *Europeans and Mongols*, pp. 153–5 (Appendix 1), who takes this as Belgorod, near Kiev. The identification with Peter Akherovich, first made in 1927 by Tomashevskii and cited in Richard, *La papauté*, p. 67, n.10, is purely conjectural.
4. Dörrie, p. 194.
5. See the introduction to the Menestò edn, pp. 50–2.
6. Martiniano Roncaglia, 'Frère Laurent de Portugal O.F.M. et sa légation en Orient (1245–1248 env.)', *Bollettino della badia greca di Grottaferrata*, n.s., 7 (1953), pp. 33–44; Richard, *La papauté*, pp. 70–1, n.26.
7. Texts in Lupprian, pp. 141–9 (nos. 20, 21); tr. in Dawson, *Mongol Mission*, pp. 73–6.
8. PC, ix, 8, pp. 306–7 (tr. Dawson, pp. 53–4). SSQ, p. 21 (= VB, xxxii, 2). Richard (n.1 ibid.) was uncertain whether Ascelin's party carried *Dei patris immensa*, but in his reply to Baichu, 22 Nov. 1248, the pope mentions having sent envoys to him in order that they might expound the faith: Lupprian, p. 198 (no. 35).
9. Niccolò di Calvi, 'Vita Innocentii IV', in Alberto Melloni, *Innocenzo IV. La concezione e l'esperienza della cristianità come regimen unius personae* (Genova, 1990), appendice, pp. 257–93 (here p. 270).
10. PC, ix, 52, pp. 332–3 (tr. Dawson, pp. 71–2).
11. Ibid., ix, 18, 46, 49, pp. 312, 329, 331 (tr. Dawson, pp. 57, 69, 71). See Marian Plezia, 'L'apport de la Pologne à l'exploration de l'Asie centrale au

milieu du XIIIᵉ siècle', *Acta Poloniae Historica* 22 (1970), pp. 18–35 (here pp. 20–1).

12. Donald Ostrowski, 'Second-redaction additions in Carpini's *Ystoria Mongalorum*', in *Adelphotes: A Tribute to Omeljan Pritsak by His Students* (Cambridge, MA, 1990 = *HUS* 14:3–4), pp. 522–50.
13. 'Annales S. Pantaleonis', p. 542. Benedict, §9, p. 139 (tr. Dawson, p. 81).
14. Gregory G. Guzman, 'The encyclopedist Vincent of Beauvais and his Mongol extracts from John of Plano Carpini and Simon of Saint-Quentin', *Speculum* 49 (1974), pp. 287–307.
15. SSQ, pp. 95–6 (= VB, xxxii, 40); see also p. 105 (= VB, xxxii, 46).
16. And not the general Eljigidei (below), as often supposed. Simon calls him 'Anguca', which is far more likely to be a corruption of Arghun Aqa's name. According to the *Yüan shih*, Eljigidei did not leave the qaghan's headquarters until autumn 1247: see P. Jackson, 'Arḡūn Aqa', *Enc.Ir.*
17. SSQ, pp. 113–17 (= VB, xxxii, 51–2).
18. *Reg. Inno. IV*, no. 4682 = Lupprian, pp. 197–8 (no. 35).
19. Persian text in Pelliot, 'Les Mongols et la papauté', pp. 15–16 (tr. in De Rachewiltz, *Papal Envoys*, pp. 213–14).
20. PC, ix, 8, p. 306 (tr. Dawson, p. 53).
21. Lupprian, pp. 147, 148.
22. WR, xxviii, 2, p. 244 (tr. Jackson and Morgan, p. 172). Ruotsala, *Europeans and Mongols*, p. 107.
23. The phrase 'about making peace with us' is omitted in the Persian original: see Pelliot, 'Les Mongols et la papauté', p. 15 (tr. in De Rachewiltz, *Papal Envoys*, p. 213). But it is explicit in the Latin version, *pro pace habenda nobiscum*: Benedict, §13, pp. 142–3 (tr. Dawson, p. 83); Salimbene de Adam, *Cronica*, ed. Giuseppe Scalia, 2 vols, CCCM 125–125A (Turnhout, 1998–9), I, p. 313. Michael Weiers, 'Von Ögödei bis Möngke – Das mongolische Großreich', in Weiers, ed., *Die Mongolen. Beiträge zu ihrer Geschichte und Kultur* (Darmstadt, 1986), p. 202.
24. PC, ix, 38, pp. 323–4 (tr. Dawson, pp. 65–6). Cf. his description of the meagre rations given to those who arrived empty-handed: v, 23, p. 268 (tr. Dawson, pp. 27–8).
25. Ibid., ix, 11 and 14, pp. 308, 310 (tr. Dawson, pp. 54–5, 56).
26. Benedict, §5, p. 137 (tr. Dawson, p. 80). Carpini is silent on this, though he mentions the practice as one to which envoys are subject: PC, iii, 3–4, pp. 236–7 (tr. Dawson, pp. 9–10).
27. SSQ, pp. 98–104 (= VB, xxxii, 42–45). On the significance of these incidents, see Ruotsala, *Europeans and Mongols*, pp. 83–4.
28. See, e.g., De Rachewiltz, *Papal Envoys*, p. 88.
29. SSQ, pp. 104–7 (= VB, xxxii, 46–47); cf. also p. 96 (= VB, xxxii, 40).
30. PC, ix, 18, p. 312 (tr. Dawson, p. 57).
31. Ibid., prologue, 2–3, p. 228 (tr. Dawson, pp. 3–4).
32. Ibid., ix, 31, p. 319 (tr. Dawson, p. 62); cf. also iv, 5, pp. 246–7 (tr. Dawson, p. 15).
33. Benedict, §12, pp. 140–1 (tr. Dawson, pp. 82–3).
34. PC, vii, 9, pp. 289–90 (tr. Dawson, p. 41).

35. Ibid., ix, 17, p. 311 (tr. Dawson, p. 57).
36. Ibid., viii, 2, p. 294 (tr. Dawson, p. 44); cf. also ix, 38, p. 323 (tr. Dawson, p. 65).
37. Ibid., viii, 5, p. 295 (tr. Dawson, p. 45).
38. Salimbene, *Cronica*, I, p. 317.
39. PC, viii, 3, p. 294 (tr. Dawson, p. 44).
40. Ibid., vii, 11–12, pp. 291–2 (tr. Dawson, pp. 42–3). SSQ, pp. 35–6, 47 (= VB, xxx, 75 and 84).
41. PC, v, 18, vii, 2, and viii, 2, pp. 264, 284–5, 293 (tr. Dawson, pp. 25, 38, 43–4).
42. Ibid., viii, 3, p. 294 (tr. Dawson, p. 44).
43. Ibid., iv, 6, and viii, 3, pp. 247, 294–5 (tr. Dawson, pp. 16, 44). On Mongol duplicity, see more briefly SSQ, p. 39 (= VB, xxx, 77).
44. PC, viii, 6, p. 296 (tr. Dawson, p. 45).
45. Ibid., viii, 3, p. 295 (tr. Dawson, p. 44). SSQ, pp. 31, 32 (= VB, xxx, 71), on their size and strength.
46. PC, viii, 14, p. 301 (tr. Dawson, p. 49). SSQ, p. 52 (= VB, xxx, 87).
47. PC, v, 12, 13, vii, 10, and viii, 12, pp. 258–9, 260, 290–1, 300 (tr. Dawson, pp. 22–3, 41–2, 48–9).
48. SSQ, p. 52 (= VB, xxx, 87).
49. PC, viii, 9, p. 298 (tr. Dawson, p. 47). SSQ, pp. 39, 45, 77–8 (= VB, xxx, 77, 82, and xxxi, 149).
50. PC, viii, 2, pp. 293–4 (tr. Dawson, p. 44). SSQ, pp. 52, 74, 98 (= VB, xxx, 87, xxxi, 146, and xxxii, 41).
51. PC, v, 19, p. 264 (tr. Dawson, pp. 25–6). The figure seems to be linked with the same number given later on, when Carpini is speaking of the next campaign against Hungary and Poland; the troops' orders are to fight without a break for eighteen years: ibid., viii, 4, p. 295 (tr. Dawson, p. 44); TR, §33, p. 22. See Ostrowski, 'Second-redaction additions', p. 542.
52. WR, xxi, 2, p. 219 (tr. Jackson and Morgan, p. 139).
53. Ostrowski, 'Second-redaction additions', pp. 549–50; for specific examples, see pp. 543 (re PC, v, 34, on the Mongol threat in Syria), 546 (re vi, 11, regarding their highly effective plundering tactics), 548 (re v, 27, on the fate of the population of Kiev). I differ from Ostrowski in my reluctance to accept that all the second-redaction additions which materially affect the sense are the work of a later writer rather than Carpini himself. See also Klopprogge, *Ursprung*, pp. 216–19.
54. Adam Marsh, 'Epistolae', in J.S. Brewer, ed., *Monumenta Franciscana*, RS (London, 1858), p. 376. For a brief survey of the purpose of the missions of 1245–7, see Peter Jackson, 'Early missions to the Mongols: Carpini and his contemporaries', *The Hakluyt Society. Annual Report for 1994*, pp. 14–32.
55. HDFS, VI, pp. 263, 265–7. See also *MGHEp.*, II, pp. 78–9 (no. 110, 30 April 1245), from which it is clear that he had already been in Europe for some months.
56. Dörrie, p. 190.
57. Pelliot, 'Les Mongols et la papauté', pp. 36–40.

58. Gregory G. Guzman, 'Simon of Saint-Quentin as historian of the Mongols and Seljuk Turks', *Medievalia et Humanistica* 3 (1972), pp. 155–78.
59. PC, prologue, 2, p. 227 (tr. Dawson, p. 3); cf. also ix, 2, p. 302 (tr. Dawson, p. 50).
60. Ibid., prologue, 1, p. 227 (tr. Dawson, p. 3).
61. Niccolò di Calvi, 'Vita Innocentii IV', pp. 269–70.
62. CICO, IV:1, pp. 48–9 (no. 21); for the full text, see pp. 43–8 (no. 20). Richard, *La papauté*, pp. 45, 59.
63. See Wilhelm de Vries, S.J., 'Innozenz IV. (1243–1254) und der christliche Osten', *OKS* 12 (1963), pp. 113–31.
64. Lupprian, pp. 155–7, 170–2 (nos. 23, 26).
65. Ibid., p. 174 (no. 27).
66. 'Annales Stadenses', *MGHS*, XVI, p. 370. Cf. also 'Annales S. Pantaleonis', p. 540; and *CM*, IV, p. 566, where the aim is supposedly a truce to last until the arrival of the Seventh Crusade.
67. Lupprian, pp. 150–4 (no. 22) = *CM*, IV, pp. 566–8.
68. CICO, IV:1, pp. 95–102 (nos. 52, 53). On Simeon, see Von den Brincken, *Die „Nationes Christianorum Orientalium"*, pp. 298–9.
69. Lupprian, p. 163 (no. 24).
70. CICO, IV:1, p. 96 (no. 52); see also *CM*, VI, p. 115.
71. Less explicitly in a letter to Louis IX of France, at that time preparing for his crusade: for these two letters of Simeon, see Pierre-Vincent Claverie, 'Deux lettres inédites de la première mission en Orient d'André de Longjumeau (1246)', *BEC* 158 (2000), pp. 283–92 (here pp. 290–2).
72. Richard, *La papauté*, pp. 60, 75.
73. PC, ix, 3, p. 304 (tr. Dawson, p. 51). Zatko, p. 41.
74. PC, ix, 48, p. 330 (tr. Dawson, p. 70).
75. CICO, IV:1, pp. 69–70 (no. 28). For these negotiations, see Bolesław Szcześniak, 'The mission of Giovanni de Plano Carpini and Benedict the Pole of Vratislavia to Halicz', *JEH* 7 (1956), pp. 12–20.
76. CICO, IV:1, pp. 66–7 (no. 26a); for the full text, cf. p. 65 (no. 26). The editors assume that the addressee was Daniil, but cf. Zatko, pp. 41–2. On Iaroslav's background, see Fennell, *Crisis*, pp. 98–9.
77. CICO, IV:1, pp. 110–11 (no. 59).
78. PC, ix, 31, 37, 49, pp. 319, 323, 331 (tr. Dawson, pp. 62, 65, 70). The rumour about poison is reported also in the Galician chronicle: *PSRL*, II, col. 808 (tr. Perfecky, p. 58).
79. Zatko, p. 47. For doubts about Iaroslav's conversion, see Georges Rochcau, 'Innocent IV devant le péril tatar: ses lettres à Daniel de Galicie et à Alexandre Nevsky', *Istina* 6 (1959), pp. 167–86 (here pp. 178–9).
80. PC, ix, 37, p. 323 (tr. Dawson, p. 65).
81. CICO, IV:1, p. 117 (no. 65).
82. Ibid., pp. 108, 112 (nos. 57, 59); and cf. p. 109 (no. 58) to the Teutonic Knights on this subject.
83. MOL, DL 72302 (22 April 1244 = *CDH*, IV:1, p. 336; *AUO*, VII, p. 164, no. 107; and *HO*, IV, p. 29, no. 12). Jaroslav Stepaniv, 'L'époque de Danylo Romanovyč (milieu du XIIIe siècle) d'après une source karaïte', *HUS* 2 (1978),

pp. 334–73 (here pp. 354–6), adduced fresh evidence to support this early visit to Batu; but Senga, 'IV. Béla', p. 590, n.27, is sceptical.

84. Hans Patze, 'Der Friede von Christburg vom Jahre 1249', *Jahrbuch für die Geschichte Mittel- und Ostdeutschlands* 7 (1958), pp. 39–91, repr. (with 'Nachwort') in Helmut Beumann (ed.), *Heidenmission und Kreuzzugsgedanke in der deutschen Ostpolitik des Mittelalters*, Wege der Forschung 7 (Darmstadt, 1963), pp. 417–85.

85. PC, ix, 4 and 10, pp. 304, 308 (tr. Dawson, pp. 52, 54, adopts the incorrect reading 'Ruthenians').

86. *PSRL*, II, coll. 816–17 (tr. Perfecky, pp. 62–3). CICO, IV:2, p. 8 (no. 7a). See generally Michał Giedroyć, 'The arrival of Christianity in Lithuania: early contacts (thirteenth century)', *OSP*, n.s., 18 (1985), pp. 1–30 (here pp. 17–26); Christiansen, *Northern Crusades*, pp. 140–1; Anti Selart, 'Confessional conflict and political co-operation: Livonia and Russia in the thirteenth century', in Murray, *Crusade and Conversion*, pp. 151–76 (here pp. 166–7).

87. Aalto, 'Swells of the Mongol-storm', pp. 13–14. Fennell, *Crisis*, pp. 107–8.

88. 'Kronika Wielkopolska' (down to 1273; written 1295), *MPH²*, VIII, p. 113. The date 1269/74 given for Ruthenia's subjection to the Mongols by Michael B. Zdan, 'The dependence of Halych-Volyn' Rus' on the Golden Horde', *SEER* 35 (1956–7), pp. 505–22 (here p. 517), is therefore too late. The Galician chronicle does not mention their participation.

89. *PSRL*, II, col. 809 (tr. Perfecky, p. 59).

90. Zatko, pp. 50–1.

91. Oscar Halecki, 'Diplomatie pontificale et activité missionnaire en Asie aux XIIIe–XVe siècles', in *XIIᵉ Congrès international des sciences historiques, Vienne, 29 août–5 septembre 1965. Rapports*, II. *Histoire des continents* (Vienna, [1966]), pp. 5–32 (here pp. 10–11).

92. *CM*, V, pp. 37–8, where the proposal comes from the Mongol envoys; cf. Matthew Paris, *Historia Anglorum*, ed. Sir Frederic Madden, RS, 3 vols (London, 1866–9), III, pp. 38–9, where it allegedly emanates from the pope. The idea of an alliance against the Muslims is found, e.g., in Davide Bigalli, *I Tartari e l'Apocalisse. Ricerche sull'escatologia in Adamo Marsh e Ruggero Bacone* (Firenze, 1971), p. 59 (Ascelin's mission), and in Reichert, *Begegnungen*, pp. 71–2.

93. PC, v, 10, pp. 257–8 (tr. Dawson, p. 22).

94. Jean Dauvillier, 'L'expansion de l'Eglise syrienne en Asie centrale et en Extrême-Orient', *L'Orient Syrien* 1 (1956), pp. 76–87; idem, 'Les Arméniens en Chine et en Asie centrale au Moyen Age', in *Mélanges de sinologie offerts à M. Paul Demiéville*, II (Paris, 1974), pp. 1–17; idem, 'Byzantins d'Asie centrale et d'Extrême-Orient au Moyen Age', in *Mélanges Martin Jugie* (Paris, 1953 = *REB* 11), pp. 62–87; all repr. in Dauvillier, *Histoire et institutions des Eglises orientales au Moyen Age* (London, 1983). Erica Hunter, 'Syriac Christianity in Central Asia', *ZRGG* 44 (1992), pp. 362–8, gives a brief overview of the Jacobites and Nestorians.

95. For the role of eastern Christians in diplomatic contacts between the Mongols of Iran and the Franks, see Jean Richard, 'D'Älǧigidäi à Ġazan: la continuité

d'une politique franque chez les Mongols d'Iran', in Aigle, *L'Iran*, pp. 57-69 (here pp. 58-61), and repr. in Richard, *Francs et Orientaux*.

96. PC, ix, 43, p. 327 (tr. Dawson, p. 68).

97. Ibid., iii, 5, p. 238 (tr. Dawson, p. 10).

98. *CM*, VI, p. 114. SSQ, p. 47 (= VB, xxx, 84).

99. *CM*, VI, p. 115. Andrew also transmitted this rumour to Thomas of Cantimpré, but probably following his second mission to the Mongols (see above, pp. 99, 101): *Thomae Cantipratani . . . miraculorum et exemplorum memorabilium sui temporis libri duo*, II:liv, 14, ed. G. Colvenerius (Douai, 1605), pp. 526-8. For Simeon, see *CM*, VI, pp. 113, 116; SSQ, p. 30 (= VB, xxx, 70).

100. Jean Richard, 'La lettre du Connétable Smbat et les rapports entre Chrétiens et Mongols au milieu du XIIIème siècle', in Dickran Kouymjian, ed., *Études arméniennes in memoriam Haïg Berbérian* (Lisbon, 1986), pp. 683-96 (here pp. 688-92), and repr. in Richard, *Croisades et états latins*, gives a better text than does D'Achéry, III, p. 626. The gist of Smbat's letter was incorporated in VB, xxxii, 92.

101. D'Achéry, III, pp. 625-6, for Eljigidei's letter; p. 627, for his and Güyüg's Christian faith (printed text checked against BN ms. lat. 3768 (here fos. 77v-78r, 79v). See further P. Jackson, 'Eljigidei', *Enc.Ir.*

102. VB, xxxii, 91: *cui consonabant et alie quedam littere que paulo ante dicto regi a rege Cypri . . . fuerant presentatae.*

103. *CM*, V, pp. 80, 87; see VI, pp. 163-5, for the letter.

104. Brewer, *Monumenta Franciscana*, p. 428.

105. For Andrew's second mission, see Pelliot, 'Les Mongols et la papauté', pp. 188-92, 204-14; for its members, ibid., pp. 176-87.

106. WR, i, 7, pp. 168-9 (tr. Jackson and Morgan, p. 67).

107. Ibid., xxxvi, 6-12, pp. 307-9 (tr. Jackson and Morgan, pp. 248-50). For Louis's letter and its unintended consequences, see Jean Richard, 'Sur les pas de Plancarpin et de Rubrouck: la lettre de saint Louis à Sartaq', *JS* (1977), pp. 49-61 (here pp. 55-60), repr. in his *Croisés*; also WR, tr. Jackson and Morgan, introduction, pp. 43-4. Weiers, 'Von Ögödei', p. 210, suggests that Möngke omitted any demand for tribute, to avoid giving the impression that Hülegü's expedition threatened the West.

108. WR, xvi, 5, p. 205 (tr. Jackson and Morgan, p. 120).

109. Ibid., xviii, 1, p. 209 (tr. Jackson and Morgan, p. 126); cf. also i, 7, p. 169 (tr. p. 68).

110. Kirakos Ganjakec'i, p. 310.

111. To the sources cited in Spuler, *Die Goldene Horde*, p. 33, add Bar Hebraeus, tr. Budge, *Chronography*, p. 398; Juwaynī, I, p. 223 (tr. Boyle, I, p. 268); and Jūzjānī, II, p. 217 (tr. Raverty, II, p. 1291).

112. WR, xvi, 5, p. 205 (tr. Jackson and Morgan, p. 120). Jean Richard, 'The Mongols and the Franks', *JAH* 3 (1969), pp. 45-57 (here pp. 49-50), repr. in his *Orient et Occident*.

113. Thomas T. Allsen, *Mongol Imperialism. The Policies of the Grand Qan Möngke in China, Russia, and the Islamic Lands, 1251-1259* (Berkeley and Los Angeles, 1987), pp. 121-2. John Fennell, *A History of the Russian Church to 1448* (Harlow, 1995), pp. 189-96. For taxation of the economic operations of the

'religious', see Erich Haenisch, *Steuergerechtsame der chinesischen Klöster unter der Mongolenherrschaft* (Leipzig, 1940), pp. 23, 45–6. There is a good overview of Chinggis Khan's 'religious policy' in Ratchnevsky, *Genghis Khan*, pp. 197–8; and see more generally, Jean-Paul Roux, 'La tolérance religieuse dans les empires turco-mongols', *RHR* 203 (1986), pp. 131–68 (here pp. 159–65).

114. Kirakos Ganjakec'i, p. 295.

115. Juwaynī, I, pp. 213–14 (tr. Boyle, I, p. 259). Bar Hebraeus, tr. Budge, *Chronography*, p. 411: I have translated as 'status' the word *ḳarn*, which Budge renders as 'horn'.

116. Jūzjānī, II, pp. 171–5 (tr. Raverty, II, pp. 1157–63). *Yüan shih*, chap. 125, cited in Jagchid and Hyer, p. 178.

117. *Yüan shih*, chap. 38, cited in G. Devéria, 'Notes d'épigraphie mongole-chinoise', *JA*, 9e série, 8:2 (1896), pp. 94–128, 395–443 (here pp. 419–20). Juwaynī, I, p. 84, and III, pp. 8–9 (tr. Boyle, I, p. 108, and II, pp. 552–3).

118. Ibid., III, pp. 79–80 (tr. Boyle, II, pp. 600–1). Jūzjānī, II, p. 179 (tr. Raverty, II, p. 1181).

119. Hsiang-mai, *Chih-yüan pien-wei lu* (1291), tr. in P.Y. Saeki, *The Nestorian Documents and Relics in China*, 2nd edn (Tokyo, 1951), p. 495, app. XV(A). Elizabeth Endicott-West, 'Notes on shamans, fortune-tellers and *yin-yang* practitioners and civil administration in Yüan China', in Amitai-Preiss and Morgan, *Mongol Empire*, pp. 224–39 (here p. 227).

120. Richard Foltz, 'Ecumenical mischief under the Mongols', *CAJ* 43 (1999), pp. 42–69.

121. WR, xxix, 15, p. 256 (tr. Jackson and Morgan, p. 187).

122. Ibid., xvii, 2, p. 206 (tr. Jackson and Morgan, p. 122).

123. Juwaynī, I, pp. 28–9 (tr. Boyle, I, p. 39). See Lionel J. Friedman, 'Joinville's Tartar visionary', *Medium Aevum* 27 (1958), pp. 1–7 (though he was unaware that Juwaynī was Bar Hebraeus's source). For Teb-Tenggeri, see Ratchnevsky, *Genghis Khan*, pp. 98–101.

124. Rashīd al-Dīn, I, pp. 166–7 (tr. Thackston, I, p. 90). Hayton, iii, 1 and 6, Fr. text pp. 148, 152, Latin text pp. 284, 287.

125. Bar Hebraeus, *Chronicon ecclesiasticum*, ed. and tr. J.B. Abbeloos and T.J. Lamy, 3 vols (Louvain, 1872–7), III, coll. 279–81. Hunter, 'Conversion of the Kerait'.

126. Bar Hebraeus, *Chronicon ecclesiasticum*, II, col. 756.

127. Jean Maurice Fiey, O.P., 'Chrétiens syriaques entre croisés et Mongols', in *Symposium syriacum 1972, célébré dans les jours 26–31 octobre 1972 à l'Institut Pontifical de Rome. Rapports et communications*, Orientalia Christiana Analecta 197 (Rome, 1974), pp. 327–41.

128. WR, xxviii, 8, p. 246 (tr. Jackson and Morgan, pp. 174–5).

129. Lupprian, pp. 209–12 (no. 39). Niccolò di Calvi, 'Vita Innocentii IV', pp. 288–9, where the envoy is simply *quidam Armenus clericus*.

130. For the uncertain chronology of these events, see Pelliot, *Notes sur l'histoire de la Horde d'Or*, pp. 29, 34–44.

131. CICO, IV:1, p. 148 (no. 86).

132. Rubruck lists the states that had submitted to the Mongols at i, 5, pp. 167–8 (tr. Jackson and Morgan, pp. 65–6).

133. Senga, 'Ungarisch-bulgarische Beziehungen', p. 78. John V.A. Fine, Jr, *The Late Medieval Balkans. A Critical Survey from the Late Twelfth Century to the Ottoman Conquest* (Ann Arbor, MC, 1987), p. 155. Its tributary status is mentioned in a letter of Béla IV (*VMH*, I, p. 231, no. 440 = *DIR*, I:1, p. 260, no. 199, both *ad annum* 1254; for the correct date, 1247, see chap. 3, n.51).

134. For Georgia at this time, see W.E.D. Allen, *A History of the Georgian People* (London, 1932), pp. 112–14.

135. SSQ, p. 86 (= VB, xxxii, 29); and see n.3 ibid.

136. WR, xxxiii, 3, p. 290 (tr. Jackson and Morgan, p. 227). See Jean Richard, 'Byzance et les Mongols', *BF* 25 (1999), pp. 83–100 (here pp. 86–7), repr. in his *Francs et Orientaux*; more generally M.A. Andreeva, 'Priem tatarskikh poslov pri nikeiskom dvore', in *Sbornik statei posviashchennykh pamiati N.P. Kondakova* (Prague, 1926), pp. 187–200.

137. Richard, 'À propos de la mission de Baudouin de Hainaut'.

138. Anne-Marie Eddé, *La principauté ayyoubide d'Alep (579/1183–658/1260)*, FIS 21 (Stuttgart, 1999), p. 165. Juwaynī, I, p. 205 (tr. Boyle, I, p. 250), calls him the sultan's brother, and SSQ, p. 112 (= VB, xxxii, 50), his uncle. See PC, v, 34, p. 274 (tr. Dawson, p. 32); the majority of mss. wrongly read Damascus for Aleppo.

139. Andrew of Longjumeau, in *CM*, VI, p. 114. SSQ, p. 93 (= VB, xxxii, 34).

140. *CM*, IV, p. 547.

141. *CGOH*, II, p. 673 (no. 2482).

142. *MGHEp.*, II, pp. 3–4 (no. 2) = *VMH*, I, pp. 187–8 (no. 348).

143. CICO, IV:1, pp. 55–6 (no. 23).

144. ASV, Reg. Vat. 21, fo. 8r (= Lange and Unger, *Diplomatarium Norvegicum*, I, pp. 21–2, no. 27; *CDH*, IV:1, p. 303).

145. Frederick: *MGHEp.*, II, p. 235 (no. 309, 18 March 1247) = *VMP*, I, pp. 44–5 (no. 90); Abulafia, *Frederick II*, p. 385. Constantinople: Societas literaria Poznaniensis, eds, *Kodeks dyplomatyczny wielkopolski*, 2 vols (Poznań, 1877–8), I, pp. 207–9 (nos. 246–7).

146. *VMH*, I, pp. 203–4 (no. 379, 4 Feb. 1247). For the alarms at this point, see also *CM*, IV, p. 546; Boniface, archbishop of Canterbury, to Peter of Savoy, ibid., VI, p. 133.

147. *VMH*, I, pp. 231–2 (no. 440) = *DIR*, I:1, pp. 261–2 (no. 199); and for the date, see n.133 above.

148. *CDRB*, IV, pp. 584–5 (no. 466). *PUB*, I:1, pp. 216–17 (no. 289).

149. *PUB*, I:2, pp. 51–3 (no. 59).

150. WR, xxxii, 4, p. 287 (tr. Jackson and Morgan, pp. 222–3), mentioning two brothers, possibly because Hülegü was initially accompanied by his brother Sübe'etei, who died en route: see Juwaynī, III, pp. 90, 98 (tr. Boyle, II, pp. 607, 612).

151. *CM*, V, p. 655.

152. *Reg. Alex. IV*, II, pp. 531–2 (no. 1726) = *MGHEp.*, III, p. 415 (no. 450). André Duchesne, ed., *Historiae Francorum Scriptores*, V (Paris, 1649), p. 272.

chapter 5

THE HALTING OF THE
MONGOL ADVANCE

Tensions within the Mongol imperial system

I f princely strife played an uncertain role in the Mongols' retreat from
Eastern Europe in 1242 (above, pp. 72–3), it is undoubtedly one
reason behind their failure to return in force for some time. For all the
efficiency and discipline of the Mongol military machine, and the striking loyalty of the nomads to Chinggis Khan's dynasty, the empire he
had founded was characterized by certain tensions. First, the boundary
between the qaghan's sphere of authority and that of his kinsmen was
increasingly blurred. In conformity with steppe tradition, the Mongol
conquests were regarded as the property of the imperial family as a
whole. One expression of this idea was the *tama* (or *tamma*) system,
whereby troops were selected, on a basis of perhaps two or three in
every hundred, and despatched to the frontiers to make fresh conquests
and to act as garrison troops: these comprised units supplied by the
various branches of the imperial family and representing their interests.[1]
Another was the allocation of specific grazing-grounds and groups of
nomadic subjects – the complex termed *ulus* in our sources – to each
member of the dynasty. Although the sedentary territories, like northern
China, were not apportioned in this manner but were under the qaghan's
direct rule, they were run by 'joint satellite administrations' comprising
both his representatives and those of his relatives (above, p. 41); and
individual princes and princesses were granted particular towns as
appanages, the revenues of which were forwarded to them by the qaghan's
officials. Naturally the qaghan's kinsfolk were ever on the alert for
opportunities to extend their possessions and influence at his expense.[2]

The second source of tension was the absence of fixed rules for the
succession to the qaghanate. It is important to distinguish between the
principles determining the inheritance of pasturelands among the Eurasian nomads and those governing the succession to the headship of the

empire as a whole. A prince's original territory – the 'hearthland', as it was known – passed to his youngest son by his chief wife.[3] If Juwaynī is to be believed, the older sons inherited grazing-grounds at a greater distance from the hearthland according to seniority. Thus Tolui, as the youngest son, received his father's original encampment (*yurt*) on the Onon and Kerülen rivers; the third son, Ögödei, and the second, Chaghadai, were granted lands in Central Asia; while Jochi, as the eldest, was given 'the land from Qayaligh and Khwārazm as far as Saqsīn and Bulghār and from that side as far as the hooves of Mongol horses had trodden'.[4] We shall return to these territorial dispositions later.

The transmission of the imperial dignity proceeded along quite different lines. We are told that the great conqueror had designated his third son Ögödei as his successor, although this has recently been questioned.[5] Ögödei was eventually elected by the princes in 1229, despite some opposition from Tolui, who had acted as regent of the empire since their father's death. But this was the last occasion on which designation by the deceased sovereign proved effective, and henceforth the princes reverted to the time-honoured practice of choosing one of their number who was more senior or who appeared more competent – a system for which the late Professor Joseph Fletcher borrowed from the Celtic world the label 'tanistry'.[6] Ögödei's desire to be succeeded by a younger son or by his grandson Shiremün was disregarded, and the throne passed to Güyüg. We do not know whom (if anyone) Güyüg designated, but his eventual successor was not a descendant of Ögödei but Möngke, Tolui's eldest son, who headed the youngest branch of Chinggis Khan's progeny. Whether this represented a breach of some earlier agreement, whereby the qaghanate was to remain in Ögödei's or in Güyüg's line, we cannot be sure; both claims appear in the sources.[7] There is evidence that following the transfer of the qaghanate to Tolui's line in 1251 the 'Secret History' was doctored in order to suggest that Chinggis Khan and Ögödei had foreseen the unsuitability of the latter's progeny.[8]

The five-year interregnum between Ögödei's death and Güyüg's election in 1246 did not necessarily entail the suspension of hostilities on the empire's frontiers: there were operations in China in 1244, and we have seen how Baichu began a new offensive in the Near East two years previously. But the long interval bears eloquent witness to the discord within the imperial dynasty. From what the Carpini mission was told, Güyüg planned to unleash a fresh expedition against the West (above, p. 91). Yet already in 1247, during his return journey, Carpini had heard of the antagonism between Batu and the new qaghan, and the author of the 'Tartar Relation' suggested that this might afford the Latin world a respite for many years to come.[9] Güyüg's brief reign

(1246–8) witnessed no campaigns of importance against external enemies. Instead, he sought to reduce the power of Batu, who had asserted his control over Baichu and his army. The noyan Eljigidei, sent to Persia with fresh troops and an ostensible commission to guard the Caucasus and Armenia against outside interference, was secretly instructed to remove Batu's representatives there; Baichu was superseded by Eljigidei himself. Güyüg was slowly moving westwards in person against his old rival at the time of his death in Central Asia in April 1248.[10]

Güyüg's premature death, which Rubruck later heard had come about either through poison or during a violent brawl with Batu's brother Shiban,[11] was followed by another interregnum, lasting three years. The regime of Güyüg's widow Oghul Qaimish, who had received Andrew of Longjumeau (see p. 99), was swept away when Batu secured the election of Möngke (1251–9). The new reign began with a purge of those who had opposed Möngke's accession. The majority of the descendants of Ögödei and Chaghadai were killed or exiled to the front in China, and their subjects and pasturelands were redistributed, mainly to Batu and his brothers or to the qaghan's own family; many of their prominent supporters, including Eljigidei, were executed.[12] Vague rumours of these upheavals reached France and even St Albans (through the intermediary of Armenian visitors).[13] It was important for the new regime, established at the cost of such violence within the ranks of the Chinggisid dynasty, to consolidate its authority by renewing the programme of imperial expansion.

The Mongol invasion of Syria

To rally support behind his regime, Möngke in 1252–3 launched campaigns both in the Far East and in south-west Asia. While he, together with his brother Qubilai (the future qaghan), carried the war deeper into Sung China, he despatched to Persia his third brother Hülegü, at the head of a considerable force, with authority over all Mongol troops already operating in the region.[14] As in previous expeditions, Hülegü's army was raised by a levy from the central forces (in this case, two men in every ten), and included contingents supplied by other branches of the dynasty, those led by Jochid princes from the Golden Horde territories being especially prominent. There was possibly some dissatisfaction at Mongol headquarters with the lack of progress made by Baichu, since Rashīd al-Dīn depicts a stormy interview following Hülegü's arrival, in which the general was upbraided for his inactivity.[15] Baichu and his forces were ordered to move west, into the Seljük Sultanate of Rūm, currently disputed between two of the sons of Kaykhusraw II; the

Mongols defeated Sultan 'Izz al-Dīn Kaykā'ūs, at Aqsarai (1256) and recognized as ruler his younger brother, Rukn al-Dīn Qilich Arslan.[16] Meanwhile Hülegü took and destroyed the majority of the strongholds of the Ismā'īlī Assassins in northern Persia, and their last Master was put to death (1256). Next it was the turn of the 'Abbasid Caliph in Baghdad. After a siege of several weeks, the city was stormed and sacked on 6 February 1258, and the Caliph al-Musta'ṣim, his sons and most of his suite were executed. Hülegü's forces then pushed forward into north-ern Syria, where Aleppo was taken by assault (24 January 1260).[17] Its Ayyubid ruler, al-Nāṣir Yūsuf, who resided at Damascus, panicked and fled southwards, with the result that the city surrendered to the Mongol general Kitbuqa in March. During the next few months Mongol troops raided Hebron, Ascalon and Jerusalem, sacked Nablus, and received the surrender of Ba'labakk and 'Ajlūn; the Ayyubid princes of Ḥimṣ, al-Ṣubayba and Karak all submitted. A contemporary Muslim author reports that the Franks were now virtually hemmed in on the coast, with a Mongol squadron based at Gaza to prevent them receiving any assist-ance from Egypt.[18]

By this time Hülegü had withdrawn with most of his army and was on his way to Azerbaijan, leaving Kitbuqa with only a rump force of perhaps ten or twenty thousand men to complete the subjugation of Syria and to garrison the new conquests. The retreat has traditionally been ascribed to the news of the death of the qaghan Möngke while besieging a fortress in China on 11 August 1259. There is a striking parallel with Batu's retreat from Eastern Europe following Ögödei's death. In this case too, there are grounds for believing that the with-drawal was dictated by ecological considerations. In a letter to the French King Louis IX in 1262, Hülegü himself would claim that he had left Syria because the grasslands there and his provisions were alike exhausted and because, moreover, it was the Mongols' practice to move to cooler uplands for the summer.[19] The departure of the majority of Mongol troops from Syria thus takes on the semblance almost of a matter of routine. But it is necessary, perhaps, to approach this evidence with circumspection, since Hülegü, in the act of seeking Frankish mili-tary cooperation against the Mamlūks, would have had an interest in keeping silent about other, more pressing reasons for his retreat. There are hints in Western sources that he saw himself as a candidate for the imperial dignity;[20] and as we shall see (below, pp. 125–6), he would shortly be engaged in full-scale conflict in the Caucasus with his cousins of the Golden Horde.

At the time of the attack on Aleppo, Mongol raiders had entered the principality of Antioch and the county of Tripoli. The city of Antioch, whose dilapidated condition Rubruck had noticed five years previously,[21] surrendered and accepted a Mongol resident. Prince Bohemond VI, perhaps under the influence of his father-in-law King Het'um of Lesser Armenia, waited upon Hülegü in person and was allowed to reach a settlement that covered his county of Tripoli as well.[22] He participated in the Mongol campaign against Ba'labakk, which he hoped to obtain from Hülegü,[23] and may have ridden into Damascus with the Mongol army; though the story that he converted the Great Mosque into a church is demonstrably apocryphal.[24] Mongol overlordship brought certain benefits in its wake. In return for Bohemond's submission and military support, districts in the Orontes valley – Kafr Bilmīs, Dayrkūsh and Kafr Dubbīn – which the Muslims had taken at an earlier date were now restored to the principality of Antioch.[25]

The Franks further south, in the kingdom of Jerusalem, however, were not ready to yield to the conquerors. In the absence of a strong central authority, power was fragmented. Since 1257 the barons and the Military Orders had been split, having taken sides in the War of Saint-Sabas between the Venetians and the Genoese. In 1258 Bohemond had foisted on them a new regent, in the person of his sister, the widowed Queen Plaisance of Cyprus, and a pro-Venetian policy: the Genoese had been driven from Acre, and it was important to remain on the winning side. But more recently nobles hostile to Bohemond from the county of Tripoli had taken refuge at Acre and were now to be found among the principal officers of the kingdom.[26] Moreover, his conciliatory attitude towards the Mongols had incurred a ban of excommunication by the papal legate Thomas Agni di Lentino, bishop of Bethlehem, which was still under consideration by Pope Urban IV in 1263.[27] In the wake of the fall of Aleppo, the regime at Acre had sent Agni's chaplain, David of Ashby, to Hülegü's camp to ascertain his intentions.[28] Now, as the Mongols ravaged the Palestinian hinterland, the Frankish government issued frantic appeals to the West: letters requesting urgent assistance reached Henry III of England, Louis IX of France, his brother Charles of Anjou and other Latin rulers in the Mediterranean region.[29] Meanwhile they temporized, despatching envoys and gifts to Kitbuqa on at least two occasions;[30] though they did not comply with his order to dismantle the walls of their fortresses.[31]

In August 1260 Kitbuqa lost patience, and his forces sacked the city of Sidon.[32] The outrage provoked such indignation in Acre that when the Mamlūk Sultan of Egypt, Sayf al-Dīn Quṭuz, advanced northwards to attack the Mongols and requested safe-conduct through Latin territory, many of the Franks were ready to fight alongside the Egyptians. The gist of the ensuing debate has apparently been preserved for us by the so-called 'Rothelin' continuation of William of Tyre's history. The advice of the Master of the Teutonic Knights, Anno von Sangerhausen, carried the day. The Franks could ill afford to lose warriors by participating in the conflict, and there was no guarantee, in the event of a Mamlūk victory, that Quṭuz would not subsequently turn against them; they should instead conserve their resources. In the event, the Franks confined themselves to furnishing supplies for the sultan's troops.[33]

On 3 September 1260 the Egyptian army did battle with Kitbuqa at 'Ayn Jālūt in Galilee.[34] The Mamlūk army equalled, or perhaps surpassed, the Mongols in number, and their victory was assured by the defection of the Ayyubid prince of Ḥimṣ. Kitbuqa himself was killed, probably in the fighting; there is a less reliable tradition retailed by Rashīd al-Dīn, according to which he was captured and executed after taunting Quṭuz by contrasting his own loyal service to his master with the Mamlūks' faithlessness and regicide.[35] A smaller Mongol force that entered northern Syria in December to avenge Kitbuqa was easily crushed near Ḥimṣ, and Hülegü himself was unable to return to the offensive in view of the outbreak of conflict within the Mongol dominions.

The effect of the brief Mongol occupation, followed by the defeat at 'Ayn Jālūt, had been simply to create a power-vacuum west of the Euphrates which was filled by the victorious Mamlūks, as one Western observer, at least, realized.[36] The former ruler, al-Nāṣir Yūsuf, who had been captured by the Mongols, was executed on Hülegü's orders as soon as news arrived of the disaster that had overtaken Kitbuqa. His territories, Aleppo and Damascus, now came under direct Mamlūk rule; other principalities in Syria, notably Ḥimṣ and Ḥamā, were in the hands of Ayyubid rulers who were the Egyptian Sultan's allies and protégés. Ironically, Quṭuz did not live to enjoy the fruits of his victory. The triumphal reception in Cairo that would have been his was reserved instead for his lieutenant Rukn al-Dīn Baybars al-Bunduqdārī, who murdered him en route for Egypt in October and usurped the throne.

Like the invasion of Europe in 1241–2, the advance of Hülegü's forces towards the eastern Mediterranean coast had provoked the greatest alarm in the West; and again the practical response proved inadequate. Some crusaders, among them the bishop of Marseilles, reached the Holy Land in the autumn of 1260; it is possible that King Jaime I of Aragon planned to bring military aid, but was prevented from sailing by adverse weather.[37] Pope Alexander IV ordered the summoning of provincial synods in the spring of 1261, from which delegates should be deputed to attend a general council in July. But the agenda did not just include the Mongol threat and the action to be taken against those, like Bohemond VI, Het'um and the Rus' Grand Prince Alexander Nevskii, who had submitted to the invaders; it also embraced the security of the Latin empire of Constantinople and the problem posed by Frederick II's son Manfred in the kingdom of Sicily.[38] The provincial councils met, and we know that Louis IX presided over one in Paris at Easter 1261, which decreed prayers, processions, and penalties for blasphemy, and prohibited tournaments for two years.[39] But the pope died in May 1261, before the general council could meet and prior to the arrival of a high-ranking delegation from the Holy Land, headed by the archbishop of Tyre.[40] In July, moreover, the Greek recovery of Constantinople threw all other crises into eclipse. When Pope Alexander's successor, Urban IV, came to renew the crusade for the defence of the Holy Land against the Mongols in the spring of 1262,[41] it would be just one of a number of crusading projects that competed for his attention.

A lost opportunity? The choice facing the Latin East in 1260

The failure of the Frankish regime at Acre to ally with the Mongols against the Mamlūks in 1260 has been seen as an act of extreme shortsightedness in view of the subsequent ability of Baybars and his successors to reduce Latin strongholds piecemeal and to destroy in turn the principality of Antioch (1268), the county of Tripoli (1289) and lastly the kingdom of Jerusalem (1291). Support for Kitbuqa, it is argued, would have brought about the destruction of the Mamlūk Sultanate and thereby secured a reprieve for the Latin settlements on the eastern Mediterranean coast. More will be said on this subject in the context of later negotiations between Western European powers and Mongol Persia (chapter 7); for the moment, we shall focus on the choice confronting the Syrian Franks in 1260.

The idea of the lost opportunity rests upon two premisses: that Hülegü's Mongols were anti-Muslim and pro-Christian, and that we can read back into the circumstances of 1260 the readiness to court Latin friendship that he and his successors were to display from 1262 onwards. In large measure, these misapprehensions are sustained by the fact that in the Near East the chief political powers with which the Mongols were in conflict were Muslim. Contemporary Muslims and eastern Christians alike sometimes equated the Mongol conquest with the triumph of the non-Muslim subject population, the *dhimmīs* or 'protected peoples', some of whom were promoted to office under the new regime. Thus a Muslim author lamenting the Mongol sack of Baghdad speaks (figuratively, perhaps) of the cross raised over the *minbars* and of authority in the hands of those who used to wear the *zunnār* (girdle), i.e. the *dhimmīs*.[42] Both Kitbuqa and Hülegü's chief wife, Doquz Khatun, were Nestorians, and Doquz Khatun is credited by eastern Christian sources with great services to her coreligionists. Yet to be beguiled by the view of oriental Christians that Hülegü and Doquz Khatun were a second Constantine and Helena[43] is to forget that the Muslim subjects of the Qara-Khitan in Central Asia in 1218 had greeted the Mongols as liberators from the oppression of Küchlüg's troops (above, p. 43). In any case, the personal inclinations of individual Mongols did not necessarily determine policy. Juwaynī comments that, although certain princes and generals had adopted a particular religion, they were careful to observe Chinggis Khan's *yasa* decreeing equal treatment for all faiths; and a Muslim author whose family were living in Damascus in 1260 tells us that Kitbuqa had not displayed his sympathy for Christianity, out of deference to Chinggis Khan's law.[44] When an edict arrived from Hülegü late in August 1260 granting them freedom of worship, the Christians of Damascus responded with a triumphalism that placed their Muslim fellow citizens under a severe strain. But Hülegü's edict extended the same concession to Jews, 'Magians' (Zoroastrians) and idolators (presumably Buddhists).[45]

The primary concern of Mongol princes and generals was not the emancipation of any particular religious community, but the extension of their sovereignty over all other peoples in accordance with Heaven's mandate to Chinggis Khan. The programme of world-conquest would be conveniently shelved by Hülegü and his successors once it became clear that they could make headway against the Mamlūks only with Western assistance; and we must bear this in mind when using sources that date from this later era, beginning with Hülegü's letter to Louis IX in 1262. Particular caution is required in approaching the crusade treatise, *La flor des estoires de la terre d'orient*, which the expatriate Armenian prince Hayton (Het'um) of Gorigos (Corycus), a nephew of King Het'um I, wrote in 1307 at the behest of Pope Clement V. Both these sources would find the attack on Sidon especially embarrassing. Hülegü told King Louis that his troops had exceeded their orders; Hayton blamed the Franks of Sidon for provoking Kitbuqa with an audacious raid on the Mongol-occupied hinterland in which the general's nephew was killed.[46] Yet Hülegü's letter was designed to elicit the French king's assistance. And although Julian, the lord of Sidon, was an irresponsible hothead, and although evidence exists for Frankish military activity at this time (below, p. 122), Hayton was quite simply a propagandist who sought to foster Latin–Mongol cooperation in the interests of his native Lesser Armenia by rewriting the events of 1260 and presenting Hülegü's conduct in a more favourable light.[47] Significantly, the only Western account of those events which depicts the Syrian Franks as hoping for Mongol assistance against the Muslims is a late one that is otherwise heavily dependent on Hayton.[48]

The decision taken by the Frankish lords at Acre in 1260 to adopt a position of benevolent neutrality towards the Mamlūks was the only rational choice in the circumstances. Firstly, the Mongols, by any standard, represented a formidable threat. They had no allies, only subjects or enemies. What they offered the Latin states in Syria and Palestine was no form of coalition on equal terms, but simply a choice between annihilation and the acceptance of their overlordship. We have seen that the papal embassies of 1245–7 had left the West in no doubt regarding the character of that overlordship. In Latin Syria it would have entailed a general levelling-out of the various groups that made up the population: the Franks would have forfeited their status as the ruling élite and would have been forced to share power with those whom they viewed as schismatics. This is clear from what transpired in 1260 in Antioch, the one Frankish state to accept a Mongol 'resident'. Here the Greek Orthodox patriarch, who had been excommunicated by his Latin counterpart and repeatedly exiled from the city by the secular authorities, was reinstated on Hülegü's express orders.[49] Judging from developments in neighbouring Muslim territories during the Mongol occupation, moreover, the Franks would further have been obliged to share power with representatives of non-Christian groups – Jews and Muslims. To condemn them for recoiling before such a prospect is to demand a capacity for ecumenicism and inter-faith dialogue that would not merely have been anachronistic in 1260 but has surfaced only as recently as the twentieth century.

In the second place, the Franks were clearly aware of their own limitations. Since the disaster at La Forbie in 1244, they had been too weak to participate in the struggles between Muslim powers in Syria, except when reinforced by a crusading army. As the Templar Master, Thomas Bérard, wrote to the West in 1260, there were only three strongholds in the kingdom, other than Acre and Tyre, that could hold out against a Mongol attack.[50] For this reason it made sense to allow Quṭuz to relieve them of the Mongol menace, at no cost to themselves; and the appreciative reception given in Western Europe to the news of the Mamlūk victory reflects the sense that the Sultan was fighting not just his own but the Franks' battle also.[51] Nor was it by any means self-evident that in assisting the Mamlūks the Franks were nurturing the power that would destroy them. Anybody observing the course of Egyptian history in the previous decade could have been forgiven for concluding that the nascent Mamlūk state was highly unstable. Quṭuz, who had ascended the throne as recently as 1259, was the fourth sovereign since the Mamlūk usurpation in 1250. No one could have foreseen that he would be supplanted, within a month of his victory at 'Ayn Jālūt, by a sultan who would be able to embark upon the systematic reduction of Latin Syria. Still less could it have been predicted at this point that Baybars's task would be greatly facilitated by Mongol inactivity – that Hülegü would not again move into Syria in force and that consequently the Franks would be unable to play off two powerful neighbours against each other.

Since they were unconscious of any advantage to be gained by submitting to Kitbuqa, it is worth pausing to observe how the Franks of the kingdom of Jerusalem did perceive their own interests. The rapid collapse of al-Nāṣir Yūsuf, whose army reputedly stood at 150,000 men, evidently made a profound impact on them; but it engendered hope as well as apprehension. As they assured Charles of Anjou, the current situation in Syria could be seen to offer an unprecedented chance to recover all the territory of the kingdom of Jerusalem that had been lost to Saladin, if only help arrived soon from Western Europe.[52] Three years later Thomas Agni, the Masters of the Military Orders and Geoffrey de Sargines, regent of the kingdom, reminded Henry III of England that they had continually brought the power-vacuum in Syria to the attention of Western rulers.[53] Their perspective had been shared by no less a figure than Pope Urban IV, who (as Jacques Pantaléon, patriarch of Jerusalem) had left the Holy Land as recently as 1259: in a letter to the French king's brother Alphonse of Toulouse in 1263, he admits that he too had been dazzled by the opportunities which seemed to be on offer.[54]

Some among the Syrian Franks in 1260 were even ready to act without waiting for Western reinforcements. Kitbuqa's sack of Sidon was doubtless a reprisal for the audacity of its lord, after al-Nāṣir's flight, in occupying the whole of the region, the revenues of which had been divided since 1254 between the Franks and the Muslims.[55] After the Mongols' expulsion from Syria, a significant force from Acre, assisted by Templar contingents drawn from the Order's principal strongholds, would launch an ambitious but disastrously unsuccessful raid on the Jawlān (Golan) region in February 1261.[56] Expansion – rather than incorporation in the world-empire of the pagan Mongols – was the opportunity that seemed to beckon in 1260 to the Latin establishment in the east. Nor was this kind of opportunism confined to those in the anti-Mongol camp. In the wake of 'Ayn Jālūt, Bohemond of Antioch occupied Laodicea (Lattakiya), thereby linking up the principality and his county of Tripoli.[57] Frankish aspirations thus belonged squarely in the same tradition as the policies of popes, like Honorius III and Innocent IV, who had sought to capitalize on the Mongol threat since the 1220s.

The Mongol invasion of Eastern Europe in 1259

While the Franks of Syria and Palestine were facing a new antagonist and receiving deliverance at the hands of an old one, their *confrères* in Eastern Europe were once again experiencing the terrors of a Mongol invasion. Independently of Hülegü's operations, Batu's brother Berke, who had succeeded as ruler of the Mongols of the Golden Horde in 1256/7, launched a savage attack on Poland in 1259. The Mongol general Boroldai devastated Cracow and Sandomir, the territories of Bolesław the Chaste, and sacked the town of Sandomir before withdrawing into the steppes.[58] The Polish annals lay considerable stress on the removal of large numbers of enslaved captives.[59] The campaign attracts less notice from chroniclers writing in neighbouring Germany than either Batu's invasion of 1241–2 or the near-contemporary events in Syria;[60] but conversely the impression given is that on this occasion the Mongols were concerned to deliver a heavier blow against Poland than they had previously. In the verdict of one Polish annalist, the attack exceeded in its ferocity even the visitation of 1241.[61] These forces, or possibly others acting in conjunction with them, were also responsible for the devastation of Lithuania and for an assault on Prussia in 1259/ 60, which inflicted heavy losses on the Teutonic Knights.[62] A significant number of crusaders may have assembled in Prussia by March 1260, when Pope Alexander placed them under the authority of the Teutonic Order's *Landmeister* there. In August the pope urged the Order to prepare to move to the Poles' assistance in the event of another Mongol attack. But in the following spring he had to authorize the crusade instead to suppress a major revolt by the Order's Prussian subjects, a directive repeated in 1262 by his successor Urban IV.[63]

In 1260, or early in 1261, Berke followed up the attack on Poland by sending an embassy to Paris to demand the submission of Louis IX. Our sole source for this mission dates it in 1262, and modern scholars have accordingly confused it with the Mongol embassy which brought the French king Hülegü's proposal for concerted action against the Mamlūks, dated April of that year (below, p. 166).[64] But we are told explicitly that Louis forwarded the envoys to Pope Alexander IV, who died in May 1261, and the few details we are given leave no doubt that the missive they carried was not couched in amicable tones as was Hülegü's letter, but was an ultimatum threatening an invasion of France if Louis did not acknowledge Mongol overlordship.[65] It surely came from Berke and heralded the next Mongol advance into the heart of Europe. Since 1259 Berke had been exerting pressure on Béla IV of Hungary to enter into a marriage alliance with the Mongols, and join them in a campaign against his Latin neighbours, or suffer another attack upon his kingdom.[66] That the khan was unable to put either threat into execution was due to the outbreak of civil war within the Mongol world.

The end of the unitary Mongol empire

It was only natural that Muslims should hail the Mamlūk victory at 'Ayn Jālūt as a watershed. Following a period in which a pagan power had ravaged many of the core regions of the *Dār al-Islām* and destroyed the 'Abbasid Caliphate, the effects of Kitbuqa's defeat on the Islamic world were all the more heartening. For Abū Shāma, writing in Damascus a few years later, it demonstrated how for every pestilence there was an antidote of its own kind: the Mongols had met defeat at the hands of another people of the steppe, since the roots of the Mamlūks lay among the nomadic Qipchāq.[67] Yet for all the psychological impact of the engagement, it was not local reverses like 'Ayn Jālūt that halted the Mongol advance in the Near East, but events in distant Mongolia.

Following the death of Möngke in August 1259, two of his younger brothers had emerged as candidates for election to the qaghanate:[68] Qubilai, on campaign in China, and Arigh Böke, whom Möngke had left in charge at Qaraqorum and who, his supporters alleged, was the designated successor.[69] For a time the two men engaged in a wary exchange of messages, but finally Qubilai took the decisive step of allowing himself to be elected at a rump assembly of princes and generals in K'ai-p'ing in May 1260. Arigh Böke's supporters reacted by proclaiming him as qaghan in September–October.[70] Qubilai had already negotiated a suspension of hostilities with the Sung empire in southern China in order to free his hand to deal with his brother,[71] and a four-year struggle now erupted in the Far East, which ended only with Arigh Boke's submission and death in 1264. The details of this war do not concern us; what does is the fact that other important members of the imperial dynasty were drawn in. Not merely did each claimant try to intrude one of his own princely supporters into the Chaghadayid *ulus* in Central Asia, but the conflict also spread further west, since Berke supported Arigh Böke and Hülegü, perhaps after an initial hesitation, declared for Qubilai.

The interests of Hülegü and of the Golden Horde were already at variance even prior to the outbreak of civil war in the Far East. Although we have no narrative sources from the Golden Horde lands themselves, authors writing in the Mamlūk empire – a polity which was in diplomatic contact with Berke and his successors from 1262 onwards – clearly believed that Hülegü and the Muslim Berke had fallen out, firstly, over the attack on Baghdad and the murder of the Caliph (1258) and, secondly, over the division of spoils from Persia. Hülegü is alleged to have executed the envoys sent by Berke to claim his share. The time-lapse of three years renders it improbable that the assault on the Caliphate played a major part in the estrangement; but the division of spoils was undoubtedly important.[72] According to the Mamlūk encyclopaedist Ibn Faḍl-Allāh al-ʿUmarī (d. 1349), whose informants were traders from the Iranian world, Chinggis Khan had allocated to his eldest son Jochi not only the Pontic steppe but also Arrān, Tabrīz, Hamadān and Marāgha.[73] This is rather what we might expect, given Juwaynī's statement that Jochi's *ulus* extended in the west 'as far as the hooves of Mongol horses had trodden' (above, p. 114), because these regions had been traversed in the course of Jebe and Sübeʾetei's expedition in 1222–3. There is also a good deal of testimony in sources from Khurāsān and from Anatolia that before Hülegü's arrival Batu and his representatives had wielded considerable authority in northern Persia.

It is, of course, possible that any arrangements favourable to the Golden Horde were abrogated when Möngke despatched Hülegü to south-western Asia and that the qaghan intended this to mark a fresh dispensation, with the creation of a new *ulus*. What we are told of the terms of Hülegü's commission, however, is itself equivocal. Rashīd al-Dīn, writing under Hülegü's great-grandson Ghazan, alleges that Möngke had intended his brother and the latter's descendants to rule over Iran in perpetuity, just as they were doing, but that he had publicly concealed his purpose and ordered Hülegü to return to Mongolia when his task was accomplished.[74] But far from representing an act of subter-fuge, the qaghan's instructions might suggest, rather, that he regarded his brother merely as his commander-in-chief in Persia and that the establishment of the Ilkhanate was no part of his plan. This seems to be the testimony, again, of al-ʿUmarī's informants, who claim that at some point after the fall of Baghdad Hülegü settled where he was, rebelled and proclaimed his independence.[75] The 'rebellion' included the arrest and execution of the Jochid princes who had taken part in the cam-paigns of 1256–60 under his command – the men described as envoys in the earlier Mamlūk accounts – and the massacre of their troops.[76] We shall probably never attain a full understanding of the events of these few years; but the balance of the evidence is that conflict broke out in the westernmost regions of the Mongol empire because Hülegü had misappropriated territories in north-western Persia which were tradi-tionally held to belong to Jochi's *ulus*.

There now ensued a duel for these regions which outlasted the Ilkhans themselves and was still intermittently in progress in the 1390s, during the era of Temür (Tamerlane). Berke's response to the execution of his kinsmen was, firstly, to launch an attack upon Hülegü's troops south of the Caucasus, and secondly to enter into diplomatic relations with his fellow Muslims in Mamlūk Egypt. Some of his troops who had escaped slaughter at the hands of Hülegü's forces had fled into Syria, where they were given asylum by the Mamlūk authorities and subsequently enrolled in the sultan's army.[77] Berke himself wrote to Baybars in 1262, complaining of Hülegü's conduct and appealing to the Mamlūk Sultan, on the basis of their common faith, to prosecute the holy war against his infidel cousin in Iran.[78] This was the first occasion, it should be noticed, when a Mongol prince showed himself ready to enter into friendly relations with an external (and still unsubdued) power on the grounds of their shared hostility towards fellow Mongols. Baybars responded with alacrity, and right down into the fourteenth century embassies were exchanged between Cairo and the khan's headquarters on the Volga.[79] Egypt benefited in addition from the recent fall of Constantinople to Michael Palaeologus in 1261 and the end of the Frankish and Venetian regime that had dominated the Bosphorus. The newly-restored Byzantine government was ready to cooperate with Baybars by permitting the shipment through the straits of Qipchāq Turkish slaves from the Pontic steppe, a task willingly assumed by its Genoese allies, with the result that the Mamlūk Sultanate was guaranteed a steady supply of fresh military recruits.[80] The understanding between the Mongols of the Golden Horde to the north and his Mamlūk enemies beyond the Euphrates acted as a vital brake upon Hülegü's ambition to expand his dominions into Syria. He too was compelled to look around for potential allies, and he naturally turned to the Mamlūks' principal enemies, the rulers of the Latin West, beginning with Louis IX of France in 1262.

Hülegü's campaigns of 1259–60 in Syria, and perhaps too the almost simultaneous invasion of Poland by Berke's forces, were therefore the last military operations to be mounted by armies gathered on the qaghan's orders and representing the united empire. By the time Arigh Böke submitted to Qubilai in 1264, that empire had dissolved into at least four distinct khanates: the Golden Horde; the Ilkhanate; the Chaghadayid khanate; and the dominions of the qaghan in China and what is now Mongolia. To maintain the struggle against Arigh Böke, Qubilai had been obliged to fall back upon the resources of northern China; Qaraqorum had been in the hands of his rival. But even after Arigh Böke's overthrow Qubilai resided at Shang-tu (formerly K'ai-p'ing) and at the newly-built capital Ta-tu (formerly Chung-tu; close to the site of modern Beijing), which the Mongols called Khanbaligh ('the Khan's town'). The choice threw into sharper relief the vast distances separating the qaghan's power-base from the westernmost marches of the Mongol world.[81]

Qubilai's victory over his brother enabled him to resume the conquest of Sung China, which was completed in 1279 and by which the Mongols became the first steppe power to rule over the entire country. But it did not win him the recognition throughout the empire which he desired. Marco Polo's bland assurance to his readers, that the Mongol empire was Qubilai's by right as well as force of arms,[82] reflects little more than the official stance of the Yüan court he served. Apart from a *rapprochement* in 1283–4 (below, p. 198), which may have been short-lived, the khans of the Golden Horde remained aloof, refusing to accept Qubilai. His Chaghadayid nominees turned against him, recreating Chaghadai's *ulus* within its pre-1251 boundaries and further securing the revenues of the neighbouring sedentary region of Transoxiana that should have gone to the qaghan. From 1269 Qubilai was also confronted in Central Asia by another rival in the person of Ögödei's grandson Qaidu. Appealing, perhaps, to the tradition that the qaghanate should remain in Ögödei's line, Qaidu was able to rally the princes of the lines of Ögödei and Chaghadai and from 1271 onwards acted as an over-khan in the region, nominating the Chaghadayid khans himself. He was never able to achieve more than local triumphs over Qubilai's armies, notably the conquest of the client Uighur principality in the 1280s and the brief occupation of Qaraqorum in 1289; but he successfully resisted Qubilai's attempts to reduce Central Asia to obedience, and he remained a thorn in the side of the qaghans in the Far East right down to his death in 1303.[83] It was not until 1304, when his son and successor Chapar was induced by his Chaghadayid confederates to submit to Qubilai's grandson, the qaghan Temür Öljeitü, that the Mongol world again acknowledged a single paramount sovereign for the first time since 1259 – and even then imperial authority rested on nothing like the same foundations as that of Chinggis Khan and his first three successors.

Qubilai's authority was acknowledged only by fellow Toluids, his brother Hülegü and his descendants in Iran. The title 'Ilkhan' borne by these princes, which does not materialize in the sources until after 1260, appears to mean 'subordinate khan'.[84] Qubilai issued a patent conferring on Hülegü rulership of all the territories west of the Oxus,[85] and similar patents were bestowed upon Hülegü's successors, following the enthronement of each new Ilkhan, down to the reign of Ghazan (1295–1304);

on occasions, senior figures in the Ilkhanid administration received Chinese titles.[86] The qaghan and his Ilkhanid allies were of course too far distant to give each other substantial military assistance in their conflicts with the other Mongol states. But Toluid solidarity meant that they exchanged frequent embassies; it was also responsible for the exchange of skilled personnel, men versed in astronomy, the natural sciences, and technology of various kinds, including military technology.[87] One high-ranking Mongol commander who travelled from China to Persia at the qaghan's behest, and stayed in Western Asia for the remainder of his life, was Rashīd al-Dīn's informant, Bolad Chingsang.

Our survey of events has brought us to 1262, a year in which the Mongols confronted the Latin world on the borders of Poland and Hungary, continued to require the unqualified submission of Western monarchs, and – despite their recent defeat in the Near East – loomed as a more distant menace beyond the Euphrates. At this point they had not abandoned their design of incorporating into their world-empire peoples who had not yet yielded to them. To nobody in the West did they appear as the Heaven-sent allies that they were to become later. How they were in fact viewed in Western eyes, and what caused opinion to begin to change after 1260, are the subject of the next two chapters.

Notes

1. Jean Aubin, 'L'ethnogénèse des Qaraunas', *Turcica* 1 (1969), pp. 65–94 (here pp. 74–5).
2. Jackson, 'From *ulus* to khanate', pp. 17–23.
3. As WR, vii, 4, p. 185 (tr. Jackson and Morgan, p. 92), noticed.
4. Juwaynī, I, pp. 31–2 (tr. Boyle, I, p. 42). The location of Saqsīn is uncertain: see Pelliot, *Notes sur l'histoire de la Horde d'Or*, pp. 165–74.
5. Dorothea Krawulsky, 'Das Testament von Chinggis Khan: Eine quellenkritische Studie zum Thema Legitimation und Herrschaft', in her *Mongolen und Ilkhâne – Ideologie und Geschichte. 5 Studien* (Beirut, 1989), pp. 65–85.
6. Joseph Fletcher, 'Turco-Mongolian monarchic tradition in the Ottoman Empire', in I. Ševčenko and F.E. Sysyn, eds, *Eucharisterion. Essays Presented to Omeljan Pritsak* (Cambridge, MA, 1979–80 = HUS 3–4), pp. 236–51 (here pp. 237–42), and idem, 'The Mongols: ecological and social perspectives', HJAS 46 (1986), pp. 11–50 (here pp. 17, 24–8); both repr. in Fletcher, *Studies on Chinese and Islamic Inner Asia*, ed. Beatrice Forbes Manz (Aldershot, 1995).
7. Ögödei's line: SH, § 255, tr. De Rachewiltz, I, pp. 187–8 (and see notes at II, pp. 923, 935–7); Rashīd al-Dīn, I, p. 69 (tr. Thackston, I, p. 39); Waṣṣāf, *Tajziyat al-amṣār wa-tazjiyat al-aʿṣār* (in a section completed c.1298), lithograph edn (Bombay, 1269 H./1853, repr. Tehran, 1338 H. solar/1959–60),

p. 66. Güyüg's line: Rashīd al-Dīn, II, p. 806 (tr. Thackston, II, p. 393). Both: Juwaynī, III, pp. 21–2 (tr. Boyle, II, p. 562).

8. Allsen, *Mongol Imperialism*, pp. 39–42. For other *ex post facto* attempts at such legitimation, see Herbert Franke, *From Tribal Chieftain to Universal Emperor and God: The Legitimation of the Yüan Dynasty*, Sitzungsberichte der Bayerischen Akademie der Wissenschaften, phil.-hist. Kl. (Munich, 1978), pp. 22–4, repr. in Franke, *China under Mongol Rule* (Aldershot, 1994).

9. TR, § 30, p. 21.

10. Jackson, 'Dissolution', p. 200. For Baichu, see ibid., p. 216; also Jackson, 'Bāyjū', and 'Eljigidei', *Enc.Ir.* Ibn al-ʿAmīd (d. *c.*1272), *Kitāb al-majmūʿ al-mubārak*, ed. Claude Cahen, 'La «Chronique des Ayyoubides» d'al-Makīn b. al-ʿAmīd', *BEO* 15 (1955–7), pp. 108–84 (here p. 130), and tr. Anne-Marie Eddé and Françoise Micheau, *Al-Makīn ibn al-ʿAmīd. Chronique des Ayyoubides (602–658/1205–6–1259–60)*, DRHC 16 (Paris, 1994), p. 25, mentions his subordination to Batu.

11. WR, xxvii, 6, p. 241 (tr. Jackson and Morgan, p. 167).

12. Allsen, *Mongol Imperialism*, pp. 22–7, 30–4.

13. John of Garlande, *De triumphis*, p. 140: *Tartarei perimunt se, rege iubente*. For the Armenians, see *CM*, V, p. 340; they are mentioned earlier (V, p. 116) as having arrived in England in 1250.

14. For an overview of this campaign, see Boyle, 'Dynastic and political history of the Īlkhāns', in *CHI*, V, pp. 340–52.

15. Rashīd al-Dīn, II, pp. 993–4 (tr. Thackston, II, pp. 486–7).

16. Cahen, *Formation of Turkey*, pp. 184–6.

17. For the Syrian campaign of 1260, see Reuven Amitai-Preiss, *Mongols and Mamluks. The Mamluk-Īlkhānid War, 1260–1281* (Cambridge, 1995), pp. 26–35.

18. Ibn Wāṣil, *Mufarrij al-kurūb fī akhbār banī Ayyūb* (1261), BN ms. arabe 1703, fo. 154r.

19. Paul Meyvaert, 'An unknown letter of Hulagu, Il-khan of Persia, to King Louis IX of France', *Viator* 11 (1980), pp. 245–59 (here p. 258). David O. Morgan, 'The Mongols in Syria, 1260–1300', in Peter W. Edbury, ed., *Crusade and Settlement. Papers Read to the First Conference of the Society for the Study of the Crusades and the Latin East and Presented to R.C. Smail* (Cardiff, 1985), pp. 231–5.

20. 'Menkonis chronicon', *MGHS*, XXIII, p. 549: *sperans se dominium suscepturum, ulterius non processit . . .* Hayton, iii, 21–22, Fr. text p. 172, Latin text p. 303, alleges (probably in error) that Hülegü was invited to take the throne.

21. WR, xxxviii, 18, p. 329 (tr. Jackson and Morgan, p. 275).

22. C.V. L[anglois], 'Lettre à Charles d'Anjou sur les affaires de Terre Sainte (Acre, 22 avril 1260)', *BEC* 78 (1917), pp. 487–90 (here p. 489).

23. al-Yūnīnī (d. 1326), *al-Dhayl ʿalā' Mirʾāt al-zamān*, 4 vols (Hyderabad, A.P., 1374–80 H./1954–61), III, p. 92; he claims to have seen Bohemond there. Amitai-Preiss, *Mongols and Mamluks*, p. 31. For the request for Baʿlabakk, see also the later mention *ad annum* 687 H./1289: ed. Antranig Melkonian, *Die Jahre 1287–1291 in der Chronik al-Yūnīnīs* (Freiburg i.Br., 1975), Ar. text p. 32 (German tr. p. 78).

24. 'Gestes des Chiprois', § 303, *RHCDA*, II, p. 751, and tr. Paul Crawford, *The 'Templar of Tyre'. Part III of the 'Deeds of the Cypriots'*, CTT 6 (Aldershot, 2003), pp. 34–5. Dominique Sourdel, 'Bohémond et les chrétiens à Damas sous l'occupation mongole', in Michel Balard *et al.*, eds, *Dei gesta per Francos. Études sur les croisades dédiées à Jean Richard* (Aldershot, 2001), pp. 295–9.

25. Ibn Shaddād (d. 1285), *al-A'lāq al-khaṭīra fī dhikr umarāʾ al-Shām wa l-Jazīra*, BL ms. Add. 23,334, fo. 54r–v. Claude Cahen, *La Syrie du Nord à l'époque des croisades et la principauté franque d'Antioche* (Paris, 1940), p. 706; for the location of these places, see ibid., pp. 159–61.

26. Peter Jackson, 'The crisis in the Holy Land in 1260', *EHR* 95 (1980), pp. 481–513 (here p. 504). For the War of St Sabas, see Peter Edbury, *John of Ibelin and the Kingdom of Jerusalem* (Woodbridge, 1997), pp. 91–4, 96.

27. *Reg. Urbain IV*, II, p. 134 (no. 292).

28. Clovis Brunel, 'David d'Ashby auteur méconnu des *Faits des Tartares*', *Romania* 79 (1958), pp. 39–46 (here p. 40).

29. The surviving letters are listed in Jackson, 'Crisis', p. 487, n.1; see also pp. 490–2. Others are mentioned in 'Hermanni Altahensis annales', p. 402; 'Annales monasterii de Burton', p. 493; *Flores historiarum*, ed. H.R. Luard, RS, 3 vols (London, 1890), II, pp. 451–2: *omnibus aliis circa mare Graecorum potentibus*.

30. Baybars al-Manṣūrī al-Dawādār (d. 1325), *Zubdat al-fikra fī taʾrīkh al-hijra*, ed. D.S. Richards, Bibliotheca Islamica 42 (Beirut, 1419 H./1998), p. 50. al-Dhahabī, *Taʾrīkh al-Islām 651–660*, ed. 'Umar 'Abd al-Salām Tadmurī (Beirut, 1419 H./1999), p. 55.

31. Ibn al-'Amīd, p. 173 (tr. Eddé and Micheau, p. 116).

32. 'Gestes des Chiprois', pp. 751–2, § 303 (tr. Crawford, p. 35). The news reached Damascus early in Ramaḍān/in mid-August: Abū Shāma (d. 1267), *al-Dhayl 'alā l-Rawḍatayn*, ed. M.Z. al-Kawtharī as *Tarājim rijāl al-qarnayn al-sādis wa l-sābiʿ* (Cairo, 1366 H./1947), p. 207.

33. 'Continuation de Guillaume de Tyr, de 1228 à 1261, dite du manuscrit de Rothelin', *RHCOcc.*, II, p. 637, and tr. Janet Shirley, *Crusader Syria in the Thirteenth Century*, CTT 5 (Aldershot, 1999), pp. 118–19. Jackson, 'Crisis', pp. 506–7.

34. For the location, see Reuven Amitai-Preiss, '"Ayn Jālūt revisited', *Tārīḫ* 2 (1991), pp. 119–50.

35. Rashīd al-Dīn, II, pp. 1032–3 (tr. Thackston, II, pp. 505–6). On the size of the respective armies, see John Masson Smith, Jr, '"Ayn Jālūt: Mamlūk success or Mongol failure?', *HJAS* 44 (1984), pp. 307–45 (here pp. 308–13).

36. 'Annales S. Justinae Patavini', *MGHS*, XIX, p. 192.

37. Jaime I, *Llibre dels fets*, § 487, tr. Damian Smith and Helena Buffery, *The Book of Deeds of James I of Aragon*, CTT 10 (Aldershot, 2003), p. 340 and n.56. For the bishop, see Richard, 'Mongols and the Franks', p. 51 and n.26; for attempts to organize the crusade, Maier, *Preaching the Crusades*, p. 85.

38. Gui de Basainville, Templar *visitor in partibus cismarinis*, to Franco de Borno, preceptor in Aquitaine, in *Monumenta Boica*, XXIX:2 (Munich, 1831), p. 200. 'Annales monasterii de Burton', pp. 495–9. 'Hermanni Altahensis annales', p. 402. Pierre Toubert, 'Les déviations de la Croisade au milieu du XIIIᵉ siècle: Alexandre IV contre Manfred', *MA* 69 (1963), pp. 391–9. Jean Richard, 'La

croisade de 1270, premier «passage général»?', *CRAIBL* (1989), pp. 510–23 (here pp. 512–13), repr. in his *Croisades et états latins.*

39. Guillaume de Nangis, 'Gesta Ludovici', p. 412.
40. Urban IV to Alphonse of Poitou, 11 June 1263, AN, J448/79; also to the archbishop of Reims, same date, in *LTC*, IV, p. 64 (no. 4849).
41. *LTC*, IV, pp. 36–7 (no. 4753, 18 April 1262). Ildefonso Rodriguez R. de Lama, ed., *La documentacion pontificia de Urbano IV (1261–1264)* (Rome, 1981), pp. 84–6 (no. 42, 15 May 1262). At this point recruitment for the anti-Mongol crusade was first extended to Spain: José Manuel Rodríguez García, 'Henry III (1216–1272), Alfonso X of Castile (1252–1284) and the crusading plans of the thirteenth century (1245–1272)', in Björn K.U. Weiler, ed. (with Ifor W. Rowlands), *England and Europe in the Reign of Henry III (1216–1272)* (Aldershot, 2002), pp. 99–120 (here n.74 at p. 117). For subsequent papal references to the Mongol threat in Syria, see AN, J451/3 (4 July 1262, to the Portuguese hierarchy), J451/4 (7 July 1262, to the Norwegian hierarchy), J451/6 (19 Feb. 1263), J448/80 (25 April 1263, to the archbishop of Tyre).
42. Joseph de Somogyi, 'A *Qaṣīda* on the destruction of Baghdād by the Mongols', *BSOS* 7 (1933–5), pp. 41–8 (text at p. 44, tr. p. 45). The verses are preserved in al-Dhahabī, *Ta'rīkh al-Islām 651–660*, p. 38.
43. Step'annos Orbelean (d. 1304), *Patmut'iwn nahangin Sisakan*, tr. M.F. Brosset, *Histoire de la Siounie*, 2 vols (St Petersburg, 1864–6), I, pp. 234, 235. J.M. Fiey, 'Iconographie syriaque: Hulagu, Doquz Khatun . . . et six ambons?', *Le Muséon* 88 (1975), pp. 59–64.
44. al-Yūnīnī, II, p. 35. For Mongol evenhandedness, see Juwaynī, I, pp. 18–19 (tr. Boyle, I, p. 26).
45. Ghāzī b. al-Wāsiṭī (d. 1312), *Kitāb al-radd 'alā' ahl al-dhimma*, ed. and tr. Richard Gottheil, 'An answer to the Dhimmis', *JAOS* 41 (1921), pp. 383–457 (text pp. 407–8, tr. pp. 445–6). Sourdel, 'Bohémond'.
46. Meyvaert, pp. 258–9 and n.83. Hayton, iii, 24, Fr. text p. 174, Latin text pp. 304–5.
47. Bertold Spuler, *Die Mongolen in Iran. Politik, Verwaltung und Kultur der Ilchanzeit, 1220–1350*, 4th edn (Leiden, 1985), p. 192. S.M. Mirnyi, '«La Flor des Estoires de Terres d'Orient» Gaitona kak istoriko-geograficheskii istochnik po vostoku i po istorii Mongolov', *Sovetskoe Vostokovedenie* (1956), no. 5, pp. 72–82. Wolfgang Giese, 'Asienkunde für den kreuzfahrenden Westen. Die „Flos historiarum terre orientis" des Hayto von Gorhigos (O.Praem.) aus dem Jahre 1307', in Gert Melville, ed., *Secundum regulam vivere. Festschrift für P. Norbert Backmund O.Praem.* (Windberg, 1978), pp. 245–64 (here pp. 249–63). For further motives, see Glen Burger, 'Cilician Armenian métissage and Hetoum's *La Fleur des histoires de la terre d'Orient*', in Jeffrey Jerome Cohen, ed., *The Postcolonial Middle Ages* (Basingstoke, 2000), pp. 67–83.
48. 'Iohannis Longi Chronica S. Bertini', *MGHS*, XXV, p. 850 (the author d. in 1383).
49. Langlois, 'Lettre à Charles d'Anjou', p. 490. Jackson, 'Crisis', p. 494.
50. Bérard's letter, as reproduced by Gui de Basainville, in *Monumenta Boica*, XXIX:2, p. 200; see also Jackson, 'Crisis', p. 492.

51. 'Menkonis chronicon', p. 549: *eosque vicit viriliter et potenter.* 'Annales S. Justinae Patavini', p. 191: *eos viriliter superavit.* 'Annales S. Rudberti Salisburgenses', p. 795: *Deo dante ipsos vicit.*

52. Langlois, 'Lettre à Charles d'Anjou', p. 490. For al-Nāṣir's army, see Thomas Bérard to Amadeus, Templar preceptor in England, 4 March [1260], in 'Annales monasterii de Burton', pp. 492–3.

53. Pierre Chaplais, ed., *Diplomatic documents preserved in the Public Record Office*, I. *1101–1272* (London, 1964), pp. 264–5 (no. 385, 4 April 1263) = Rymer, I:2, p. 54 (*ad annum* 1260, but the Indiction is given correctly as *sexta*).

54. *LTC*, IV, pp. 71–4 (no. 4866, 6 Sept. 1263). The papal letter clearly echoes that of 4 April 1263 (see n.53).

55. Ibn Shaddād, *al-A 'lāq al-khaṭīra*, ed. Sāmī Dahhān, *Liban, Jordanie, Palestine. Topographie historique d'Ibn Šaddād* (Damascus, 1382 H./1963), p. 100. Humphreys, *From Saladin to the Mongols*, pp. 325, 355.

56. Abū Shāma, p. 212. Jackson, 'Crisis', p. 509.

57. Ibn 'Abd al-Ẓāhir (d. 1292), *al-Rawḍ al-zāhir fī sīrat al-malik al-Ẓāhir*, ed. 'Abd al-'Azīz al-Khuwayṭir (Riyāḍ, 1396 H./1976), p. 300.

58. The fullest accounts are in 'Rocznik kapituły krakowskiej' (down to 1266), *MPH²*, V, pp. 87–8 = 'Annales capituli Cracoviensis', *MGHS*, XIX, pp. 600–1; 'Kronika wielkopolska', pp. 113–14 = 'Annales capituli Posnaniensis', *MGHS*, XXIX, p. 460; and *PSRL*, II, coll. 852–5 (tr. Perfecky, pp. 79–80), which alone names the Mongol commander.

59. 'R.', abbot of 'Quda', to 'N.', abbot of Welehrad in Moravia [1259], ed. W. Wattenbach, in *NA* 2 (1877), p. 626. 'Rocznik kapituły krakowskiej', p. 88 = 'Annales capituli Cracoviensis', pp. 600–1. 'Rocznik krótki' (to 1283), *MPH²*, V, p. 242 = 'Annales Cracovienses breves', *MGHS*, XIX, p. 666. 'Kronika wielkopolska', p. 114 = 'Annales capituli Posnaniensis', p. 460. 'Rocznik Traski' (1340s), *MPH*, II, p. 839 = 'Annales Polonorum (i)', *MGHS*, XIX, p. 634. 'Rocznik małopolski' (14th cent.), *MPH*, III, p. 170 = 'Annales Polonorum (iv)', *MGHS*, XIX, p. 635. Less contemporary: 'Annales Vratislavienses antiqui', *MGHS*, XIX, p. 528; 'Rocznik Świętokrzyski', *MPH*, III, p. 73 = 'Annales Sancti Crucis Polonici', *MGHS*, XIX, p. 681.

60. 'Annales Mellicenses. Continuatio Lambacensis', p. 560. 'Annales Sancti Rudberti Salisburgenses', p. 795, reports an apocryphal victory over the invaders by the Polish dukes in alliance with the Teutonic Knights.

61. 'Rocznik kapituły krakowskiej', p. 88 = 'Annales capituli Cracoviensis', p. 601. Cf. also the letter of 1259 referred to in n.59 above, and that of the abbot of Wonchok, in Oswald Redlich, ed., *Eine Wiener Briefsammlung zur Geschichte des deutschen Reiches* (Vienna, 1894), pp. 7–8 (no. 8).

62. Lithuania: *CDRB*, V:1, pp. 364–5 (no. 235, 9 Sept. 1260); the Mongols had been active in the lands of the Jądwings in 1258, *PSRL*, II, coll. 847–8 (tr. Perfecky, p. 77). Prussia: 'Annales Mellicenses. Continuatio Zwetlensis tertia', *MGHS*, IX, p. 644; the fighting is possibly referred to in a papal letter of Dec. 1259, *PUB*, I:2, pp. 73–4 (no. 82).

63. *PUB*, I:2, pp. 84–6, 98–9, 111, 128 (nos. 98, 99, 109, 134, 154). Christiansen, *Northern Crusades*, p. 107. Jürgen Sarnowsky, 'The Teutonic Order confronts Mongols and Turks', in Malcolm Barber, ed., *The Military Orders. Fighting for*

the Faith and Caring for the Sick (Aldershot, 1994), pp. 253–62 (here pp. 256–7). Maier, *Preaching the Crusades*, pp. 90–1.

64. Jean Richard, 'Une ambassade mongole à Paris en 1262', *JS* (1979), pp. 295–303, repr. in Richard, *Croisés*. Schmieder, *Europa*, p. 92.
65. 'Chronica minor auctore Minorita Erphordiensi', *MGHS*, XXIV, p. 202.
66. *VMH*, I, pp. 239–40 (no. 454).
67. Abū Shāma, p. 208. See the comments of David Ayalon, 'The European-Asiatic steppe: a major reservoir of power for the Islamic world', in *Trudy XXV mezhdunarodnogo kongressy vostokovedov, Moskva 1960*, II (Moscow, 1963), pp. 47–52 (here pp. 49–50), repr. in Ayalon, *The Mamlūk Military Society* (London, 1979).
68. For what follows, see Jackson, 'Dissolution', pp. 227–35; Morris Rossabi, *Khubilai Khan. His Life and Times* (Berkeley and Los Angeles, 1988), pp. 53–62.
69. Jamāl al-Qarshī (writing in Central Asia *c.*1303), *Mulḥaqāt al-Ṣurāḥ*, partial ed. in V.V. Bartol'd, *Turkestan v epokhu mongol'skogo nashestviia*, 2 vols (St Petersburg, 1898–1900), I (texts), p. 138. Bar Hebraeus, tr. Budge, *Chronography*, p. 439, and *Mukhtaṣar*, p. 491. Ibn al-'Amīd, p. 173 (tr. Eddé and Micheau, p. 115).
70. Shawwāl 658 H., according to Jamāl al-Qarshī, pp. 137–8: in Jackson, 'Dissolution', p. 229, n.187, I erroneously gave the equivalence as June–July 1260, which is in fact the date furnished in the *Yüan shih*.
71. Dietlinde Schlegel, 'Koexistenz oder Annexionskrieg? Kublai Khans Politik gegenüber dem Sung-Reich 1256–1276', *Saeculum* 19 (1968), pp. 390–405 (here pp. 397–402).
72. For what follows, see David Ayalon, 'The Great *Yāsa* of Chingiz Khān: a reexamination. Part B', *SI* 34 (1971), pp. 151–80 (here pp. 174–6), repr. in Ayalon, *Outsiders in the Lands of Islam: Mamlūks, Mongols and Eunuchs* (London, 1988); Jackson, 'Dissolution', pp. 208–27 *passim*.
73. Ibn Faḍl-Allāh al-'Umarī, *Masālik al-abṣār fī mamālik al-amṣār*, ed. and tr. Klaus Lech, *Das mongolische Weltreich: Al-'Umarī's Darstellung der mongolischen Reiche in seinem Werk...*, AF 22 (Wiesbaden, 1968), text p. 15 (German tr. p. 100).
74. Rashīd al-Dīn, II, p. 977 (tr. Thackston, II, p. 479). See Jackson, 'Dissolution', pp. 221–2; Dorothea Krawulsky, 'Die Dynastie der Ilkhâne: Eine Untersuchung zu Regierungsbeginn, Dynastie- und Reichsname', in her *Mongolen und Ilkhâne*, p. 90, is similarly sceptical about Möngke's 'secret' design. But for a different view, see Thomas Allsen, *Culture and Conquest in Mongol Eurasia* (Cambridge, 2001), pp. 20–2.
75. al-'Umarī, *Masālik*, ed. and tr. Lech, text p. 2 (German tr. p. 91).
76. For the details, given by Rashīd al-Dīn, I, p. 738, and II, pp. 1034, 1044 (tr. Thackston, II, pp. 362, 506, 511), and by Armenian historians, see Boyle, 'Dynastic and political history', pp. 352–3; Jackson, 'Dissolution', pp. 226–7, 232–3.
77. David Ayalon, 'The Wafidiya in the Mamluk kingdom', *Islamic Culture* 25 (1951), pp. 81–104, repr. in Ayalon, *Studies on the Mamlūks of Egypt (1250–1517)* (London, 1977).

78. Ayalon, 'Great *Yāsa*', pp. 167–73.

79. S. Zakirov, *Diplomaticheskie otnosheniia Zolotoi Ordy s Egiptom (XIII–XIV vv.)* (Moscow, 1966).

80. J.J. Saunders, 'The Mongol defeat at Ayn Jalut and the restoration of the Greek empire', in his *Muslims and Mongols*, ed. G.W. Rice (Canterbury, N.Z., 1977), pp. 67–76.

81. John W. Dardess, 'From Mongol empire to Yüan dynasty: changing forms of imperial rule in Mongolia and Central Asia', *Monumenta Serica* 30 (1972–3), pp. 117–65 (here pp. 131–2).

82. *DM*, p. 406/MP, I, pp. 192–3 (tr. Ricci, p. 103).

83. The standard work is now Michal Biran, *Qaidu and the Rise of the Independent Mongol State in Central Asia* (Richmond, Surrey, 1997). For brief introductions, see W. Barthold, *Four Studies on the History of Central Asia*, tr. V. and T. Minorsky, 3 vols (Leiden, 1956–62), I, pp. 124–9, and Pelliot, *Notes on Marco Polo*, I, pp. 124–9.

84. Reuven Amitai-Preiss, 'Evidence for the early use of the title *īlkhān* among the Mongols', *JRAS*, 3rd series, 1 (1991), pp. 354–61. Allsen, *Culture and Conquest*, pp. 21–2. Idem, 'Changing forms of legitimation in Mongol Iran', in Seaman and Marks, *Rulers from the Steppe*, pp. 223–41 (here p. 227). The meaning 'peaceful khan' (i.e. who had imposed peace on Iran) adopted by Krawulsky, 'Die Dynastie', pp. 95–8, is apparently based on a false etymology: see Marcel Erdal, 'Die türkisch-mongolischen Titel *elχan* und *elči*', in Barbara Kellner-Heinkele, ed., *Altaica Berolinensia: The Concept of Sovereignty in the Altaic World. Permanent International Altaistic Conference, 34th Meeting, Berlin 21–26 July, 1991*, AF 126 (Wiesbaden, 1993), pp. 81–99 (here pp. 85–7).

85. Rashīd al-Dīn, II, pp. 880, 1047 (tr. Thackston, II, pp. 429, 512): the date is unclear.

86. Thomas T. Allsen, 'Notes on Chinese titles in Mongol Iran', *MS* 14 (1991), pp. 27–39.

87. Allsen, *Culture and Conquest, passim*.

chapter 6

IMAGES OF THE ENEMY[1]

The Mongols' image of the Franks

For those who seek an insight into the Mongol view of the Western
world, there are only two avenues – both somewhat indirect, given
the absence of any Mongolian narrative source that details the invasion
of Europe. One way entails gleaning what we can from sources composed by the Mongols' subjects, notably Chinese material and the
universal history of the Ilkhanid statesman Rashīd al-Dīn, which includes a section on the Franks (1305/6). The other route is through
the accounts of the Latin visitors to the Mongol empire. Some of the
material they supply is problematic. To take one example, the way in
which the Mongols are said to anticipate a final defeat at Frankish hands
within a certain period owes far more, as we shall see, to Western
exegesis of apocalyptic texts than it does to conversations in the steppe.

There are indications, nevertheless, that in the 1240s the Mongols
conceived of Latin Christendom as a single power, of considerable size.
According to the 'Tartar Relation', they thought of it as comprising the
western half of the inhabited world.[2] The qaghan Güyüg's letter to
Innocent IV (1247) suggests that the Mongols initially saw the Pope as
the emperor or overlord of a number of lesser rulers;[3] though subsequently Hülegü assured one of these kinglets, Louis IX of France (1262),
that they had learned the Pope's true priestly status.[4] In 1255 Rubruck
observed that if the Mongols heard the Pope was preparing to unleash a
crusade against them they would all take to their heels and retire into
the wilderness from which they had come.[5] It is tempting to discount
this statement – like the claims of Carpini and Simon of Saint-Quentin
that the Mongols stood in some awe of Frankish might – as tendentious
and indeed chauvinistic, designed partly to inspire determined resistance
in the event of a future attack (above, p. 92). But, as we saw, such
views are echoed by authors within the Mongol empire (p. 73); while a

Chinese source dating from 1263, and apparently based on a report sent by Hülegü to Möngke in 1258, describes the Franks as very fine warriors.[6] Contemporary Muslim geographers, moreover, transmit the image of a powerful European king periodically launching formidable expeditions against Syria and Palestine, and it may be that this had been communicated to the Mongols during their advance through south-west Asia.[7]

On the other hand, the Mongols' sense of their own superiority was in no way modified, since they regarded all Westerners as future subjects.[8] And early Latin visitors leave us in no doubt that their Mongol hosts held them in the greatest contempt. This was seemingly not so much because they represented sedentary culture as because they were members of Mendicant Orders, who were devoted to poverty and abstinence, who brought only meagre gifts for the qaghan, and who exhorted their hosts to accept Christianity. 'You urge us to become Christians and to be dogs like you', Ascelin's party were told at Baichu's encampment; 'is not your Pope a dog, and are not all you Christians dogs?'[9] And Rubruck's guide on the route from Batu's headquarters to the qaghan, before he recognized that the friars could be useful through their prayers, was disgusted at having to escort such wretched people.[10] Both at Batu's encampment and at Möngke's headquarters, where the party arrived in December, the friars' appearance with bare feet, says Rubruck, presented quite a spectacle for the crowd that had gathered; on the latter occasion they were asked whether they had no use for their feet.[11] Clearly the Western religious provoked a very different response from the Western warrior.

Contemporary writers and public opinion in the West

For the impact of the Mongol attack of 1241 on what might be called 'public opinion' in the Latin West, the sources are rather more plentiful. They comprise the few authors, like Thomas of Spalato and Roger of Várad, whose narratives describe the onslaught at first hand; the notables who issued the appeals for help that have come down to us; major figures like the pope and the Emperor Frederick II who responded to such appeals; monastic and clerical annalists who commented on the invasion in greater or lesser depth; and model sermons which refer to the Mongols (as yet a relatively under-exploited source).[12] As a means of eliciting public opinion, these sources are not entirely satisfactory. In the first place, to attempt a systematic exposition of Western views about the Mongols risks lending a spurious coherence to ideas that may in fact have been half-formed, transient and mutually contradictory. And secondly, we cannot be sure how much impact any particular letter or chronicle had. It might be expected, for example, that the Emperor's encyclical of 3 July 1241, which according to Richard of San Germano was sent to several of his fellow monarchs,[13] did much to shape opinion, indirectly or otherwise. But even Matthew Paris, who in the early 1240s certainly felt a good deal of sympathy for Frederick, admits that the Emperor's proposals were greeted with suspicion and that his enemies charged him with inciting the Mongol attack in order to extend his suzerainty over Béla IV.[14] So too the influence of a narrative source might bear no relation whatever to its value for scholars in the twenty-first century (and in what follows, I have tried to distinguish annalists who are not manifestly interdependent from those who clearly did no more than copy their material). Matthew Paris, as we saw, assembled a dossier of information on the Mongols; but only a few manuscripts of the *Chronica majora* have survived, suggesting that it did not circulate widely. On the other hand, a set of annals – say, in Germany – might enjoy a wide currency, evident from the fact that it was borrowed, within a mere decade or two, by a number of other monastic chronicles; yet it might contain only the most cursory reference to the Mongol invasion of 1241–2. Not only do many annalists dismiss that invasion in a single laconic entry, but several neglect to mention it at all.[15]

Within fifteen years of the attack a number of Western Europeans had visited the Mongol world. Although the earliest reports outlining the Mongol threat, produced by the friars Richardus in *c*.1235 and Julian in 1237–8, seem to have been known to Matthew Paris within a few years,[16] it was the Franciscan and Dominican envoys of Pope Innocent IV, returning in 1247–8, who made available a significant corpus of more or less accurate information on Mongol society and its customs, in the reports of Carpini and of Simon of Saint-Quentin. For the next sixty years – until the appearance of the frequently-cited and much-copied *La flor des estoires* of Hayton of Gorigos (1307) and, to a lesser degree, of Marco Polo's book – they would have no equal. Initially, at least, Carpini's experiences reached a wide public. As we have seen (p. 88), incomplete versions of his report were circulating even before the party rejoined Pope Innocent at Lyons in October 1247. Salimbene, who subsequently met Carpini at Sens in 1248, gives the impression that he was then virtually engaged on a lecture tour.[17] Thereafter, it is possible that his report would have slid into obscurity had not Vincent of Beauvais incorporated sizeable extracts in his *Speculum historiale* (*c*.1253), one of the most popular works of the Middle Ages. Vincent did the same with Simon of Saint-Quentin's *Historia* (which has not survived in its original form), thus ensuring that the material the two reports contained was transmitted over time to an extensive readership.

Their contemporaries were less fortunate. Only a brief summary of the first mission of Andrew of Longjumeau has come down to us, and what little we know of the course of his second, on behalf of Louis IX, is derived from Joinville and from Rubruck. Rubruck's own report to King Louis was a commendably full document; but it would languish in relative obscurity for over three centuries. Indeed, only the English Franciscan Roger Bacon is known to have read it. He met Rubruck, probably during a visit to Paris in 1256–7, and had the opportunity to collate his own text of the *Itinerarium* with the friar's oral statements. Whether Bacon's copy was the book *de vita et moribus Tartarorum*, approximately the length of a psalter, which the chronicler John of Wallingford (d. 1258) says was presented to Simon de Montfort in 1257, we cannot tell.[18] In any event, Bacon duly inserted citations from Rubruck's book, sometimes with specific attribution, in his own *Opus maius* (*c.*1267),[19] though this too barely circulated. Two other reports dating from this early period are lost. The single known manuscript of David of Ashby's *Les fais des Tartares*, written probably in advance of the Second Council of Lyons (1274), was destroyed in a fire in 1904. Of the *De ortu Tartarorum*, dated 1255, which has been persuasively attributed to the Dominican Jacek Odrowąż (St Hyacinth; d. 1257), only the preface has survived (and makes minimal reference to the Mongols); the main text was possibly never written.[20]

An alien people

The devastation of Poland, Moravia and Hungary in 1241–2 largely dispelled any notion that the Mongols were the forces of a Christian 'King David' or Prester John, as had been assumed on the first news of the attacks by Chinggis Khan's forces on the Islamic world. It is true that the earlier optimism is echoed in the rumours that their goal was to retrieve from Cologne the bones of the Three Kings; it was for this reason that the Mongols were sometimes called 'Tarsenses' (i.e. people of 'Tarse', as the country of the Magi was traditionally known).[21] Such reports would persist even as late as the Mongol attack on Hungary in 1285.[22] But speculation of this kind was dwarfed by the numerous reports depicting the invaders as hostile and bloodthirsty barbarians.

The Mongols occupied no place in the Western scriptural and ency-clopaedic tradition. They had taken a mere two decades to burst upon the West's horizons from nowhere – an unknown race from an unknown and far distant region.[23] 'Where had such a people lain hidden?' asked Matthew Paris.[24] The most precise answer given to this question was that they had come 'from the furthest parts of Scythia'.[25] It was tempting to identify them with more familiar enemies. As we saw (p. 63), some observers confused the Mongols who ravaged Hungary in 1241 with the Cumans. For others, the newcomers were Saracens,[26] a term normally reserved for the Muslims (though occasionally applied to the pagans of north-eastern Europe). One annalist, doubtless bemused by the rapid succession of events in Syria, made the Khwarazmian sack of Jerusalem in 1244 the work of the Mongols.[27] Various etymologies were proposed for the name Tartar, by which the invaders were known in the West. One was that it was derived from a river in their homeland; Matthew Paris, for his part, linked it with the islands of Tarachonta, where the eighth-century geographer Aethicus Ister claimed that Gog and Magog had built a city.[28]

Emerging from the vast wilderness that apparently extended for hundreds of miles to the east, the conquerors seemed to belong, as Rubruck would put it, to 'some other world'.[29] In ecological terms it was a world not totally unheard-of in the West; but its character was alien, and contemporary observers borrowed the vocabulary previously applied to other steppe nomads like the tenth-century Hungarians or the Cumans. For many, first and foremost, they were barbarians.[30] Both Carpini and Rubruck apply the word to them at an early stage in their reports, although they do not employ it frequently.[31] Simon of Saint-Quentin dismissed as 'beastly humans' the Mongols in Baichu's camp who could not grasp the doctrine of papal primacy, despite the efforts of Ascelin's party to expound it to them.[32] They knew nothing of weaving, and were clothed in the skins of animals.[33] They did not practise agriculture, and had neither villages nor towns.[34] Rubruck saw no building, other than the imperial 'capital', Qaraqorum, and only one village in the course of his return journey; in fact, he learned that the conquerors had destroyed towns in Central Asia in order to extend the area of pasturage for their livestock.[35] 'Nowhere have they any lasting city', he begins his survey of Mongol society, in terms borrowed from the Epistle to the Hebrews (xiii, 14); 'and of the one to come they have no knowledge'.[36] We should note the subtle connection here between pastoral nomadism and the lack of rootedness in any salvific belief. Influenced by St Augustine, European Christians in the Middle Ages, as in a later phase of contact with the outside world, turned to the city as the natural image of both the earthly and the heavenly community.[37]

A number of writers, beginning with Henry of Livonia only a few years after the Mongols' first appearance in the Pontic steppe and their victory over the Rus' near the Kalka River in 1223, commented that they were unfamiliar with bread, and devoured raw meat instead.[38] Thomas of Spalato noted that the Mongols abhorred bread, and believed that they drank a concoction of mare's milk and blood.[39] The papal envoys in turn drew attention to the fact that the Mongols did not eat bread, herbs or vegetables.[40] Rubruck observed that they did not know how to catch fish and had no interest in fish other than those so large that they could eat their flesh like mutton.[41] They had no wine of their own and were dependent on what was imported into the steppe; instead they drank fermented mare's milk (*qumis*), especially in the summer, wine made from rice or millet, or meat broth.[42] The absence of, or relative disregard for, the three elements – bread, wine and fish – that played such a central role in the Western European diet (not to mention the Christian liturgical curriculum) was especially noteworthy.

Conversely, what the Mongols did eat comprised every kind of thing that was forbidden to Christians and fostered the image of an unclean people. A few authors writing soon after the assault on Eastern Europe, including Thomas of Spalato, mentioned that the invaders ate the flesh of clean and unclean beasts without discrimination,[43] and this refrain would be taken up by the friars. They ate all their dead animals without distinction, noticed Rubruck, specifying horses as well as oxen and sheep; but he later added that the Mongol diet included mice, marmots and certain other small animals 'which are good to eat'.[44] The papal envoys had been still more damning. Simon of Saint-Quentin alleged that the Mongols fed on dogs, cats and rats – everything, in fact, except the she-mule.[45] The unappetizing fare listed by Carpini included not merely dogs, wolves, foxes and mice, but also lice and the afterbirth of mares.[46] The Mongols' uncleanness extended beyond the components of their diet. They neglected to wash dishes or utensils, and did not employ napkins.[47] Rubruck betrays particular irritation over their habit of voiding their bowels in mid-conversation, 'moving away from us', he says, 'no further than one could toss a bean'.[48]

A few of the writers who noticed the invasion, among them Matthew Paris, accused the Mongols of eating human flesh (see Plate 1).[49] On this topic the Rus' cleric Peter and Carpini were alike cautious: the Mongols ate human beings only in emergencies, when other rations were exhausted (and, Peter assured the Council of Lyons, they invariably cooked it first).[50] Rubruck had nothing to say on the matter. But Simon of Saint-Quentin gave himself a freer rein. The Mongols engaged in cannibalism for any of three reasons: out of necessity, for sheer pleasure, and as a stratagem to instil terror into their enemies. Thus, he says, they sometimes eat captured rebels by way of punishment. Elsewhere in his report, we read of a variant form of cannibalism, since some Mongols quietly kill their elderly and infirm fathers, burn the bodies, and sprinkle the ashes over their food.[51]

Plate 1 Mongol cannibalism: Matthew Paris, *Chronica Majora*, The Parker Library, Corpus Christi College, Cambridge, ms. 16, fo. 167r (reproduced with the kind permission of the Master and Fellows).

From uncleanness it was but a short step to godlessness. The Mongols' religion, thought one annalist, was to deny Almighty God and to kill men.[52] They were 'without religion [*exlex*]', 'without faith [*perfidi*]'.[53] Carpini saw no reason to dissent. The Mongols had no religion. Although they acknowledged one God, creator of all things visible and invisible, they did not worship him with prayers or any kind of ceremony.[54] They knew nothing of everlasting life or eternal damnation.[55] The sins they recognized were 'things invented by them or by their forebears'.[56] Simon of Saint-Quentin remarked on their failure to observe abstinence on any day or at any season of the year. For him, Mongol ultimatums blasphemed by calling the qaghan 'son of God' and venerating him in God's place,[57] a charge found earlier, in Ivo of Narbonne's letter, and subsequently echoed in the Latin East during the Mongol invasion of 1260.[58] Both Carpini and Rubruck believed, erroneously, that the effigies (*ongghod*) in the Mongol encampments were idols which they worshipped, and failed to realize that these represented their ancestors, whose spirits were conjured up by the shamans.[59] The Mongols set great store by divinations, soothsaying, auguries and incantations – practices to which, says Rubruck, everyone in those parts was given.[60] In Carpini's view, they perpetrated abominations and the worship of God was brought to nothing.[61]

Shadows of the Apocalypse

The advent of a pagan nation from the east which was much more powerful and destructive than earlier steppe invaders touched the apocalyptic sensitivities of medieval Christians.[62] In their endeavours to understand the cataclysm that had befallen Eastern Europe, they naturally had recourse to the historical and geographical material, culled from Scripture and from pagan Antiquity, which was mentioned above (pp. 18–22). Some commentators adopted what might be called a broadly eschatological tone. For Roger of Várad, the Mongol onslaught was a clear sign that the world was hastening towards its end.[63] Others saw the invasion as God's chastisement for human sin (a role, it is interesting to note, that looms large in apocryphal letters generated in Western Europe even as late as the invasion of Hungary in 1285), and His chosen instrument as a people from Hell.[64] But the Mongols were seen as having a particular animus against Christianity. Their express purpose – thought many, including Pope Gregory IX and the Emperor Frederick – was to destroy the Christian Church and to annihilate Christians.[65] They showed no respect for any religious Order;[66] they slaughtered Christians without mercy and with no regard for rank, age or sex (a detail which echoes more official pronouncements, like papal encyclicals and the decree of the Lyons Council).[67] They are commonly described as satellites of Antichrist, and two of the letters incorporated in the *Chronica majora* have Chinggis Khan branding captured children on the forehead with his mark, a clear echo of the action of Antichrist (Revelation, xiii, 16).[68] The Mongols are said to be accompanied sometimes by Amazons or cannibals;[69] at other times, by heretics and by bogus or renegade Christians, who (naturally) egg them on to commit atrocities against churches and ecclesiastical personnel.[70] As the middle of the thirteenth century drew near, these ideas may have taken on a new urgency, given the tendency of disciples and admirers of Joachim of Fiore to associate the year 1260 with the advent of Antichrist.[71] It has been proposed that the Flagellant outbreak of that very year was in part a response to the Mongols' recent devastation of Poland and their invasion of Syria.[72]

The sense of foreboding is also manifest in the readiness of contemporary authors to juxtapose this grim new enemy with more familiar antagonists and 'outgroups' nearer home. The nightmare possibility of an alliance between the Muslims and Patarene heretics (Cathars) within Western Europe had been contemplated as far back as the 1190s;[73] and the advent of the Mongols induced a similar paranoia. In 1223 Caesarius of Haisterbach had listed the Mongol attack on the Rus' among a series of tribulations that had befallen Christendom, including Saladin's victories and the rise of the Cathar heresy.[74] The Emperor Frederick himself, in a letter of 1246, juxtaposed the Mongols with the Patarenes (a term which he applied to his enemies in the cities of Lombardy), doubtless as a means of enhancing his credentials as the champion of Christendom.[75] It was especially tempting to link the Mongols with heterodoxy, in view of their known practice of recruiting members of every religious sect.[76] From the 1250s onwards a few authors connected them, explicitly or otherwise, with the recent phenomenon of the Pastoureaux, a movement among the rural poor of the French-Imperial borderlands in 1251 led by a mysterious figure called the 'Master of Hungary'. The original aim was to cross the sea to bring much-needed succour to Louis IX of France, but the movement rapidly degenerated, as the undisciplined crowds, seeking scapegoats for the king's failure, turned on clergy, friars and Jews and had to be suppressed by force.[77] Two writers, in fact, suggestively move on to the Pastoureaux directly after their account of the Mongol invasion.[78] In c.1267 we find a more adventurous spirit, Roger Bacon, speculating whether the 'Master' was an agent in the service of either the Muslims or the Mongols.[79]

A more pernicious rationale would associate the Mongols with the Jews, a minority group which had come to be seen increasingly as posing an internal threat to Christians and Christendom in the course of the twelfth century.[80] The linkage was the identification of the invaders with the Ten Lost Tribes of Israel. Matthew Paris was ready to discount the inconvenient fact that the Mongols did not speak Hebrew and knew nothing of the Mosaic law (or, in his view, any other).[81] But elsewhere doubt was expressed about the equation,[82] and Thomas of Spalato for one knew that the Mongols did not practise Judaism, Islam or Christianity.[83] Unfortunately, elements in Germany were less sceptical and engaged in pogroms against the Jews in 1241, on the grounds that they were preparing to welcome the Mongols as deliverers and were attempting to ship arms to these their coreligionists in order to exact revenge for Christian persecution; the Jewish community in Frankfurt-am-Main appears to have suffered particularly vehement attacks. Despite contemporary claims,[84] it is highly unlikely that the Jews saw the Mongols in this light. What had impinged upon Christian consciousness was the widespread excitement among the Jews as the approach of the year 5000 of their era (1240) fuelled messianic expectations.[85] The fact that King David's father had been named in the *Relatio de Davide rege* of 1221 as 'King Israel' (the Latin could equally be rendered as 'King *of*

Israel')[86] may have given a further boost to such hopes among Jewish communities over the past twenty years. They are perhaps mirrored in a Latin prophecy that circulated widely in 1241, foretelling *inter alia* the Jews' deliverance from captivity.[87] At least some Latin writers, of course, were well aware that the Mongols themselves did not distinguish Jews from other religious groups; and Jews in the Near East, moreover, had felt at risk from Mongol attacks in the late 1230s along with everyone else, and would evacuate Jerusalem on the eve of the Mongol occupation in 1260.[88]

For many Western observers, the Mongols were self-evidently one of the peoples whose appearance had been prophesied by Pseudo-Methodius, just as the pagan Hungarians had been identified with Gog and Magog in the 890s.[89] According to Thomas of Spalato, many scholars began, at the time of the invasion, to examine the *Sermo* and proposed that the Mongols were the forerunners of Antichrist.[90] One was Albert Behaim, the archdeacon of Passau, who is known to have copied a text of Pseudo-Methodius's work into his book of *memorabilia*.[91] Matthew Paris was another. We have seen that he first resorted to Aethicus Ister to explain the name Tartar, but by 1245 he was certainly mindful also of Pseudo-Methodius's prophecy concerning the sons of Ishmael.[92] The list of those who were apparently convinced that the Mongols were indeed the Ishmaelites includes Henry Raspe, landgrave of Thuringia, and a Hungarian Benedictine abbot, in letters reproduced in the *Chronica majora*;[93] various annalists;[94] and the author of a prophecy in the form of a dialogue between Alexander and Aristotle which, together with Julian's report and a number of letters concerning the Mongol menace, was copied into a manuscript at Ottobeuren in 1241.[95] One circumstance favouring the equation was the destruction of the 'kingdom of Persia' (i.e. the Khwarazmian empire), which had been announced in the *Relatio de Davide rege* and in papal letters in 1221 and which, according to Pseudo-Methodius, would precede or coincide with the advent of the Ishmaelites.[96]

Since Pseudo-Methodius had foretold of the Mongols, it was natural to endow them with traits that he had applied to the Ishmaelites or the Inclosed Nations. According to the *Sermo*, for instance, the Ishmaelite persecution would last for forty-nine years, and consequently we find the Rus' cleric Peter giving this as the period of the Mongol dominion.[97] The Ishmaelites would ravage a vast territory as far as the vicinity of Rome before suffering an overwhelming defeat at the hands of the king of the Greeks or Romans, and so Rome was believed to be the Mongols' goal.[98] Peter claimed that the Mongols themselves anticipated a bitter struggle with the Romans, and Ivo of Narbonne says that one motive for their advance was to chastise the greed and arrogance of the Romans, who had at one time oppressed them.[99] Even the Emperor Frederick apparently thought that they were making for Rome.[100]

Several notices of the Mongol invasion contain formulaic descriptions of the profanation of churches – killing priests at the altars, having sexual intercourse with their womenfolk in consecrated places, dressing their women in holy garments, stabling their horses among the graves of saints – which reproduce practically *verbatim* the conduct ascribed in the *Sermo* to the Ishmaelites.[101] At times the invaders are also said to have come forth from islands; at others, to have broken out of a mountain range (sometimes called the Caspian mountains). In the former case, the islands could conceivably be 'Tarse'; but more probably the allusion in both cases is to the Inclosed Nations, as portrayed respectively by Aethicus Ister or by Pseudo-Methodius.[102] The Inclosed Nations followed a remarkably undiscriminating diet, including the flesh of dogs, mice, mares, snakes, scorpions, carrion, aborted foetuses, every kind of clean and unclean beasts, and human beings;[103] and, as we saw above, such details were readily inserted into accounts of the Mongols. The author of the 'Tartar Relation', which is closely related to the *Ystoria Mongalorum*, substituted for Carpini's phrase 'afterbirth of mares' simply the word 'afterbirth',[104] which was more evocative of the *Sermo*. Our difficulty here, of course, lies in distinguishing between those writers who imputed certain characteristics to the Mongols specifically because they saw them as the apocalyptic peoples mentioned by Pseudo-Methodius, and those who ascribed these same features to them but without any such conscious association.

The most striking evidence for Thomas of Spalato's claim that Pseudo-Methodius was recruited to make sense of the Mongol invasion is to be found in a remarkable letter dating from *c*.1239–40, even before the attack on Latin territory. Here an anonymous Hungarian bishop recounts his interrogation of two Mongol captives. The two surviving versions of the letter differ slightly, and the bishop clearly had access to information from sources other than his prisoners; a good deal of the information that emerges can be related without any difficulty to known characteristics of the Mongol war-machine.[105] Yet we are left with the overwhelming impression that Pseudo-Methodius dictated the agenda for this interview and, indeed, its outcome. In reply to a question about their origins, the prisoners said that they lived beyond some mountains and close to a river named Egog (unidentified); hence, the bishop concluded, they belonged to Gog and Magog. Asked how they had broken out of the mountains, they answered that it had taken their forebears three hundred years to remove all the trees and rocks that barred their way. The bishop enquired about their religion. They believed in nothing, they replied, and it was their intention to conquer the entire world. The bishop ascertained that the Mongol alphabet, which the prisoners alleged they had learned after emerging from the mountain barrier, was Hebrew. Those who had taught them this alphabet (in reality Uighur Buddhists) were pale men who fasted and wore long robes: the bishop inferred that these were Pharisees and Sadducees (and hence, although he does not say so explicitly, he was dealing with the Ten Lost Tribes). Were the Mongols discriminating in their diet? No: they ate frogs, dogs, snakes, and all things without distinction.

Clearly the quantity of information about the invaders that pointed towards venerable and trusted prophecy was embarrassing; the problem lay in deciding with which people to identify the Tartars. The author of the apocryphal *Epistola prudenti viro*, which was in circulation by 1246, linked them both with the Ishmaelites and with Gog and Magog.[106] One annalist, who seems already to have accepted the identification with the Ten Lost Tribes, proceeded for good measure to add the duration of the Ishmaelite domination (forty-nine years) and that specified for Gog and Magog (seven), and forecast that the Mongols' empire would last for fifty-six years.[107]

Although the Ishmaelites (where the term does not simply denote Muslims) and Gog and Magog were certainly peoples believed to exist in some distant region, their significance *at this point* could not be purely geographical. Their association, by contemporary or near-contemporary observers, with far-flung conquest and the devastation of 1241–2 carries overtones that are undeniably apocalyptic.[108] On the other hand, we should avoid overstating the dimensions of this reaction. It goes without saying that terseness, and the absence of speculation about the Mongols' origins and significance, are not necessarily an index of sophistication;[109] such accounts may simply be the work of authors less given to profound reflection. But neither the letters of Popes Gregory IX and Innocent IV nor those of the Emperor Frederick refer to the apocalyptic races; nor is any direct evidence to be gleaned from the circumstantial account of Thomas of Spalato that he saw the Mongols in this light. Even some of the more detailed annalistic notices of the invasion are devoid of apocalyptic speculation. The chronicler of St Pantaleon at Cologne tells us that he has heard much that is incredible or utterly inhuman about the origins, religion and diet of this barbarian race, but that since it is not yet confirmed he will refrain from inserting it at this juncture. He may, of course, have been deterred by the fact that Carpini's party halted in Cologne during their return journey in 1247, when Benedict dictated his relatively sober account to an anonymous cleric of the city.[110] The friars are especially conspicuous in this regard. Albert, the author of the Stade annals and a convert from the Benedictines to the Franciscan Order, had inserted a reference to Pseudo-Methodius in the early part of his survey of world history; but he makes no link whatsoever between that author and the Mongols, being content with a vague allusion to a prophecy by Hildegard of Bingen.[111] None of the friars, in fact, who wrote letters about the invaders in 1241–2 refers to apocalyptic peoples, with the single exception of the Franciscan vice-minister in Bohemia, who speaks in passing of the Mongols' ferocity as having been foretold in Scripture.[112]

Corroboration from outside the Latin world?

Generally speaking, then, many – but by no means all – Western observers saw in the Mongols what they expected to find, namely forerunners of the Last Things as prophesied in Scripture and in the *Sermo* of Pseudo-Methodius. The attraction of the appeal to eschatological literature, of course, was that it provided solace: the barbarous nations would in time be overcome, and following the destruction of the Ishmaelites, at least, there would be peace. But this does not exclude the possibility that Catholic writers found their ideas corroborated by non-Latin or non-Christian sources, or had even acquired them from that quarter. One external influence upon Latin Christians at this juncture was almost certainly the Orthodox Rus'. The Rus' equated the Mongols with the Ishmaelites just as they had earlier occupants of the steppe; and the Russian chronicle tradition begins to invoke Pseudo-Methodius from the time of the very first Mongol attack in 1223.[113] The Hungarian Friar Julian evidently owed a good deal to Rus' informants: in a clear allusion to the *Sermo*, a Rus' cleric had told him that the Mongols' ancestors were the Midianites of the Old Testament (Judges, vi–viii), who for Pseudo-Methodius had formed part of the Ishmaelite race. The exiled Rus' churchman Peter voiced this same opinion at the Council of Lyons in 1245, even naming the wilderness from which the Mongols had emerged as 'Etrev' (i.e. Pseudo-Methodius's 'Ethrib'; see above, p. 21).[114]

Recent scholarship on the Mongols' image in Europe, particularly the work of Axel Klopprogge, has done much to highlight the use that the Latin West, confronting an unknown and alien power in 1241, made of the *Sermo*, both directly and through Rus' informants. This work tends, however, to neglect other avenues by which ideas may have reached Europe and served to lend conviction to Pseudo-Methodian prophecy. What little we know of Byzantine ideas about the Mongols does not suggest that the court of Nicaea served as a conduit to Latin Christendom in this respect.[115] Among the Armenians there was apparently a perception that they were living in the last days before the advent of Antichrist, and Pseudo-Methodius enjoyed a place in their prophetic tradition; but greater weight seems to have been given to a fourth-century prophecy of St Nerses, which would attract Rubruck's notice when he passed through Greater Armenia in 1254.[116] There are, however, more promising avenues of enquiry. Modern scholars sometimes treat the West as if it were hermetically sealed from the non-Christian world; and two possible channels of information that have been ignored, I suggest, are reports current within the Islamic Near East and the Mongols' own notions about their origins.

Pseudo-Methodian and related ideas are known to have been current among the Christian community in thirteenth-century Egypt, where even Muslims were affected by them.[117] Islam's own apocalyptic literature includes a tradition (*ḥadīth*) ascribed to the Prophet, to the effect that the first sign of the Last Things would be the irruption of the 'Turks' (denoting, in this context, the steppe peoples in general): it is quoted, for example, by the chronicler Jūzjānī, who had fled before the Mongols in 1221 and who wrote in Delhi *c*.1260.[118] In Islamic cosmography, too, Gog and Magog had been enclosed by Alexander (known to Muslims as 'Dhu l-Qarnayn') behind barriers through which they would burst at the end of time (Qur'ān, xviii, 82–98).[119] Now admittedly certain Muslim authors contemporary with the first Mongol assault on the Islamic world make only oblique references to Gog and Magog in connection with the invaders. For Ibn al-Athīr (d. 1233), the Mongols were the greatest disaster to afflict civilization *other than* Gog and Magog, while 'Awfī (writing in 1232–3) saw them as the harbingers of those nations.[120]

More relevant to our discussion here, however, are ideas that were current regarding the role of the Qara-Khitan empire as a barrier obstructing the expansion of the uncivilized steppe peoples who lived further east, and consequently of the Khwārazmshāh Muḥammad in undermining the Gür-khan's power. Both Ibn al-Athīr and Juwaynī allude to the way in which the Khwārazmshāh facilitated the Mongol irruption by removing the rulers of territories in their path.[121] Other references are more specific. On his deathbed in 1200 Muḥammad's father Tekish had allegedly warned his sons never to quarrel with the Qara-Khitan. Juwaynī's version of this tale makes Tekish speak of the Qara-Khitan as a 'wall behind which were terrible foes'.[122] Juwaynī also tells us that his cousin, prior to the Mongol attack on the Khwarazmian empire, heard the Qara-Khitan likened to the 'wall of Dhu l-Qarnayn'.[123] This material is of course transmitted to us in a source that dates from as late as 1260; but the theme clearly has a longer pedigree, since it first appears in the memoirs of 'Abd al-Laṭīf al-Baghdādī, known as Ibn al-Labbād (d. 1231–2), which were preserved in the chronicle of al-Dhahabī (d. 1348). Ibn al-Labbād, who travelled in northern Syria and Anatolia in 1221–2, already speaks of the Qara-Khitan as a barrier (*sadd*) opened by the Khwārazmshāh,[124] and the image was to be employed by other writers.[125] Subsequently – by the 1250s, at least, but possibly as early as his death in 1231 – the Khwārazmshāh's son Jalāl al-Dīn came to be seen in Syria as a barrier through which the Mongols had broken.[126]

It is conceivable that these highly figurative phrases entered the Latin world from the camp of its Muslim neighbours and enemies, and that in the process the images they conveyed were transmuted back into a physical barrier, helping to focus attention on prophetic material already to hand in the West. Similarly, tales about the Mongols' cannibalism had long been current in northern Syria, for a woman allegedly told Ibn al-Labbād in Aleppo in 1222 how they had killed her two sons and drunk their blood.[127] Rumours that the Mongols were cannibals had certainly reached Baghdad by the late 1240s.[128] Muslim authors also drew attention, as their Latin contemporaries would, to the fact that the Mongols ate carrion and dogs.[129] Merchants from cities such as Mosul who were active in the commerce with the Mediterranean coast could have introduced such perceptions to Frankish Syria, in much the same way that traders had brought to Antioch the heartening rumours of King David's advance in 1221.[130]

In deciding to what extent ideas transmitted from Rus' were reinforced by stories circulating within the Islamic world, we admittedly find ourselves moving in the realm of conjecture. That the Mongols' own beliefs about their origins came to the notice of Western Christians, however, is more certain. One tradition among them was that for many generations they had inhabited a valley called Ergene Qun, confined by impenetrable mountains and forests, but had eventually broken out by melting an iron mine with bellows. This tale bears a striking similarity to the origin-myths of the early Turks in the sixth–eighth centuries. It does not figure in our earliest Mongolian source, the 'Secret History', where the account of the origins of Chinggis Khan's clan itself represents an amalgam of elements from the legendary history of the Turks and the Khitan.[131] But the story surfaces often in Rashīd al-Dīn's *Jāmiʿ al-tawārīkh* (1303–4) and fleetingly in the *Flor des estoires* of Hayton of Gorigos (1307).[132] A brief and somewhat garbled version had already reached Jūzjānī by 1260 at the very latest.[133] We cannot be sure whether Mongol elements had been present in the early Turkish legends or whether

Turkish motifs were appropriated and carried over into the later Mongol tradition.[134] These origin-myths were conceivably influenced by the Syriac version of the Alexander Romance, which was introduced to Central Asia by Nestorian Christians in, or soon after, the seventh century; and hence they sprang ultimately from the same soil as did Pseudo-Methodius.[135] What had now transpired, however, was that with the appearance of the Mongols in Eastern Europe the movement of ideas was reversed, as details of their legendary origins found their way westwards. In one case, certainly, transmission to the Latin world was direct. The Hungarian bishop interviewing Mongol prisoners got the answer he did, about breaking through a mountain barrier (p. 145 above), not merely because of the way he framed his question, but because the response he expected coincided with the Mongols' own notions about their remote past.

The contribution of the friars, 1245–55

We have seen how the friars' reports often confirmed and amplified what had been known for some years about the Mongols' diet and customs. It is time to ask whether their information and perspective differed qualitatively from those of the annalists. Klopprogge identifies a pronounced gulf between them. Whereas chroniclers describing the events of 1241–2 accounted for the Mongol attacks by reference to divine judgement or to apocalyptic prophecy, he suggests that the friars, drawing upon the methods of the school of Chartres, sought causes, rather, in human action and historical events (though not, in every case, events that a modern scholar would recognize as such), producing more down-to-earth, this-worldly explanations. The significance of an event in terms of sacred history might still be discernible; but it was no longer assigned any causative function.[136]

Now it is true that the friars' reports attempt to find rational explanations for phenomena hitherto associated with the terrifying and the monstrous. Thus Carpini, for instance, accounts for the Mongols' undiscriminating diet on the grounds of an earlier crisis in which they had been faced with a severe dearth of victuals.[137] Moreover, he may demonstrate a more accurate understanding of what Simon of Saint-Quentin portrayed as the Mongols' consumption of the cremated remains of their dead (p. 140 above), for he relates how at a burial they sacrifice and eat a horse and then burn its bones in honour of the deceased.[138] Rubruck almost unconsciously furnishes an explanation for the consumption of raw meat when he describes how the lack of suitable fuel often obliged his party to eat meat that was only semi-cooked.[139]

Yet Klopprogge's brilliant theory about the influence of Chartres grows less convincing on closer scrutiny. Even if we disregard the grave doubts that have been expressed regarding the role and significance of the School,[140] it is unlikely to have influenced the early Franciscans. In harmony with their founder's views (and in sharp contrast with the Dominicans), they avoided academic pursuits. Rubruck had probably studied in Paris (a more important intellectual centre than Chartres). But Carpini – older by a generation, and a busy administrator who had exercised responsibility in the Order almost since St Francis's own day – can hardly have spent time in a school or university,[141] although it is true that Salimbene writes of him expounding to the monks at Sens whatever in his report seemed problematic or obscure; and says not only that everyone regarded him as a man 'of a most holy life [*sanctissime vite*]' but also that he was 'well read [*litteratus*]'.[142]

The friars in general were admittedly less given to apocalyptic speculation, perhaps, than were their contemporaries. The Franciscan Adam Marsh was clearly impressed by the insights of Joachim of Fiore, and already in the 1250s Matthew Paris was accusing the Mendicants of peddling Joachite ideas.[143] Yet, as we saw, only one of the letters written by friars from Eastern Europe in 1241–2 makes any reference to the Mongols as a subject of Scriptural prophecy. Nor did the Franciscan Alexander of Bremen, in his exegetical work on the Apocalypse (completed *c*.1249), credit them with any such role: although the sole reference to them occurs in the original draft of the work, dating from 1235 (when little was known of the Tartars), it was significantly not updated in the later version.[144] The anonymous of Passau, who may have been a Dominican, says nothing of the Tartars when briefly mentioning Gog and Magog in his treatise on Antichrist, written in the 1260s.[145] And there is no denying that the friars who travelled in Mongol Asia in the period 1245–55 make little or no explicit reference to the apocalyptic peoples. In his opening paragraph, the author of the 'Tartar Relation' makes clear his belief that he was living in the final stage of history,[146] though he says no more on the subject; and this assumption, of course, did not necessarily imply a view of the Mongols as heralds of the Apocalypse. Rubruck enquired in the Caucasus region about the Jews inclosed by Alexander the Great, as Simon of Saint-Quentin and his Dominican colleagues had done seven years earlier.[147] Simon himself contrived an improbable link between Gog and the name of the qaghan Güyüg (for whom he invents an otherwise unknown brother called Magog), though it should be noted that he appeals not to Pseudo-Methodius but to Ezekiel.[148]

Such preoccupations, of course, may have been geographical rather than prophetic in character. Yet certain matters touched on in the friars' reports are simply too evocative not to have borne at least some apocalyptic content. When Simon devotes a few sentences to Mongol cannibalism, or when Carpini remarks that the Mongols eat the after-birth of mares, we can be fairly sure that they have one eye cocked on Pseudo-Methodius, since these are among the hallmarks of his unclean nations. The addiction to magic and necromancy was also reminiscent of the black arts practised by the Inclosed Peoples. It is difficult, moreover, to account for Carpini's interest in the precise number of years (forty-two, he alleges) that had elapsed since the Mongols first emerged from their homeland[149] without falling back on the Pseudo-Methodian frame of reference adopted by the Rus' cleric Peter. Rubruck, in turn, more than once draws an analogy between the Mongols and the Children of Israel.[150] Roger Bacon, having read Rubruck's report and discussed it with him, was certainly not deflected by either experience from musing about the possible identity of the Mongols with the apocalyptic Gog and Magog, though he reached no firm conclusion.[151] The Dominican author of the *De ortu Tartarorum* (1255) almost certainly viewed the Mongols through an apocalyptic lens.[152]

It is important to set the friars' reports in context. They undeniably reflect a greater degree of insight and sophistication than are to be detected in the observations of Matthew Paris and other chroniclers back in Western Europe. They asked questions, and sometimes betray dissatisfaction with the answers they received. As they passed through Mongol Asia, they picked up many a story that belonged to the 'outer world' of the societies among whom they were moving. Carpini borrowed various tales from Rus' clerics;[153] and he recounts others that are transmitted by travellers within Asia as early as the eighth century: tales of a race with ox's feet; of a people whose females were human while the males had dog's heads; of cannibalism.[154] We know that such fables enjoyed a wide circulation. Only a few years earlier a Muslim envoy from the Mongols had told the Ayyubid prince of Mayyāfāriqīn about a headless people in the Far East, close to the land of Gog and Magog, whose eyes were in their shoulders, and who lived off fish; and of another race, whose flocks were generated from seed sown in the ground.[155] Rubruck was more sceptical, perhaps. He expressed doubt about the existence of the monsters described by Isidore and Solinus,[156] and he makes no link between the Mongols and cannibalism. When, however, he heard that the Tibetans, who lay at some distance from his route, ate their dead kinsfolk as a mark of respect, he found no reason to reject something of which Solinus had written.[157] The friars were creatures of their time; and if they found no evidence for a phe-nomenon that was part of the common stock of Western folklore, their reaction was often simply to relegate it beyond their now dramatically extended geographical horizons.

Notes

1. An earlier version of the bulk of this chapter appeared as 'Medieval Christendom's encounter with the alien', *Historical Research* 74 (2001), pp. 347–69. I am grateful to the Editor for permission to reuse much of the material here.
2. TR, §2, p. 4.
3. The idea surfaces also in a variant text of Peter's report: OOLB ms. 446, fo. 267vb: *intellexerunt etiam papam maiorem esse de mundo.* On this, see Ruotsala, *Europeans and Mongols*, p. 155, n.15.
4. Meyvaert, p. 258.
5. WR, xiii, 2, p. 195 (tr. Jackson and Morgan, p. 107).
6. Emil Bretschneider, *Mediaeval Researches from Eastern Asiatic Sources*, 2 vols (London, 1910), I, p. 142. Cf. Jean Richard, 'An account of the battle of Hattin referring to the Frankish mercenaries in Oriental Moslem states', *Speculum* 27 (1952), pp. 168–77 (here pp. 173–4) repr. in his *Orient et Occident*; also his 'Mongols and the Franks', p. 50. See also below, p. 181.
7. al-Qazwīnī, *Āthār al-bilād*, p. 334; cf. also ibid., p. 388. Jackson, 'Crisis', p. 496.
8. PC, iv, 4, p. 246 (tr. Dawson, p. 15). TR, §53, pp. 32–3. WR, xxviii, 3, p. 244 (tr. Jackson and Morgan, p. 173). Cf. Ruotsala, *Europeans and Mongols*, pp. 90–1.
9. SSQ, pp. 100–1 (= VB, xxxii, 43).
10. WR, xxii, 2, p. 221 (tr. Jackson and Morgan, p. 141).
11. Ibid., xix, 5, and xxviii, 4, pp. 213, 245 (tr. Jackson and Morgan, pp. 132, 173).
12. For a promising start, see Jussi Hanska and Antti Ruotsala, 'Berthold von Regensburg, OFM, and the Mongols – medieval sermon as a historical source', *AFH* 89 (1996), pp. 425–45; Ruotsala, *Europeans and Mongols*, pp. 60–7. In appendix 2 ibid., Ruotsala prints Eudes de Châteauroux, 'Sermo in concilio pro negotio Tartarorum', which he dates (pp. 60–1 and n.2) to 1241/3 on the grounds that the pope has recently died after summoning a council and that the Mongols are depicted as an immediate threat. My own view, however, is that the sermon belongs to 1261, following the death of Alexander IV, and would have been delivered at a provincial synod in France (see p. 119 above): the reference to appeals from 'the Holy Land, Tripoli and Antioch' as well as from 'Prussia and Livonia' (see p. 123) would support this dating rather more than 1241/3.
13. Richard of San Germano, 'Chronica', p. 210.
14. *CM*, IV, pp. 119–20.
15. Klopprogge, *Ursprung*, pp. 188–93.
16. Cf. the details in Dörrie, pp. 158–9, 166, 172, 179, with *CM*, III, p. 488. For the dates of the two reports and the journeys they describe, see Dörrie, pp. 137–9, and *Mongolensturm*, pp. 71, 96.
17. Salimbene, *Cronica*, I, p. 321.

18. 'Ex cronicis Iohannis de Wallingford', *MGHS*, XXVIII, pp. 510–11; hence *Chronica Johannis de Oxenedes*, ed. H. Ellis, RS (London, 1859), p. 217 (*ad annum* 1258). Their claim that the book could be found in the *Liber additamentorum* at St Albans is surely based on a confusion with the documents gathered by Matthew Paris, though Bigalli, *I Tartari e l'Apocalisse*, p. 25, assumes that it refers to the same collection.

19. *OM*, I, p. 305; see Jarl Charpentier, 'William of Rubruck and Roger Bacon', in *Hyllningsskrift tillägnad Sven Hedin på hans 70-årsdag den 19. Febr. 1935* (Stockholm, 1935), pp. 255–67 (here p. 256). Pelliot, *Recherches*, p. 233, thought that the meeting with Bacon might have fallen 10 years after Rubruck's return from the Mongols.

20. Text in Marvin L. Colker, 'America rediscovered in the thirteenth century?', *Speculum* 54 (1979), pp. 712–26 (here pp. 720–6). See now Gunar Freibergs, 'The *Descripciones Terrarum*: its date, sources, author and purpose', in Jerzy Kłoczowski, ed., *Christianity in East Central Europe: Late Middle Ages*, Proceedings of the Commission Internationale d'Histoire Ecclésiastique Comparée, Lublin 1996, part 2 (Lublin, 1999), pp. 180–201.

21. *CM*, IV, p. 109, n.2. Ivo of Narbonne, ibid., IV, p. 276. John of Garlande, *De triumphis*, p. 108. 'Richeri Gesta', p. 310 (confusing *Tarse* with Tarsus in Cilicia). 'Gestorum Treverorum continuatio quarta', p. 403. 'Rocznik kapituły gnieźnieńskiej' (down to 1247), *MPH²*, VI, p. 5 = 'Annales capituli Posnaniensis', p. 440. 'De invasione Tartarorum fragmentum', p. 599. 'Annales Marbacenses', *MGHS*, XVII, p. 175, a passage relating to 1222, but believed to have been written after 1238: see Anna-Dorothee von den Brincken, 'Die Mongolen im Weltbild der Lateiner um die Mitte des 13. Jahrhunderts unter besonderer Berücksichtigung des „Speculum Historiale" des Vincenz von Beauvais OP', *AK* 57 (1975), pp. 117–40 (here pp. 121–2). For 'Tarse', see Sinor, 'Le Mongol vu par l'Occident', pp. 58–9; Bezzola, pp. 34–5.

22. Salimbene, *Cronica*, II, pp. 871–2, reproducing the letter; for another copy, cf. Redlich, *Eine Wiener Briefsammlung*, p. 242 (no. 245); and see also 'Annales Mantuani', *MGHS*, XIX, p. 29; Ottokar of Styria, *Reimchronik* (to 1309), vv. 23692–23700, ed. Joseph Seemüller, *Ottokars Österreichische Reimchronik*, MGH Deutsche Chroniken 5 (Hannover, 1890–3), I, pp. 312–13; John of Viktring (d. 1345/7), *Liber certarum historiarum*, ed. Fedor Schneider, SRG, 2 vols (Hannover and Leipzig, 1909–10), I, pp. 257 (recension A), 297 (recensions B, D and A2) (*ad annum* 1288).

23. 'Annales Scheftlarienses maiores', p. 341: *quedam incognita gens barbarica*. 'Annales Admuntenses. Continuatio Garstensis', p. 597: *ignota gens Tartarorum*. Otto, duke of Bavaria, to Siboto, bishop of Augsburg, in IUB ms. 187, fo. 7v: *gens barbara Tartarorum . . . de longinquis et ignotis partibus*. 'Carmina de regno Ungariae destructo', p. 604.

24. *CM*, IV, p. 120; cf. also ibid., p. 77.

25. 'Annales S. Pantaleonis', p. 535.

26. 'Annales Scheftlarienses minores', *MGHS*, XVII, p. 344: *Sarraceni dicti Tartari*. 'Balduini Ninovensis chronicon', p. 543: *quidam Sarraceni qui Tartari vulgariter appellantur*. This was presumably why Ponce of Albon thought that they avoided pork: 'Ex Historiae regum Franciae continuatione Parisiensi', p. 605.

27. 'Annales Scheftlarienses maiores', p. 342.
28. Tarachonta: *CM*, IV, p. 109, n.2 (citing the papal legate Otto), and VI, p. 497, n.1 (marginal note from BL, Cotton ms., Nero D I, fo. 85); at IV, p. 387, the link with Tarachonta in the report of the Rus' cleric Peter is an interpolation by Matthew, and does not appear in the Burton annals version (Dörrie, p. 189) or in the variant text found in OOLB ms. 446 (below, n.97). Cf. Otto Prinz, ed., *Die Kosmographie des Aethicus*, MGHQu. 14 (Munich, 1993), pp. 120–1. For the derivation from a river 'Tartar', see TS, p. 169 (tr. in *Mongolensturm*, p. 251); *CM*, III, p. 488 ('Tar'), and IV, p. 78; PC, v, 2, p. 252 (tr. Dawson, p. 19); TR, §3, p. 4.
29. WR, i, 14, and ix, 1, pp. 171, 187 (tr. Jackson and Morgan, pp. 71, 97).
30. *CM*, IV, p. 109. Emperor Frederick II to Henry III, ibid., IV, p. 112 (= *HDFS*, V, p. 1149). Jordan, Franciscan vice-minister in Bohemia, in *CM*, VI, pp. 79, 83. Dominican Bartholomew to Bishop E[gino] of Brixen, in *HDFS*, V, p. 1148. Béla IV to Conrad IV, in Böhmer, 'Briefe', p. 113. 'Annales Stadenses', p. 367. 'Annales S. Pantaleonis', p. 535. 'Gestorum Treverorum continuatio quarta', p. 404. 'Chronica minor auctore Minorita Erphordiensi', p. 199. Continuation of Gervase of Canterbury, *Gesta regum*, in William Stubbs, ed., *The Historical Works of Gervase of Canterbury*, RS, 2 vols (London, 1879–80), II, p. 179. And see n.23 above.
31. PC, ix, 5, p. 305 (tr. Dawson, p. 52). WR, as n.29 above.
32. SSQ, p. 105 (= VB, xxxii, 46).
33. Claverie, 'L'apparition', p. 612 (but read *de pellibus ovium* for *de pellibus obvium*). Emperor Frederick II to Henry III, in *CM*, IV, p. 115 = *HDFS*, V, p. 1151.
34. PC, i, 4, p. 230 (tr. Dawson, p. 5). SSQ, p. 32 (= VB, xxx, 71).
35. WR, ix, 4, xxiii, 6, and xxxvii, 1, pp. 189, 226, 312 (tr. Jackson and Morgan, pp. 99, 147, 254).
36. Ibid., ii, 1, p. 172 (tr. Jackson and Morgan, p. 72).
37. Anthony Pagden, *The Fall of Natural Man: The American Indian and the Origins of Comparative Ethnology* (Cambridge, 1982), p. 71.
38. Henry of Livonia, *Chronicon*, xxvi, 1, p. 186 (tr. Brundage, p. 205). See also *CM*, III, p. 488; 'Chronicon S. Medardi', p. 492; 'Carmina de regno Ungariae destructo', p. 601 (probably based on Carpini's report); John of Garlande, *De triumphis*, p. 109.
39. TS, p. 170 (tr. in *Mongolensturm*, p. 252).
40. PC, iv, 8, p. 248 (tr. Dawson, p. 16). SSQ, p. 32 (= VB, xxx, 71), on bread alone.
41. WR, xiii, 10, p. 197 (tr. Jackson and Morgan, p. 109).
42. Ibid., ii, 9, p. 175 (tr. Jackson and Morgan, p. 76). Cf. PC, iv, 8, p. 248 (tr. Dawson, p. 17).
43. TS, p. 170 (tr. in *Mongolensturm*, p. 252). Peter, in Dörrie, p. 191 (mares, dogs, and any other animals whatever). Ponce of Albon, in 'Ex Historiae regum Franciae continuatione Parisiensi', p. 605. 'Chronicon S. Medardi', p. 492. *CM*, IV, p. 76 (dogs). Henry Raspe, ibid., VI, p. 77 (frogs and snakes).
44. WR, iii, 1, and v, 1–2, pp. 176, 180 (tr. Jackson and Morgan, pp. 79, 84).
45. SSQ, p. 40 (= VB, xxx, 78).
46. PC, iv, 7, p. 248 (tr. Dawson, p. 16).

47. Ibid., iv, 8, pp. 248-9 (tr. Dawson, pp. 16-17); also TR, §54, p. 33. WR, vii, 1, p. 184 (tr. Jackson and Morgan, pp. 90-1).
48. Ibid., xiii, 5, p. 196 (tr. Jackson and Morgan, p. 108).
49. *CM*, III, p. 488, and IV, p. 76. Ivo of Narbonne, ibid., IV, p. 273. Henry Raspe, ibid., VI, p. 77. 'Chronicon S. Medardi', p. 492. John of Garlande, *De triumphis*, pp. 110-11. See Gregory G. Guzman, 'Reports of Mongol cannibalism in the thirteenth-century Latin sources: oriental fact or western fiction?', in Scott D. Westrem, ed., *Discovering New Worlds. Essays on Medieval Exploration and Imagination* (New York, 1991), pp. 31-68.
50. Dörrie, p. 191. PC, iv, 7, p. 248 (tr. Dawson, p. 16); cf. also TR, §54, p. 33.
51. SSQ, pp. 38, 41, 51 (= VB, xxx, 77, 78, 86).
52. 'Continuatio Sancrucensis secunda', p. 640.
53. *CM*, IV, p. 109; and cf. also ibid., pp. 77-8. Henry Raspe, ibid., IV, p. 110. Emperor Frederick II to Henry III, ibid., IV, p. 115 (= *HDFS*, V, p. 1151). Ivo of Narbonne, ibid., IV, p. 272: *gens... cui lex exlex*. Peter, in Dörrie, p. 189 (only in *CM* version). Aubry of Trois-Fontaines, 'Cronica', p. 946: *nullius sunt pietatis... nihil credunt*. 'Carmina de regno Ungariae destructo', p. 602: *gens... incredula*. Niccolò di Calvi, 'Vita Innocentii IV', p. 270: *nullius religionis et ritus*. G. Busson and A. Ledru, eds, 'Actus pontificum Cenomannis in urbe degentium', *Archives Historiques du Maine* 2 (1901), p. 499 (in a section written 1255/1272).
54. PC, iii, 2, p. 236 (tr. Dawson, p. 9); cf. TR, §39, p. 25.
55. PC, iii, 9, p. 240 (tr. Dawson, p. 12); cf. TR, §42, p. 28.
56. PC, iii, 7, p. 239 (tr. Dawson, p. 11); cf. TR, §42, pp. 27-8, ascribing these taboos to the Mongols' fear of their ancestors.
57. SSQ, pp. 34-5 (= VB, xxx, 74); cf. also p. 92 (= VB, xxxii, 34).
58. Ivo of Narbonne, in *CM*, IV, p. 275: *principia* [sic] *suarum tribuum deos vocant*. Thomas Agni di Lentino to all the faithful, 1 March 1260, in 'Menkonis chronicon', p. 548.
59. PC, iii, 2-3, pp. 236-7 (tr. Dawson, p. 9); cf. TR, §39, p. 25. WR, xxv, 9-10, p. 232 (tr. Jackson and Morgan, p. 156). See Felipe Fernández-Armesto, 'Medieval ethnography', *Journal of the Anthropological Society of Oxford* 13 (1982), pp. 275-86 (here p. 279).
60. PC, iii, 10, pp. 240-1 (tr. Dawson, p. 12). SSQ, p. 34 (= VB, xxx, 74). WR, xvii, 4, p. 207 (tr. Jackson and Morgan, p. 124).
61. PC, viii, 3, p. 294 (tr. Dawson, p. 44).
62. For a good introduction to medieval apocalyptic literature in the West, see Paul J. Alexander, 'Medieval Apocalypses as historical sources', *AHR* 73 (1968), pp. 997-1018.
63. RV, p. 552 (tr. in *Mongolensturm*, p. 140).
64. D.A. DeWeese, 'The influence of the Mongols on the religious consciousness of thirteenth century Europe', *MS* 5 (1978-9), pp. 41-78 (here pp. 47-53). Connell, 'Western views', pp. 117-19; but cf. Klopprogge, *Ursprung*, pp. 155-9. Richard, 'Ultimatums mongols', pp. 219-21. Claverie, 'L'apparition', p. 612.
65. *MGHEp.*, I, p. 723 (no. 822). Emperor Frederick II to Béla IV, in *HDFS*, V, p. 1145, and to Henry III of England, ibid., p. 1166; cf. also ibid., p. 1149

(= *CM*, IV, p. 112). Dominican Bartholomew to the bishop of Brixen, *HDFS*, V, p. 1148: *Christi fidem delere conantur*. Václav I of Bohemia, in Böhmer, 'Briefe', p. 111: *nichil aliud desiderant quam totam christianitatem abolere*. 'Annales Scheftlarienses maiores', p. 341. 'Gestorum Treverorum continuatio quarta', p. 403: *exterminium toti orbi christiano meditans*. Norman P. Tanner, ed., *Decrees of the Ecumenical Councils*, I. *Nicaea I to Lateran V* (London and Georgetown, 1990), p. 297: *christianum populum subjugare sibi vel potius perimere appetens*. Eudes de Châteauroux, sermo II, 'De invitatione ad crucem', in Christoph T. Maier, *Crusade Propaganda and Ideology. Model Sermons for the Preaching of the Cross* (Cambridge, 2000), p. 146 (tr. p. 147) (possibly dating from 1260, though Maier, pp. 25, 76, ascribes it to 1241). Cf. also 'Annales Mellicenses. Continuatio Lambacensis', p. 559: *sacerdotes cum grege Christi dispergunt*.

66. 'Annales S. Pantaleonis', p. 535. 'Annales Sancti Rudberti Salisburgenses', p. 787. Cf. also Claverie, 'L'apparition', p. 612; 'Carmina de regno Ungariae destructo', p. 606; Stubbs, *Historical Works of Gervase of Canterbury*, II, p. 179; John of Garlande, *De triumphis*, p. 111.

67. *MGHEp.*, I, p. 723 (no. 822). Béla IV to Conrad IV, in Böhmer, 'Briefe', p. 113; variant text in Hermann Baerwald, ed., *Das Baumgartenberger Formelbuch. Eine Quelle zur Geschichte des 13ᵗᵉⁿ Jahrh.*, FRAS² 25 (Vienna, 1866), p. 348. Emperor Frederick II to Henry III, in *HDFS*, V, p. 1149 (= *CM*, IV, p. 112). Tanner, *Decrees*, p. 297: *gladio ... nec aetate parcente nec sexui*. 'Relatio de concilio Lugdunensi', *MGHLeg.*, II, p. 514. MOL, DL 383 (= *CDH*, IV:2, p. 215). RV, p. 577 (tr. in *Mongolensturm*, p. 171). TS, pp. 165, 175 (tr. in *Mongolensturm*, pp. 246, 258). 'Continuatio Sancrucensis secunda', p. 640. 'Continuatio Zwetlensis tertia', *MGHS*, IX, p. 655. 'Annales Sancti Rudberti Salisburgenses', p. 787. 'Annales Stadenses', p. 367. 'Notae Altahenses', *MGHS*, XVII, p. 422. 'Rocznik kapituły krakowskiej', p. 79 = 'Annales capituli Cracoviensis', p. 598. 'Gestorum Treverorum continuatio quarta', p. 404. Ponce of Albon, in 'Ex Historiae regum Franciae continuatione Parisiensi', p. 604. 'Carmina de regno Ungariae destructo', pp. 601, 604. *CM*, IV, p. 77. Ivo of Narbonne, ibid., IV, p. 273. Jordan, Franciscan vice-minister in Bohemia, ibid., VI, pp. 81, 83. Cf. also 'Chronicon S. Medardi', p. 492; 'Kronika wielkopolska', pp. 87, 88; 'Rocznik kapituły gnieźnieńskiej', p. 5 = 'Annales capituli Posnaniensis', p. 440; Schneider, 'Ein Schreiben', p. 669; Uros, abbot of Pannonhalma, in MOL, DF 290698; Eudes de Châteauroux, 'Sermo in concilio pro negotio Tartarorum', in Ruotsala, *Europeans and Mongols*, p. 159.

68. A Hungarian bishop to the bishop of Paris, in *CM*, VI, p. 76. Henry Raspe to Henry II of Brabant, ibid., p. 78. Satellites of Antichrist: Klopprogge, *Ursprung*, pp. 183–6.

69. 'Gestorum Treverorum continuatio quarta', p. 404. Ivo of Narbonne, in *CM*, IV, p. 273.

70. 'Annales Scheftlarienses maiores', p. 341. 'Continuatio Sancrucensis secunda', p. 640. 'Gestorum Treverorum continuatio quarta', p. 404: *christianorum quoque refuge et dampnaticii*. Dominican 'R.' and Franciscan 'J.' to all Friars, in *CM*, VI, p. 82: *pessimi Christiani*. Jordan, Franciscan vice-minister in Bohemia,

and A[lbert], guardian of the convent at Prague, to Henry II of Brabant, ibid., p. 84. John of Garlande, *De triumphis*, p. 114: *Catholici falsi.*
71. Morton W. Bloomfield and Marjorie E. Reeves, 'The penetration of Joachism into northern Europe', *Speculum* 29 (1954), pp. 772–93 (here pp. 777–9, 787–8). Marjorie Reeves, *The Influence of Prophecy in the Later Middle Ages. A Study in Joachimism* (Oxford, 1969), pp. 46–8.
72. Gary Dickson, 'The Flagellants of 1260 and the crusades', *JMH* 15 (1989), pp. 227–67 (here pp. 248–51).
73. Marjorie E. Reeves, 'History and prophecy in medieval thought', *Medievalia et Humanistica* 5 (1974), pp. 51–75 (here p. 61).
74. Caesarius of Haisterbach, *Dialogus miraculorum*, x, 47, ed. Joseph Strange, 2 vols (Cologne, 1851), II, pp. 250–1; tr. H. von E. Scott and C.C. Swinton Bland, *Caesarius of Heisterbach (1220–1235). The Dialogue on Miracles*, 2 vols (London, 1929), II, pp. 210–11.
75. *HDFS*, VI:1, p. 257.
76. Peter, in Dörrie, p. 192. Cf. also 'Carmina de regno Ungariae destructo', p. 603: *heretici apercius, securius incedunt, apostate iudicium non credunt.*
77. Malcolm Barber, 'The Crusade of the Shepherds in 1251', in J.F. Sweets, ed., *Proceedings of the Tenth Annual Meeting of the Western Society for French History, 14–16 October 1982, Winnipeg* (Lawrence, KS, 1984), pp. 1–23, and repr. in Barber, *Crusaders and Heretics, 12th–14th Centuries* (Aldershot, 1995). Gary Dickson, 'The advent of the *Pastores* (1251)', *Revue Belge de Philologie et d'Histoire* 66 (1988), pp. 249–67. In the 1250s, some writers already associated this episode with the Children's Crusade as evidence of a satanic conspiracy: Dickson, 'La genèse de la Croisade des Enfants (1212)', *BEC* 153 (1995), pp. 53–102 (here p. 54).
78. 'Richeri Gesta' (after 1264), pp. 310–11. Busson and Ledru , 'Actus pontificum Cenomannis', pp. 499–500 (and see n.53 above), where the Mongol invasion seems for this purpose to be deliberately removed from its chronological context.
79. *OM*, I, p. 401. Others too suspected the 'Master' of being in the Egyptians' pay: *CM*, V, pp. 246, 252; 'Chronique de Saint-Denis', *RHGF*, XXI, p. 115.
80. See, e.g., Robert Chazan, 'The deteriorating image of the Jews – twelfth and thirteenth centuries', in Scott L. Waugh and Peter D. Diehl, eds, *Christendom and Its Discontents: Exclusion, Persecution and Rebellion, 1000–1500* (Cambridge, 1996), pp. 220–33.
81. *CM*, IV, pp. 77–8.
82. 'Richeri Gesta', p. 310.
83. TS, p. 169 (tr. in *Mongolensturm*, p. 251).
84. *CM*, IV, pp. 131–2. 'Gestorum Treverorum continuatio quarta', p. 404. 'Annales Marbacenses', p. 175 (but cf. n.21 above). John of Garlande, *De triumphis*, pp. 112–13.
85. Sophia Menache, 'Tartars, Jews, Saracens and the Jewish–Mongol "plot" of 1241', *History* 81 (1996), pp. 319–42 (here pp. 334–8). Israel Jacob Yuval, 'Jewish Messianic expectations towards 1240 and Christian reactions', in Peter Schäfer and Mark R. Cohen, eds, *Towards the Millennium: Messianic Expectations from the Bible to WACO* (Leiden, 1998), pp. 105–21 (I owe this reference to

Reuven Amitai). The principal sources are *CM*, IV, pp. 131–3, and 'Annales Erphordenses', p. 34 (the Mongols not mentioned, but the outbreak at Frankfurt dated 24 May 1241). For a faint echo of the significance of 1240, see 'Chronicon rhythmicum Austriacum', *MGHS*, XXV, p. 360.

86. Jacques de Vitry, *Epistolae*, pp. 141, 142. Klopprogge, *Ursprung*, p. 177.

87. Robert E. Lerner, *The Powers of Prophecy: The Cedar of Lebanon Vision from the Mongol Onslaught to the Dawn of the Enlightenment* (Berkeley and Los Angeles, 1983), p. 16 (Latin text at p. 200: *filii Israel liberabuntur de captivitate*).

88. No distinction: Henry Raspe to Henry II of Brabant, in *CM*, VI, p. 77; Stubbs, *Historical Works of Gervase of Canterbury*, II, p. 179; cf. also Robert, patriarch of Jerusalem, to Innocent IV, 1244, in 'Annales monasterii de Burton', p. 258; Menache, 'Tartars', p. 338. Jews in the Near East: S.D. Goitein, 'Glimpses from the Cairo Geniza on naval warfare in the Mediterranean and on the Mongol invasion', in *Studi orientalistici in onore di Giorgio Levi della Vida* (Rome, 1956), I, pp. 393–408 (here pp. 398–401, 407–8); Benjamin Kedar, 'The Jewish community in Jerusalem in the 13th century', *Tarbiz* 41 (1971–2), pp. 82–94 [in Hebrew, with English résumé].

89. This notion had been refuted in *c*.900 by an author sometimes called Remigius: 'Incerti scriptoris epistola ad episcopum Virdunensem', in A.F. Gombos, ed., *Catalogus fontium historiae Hungaricae*, 4 vols with continuous pagination (Budapest, 1937–43), II, pp. 1236–7. See Hansgerd Göckenjan, 'Die Landnahme der Ungarn aus der Sicht der zeitgenössischen ostfränkisch-deutschen Quellen', *UAJ*, n.F., 13 (1994), pp. 1–17.

90. TS, p. 171 (tr. in *Mongolensturm*, p. 253).

91. Thomas Frenz and Peter Herde, eds, *Das Brief- und Memorialbuch des Albert Behaim*, MGH Briefe des späten Mittelalters 1 (Munich, 2000), pp. 134–78 (no. 43). On the author, see Frenz, 'Apokalypse als Geschichtserklärung. Neuere Forschungsergebnisse über den Passauer Domdekan Albert Behaim († 1260)', *Ostbairische Grenzmarken. Passauer Jahrbuch für Geschichte, Kunst und Volkskunde* 32 (1990), pp. 48–55. Below, I have added references to Albert's text alongside that of the *Sermo*, from which it often differs in minor respects.

92. *CM*, VI, p. 497, n.1 (from BL, Cotton ms. Nero D I, fo. 85).

93. Ibid., VI, p. 78.

94. 'Gestorum Treverorum continuatio quarta', p. 403. 'Annales Scheftlarienses maiores', p. 341. 'Chronicon S. Medardi', p. 491. 'Annales monasterii de Theokesberia', p. 118. *Flores historiarum*, II, p. 267. Klopprogge, *Ursprung*, p. 174. See also Jacob of Maerlant, *Alexanders Geesten* (*c*.1260), ed. F.-A. Snellaert, 2 vols (Brussels, 1860–1), II, p. 85, vv. 1183–1201 (I owe this reference to Peter Hoppenbrouwers).

95. IUB ms. 187: the dialogue is at fo. 8r–v (here 8r). On this ms., see Walter Neuhauser, *Katalog der Handschriften der Universitätsbibliothek Innsbruck, Teil 2* (Vienna, 1991), pp. 174–7; Lerner, *Powers of Prophecy*, pp. 11–13.

96. Sackur, pp. 80, 82 (Frenz and Herde, pp. 159–60, 162). For the recent overthrow of 'Persia' or the 'king of the Persians', see Jacques de Vitry, *Epistolae*, pp. 141–4; Oliver of Paderborn, *Historia Damiatina*, §§55 and 76, in H. Hoogeweg, ed., *Die Schriften des kölner Domscholasters, späteren Bischofs von Paderborn und Kardinal-Bischofs von S. Sabina Oliverus*, Bibliothek des

litterarischen Vereins in Stuttgart 202 (Tübingen, 1894), pp. 258, 273–4, and tr. in Edward Peters, ed., *Christian Society and the Crusades 1198–1229* (Philadelphia, 1971), pp. 112–13, 129; Zarncke, 'Zur Sage', p. 612; Ralph of Coggeshall, p. 190; Aubry of Trois-Fontaines, 'Cronica', p. 911. A Christian Egyptian author, recounting the events of 1221, similarly calls the Khwārazmshāh *malik al-furs* ('king of the Persians'): *Siyar al-abā' al-baṭārika*, ed. and tr. Khs-Burmester and Khater, IV:1, text p. 35, tr. p. 73.

97. The figure appears in the report of 'Petrus archiepiscopus de Belgrab in Ruscia super facto tartarorum', OOLB ms. 446, fo. 267vb, cited by Ruotsala, *Europeans and Mongols*, pp. 154–5; though abridged, this text may well be closer to the original here than the versions edited by Dörrie, which have 39 years (see 'Drei Texte', p. 193). For Pseudo-Methodius's data, see n.107 below.

98. Julian, in Dörrie, p. 178 (tr. in *Mongolensturm*, p. 107). TS, p. 171 (tr. in *Mongolensturm*, p. 253). For Rome and the king of the Romans, see Sackur, p. 80: *consurgent . . . adversus Romanorum imperium filii Hismahel . . . et contradicunt regno Romanorum*; p. 83: *Romania corrumpitur et in occisione erit* (Frenz and Herde, pp. 159, 163); cf. also pp. 68–9, 89–91 (Frenz and Herde, pp. 147–8, 170–1).

99. Peter, in Dörrie, p. 193. Ivo of Narbonne, in *CM*, IV, p. 276.

100. Frederick II to the Roman Senate, in *HDFS*, V, p. 1140.

101. Sackur, pp. 85–6 (Frenz and Herde, p. 166). On the chroniclers, see Klopprogge, *Ursprung*, pp. 173–4; idem, 'Das Mongolenbild im Abendland', in Stephan Conermann and Jan Kusber, eds, *Die Mongolen in Asien und Europa* (Frankfurt-am-Main, 1997), pp. 81–101 (here p. 98).

102. Islands: *The Chronicle of Bury St. Edmunds (1212–1301)*, ed. and tr. Antonia Gransden, Nelson's Medieval Texts (London, 1964), p. 10 (section written by John of Taxter, d. *c*.1265). Mountains: *CM*, III, p. 488, and IV, p. 76; 'F.', abbot of St Mary's in Hungary, ibid., VI, p. 79; *OM*, I, p. 268, and II, p. 234. For the islands of Tarse, see Sinor, 'Le Mongol vu par l'Occident', p. 58.

103. Sackur, pp. 72–3, 92 (Frenz and Herde, pp. 152, 173).

104. TR, §54, p. 33: *adluv(i)ones*. Carpini's text had read *abluviones iumentorum*.

105. For what follows, see especially Klopprogge, *Ursprung*, pp. 162–8; Johannes Fried, 'Auf der Suche nach der Wirklichkeit: die Mongolen und die europäische Erfahrungswissenschaft im 13. Jahrhundert', *HZ* 243 (1986), pp. 287–332 (here pp. 299–301). The two versions of the letter are in *CM*, VI, pp. 75–6, and 'Annales de Waverleia', *AM*, II, pp. 324–5. Cf. also Bigalli, *I Tartari*, pp. 64–9; Klopprogge, 'Das Mongolenbild', pp. 96–9; Schmieder, *Europa*, pp. 207, 260; and for the date, Bezzola, p. 54 and n.198.

106. C.S.F. Burnett, 'An apocryphal letter from the Arabic philosopher al-Kindi to Theodore, Frederick II's astrologer, concerning Gog and Magog, the Enclosed Nations, and the scourge of the Mongols', *Viator* 15 (1984), pp. 151–67 (here pp. 164, 166; for the date, see pp. 155, 158). Charles Burnett and Patrick Gautier Dalché, 'Attitudes towards the Mongols in medieval literature: the XXII kings of Gog and Magog from the court of Frederick II to Jean de Mandeville', *Viator* 22 (1991), pp. 153–67 (here p. 160).

107. Klopprogge, *Ursprung*, p. 174, citing 'Gestorum Treverorum continuatio quarta', p. 403. For the respective figures for the domination of the Ishmaelites

IMAGES OF THE ENEMY

and of the unclean peoples, see Sackur, p. 69: *usque ad numerum temporum
ebdomadarum VII*; ibid., p. 92: *post ebdomada vero temporis* (Frenz and Herde,
pp. 148, 173), where Pseudo-Methodius's 'week' = seven years.

108. *Pace* Schmieder, *Europa*, p. 207. Her comments are more appropriate when
applied to authors who wrote some decades later: see ibid., pp. 263–8. For
an example of *Ismahelite* as Muslims, see RV, p. 582 (tr. in *Mongolensturm*,
p. 179; and see ibid., p. 220, n.208), who lists them among the races within
the Mongol army; more generally, Smail Balić, 'Der Islam im mittelalterlichen
Ungarn', *SOF* 23 (1964), pp. 19–35.

109. Anna Rutkowska-Plachcinska, 'L'image du danger tatar dans les sources
polonaises', in *Histoire et société. Mélanges offerts à Georges Duby*, Textes réunis
par les médiévistes de l'Université de Provence 4 (Aix–en–Provence, 1992),
pp. 87–95 (here pp. 87–8).

110. 'Annales S. Pantaleonis', pp. 535–6; for the Franciscans' visit, see p. 542.

111. 'Annales Stadenses', p. 331 (ibid., pp. 284, for Pseudo-Methodius, and 367
for the Mongol invasion). Martin Haeusler, *Das Ende der Geschichte in der
mittelalterlichen Weltchronistik* (Köln and Vienna, 1980), p. 69.

112. *CM*, VI, p. 80.

113. *Novgorodskaia pervaia letopis' starshego i mladshego izvodov*, ed. A.N. Nasonov
(Moscow and Leningrad, 1950), pp. 61, 264 (tr. Michell and Forbes, *Chronicle
of Novgorod*, p. 64). Leonid S. Chekin, 'The Godless Ishmaelites: the image of
the steppe in eleventh-thirteenth-century Rus'', *Russian History* 19 (1992),
pp. 9–28 (here pp. 12–13, 20–3).

114. Dörrie, pp. 181, 188 (here the version of Peter's report in OOLB ms. 446
reads *Hertruch*), 190. Von den Brincken, 'Die Mongolen im Weltbild',
p. 122. Klopprogge, *Ursprung*, pp. 175–6.

115. G. Graf, 'Die Tataren im Spiegel der byzantinischen Literatur', in A. Scheiber,
ed., *Emlékkonyv Heller Bernát Professzor hetvenedik szuletésnapjára* (Budapest,
1941), pp. 77–85. But for criticism of this piece, see Bezzola, p. 9, n.7.

116. Kirakos Ganjakec'i, p. 193 (in a section completed by 1241). For St Nerses'
prophecy, see ibid., pp. 6, 194; Galstian, *Armianskie istochniki o Mongolakh*,
pp. 45–6, 47, 71, 103; WR, xxxviii, 3, pp. 322–3 (tr. Jackson and Morgan,
pp. 266–7); Robert W. Thomson, 'The crusaders through Armenian eyes', in
Angeliki E. Laiou and Roy Parviz Mottahedeh, eds, *The Crusades from the
Perspective of Byzantium and the Muslim World* (Washington, 2001), pp. 71–
82 (here pp. 73–8).

117. Remke Kruk, 'History and apocalypse: Ibn al-Nafîs' justification of Mamluk
rule', *Der Islam* 72 (1995), pp. 324–37 (here pp. 329–31).

118. Jūzjānī, II, pp. 92–4, 98 (tr. Raverty, II, p. 935, abridged). Several such
traditions are collected in David Cook, 'Muslim apocalyptic and *Jihād*', *JSAI*
20 (1996), pp. 66–104 (here pp. 96–101).

119. E. Van Donzel and Claudia Ott, 'Yādjūdj wa-Mādjūdj', *Enc.Isl.*² André Miquel,
La géographie humaine du monde musulman jusqu'au milieu du 11ᵉ siècle, II.
Géographie arabe et représentation du monde: la terre et l'étranger, Civilisations
et sociétés 37 (Paris, 1975), pp. 497–511. DeWeese, *Islamization*, pp. 287–9.
See Ruth I. Meserve, 'The inhospitable land of the barbarian', *JAH* 16 (1982),
pp. 75–82, for further material.

120. Ibn al-Athīr, XII, p. 359; tr. in Bertold Spuler, *History of the Mongols*, tr. Helga and Stuart Drummond (London, 1972), p. 30. 'Awfī, *Jawāmi' al-ḥikāyāt*, BL ms. Or. 4392, fo. 127v.

121. Ibn al-Athīr, XII, p. 361 (tr. in Spuler, *History of the Mongols*, p. 32). Juwaynī, I, p. 52 (tr. Boyle, I, p. 70). For a variation on this theme, see Paul, 'L'invasion mongole', p. 46 and n.30.

122. Juwaynī, II, p. 89 (tr. Boyle, I, p. 357); cf. also I, p. 52 (tr. Boyle, I, p. 70). Jūzjānī, I, p. 302 (tr. Raverty, I, p. 244), mentions the advice, but omits the metaphor of the wall.

123. Juwaynī, II, pp. 79-80 (tr. Boyle, I, p. 347).

124. al-Dhahabī, *Ta'rīkh al-Islām 611-620*, ed. Tadmurī (Beirut, 1417 H./1997), p. 366; for the text, see also Claude Cahen, '''Abdallaṭīf al-Baghdādī, portraitiste et historien de son temps: extraits inédits de ses mémoires', *BEO* 23 (1970), pp. 101-28 (here p. 117); tr. in Cahen, '''Abdallaṭīf al-Baghdādī et les Khwārizmiens', in C.E. Bosworth, ed., *Iran and Islam: In Memory of the Late Vladimir Minorsky* (Edinburgh, 1971), pp. 149-66 (here p. 152).

125. Ibn Abi l-Ḥadīd, *Sharḥ Nahj al-balāgha* (1245/1251), partially ed. and tr. Mukhtār Jabalī, *Les invasions mongoles en Orient vécues par un savant arabe* (Paris, 1995), Ar. text p. 23: *mulūk al-khiṭā kānū wiqāyat ᵃⁿ lahu min hā'ulā'i* (French tr. pp. 22-3). Ibn Wāṣil, *Mufarrij al-kurūb* (1261), ed. Jamāl al-Dīn al-Shayyāl *et al.*, 5 vols (Cairo, 1953-77), III, p. 38.

126. Sibṭ Ibn al-Jawzī (d. 1257), *Mir'āt al-zamān fī ta'rīkh al-a'yān*, VIII:2 (Hyderabad, A.P., 1371 H./1952), p. 671, claiming that the Ayyubid prince al-Ashraf Mūsā reacted thus on the news of Jalāl al-Dīn's death. Ibn Wāṣil, IV, p. 296.

127. al-Dhahabī, *Ta'rīkh al-Islām 611-620*, p. 50 (Cahen, '''Abdallaṭīf al-Baghdādī, portraitiste', p. 127).

128. Ibn Abi l-Ḥadīd, text p. 39 (tr. p. 41): his informant was a merchant from Khurāsān whose brother had been in the Khwārazmshāh's service.

129. Ibn al-Athīr, XII, p. 360 (tr. in Spuler, *History of the Mongols*, p. 31); hence Ibn Abi l-Ḥadīd, text p. 27 (tr. pp. 26-7).

130. Jacques de Vitry, *Epistolae*, p. 149. Jean Richard, 'La confrérie des Mosserins d'Acre et les marchands de Mossoul au XIIIe siècle', *L'Orient Syrien* 11 (1966), pp. 451-60 (here p. 455), repr. in Richard, *Orient et Occident*. Von den Brincken, *Die „Nationes Christianorum Orientalium"*, p. 333.

131. Käthe Uray-Kőhalmi, 'Synkretismus im Staatskult der frühen Dschingisiden', in W. Heissig and H.J. Klimkeit, eds, *Synkretismus in den Religionen Zentralasiens*, Studies in Oriental Religions 13 (Wiesbaden, 1987), pp. 136-58.

132. Rashīd al-Dīn, I, pp. 43-4, 145-51, 157, 192, 218 (tr. Thackston, I, pp. 25-6, 79-81, 84, 102, 114). Hayton, iii, 7, Fr. text p. 153, Latin text p. 288.

133. Jūzjānī, II, p. 99 (tr. Raverty, II, p. 937): here the emergence from enclosed mountains is placed early in Chinggis Khan's career.

134. Denis Sinor, 'The legendary origin of the Turks', in E.V. Žygas and P. Voorheis, eds, *Folklorica. Festschrift for Felix J. Oinas*, IUUAS 141 (Bloomington, IN, 1982), pp. 223-57 (here pp. 242-3, 247-9), and repr. in Sinor, *Studies*. DeWeese, *Islamization*, pp. 273-87.

IMAGES OF THE ENEMY

135. John Andrew Boyle, 'The Alexander legend in Central Asia', *Folklore* 83 (1974), pp. 217–28 (here pp. 222–3), repr. in Boyle, *Mongol World-Empire*; idem, 'Alexander and the Mongols', *JRAS* (1979), pp. 123–36. But as DeWeese, *Islamization*, p. 274, n.79, points out, the application of the legend to the Turks must predate any Nestorian influence.

136. Klopprogge, *Ursprung*, pp. 11, 206–7, 237–57, and 'Das Mongolenbild', pp. 99–101. Cf. also the brief comments of Johannes Fried, *Aufstieg aus dem Untergang. Apokalyptisches Denken und die Entstehung der modernen Naturwissenschaft im Mittelalter* (Munich, 2001), pp. 78–9.

137. PC, v, 17, pp. 263–4 (tr. Dawson, p. 25). Klopprogge, *Ursprung*, p. 221.

138. PC, iii, 12, p. 242 (tr. Dawson, p. 13). See John Andrew Boyle, 'A form of horse sacrifice amongst the thirteenth- and fourteenth-century Mongols', in *Proceedings of the VIIth meeting of the Permanent International Altaistic Conference 29 Augustus–3 September 1964* (Wiesbaden, 1965 = *CAJ* 10), pp. 145–50, and repr. in Boyle, *Mongol World-Empire*.

139. WR, xxii, 1, p. 221 (tr. Jackson and Morgan, p. 141).

140. See Sir Richard Southern, *Scholastic Humanism and the Unification of Europe*, I. *Foundations* (Oxford, 1995), pp. 58–101.

141. The few known biographical details about Carpini are given in Menestò's edition, pp. 50–2. See Heinrich Euler, 'Die Begegnung Europas mit den Mongolen im Spiegel abendländischer Reiseberichte', *Saeculum* 23 (1972), pp. 47–58 (here pp. 49–51), for a comparison of the two men.

142. Salimbene, *Cronica*, I, pp. 312, 313, 321.

143. *CM*, V, p. 599. Haeusler, p. 62. Ruotsala, *Europeans and Mongols*, pp. 94–9. For Adam, see Davide Bigalli, 'Giudizio escatologico e tecnica di missione nei pensatori francescani: Ruggero Bacone', in *Espansione del francescanesimo tra Occidente e Oriente nel secolo XIII. Atti del VI Convegno internazionale, Assisi, 12–14 ottobre 1978* (Assisi, 1979), pp. 151–86 (here pp. 159–60).

144. Alexander Minorita, *Expositio in Apocalypsim*, ed. Alois Wachtel, MGHQu. 1 (Weimar, 1955), p. 433; cf. also p. 451 (cited by Schmieder, *Europa*, pp. 260 and n.330, 262, n.344, and 266, n.348). On the successive versions of this work, see Sabine Schmolinsky, *Der Apokalypsenkommentar des Alexander Minorita. Zur frühen Rezeption Joachims von Fiore in Deutschland*, MGH Studien und Texte 3 (Hannover, 1991), pp. 31–52 (pp. 35–6 for the *Thatari*).

145. Alexander Patschovsky, *Der Passauer Anonymus: ein Sammelwerk über Ketzer, Juden, Antichrist aus der Mitte des 13. Jahrhunderts*, MGH Schriften 22 (Stuttgart, 1968), esp. p. 162.

146. TR, §1, p. 3: *que in fine iam clarescunt seculorum. . . .*

147. WR, xxxvii, 20, p. 319 (tr. Jackson and Morgan, p. 261). SSQ, p. 55 (= VB, xxx, 89).

148. Ibid., pp. 90, 92 (= VB, xxxii, 32 and 34).

149. PC, v, 19, p. 264 (tr. Dawson, pp. 25–6). SSQ, p. 27 (= VB, xxx, 69), dated the beginning of Mongol domination in the year 1202.

150. WR, xix, 4, and xxi, 10, pp. 213, 232 (tr. Jackson and Morgan, pp. 131, 156). DeWeese, 'Influence', pp. 56–7, sees this merely as symptomatic of the more positive view of the Mongols that was emerging.

151. *OM*, I, pp. 268–9, and II, pp. 234–5; at I, p. 363, he seems to accept Rubruck's belief that Methodius's prophecy about the Ishmaelites had been fulfilled in the Saracens. Bacon, *Opus tertium*, partial ed. A.G. Little (Aberdeen, 1912, repr. Farnborough, 1966), p. 12. See more generally Reeves, *Influence of Prophecy*, pp. 46–8; Bigalli, 'Giudizio escatologico', pp. 168–70.

152. Freibergs, *'Descripciones Terrarum'*, pp. 196, 198.

153. Chekin, 'Godless Ishmaelites', pp. 14–16, 24.

154. Jackson, 'Medieval Christendom's encounter', p. 368. For an island in present-day Indonesia inhabited by a race of human females and dog-headed males, see the 6th-century *Liang shu*, quoted in Pelliot, *Notes on Marco Polo*, II, p. 724.

155. Sibṭ Ibn al-Jawzī, *Mir'āt*, VIII:2, pp. 733–4 (*ad annum* 638 H./1240–1): the brief lacuna in the text is to be filled from al-Jazarī (d. 1339), *Ḥawādith al-zamān*, Forschungs- und Landesbibliothek Gotha, ms. Orient. A1559, fo. 75v, who is here citing the Sibṭ *verbatim*.

156. WR, xxix, 46, p. 269 (tr. Jackson and Morgan, p. 201).

157. Ibid., xxvi, 3, p. 234 (tr. Jackson and Morgan, p. 158); hence *OM*, I, p. 371. Cf. Solinus, *Collectanea rerum*, xv, 13, ed. Th. Mommsen, 2nd edn (Berlin, 1958), p. 84; also PC, v, 14, pp. 260–1 (tr. Dawson, p. 23). For a report that the Mug-lig, or Ke'u-li, ate their dead parents, see Jacques Bacot, 'Reconnaissance en Haute Asie septentrionale par cinq envoyés ouigours au VIIIᵉ siècle', *JA* 244 (1956), pp. 137–53 (here p. 145); for their localization (in Korea), Gerard Clauson, 'À propos du manuscrit Pelliot tibétain 1283', *JA* 245 (1957), pp. 11–24 (here pp. 19–20).

chapter 7

AN ALLY AGAINST ISLAM: THE MONGOLS IN THE NEAR EAST

In the light of their attacks on Latin territory in 1241–4 and in 1259–60, the Mongols had emerged quite simply as the greatest threat confronting Catholic Christendom, so that in 1260 the Frankish leaders at Acre had chosen to cooperate with the more familiar Muslim demon as a means of staving off an attack by Hülegü's forces. But beginning in 1262, in the wake of the dissolution of the Mongol empire, Hülegü and his successors made a series of overtures designed to gain Latin collaboration in the war against the Mamlūks. These diplomatic contacts, which continued into the early fourteenth century, were made with the popes and with Western European sovereigns, particularly the French and English kings and sometimes also those of Aragon and Sicily.[1] Only minimally and rarely did they involve the Near Eastern Franks, who were now a negligible quantity. In any case, the Mamlūk Sultans Baybars (1260–77) and Qalāwūn (1279–90), informed of these negotiations between their enemies by their highly efficient intelligence network,[2] were encouraged to embark on the reduction of the Latin outposts in Syria and Palestine, a process completed in 1291.

The Ilkhans' quest for a synchronized attack

There is no doubt that Hülegü was concerned to avenge 'Ayn Jālūt, and indeed to prosecute his dynasty's traditional mission by reducing Syria and Egypt.[3] The fact that the Mamlūks originated among the nomadic Qipchāq, and hence would have been classed as refugee 'slaves' of the Mongols (above, p. 60), may have given added edge to the struggle.[4] Yet the collapse of the Mongol empire had left Hülegü in an exposed position. To his rear were hostile kinsmen who coveted his territories: it is not surprising that he and his successors tended to reside in the steppelands of Azerbaijan and the Transcaucasus, close to the frontier with the Golden Horde. The existence of an independent Mamlūk

Sultanate, moreover, served as an incitement to Muslim client rulers within his own dominions to intrigue with the Mamlūks and even to rise in revolt, as the prince of Fārs (in south-western Persia) did in 1263.[5] In the circumstances, it was necessary to look around for external allies.

In April 1262, less than two years after Kitbuqa's overthrow, Hülegü wrote to Louis IX, announcing his intention to attack the Mamlūks and proposing that the French monarch send his fleet to blockade Egypt by sea.[6] It is unclear whether the letter, of which the only known manuscript has survived in Vienna, ever reached Paris. A report by Ilkhanid envoys to the Second Council of Lyons in 1274 would allege that Hülegü had sent ambassadors to Pope Urban IV and to 'all kings and princes overseas', but that – like Sartaq's envoy in 1254 (p. 102 above) – the party had been intercepted in Sicily. King Manfred, against whom the pope was then organizing a crusade to deprive him of his kingdom and who was in contact with the Mamlūk regime,[7] packed the Mongol embassy off by ship.[8] According to Urban IV's letter to Hülegü, *Exultavit cor nostrum* (undated but belonging to 1263/4), a certain John the Hungarian had arrived, claiming to be the Ilkhan's envoy and alleging that Hülegü was greatly attached to the Christian faith and contemplated baptism; but he carried no letters of accreditation.[9] Conceivably John was one of the envoys whose effects had been confiscated by Manfred; yet although he is mentioned by name in Hülegü's letter to King Louis, he is not there described as its bearer. We cannot be sure, therefore, that all these details relate to one and the same embassy.

Urban had particular reason to welcome John's revelations, since he had learned that the Mamlūk Sultan Baybars had broken his truce with the Franks and was threatening Acre.[10] In the absence of any credentials supporting John's story, *Exultavit cor nostrum* was cautiously welcoming, and added that Urban was instructing Guillaume d'Agen, the newly-elected patriarch of Jerusalem and papal legate in the east, to investigate further.[11] Yet we do not know the sequel to *Exultavit cor nostrum*. Although a papal bull of January 1264 focuses on the Egyptian threat and makes no mention of the Mongols whatever,[12] it is noteworthy that in July of that year – surely after John the Hungarian brought news of Hülegü's desire to embrace Christianity – Urban was still referring to the Mongols in the Near East as a formidable enemy in the same breath as Mamlūk Egypt.[13] Not until Clement IV's pontificate (1265–8), it seems, did the Curia begin to entertain the possibility that the Ilkhan might serve as an ally against Baybars.[14] Interestingly enough, there is evidence that this contingency was contemplated more widely from about the same time, since the Book of Sidrach, which dates from some point after 1268, includes a prophecy that the Mongols would not merely defeat the Muslims but would in time become friends of the Franks.[15]

Contact was apparently resumed by Hülegü's son and successor Abaqa (1265–82). Learning of the projected crusade (the Eighth) against Egypt, he despatched envoys late in 1266 or early in 1267 both to Pope Clement and to Jaime I of Aragon, who had taken the cross and whose plans were the most advanced.[16] From Clement's response, it is clear both that Abaqa had written at least once before and that he had just learned of Manfred's overthrow by a crusading army under Charles of Anjou. In his reply to the pope, dated 1268, the Ilkhan explained apologetically that his previous missive had been written in Mongolian because his Latin secretary was absent from court, and promised to send troops under his brother Ejei to aid the Christians.[17] He may have been spurred on by the recent Mamlūk capture of Antioch (May 1268), whose prince, it will be recalled, had been tributary to the Ilkhan since 1260; a Mongol 'resident' (basqaq, shiḥna) was still based there when the city fell.[18] Unfortunately the envoys chanced to meet ambassadors from Baybars in Genoa, and a full-blown skirmish ensued in the city's main square before the Genoese separated the combatants. One purpose of the Mongol embassy of 1268 was to meet Louis IX, who had just taken the cross, and his brother Charles of Anjou, king of Sicily.[19]

In the event the Aragonese expedition foundered in a storm in the Western Mediterranean in the autumn of 1269, and the French crusade in 1270 was diverted to Tunis, where yet another embassy from Abaqa arrived to find that Louis had just died and his son and successor Philip III was preparing to reembark for France.[20] Only the English contingent, under the Lord Edward (the future Edward I), sailed on from Tunis and made contact with the Mongols. In September 1271 Abaqa asked Edward to coordinate his activities with those of the Mongol general Samaghar, whom he was sending against the Mamlūks. But in fact the Mongol force that raided as far as Ḥārim and Afāmiyya in October was relatively modest in size, and retreated on Baybars' rapid advance. The Sultan was able to prevent any junction of his enemies; Edward's simultaneous attack on Qāqūn (Caco) in September was a feeble affair, and he left Palestine in September 1272 without any effective military collaboration between crusaders and Mongols having taken place.[21]

Abaqa next sent a delegation to the Council of Lyons, which had been summoned by Pope Gregory X for 1274. The unscheduled arrival of the Mongol envoys created a great stir, particularly when their leader, and possibly members of his suite, voluntarily underwent a public baptism. They were escorted by David of Ashby who, as chaplain to Thomas Agni, bishop of Bethlehem and papal legate in Palestine, had been despatched to Hülegü in 1260 and had remained with the Mongols ever since. Abaqa's Latin secretary Richardus delivered a report, to which reference has already been made (p. 166), outlining the course of Western–Ilkhanid relations under Hülegü and his son, and assured the assembly of his master's continued determination to drive the Mamlūks from Syria.[22] *Les fais des Tartares*, David of Ashby's account of the Mongols, was probably submitted to the Council. Although the only known manuscript is now lost, the chapter on Mongol methods of waging war has survived in transcript; it was doubtless written with joint military action in mind.[23]

Another embassy to Europe in 1276–7, headed by the brothers John and James Vassalli, who are described by a French chronicler as Georgians but were probably Greeks, likewise bore no fruit. From Philip III's court John crossed to England, and conveyed the Ilkhan's apology for the failure to collaborate in 1271 to King Edward I,[24] whom David of Ashby had already visited after the Council, early in 1275.[25] When the ambassadors left Europe in 1277 after being received by the short-lived Pope John XXI, they were accompanied by envoys to Abaqa from Charles of Anjou, who had just purchased a claim to the kingdom of Jerusalem and had sent troops to take over the government at Acre. The content of his message, and the purpose and outcome of another embassy which he despatched to the Ilkhan in 1278, are alike unknown.[26]

Abaqa made no attempt to profit from the removal of Baybars, who died at Damascus in 1277 on the way back from an invasion of Anatolia. A relatively minor raid was launched on Aleppo in the late summer of 1280,[27] and it was not until 1281 that the Mongols moved into northern Syria in strength under the Ilkhan's brother Möngke Temür. Prior to this, Abaqa made a last bid to secure Western European cooperation by sending an embassy to Edward I.[28] Troops and provisions had also been demanded from Acre in the summer of 1280,[29] and both Bohemond VII of Tripoli and King Hugh III of Cyprus were urged to join forces with the Mongols. But Hugh's arrival was delayed, and the new Mamlūk Sultan Qalāwūn was able to position his army between Möngke Temür and the Franks on the coast; it seems that only some Hospitallers from Margat (Marqab) participated in the campaign.[30] Although the ensuing engagement near Ḥimṣ on 30 October 1281 was indecisive and the Sultan's army was badly mauled, most of the Mongols dispersed in search of plunder and Möngke Temür had to relinquish the field to the Mamlūks.[31] Both he and the Ilkhan died in the following year.

The brief reign of Abaqa's brother and successor Tegüder, who had adopted Islam and assumed the name of Aḥmad (1282–4), was marked by the opening of negotiations with Egypt. Dr Allouche has shown that this step was rather less revolutionary than it appears and that Aḥmad's letters to Qalāwūn were just as uncompromising as the previous ultimatums. Far from abandoning his predecessors' expansionist designs and seeking a peaceful *modus vivendi*, as was once thought, the new Ilkhan was making a fresh endeavour to secure the Mamlūks' submission, on the grounds that they could now have no objection to acknowledging the sovereignty of a fellow Muslim.[32] This policy, which met with a cool response from Qalāwūn, was in any case jettisoned when Aḥmad was overthrown and killed by his nephew, Abaqa's son Arghun. In his correspondence with Western rulers Arghun would take care to portray his uncle, unfairly perhaps, as a ruler whose Islamic faith had led him to turn his back upon tradition.[33] News reached Europe that a Muslim ruler had been supplanted by one who was favourable to the Christians.[34]

The *débâcle* of 1281 conceivably persuaded Arghun that victory over the Mamlūks would elude him unless he enjoyed the cooperation of the Latin West.[35] Like his father, he made strenuous attempts to court the Catholic world, sending four missions to Europe in the course of a brief reign (1284–91).[36] The first (1285), which was accompanied by an envoy from Qubilai named ʿĪsā Kelemechi, brought Pope Honorius IV a letter (in barbarous Latin) offering to divide 'the land of Sham, namely Egypt' with the Franks following the 'removal' of the Saracens who lay between Arghun's dominions and the West.[37] The next embassy, which arrived in the summer of 1287, during the vacancy in the Holy See following Honorius's death, was headed by the Nestorian monk Rabban Ṣawma, a close associate of the Patriarch Yahballaha III. Rabban Ṣawma, who occupied the time until the election of Nicholas IV in 1288 with visits to Philip IV of France and to Edward I of England at Bordeaux, was treated with great distinction but left only with many assurances of support and no promise of concrete assistance.[38] In 1289–90 a third embassy from Arghun waited upon the pope, Philip and Edward, and undertook to rendezvous with the French king outside Damascus in February 1291.[39] A last mission, which arrived in the summer of 1290, was still in Europe late in August 1291, when Pope Nicholas heard the appalling news of the fall of Acre and the other remaining bastions of Frankish rule in Palestine. He wrote at once to Arghun exhorting him to be baptized and to move against the Mamlūks; but the Ilkhan had died some months previously (9 March 1291).[40] The pope himself died in the following year, without having launched the crusade he longed for.

For all his efforts, the joint operations Arghun desired had failed to come about. Only a contingent of 800 Genoese arrived, whom he employed in 1290 in building ships at Baghdad with a view to harassing Egyptian commerce at the southern approaches to the Red Sea. As

Genoese policy since 1261 had centred on cooperation with the Mamlūks (above, p. 126), this represented a major realignment, provoked, it seems, by Sultan Qalāwūn's crushing defeat of the Armenians in 1285 and by the simultaneous emergence of a Venetian threat to Genoese interests in the Black Sea. In any event, the project came to nothing when the Genoese government backed down and disowned it, making a new treaty with the Egyptian Sultan, and the sailors split into factions and slaughtered each other at Baṣra.[41]

Although Edward I's envoy Geoffrey de Langley visited the court of Arghun's brother and successor, Gaikhatu, in 1292,[42] neither Gaikhatu (1291–5) nor his cousin, Baidu (1295), is known to have sent an embassy to the West, and contact with Europe was resumed only under Arghun's son Ghazan (1295–1304). Ghazan, paradoxically, was a Muslim convert, having been induced to profess Islam by the prominent amir Nawrūz, to whom he owed his enthronement. Encouraged by the in-fighting among the Mamlūk élite, and goaded also by Egyptian campaigns against Lesser Armenia and by the sultan's support for a disaffected Mongol noyan in Anatolia, he first took the field in the winter of 1299. In the Ḥimṣ region on 22 December, the Ilkhanid army inflicted a crushing defeat on the Mamlūk Sultan, Qalāwūn's young son al-Nāṣir Muḥammad, who fled back to Egypt. The whole of Syria and Palestine, evacuated by their Mamlūk garrisons, lay open to the Mongols, who entered Damascus on 31 December. But Ghazan's forces in turn withdrew early in February 1300, leaving the country to be reoccupied by the Mamlūks. In a second campaign, beginning in the late autumn, the Ilkhan reached the vicinity of Aleppo by January 1301. But on this occasion the winter rains rendered the terrain unsuitable for an engagement, and the Mongol van under Qutlugh Shāh ventured no further than Qinnasrīn. Extricating his troops from the mud with some difficulty, Ghazan retired into Mesopotamia in February.[43] His third and last Syrian campaign, in the spring of 1303, was a disaster. The Ilkhan himself retired soon after crossing the Euphrates, leaving his army under the command of Qutlugh Shāh, who was defeated by the Mamlūks at Marj al-Ṣuffār, near Damascus, on 20 April.[44] In the autumn, while preparing a fourth invasion of Syria in order to avenge this humiliation, Ghazan fell ill. He died on 11 May 1304.

Whereas Abaqa had committed himself to an attack upon the Mamlūks only after several attempts to secure Western cooperation, Aḥmad had sought the Mamlūks' submission without any recourse to the West at all, and Arghun had persisted in the quest for a Western alliance right down to his death without ever taking the field against the mutual enemy, Ghazan adopted a different policy. He had already embarked upon his first invasion of Syria when he entered into contact with the Latin world, sending embassies to King Henry II of Cyprus and to Pope Boniface VIII. The king of Cyprus made some attempt to mount his own operations in harmony with the Mongols' movements. In the autumn of 1299 he sent two galleys to occupy Botrun and to rebuild the fortress of Nephin, while a larger fleet of sixteen galleys made what amounted to no more than a demonstration at Rosetta and outside the harbour of Alexandria before touching briefly at Acre, Tortosa and Maraclea. More serious was the expedition led in 1300, in response to another appeal from Ghazan, by the king's brother Amaury, titular lord of Tyre and Constable of the kingdom of Jerusalem – the first attempt since 1291 to restore the Latin settlement in the Holy Land and to coordinate military activity with the Ilkhan's forces. The Templar Master, Jacques de Molay, seems to have been particularly enthusiastic about the campaign.[45] At the head of a combined force of Cypriot knights and Templars, Amaury occupied the small island of Ruad (Arwād), off the coast near Tortosa; but Qutlugh Shāh's army did not appear and the Cypriots withdrew. In 1302, after a brave resistance, the small Templar garrison on Ruad was compelled to surrender to a Mamlūk army.[46]

We can infer that Ghazan was losing patience with Western rulers from his letters to Henry II of Cyprus in 1299 and to Edward I in 1302, both of which mention repeated failures to respond to Ilkhanid requests for military action.[47] And it was several years before his brother Öljeitü (1304–16) embarked on aggression against the Mamlūks. Almost at the beginning of his reign, he received a joint embassy from the qaghan, Qubilai's successor Temür, and the Mongol rulers of Central Asia, informing him that they had made peace (above, p. 127). Shortly afterwards, Toqto'a, the khan of the Golden Horde, sent envoys to the Ilkhan to indicate his adhesion to this general settlement. Öljeitü was quick to pass on the good news to the pope and the kings of France and England. His letter of 1305 to Philip IV of France, which alone has survived, announces the end of the hostilities that had raged for forty-five years (i.e. since the death of Möngke in 1259) and the recognition of Temür as sovereign throughout the Mongol world; the Ilkhan also expressed his satisfaction that Western European rulers were likewise now at peace and hinted at the consequences for their mutual enemies.[48] Pope Clement V was sufficiently encouraged to speak in 1307 of the Ilkhan's restitution of the Holy Land to Western hands as a strong possibility;[49] and a second embassy from Öljeitü in that year cheered him 'like spiritual sustenance'.[50] But the Ilkhan's primary concern, it appears, was to deal with opponents nearer home, in northern and eastern Persia,[51] and it was not until 1312 that he attacked the Mamlūk empire, investing the fortress of al-Raḥba on the Euphrates; this campaign too was a failure.[52] Whether the last known embassy from Öljeitü to a Western monarch (Edward II) in 1313[53] was connected with it, we do not know; but in 1320 his young son and successor, Abū Saʿīd, made peace with the Mamlūks.

In many respects, the Mongol occupation of Syria in 1299–1300 represents the high water-mark of Mongol–Latin relations. However ephemeral, it caused a great stir in Western Europe. There was nothing particularly novel about this. Rumour had already made the 'king of the Tartars' in person attend the Second Council of Lyons, where he was allegedly baptized and received a crown at the pope's hands.[54] Over-optimistic reports had likewise circulated in connection with Baybars' invasion of Anatolia and his death in 1277 (supposedly at the hands of the Mongols, who had then reconquered the Holy Land),[55] and with Möngke Temür's campaign in 1281, when a cluster of chroniclers registered the sultan's defeat and capture and the Mongol reoccupation of Antioch *ad annum* 1282.[56] A story had surfaced in *c.*1280 about the birth to the Ilkhan's wife, a daughter of the Armenian king, of a monstrous child, which at baptism became completely normal, whereupon the Ilkhan converted to Christianity and went on to wrest Jerusalem from the Mamlūks; in 1299–1300 this tale would be repeated in connection with both Ghazan and his brother.[57] In 1288 and 1293 even more fantastic reports are found in the Hagnaby chronicle regarding Mongol victories over the Muslims: on the latter occasion (when rumour may have grossly distorted an Egyptian retreat following the capture of Qalʿat al-Rūm in 1292) the Sultan's brother was allegedly captured and Muslim prisoners forwarded as gifts to various Western monarchs, including Edward I.[58]

Ghazan's operations in 1300, however, achieved the greatest prominence of all, in part because, as Dr Sylvia Schein has indicated, they coincided with the Jubilee Year proclaimed in Rome by Pope Boniface VIII.[59] The Mongol campaign rapidly acquired the flavour of an epoch-making Christian triumph in which the Ilkhan appeared to fulfil the role that had long awaited Prester John. Word spread that the kings of 'Greece', Armenia and Cyprus had recovered the Holy Sepulchre with Tartar assistance.[60] The false rumour retailed by the doge of Venice,[61] that the Egyptian Sultan had been taken prisoner, seems swiftly to have turned into a report of his death. The Ilkhan had also signalled his capture of Jerusalem by being baptized.[62] It was even reported that following the occupation of Damascus and the return of the entire Holy Land to the Christians he had gone on to conquer Egypt.[63] Some of these tales may have been spread by Frankish prisoners who had escaped from Mamlūk captivity. The Armenian king was supposed to have sent a message to Henry of Cyprus with a knight who had been liberated at the fall of Damascus; and the alleged release by the Sultan of a knight who had been a prisoner in Cairo for several years was turned into the work of the victorious Ilkhan.[64] Other stories may have originated with Latin merchants who had been in Alexandria and Damietta and who declared that Ghazan was certain to conquer Egypt.[65] The Mongol liberation of the Holy City, of course, furnished the opportunity for Pope Boniface and Western chroniclers alike to castigate Latin princes by claiming that God had preferred a pagan ruler as His instrument.[66]

The mechanics of Ilkhanid diplomacy

In their successive attempts to secure assistance from the Latin world, the Ilkhans took care to select personnel who would elicit the confidence of Western rulers and to impart a Christian complexion to their overtures. Rabban Ṣawma was only one of a number of Nestorian clerics who were included in Ilkhanid embassies: Solomon Arkaun (Mong. *erke'ün*, 'priest'), the bearer of Abaqa's letter in 1268; 'Īsā *kelemechi* ('the interpreter') in 1285; and 'Saabedin', who accompanied Ṣawma in 1287 and who later visited Europe as part of the embassies of 1290 and 1302.[67] But expatriate Franks also played an increasingly important role. The scribe and Latin interpreter (*notarius... ac interpretes Latinorum*) Richardus, who accompanied the possibly abortive embassy of 1262, and who subsequently drafted the report of Abaqa's envoys to the Council of Lyons in 1274, may be identical with the Latin secretary whose temporary absence from court in 1267 had prevented the Ilkhan's chancery from writing in Latin.[68] In the last twenty years, Genoese were especially prominent, like Tommaso *Banchrinus* ('the Banker') de' Anfossi, who accompanied Arghun's first mission in 1285, or Buscarello de' Ghisolfi, a member of the Ilkhan's guard, who brought Arghun's letters of 1289 and 1290 and Ghazan's of 1302. Öljeitü's letter in 1307 was delivered by Tommaso Ugi of Siena, his *ildüchi* ('sword-bearer').[69] Ghazan additionally sought to instil confidence into Western rulers by appointing to oversee the Christian resettlement of the Holy Land his Pisan agent Isolo ('Chol') da Anastasio, who carried his letter to King Henry of Cyprus and of whose existence the Papacy had been aware for several years, since Nicholas IV had addressed a letter to him as far back as 1289.[70]

During Abaqa's reign, Ilkhanid embassies to Latin rulers were accompanied by the envoys of other Christian princes. His missions to Jaime I of Aragon in 1268–9, to Louis IX in 1269, and to the crusading army in

Tunisia in 1270 arrived with the ambassadors of the Byzantine Emperor Michael VIII Palaeologus, whose illegitimate daughter was one of his wives;[71] and his envoys joined the Council of Lyons not long after the delegation from Byzantium. Michael, who in the late 1260s had been a client, rather, of the Golden Horde, was a recent addition to the Ilkhan's orbit. Clearly it was hoped, by associating him with the Mongol mission, to enhance its Christian credentials; though the Emperor, threatened by the plans of Louis's brother, Charles of Anjou, to restore the Latin empire of Constantinople, had his own reasons for courting the French king.[72] In 1277 the Vassallis brought, in addition to Abaqa's own letters, one for Edward I from the Ilkhan's protégé, King Leo III of Lesser Armenia.[73] Although Armenian envoys are not known to have travelled west with Mongol embassies on subsequent occasions, the Armenian kings remained in contact with Edward, addressing five appeals to him between the fall of Acre in 1291 and 1307.[74] Since the elimination of Latin Syria, Lesser Armenia, as Pope Boniface VIII reminded the English and French monarchs in 1298,[75] was in the front line of Mamlūk attack.

The Ilkhans' letters emphasized their good will towards the West and their favourable treatment of their eastern Christian subjects. At the very outset, in 1262, Hülegü described himself as 'kindly exalter of the Christian faith'.[76] Abaqa too claimed to love Christians and to protect their churches,[77] while Arghun, in his first letter in 1285, drew attention to Chinggis Khan's edict which, he alleged, exempted Christians from tribute and made them 'free' in his territory.[78] The Ilkhan was here guilty of precisely the same dissimulation as Eljigidei had been in 1248 (see pp. 99–100), since the exemption, firstly, applied not to Christians at large but only to priests and monks, and in the second place covered not just Christian holy men but also the 'religious class' within every other confessional group. The return of Jerusalem and the rest of the Holy Land to Latin rule also formed part of these Ilkhanid initiatives. Hülegü informed Louis IX that he had handed over the Holy City to the Franks already, during the brief Mongol occupation in 1260 (although, as we have seen, this is nowhere indicated in any of the Muslim sources, still less in the Frankish appeals for help to the West), and the claim was reiterated in 1274 by Abaqa's envoys, who also alleged that he and his father had regularly freed Christian slaves and had them escorted to the Mediterranean coast.[79] Arghun offered to restore Jerusalem to the Franks after its recovery from the Muslims.[80]

Sometimes a pope's reply reveals that Mongol ambassadors sometimes amplified the Ilkhans' letters by word of mouth, stressing their master's sympathy towards Christianity and his desire for baptism.[81] We are fortunate to have a written copy of Buscarello's oral statements to Philip IV in 1289. Buscarello assured the French king that, after the Mamlūk capture of Tripoli earlier that year, the Ilkhan had angrily executed four of his principal Muslim amirs for expressing pleasure at the news.[82] Abaqa's envoys at Lyons had reminded their audience that Hülegü's chief wife Doquz Khatun – like Sorqaqtani, a Nestorian and a princess of the former royal dynasty of the Kereyid – was a daughter of Prester John. They further alleged that Hülegü had revealed to David of Ashby many intimate secrets of his heart, which he had never vouchsafed to anyone else, regarding his conversion to the faith and his baptism.[83]

Information of this kind could serve to distract the popes from the ambassadors' diplomatic goals. In 1277 the Vassallis asked John XXI to send suitable personnel to instruct both the Ilkhan and his uncle, the qaghan Qubilai, in the faith, so that the sole result of their embassy was a Franciscan mission to China, bearing letters from the pope's successor, Nicholas III, in which Abaqa and Qubilai were invited to embrace Christianity and the Ilkhan was requested to use his good offices with his uncle.[84] Arghun's envoys in 1289 told Nicholas IV of Qubilai's attachment to the Roman Church and the Latins in general, and (allegedly on the Ilkhan's behalf) urged the pope to despatch Western *religiosi* to China[85] – thus prompting in turn the mission of the Franciscan John of Montecorvino. We shall see later (chapter 10) that such requests sprang not so much from any specific leanings towards Christianity as from a desire to acquire new techniques from religious 'specialists' of every kind. During Arghun's reign, the impression that the Ilkhan was on the verge of becoming a Christian was conveyed in such a way as to set in motion a diplomatic *pas-de-deux*. Rabban Ṣawma having assured the Cardinals in 1287 that the Ilkhan wished to be baptized in Jerusalem once it was taken from the Mamlūks, Nicholas IV urged Arghun to be baptized at once: this was not a step to be postponed, and God would be more likely to smile upon the campaign.[86] Arghun effectively disowned Ṣawma's claim by querying whether baptism was necessary at all.[87]

The Ilkhans and Christianity

We have already examined the religious attitudes of members of the Mongol imperial dynasty, and the alleged Christian leanings of the Ilkhans in particular will now be considered. As we have seen (pp. 97–102), from a relatively early date stories had been current in eastern Christian circles about the conversion of prominent Mongols – stories which, with the possible exception of those surrounding Sartaq, were always overblown. Similar hopes were centred on Hülegü, especially in the wake of the sack of Baghdad, where the Christian population appears to have escaped the general massacre.[88] From c.1262, at least, it looks as if the Ilkhan encouraged such sentiments and promoted a widespread myth of his own Christian leanings. In much the same way as he spoke to David of Ashby about his sympathy towards Christianity, so he appeared to open his heart to the Armenian historian Vardan Arewelc'i, who visited his court in 1264. Hülegü told Vardan and his companions that he had been a Christian since birth, through the influence of his mother Sorqaqtani. Vardan assured him that Christian clergy 'by land and by sea' were praying for him. But by his death in the following year, we are told, Hülegü had been led astray by the 'astrologers and priests of some images called Šakmonia', i.e. Buddhist lamas (toyins). The Buddhists even persuaded him to build an idol-temple, where he prayed and where 'they worked whatever witchcraft they desired upon him'.[89] Vardan's contemporary, Kirakos Ganjakec'i (d. c.1272), says that Doquz Khatun tried in vain to wean him away from his dependence on the toyins.[90] Hülegü was the last Ilkhan, in fact, to be buried according to traditional Mongol custom, whereby even live female slaves were interred alongside their master to serve him in the afterlife.[91] It was perhaps for this reason that when, according to Vardan, Doquz Khatun asked the clergy to celebrate Mass for her husband's soul, the Armenians refused, though the Nestorians complied.[92]

Such expectations of imminent conversion did not, apparently, attach themselves to Hülegü's successors; but apart from Aḥmad-Tegüder they gained a reputation for being at least well-disposed towards Christians. Arghun, in particular, is described by the Dominican missionary Ricoldo of Montecroce as 'a man given to the worst villainy, but for all that a friend to the Christians'.[93] Yet once again, as in the case of earlier Mongol sovereigns, the evidence is equivocal. Arghun is known to have made the pilgrimage to the shrine of Abū Yazīd at Bisṭām to pray for victory over his uncle; he frequented the company of Buddhist lamas, and died from the effects of a life-prolonging drug which one of them had prescribed.[94] Rashīd al-Dīn charges Baidu with excessive favour towards Christians, and Hayton apostrophizes him as 'a good Christian'; but more than one Christian source depicts even Baidu as a late convert to Islam.[95] Ramón Lull claimed that during his stay in the Near East he had heard rumours of Ghazan's desire for a more certain knowledge of Christianity; he had become a Muslim, allegedly, when this knowledge was not forthcoming.[96] This is surely wishful thinking, but it echoes earlier reports of conversations between Christians and Ghazan's great-grandfather Hülegü. Öljeitü had a rather more 'turbulent conversion history': in the course of a comparatively short career, he was believed to be in turn a Nestorian, a Buddhist, a Sunnī Muslim of first the Hanafī and then the Shāfiʿī school, and a Twelver Shīʿī, before possibly reverting to Sunnism.[97] Apart from his baptism in 1291, which brought an overjoyed response from Nicholas IV (the prince was named Nicholas in the pope's honour),[98] all these tergiversations apparently passed unnoticed in the Latin West. No envoy from either Ghazan or Öljeitü informed the pope or any Western monarch that his master was a Muslim convert, with the ludicrous result that in 1307 Edward II wrote to Öljeitü applauding his intention of 'extirpating the abominable sect of Mahomet'.[99]

In any case, the careers of Ghazan and Öljeitü demonstrate that personal religious preferences exerted little or no influence on foreign policy. Hayton, it is true, admits that Ghazan had been converted to Islam and that in the opening months of his reign he had treated Christians with great harshness; but this is blamed on unnamed Muslim amirs who had since been executed for treason, i.e. Nawrūz and his brothers, who had fallen from grace in 1297. And Hayton further proceeds to make out that Ghazan thereupon became pro-Christian and anti-Muslim.[100] This is both to misrepresent the Ilkhan's personal stance and to confuse domestic with foreign affairs. The repressive measures taken against Christians in the first two years of the reign were indeed discontinued in 1297; but Ghazan's attitude towards territorial aggrandisement at the expense of the Mamlūks was consistent throughout the reign and was essentially that of his predecessors.[101] Öljeitü's harsh proceedings against his Christian subjects[102] did not prevent him from making war on Egypt.

We have seen how the Franks of Palestine are accused of failing to profit from a Mongol alliance in 1260 and opting instead for their own ruin by assisting the Mamlūks. A more extravagant development of this idea sees a Mongol–Frankish *entente* as administering such a blow to Islam that Christianity would have become, and remained, the dominant religion in the Near East. That the alliance did not come to pass, the argument tends to run, was the responsibility of the West. This verdict is already foreshadowed in works dating from the fourteenth century, largely under the influence of Hayton of Gorigos. Thus Jean Le Long (d. 1383) suggests, in his reworking of Hayton's treatise, that the Tartars for the most part jettisoned Christianity and embraced Islam because, while they themselves were engaged in a titanic struggle with the Muslims, the Christians of the West did little or nothing to aid the Holy Land.[103] A glance at the history of the Golden Horde hardly inspires confidence in such an analysis. There the Mongol khans adopted, not the faith of their Rus' tributaries, but Islam – the religion of the wealthiest and culturally most advanced of their territories, Khwārazm. The

Ilkhans, governing an overwhelmingly Muslim population in the still more prosperous regions of Persia and Iraq, were bound in any eventuality to tread the same path.

The Mongols and Syria: ecological considerations

Evidently the Latin Christians' domination of the sea-lanes provided a major incentive for Hülegü and his successors to court their assistance. There was, however, another powerful reason for the Ilkhans' desire to enlist Western military aid – the nature of the terrain. Although Professor Amitai argues that the logistical difficulties of operating in Syria may have been overstated,[104] the region clearly afforded only limited pasturage for a large army of Inner Asian horsemen. Muslim writers had commented on the relative dearth of grassland in Syria in 1216, a few years before the advent of the Mongols, when the citizens of Aleppo stood in fear of an invasion by the nomadic Qipchāq cavalry of the Khwārazmshāh.[105] Hülegü himself alluded to the problem in his letter of 1262 to Louis IX: he had withdrawn the bulk of his army from Syria two years earlier, not merely because the season required the Mongols to move to cooler uplands but additionally because both provisions and grass were almost exhausted.[106] It was surely for this reason that, whereas in an earlier period both in Eastern Europe and in northern China the Mongols' horses were quite unused to fodder and depended on grass,[107] during Ghazan's campaigns the Ilkhan's army was accompanied by great numbers of camels carrying fodder for its mounts.[108] Even so, the 'Templar of Tyre' ascribed Ghazan's slow pursuit of the defeated Mamlūk army in 1299 to a shortage of grass which weakened his horses.[109] The hot season, moreover, presented further problems. We have seen (p. 74) how in northern Syria in the summer of 1244 the Mongols' horses suffered damage to their hooves; and both Fidenzio of Padua and Hayton mention that the strength of the summer heats prevented the Mongols from staying in the country.[110] It seems that the region threw up more hazards for the Ilkhans' cavalry than merely a dearth of pasturage.

In China, a country likewise ill-suited to nomadic cavalry operations, the Mongols circumvented the difficulty by employing Chinese infantry in large numbers. In Syria and Palestine, they proposed to overcome a parallel problem by recruiting an ally whose forces were seemingly more at home in the terrain. The horses which were offered to Western crusading leaders – 20, or 30,000 to Philip IV by Buscarello in 1289, 100,000 to the same ruler by Öljeitü's envoys in 1305, and (possibly) 200,000 to Clement V by Tommaso *ildüchi* two years later – were presumably not the Inner Asian ponies that the Mongols themselves traditionally rode, but larger animals capable of carrying a heavily-mailed Frankish knight.[111]

The problems of collaboration

Why, then, did the diplomatic contacts between the Ilkhanate and the West fail to lead anywhere? In the first place, the very circumstance that impelled the Ilkhans to solicit Latin help – conflict within the Mongol world – also undermined their efforts to avenge 'Ayn Jālūt. In 1270 the Chaghadayid khan Baraq, supported by Qaidu, had devastated Abaqa's eastern provinces, an outrage to which the Ilkhan retaliated in 1273–4 with the sack of Bukhārā.[112] During Ghazan's second Syrian campaign in 1300–1, Chaghadayid forces exploited his absence by ravaging Fārs (though Hayton exaggerates when he claims that invasions by Qaidu's forces compelled the Ilkhan to withdraw from Syria on two occasions).[113] And to the north, the khans of the Golden Horde were ever alert for opportunities to attack Ilkhanid Azerbaijan. In blaming Abaqa's past failure to move against Egypt on the fact that Mongol Persia was surrounded by mighty enemies,[114] his representatives in 1274 were not altogether disingenuous.

It is important, secondly, that we do not consider the Latin response in isolation from the difficulties that beset the crusade to the east in the latter half of the thirteenth century. To judge from the attention vouchsafed by successive popes, Western monarchs and publicists, we may well doubt whether enthusiasm for the crusade to the Holy Land really was in a state of decline.[115] But antipathies and conflicts within the Latin world, particularly after the Sicilian Vespers and the onset of the Angevin–Aragonese war in 1282–3, could only serve to distract precisely those rulers to whom the Franks in Syria and Palestine – and of course the Ilkhans – addressed their appeals. This was brought vividly home to Rabban Ṣawma in 1287, when from the roof of his lodgings in Naples he witnessed the Aragonese trouncing the Angevin fleet in the bay below.[116] Contemporary opinion within Europe saw the persistence of strife among Western monarchs as a major impediment to crusading efforts. Marino Sanudo would link the loss of the Holy Land with the 'War of the Vespers', and Edward I, in his letter of 1303 to Ghazan, was doubtless sincere in blaming such conflict for the failure of Latin princes to launch the desired attack on Egypt during the past three decades.[117]

Even without such domestic distractions, the promotion of a major expedition to the east, representing the combined efforts of Latin Christian powers, was a time-consuming and cumbersome business.[118] This Edward I implicitly acknowledged in 1275 by his inability to tell Abaqa when the crusade would arrive in Palestine because the pope had not yet set a date, and in 1290 by his promise to inform Arghun once the pope consented to his departure.[119] The pope for his part had to tell the Ilkhan in 1267 that he would notify him of the timetable once he had consulted the various monarchs.[120] When Arghun in the summer of 1289 appointed a rendezvous with the French king outside Damascus in the early months of 1291, he envisaged a schedule to which no major crusade could have adhered. In some measure this was due to the increasingly intricate nature of crusade planning. By the Second Council of Lyons, crusade strategists were coming to believe – and Pope Gregory X accepted – that successful operations against the Mamlūks raised logistical problems which had not been anticipated at the time of Louis IX's invasion of Egypt in 1249–50 and which demanded more complex solutions than anyone had hitherto envisaged. From around the time of the Council, the crusade came to be viewed as a two-stage affair, involving a preliminary, small-scale expedition (*passagium particulare*) designed to secure a bridgehead, with a second and much larger force (*passagium generale*) following it, perhaps two years or so later.[121] Not all the authors of crusade treatises over the next few decades made use of this distinction in their works; but there is little doubt that the popes, and the Latin monarchs who were now seen as indispensable to the crusade against the Mamlūks, embraced it. One problem, therefore, lay in deciding at which juncture cooperation with the Ilkhan's forces should occur. Another was the lack of any Frankish base on the Syro-Palestinian coast after 1291. Had the Mamlūk Sultans left a single bastion in Christian hands – wrote a well-informed observer some decades later – the Latins would have been able to inflict considerable damage on the Muslims at the time of Ghazan's incursions.[122]

The ultimate aims of Ilkhanid policy

On the other hand, we should not lose sight of the character of Mongol diplomacy, as noticed in chapter 2. It is striking that court historians in Mongol Iran – Rashīd al-Dīn and Waṣṣāf – make no mention whatsoever of the Ilkhans' dealings with the Christian West; in fact, they barely allude to the Franks at all.[123] We might have ascribed these authors' silence to nothing more than the proverbial lack of Muslim interest in Frankish affairs throughout the Middle Ages and beyond. But such unconcern would be especially surprising in Rashīd al-Dīn, whose name appears on the seal on the reverse of Ghazan's letter of 1302 to Boniface VIII[124] and whose *Jāmiʿ al-tawārīkh* included a section on the history of the Franks. An alternative explanation is that Ilkhanid contacts with the

Latin world were simply embarrassing. Writing for a prince who styled himself 'Sovereign of Islam' (*Pādishāh-i Islām*), neither Rashīd al-Dīn nor Waṣṣāf could afford to draw attention to negotiations which were designed to obtain infidel assistance against Ghazan's coreligionists in the Mamlūk Sultanate.[125]

Another reason for the reticence of these Ilkhanid authors is that the overtures to still independent Latin rulers appeared to entail the abandonment of the Mongol programme of world-conquest – or, rather, they required its suspension. In this context we should recall the conciliatory tone adopted by the embassy of the Mongol general Eljigidei to Louis IX, then in Cyprus on crusade: as we saw (p. 99), this nurtured the idea that important figures in the Mongol high command, including the qaghan Güyüg, were Christians. Eljigidei's cordial letter, wishing Louis well in his expedition and containing no demand for submission, differed markedly in tone from the ultimatums hitherto sent to Western potentates by the Mongols; though his intercession on behalf of eastern Christians required the Franks, in effect, to comply with one of the *yasas* promulgated by Chinggis Khan.[126] It was the oral statements of Eljigidei's envoys, however, which gave rise to the most optimistic assessments. They told Louis that their master planned an attack on Baghdad in the summer of 1249, and asked him to direct his crusade against Egypt so that the Caliph would receive no help from that quarter. Yet for all the excitement generated in Western Europe, some in the crusading army expected no good to come of the exchange of embassies;[127] and at least one contemporary observer was sufficiently astute to see that the Mongols were apprehensive about the crusaders' objective and that their purpose was to deflect the crusade away from territories, like Aleppo and Anatolia, which lay within their current sphere of operations (and towards Egypt, in which they had no immediate interest). In his view, the assurances about the Christian faith of leading Mongols were merely part of the ploy.[128] Eljigidei's overture to King Louis was surely an example of the conciliatory tactics by which the Mongols aimed to disarm the suspicions of distant rulers, and to which Carpini had drawn attention (above, p. 47).

All that had changed since 1248, in terms of purpose, was that the Latins were required to attack the same enemy, rather than to distract a different one. No more than Eljigidei had the Ilkhans discarded the Mongol programme of world-conquest.[129] Here the attitudes of Ilkhanid court historians are informative. It is noteworthy that Rashīd al-Dīn, when mentioning foreign nations, still thinks it worthwhile to say whether or not they are 'in rebellion' against the qaghan.[130] Waṣṣāf, describing the Central Asian Mongols' overture to the qaghan Temür in 1304 which brought about a general peace in the Mongol world, has them list the external enemies on whom the various khanates should concentrate their attention, rather than engaging in internecine wars. Those confronting the Ilkhanate are said to comprise North Africa (*Maghrib*), Egypt, Rūm (probably the Byzantine empire) and, most significantly, the Franks.[131] The Ilkhans' own sentiments are harder to elicit. Ghazan's boast in 1300 to the Mamlūk Sultan that the contingents ranged under his banner now included Franks[132] was doubtless part of normal diplomatic swagger. But the surviving letters which Hülegü's successors addressed to Western princes generally employ the language of command rather than entreaty.[133] And that the old claims had still not been jettisoned even in relation to Latin Christendom also emerges from two of these letters – the one dating from the very beginning of negotiations with the Franks, the other from their final phase.

Though no ultimatum of the kind to which the West had grown accustomed, Hülegü's letter of 1262 nevertheless contains a sonorous restatement of Heaven's mandate to Chinggis Khan. It begins with the opening words of the Epistle to the Hebrews (i, 1):

God, Who at sundry times and in divers manners spoke in time past unto the fathers by the Prophets, hath in these last days spoken unto . . .

But Hülegü then continues:

our grandfather Chinggis Khan through Teb-Tenggeri, his kinsman, disclosing to him events which would miraculously come to pass in future times and declaring to him through the said Teb-Tenggeri: 'I am the one all-powerful God in the highest, and I have set thee to be lord over the nations and kingdoms and to be ruler of the whole earth, to root out and to pull down, to destroy and to throw down, to build and to plant . . .'.[134]

With yet another (slightly adapted) quotation here, from Jeremiah (i, 10), the Ilkhanid chancery was engaged in an audacious bid to recruit Judaeo-Christian Holy Writ into the service of the Mongol world-order, by embedding within it the transmission of Heaven's mandate to Chinggis Khan through the shaman Teb-Tenggeri. Possibly this was the work of Christian scribes, though it was almost certainly done with the Ilkhan's own sanction. Hülegü then devotes considerable space to a catalogue of rulers who had resisted the Mongols and had accordingly been crushed. The proposal, at the end of the letter, to attack Egypt by sea is somewhat peremptory,[135] as if Hülegü is well aware that Louis has at no time gone through the proper formalities of submission but, given the urgency of the situation, is not minded to press the point.

In the second letter, written to Louis's grandson Philip IV in 1304, the Ilkhan Öljeitü announces the general reconciliation of the Mongol khanates in vivid language with his statement that their postal relay-stations were now linked up once more 'from Nangiyas [i.e. Southern China], where the sun rises, as far as the Ocean Sea [*talu dalai*]'. This last phrase long puzzled commentators, but – as Professor Sinor demonstrated – it denotes, not the Mediterranean (which might have been described as one border of the Ilkhanate), but the Ocean which was believed to surround the Eurasian land-mass. Öljeitü's phrasing, in other words, indicated that Mongol dominion extended to the world's very limits. This was not a notion of reality to which any Catholic ruler could assent; and the phrase was tactfully omitted from the two Italian translations made at Philip's court by the Europeans who accompanied the embassy. Edward II of England, too, was led to believe that the letter described Mongol rule as extending to 'the frontiers of Outremer'.[136]

Here, then, we have two letters, whose dates frame the era of Ilkhanid–Western negotiations and in which the idea of world-domination, though muted, is still in evidence. More importantly, the second letter was written in the immediate aftermath of the reunion of the Mongol empire, when at least one court historian in the Ilkhanate includes the Franks among the powers whom Hülegü's descendants would now be free to attack. We cannot exclude the strong possibility that, had the newly-restored Mongol unity persisted, and had a successful alliance with the West achieved the destruction of the Mamlūk Sultanate, the Ilkhans would then have turned upon the Franks of Cyprus and Greece. There would have been nothing particularly incongruous about this, of course: it was by such methods that the Mongol empire had grown under Chinggis Khan and his immediate successors.

Reservations in the West

One last reason for the unproductive character of Western–Ilkhanid diplomacy was surely the reserve with which the Mongols were viewed in Western Europe. This was in part, of course, the legacy of the ultimatums and of the devastation perpetrated in 1241–2. And it is worth noting that there appears to have been a considerable delay before writers in the Latin West became aware of the disintegration of the unitary Mongol empire and learned to distinguish between the Ilkhans' policy, which involved working with the Catholic powers, and that of their cousins and enemies in the Golden Horde, who continued to menace Poland and Hungary. Matthew Paris, as we saw, had heard of the Mongols' internal crisis of 1250–1. Thereafter, however, we find remarkably little reference in Latin sources to the strife among Mongol princes. The author of the *Flores historiarum* knew only that the Mongols of Persia had been prevented from joining the Lord Edward in 1271 because of losses owing to 'internal oppression'.[137] Roger Bacon seems to have been the sole author who was aware of these internecine conflicts, which he attributed to the divisions of territory among the princes made by Möngke and which for him explained the Mongols' failure to conquer the world.[138] Otherwise Polo and Hayton are the earliest writers frankly to describe the wars among the khanates.[139] On occasions, Ilkhanid envoys alluded to their master's embarrassments, as Abaqa's envoys did in 1274. But it was incumbent upon them to broach the subject delicately: a forthright exposition of the difficulties might further have discouraged Western rulers from relying upon a Mongol alliance.

It is true that two early fourteenth-century writers, reflecting on the Mongol pretensions of a bygone age, drew highly positive conclusions. In their eyes, Eljigidei's embassy in 1248–9 had marked the onset of friendlier relations; the Mongols had surely demonstrated their sincerity in courting the West by the fact that their overtures had begun when their mood was actually more uncompromising than now.[140] But a greater number of Western voices recalled Mongol excesses. The Mongols believed that they were the true masters of the world, wrote Ricoldo of Montecroce in the 1290s, and that the whole world had been created for their enjoyment and was under an obligation to present them with tribute and gifts; and his verdict was echoed a few years later by the author of the *Memoria Terrae Sanctae*.[141] Even Hayton – the most enthusiastic advocate of Western–Mongol collaboration, as we saw (p. 120) – felt bound to say that the Ilkhan would not readily listen to European advice and to enter a *caveat* that the two allied armies should follow different routes, because if they came into close proximity the crusaders would find Mongol bluster and arrogance intolerable.[142] Perhaps a similar perception had prompted the author of the *Via ad Terram Sanctam*, which betrays more sympathy than the *Memoria* for the Mongol alliance, to recommend that the two forces avoid contact.[143]

On balance, if the numerous recovery treatises composed from c.1290 onwards are an index of public opinion in the Latin West, the idea of active cooperation with the Mongols found little favour there. The space allowed to the Ilkhan's forces in these projects is relatively limited; in some they are not referred to at all. Where they are mentioned, the author is usually readier to notice their eagerness for collaboration than to recommend it himself. Fidenzio of Padua, writing in 1290/1, had been an exception. He took it almost for granted that if crusaders followed the land route across Anatolia the Turks would not dare to harass them out of deference to the Ilkhan's authority; and he believed that the Ilkhan would send aid to a crusading army in Syria.[144] But most authors took a less sanguine view. It is possibly significant that the Mongol alliance does not figure in the crusading proposals drawn up in 1306 by the Masters of the Temple and the Hospital, Jacques de Molay and Foulques de Villaret, at the request of Pope Clement V. These and other authors writing after 1303, of course, may have omitted the Mongols from their calculations on the grounds that the Ilkhan's forces had so far made a poor showing against the Egyptian army. Already a treatise by King Charles II of Naples (c.1295) had alluded to the Mongols only in the context of their three defeats at Mamlūk hands;[145] and in 1318 Guillaume Adam would ascribe the Mongols' victories over the Egyptians purely to the Georgian troops who fought alongside them.[146]

Although a slightly later memorandum drafted by Villaret (1307/8) does envisage a Mongol invasion of Syria, there is no explicit reference to cooperation. Rather, he proposes a Frankish assault on Egypt when the Mamlūk army is distracted by the Mongol attack, and deprecates the course of action adopted in 1300, when the Franks had made for Tortosa, Egypt had been left unharmed, and the Mamlūks (he alleges) had rejoiced.[147] This same strategy of attacking the Nile delta would be advocated by King Henry II of Cyprus in c.1311, on the grounds that the Sultan's troops in Syria would not dare move to Egypt's assistance, for fear of a Mongol invasion.[148] The role that these two documents reserve for the Ilkhan's army is an ancillary – indeed, almost an incidental – one. More underlies this, perhaps, than attachment to the long-established 'Egyptian strategy', and objections to a landing in Lesser Armenia on the grounds that the climate was insalubrious or that the Armenians were useless allies. Such objections were certainly voiced.[149] But it is noteworthy that one Western writer, describing the Hospitallers' refusal to participate in the Ruad expedition, makes them complain of being deceived by Ghazan's promises in the past;[150] and doubtless Molay, Villaret and King Henry were all disillusioned by the Mongols' failure to move to the rescue of the Frankish bridgehead in 1300–1[151] – this despite the fact that the Mongol general Qutlugh Shāh ascribed the retreat on that occasion to Ghazan's illness, as would Hayton later.[152]

But the Latins' reticence very probably sprang from another consideration also. It was fuelled, that is, by the Mongol tactics of subterfuge with which the West had been familiar for some decades. When Pope Alexander IV wrote in 1260 of the Mongol practice of simulating friendship towards Christians,[153] he must have had in mind the disappointing outcome of Eljigidei's overture to Louis IX. His view certainly found literary corroboration in the accounts of Carpini and Simon of Saint-Quentin, which Vincent of Beauvais's encyclopaedia had done so much to publicize. Small wonder that suspicions were voiced about Ilkhanid intentions. Alfonso X of Castile is supposed to have warned King Jaime of Aragon against the Mongols in 1269: they were, he said, 'a very deceitful people'.[154] 'God knows whether they were genuine envoys or spies', wrote Guillaume de Nangis of the Vassalli brothers in 1276.[155] Scepticism was expressed, too, about the motives of the Mongol envoys baptized at Lyons in 1274.[156] The Latins had to weigh the possibility that Arghun's alleged eagerness for baptism might be just another attempt to dupe them. And even authors who favoured cooperation with the Ilkhan's forces – Fidenzio and the later writer Garcia d'Ayerve, bishop of Leon (1319) – were under no misapprehensions about the impulse behind Ilkhanid diplomacy: the Mongols simply hated the Mamlūks more than the Franks.[157] The evidence reviewed above suggests that these suspicions were justified.

Notes

1. These are conveniently surveyed in J.A. Boyle, 'The Ilkhans of Persia and the princes of Europe', *CAJ* 20 (1976), pp. 25–40; in Schmieder, *Europa*, pp. 89–109 (with a calendar of embassies at pp. 328–35); and in Richard, 'D'Älğigidäi à Ġazan', pp. 62–6. For England, see L. Lockhart, 'The relations between Edward I and Edward II of England and the Mongol Īl-khāns of Persia', *Iran* 6 (1968), pp. 23–31; for Naples, G.M. Monti, 'I tre primi sovrani angioini e i Tartari', in his *Da Carlo I a Roberto di Angiò. Ricerche e documenti* (Trani, 1936), pp. 17–36.
2. Reuven Amitai, 'Mamlūk espionage among Mongols and Franks', in B.Z. Kedar and A.L. Udovich, eds, *The Medieval Levant. Studies in Memory of Eliyahu Ashtor (1914–1984)* (Haifa, 1988 = *AAS* 22), pp. 173–81.
3. Reuven Amitai-Preiss, 'Mongol imperial ideology and the Ilkhanid war against the Mamluks', in Amitai-Preiss and Morgan, *Mongol Empire*, pp. 57–72. See also Amitai-Preiss, *Mongols and Mamluks*, pp. 230–3.
4. Charles J. Halperin, 'The Kipchak connection: the Ilkhans, the Mamluks and Ayn Jalut', *BSOAS* 63 (2000), pp. 229–45. For another reference to the Cumans as the Mongols' slaves, see *Novgorodskaia pervaia letopis'*, p. 265 (tr. Michell and Forbes, *Chronicle of Novgorod*, p. 65).
5. Spuler, *Die Mongolen in Iran*, p. 119; other examples in Amitai-Preiss, *Mongols and Mamluks*, pp. 151–2.
6. Meyvaert, p. 259.
7. Ibn Wāṣil, IV, p. 248, describes how he himself headed an embassy from Baybars to Manfred in 659 H./1261; tr. in Francesco Gabrieli, *Arab Historians of the Crusades* (London, 1969), p. 277. See further Reuven Amitai-Preiss, 'Mamluk perceptions of the Mongol-Frankish rapprochement', *MHR* 7 (1992), pp. 50–65 (here p. 53).
8. Lupprian, p. 230 (no. 44) = Burkhard Roberg, 'Die Tartaren auf dem 2. Konzil von Lyon 1274', *Annuarium Historiae Conciliorum* 5 (1973), pp. 241–302 (here p. 300). Schmieder, *Europa*, p. 328, n.1, offers a different

reconstruction, identifying Hülegü's embassy with that which brought an ultimatum to Paris in 1262 (above, pp. 123–4).

9. Lupprian, pp. 217, 219 (no. 41). This letter, the two halves of which had become separated (*Reg. Urbain IV*, nos. 2868, 2814 *bis*), was redated to 1264 by Jean Richard, 'Le début des relations entre la papauté et les Mongols de Perse', *JA* 237 (1949), pp. 291–7, repr. in Richard, *Les relations*; but cf. n.11 below.

10. *LTC*, IV, pp. 71–4 (no. 4866, 6 Sept. 1263).

11. Lupprian, p. 219 (no. 41): the *terminus a quo* is here given as 23 May 1263, when Guillaume received legatine status (*Reg. Urbain IV*, no. 241). He reached Palestine on 25 Sept. 1263: 'L'estoire de Eracles empereur', *RHCOcc.*, II, p. 447. See Yves Dossat, 'Guillaume II, évêque d'Agen, patriarche de Jérusalem', in *Islam et chrétiens du Midi (XIIe–XIVe s.)*, Cahiers de Fanjeaux 18 (Toulouse, 1983), pp. 77–114 (here pp. 91–2).

12. *LTC*, IV, pp. 81–3 (no. 4893).

13. *Reg. Urbain IV*, III, p. 419 (no. 867, 18 July 1264); cf. ibid., p. 421 (no. 869, 17 July 1264) = *LTC*, IV, p. 103 (no. 4949).

14. *Reg. Clem. IV*, I, p. 392 (no. 1131, 1 Oct. 1266): *contra Saracenos adjuvantibus Tartaris* (though the context is a *reductio ad absurdum*: whether they or other non-Latin allies against the Muslims were thereby entitled to the indulgence). Eudes de Châteauroux had come to see the Mongols as potential allies by the late 1260s: Ruotsala, *Europeans and Mongols*, p. 67.

15. Möhring, *Der Weltkaiser*, pp. 200–1 and nn.158–9, corrects Schmieder, *Europa*, pp. 269–71, who assumed that the work was eastern Christian in origin and dated the French version to *c*.1260.

16. For what follows, see Richard, 'La croisade de 1270'.

17. Lupprian, pp. 221–2 (no. 42). Eugène Card. Tisserant, 'Une lettre de l'Ilkhan de Perse Abaga adressée au Pape Clément IV', *Le Muséon* 59 (1946), pp. 547–56 (here pp. 555–6) = Lupprian, pp. 224–5 (no. 43). Abel-Rémusat, 'Mémoires', *MAIBL* 7 (1824), p. 339, was surely wrong to assume that Abaqa's pleasure at Manfred's overthrow was insincere: the Sicilian king had obstructed the Ilkhan's diplomatic traffic with the West.

18. Ibn 'Abd al-Ẓāhir, *Rawḍ*, p. 308. 'Cronica S. Petri Erfordensis moderna', p. 405; hence 'Cronica Reinhardsbrunnensis', *MGHS*, XXX, p. 625. Amitai-Preiss, 'Mamluk perceptions', p. 57.

19. 'Cronica S. Petri Erfordensis moderna', p. 405; hence 'Cronica Reinhardsbrunnensis', p. 625. *Annali Genovesi di Caffaro e de' suoi continuatori dal MXCIX al MCCXCII*, ed. L.P. Belgrano *et al.*, Fonti per la Storia d'Italia, 5 vols (Rome, 1890–1929), IV, p. 115.

20. 'Chronicon Hanoniense quod dicitur Balduini Avennensis', *MGHS*, XXV, p. 463; text also in *RHGF*, XXI, p. 177. 'Chronique de Primat, traduite par Jean de Vignay', *RHGF*, XXIII, p. 73, is briefer. Reinhold Röhricht, 'Der Kreuzzug des Königs Jacob I. von Aragonien', *MIOG* 11 (1890), pp. 372–95 (here pp. 373–4).

21. Arnold FitzThedmar, *Liber de antiquis legibus*, ed. Thomas Stapleton, CS, 3rd series, 25 (London, 1846), p. 143. Lockhart, p. 24. Amitai-Preiss, *Mongols and Mamluks*, pp. 98–9, 125–6. For the crusade, see generally Michael Prestwich, *Edward I* (London, 1988), pp. 74–9.

22. Lupprian, pp. 229–30 (no. 44) = Roberg, pp. 298–300. Jean Richard, 'Chrétiens et Mongols au Concile: la Papauté et les Mongols de Perse dans la seconde moitié du XIIIe siècle', in *1274 année charnière*, pp. 31–44 (here pp. 37–8), repr. in Richard, *Croisés*.
23. A. Scheler, 'Notices et extraits de deux manuscrits français de la Bibliothèque Royale de Turin', *Le Bibliophile Belge*, 3e série, 2 (1867), pp. 1–33 (here pp. 26–8). Brunel, 'David d'Ashby', pp. 40–3. Richard, 'Chrétiens et Mongols', p. 38.
24. *Chronica Johannis de Oxenedes*, p. 250. *Chronicle of Bury St. Edmunds*, p. 63.
25. Edward I to Abaqa, 26 Jan. 1275, in Rymer, I:2, p. 144.
26. Monti, pp. 22–3. Rudolf Hiestand and Hans Eberhard Mayer, 'Ein Bischof von Odense bei den Tataren', *DA* 58 (2002), pp. 219–27 (esp. pp. 224–6).
27. Amitai-Preiss, *Mongols and Mamluks*, pp. 183–4, 185.
28. *Chronica Johannis de Oxenedes*, p. 256. Bartholomew Cotton (d. *c.*1298), *Historia Anglicana*, ed. H.R. Luard, RS (London, 1859), p. 160. *Chronicle of Bury St. Edmunds*, p. 72. Schmieder, *Europa*, p. 330.
29. Geoffrey, bishop of Hebron, to Edward I, 5 Oct. 1280, in Rymer, I:2, p. 189.
30. *Chronicle of Bury St. Edmunds*, pp. 76–7. Bartholomew Cotton, *Historia Anglicana*, p. 163, and *Chronica Johannis de Oxenedes*, p. 260, both date the battle in 1282. 'Annales Colmarienses maiores', *MGHS*, XVII, p. 208, mentions a victory by the Hospitallers alone. 'Gestes des Chiprois', p. 786, §407 (tr. Crawford, p. 78), says merely that Syrian Frankish knights took part.
31. On the campaign of 1281, see Amitai-Preiss, *Mongols and Mamluks*, pp. 187–201. For Mongol dealings with the Syrian Franks, see the letter of the Hospitaller Joseph de Cancy to Edward I, 31 March 1282, in *CGOH*, III, p. 425 (no. 3782), and tr. in William Basevi Sanders, *A Crusader's Letter from 'the Holy Land' [1281]*, PPTS 5:5 (London, 1888), p. 7; Nicholas of Lorgne, Master of the Hospital, to Edward I, 5 March 1282, in Ch. Kohler and C.-V. Langlois, 'Lettres inédites sur les croisades (1275–1307)', *BEC* 52 (1891), pp. 46–63 (here pp. 60–1 = *CGOH*, III, pp. 423–4, no. 3781).
32. Adel Allouche, 'Tegüder's ultimatum to Qalawun', *IJMES* 22 (1990), pp. 437–46. Reuven Amitai, 'The conversion of Tegüder Ilkhan to Islam', *JSAI* 25 (2001), pp. 15–43 (here pp. 30–3).
33. Lupprian, p. 246 (no. 49).
34. Salimbene, *Cronica*, II, pp. 811–12 (Reichert, *Begegnungen*, pp. 129–30, wrongly takes this passage to refer to the war in Mongolia between Qubilai and his Christian kinsman Nayan); hence 'Alberti Milioli notarii Regini Liber de temporibus', *MGHS*, XXXI, p. 565.
35. So according to the biography of Mar Yahballaha III, tr. E.A. Wallis Budge, *The Monks of Kûblâi Khân Emperor of China* (London, 1928), p. 165.
36. For these relations, see J.-B. Chabot, 'Notes sur les relations du roi Argoun avec l'Occident', *ROL* 2 (1894), pp. 566–629; Lupprian, pp. 77–82.
37. Lupprian, pp. 245–6 (no. 49). 'Sham', strictly speaking, denoted Syria and Palestine.
38. This mission is described in Budge, *Monks of Kûblâi Khân*, pp. 165–97. See further Morris Rossabi, *Voyager from Xanadu. Rabban Sauma and the First Journey from China to the West* (New York, 1992), pp. 99–171.

39. Antoine Mostaert and Francis Woodman Cleaves, eds, *Les lettres de 1289 et 1305 des ilkhan Aṛγun et Öljeitü à Philippe le Bel*, Harvard-Yenching Institute, Scripta Mongolica Monograph Series 1 (Cambridge, MA, 1962), p. 18.

40. Rymer, I:3, p. 76; cf. Lupprian, pp. 270–1, 275–6 (nos. 60, 62). Boyle, 'Ilkhans of Persia', p. 36. See generally Franco Cardini, 'Niccolò IV e la Crociata', in E. Menestò, ed., *Niccolò IV: un pontificato tra Oriente ed Occidente. Atti del Convegno internazionale di studi in occasione del VII centenario del pontificato di Niccolò IV, Ascoli-Piceno 14–17 dicembre 1989* (Spoleto, 1991), pp. 135–55.

41. Jean Richard, 'European voyages in the Indian Ocean and Caspian Sea (12th–15th centuries)', *Iran* 6 (1968), pp. 45–52 (here p. 49); idem, 'Les navigations des Occidentaux sur l'Océan Indien et la mer Caspienne (XIIᵉ–XVᵉ siècles)', in M. Mollat du Jourdain, ed., *Sociétés et compagnies de commerce en Orient* (Paris, 1970), pp. 353–63 (here pp. 359–60), and repr. in Richard, *Orient et Occident*. For a persuasive reconstruction of the context and significance of the incident, see Virgil Ciocîltan, 'Genoa's challenge to Egypt (1287–1290)', *RRH* 32 (1993), pp. 283–307; also Şerban Papacostea, 'Gênes, Venise et la mer Noire à la fin du XIIIᵉ siècle', *RRH* 29 (1990), pp. 211–36.

42. D.O. Morgan, 'Langley, Geoffrey of', *Dictionary of National Biography*, new edn.

43. On these campaigns, see Boyle, 'Dynastic and political history', pp. 387–9; Irwin, *Middle East*, pp. 99–101. For the first, see also Reuven Amitai, 'Whither the Ilkhanid army? Ghazan's first campaign into Syria (1299–1300)', in Di Cosmo, *Warfare*, pp. 221–64 (here pp. 225–53).

44. Boyle, 'Dynastic and political history', pp. 393–4.

45. Jacques de Molay to Jaime II of Aragon, 8 Nov. [1301], in Heinrich Finke, ed., *Papsttum und Untergang des Templerordens*, 3 vols (Münster, 1907), II. *Quellen*, pp. 3–4 (no. 3).

46. For a full account of these various operations, see Peter W. Edbury, *The Kingdom of Cyprus and the Crusades, 1191–1374* (Cambridge, 1991), pp. 104–6.

47. Henry of Cyprus: Andrea Dandolo, 'Chronica', appendix I, p. 396; *Chronique d'Amadi*, ed. René de Mas Latrie (Paris, 1891), p. 234. Edward I: Rymer, I:4, p. 22.

48. Mostaert and Cleaves, *Les lettres*, pp. 56–7. Öljeitü would have learned of the Peace of Caltabellotta (1302) from Edward I's letter of 12 March 1303 to Ghazan: Rymer, I:4, p. 22. It is referred to also in Rashīd al-Dīn's history of the Franks (1303/4): Karl Jahn, ed., *Die Frankengeschichte des Rašīd ad-Dīn*, 2nd edn (Vienna, 1977), facsimile of Persian text, Topkapı Sarayı, Istanbul, ms. Hazine 1653, fol. 421r (German tr. pp. 92–3); cf. also the reference to peace in Hayton, iv, 12, Fr. text p. 236, Latin text p. 350.

49. *Reg. Clem. V*, III, p. 168 (no. 2269). For his crusading policy, see Sophia Menache, *Clement V* (Cambridge, 1998), pp. 101–19.

50. *Reg. Clem. V*, III, pp. 331–2 (no. 3549, 1 March 1308). For the Mongol embassy's passage through Limoges in 1307, see 'Anonymi S. Martialis chronicon ad annum MCCCXX continuatum', *RHGF*, XXI, p. 811.

51. See Jackson, *Delhi Sultanate*, p. 225.

52. Boyle, 'Dynastic and political history', p. 403.

53. PRO, E/101, 375/8, cited by Robert Sabatino Lopez, 'Nuove luci sugli Italiani in estremo oriente prima di Colombo', in his *Su e giù*, pp. 81-135 (here p. 87, n.11).
54. Soranzo, p. 222 and n.1.
55. William Rishanger, 'Chronica', in Henry Thomas Riley, ed., *Willelmi Rishanger, quondam monachi S. Albani, et quorundam anonymorum Chronica et Annales*, RS (London, 1865), p. 89 (*ad annum* 1276). *Chronica Johannis de Oxenedes*, p. 250.
56. Ibid., p. 260. Bartholomew Cotton, *Historia Anglicana*, p. 163. *Chronicle of Bury St. Edmunds*, pp. 76-7. Cf. also 'Continuatio Praedicatorum Vindobon-ensium' (*c*.1283), *MGHS*, IX, p. 731. Antioch: 'Annales Colmarienses maiores', p. 209. A few sources, however, were aware that the Mamlūks rallied and repulsed the Mongols: 'Continuatio Pontificum Romana' (soon after 1287), *MGHS*, XXII, p. 478; Guillaume de Nangis, 'Gesta Philippi tertii Francorum regis'/'Vie de Philippe III', *RHGF*, XX, Latin text p. 520, Fr. text p. 521, and 'Chronicon', ibid., p. 568.
57. 1280: 'Annales S. Rudberti Salisburgenses', p. 806; greatly embellished by Ottokar of Styria, *Reimchronik*, vv. 19097-19351, ed. Seemüller, I, pp. 253-6. 1299: William Rishanger, 'Chronica', pp. 189-90; *Flores historiarum*, III, pp. 107-8. 1300: Heinrich Finke, ed., *Acta Aragonensia*, 3 vols (Berlin and Leipzig, 1908-22), II, p. 747 (no. 464: the editor dates this letter to 1307). Cf. Giovanni Villani, *Cronica*, viii, 35, ed. Francesco Gherardi Dragomanni, 4 vols, Collezione di storici e cronisti italiani editi ed inediti 1-4 (Firenze, 1844), II, pp. 36-7 (no date, and putting Ghazan at the centre of the story).
58. Hagnaby chronicle, BL Cotton ms. Vespasian B XI, fos. 32v, 34v. The prisoners are said to have reached Edward's court *circa festum assumptionis beate Marie*, i.e. 15 Aug. 1293. For the Qal'at al-Rūm campaign, see Boyle, 'Dynastic and political history', p. 373.
59. For what follows, see Sylvia Schein, '*Gesta Dei per Mongolos* 1300: the genesis of a non-event', *EHR* 94 (1979), pp. 805-19.
60. 'Hermanni Altahensis continuatio tertia', *MGHS*, XXIV, p. 56.
61. Andrea Dandolo, 'Chronica', p. 397. 'Martini continuationes Anglicae Fratrum Minorum', *MGHS*, XXIV, p. 258.
62. 'Annales Weissenaugienses brevissimi', *MGHS*, XXX, p. 724.
63. 'Annales Frisacenses', p. 67. 'Gesta Boemundi archiepiscopi Treverensis', *MGHS*, XXIV, p. 483. Schein, '*Gesta Dei*', pp. 806, 814. A letter of Jacopo di Ferrara, 14 Feb. 1300, in the Hagnaby chronicle, fo. 49r, says merely that the Tartars intend to go on to Egypt.
64. J.W. Willis Bund, ed., *Episcopal Registers, Diocese of Worcester. Register of Bishop Godfrey Giffard, September 23rd, 1268, to August 15th, 1301*, 2 vols (Oxford, 1902), II, p. 500 (*ad annum* 1298). Rishanger, 'Annales regis Edwardi Primi', in Riley, *Willelmi Rishanger*, pp. 443, 444. *Annales Caesarienses*, ed. Georg Leidinger, in *Sitzungsberichte der Königlich Bayerischen Akademie der Wissenschaften, philos.-philol. und hist. Klasse* (Munich, 1910), p. 36. Sylvia Schein, *Fideles Crucis. The Papacy, the West, and the recovery of the Holy Land 1274-1314* (Oxford, 1991), p. 167.
65. 'Gestes des Chiprois', p. 847, §608 (tr. Crawford, p. 154).

66. 'Gesta Boemundi', pp. 481–2. Schein, 'Gesta Dei', p. 816.
67. Solomon: Tisserant, p. 556 = Lupprian, p. 225 (no. 43). 'Saabedin': ibid., p. 248 (no. 50); Rymer, I:3, p. 76; Hieronymus Golubovich, 'Epistola syriaca Dionysii episcopi Taurisiensis ad Bonifatium VIII (1302)', *AFH* 18 (1925), pp. 351–5. See also Richard, 'D'Älğigidäi à Ġazan', p. 64. *Erke'ün*: Gerhard Doerfer, *Türkische und mongolische Elemente im Neupersischen*, 4 vols (Wiesbaden, 1963–75), I, pp. 123–5.
68. Lupprian, p. 221 (no. 42).
69. Jacques Paviot, 'Buscarello de' Ghisolfi marchand génois intermédiaire entre la Perse mongole et la Chrétienté latine (fin du XIIIme–début du XIVme siècles)', in *Storia dei Genovesi*, XI (Genova, 1991), pp. 107–17. Michel Balard, 'Sur les traces de Buscarello de' Ghisolfi', in Balard *et al.*, *Dei gesta*, pp. 71–8. Tommaso de' Anfossi: Luciano Petech, 'Les marchands italiens dans l'empire mongol', in his *Selected Papers on Asian History*, Serie Orientale Roma 60 (Rome, 1988), pp. 161–86 (here pp. 174–5); this is an updated version of an article in *JA* 250 (1962). Tommaso Ugi: ibid., pp. 181–2, and *Reg. Clem. V*, III, pp. 331–2 (no. 3549).
70. *Chronique d'Amadi*, p. 236. Jean Richard, 'Isol le Pisan: un aventurier franc gouverneur d'une province mongole?', *CAJ* 14 (1970), pp. 186–94, repr. in Richard, *Orient et Occident*.
71. Aragon: Jaime I, *Llibre dels fets*, §482, pp. 337–8. Paris: 'Cronica S. Petri Erfordensis moderna', p. 405 (hence 'Cronica Reinhardsbrunnensis', p. 625); *Annali Genovesi*, IV, p. 115. Tunis: 'Chronicon Hanoniense', p. 463 (= *RHGF*, XXI, p. 177). 'Chronique de Primat', p. 73, does not suggest that the Greeks and Mongols formed part of the same embassy in 1270.
72. Louis Bréhier, 'Une ambassade byzantine au camp de saint Louis devant Tunis (août 1270)', in *Mélanges offerts à M. Nicolas Iorga par ses amis de France et des pays de langue française* (Paris, 1933), pp. 139–46.
73. Kohler and Langlois, 'Lettres inédites', p. 56.
74. Simon Lloyd, *English Society and the Crusade 1216–1307* (Oxford, 1988), pp. 27, 251–2, 255. A letter from Het'um II to Edward on the fall of Acre (1291) appears in Bartholomew Cotton, *Historia Anglicana*, pp. 219–23; it is preserved also in BL Royal ms. 12 D XI, fo. 15v (with Edward's reply at fos. 16v–17), and in Lambeth Palace Library ms. 221, fo. 225v.
75. Rymer, I:3, p. 204. Georges Digard *et al.*, eds, *Les registres de Boniface VIII*, 4 vols (Paris, 1884–1939), II, col. 174 (no. 2654).
76. Meyvaert, p. 253.
77. Tisserant, p. 556 = Lupprian, p. 224 (no. 43). Lupprian, p. 230 (no. 44) = Roberg, p. 300.
78. Lupprian, p. 246 (no. 49).
79. Meyvaert, p. 258. Lupprian, p. 229 (no. 44) = Roberg, p. 299.
80. Mostaert and Cleaves, *Les lettres*, p. 18.
81. Lupprian, pp. 221, 248 (nos. 42, 50).
82. Chabot, p. 611.
83. Lupprian, p. 229 (no. 44) = Roberg, pp. 299–300.
84. Lupprian, pp. 234–6 (no. 46), 238–41 (no. 47).
85. Ibid., p. 256 (no. 54).

86. Ibid., pp. 253–4 (no. 53).

87. Ibid., p. 266 (no. 57).

88. For more detail, see Peter Jackson, 'Hülegü Khan and the Christians: the making of a myth', in Jonathan Phillips and Peter Edbury, eds, *The Experience of Crusading*, II. *Defining the Crusader Kingdom* (Cambridge, 2003), pp. 196–213; more generally, idem, 'The Mongols and the faith of the conquered', in Reuven Amitai and Michal Biran, eds, *Mongols, Turks and Others: Eurasian Nomads and the Sedentary World* (Leiden, 2005), and chap. 10 below.

89. Vardan Arewelc'i, *Hawak'umn patmut'ean*, tr. Robert W. Thomson, 'The historical compilation of Vardan Arewelc'i', *Dumbarton Oaks Popers* 34 (1989), pp. 125–226 (here pp. 220–1).

90. Kirakos Ganjakec'i, pp. 333–4. For Hülegü and the Buddhists, see Samuel N. Grupper, 'The Buddhist sanctuary-vihāra of Labnasagut and the Il-qan Hülegü: an overview of Il-qanid Buddhism and related matters', *AEMA* 13 (2004), pp. 5–77.

91. Waṣṣāf, p. 52. Morgan, *Mongols*, p. 158.

92. Vardan Arewelc'i, p. 222. Spuler, *Die Mongolen in Iran*, p. 177.

93. Ricoldo of Montecroce, *Liber peregrinationis*, ed. J.C.M. Laurent in *Peregrinatores medii aevi quatuor*, 2nd edn (Leipzig, 1873), p. 121: *homo pessimus in omni scelere, amicus tamen Christianorum*. Cf. also 'Gestes des Chiprois', p. 843, §591 (tr. Crawford, p. 149).

94. Rashīd al-Dīn, II, p. 1137 (tr. Thackston, III, p. 554). P. Jackson, 'Arḡūn Khan', *Enc.Ir.*

95. Rashīd al-Dīn, tr. Thackston, III, p. 622 (not in Rawshan and Mūsawī edn). Hayton, iii, 37–8, Fr. text pp. 189–90, Latin text p. 315. Brosset, *Histoire de la Siounie*, I, p. 260. Continuator of Bar Hebraeus, tr. Budge, *Chronography*, p. 505.

96. Ramón Lull, 'De fine' (1305), i, 5, in Alois Madre, ed., *Raimundi Lulli opera Latina*, IX, CCCM 35 (Turnhout, 1981), p. 267.

97. Judith Pfeiffer, 'Conversion versions: Sultan Öljeytü's conversion to Shi'ism (709/1309) in Muslim narrative sources', *MS* 22 (1999), pp. 35–67 (esp. pp. 36–7, 43).

98. Lupprian, pp. 272–3 (no. 61).

99. Rymer, I:4, pp. 100–1.

100. Hayton, iii, 39, Fr. text p. 191, Latin text p. 316. The version of events in 'Gestes des Chiprois', p. 844, §§593–4 (tr. Crawford, p. 150), is very similar.

101. For Ghazan's shifting religious policies, see Jean Aubin, *Émirs mongols et vizirs persans dans les remous de l'acculturation*, Studia Iranica, cahier 15 (Paris, 1995), pp. 61–6.

102. David Bundy, 'The Syriac and Armenian Christian responses to the Islamification of the Mongols', in John Victor Tolan, ed., *Medieval Christian Perceptions of Islam: A Book of Essays* (New York and London, 1996), pp. 33–53 (here pp. 40–1).

103. 'Iohannis Longi Chronica S. Bertini', p. 850.

104. Amitai-Preiss, *Mongols and Mamluks*, pp. 225–9, arguing against Smith, ''Ayn Jālūt', pp. 328–44.

105. Cahen, ''Abdallaṭīf al-Baghdādī, portraitiste', p. 118 (tr. in Cahen, ''Abdallaṭīf al-Baghdādī et les Khwārizmiens', p. 153); text in al-Dhahabī, *Ta'rīkh al-Islām 611–620*, p. 367. Morgan, 'Mongols in Syria', p. 234.

106. Meyvaert, p. 258.

107. Sinor, 'Horse and pasture', pp. 177–9.

108. Morgan, 'Mongols in Syria', p. 233. Amitai, 'Whither the Ilkhanid army?', pp. 229–30.

109. 'Gestes des Chiprois', p. 847, §609 (tr. Crawford, p. 154).

110. Fidenzio of Padua, 'Liber recuperationis Terrae Sanctae', in *BBTS*, II, p. 53. Hayton, iii, 41, and iv, 21, Fr. text pp. 198, 245, Latin text pp. 320, 357; hence Marino Sanudo, *Liber secretorum*, II:ii, 2, p. 37 (adding a dearth of grass). See also Amitai-Preiss, *Mongols and Mamluks*, p. 229, and 'Whither the Ilkhanid army?', p. 259.

111. 1289: Chabot, p. 611. 1305/7: *Reg. Clem. V*, III, p. 332 (no. 3549), has 200,000; but John Burgundi to Jaime II of Aragon, 26 June 1307, in Finke, *Papsttum*, II, p. 38 (no. 25), shows that only 100,000 of these were meant for the crusaders; the rest would be carrying Mongol warriors. See further Amitai, 'Whither the Ilkhanid army?', pp. 253–4.

112. Spuler, *Die Mongolen in Iran*, pp. 61–3.

113. 1300: Rashīd al-Dīn, II, p. 1109, with *Abaqa Khān*, but two mss. read *Pādishāh-i Islām*, i.e. Ghazan (tr. Thackston, III, p. 540); Hayton, iii, 41, Fr. text p. 196, Latin text p. 319 (both with 'Baido'). 1303: ibid., iii, 42, Latin text p. 321, variant reading of mss. D, E and F (the main text, like the French, p. 200, reads 'Baydo'). Marino Sanudo, *Liber secretorum*, III:xiii, 8, p. 240, mentions only the attack of 1300, and reads 'Caydo'.

114. Lupprian, p. 230 (no. 44).

115. As proposed, e.g., by Schmieder, *Europa*, pp. 104, 109. For the contrary view, see Elizabeth Siberry, *Criticism of Crusading 1095–1274* (Oxford, 1985).

116. Budge, *Monks of Kúblái Khân*, p. 171.

117. Sanudo to Philip VI of France (1334), in Kunstmann, 'Studien', p. 803. Rymer, I:4, p. 22. For the emphasis on peace 'behind the lines', see Björn Weiler, 'The *Negotium Terrae Sanctae* in the political discourse of Latin Christendom, 1215–1311', *International History Review* 25 (2003), pp. 1–36 (here pp. 1–23). The failure to resettle the Holy Land in 1300 was blamed in part on warfare within Christendom: 'Martini continuationes Anglicae Fratrum Minorum', p. 258. Cf. also Fidenzio of Padua, p. 16.

118. See Lloyd, *English Society*, especially chaps. 1–2.

119. 1275: Rymer, I:2, p. 144. 1290: Chabot, p. 616; *Calendar of Close Rolls. Edward I*, III. *1288–1296* (London, 1904), p. 145.

120. Lupprian, p. 222 (no. 42); and cf. p. 232 (no. 45: 13 March 1275).

121. Norman Housley, *The Later Crusades, 1274–1580. From Lyons to Alcazar* (Oxford, 1992), pp. 12–13.

122. Ibn Faḍl-Allāh al-'Umarī, *Masālik*, partial ed. and tr. M. Amari, 'Al 'Umarî, Condizioni degli Stati cristiani dell'Occidente secondo una relazione di Domenichino Doria da Genova', *Atti della R. Accademia dei Lincei, serie terza, Memorie della classe di scienze morali, storiche e filologiche* 11 (Rome, 1883), pp. 67–103 (Arabic text pp. 102–3, tr. p. 87).

123. Rashīd al-Dīn's 'correspondence' (*mukātibāt*), which does contain references to Mongol–Frankish relations, appears to be an apocryphal collection dating from the 15th century: A.H. Morton, 'The letters of Rashīd al-Dīn: Īlkhānid fact or Timurid fiction?', in Amitai-Preiss and Morgan, *Mongol Empire*, pp. 155–99. For a spirited but unconvincing attempt at rehabilitation, see Abolala Soudavar, 'In defense of Rašid-od-din and his letters', *Studia Iranica* 32 (2003), pp. 77–120.

124. Mostaert and Cleaves, 'Trois documents', pp. 478–81.

125. Morgan, *Mongols*, p. 194, dismisses this hypothesis as 'unduly conspiracy minded'. On Muslim disdain for the Franks, see ibid., pp. 192–4; Bernard Lewis, 'Ifrandja', *Enc.Isl.*²; Boyle, 'Ilkhans of Persia', pp. 25–7; though for an exception, see n.122 above.

126. Richard, 'Ultimatums mongols', pp. 217–18.

127. Guy, a household knight of the viscount of Melun, 1249, in *CM*, VI, p. 161. See also John of Garlande, *De triumphis*, p. 128: *Tartareae gentis rex sacro fonte renasci poscit, sed caveat Gallica turma dolos.*

128. SSQ, pp. 97–8 (= VB, xxxii, 41): some of this may represent parenthetical comment by VB himself.

129. Like Amitai-Preiss, 'Mongol imperial ideology', pp. 62–72, I differ here from Richard, 'Mongols and the Franks', p. 56, and 'D'Älğigidäi à Gazan', p. 67, who believes that Hülegü's successors abandoned this policy.

130. E.g. Hungary: Rashīd al-Dīn, I, p. 667 (tr. Thackston, II, p. 326); Japan and 'Lūchak and Khaynām [Hainan?]': ibid., II, pp. 911–12 (tr. II, p. 446). For Lūchak (Marco Polo's 'Logiak', somewhere in S.E. Asia), see Pelliot, *Notes on Marco Polo*, II, pp. 767–70.

131. Waṣṣāf, p. 454.

132. Baybars al-Manṣūrī, *Zubdat al-fikra*, p. 336.

133. Schmieder, *Europa*, p. 94, n.102.

134. Meyvaert, p. 252. For Teb-Tenggeri, see Ratchnevsky, *Genghis Khan*, pp. 98–101.

135. Meyvaert, pp. 253, 257–8.

136. Mostaert and Cleaves, *Les lettres*, pp. 56, 72–4. Rymer, I:4, p. 93. Denis Sinor, 'The mysterious "Talu Sea" in Öljeitü's letter to Philip the Fair of France', in John G. Hangin and Urgunge Onon, eds, *Analecta Mongolica Dedicated to the Seventieth Birthday of Professor Owen Lattimore*, Mongolia Society Occasional Papers 8 (Bloomington, IN, 1972), pp. 115–21, and repr. in Sinor, *Inner Asia*.

137. *Flores historiarum*, III, p. 29: *intestina tirannide perierunt.* This notice is conceivably just an anachronistic echo of the upheavals of 1251.

138. OM, I, p. 369: *qui regnum divisit istis principibus Tartarorum, qui nunc regnant et discordant ab invicem*; p. 370: *Quae* [i.e. *gens Moal*] *si esset concors . . .*; p. 400: *Nisi enim Dominus . . . permitteret seminari discordias inter eos frequentes, jam totum mundum occupassent.*

139. Antony Leopold, *How to Recover the Holy Land. The Crusade Proposals of the Late Thirteenth and Early Fourteenth Centuries* (Aldershot, 2000), p. 112. Schmieder, *Europa*, p. 89, believes Western observers swiftly came to distinguish the Ilkhans from the Golden Horde khans. Yet they may still not have been fully aware of the hostility between the two powers.

140. Guillaume Adam, 'De modo Sarracenos extirpandi', *RHCDA*, II, p. 535. 'Directorium ad passagium faciendum' (possibly by Raymond Étienne, *c*.1332), ibid., p. 504.
141. Ricoldo, *Liber peregrinationis*, pp. 114–15. *Memoria Terrae Sanctae*, in Kohler, 'Deux projets', p. 447.
142. Hayton, iv, 27, Fr. text p. 251, Latin text p. 361.
143. *Via ad Terram Sanctam*, in Kohler, 'Deux projets', p. 431.
144. Fidenzio of Padua, pp. 51, 57; cf. also ibid., p. 53.
145. G.I. Brătianu, 'Le Conseil du roi Charles', *RHSEE* 19 (1942), pp. 291–361 (here p. 353; and see the editor's comments at pp. 297, 308).
146. Guillaume Adam, 'De modo Sarracenos extirpandi', pp. 534–5.
147. Benjamin Z. Kedar and Sylvia Schein, 'Un projet de «passage particulier» proposé de l'Ordre de l'Hôpital, 1306–1307', *BEC* 137 (1979), pp. 211–26 (here p. 226). This document does not, as the editors claim (ibid., p. 215), envisage 'cooperation' with the Mongols. For the date, see Alain Demurger, 'Les ordres militaires et la croisade au début du XIVe siècle: Quelques remarques sur les traités de croisade de Jacques de Molay et de Foulques de Villaret', in Balard *et al.*, *Dei gesta*, pp. 117–28 (here pp. 124–6).
148. 'Mémoire sur les moyens de reconquérir la Terre Sainte', in Comte Louis de Mas Latrie, *Histoire de l'île de Chypre sous la maison de Lusignan*, 3 vols (Paris, 1852–61), II, p. 124.
149. Climate: ibid., p. 122; Marino Sanudo, *Liber secretorum*, II:ii, 2, p. 37; Jacopo d'Acqui, in A.A. Michieli, 'Il Milione di Marco Polo e un cronista del 1300', *La Geografia* 12 (1924), pp. 153–66 (here p. 161). Armenians: John Critchley, *Marco Polo's Book* (Aldershot, 1992), pp. 69–70. Both: Jacques de Molay, 'Consilium', in Étienne Baluze, ed., *Vitae paparum Avenionensium*, new edn by G. Mollat, 4 vols (Paris, 1914–27), III, pp. 146–7. The *Via ad Terram Sanctam* and the *Memoria* favour a landing in Armenia but draw attention to the summer heat: Kohler, 'Deux projets', pp. 428, 451. See generally A.T. Luttrell, 'The Hospitallers' interventions in Cilician Armenia: 1291–1375', in Boase, *Cilician Kingdom*, pp. 118–44 (here pp. 123–4); and on the 'Egyptian strategy', J.J. Saunders, *Aspects of the Crusades*, 2nd edn (Christchurch, N.Z., 1968), pp. 37–51.
150. 'Excerpta e Memoriali historiarum, auctore Iohanne Parisiensi, sancti Victoris Parisiensis canonico regulari', *RHGF*, XXI, p. 640 (the author d. *c*.1351).
151. Leopold, p. 115.
152. 'Gestes des Chiprois', p. 850, §622 (tr. Crawford, p. 157). Hayton, iii, 41, Fr. text p. 199, Latin text p. 321.
153. Rymer, I:2, p. 60: *simulant se ad Christianos privatae affectionis habere propositum*. The letter is also found in 'Annales monasterii de Burton', p. 497.
154. Jaime I, *Llibre dels fets*, §476, tr. p. 335.
155. Guillaume de Nangis, 'Chronicon', p. 565; see also his 'Gesta Philippi tertii'/ 'Vie de Philippe III', pp. 510/511.
156. 'Chronique de Primat', p. 91.
157. Fidenzio of Padua, p. 57. For Garcia, see Schmieder, *Europa*, p. 113.

chapter 8

FROM CONFRONTATION
TO COEXISTENCE:
THE GOLDEN HORDE

Kingdoms divided

In December 1273 a report by Bishop Bruno of Olmütz (Olomouc), submitted to Pope Gregory X in advance of the Second Council of Lyons, painted a depressing picture of the eastern regions of Latin Europe. Hungary was gravely afflicted by the turbulence of the pagan Cumans. Its queen (Elizabeth, the consort of István V) was a Cuman, and two of her daughters were betrothed to rulers from among the schismatic Rus'. Poland was under constant pressure from the pagan Lithuanians. It was through these territories that the Mongols had mounted attacks in the past, and they would surely do so again. The German princes were united only in their determination to have no master, and were incapable of defending the Christian cause in Europe or the Holy Land.[1]

This last swipe at the Germans might have led Bruno on to the tendency of Latin rulers in general to fight one another rather than unite against the pagan enemy. Poland was progressively fragmented, as the various branches of the Piast dynasty carved Silesia, Mazovia and Kujavia into ever smaller duchies. Only Great and Little Poland seemed exempt from this fissiparous process; but the extinction of their two ruling lines – with the deaths of Bolesław V ('the Chaste') of Cracow in 1279 and of Przemysław II of Great Poland in 1296 – unleashed struggles for the inheritance among their surviving kinsmen. These troubles profited Poland's neighbours, the Teutonic Knights and the margraves of Brandenburg, and encouraged the Bohemian king, Václav II (1278–1305), first to extend his suzerainty over several Polish duchies and then to occupy Cracow and secure his own coronation as king of Poland in 1300. Not until Václav's death, followed by that of his young son Václav III and the extinction of the Přemyslid dynasty in 1306, did Władysław Łokietek ('the Short'), of the Kujavian line, embark in earnest on the slow *rassemblement* of Piast Poland. He was finally crowned king in 1320. It is a measure of the difficulties confronting him that his most urgent priority was not to defend the kingdom against pagan neighbours but to check the expansion of Bohemia under its new sovereign, John of Luxemburg (1310–46), and to recover the city of Danzig (Gdańsk) and the rest of Pomerellia (Pomorze), which had been bequeathed to Przemysław II in 1296 and which the Teutonic Knights had misappropriated in 1308.[2]

Hungary too, as Bruno noticed, had other troubles. Béla IV had again recruited several Cuman bands into his service in 1246, and had secured their allegiance by marrying his son and heir István to the daughter of one of their khans. But from the 1250s he was in conflict with King Ottokar II of Bohemia, who in 1246 had inherited the extensive lands of the Babenberg dukes of Austria; and during the last decade of his reign he was at odds with István, to whom he had granted the royal title and a share of the kingdom. In 1270 Bernard, abbot of Montecassino, recently returned from a mission to the Hungarian court to arrange marriages between two of István V's children and the offspring of Charles of Anjou, king of Sicily, could still comment favourably on Hungarian military strength.[3] But after the brief reign of István V (1270–2) the throne passed to his young son László IV ('the Cuman', 1272–90), whose minority was dominated by civil war between rival baronial families. Although the king provoked the resentment of the Hungarian nobility by his dependence on his mother's often pagan relatives, this did not prevent a Cuman revolt in the early 1280s. Nor did the energy with which he crushed the insurgents dissipate the mounting rumours that he consorted with pagans and had repudiated his wife, Charles of Anjou's daughter Elizabeth (Isabella), in favour of two Cuman concubines. These reports reached Rome through the agency of Lodomer, archbishop of Esztergom, and brought down upon László a series of rebukes from Popes Honorius IV and Nicholas IV, who did not scruple to communicate to other monarchs their fears that Hungary was reverting to paganism.[4]

When, on László IV's murder in 1290, the crown passed to a cousin, András III, rival candidates appeared in the form of Charles Martel, a grandson of Charles I of Anjou and a son of the late king's sister, and Václav II of Bohemia, whose mother was a granddaughter of Béla IV. The Hungarian nobility was divided. Charles Martel adopted the title 'King of Hungary' at once, as after his demise (1295) did his son Charles Robert ('Carobert'); Václav entered the country at the head of an army on András III's death (1301) and assumed the government on his son's behalf. At the beginning of the fourteenth century Václav was styling himself king of Bohemia, Hungary and Poland. His death in 1305, and that of Václav III in 1306, put an end to these grandiose designs; but it was only in 1309 that the Angevin Carobert finally secured the Hungarian crown.

The Curia was well aware of the perils of disunity. As far back as 1247 Carpini had warned that intelligence of Western dissensions would encourage the Mongols to attack, and in a sermon in 1261 Eudes de Châteauroux spoke of Christian disunity opening a path for them.[5] The war between Hungary and Bohemia was a cause for particular concern. In 1254 Innocent IV had expressed anxiety lest the quarrel between Béla and Ottokar might result in the subjection of Christian peoples to pagan rule.[6] Urban IV hoped in 1262 that peace could be preserved between the Hungarian and Bohemian monarchs, in order that the faithful of those parts might be strengthened in their efforts to resist the Mongols.[7] In the previous year, in a letter to Richard of Cornwall, one of the two claimants to the imperial throne, he had lamented the wretched state of Christendom, shaken as it was by conflicts that were 'more instinctual than internal' and assailed from outside by fierce peoples, especially the Tartars.[8]

The Latin world might have counted itself fortunate that after 1261–2 the Golden Horde itself was embroiled in war on its other borders – especially south of the Caucasus, where the territories disputed with the Ilkhans, it has been suggested, were more important to Berke and his successors than were the Rus' lands (or, by extension, Latin Europe).[9] We know less than we should like about the internal history of the Horde or its relations with other Mongol states; but one episode suggests that the rhythm of Mongol activity on the European frontier can be linked in with developments elsewhere. Since Berke's time the khans had refused to recognize the qaghan Qubilai, allying themselves with Qaidu and his confederates. Thus in 1268, when a group of princes operating in Central Asia on Qubilai's behalf mutinied and arrested the qaghan's son Nomoghan, they sent him to the khan of the Golden Horde, Möngke Temür (1267–81). In 1283, however, Möngke Temür's brother and successor, Töde Möngke (1281–7), made his peace with Qubilai, returned his son to him, and acknowledged his supremacy.[10] It may have been this development that prompted the Ilkhan Aḥmad-Tegüder, in his second letter to the Mamlūk Sultan in 1283 (above, pp. 168–9), to refer to the unity of the Mongol princes.[11] The Jochids' *rapprochement* with the Yüan empire and the Ilkhanate did not apparently last many years. But it perhaps gave the Golden Horde additional security in both the south and the east, releasing forces for a more forward policy in Europe; it would thus explain in part the surge of military activity from the mid 1280s – including major attacks on Bulgaria, Hungary and Poland (see below, pp. 203–5) – which has been described as 'the second Tatar-Mongol invasion of Central and South-Eastern Europe'.[12]

Otherwise, the khans followed a more defensive policy. They were on occasions opportunistic, intervening when their Latin neighbours were in difficulties, but it seems that they launched their heaviest attacks when these outside powers had the temerity to encroach upon the Mongol sphere of influence. And divisions within the Mongol world often dictated restraint. This was certainly the case after the rise of the Jochid prince Noghai, a great-nephew of Berke, who forged for himself a virtually autonomous principality in the south-western marches of the Golden Horde's dominions. His position naturally aroused the suspicions of the khan at Sarai. Noghai had cooperated on campaign in Eastern Europe with Möngke Temür's nephew Töle Buqa ('Teleboga' in Latin sources), and was instrumental in his accession as khan (1287–90). But when the two men quarrelled, Noghai assisted Möngke Temür's son Toqto'a to overthrow him in 1290. After Noghai himself took the title of khan from 1296/7, he and Toqto'a (1290–1312) in turn fell out, and another civil war ensued, which ended with Noghai's defeat and death in 1299/1300.[13] Around the same time Toqto'a became embroiled in the politics of the White Horde. This is the name given to the eastern wing of the Jochid *ulus*, located in the steppelands north of the Aral Sea and ruled by the line of Orda, Batu's elder brother. Toqto'a's championship of its khan against a rival who was supported by Qaidu and the Chaghadayids,[14] meant that troops were siphoned off, to participate in the struggle, which might otherwise have been available for campaigns in Hungary and Poland.

Propaganda and posture

In 1273 Bruno of Olmütz saw the Bohemian kingdom as Christendom's sole bulwark against the pagan menace in Eastern Europe.[15] As a subject of King Ottokar, and perhaps also as an advocate of his candidature for the imperial throne, the bishop might have been expected to take this view;[16] but partisanship of this kind was by no means confined to Bohemia. When Ottokar fell in battle against the combined forces of the Emperor-elect Rudolf I and the Hungarians in 1278, it was an Austrian annalist who remarked that even the Tartars had known him as 'the Iron King'.[17]

Yet Ottokar, who so distinguished himself on crusade against the pagan Prussians, is not known ever to have crossed swords with the

Mongols. Under the year 1277, the annals of Niederaltaich describe how, over a period of twenty-four years, he had defended his territories against the incursions of Hungarians, Cumans and Tartars, with strenuous effort and at considerable expense both in money and in the lives of his subjects.[18] This is probably nothing more than second-hand Bohemian propaganda. Although his war with Béla IV in 1260 virtually coincided with the threat of a Mongol attack on Hungary, Ottokar complained to the pope that Béla had attacked him at the head of forces which included pagan Cumans and Mongols, as well as Muslims ('Ishmaelites') and schismatics such as Greeks, Bulgarians and Bosnians.[19] It would become a standard charge against Hungary's rulers, but similar accusations were levelled elsewhere. In much the same way the bishop of Breslau (Wrocław) a few years later would denounce Bolesław the Chaste for entering Silesia at the head of countless thousands of 'Ruthenians, Cumans and Lithuanians'.[20] It was always useful to stigmatize the enemy as one who employed pagans and schismatics. The army which Ottokar himself mustered against the German king in 1276 was rumoured to include infidels – possibly even Mongols.[21]

A later Bohemian chronicler alleged that the Tartar ruler stood in such awe of Ottokar's power that he sent the king rich gifts and addressed him as a beloved brother.[22] Simply another dose of uncritical adulation, perhaps; but it has an authentic ring, if we recall how the Mongols tried to detach more distant states from neighbours whom they were planning to attack. Berke had tried to ensnare Béla in an alliance in 1259 (above, p. 124). Ottokar too is known to have received envoys from the Mongols.[23] The fact that they also despatched an embassy to his son and successor, Václav II, in 1293[24] – a year in which they invaded Poland (below, p. 206) – suggests that the Golden Horde was aware of his hostility towards Władysław Łokietek (as also, no doubt, his candidacy for the Hungarian throne in opposition to András III) and sought his neutrality or his cooperation.

For their part, the Hungarian monarchs from Béla IV onwards had a vested interest in presenting their country as a 'front-line' state burdened with the responsibility of defending the whole of Christendom. Béla sought to exploit this image, of course, during the war with Bohemia, which, he claimed, had rendered his borders more attractive to the Mongols.[25] His amazement in 1247 that the pope permitted Louis IX to leave Europe on crusade when Hungary was under threat (above, p. 104) might have been mere haggling over resources. As Nora Berend has shown, however, the king's aim in promoting the idea that his realm was a bulwark was also to extort from the Curia concessions relating to the church within Hungary.[26] The propaganda campaign seems to have been effective. When the Dominican Master-General, Humbert of Romans, drafted his *Opus tripartitum* for Gregory X in 1273, he observed that the Tartars no longer did Christians any injury except in Hungary[27] – a verdict that scarcely did justice to Poland's experience in 1259. The notion of a kingdom that was perilously exposed to infidel attack was well established by the beginning of the fourteenth century, when Pope Boniface VIII contrasted Hungary's once flourishing condition with its present wretched state.[28]

The posture adopted by Béla IV and István V did not mean that their claims were completely unfounded; but the reality was undoubtedly more complex than either their self-portrayal or the accusations of their enemies. Béla and his son were engaged in the difficult exercise of balancing their role as faithful sons of the Church against a pressing need to appease their new and formidable pagan neighbour. As Alexander IV had done before him, Urban IV strongly tried to discourage them from reaching some kind of diplomatic accommodation with the Golden Horde.[29] But royal charters reveal that papal admonitions were ineffective. Béla is known to have received envoys from the Mongols in 1263/4.[30] In 1270 István rewarded a noble for faithful services that included two missions to the khan with the purpose of deflecting a Mongol attack.[31] The fact that these diplomatic overtures bore fruit makes it likely that Hungary – denied military assistance in the crisis of 1241–2 and during subsequent alarms – opted to protect itself in the 1260s by paying tribute to the Golden Horde. In 1288 the hostile archbishop of Esztergom would accuse László IV of entering into a compact of submission to the Mongols:[32] if indeed the charge was justified, the king was simply following the precedents set by his father and grandfather.

The Mongols and client states

In much of Eastern Europe, the Mongol threat was indirect. Here the Golden Horde could be seen as a malign power drawing into its embrace states that would otherwise have succumbed to Latin pressure and acknowledged Christian overlordship and the primacy of Rome. In the Baltic region, where the Teutonic Knights and the Poles already faced pagan Prussians and Lithuanians in addition to the Mongols,[33] the situation appeared all the more delicate in view of the large numbers of neophytes who needed at all costs to be preserved from a pagan conquest. Occasionally a rumour is transmitted, as in 1263, of an engagement between the Mongols and the Teutonic Knights.[34] But we know little about clashes between the Mongols and the Knights. The chief reason is that on this northerly frontier the Golden Horde acted alongside or through proxies like the Rus' princes or the Lithuanians. Papal bulls that mention simply pagans or schismatics may in fact be referring to local, more traditional enemies, acting at the khan's instigation or bolstered by a Mongol force.

The Prussian chronicles, which begin in the 1320s, provide sparse detail for the earlier period, and some encounters are known to us only from Rus' sources. In 1269, for instance, the 'great *basqaq*' *Amraghan and 'many Tatars' joined the army assembled by Nevskii's brother and successor, Iaroslav of Vladimir-Suzdal', and the Germans were so cowed that they sent gifts to the Mongols and abandoned the region of Narva.[35] The Mongols also lent assistance to Daniil's progeny in Ruthenia, who had been tributary to the Golden Horde since the 1250s, had participated in the Mongol campaign of 1259 against Poland, and continued to engage in periodic hostilities with the Poles on their own account.[36] Thus early in 1281 Leszek the Black of Cracow and Sandomir defeated near Goslicz a Mongol force which had entered his territory in support of Daniil's son Lev I;[37] and in 1302 the army with which Lev's son Iury I failed to raise a Polish siege of Lublin included Lithuanians and Mongols.[38]

The Lithuanians' relations with the Golden Horde are less well documented than those of Rus'. As we saw, their territory had been devastated in 1258/9 (above, p. 123), and they were probably tributary to the khan in the 1260s, when reports reached the Curia that they were in league with the Mongols.[39] This is still more likely to have been the case in the early fourteenth century, as Lithuania began to absorb various principalities in western Rus', such as Polotsk. It is noteworthy that, when in 1323 the Lithuanian Grand Duke Gediminas took Kiev and installed there as prince his brother Fedor, there was no question of discontinuing the principality's tribute to the khan: we find Fedor on campaign a few years later, with a Mongol *basqaq* in his entourage.[40]

Further south, in the Balkans, the situation was similar and Noghai's influence was felt particularly keenly. One of the initial effects of Mongol operations in the 1240s had been temporarily to put a brake on Nicaean Greek aggression against the Latin empire.[41] But the Latins had less reason to be grateful within thirty years, when the Byzantine empire, newly re-established with the capture of Constantinople (1261), lay within the penumbra of Mongol overlordship. The Emperor Michael VIII had endeavoured to maintain friendly relations both with the Ilkhans in Iran and with the Golden Horde. In c.1264, however, Berke sent an army to attack Thrace and secure the release of the exiled Seljük Sultan Kaykā'ūs, whom the Emperor had incarcerated; and from 1273 Michael allied with Noghai, giving him an illegitimate daughter in marriage and using him as a means of putting pressure on Bulgaria when its king menaced the empire's northern frontier in 1273 and 1279.[42] When Michael died in 1282, he had just welcomed in Constantinople a band of Mongol auxiliaries whom Noghai had sent to assist him against the despot of Thessaly; if we can trust the Byzantine chronicler Pachymeres, they mourned the Emperor as wholeheartedly as did his own people.[43]

Thereafter, however, relations between the Mongols of the Pontic steppe and the Byzantine empire cooled markedly. As the result of a major campaign against Bulgaria in 1284/5, Sāqchī (Isaccea), in the Dobrudja region, came under Mongol overlordship and coins were struck there in the khan's name; direct rule was imposed at some point before 1296/7, when the town became the centre of Noghai's new khanate.[44] These developments brought Mongol power uncomfortably closer to Constantinople. There were inroads in 1284/5 and 1297; and although Michael's son and successor, Andronicus II, gave daughters in marriage both to Toqto'a and to his successor Uzbek (1312–41), this did not prevent the latter mounting a series of Mongol attacks on Thrace during the emperor's final years (1320, 1321, 1324). From some point in the late 1330s the Byzantine port of Vicina Macaria in the Danube estuary underwent occupation by the Golden Horde.[45] In 1341, just prior to Uzbek's death, Andronicus III had to send an embassy to deflect a major attack by the khan's forces on Constantinople.[46] For a number of Western commentators writing in the early fourteenth century, before the rise of the Ottoman Turks, the Tartars threatened Byzantium's very survival.[47] Muslim observers formed a similar impression, for a few years later the encyclopaedist Ibn Faḍl-Allāh al-'Umarī was told of the Byzantine Emperor's repeated efforts to appease the khan.[48]

Bulgaria's subjugation by the Mongols in 1242 had proved shortlived. The Hungarians occupied the city of Vidin in the 1260s and brought the Bulgarian kingdom under Hungarian suzerainty; but these gains lapsed early in the minority of the young László IV.[49] A Byzantine chronicler comments that the Mongols were daily raiding Bulgaria in the 1270s.[50] In 1280 its king – George Terter, a noble of Cuman extraction – acknowledged the khan's overlordship and married Noghai's daughter, and the Mongols extended their authority also over the minor dynasts who ruled in Vidin and Branichevo. Serbia too recognized Mongol overlordship in or soon after 1291, and its king had to send his son as a hostage to Noghai's headquarters. When George Terter was expelled by a local boyar in c.1295, the Mongols launched another invasion of Bulgaria. Even Noghai's downfall did not materially affect Mongol influence in the region, since a son of Toqto'a was now stationed in Sāqchī and along the Danube as far as the 'Iron Gate'.[51]

Noghai's fugitive son Cheke, who had briefly made himself master of Bulgaria (1300–1), was captured by George Terter's son Svetoslav and murdered on the orders of Toqto'a; Svetoslav took over and acted as the khan's dutiful subordinate.[52] In 1308 an anonymous survey of south-eastern Europe could accordingly still describe Bulgaria as tributary to the Tartars.[53] Within two decades or so, yet another vehicle of Mongol influence emerged, in the principality of Wallachia. The Vlach prince Basaraba, who bore a Cuman name (though not necessarily himself of Cuman descent), could count on support from the Golden Horde in defying the Hungarian king from at least 1330 onwards.[54]

The Mongol threat to the Latin West down to 1323

In its interventions in each of these areas, the Golden Horde was active on behalf of, or exerting pressure upon, schismatic rulers, and hence constituted an additional obstacle to the ambitions of popes and Western secular princes. But to what extent did the Mongols threaten the security of Latin states themselves? The incidence of Mongol raiding during the first two decades after 1260 is difficult to gauge: as we saw, even when the Tartars are expressly mentioned this does not necessarily indicate operations by the forces of the Golden Horde. Hungary may have suffered a series of raids from the Horde after 1272, since András III's charter of liberties (1291) tells how the Mongols and Cumans had taken advantage of the minority of his predecessor, László IV, to attack the kingdom on frequent occasions.[55] For what it is worth, Rashīd al-Dīn's informants around the turn of the century were likewise under the impression that Noghai had launched repeated inroads into Hungary.[56]

These were probably only minor raids; but the mid-1280s appear to have witnessed a shift in policy, with major attacks upon both Hungary and Poland in succession, which as we saw coincided with advances in the Balkans and should possibly also be viewed against the background of the Golden Horde's relations with other Mongol powers. In Hungary, the dispute between King László and the Church, and subsequently the upheavals caused by the Cuman revolt, furnished new opportunities for the Mongols to exploit, and in the fourteenth century it was believed that they had been summoned by elements among the defeated Cumans who had taken refuge among them.[57] The khan may also have been provoked by King László's action, during the campaign to suppress the Cumans, in leading his forces into what would later become Wallachia – in the sonorous words of his charter, 'beyond the mountains, around the confines and frontiers of the Tartars, which none of our predecessors had penetrated'.[58]

If the Mongol invasion of Hungary at the onset of Lent 1285 was not on the scale of 1241–2, it was nevertheless a major enterprise. It was led by two prominent figures – Noghai and the future khan Töle Buqa – and was accompanied by Lev Daniilovich and others from among their Rus' satellites.[59] Even though the figures given by German annalists smack of hyperbole,[60] the language of Hungarian charters certainly indicates that the numbers involved were considerable.[61] The invaders ravaged as far as the Danube and entered Pest; and László's consort Elizabeth, from the safety of the walls of Buda, witnessed a spirited and effective sally by members of her household.[62] The Mongols may still have been present in the kingdom in June.[63] Although László himself headed an expedition into Transylvania from May to August, he probably did no more than harass their withdrawal;[64] according to a contemporary letter and reports that reached Germany, it was the local troops – Saxons, Vlachs and Székely, the last fighting as light cavalry – who cut off their retreat in Transylvania and inflicted on them a serious reverse.[65] Polish sources allege that the Mongols also suffered considerably from famine and some kind of epidemic.[66]

In 1287 Noghai and Töle Buqa invaded Poland; according to the fourteenth-century *Vita* of St Kynga (Kunigunde, widow of Bolesław the Chaste), they were in the country from 6 December until early February 1288.[67] Töle Buqa failed to take Sandomir, while Noghai headed a similarly unsuccessful attack upon Cracow, which Polish annals place around Christmas.[68] For their spirited resistance the citizens of Cracow would later be rewarded by Leszek the Black with tax exemptions.[69] We learn more about the campaign from a charter of László IV of Hungary, dated 1288, in which the king rewarded György, son of Szymon, for his services.[70] While Leszek sought refuge in Hungary from the Mongols, his kinsman László had despatched a corps of Hungarian troops under György to aid the Poles. György engaged a force of about a thousand Mongols near Sandecz (now Stary Sącz), killing their commander.[71] In February 1288 Leszek in turn expressed his gratitude by giving György a *villa* in Sandecz.[72] It was perhaps in reprisal for the aid given by László that the Mongols attacked the Szepes (Zips) region of Hungary later in the year, albeit on a smaller scale; here György again distinguished himself.

During those years when the Golden Horde was prey to civil war between Töle Buqa and Noghai (1290–1) or between the latter and Toqto'a (1298–9), the Latin world seems to have been spared Mongol raids; but they recommenced each time the Mongols' internal conflicts had been resolved. A diploma of András III relates how, around winter in the second year following his coronation (i.e. 1291–2), the Mongols raided the Mačva ('Macho') region and he had despatched troops against them. This incursion, from the south, indicates that Noghai's forces were now using Bulgaria, or perhaps Serbia, as a base to attack Hungary (above, p. 203).[73] A charter of 1296 refers to a recent raid on Hungary, though it furnishes scant detail and in any case could conceivably refer to the inroad of 1291–2.[74] There is documentary evidence, lastly, of a Mongol attack on the Leles region in Zemplén (in present-day Slovakia) in 1305.[75] As for Poland, Mongol troops are found ravaging Sandomir in 1293, doubtless profiting from Łokietek's war with King Václav of Bohemia.[76] After this episode, no more Mongol incursions into Poland are mentioned until Uzbek's reign (1312–41).

Frontier conditions and mentalities

If, by the last decades of the thirteenth century, Ilkhanid diplomacy was turning the Mongols of Persia into potential allies, no such aura attached to those of the Golden Horde. In Europe fear of the Mongols was widespread, surfacing on one occasion in the most incongruous of places. During a widespread popular rising in the Utrecht region in 1274, it was apparently natural for the citizens, confronted by an unexpected and formidable attack by the rebels, to assume that the assailants were the Tartars.[77] As late as 1330 Marino Sanudo, like some latter-day Carpini, was warning that the divisions in the Latin world would enable the Mongols to advance into France, Germany and Italy.[78] In Eastern Europe, apprehensions of an imminent Mongol attack reverberated along a vast frontier – Latin Christendom's longest land frontier with a pagan enemy. In 1286 the Teutonic Knights evacuated four of their Prussian strongholds on reports of the Mongols' approach, sparked off, in all likelihood, by the preparations to invade Poland.[79] The same invasion of Poland in 1340–1 (below, p. 210) that spawned rumours of an attack on Brandenburg also elicited an urgent appeal to the pope on the part of Prussian bishops and prompted a papal collector in western Hungary to despatch his funds to the greater security of Zagreb.[80] The manner in which, alongside this Mongol campaign, contemporary chroniclers describe a near-simultaneous attack on Christian Spain by the Muslim ruler of Granada and his Moroccan allies and an Ottoman Turkish advance against the Greeks, suggests a general sense of crisis. Late in August 1340 Pope Benedict XII himself juxtaposed these other enemies with the Mongol threat in a letter urging the French king to make peace with Edward III.[81]

The Hungarians alone shared an eastern and south-eastern border with the Mongol world that extended for hundreds of miles. For them, the 'frontier' was likely to be a yawning wilderness, from which the enemy might appear with no warning. In 1264 Pope Urban IV assigned the parish of Wynch (Felvincz, in Aranyos) to the archdeacon of Szatmár (now Satu Mare in Rumania), on the grounds that he was based 'in the furthest part of the realm of Hungary, so that between him and the Tartars' territory there is absolutely no human habitation'.[82] The city of Milcov, once the centre of a bishopric, was described as ruined and devoid of Christian inhabitants in 1278.[83] These eastern regions were bleak terrain for Latin forces. When the Hungarian King Louis (Lájos) crossed the Carpathians early in April 1352, on his way back from a campaign against the Lithuanians and Mongols, his horses had to feed on branches and for an entire week the men ate nothing but beans. According to the Franciscan János of Eger, the king's confessor, who has left us an account of this expedition, he and a colleague were so weakened by hunger that they were unable to mount or dismount without help.[84] The climate did not necessarily smile upon the enemy either, of course. During the Mongol retreat from Hungary in 1285, Noghai made off to the safety of his winter quarters, but Töle Buqa's troops were decimated in the freezing cold and were reduced to eating their mounts, dogs and dead comrades. The Volynian Chronicle has him arrive back with few survivors of his original force after crossing the Carpathians.[85]

Documents from thirteenth-century Hungary bear vivid testimony to the psychological impact of Mongol inroads. Nora Berend has drawn attention to the way in which the experience of 1241–2 had seared itself on the Hungarian collective memory, to the extent that it inaugurated a new semi-official chronology. Throughout the rest of his reign Béla IV's chancery employed phrases like 'at the time of the Tartar persecution' or 'at the pestilential advent of the Tartars'; and the simple words 'at the time of the Tartars' became entrenched in the language of record.[86] During the process for the canonization of Béla's daughter Margaret in 1276, a number of witnesses established their ages by reference to the Mongol invasion.[87] Subsequent onslaughts intensified the sense of disruption and loss, particularly that of 1285, which passed into Hungarian historiography as 'the second Tartar assault' and obliged chancery scribes to devise phrases like 'the time of the first' (or 'former') 'Tartars' – or even, in one case, 'the main Tartars' – for the invasion of 1241.[88] In Poland the emotional imprint of Mongol devastation is less clearly discernible; but it manifests itself, perhaps, in the way that annalists regularly couple the name of Duke Henry II of Lower Silesia, for some years after 1241, with the poignant formula 'who was slain by the Tartars'.[89]

There is no shortage of documentary evidence for the material and economic damage perpetrated by Mongol attacks after 1242. In 1296 the church of St Mary in Sandomir, which had been burned down in 1259, was still not fully rebuilt, and Pope Boniface VIII granted indulgences to anybody who assisted in the task.[90] Pope Clement VI was told in 1343 that the abbey of St Andrew near Visegrád (in western Hungary), which had flourished before the Tartar invasions, had housed no monks for more than forty years.[91] At some point in the later 1280s László IV remitted half the revenue due from the inhabitants of Beszterce (Bistritz), 'in very great measure annihilated or impoverished by the devastation and burnings of the Tartars'.[92] Whether mounting lightning raids or, as in 1285, wide-ranging campaigns of devastation, the enemy were intent on acquiring able-bodied captives in large numbers, and Hungarian charters regularly give great prominence to the liberation of some thousands of their unhappy countrymen by those notables who defeated the Mongols.[93] Serfs whom the invaders abducted, but who subsequently escaped back to their homes without the aid of a ransom, were legally free in the duchy of Sandomir, though an appeal addressed to Pope John XXII in 1327 suggests that their lords (in this case the church of Sandomir) were but imperfectly acquainted with this custom.[94] Arrangements were made, presumably, for the ransoming of Christian prisoners (and would have imposed an additional burden on local communities); but regrettably the only extant charter documenting such efforts, in Hungary, is an eighteenth-century forgery.[95]

Naturally the Mongols were not the only agents of destruction and sacrilege in Hungary. Many elements within the kingdom profited from the upheavals caused by the Mongol attacks to misappropriate ecclesiastical property, so that Clement VI would complain in 1344 that more than forty Benedictine houses had been illegally occupied over the past hundred years.[96] In 1277 the archbishop of Kalocsa recounted the bloodthirsty career of a Saxon rebel whom he accused of adopting 'Tartar' practices;[97] and eight years later King László himself referred to the mutual strife of the Hungarians in the same breath as Tartar and Cuman attacks.[98] For a Hungarian cleric writing in 1321, past decades were an era of wickedness characterized by 'both Tartar invasion and oppression by the tyrants of the land' – a situation that, in his view, Divine Grace combined with King Carobert's energies had done much to ameliorate.[99] Other churchmen were less ready to discriminate among Hungary's various afflictions and less fulsome about the king's role. Protesting to Pope Benedict XII in 1338 about Carobert's erosion of ecclesiastical rights, the kingdom's prelates spoke of the vulnerability of their churches. Their sole means of resisting the encroachments of the lay power was to produce written privileges which had in fact been destroyed by fire in the course of two Tartar invasions.[100] There were those in Eastern Europe who had clearly learned to turn Mongol visitations to good account.

The war over Ruthenia

Both László IV and András III cooperated with the Polish dukes Leszek and his brother Władysław Łokietek in the 1280s and 1290s against other enemies besides the Mongols,[101] and these close relations were maintained into the Angevin era. Łokietek gave his sister Elizabeth in marriage to King Carobert in 1320, and under his son and successor, Casimir III 'the Great' (1333–70), the alliance served as a cornerstone of Polish foreign policy. As it became apparent that Casimir would leave no direct male heir, and that on his death the throne would pass to his nephew, Carobert's son Louis I of Hungary (1342–82), Hungary's Angevin rulers had a growing stake in Poland's territorial integrity. The two powers shared additional concerns about the aggrandizement of the Luxemburg dynasty in Bohemia. They were also both still menaced by the Mongols, and for much of the fourteenth century it is possible to treat of Polish and Hungarian relations with the Golden Horde together, particularly in relation to successive crises in Ruthenia.

Daniil's descendants fulfilled in some degree the role which Pope Innocent IV had envisaged for their illustrious ancestor in the mid-thirteenth century (above, p. 95). While paying tribute to the Golden Horde, they also maintained amicable ties with Poland's principal rival in the north, the Teutonic Order. In an agreement of 1316, Lev I's grandsons, Lev II and Andrei, spoke of the friendship between their predecessors and the Knights, and assured them of their readiness to protect the Order's territories against the Mongols or any other aggressor.[102] But in 1322/3 the brothers both perished, possibly in armed conflicts against the Lithuanians,[103] and with them the Riurikid line in Ruthenia died out. Władysław Łokietek saw this as a crisis which would bring the Mongols into Poland in defence of their vital interests, and in May 1323 wrote a pressing appeal to Pope John XXII.[104] The pope was then heavily embroiled in a dispute with the Emperor Louis IV.[105] Whatever his response, which has not survived, he may not have authorized a crusade against the Mongols until June 1325.[106] By that juncture a crisis had been averted through the enthronement of the Mazovian prince Bolesław, whose mother was a sister of the dead princes and who cemented his rule by converting to the Orthodox rite and assuming the style of Iury II.[107] Although like his uncles he made a compact with the

Teutonic Order in 1327 on the basis of their common hostility to the Mongols, he appears to have maintained the tribute which his predecessors rendered to the Golden Horde.[108]

When Bolesław-Iury was murdered in March or April 1340 by boyars who resented his Latinizing policies, he left no issue; his heirs were his two brothers, who ruled in Mazovia. Casimir III, in concert with his ally Carobert, responded swiftly. In the course of two campaigns, in which he was joined by troops from Hungary,[109] he occupied Lwów, seized the late prince's treasure, and asserted his authority over the principality of Galicia. The Mongols, summoned by Galician boyars who hoped thereby to avoid Latin rule, reacted in the winter of 1340–1 by devastating the region of Sandomir and mounting an abortive siege of Lublin, before Casimir checked them on the Vistula.[110] According to a Bohemian chronicler, they were compelled to retreat by the harsh cold and heavy snow;[111] while Uzbek's attacks on Byzantium (above, p. 203) and the Chaghadayids in 1341, followed by his death early in the following year and a disputed succession,[112] must have distracted the Golden Horde from further campaigning in Poland. Casimir had been reduced to detaching a leading boyar, Dmitrii Diet'ko, from the Mongols and for a time recognizing him virtually as an independent prince in Galicia. Volynia, which the Lithuanian prince Liubartis had seized around this time, possibly on the khan's behalf, lay beyond his reach. But the Golden Horde never succeeded in bringing Galicia back within its orbit, and from 1349, at least, Casimir styled himself *Polonie et Russie rex*.

Spasmodic war between Casimir and the Mongols continued well into the 1350s, and may have been terminated only by the dissolution of the khanate in the civil war that followed the death of Uzbek's grandson Berdībek in 1359. By this time Poland's enemies in the east were acting in concert. Just as from the late 1340s the Lithuanian Grand Duke Algirdas was ready to seek Mongol assistance in his conflict with Moscow,[113] so the Golden Horde appeared a serviceable ally in his struggle with Poland. By 1351 Clement VI was aware of an alliance (*confederatio*) between Lithuania and the Mongols, and in this same year the Lithuanians devastated the Lwów region.[114] In March 1352, when the Golden Horde and its Rus' allies ravaged Polish territory and captured an unnamed city (probably Lublin), one source indicates that this invasion was mounted in support of the Lithuanians.[115] When Louis of Hungary, who had already joined forces with Casimir on an expedition against the Lithuanians in 1351, led Hungarian and Polish troops on another campaign into Ruthenia in the late winter of 1352, he secured the nominal submission of the Lithuanian castellan of Belz; but the fortress is described as being 'in the neighbourhood of the Tartars' and his army was shadowed by the Mongols and the Rus' as he withdrew.[116] In November 1354 Pope Innocent VI, authorizing crusade preaching, spoke of Mongol assaults on Poland over the previous three years, but duly named the Lithuanians alongside the Mongols as targets of the planned crusade.[117]

That Casimir himself came to see Lithuania as a more formidable enemy than the Mongols is clear from a marked shift in his relations with the Golden Horde. He may have flirted briefly with the khan's envoys in 1349, with a view to his operations against Liubartis later that year.[118] The forfeiture of several important towns in Ruthenia during the Lithuanian campaign of 1350 furnished a stronger incentive to make use of the Mongols. Certainly Casimir was in league with them by 1356 when, in a vain request for the Teutonic Order's assistance against the Lithuanians, he assured the *Hochmeister* that he had also secured the services of seven Mongol 'princes'.[119] The Knights, who had themselves effected a *rapprochement* with Lithuania, duly reported to Avignon in 1357 that the Polish king had submitted to the Golden Horde and undertaken to pay tribute, thus bringing down on Casimir a rebuke from Pope Innocent VI.[120] The seven Mongol princes surely commanded auxiliaries sent by the khan to assist his new client. During these years, confrontation with the Golden Horde alternated with bouts of negotiation. In 1363 the king asked Pope Urban V to provide a benefice for a cleric whose energies had been taxed 'on numerous occasions in our embassies to the emperor of the infidel Tartars in order to make truces for the repose of Christendom'.[121] Just as in the 1260s the Hungarian court had negotiated with the Golden Horde for the sake of survival, so now the Polish king, in order to outflank and defeat the Lithuanians, had evidently been prepared to outbid them for Mongol support.

Yet despite such lapses, Poland under Casimir was beginning to acquire the status long aspired to by Hungary, that of a barrier (*antemurale*) against pagan aggression.[122] Whereas after *c.*1354 Hungarian policy under Louis I became increasingly oriented towards the kingdom's southern neighbours, the heretics and schismatics of Bosnia, Serbia, Wallachia and Bulgaria, and by the last years of the century was focused on the Ottoman Turkish advance in the Balkans,[123] conflict with both the Horde and Lithuania continued to play a part in Polish policy down until Casimir's death in 1370 and beyond, during Louis's own reign in Poland (1370–82). Thus Urban V, responding in 1363 to another request from Casimir, granted indulgences to any of the faithful who, over the next twelve years, aided him against the Tartars and the Lithuanians in the defence of his kingdom.[124] In 1376 Louis's representative in Galicia,

Duke Władysław of Opole, asked Pope Gregory XI to transfer to Lwów the seat of the archbishop of Halicz (Halych), a town which lacked walls and was too remote and exposed, lying as it did between the Tartars and the Lithuanians.[125] As we shall see, however, by this date mention of the Mongols was little more than a formal requirement.

In Hungary, King Carobert does not seem to have been unduly troubled by Mongol attacks. During a campaign against an unspecified rebel (most probably the Wallachian prince Basaraba) in the summer of 1324, he despatched a reconnaissance force into Mongol territory, perhaps with a view to the Mongol reaction to events in Ruthenia; two Mongol youths captured on this occasion were despatched as a gift to Pope John XXII in 1325.[126] The Mongol incursion into Hungary in 1326, mentioned only by a chronicler writing in distant Prussia,[127] was doubtless made in reprisal. Apart from this, the only other report of a Mongol invasion in Carobert's reign is the vague rumour of an imminent attack, transmitted to the Venetian Senate in the spring of 1340,[128] which may in fact echo the king's efforts to assist his uncle Casimir in Galicia (above, p. 210).

Modern scholars have inferred a series of Mongol invasions, in 1332, 1334 and 1338, from references in contemporary papal correspondence.[129] In striking contrast with the attacks of 1241–2 and 1285–8 and even with several lesser raids, however, these inroads have left no impression in the numerous royal and other charters that have come down to us. Nor, with one exception, does any of the papal letters in question offer direct evidence of Mongol invasions of Hungary at this time. John XXII's bull of 1332, authorizing the recreation of the defunct bishopric of Milcov, simply refers to the visitation of 1241, which had been responsible for the destruction of the see.[130] Other letters are highly unspecific regarding the enemy, as when Benedict XII in 1335 expressed his joy at Carobert's recent victory over pagan foes.[131] Moreover, the popes tended, when mentioning the Hungarian king's incessant conflicts with his non-Catholic neighbours, to give pride of place to schismatics. Thus John in 1332 referred only to hostilities with 'Ruthenians [presumably Rus'] and other schismatics and infidels', and Benedict in 1339 made no explicit allusion to the Mongols among Carobert's pagan enemies.[132] The exception to this general pattern, a letter of 1331 in which John felicitates Carobert on a recent victory over the Tartars, may refer to a genuine engagement, perhaps just prior to the king's disastrous Wallachian campaign in 1330.[133]

In King Louis's reign we have more reliable indications of Mongol attacks upon Hungary. One is known to have occurred in, or not long before, 1348.[134] In the spring of 1352 troops were being raised to fight the Mongols and the pope was informed of a recent attack which may have formed part of their operations against Poland.[135] In the following year, when Louis, fearing another Mongol invasion, ordered all the kingdom's fortresses to be repaired, the Transylvanian stronghold of Várhegy (in the county of Sáros; now Délulŭ-Cetăţii in Rumania) was said to have been damaged in the latest Mongol attack.[136] But the Hungarian kingdom was now strong enough to take the offensive. In February 1345 the *ispan* of the Székely (and future voivode of Transylvania), András Lachkfi, entered Mongol territory and defeated and captured a Mongol commander named *Otlamish, who was married to the khan's sister. The following year witnessed another victorious campaign by the Székely, as a result of which the surviving Mongols are said to have fallen back upon the Black Sea coast.[137] In the wake of these triumphs, Clement VI seems again to have tried to reestablish the bishopric of Milcov, though without effect, since Innocent VI, nominating yet another bishop in 1353, spoke of the see as long vacant.[138]

The crusade against the Mongols

The struggle for Ruthenia from 1340 marks the point at which crusading machinery begins to be applied to the Polish and Hungarian theatres of war on a regular basis. In analysing papal crusading policy, we have to distinguish different levels of concession: the grant to individuals of a spiritual privilege, i.e. the indulgence or full pardon for sins, often equated expressly with the indulgence conferred on those who went to fight in the Holy Land; the authorization of crusade preaching (over a geographical area which might well vary considerably) on behalf of one or more Christian kingdoms; and the grant of ecclesiastical revenues to a Christian ruler to support a campaign.

Popes authorized remarkably few crusades against the Mongols in Eastern Europe after 1261. In June 1265 Clement IV, alerted by Béla to the danger of an imminent attack, ordered the crusade to be preached against the Mongols in Hungary, Bohemia, Poland, Brandenburg, Austria, Styria and Carinthia.[139] In 1288 Nicholas IV, in a letter that was chiefly concerned with the charges of sub-Christian behaviour against King László, ordered crusade preaching in Hungary, Poland and Bohemia should the Mongols make any attempt against Christian peoples.[140] Apart from these, it seems that the Curia issued no other bulls for the crusade against the Mongols until the second quarter of the fourteenth century.[141]

In 1340 Casimir, anticipating a Mongol reaction to his operations in Galicia, took the precaution of seeking aid from Pope Benedict XII, who in August ordered Polish prelates to arrange for the crusade against the Mongols to be preached in Poland, Hungary and Bohemia.[142] Benedict was keen to reach a settlement: soon afterwards, in a letter to Uzbek that related primarily to Catholic missionary activity in his dominions, he urged the khan to abandon his hostile intentions and undertook to make amends should the Hungarian and Polish kings prove to have done him any unwarranted injury.[143] Benedict's successors adopted a less irenic stance. In 1343 Clement VI granted Casimir a tenth of the revenues of the archbishop of Gnieźno and his suffragans for two years, on the grounds that the Polish kingdom was under frequent attack by Tartars, Rus' and Lithuanians.[144] From March 1351 he granted a further tenth for four years, and ordered the Polish prelates to institute crusade preaching in Poland, Hungary and Bohemia in order to defend Poland against the Tartars. Innocent VI renewed the grant in 1355 for another four years.[145]

On the basis of the distinction drawn above with regard to papal crusading policy, it seems that in the eyes of the Curia the Hungarian monarchs had less reason than the Poles to expect a Mongol attack. Certainly the papal response to the Mongol threat to Hungary (as opposed to the conflict in Ruthenia) seems remarkably tepid. In 1325 John XXII refused Carobert's request for a subsidy from neighbouring kingdoms, on the grounds that no precedent existed for such a grant.[146] In another bull he responded to a letter from Carobert which had evidently rehearsed his kingdom's sufferings over the decades at the hands of the Tartars. Recognizing the Hungarians' tribulations, the pope was prepared to grant all who died fighting in defence of the faith in Hungary or in neighbouring regions, against Tartars, other pagans, or schismatics, full pardon of their sins.[147] A later bull, in 1334, repeated this concession – and the tribulations – *verbatim*; Carobert himself was included, a privilege reissued in 1339 by Benedict XII.[148]

But the papacy went no further. It is true that John XXII called Carobert an 'athlete of Christ', that for Benedict XII he was striving to be a wall of defence (*murum defensionis*) for Christian peoples, and that Innocent VI, granting King Louis a tenth in 1356 for the war against the papacy's local opponents in Italy, would praise him for having kept the Tartars at bay; true also that Clement VI awarded Louis any lands he might wrest from pagans or schismatics.[149] Significantly, however, Clement's grant of a four-year tenth to Louis in 1352 was the first time that a pope had assigned substantial crusading revenues to a Hungarian monarch. The purpose on that occasion was not to promote a crusade but to reimburse the king for the heavy expenditure he had incurred in withstanding Mongol attacks; and even this has the appearance of a *quid pro quo*, since Clement seems to link the concession with Louis's recent release of some distinguished Neapolitan prisoners.[150] The terminology employed in papal bulls suggests a consistent distinction, if not one that is altogether clear. The Hungarian kings and those who died fighting the Mongols within their dominions were offered 'full pardon for their sins' (*plenam veniam peccatorum*); the Polish king and those who rallied to his banner were usually vouchsafed 'that indulgence which was granted by our predecessors to those who cross to the Holy Land'. Most importantly of all, no Avignon pope authorized a crusade for the defence of Hungary (as opposed to preaching within Hungary for the defence of Poland).

What is the explanation for this seemingly cavalier treatment? By 1352, certainly, the papacy was trying to draw Louis into its own struggles in central Italy and may well have been reluctant to let him become too embroiled on his eastern frontier. But the Italian embarrassments date from too late a stage to account for the papal stance in the 1340s. Favour towards Poland has to be seen, perhaps, against the background of the Curia's satisfaction at the restoration of the Polish monarchy in 1320 and frustration at its own incapacity to secure justice for the Polish king from the Teutonic Knights; it is also likely that the papacy gave priority to campaigns which would guarantee the retention of freshly-annexed Orthodox Galicia. There is of course an additional, simpler, and more obvious, explanation: namely, that popes had come to attach less weight to Hungary's situation than to the danger facing Poland, despite – or even, perhaps, because of – the calls for help that had reached them with remorseless regularity ever since the time of Béla IV.[151]

The effectiveness of crusading appeals is quite another matter. The crusades for the defence of Poland failed to attract the international support that the papacy intended. The most spectacular claims surround the expedition which Benedict XII summoned on Casimir's behalf in 1340, when two chroniclers speak of large numbers of crusaders moving to the Poles' assistance. But other sources suggest that Casimir's appeals to his Latin neighbours had fallen on deaf ears. In a letter of June 1341 Benedict himself would acknowledge that Casimir had not received the reinforcements he needed.[152] According to John of Winterthur, the Emperor Louis IV observed: 'Since they are powerful and mighty kings, let them defend themselves against infidel attack.' Louis's relations with the Polish king at this time were admittedly chilly.[153] But in considering the question of German non-participation, we cannot fail to be struck by the contrast with the crusading reinforcements available every winter to the Teutonic Knights in Prussia and Livonia.

The decline of the Golden Horde and the rise of Lithuania

Two circumstances combined to make the anti-Mongol crusade redundant in Eastern Europe. One was Mongol collapse; the other was the escape of Lithuania from the khans' orbit and its *rapprochement* with Poland. The Golden Horde may already have been gravely weakened by the onset, in 1346, of the Black Death which, in the verdict of one Hungarian chronicler, had inflicted such losses on the Tartars that Louis I was able to embark on his invasion of Naples with equanimity.[154] Then, following the deaths of Jānībek (1357) and his son Berdībek (1358/9), the khanate sank into prolonged internecine war, in which sometimes as many as three or four khans vied for recognition by the amirs and for possession of major centres like Sarai, Qirim (Krim) and Azāq. In the core Golden Horde territories, princes of Batu's line (which may have died out during the 1360s) had to compete with the progeny of his brothers, and from the 1370s onwards the khans of the 'White Horde', descendants of Jochi's sons Orda and Toqa Temür, also entered the lists; Orus Khan of the White Horde, who had already appropriated Khwārazm, took Sarai itself in 1374/5.[155] For much of the period 1360–80 the dominant figure in the western Pontic steppe was the amir Mamai, who made and unmade khans and contrived to maintain some kind of suzerainty over the Rus' princes, though he seems never to have been in a position to intervene in Polish or Lithuanian affairs. In any case he suffered a humiliating defeat at the hands of the prince of Moscow at Kulikovo Pole in 1380 and was shortly overthrown by Toqtamish, a kinsman of Orus Khan who had recently supplanted the latter's son as khan of the White Horde.[156] Toqtamish briefly reunited the Golden Horde, and from this point onwards the two Jochid polities nominally formed a single khanate.

Toqtamish, a more powerful figure who reimposed overlordship on Moscow (1382), threatened to make the Mongols again a force to be reckoned with in the politics of Eastern Europe. Yet, like so many previous khans, he manifested a greater interest in Khwārazm and the lands south of the Caucasus than in those to the west of the Pontic steppe. Although indebted for his sovereignty in the White Horde to the Turco-Mongol conqueror Temür-*i Lang* ('the Lame'; hence 'Tamerlane'), whose dominions extended from Central Asia to Iraq, he turned against his benefactor, and launched audacious attacks upon Azerbaijan in 1385–6 and upon Transoxiana in 1387–8. Temür retaliated with two campaigns (1391 and 1395–6) in which he crushed Toqtamish and ruthlessly sacked the khanate's principal towns, Sarai, Qirim, Astrakhan and Bulghār; Toqtamish was replaced with another descendant of Toqa Temür named Temür Qutlugh.[157] Henceforth it was as a fugitive seeking to regain power from Temür's nominees that he influenced the politics of the Latin world.

The impact of these upheavals is clearly visible along the Golden Horde's western frontiers. In March 1373 Pope Gregory XI, authorizing preparations for a crusade against the Ottomans, extended it to include the Tartars, with whom, he was told, the Turks had negotiated an alliance;[158] but two weeks later he was writing of the Mongol threat to Hungary in terms that suggest it was a thing of the past, superseded by the Turkish menace.[159] On the south-western periphery of the Horde's territory, the Vlach principalities of Wallachia and Moldavia were emancipated from Mongol overlordship; Moldavia instead accepted Polish suzerainty in 1387.[160] In several ports along the Black Sea coast, a series of treaties between 1380 and 1387 replaced the khan's sovereignty with that of Genoa (below, p. 306).[161] Around the Danube estuary a *de facto* autonomous principality briefly emerged under 'Demetrius, *princeps Tartarorum*'; but Demetrius, whose merchants were the subject of a commercial agreement with Louis I in 1368, may have lost his southernmost territory in the Dobrudja to a local despot named Dobrotich, who owed a loose allegiance to the Byzantine Emperor.[162] Louis himself was able to occupy part of Bulgaria in 1365, and for a time thereafter its king paid tribute to Hungary.[163]

It was the Mongols' former clients and allies in pagan Lithuania who were best placed to profit from the situation. The Grand Duke Algirdas had already exploited the Golden Horde's troubles in *c.*1362 when, in a campaign that pushed deeper into Mongol territory than any previous expedition, he defeated the khan's forces at the battle of the 'Blue Waters'; subsequently he built up his influence in Podolia through the agency of the sons of his brother Koriatas.[164] On his death in 1377 Algirdas was succeeded by his eldest son Jogailo (Jagiello), who in 1386 married Louis's younger daughter Jadwiga (Hedwig), was officially baptized a Christian, and was crowned king of Poland as Władysław II. His authority in Lithuania was at first disputed by his uncle Kiestutis and then, following Kiestutis's death (1382), by the latter's son Vytautas (Witold), but in 1392 the cousins reached an agreement which inaugurated an era of close cooperation. Jogailo effectively left Vytautas in control of Lithuania as Grand Duke, but seconded him in his struggle with the Teutonic Order and with the Golden Horde.

The Lithuanian ruling dynasty's dalliance with the notion of baptism had been fitfully in progress since the 1250s, and under the Grand Duke Gediminas (1315–41/2) had become a vital tool of diplomacy. In 1324 it had even encouraged Pope John XXII to write to Gediminas to ask him to help defend Christendom from the infidel (by which he surely meant the Mongols).[165] Even before his rise to power, Vytautas had proved an able exponent of what was by then the traditional Lithuanian policy *vis-à-vis* the papacy. Gregory XI, who as recently as 1373 had appealed to Algirdas, Kiestutis and other Lithuanian princes to accept Christianity and had urged King Louis to spare no efforts to bring this about, commended Vytautas in 1378 for his efforts against the Tartars and for his persistence in the unity of the Christian faith and obedience to the Holy See, and granted him the right to have his personal confessor absolve him of his sins on his deathbed.[166] A pagan member of a pagan dynasty that less than thirty years earlier had been in league with the Mongols was now being fêted by the Holy See as if he were a faithful Catholic.

If the Lithuanian rulers were at last being incorporated in the family of Christian princes, there was another side to their diplomacy. The fact that Władysław-Jogailo had received a crusading indulgence from the Roman Pope Urban VI in 1388 for his war against the Turks and Tartars[167] did not prevent him in 1393 from making a pact with Toqtamish by which he undertook to pay tribute in return for a grant of Rus' territory.[168] And after Temür's campaigns into the Pontic steppe, Poland and Lithuania were the obvious external powers to which Toqtamish could turn. He threw himself on Vytautas's mercy and was settled with his followers in the neighbourhood of Vilnius and Troki (1397).[169] A large body of his former troops are known to have abandoned him in 1397/8 and pushed south into the Balkans to enter the service of the Ottoman Sultan Bāyezīd, who subsequently grew suspicious of their leaders, however, and had them executed.[170] They were not the only Mongol group operating in south-eastern Europe. Early in 1402, we are told, a coalition comprising King Sigismund of Hungary, the Wallachian voivode Mircea and the Tartars took advantage of the Sultan's difficulties in order to encroach upon his territories.[171] We do not know which Golden Horde khan these particular Tartars represented: they may have been the 'White Tartars' at whose hands the Hungarian and French troops fleeing northwards in the wake of their defeat by the Ottomans at Nicopolis in 1396 had allegedly suffered no harm.[172] Whatever the case, the episode parallels the situation further north where, over the next twenty years or so, Lithuania and Poland were allied with Toqtamish's sons against Temür Qutlugh and his successors, who were supported by the new strong man, the amir Edigü (or Edigei).

Vytautas and his allies suffered a signal check in an engagement on the Vorskla, a tributary of the Dnieper (12 August 1399), which effectively curtailed the Lithuanian Grand Duke's plans to further his hegemony in Eastern Europe.[173] Toqtamish, who had deserted the Lithuanians in the heat of battle, fled in 1401 into western Siberia, where he was eventually run to ground and killed in 1405/6 by the troops of Temür Qutlugh's successor Shādībek.[174] The Castilian envoy Ruy González de Clavijo, travelling through Persia and Transoxiana in 1404, heard a rumour that Toqtamish was in friendly contact with his old enemy Temür and was seeking the latter's support against Edigü.[175] Whatever the truth of this, the alliance with Toqtamish's line neverthe-less held good and served Vytautas well. Toqtamish's sons, headed by Jalāl al-Dīn, first took refuge with the prince of Moscow and then, dislodged during an abortive attack on the city by Edigü (1408), moved into Vytautas's territory and were settled successively near Kiev and in the vicinity of Troki, where the Burgundian knight Ghillebert de Lannoy noticed their presence a few years later.[176]

It is a measure of the Golden Horde's weakness that Edigü and his protégés were not merely unable or unwilling to follow up the victory of 1399, but in the wake of the Moscow campaign even made unsuccessful overtures to Vytautas with a view to gaining Lithuanian support against their rivals. Instead the Grand Duke assisted successively Jalāl al-Dīn (1412) and, following his overthrow by Edigü, another of Toqtamish's sons, Kerim Berdī (1413/14), to establish themselves as khans over part of the Horde's territory. In 1418 yet a third brother who currently enjoyed Vytautas's backing defeated Edigü and obliged him to flee into the Crimea, whence he made peace with the Grand Duke shortly before his death (1419). Edigü was the last figure to wield anything like strong authority in the Golden Horde;[177] certainly none of the numerous khans who presided over its disintegration into the khanates of the Crimea, Astrakhan, Kazan and Kasimov in the mid-fifteenth century was a worthy successor.

The princes of the Golden Horde continued to play a useful role in the politics of Christian Eastern Europe. During Jalāl al-Dīn's brief reign as khan (1411–12), Sigismund of Hungary sought his alliance, as part of his vendetta against the Venetians in the Black Sea.[178] When Vytautas and Władysław-Jogailo inflicted a decisive defeat on the Teutonic Knights at Tannenberg (15 July 1410), they had the support not only of Rus' troops but also of a Mongol contingent headed by Jalāl al-Dīn and representing Toqtamish's heirs.[179] It is unclear how far the rest of Latin Christendom was aware of these alliances until the Teutonic Order's proctors, in the full glare of the Council of Constance (1414–15), denounced the Poles for using pagans in this fashion.[180] Certainly, around the turn of the century the papacy had been very ill-informed about the situation. In 1398 the Roman Pope, Boniface IX, had ordered crusade preaching in Poland, Lithuania and neighbouring territories for the war against 'Tartars, pagans, Turks and other barbarian nations'; and on the news of the disaster on the Vorskla he authorized the collection of an ecclesiastical tenth to defend Władysław-Jogailo against Tartar invasion – on neither occasion aware, it seems, that the conflict was at least in part between two Mongol factions and that the Poles were allied with one of them.[181]

The Grand Duke of Lithuania was just one, if perhaps the most successful, of a number of princes who were now in a position to meddle in the internal affairs of the Golden Horde and to enlist or discard the military support of Mongol princes at will. Like their cousins the Ilkhans, the khans of Jochi's line had moved from being the scourge of Christian peoples to being seen as possible allies, but with an important difference. Whereas in the Near East the projected Ilkhanid–Latin alliance was designed in part to serve the interests of the Mongol rulers themselves in bringing down their most formidable external enemy, the Mamlūk empire, in Eastern Europe cooperation was sought by displaced or insecure rulers with a view to destroying their rivals among Jochi's numerous descendants. They had been reduced, moreover, to serving as an auxiliary in the conflicts of others.[182] The Mongols were no longer the dominant power in this region, but simply one among several more evenly-matched elements – Poland, Lithuania, Moscow and other Rus' principalities, the Teutonic Knights – which competed for tribute and territory.

Notes

1. Bruno of Olmütz, 'Relatio de statu ecclesiae in regno Alemanniae (1273. Dec. 16.)', §§4–5, *MGHLeg.*, III, pp. 590–1 (no. 620); also in *CDRB*, V:2, pp. 371–2 (no. 719).
2. Paul W. Knoll, *The Rise of the Polish Monarchy: Piast Poland in East Central Europe, 1320–1370* (Chicago, IL, 1972), pp. 14–41.
3. *AUO*, VIII, pp. 316–17 (no. 212), cited in Engel, *Realm of St Stephen*, pp. 107–8.
4. For a balanced survey of the reign, see Berend, *At the Gate*, pp. 171–83; and her remarks in 'How many medieval Europes? The "pagans" of Hungary and regional diversity in Christendom', in Peter Linehan and Janet L. Nelson, eds, *The Medieval World* (London, 2001), pp. 77–92 (here pp. 88–9).
5. *PC*, viii, 6, and ix, 44, pp. 296, 327–8 (tr. Dawson, pp. 45, 68). Eudes de Châteauroux, 'Sermo in concilio', in Ruotsala, *Europeans and Mongols*, p. 160: *discordie inter christianos parant viam tartaris*; for the date, see above, p. 153, n.12.

6. *VMH*, I, p. 227 (no. 431) = *MGHEp.*, III, p. 238 (no. 273) = *CDRB*, V:1, pp. 57–8 (no. 20). For Bohemian–Hungarian relations during this period, see Jörg K. Hoensch, *Přemysl Otakar II. von Böhmen. Der goldene König* (Graz, Vienna and Köln, 1989), pp. 44–8, 112–20.

7. *MGHEp.*, III, p. 482 (no. 518, 20 April 1262) = *CDRB*, V:1, p. 480 (no. 321). See also Urban to Béla IV, in Hans Martin Schaller, 'Eine kuriale Briefsammlung des 13. Jahrhunderts mit unbekannten Briefen Friedrichs II. (Trier, Stadtbibliothek, Cod. 859/1097)', *DA* 18 (1962), pp. 171–213 (here p. 208, no. 12), repr. in his *Stauferzeit*, pp. 283–328 (here p. 323).

8. *MGHEp.*, III, p. 548 (no. 560/1, 27 Aug. 1263) = *MGHLeg.*, II, p. 531 (no. 405).

9. Sinor, 'Les relations', p. 59. Charles J. Halperin, 'Russia in the Mongol empire in comparative perspective', *HJAS* 43 (1983), pp. 239–61.

10. For these events, see Biran, *Qaidu*, pp. 63–5; Th.T. Allsen, 'The Princes of the Left Hand: an introduction to the history of the *ulus* of Orda in the thirteenth and early fourteenth centuries', *AEMA* 5 (1985 [1987]), pp. 5–40 (here pp. 20–1). The principal Persian sources are Rashīd al-Dīn, II, pp. 896–7 (tr. Thackston, II, p. 438; tr. Boyle, *Successors*, p. 269), and Waṣṣāf, p. 67. Nomoghan arrived back in Khanbaligh on 26 March 1284: *Yüan shih*, chap. 13, cited in Pelliot, *Notes on Marco Polo*, II, p. 796.

11. Ibn 'Abd al-Ẓāhir, *Tashrīf al-ayyām wa l-ʿuṣūr fī sīrat al-malik al-Manṣūr*, ed. Murād Kāmil (Cairo, 1961), p. 70. Allouche, p. 443, sees this merely as 'diplomatic bluff'.

12. Şerban Papacostea, cited in Ernest Oberländer-Târnoveanu, 'Byzantino-Tartarica – le monnayage dans la zone des bouches du Danube à la fin du XIIIᵉ et au commencement du XIVᵉ siècle', *MN* 2 (1995–6), pp. 191–214 (here p. 210).

13. On Noghai, see N.I. Veselovskii, *Khan iz temnikov Zolotoi Ordy. Nogai i ego vremia*, Zapiski Rossiiskoi Akademii Nauk, 8e série, 13:6 (Petrograd, 1922); more briefly, Spuler, *Die Goldene Horde*, pp. 64–77. For his assumption of the title of khan, see Ernest Oberländer-Târnoveanu, 'Numismatical contributions to the history of south-eastern Europe at the end of the 13th century', *RRH* 26 (1987), pp. 245–58 (here pp. 252–5); cf. also Lăčezar Lazarov, 'Sur un type de monnaies en cuivre avec la tamgha de Nogaj', *BHR* 25:4 (1997), pp. 3–11.

14. Biran, *Qaidu*, pp. 65–6. Allsen, 'Princes of the Left Hand', pp. 22–3.

15. Bruno of Olmütz, 'Relatio de statu', p. 591 = *CDRB*, V:2, p. 372.

16. Housley, *Later Crusades*, p. 322. Weiler, '*Negotium Terrae Sanctae*', p. 28. But see Jaroslav Goll, 'Zu Brunos von Olmütz Bericht an Papst Gregor X. (1273)', *MIOG* 23 (1902), pp. 487–90.

17. 'Cronica S. Petri Erfordensis moderna', p. 417. For the treatment of Ottokar by the chroniclers, see generally František Graus, 'Přemysl Otakar II. – sein Ruhm und sein Nachleben. Ein Beitrag zur Geschichte politischer Propaganda und Chronistik', *MIOG* 79 (1971), pp. 57–110.

18. 'Hermanni Altahensis annales', p. 410.

19. *CDH*, IV:3, pp. 15–17 = *DIR*, I:1, p. 287 (no. 211); and cf. also 'Annales Otakariani', *MGHS*, IX, pp. 184–5.

20. Societas literaria Poznaniensis, *Kodeks diplomatyczny wielkopolski*, I, pp. 571, 572 (nos. 611, 612).

21. 'Thomae Tusci Gesta imperatorum et pontificum' (down to 1278), *MGHS*, XXII, p. 525.

22. František of Prague (*c*.1353), 'Chronica Pragensis', *FRB*, IV, p. 351 = 'Continuatio Francisci Pragensis', in Johann Loserth, ed., *Die Königsaaler Geschichts-Quellen mit den Zusätzen und der Fortsetzung des Domherrn Franz von Prag*, FRAS[1] 8 (Vienna, 1875), p. 542.

23. For a letter from Ottokar requesting safe-conduct for returning Mongol envoys, see Franz Palacky, ed., *Über Formelbücher, zunächst in Bezug auf böhmische Geschichte*, 2 vols (Prague, 1842-7), II, p. 14 (no. 1).

24. Heinrich von Heimburg (born 1242), 'Annales', *MGHS*, XVII, p. 718 = 'Letopisové Jindřicha Heimburského', *FRB*, III, p. 320.

25. MOL, DL 540 (7 Jan. 1263 = *CDH*, IV:3, p. 101).

26. Berend, *At the Gate*, pp. 163-71; also her 'Hungary, the "Gate of Christendom"', in David Abulafia and Nora Berend, eds, *Medieval Frontiers: Concepts and Practices* (Aldershot, 2002), pp. 195-215 (here pp. 208-15).

27. Humbert of Romans, 'Opusculum tripartitum', i, 5, in Orthuinus Gratius, *Fasciculum rerum expetendarum et fugiendarum*, new edn by Edward Brown, 2 vols (London, 1690), II, p. 187: *ita longe sunt a multitudine Christiana, quod adhuc parum nocuerunt eis nisi solum in Hungaria*. For this work, see Edward Tracy Brett, *Humbert of Romans. His Life and Views of Thirteenth-Century Society* (Toronto, 1984), pp. 176-94.

28. *VMH*, I, p. 387 (no. 621, 17 Oct. 1301) = *DIR*, I:1, p. 557 (no. 444). See also *VMH*, I, pp. 388, 392 (nos. 622, 628) = *DIR*, I:1, pp. 558, 560 (nos. 445, 446).

29. *VMH*, I, pp. 264-5 (nos. 483, 484, 28 Jan. 1264) = *AUO*, III, p. 84 (no. 57). For Alexander IV, see *VMH*, I, p. 240 (no. 454).

30. MOL, DL 104886 (8 April 1264 = *HO*, VIII, p. 96, no. 76): they are named as *Vybar filiu[s] Beubarch* [?], Abachi and Tamachi.

31. MOL, DL 104888 (10 Dec. 1270 = *AUO*, XII, p. 7, no. 3; *DIR*, I:1, pp. 347-8, no. 258); cf. also DL 67344 (*anno* 1268 = *HO*, VIII, p. 111, no. 89). The first mission alone is mentioned in DL 100036 (*anno* 1263, late copy of a transcript dated 1271 = Györffy, 'Adatok', p. 7, no. 12). Cf. Sinor, 'Les relations', p. 58.

32. Lodomer to Pope Nicholas IV, 8 May 1288, in János Karácsonyi, 'A mérges vipera és az antimoniális. Korkép Kún László király idejéből', *Századok* 44 (1910), pp. 1-24 (here pp. 3, 4, 7, 8). Lodomer to the clerics and nobles of Hungary, 1288, ibid., pp. 8, 10-11. Cf. the comments of Berend, *At the Gate*, pp. 176-7.

33. See Rutkowska-Plachcinska, 'L'image du danger tatar', pp. 87-8.

34. *PUB*, I:2, p. 160 (no. 207). Sarnowsky, 'Teutonic Order', p. 257, n.21, assumes that this refers to the events of 1260.

35. *PSRL*, X. *Patriarshaia ili Nikonovskaia letopis'*, p. 147; tr. Serge A. and Betty Jean Zenkovsky, *The Nikonian Chronicle*, 5 vols (Princeton, NJ, 1984-9), III, p. 45. Fennell, *Crisis*, pp. 128-9. Nazarova, 'Crusades against Votians', p. 195.

36. Zdan, pp. 517–18.
37. *PSRL*, II, coll. 881–2 (tr. Perfecky, p. 92). 'Rocznik Traski', p. 847 = 'Annales Polonorum (i)', p. 644, and 'Rocznik małopolski', p. 181 = 'Annales Polonorum (iv)', pp. 645, 647, both date the battle near Goslicz on 23 Feb. 1280. 'Annales Sandivogii' (to 1360), *MGHS*, XXIX, p. 429. Spuler, *Die Goldene Horde*, p. 59, places the beginning of these hostilities in 1279.
38. 'Rocznik Traski', p. 853 = 'Annales Polonorum (i)', pp. 652, 654. 'Annales Sandivogii', p. 429. On this episode, see Gotthold Rhode, *Die Ostgrenze Polens. Politische Entwicklung, kulturelle Bedeutung und geistige Auswirkung*, I. *Im Mittelalter bis zum Jahre 1401* (Köln and Graz, 1955), pp. 112–13, 120.
39. *PUB*, I:2, p. 166 (no. 222, 4 June 1264) = CICO, V:1, p. 41 (no. 11) = *CDRB*, V:1, p. 614 (no. 413). *VMP*, I, p. 79 (no. 151, 20 Jan. 1268) = *PUB*, I:2, p. 197 (no. 279) = *CDRB*, V:2, pp. 96–7 (no. 538). *VMP*, I, p. 80 (no. 154, 26 Jan. 1268) = *PUB*, I:2, p. 199 (no. 281) = *CDRB*, V:2, pp. 100–1 (no. 541).
40. *Basqaq*: S.C. Rowell, *Lithuania Ascending: A Pagan Empire within East-Central Europe, 1295–1345* (Cambridge, 1994), pp. 100, 112–13; J. Pelenski, 'The contest between Lithuania-Rus' and the Golden Horde in the fourteenth century for supremacy over eastern Europe', *AEMA* 2 (1982), pp. 303–20 (here pp. 307–8), repr. in his *The Contest for the Legacy of Kievan Rus'* (Boulder, CO, 1998), pp. 131–50 (here p. 134). For early Lithuanian expansion, see generally Rowell, *Lithuania Ascending*, pp. 82–7, 94–111.
41. As pointed out by Maier, *Preaching the Crusades*, p. 78.
42. Georgios Pachymeres (d. shortly after 1307), *De Michaele et Andronico Palaeologo*, v, 3–4, ed. Albert Failler and tr. Vitalien Laurent, *Georges Pachymérès. Relations historiques*, 5 vols (Paris, 1984–2000), II, pp. 443–9 (French tr. pp. 442–8). For Berke's attack, see Marius Canard, 'Un traité entre Byzance et l'Égypte au XIIIᵉ siècle et les relations diplomatiques de Michel VIII Paléologue avec les sultans mamlûks Baibars et Qalâ'ûn', in *Mélanges offerts à Gaudefroy-Demombynes par ses amis et anciens élèves* (Cairo, 1935–45), pp. 197–224 (here pp. 211–19).
43. Pachymeres, vi, 34–6, ed. Failler and Laurent, II, pp. 659, 664, 666 (French tr. pp. 658, 665, 667).
44. Ernest Oberländer-Târnoveanu, 'Un atelier monétaire inconnu de la Horde d'Or sur le Danube: Sāqčy-Isaccea (XIIIe–XIVe siècles)', in *Actes du XIe Congrès International de Numismatique organisé à l'occasion du 150e anniversaire de la Société Royale de Numismatique de Belgique, Bruxelles, 8–13 septembre 1991*, 4 vols (Louvain-la-Neuve, 1993), III, pp. 291–304. Idem, 'Byzantino-Tartarica', pp. 209–11.
45. Angeliki E. Laiou, *Constantinople and the Latins. The Foreign Policy of Andronicus II 1282–1328* (Cambridge, MA, 1972), pp. 37, 281, 291, 297. Spuler, *Die Goldene Horde*, p. 74. V. Laurent, 'Le métropolite de Vicina Macaire et la prise de la ville par les Tartares', *RHSEE* 23 (1946), pp. 225–32; but cf. Şerban Papacostea, 'De Vicina à Kilia. Byzantins et Génois aux bouches du Danube au XIVᵉ siècle', *RESEE* 16 (1978), pp. 65–79 (here pp. 69–70); Dennis Deletant, 'Genoese, Tatars and Rumanians at the mouth of the Danube in the fourteenth century', *SEER* 62 (1984), pp. 511–30 (here pp. 516–17).

46. V. Laurent, 'L'assaut avorté de la Horde d'Or contre l'empire byzantin (Printemps-été 1341)', *REB* 18 (1960), pp. 145–62. Raymond-Joseph Loenertz, O.P., 'Notes d'histoire et de chronologie byzantines, II. Dernière ambassade grecque à la Horde d'Or (1341)', in Loenertz, *Byzantina et Franco-Graeca*, ed. Peter Schreiner (Rome, 1970), pp. 426–30. Papacostea, 'De Vicina', p. 70.

47. Ramón Lull, 'Liber de acquisitione Terrae Sanctae' (1309), ed. P.E. Kamar, *Studia Orientalia Christiana Collectanea* 6 (1961), p. 130; tr. in Norman Housley, *Documents on the Later Crusades 1274–1580* (Basingstoke and London, 1996), p. 48. Sanudo to the bishop of Ostia (1330), in Kunstmann, 'Studien', p. 781; also a mention of Greek fears in his letter to Philip VI of France (1334), ibid., p. 804. 'Directorium ad passagium faciendum', pp. 449–51.

48. Ibn Faḍl-Allāh al-'Umarī, *Masālik*, ed. Lech, pp. 74–5 (German tr. pp. 141–2); text also in *SMIZO*, I, p. 214 (Russian tr. p. 236). Dimitri A. Korobeinikov, 'Diplomatic correspondence between Byzantium and the Mamlūk Sultanate in the fourteenth century', *Al-Masāq* 16:1 (2004), pp. 53–74 (here pp. 58, 61).

49. For what follows, see generally Victor Spinei, 'Aspekte der politischen Verhältnisse des Gebietes zwischen Donau und Schwarzem Meer zur Zeit der Mongolenherrschaft (XIII–XIV Jahrhundert)', *Dacoromania* 3 (1975–6), pp. 29–38 (here pp. 31–2); Ilka Petrova, 'Nordwestbulgarien in der ungarischen Politik der Balkanhalbinsel im 13. Jahrhundert', *BHR* 11 (1983), pp. 57–65; Fine, *Late Medieval Balkans*, pp. 170–84, 195–9. The standard work on Mongol–Bulgarian relations is still P. Nikov, *Tatarbolgarskite otnosheniia prez srednite vekove s ogled k'm tsaruvaneto na Smiletsa*, Godishnik na Sofiiskiia Universitet, I. Istoriko-filoologicheski fakultet 15–16 (Sofia, 1919–20); abstract in Gaston Cahen, 'Les Mongols dans les Balkans', *RH* 146 (May–Aug. 1924), pp. 55–9.

50. Pachymeres, vi, 3, ed. Failler and Laurent, II, p. 551 (French tr. p. 550).

51. Baybars al-Manṣūrī, *Zubdat al-fikra*, p. 355. al-Nuwayrī (d. 1332), *Nihāyat al-arab fī funūn al-adab*, 33 vols (Cairo, 1923–98), XXVII, p. 373 (with ṢN'JY in error for ṢQJY). Both texts also in *SMIZO*, I, pp. 93, 139 (Russian tr. pp. 117, 161).

52. Spuler, *Die Goldene Horde*, pp. 77–8. Oberländer-Târnoveanu, 'Numismatical contributions', pp. 256–8. The versions of this episode found in the Greek and Arabic sources differ markedly.

53. Olgierd Górka, ed., *Anonymi descriptio Europae orientalis »imperium Constantinopolitanum, Albania, Serbia, Bulgaria, Ruthenia, Ungaria, Polonia, Bohemia« anno MCCCVIII exarata* (Cracow, 1916), pp. 39–40 (§85). See also the treatise (after 1313) examined by Patrick Gautier Dalché, 'Une géographie provenant du milieu des marchands toscans (début XIVᵉ siècle)', in *Società, istituzioni, spiritualità. Studi in onore di Cinzio Violante*, I (Spoleto, 1994), pp. 433–43 (here p. 439).

54. M. Alexandrescu-Dersca, 'L'expédition d'Umur Beg d'Aydin aux bouches du Danube (1337 ou 1338)', *Studia et Acta Orientalia* 2 (1959 [Bucarest, 1960]), pp. 3–23 (here pp. 16–19). P.P. Panaitescu, 'Mircea l'Ancien et les Tatares', *RHSEE* 19 (1942), pp. 438–48 (here pp. 439–40). For other evidence of Mongol domination in the region, see Victor Spinei, *Moldavia in the 11th–*

14th Centuries, tr. Liliana Teodoreanu and Ioana Sturza ([Bucarest], 1986), pp. 124–7.

55. MOL, DL 30586 (= *CDH*, VII:2, p. 141; *UBGD*, I, p. 173, no. 242). Where the printed texts show a lacuna after *Tartari*, the words *et Cumani* are faintly discernible in the original. Cf. also Humbert of Romans, as cited in n.27 above.

56. Jahn, *Die Frankengeschichte*, Tafeln 44–45, facsimile of Persian text, Topkapı Sarayı, Istanbul, ms. Hazine 1653, fo. 415r–v (German trans., p. 53).

57. 'Chronici Hungarici compositio saeculi XIV' (down to 1343), *SRH*, I, p. 472. 'Chronicon Zagrabiense' (1334/1354), ibid., p. 213. We know from Simon of Kéza (*c.*1282) that some of the defeated Cumans had fled to 'the barbarian peoples': 'Gesta Hungarorum', §75, in *SRH*, I, p. 187, and also ed. and tr. László Veszprémy and Frank Schaer, *Simon of Keza. Deeds of the Hungarians* (Budapest, 1999), p. 156 (tr. p. 157). Kosztolnyik, *Hungary*, p. 285.

58. MOL, DF 277873 (*anno* 1288): *cum . . . de finibus et terminis tartarorum quos nemo predecessorum nostrorum peragraverat ultra alpes . . . accessissemus* (= *CDH*, V:3, p. 410; *DIR*, I:1, p. 485, no. 390; *EO*, p. 274, no. 438). The campaign is also mentioned in DF 251669 (27 June 1286, confirmation dated 25 Aug. 1291): *in diversis expedicionibus . . . specialiter ultra alpes in confinio tartarorum* (= *CDH*, V:3, p. 316; *HO*, VI, p. 316, no. 229). Spuler, *Die Goldene Horde*, p. 66, proposes that the Mongols attacked because disease among their cattle made it necessary to restock with booty and victuals.

59. *PSRL*, II, col. 888 (tr. Perfecky, p. 95). 'Annales Augustani minores', *MGHS*, X, p. 10: *invaserunt circa purificationem et terram per totam quadragesimam potenter occupantes*. Polish sources date the onset of the invasion in 1284: 'Rocznik Traski', p. 850 = 'Annales Polonorum (i)', p. 648; 'Rocznik małopolski', p. 183 = 'Annales Polonorum (iv)', p. 649. See generally György Székely, 'Egy elfeledett rettegés: a második tatárjárás a magyar történeti hagyományokban és az egyetemes összefüggésekben', *Századok* 122 (1988), pp. 52–88.

60. The Mongol army extended over eleven miles: 'Continuatio Altahensis', *MGHS*, XVII, p. 414. 'Annales S. Rudberti', p. 809, allege that their camp measured 6 × 10 *rastae* [?]. A letter of Benedict, provost of Esztergom, gives the inflated figure of 200,000: MOL, DF 286314, fo. 119v (= *MES*, II, p. 419, no. 434; *EO*, p. 264, no. 407).

61. MOL, DL 1229: *potencialiter cum omni ipsorum multitudine* (= *CDH*, V:3, p. 399); DL 1298: *cum omni milicia ipsorum* (= *AUO*, XII, p. 497, no. 413); same phrase in DF 253331 (= *AUO*, V, p. 20, no. 13; *UBGD*, I, p. 169, no. 239). See also DL 28502: *maximam partem regni nostri vastibus diris et spoliis peragrasset* (= *CDH*, V:3, pp. 452–3; *UBGS*, p. 148, no. 151; *MES*, II, p. 254, no. 233; *SO*, I, p. 22, no. 18; *DIR*, I:1, p. 488, no. 393).

62. *CDH*, VII:2, p. 110. For the advance as far as Pest, see 'Chronici Hungarici compositio', p. 472.

63. MOL, DL 105994 (14 June 1285): *in praesenti persecucione Tartarorum* (= *CDH*, V:3, p. 301; *MES*, II, p. 197, no. 177).

64. *AKO*, nos. 3361–2, 3372, 3374–5, 3387: he was in Gyulafehérvár by 27 May, in Szepes by 21 July, in Szerencs by 1 Aug., in Sarus by 14 Aug., and at

Zólyom by 11 Sept. Salimbene, *Cronica*, II, p. 871, heard that the Mongols had made peace with the king.

65. Benedict, provost of Esztergom, in MOL, DF 286314, fo. 119v (= *MES*, II, p. 419, no. 434; *EO*, pp. 263–4, no. 407). 'Annales S. Stephani Frisingenses' (down to 1412, but written up more or less contemporarily), *MGHS*, XIII, p. 57. See also DL 28572 (27 May 1285, 15th-cent. copy of a transcript dated 1317 = *SO*, IV, p. 2, no. 657). On the Székely, see Engel, *Realm of St. Stephen*, pp. 115–17.

66. 'Rocznik Traski', p. 850 = 'Annales Polonorum (i)', p. 648. 'Rocznik małopolski', p. 183 = 'Annales Polonorum (iv)', p. 649.

67. 'Vita et miracula Sanctae Kyngae ducissae Cracoviensis', *MPH*, IV, p. 715.

68. 'Kalendarz katedry krakowskiej', MPH^2, V, p. 194: *ix kalendas – vigilia Domini nostri Jesu Christi*. 'Rocznik poznański I' (to 1288, with mid-14th-century additions), MPH^2, VI, p. 130: *circa natale Domini* (but *ad annum* 1288) = 'Annales Posnanienses', *MGHS*, XXIX, p. 470. 'Rocznik Traski', p. 852 = 'Annales Polonorum (i)', p. 650, gives simply 1287. For the names of the Mongol commanders, and their failure before Cracow and Sandomir, see also *PSRL*, II, coll. 891–5 (tr. Perfecky, pp. 96–8).

69. Franciszek Piekosiński, ed., *Kodeks dyplomatyczny miasta Krakowa, I. 1257–1506*, MMAH 5 (Cracow, 1879), pp. 4–5 (no. 2).

70. For what follows, see MOL, DL 57222 (= *CDH*, V:3, pp. 394–6); Gyula Pauler, *A magyar nemzet története az Árpádházi királyok alatt*, 2 vols (Budapest, 1899), II, pp. 398–9.

71. 'Rocznik małopolski', pp. 184/185 = 'Annales Polonorum (ii)', p. 650, and '(iii)', p. 651: Polish annals put the invaders at Sandecz in 1288. St Kynga was a nun there: MOL, DF 258823 (*anno* 1289 = *CDH*, V:3, pp. 463–4; *HO*, VI, p. 344, no. 249).

72. Franciszek Piekosiński, ed., *Kodeks dyplomatyczny małopolski, I. 1178–1386*, MMAH 3 (Cracow, 1876), pp. 133–4 (no. 113: *in die Cinerum* 1287, i.e. 10 Feb. 1288) = *CDH*, V:3, p. 384.

73. MOL, DL 40217 (10 Nov. 1293 = *AKO*, no. 3951; extract in *EO*, pp. 300–1, no. 522), not available to Pauler, II, p. 449. He therefore dated the invasion in 1297 on the basis of DF 285245 (13 July 1298, confirmation dated 13 Oct. 1307 = *AUO*, XII, p. 617, no. 492), which clearly refers to the same attack on 'Macho'.

74. *CDH*, VII:4, p. 237 (no. 244): *nuper Tartari regnum Hungariae invaserant*.

75. MOL, DL 69658 and DL 69939 = Vincent Sedlák, ed., *Regesta diplomatica nec non epistolaria Slovaciae*, 2 vols (Bratislava, 1980–7), I, pp. 239, 260 (nos. 518, 572): both documents refer to events of 1307, *tercio anno post exitum Tartarorum*, i.e. two [not three] years after the Tartars' departure.

76. 'Rocznik Traski', p. 852 = 'Annales Polonorum (i)', p. 652. 'Rocznik małopolski', pp. 184/185 = 'Annales Polonorum (iii, iv)', p. 653. The link is clearer in Ján Długosz, *Historia Polonica* (late 15th cent.), ed. Ignaz Żegota Pauli and Alexander Przezdziecki, 5 vols (Cracow, 1873–8), II, p. 519.

77. Jan van Beke, *Chronographia* (*c.*1346), ed. H. Bruch (The Hague, 1973), p. 221 (I owe this reference to Peter Hoppenbrouwers).

78. Sanudo to the bishop of Ostia (1330), in Kunstmann, 'Studien', pp. 779–81; see also his letter to Philip VI of France (1332), ibid., pp. 797–8.

79. 'Annales terrae Prussicae' (soon after 1340), *MGHS*, XIX, p. 692 = 'Chronica terrae Prussiae', *MPH*, IV, p. 37.

80. *MPV*, I, p. 419 (no. 208, Feb. 1340/1). *PUB*, III:1, pp. 240–1 (no. 345). John of Winterthur (d. after 1348), *Cronica*, ed. Friedrich Baethgen, SRG² 3 (Berlin, 1924), p. 184, reports Mongol attacks upon Hungary, Brandenburg and Prussia. John of Cornazzano, 'Historia Parmensis', in *Monumenta historica ad provincias Parmensem et Placentinam pertinentia*, VIII. *Chronica Parmensia a sec. XI ad exitum sec. XIV* (Parma, 1858), p. 379, thought that the Mongols were trying to enter Bohemia, Poland and Hungary. See also p. 212 and n.128 below.

81. František, 'Chronica Pragensis', pp. 428–9 = 'Continuatio Francisci Pragensis', pp. 562–3. Galvano Fiamma, 'Opusculum de rebus gestis ab Azone, Luchino, et Johanne Vicecomitibus' (to 1342), *RIS²*, XII, p. 39, §14. Georges Daumet, ed., *Bénoît XII (1334–1342). Lettres closes, patentes et curiales se rapportant à la France* (Paris, 1899–1920), col. 475 (no. 763). Schmieder, *Europa*, p. 179.

82. *UBGS*, p. 82 (no. 82) = *UBGD*, I, p. 90 (no. 103).

83. CICO, V:2, pp. 59–60 (no. 27) = *VMH*, I, p. 337 (no. 552) = *DIR*, I:1, pp. 429–30 (no. 345): all the editions read *multo* in error for *milco*.

84. János's detailed chronicle of the years 1345–55 was incorporated in the 'Chronicon Dubnicense' (*c.*1476): Flórián Mátyás, ed., *Historiae Hungaricae fontes domestici*, 4 vols (Leipzig, 1881–5), III, pp. 165–6. On the author, see J. Horváth, 'Die ungarischen Chronisten der Angiovinenzeit', *Acta Linguistica Academiae Scientiarum Hungaricae* 21 (1971), pp. 321–77 (here pp. 375–7).

85. *PSRL*, II, coll. 890–1 (tr. Perfecky, p. 96); for the weather, see also 'Continuatio Altahensis', p. 414; Ottokar of Styria, *Reimchronik*, I, p. 313 (vv. 23706–23759), and hence John of Viktring, *Liber certarum historiarum*, I, pp. 257 (recension A), 297–8 (recensions B, D and A2). Baybars al-Manṣūrī, *Zubdat al-fikra*, pp. 260–1; al-Nuwayrī, *Nihāyat al-arab*, XXVII, p. 366 (but with *al-Karak* for *al-Karal*; on the name 'Kerel'/'Keler' for Hungary, see above, p. 75, n.3); texts also in *SMIZO*, I, pp. 84, 135 (Russian tr., pp. 106, wrongly identifying *KRL* as Cracow, and 156). Both Mamlūk authors date the campaign in 686 H./1287–8, confusing it with the later attack.

86. Berend, *At the Gate*, pp. 37–8. For examples from László IV's reign, see, e.g., Erzsébet Látkóczki Kondorné, ed., *Árpád-kori oklevelek a Heves megyei levéltárban* (Eger, 1997), nos. 28, 30, 31, 34.

87. Collegium historicum Hungarorum Romanum *et al.*, eds, *Monumenta Romana episcopatus Vesprimiensis. A veszprémi püspökszeg Római oklevéltára*, 4 vols (Budapest, 1896–1907), I, pp. 339, 344, 347, 349, 381.

88. MOL, DF 238633 (10 April 1288): *a tempore . . . introitus antiquorum tartarorum* (= *AUO*, IV, p. 311, no. 200); DL 29106 (26 Jan. 1304, transcribed in a document of 1307): *a tempore antiquorum tartharorum* (= *UBGD*, I, p. 229, no. 300); DL 1287 (25 July 1290): *ante adventum priorum tartarorum* (= *HO*, VIII, p. 283, no. 230); DL 95050 (*anno* 1291): *a tempore*

priorum tartarorum (= *CDH*, VI:1, p. 126); DL 40468 (5 Feb. 1302, transcribed in a document of 1325): *quarto anno post magnos tartaros.*

89. E.g. 'Rocznik kapituły gnieźnieńskiej', *MPH*[2], VI, p. 9; 'Rocznik kapituły poznańskiej', ibid., pp. 27, 41, 48; 'Kronika wielkopolska', pp. 88, 90, 95, 105, 118, 125; 'Rocznik Traski', p. 839.

90. Piekosiński, *Kodeks dyplomatyczny Małopolski*, I, pp. 153–4 (no. 128).

91. ASV, Reg. Vat. 137, fo. 156v (no. 554).

92. MOL, DF 247222 (confirmation by András III, 10 Feb. 1291, of László's own confirmation of 27 May 1290): *per vastus et incendia Tartarorum plurimum sunt destructi et depauperati* (= *AUO*, IX, p. 518, no. 289; *UBGS*, p. 138, no. 142; *UBGD*, I, p. 149, no. 211; *DIR*, I:1, pp. 462, 491, nos. 371, 397).

93. E.g. MOL, DL 57222 (*anno* 1288 = *CDH*, V:3, pp. 394, 395); DL 1229 (*anno* 1288 = *CDH*, V:3, p. 399); DL 28502 (18 Sept. 1289 = *CDH*, V:3, p. 453; *UBGS*, p. 148, no. 151; *MES*, II, p. 254, no. 233; *DIR*, I:1, p. 488, no. 393); DL 1298 (*anno* 1290 = *AUO*, XII, p. 497, no. 413); DF 262705 (22 Aug. 1298 = *CDH*, VI:2, p. 151).

94. *VMP*, I, pp. 294–5 (no. 375) = Irena Sułkowska-Kuraś and Stanisław Kuraś, eds, *Bullarium Poloniae*, 6 vols so far (Rome and Lublin, 1982–), I, p. 250 (no. 1411): the appellant's history, though complicated, hardly justified the position taken by the church of Sandomir.

95. MOL, DF 246230 (purportedly 7 Jan. 1302): see E. Lukinich, L. Gáldi, A.F. Nagy and L. Makkai, eds, *Documenta historiam Valachorum in Hungaria illustrantia usque ad annum 1400 p. Christum* (Budapest, 1941), pp. 47–9 (no. 27).

96. MOL, DF 207181.

97. MOL, DF 280223: *feritate demum usus tartarica* (= *EO*, p. 242, no. 351).

98. MOL, DF 248553 (= *CDH*, V:3, p. 289; *MES*, II, p. 200, no. 180).

99. MOL, DF 244570 (= *UBGD*, I, p. 351, no. 380).

100. CICO, VIII, pp. 55–6 (no. 30, 20 Sept. 1338). Cf. *CDH*, VIII:4, p. 323 (no. 153): *nisi privilegiorum instrumenta exhibeant quae dupplici Tartarorum excursione flammis deleta fuerant* = *AE*, XXV, p. 127 (§22).

101. *AKO*, nos. 3841, 3910. Pauler, II, pp. 388–9, 419–20.

102. *PUB*, II, pp. 108–9 (no. 157).

103. Rowell, *Lithuania Ascending*, pp. 95–7; ibid., pp. 100–11 for a thorough discussion of the sources.

104. *MPV*, I, pp. 72–3 (no. 83).

105. For the impact of this dispute on papal policy in Eastern Europe in 1323–5, see Rowell, *Lithuania Ascending*, pp. 217–21.

106. CICO, VII:2, p. 162 (no. 79, 20 June 1325) = *VMP*, I, p. 205 (no. 316). Ibid., I, p. 215 (no. 334, 1 July 1325) = *MPV*, III, pp. 240–1 (no. 186).

107. Rhode, *Die Ostgrenze Polens*, pp. 122–6. Knoll, *Rise*, p. 45.

108. Ibid., p. 123 and n.8, citing Jan of Czarnków (d. 1384), 'Kronika', *MPH*, II, p. 622; see also John of Viktring, *Liber certarum historiarum*, II, p. 218. Pope Benedict XII certainly thought the principality had paid tribute to the Mongols: CICO, VIII, p. 112 (no. 53) = *VMP*, I, p. 434 (no. 566). But Zdan, p. 521, believes it was totally independent. For the 1327 agreement, see *PUB*, II, pp. 387–8 (no. 582); more generally, Knoll, *Rise*, p. 122.

109. The recent despatch of Hungarian troops to Poland is mentioned in MOL, DL 3309 (15 May 1340 = *AO*, IV, p. 26, no. 20); see also DL 68845 (17 Sept. 1342 = *MES*, III, pp. 473–4, no. 625).
110. For these events, see Knoll, *Rise*, pp. 126–33; and cf. Rowell, *Lithuania Ascending*, pp. 264–9. The principal sources are 'Rocznik Traski', pp. 860–1 = 'Continuatio annalium Polonorum (i)', *MGHS*, XIX, pp. 661–2 (Traska tells us he was a participant); (with virtually identical wording) 'Rocznik małopolski', pp. 199–200 = 'Continuatio annalium Polonorum (iii)', *MGHS*, XIX, pp. 661–2; and Jan of Czarnków, 'Kronika', pp. 621–2. The Mongol siege of Lublin dated 1337 in 'Rocznik Świętokrzyski', *MPH*, III, p. 78 (which does not mention an attack *ad annos* 1340–1), must refer to this invasion, *pace* Knoll, *Rise*, pp. 107 (and n.100), 123 (and n.9), 125. A letter of Benedict XII summarizes recent events: CICO, VIII, pp. 111–12 (no. 53, 29 June 1341) = *VMP*, I, p. 434 (no. 566). The otherwise fanciful account by John of Winterthur, *Cronica*, pp. 181, 182–5, accounts for the Mongol invasion more or less correctly.
111. František, 'Chronica Pragensis', pp. 429, 431 = 'Continuatio Francisci Pragensis', pp. 563, 566.
112. Spuler, *Die Goldene Horde*, pp. 98–9. For the war with the Chaghadayids, see Shams al-Dīn al-Shujāʿī, *Taʾrīkh al-malik al-Nāṣir Muḥammad bin Qalāwūn al-Ṣāliḥī wa-awlādihi*, ed. and tr. Barbara Schäfer, 2 vols (Wiesbaden, 1977–85), I (text), pp. 214, 234, II (tr.), pp. 249, 268; texts also in *SMIZO*, I, pp. 254–5 (Russian tr. p. 263).
113. Spuler, *Die Goldene Horde*, pp. 105–6.
114. *MPV*, II, p. 53 (no. 80) = *VMP*, I, p. 532 (no. 702). Mathias von Neuenburg, *Chronik*, ed. Adolf Hofmeister, SRG² 4 (Berlin, 1924–36), p. 465. 'Spominki lwówskie', *MPH*, III, p. 251.
115. 'Rocznik miechowski' (in a section completed 1388?), *MPH*, II, p. 885 = 'Annales Mechovienses', *MGHS*, XIX, p. 670. Heinrich Taube von Selbach (alias Heinrich von Rebdorf; d. 1364), *Chronica imperatorum et paparum*, ed. Harry Breßlau, SRG² 1 (Berlin, 1922), pp. 102–3; excerpt also in *SRP*, II, p. 742. *Chronicon Moguntinum* (*c*.1406), ed. Karl Hegel (Hannover, 1885), p. 4. Knoll, *Rise*, p. 151. Garbled reports reached Florence in April 1352: Matteo Villani, *Cronica*, ii, 72, ed. Francesco Gherardi Dragomanni, 2 vols, Collezione di storici e cronisti italiani editi ed inediti 5–6 (Firenze, 1846), I, pp. 197–8.
116. Detailed account by János of Eger, inserted in 'Chronicon Dubnicense', pp. 163–5. For this and the 1351 campaign, see Knoll, *Rise*, pp. 149–51.
117. CICO, X, pp. 97–9 (no. 52, 4 Nov. 1354) = *VMH*, II, pp. 10–11 (no. 18); for the grant of a tenth, *VMP*, I, pp. 556–7 (no. 739, 22 Nov. 1354); *MPV*, II, pp. 75–7 (no. 113, 12 Feb. 1355).
118. 'Rocznik miechowski', p. 885 = 'Annales Mechovienses', p. 670. Rhode, *Die Ostgrenze Polens*, p. 194 and n.127. Knoll, *Rise*, p. 140.
119. *PUB*, V, pp. 197–8 (no. 349). Knoll, *Rise*, pp. 156–7 and n.55. Spuler, *Die Goldene Horde*, p. 108, views this, unnecessarily, as evidence of a split in the Mongols' ranks.

120. CICO, X, pp. 188–9 (no. 101) = *PUB*, V, p. 287 (no. 512, 24 Jan. 1357) = *VMP*, I, p. 581 (no. 776). Knoll, *Rise*, pp. 156–7; also pp. 159–60 for the Order's agreement with Lithuania.

121. *MPV*, III, pp. 400–1 (no. 421).

122. Paul W. Knoll, 'Poland as *antemurale Christianitatis* in the late Middle Ages', *CHR* 60 (1974), pp. 381–401 (here pp. 392–7); cf. also Knoll, *Rise*, pp. 174–6.

123. See generally Norman Housley, 'King Louis the Great of Hungary and the crusades, 1342–1382', *SEER* 62 (1984), pp. 192–208 (here pp. 195 ff.).

124. *MPV*, III, p. 408 (no. 432). CICO, XI, pp. 47–8 (no. 29a) = *VMP*, I, pp. 618–19 (no. 833).

125. CICO, XII, pp. 386–7 (no. 197) = *VMP*, I, p. 719 (no. 967).

126. MOL, DL 73080 (10 Oct. 1324 = *UBGD*, I, pp. 388–9, no. 427). For the duration of Carobert's campaign, see Gyula Kristó *et al.*, eds, *Anjou-kori oklevéltár. Documenta res Hungaricas tempore regum Andegavensium illustrantia 1301–1387*, 15 vols to date (Budapest and Szeged, 1990–), VIII, nos. 314, 343, 356, 375–6, 378–80, 383, 387: the king was encamped at Déva on 17 June, by the River Küküllő from 10 to 25 July, at Szében (Hermannstadt) on 10–11 Aug., and at Varas on 12–14 Aug.; he was back in Visegrád by 25 Aug. The enemy is vaguely alluded to in DL 2256 (2 Sept. 1324): *contra aemulos et infideles eiusdem domini* (= *CDH*, VIII:2, pp. 599–600; *UBGD*, I, p. 388, no. 426). For the captives, see *VMH*, I, pp. 501–2 (no. 772): *de preda regia . . . duos videlicet iuvenes Tartaros.*

127. Peter von Dusburg, *Chronica terre Prussie* (to 1326), ed. M. Töppen and tr. K. Scholz and D. Wojtecki, *Chronik des Preussenlandes*, AQ 25 (Darmstadt, 1984), p. 538; also in *SRP*, I, p. 213.

128. *MHSM*, II, p. 79 (12 June 1340): *propter invasionem, quam fecerunt Tartari versus partes suas.*

129. E.g. Spuler, *Die Goldene Horde*, p. 97 and n.67; Rhode, *Die Ostgrenze Polens*, p. 173; Knoll, *Rise*, p. 125 and n.20. See also Alexandrescu-Dersca, 'L'expédition', p. 18.

130. CICO, IX, p. 191 (no. 122b) = *CDH*, VIII:3, pp. 635–7 (no. 287) = *UBGD*, I, pp. 455–6 (no. 499). It seems to have remained a dead letter, since in the following year the pope transferred the newly-appointed bishop to the see of Nitra; and cf. below.

131. *VMH*, I, p. 605 (no. 900, 1 Aug. 1335). The letter could well refer to schismatic Bosnians or Serbs: Alexandrescu-Dersca, 'L'expédition', p. 17, n.6.

132. *VMH*, I, pp. 553–4 (no. 865, 1 June 1332). CICO, VIII, pp. 70–1 (no. 36, 17 Jan. 1339) = *VMH*, I, pp. 629–30 (no. 945) = *DIR*, I:1, pp. 656–7 (no. 523).

133. *VMH*, I, pp. 544–5 (no. 845) = *DIR*, I:1, p. 617 (no. 491). For the Wallachian campaign, see Engel, *Realm of St Stephen*, pp. 135–6.

134. MOL, DL 27426 (13 Nov. 1348, transcribed in a document of 1426 = *AO*, V, pp. 247–8, no. 125): *in quodam conflictu contra sevam gentem Tartarorum confinia regni nostri tirannice invadere attentancium habito.*

135. *VMH*, I, p. 815 (no. 1249, 15 July 1352) = *DIR*, I:2, p. 25 (no. 19): *perfidi Tartari et infideles alii regno tuo et terris ibi subiectis confines et contigui*

regnum et terras ipsas...invaserunt et invadere moliuntur. Troop-raising: *CDH*, IX:2, p. 206 = *DIR*, I:2, p. 22 (no. 16). Poland: above, p. 210 and n.115.

136. *SO*, I, pp. 62–3 (no. 48) = *DIR*, I:2, pp. 32–3 (no. 25).

137. These campaigns are described by János of Eger (above, n.84), in 'Chronicon Dubnicense', pp. 151–2; and by János of Küküllő (d. 1394), *De vita et gestis Ludovici regis Hungariae,* now lost but incorporated in both 'Chronicon Dubnicense', pp. 167–8, and *Chronicon Budense* (completed 1473), ed. J. Podhradczky (Buda, 1838), pp. 276–7. András's campaign is referred to in MOL, DF 274724 (16 Oct. 1349, transcribed in a document of 1357 = *CDH*, XI, p. 550), and DF 208867 (= *MES*, IV, p. 169, no. 137), which mentions the Rus' alongside the Tartars.

138. CICO, IX, pp. 188–9 (no. 122) = *VMH*, I, pp. 737–8 (no. 1107) = *UBGD*, II, pp. 39–40 (no. 621). Cf. CICO, X, p. 14 (no. 6, 12 Feb. 1353); and for these and still later attempts to restore the diocese, Spinei, *Moldavia*, pp. 178–81. Alfons Huber, 'Ludwig I. von Ungarn und die ungarischen Vasallenländer', *Archiv für Österreichische Geschichte* 6 (1885), pp. 1–44 (here pp. 16–18).

139. *VMH*, I, p. 280 (no. 513).

140. Ibid., I, pp. 358–9 (no. 578).

141. For a bull of 1325 wrongly dated to 1314, see n.147 below. There was a similarly long gap after 1265 (though for a different reason) in the issuance of crusading bulls to the Teutonic Knights in the Baltic region: Axel Ehlers, 'The crusade of the Teutonic Knights against Lithuania reconsidered', in Murray, *Crusade and Conversion*, pp. 21–44 (here pp. 26–9).

142. CICO, VIII, pp. 103–4 (no. 48) = *VMH*, I, pp. 637–8 (no. 958) = *DIR*, I:1, pp. 658–60 (no. 525).

143. CICO, VIII, pp. 105–6 (no. 49); full text in *VMH*, I, pp. 638–9 (no. 960) = *DIR*, I:1, p. 662 (no. 527).

144. *MPV*, I, pp. 424–8 (no. 214), 428–32 (no. 215, with 'Turks' in error for 'Tartars'). *VMP*, I, p. 146 (no. 605).

145. *MPV*, II, pp. 52–4 (no. 80, 14 March 1351) = *VMP*, I, pp. 531–3 (no. 702), for the grant of an ecclesiastical tenth. CICO, IX, pp. 281–4 (no. 180, 15 May 1351) = *VMP*, I, pp. 539–40 (no. 713), for the crusading indulgence. Ibid., I, pp. 558–9 (no. 742: 1355). Norman Housley, *The Avignon Papacy and the Crusades, 1305–1378* (Oxford, 1986), p. 69.

146. *VMH*, I, p. 501 (no. 771) = *DIR*, I:1, p. 594 (no. 470).

147. ASV, Reg. Vat. 78, fo. 66 (no. 212), wrongly attributed to Clement V, and hence dated to 1314, in *AE*, XXIV, p. 23 (§13), *CDH*, VIII:1, pp. 534–5, and *DIR*, I:1, pp. 574–5 (no. 453).

148. 1334: CICO, VII:2, p. 266 (no. 143) = *VMH*, I, pp. 600–1 (no. 894) = *DIR*, I:1, pp. 630–1 (no. 504); for the same indulgence for Carobert, ibid., p. 630 (no. 503) = *AE*, XXV, p. 12 (§26). 1339: CICO, VIII, pp. 70–1 (no. 36) = *VMH*, I, pp. 629–30 (no. 945) = *DIR*, I:1, pp. 656–7 (no. 523).

149. John: ASV, Reg. Vat. 114, fo. 156v. Benedict: CICO, VIII, p. 70 (no. 36) = *VMH*, I, p. 629 (no. 945) = *DIR*, I:1, p. 657 (no. 523). Louis: CICO, X, p. 164 (no. 87) = *VMH*, II, p. 33 (no. 61), and for the grant of territory, CICO, IX, p. 325 (no. 197) = *DIR*, I:2, p. 24 (no. 18).

150. *VMH*, I, pp. 815–16 (no. 1249, 15 July 1352) = *DIR*, I:2, pp. 25–6 (no. 19); see also *VMH*, I, pp. 816–17 (no. 1250); for the release of the Neapolitans, ibid., p. 818 (no. 1253); Housley, *Avignon Papacy*, p. 71.
151. Though Knoll, *Rise*, p. 176, suggests that even the monies promised to Poland were insufficient.
152. CICO, VIII, p. 112 (no. 53) = *VMP*, I, p. 434 (no. 566).
153. František, 'Chronica Pragensis', p. 430 = 'Continuatio Francisci Pragensis', p. 565. John of Winterthur, *Cronica*, pp. 182–3, after saying that the Emperor withheld his assistance, has crusaders from neighbouring regions overwhelming the Mongols in Hungary! According to Galvano Fiamma, 'Opusculum', p. 41, §18, the kings of Poland, Hungary and Bohemia were assisted by 'numerous Germans'. See generally Knoll, *Rise*, pp. 99–100.
154. János of Eger, in 'Chronicon Dubnicense', p. 148.
155. For this first period of civil war, see Spuler, *Die Goldene Horde*, pp. 109–27.
156. Orus was third, and Toqtamish fifth, in descent from Toqa Temür's son Uz Temür, according to the Chinggisid genealogy in *Mu'izz al-ansāb* (1426), BN ms. Ancien fonds persan 67, fos. 25v–26r (Russian tr. in *SMIZO*, II, p. 61), and adopted by D. DeWeese, 'Toḵtami<u>sh</u>', *Enc.Isl.*², in preference to the traditional descent of both Orus and Toqtamish from Orda, which is given by Spuler.
157. Fourth in descent from Toqa Temür's youngest son Kin Temür: *Mu'izz al-ansāb*, fos. 25v, 27v (Russian tr. in *SMIZO*, II, p. 63). For Toqtamish's conflict with Temür, see Spuler, *Die Goldene Horde*, pp. 129–36.
158. *VMH*, II, p. 135 (no. 271, 23 March 1373) = *DIR*, I:2, p. 201 (no. 149): *sese cum Tartaris vicinis Regno Ungarie ad invadendum ipsum Regnum . . . impietatis funiculis colligarunt*; see also *VMH*, II, p. 138 (no. 272) = *DIR*, I:2, pp. 204–5 (no. 150).
159. G. Mollat, ed., *Lettres secrètes et curiales du pape Grégoire XI (1370–1378) intéressant les pays autres que la France* (Paris, 1962–5), fasc. 1, p. 232 (no. 1651, 4 April 1373).
160. Deletant, 'Genoese, Tatars and Rumanians', pp. 525–6.
161. Alexander A. Vasiliev, *The Goths in the Crimea* (Cambridge, MA, 1936), pp. 177–82.
162. Şerban Papacostea, 'Aux débuts de l'état moldave. Considérations en marge d'une nouvelle source', *RRH* 12 (1973), pp. 139–58 (here pp. 152–7). G.I. Brătianu, 'Deux études historiques, II. Demetrius princeps Tartarorum (ca.1360–1380)', *Revue des Études Roumaines* 9–10 (1965), pp. 39–46; and cf. Deletant, 'Genoese, Tatars and Rumanians', pp. 518, 528.
163. See Engel, *Realm of St Stephen*, pp. 165–7.
164. Pelenski, 'Contest', pp. 309–11 (in his *Contest*, pp. 135–7): the river was either the Siniukha, a tributary of the Bug, or the Snyvod', on the borders of the Kiev region, Volynia and Podolia. See more generally Matei Cazacu, 'A propos de l'expansion polono-lituanienne au nord de la mer Noire aux XIVᵉ–XVᵉ siècles: Czarnigrad, la "Cité Noire" de l'embouchure du Dniestr', in Ch. Lemercier-Quelquejay, G. Veinstein and S.E. Wimbush, eds, *Passé turco-tatar, présent soviétique. Études offertes à Alexandre Bennigsen* (Paris and Louvain, 1986), pp. 99–122 (here pp. 100–5).

165. CICO, VII:2, pp. 155–7 (no. 76a) = *VMP*, I, pp. 193–5, no. 293. James Muldoon, *Popes, Lawyers and Infidels. The Church and the Non-Christian World, 1250–1550* (Liverpool, 1979), p. 87, assumes that the Mongols are intended; see also Rowell, *Lithuania Ascending*, pp. 219–20.

166. *VMP*, I, pp. 748–9 (no. 1015); ibid., p. 695 (nos. 934–5), for the letters of 1373.

167. Anatoli Lewicki, ed., *Codex epistolaris saeculi decimi quinti*, II, MMAH 12 (Cracow, 1891), p. 17 (no. 13).

168. Johann Voigt, ed., *Codex diplomaticus Prussicus*, 6 vols (Königsberg, 1836–61), VI, p. 47 (no. 42).

169. Spuler, *Die Goldene Horde*, p. 137.

170. Aurel Decei, 'Établissement de Aktav de la Horde d'Or dans l'empire ottoman, au temps de Yildirim Bayezid', in *Zeki Velidi Togan'a armağan* (Istanbul, 1950–5), pp. 77–92, amending the thesis of Panaitescu, 'Mircea l'Ancien', pp. 441–7. Peter Schreiner, ed., *Die byzantinischen Kleinchroniken*, 3 vols (Vienna, 1975–9), II, pp. 362–3.

171. Venetian report of 11 April 1402, in N. Iorga, 'Notes et extraits pour servir à l'histoire des croisades au XVᵉ siècle', *ROL* 4 (1896), pp. 25–118, 226–320, 503–622 (here pp. 248–9); also in George T. Dennis, 'Three reports from Crete on the situation in Romania, 1401–1402', *SV* 12 (1970), pp. 243–65 (here p. 248, tr. p. 259), repr. in his *Byzantium and the Franks 1350–1420* (London, 1982).

172. Dietrich von Nyem, *De scismate libri tres* (1410), ed. G. Erler (Leipzig, 1890), p. 330 (addendum from the Paderborn ms.): he thought that these Tartars were Temür's subjects.

173. On the battle and its consequences, see Pelenski, 'Contest', pp. 311–18 (in his *Contest*, pp. 137–43); but cf. Cazacu, 'A propos de l'expansion', pp. 105–6.

174. A first cousin of Temür Qutlugh: *Muʿizz al-ansāb*, fo. 27v (Russian tr. in *SMIZO*, II, p. 62). For the date, see DeWeese, 'Toktamish', p. 563. For Toqtamish's flight from Astrakhan in the summer of 1401, see Iorga, 'Notes', p. 245; Dennis, 'Three reports', p. 246 (tr. p. 254).

175. Clavijo, *Embajada a Tamorlán*, ed. Francisco López Estrada (Madrid, 1943), pp. 216–17; tr. G. Le Strange, *Embassy to Tamerlane 1403–1406* (London, 1928), pp. 299–300.

176. Anton Prochaska, ed., *Codex epistolaris Vitoldi magni ducis Lithuaniae 1376–1430*, MMAH 6 (Cracow, 1882), p. 170 (no. 393, 9 April 1409). Ch. Potvin, ed., *Oeuvres de Ghillebert de Lannoy, voyageur, diplomate et moraliste* (Louvain, 1878), p. 41; also in *SRP*, III, p. 448.

177. Spuler, *Die Goldene Horde*, pp. 136–54.

178. Hermann Heimpel, 'Zur Handelspolitik Kaiser Sigismunds', *VSWG* 23 (1930), pp. 145–56.

179. 'Franciscani Thorunensis annales Prussici', *SRP*, III, p. 314. Conrad Bitschin, 'Fortsetzung zu Peter von Dusburgs Chronik' (down to 1435), ibid., p. 484. Spuler, *Die Goldene Horde*, p. 147. On Tannenberg, see Christiansen, *Northern Crusades*, pp. 227–8; Sven Ekdahl, *Die Schlacht bei Tannenberg 1410*, I. *Quellenkritische Untersuchungen* (Berlin, 1982).

180. For the controversy at Constance, see Christiansen, *Northern Crusades*, pp. 231–41; Schmieder, *Europa*, pp. 189–92.
181. *VMP*, I, pp. 769–73 (nos. 1041–3). Sarnowsky, 'Teutonic Order', p. 258. Muldoon, *Popes*, p. 100, believes that Boniface IX, and his successors prior to the Council of Constance, were uninterested in the infidels on Latin Christendom's north-eastern frontier.
182. See the verdicts of Spuler, *Die Goldene Horde*, pp. 101, 105–6, 142–3, 150; Pelenski, 'Contest', pp. 318–20 (in his *Contest*, pp. 143–5); and Michael Weiers, 'Die Goldene Horde oder das Khanat Qyptschaq', in Weiers, *Die Mongolen*, p. 371.

chapter 9

TEMÜR[1] (TAMERLANE) AND LATIN CHRISTENDOM

———————————— ❧⟨⟨⟨⟨⟩⟩⟩⟩❧ ————————————

The rise of Temür

Although those who wrote about Temür's career during his lifetime gave no date for the conqueror's birth, a convention among his later biographers would place it in 736 H./1335–6. The year was highly emblematic: it had witnessed the death of the last undisputed Ilkhan, Abū Saʿīd, the effective collapse of the Ilkhanate, and the division of its territories among a number of largely non-Mongol dynasties.[2] Temür and his political opponents within the Mongol world acted out their lives on a stage dominated by the figure of Chinggis Khan.[3] He and his historians believed (or wanted others to believe) that he was engaged in the restoration of Chinggis Khan's world-empire.[4] Temür's own origins lay not in Ilkhanid Persia, but in the Chaghadayid khanate in Central Asia, the territory known to Western Europeans as *Medium Imperium*, 'the Middle Empire', or (much less accurately) as *Media* and *Imperium Medorum*. The history of this polity is ill-documented and more obscure than that of any of the other Mongol states, but it seems that from *c.*1340 it was split into two khanates. In the western part, comprising Transoxiana, the tribal amirs disputed power in the name of a series of feeble and ephemeral khans belonging to the lines of Chaghadai and (sometimes) of Ögödei. Here Islam had made significant advances, and the rulers were semi-sedentarized. In the east, by contrast, where Islam was only beginning to make any headway, the Chaghadayid khans retained real power and their lifestyle was characteristically that of the steppe nomad. This region was popularly called *Mughulistān* ('Mongolia'), though to their western neighbours in Transoxiana its Mongol inhabitants were known as *Jata* (allegedly 'robbers').[5]

Temür belonged to the ruling clan of the Turkicized Mongol tribe of the Barlas, which occupied the pasturelands around Shahr-i Sabz (Kish) in Transoxiana.[6] In the upheavals which followed the murder of the leading warlord and khan-maker, Qazaghan, in 1358, he first collaborated with the Chaghadayid khan of Mughulistān, who invaded and briefly subdued Transoxiana in 1361–2, and then allied with Qazaghan's grandson Ḥusayn in order to defeat and expel the invaders. It was in the course of a local conflict in eastern Persia, where the two men had taken temporary refuge, that Temür received the wounds which partially disabled him and gave rise to his sobriquet 'the Lame' (Persian -*i lang*; Turkish *aksak*). By 1370, when he broke with Ḥusayn and overthrew him, Temür had become the paramount figure in the western Chaghadayid polity.

During the next few decades Temür welded the Chaghadayid nomads into a more effective war-machine by gradually transferring administrative office and military command from the old tribal leaders to men chosen from his own personal following.[7] To cement his authority over the military, he led them in successful expeditions against external enemies: the khans of Mughulistān; the successor dynasties that had arisen from the débris of the Ilkhanate; the Sultanate of Delhi, which had defied numerous Chaghadayid attacks in the past; and the Mamlūk Sultanate of Egypt and Syria. We have seen how he intervened, too, in the politics of the White Horde, where he promoted his client Toqtamish, and was drawn into attacks on the Golden Horde when Toqtamish turned against him. Temür's policy was one of indirect rule: he replaced his vanquished enemies with princes – usually from the same dynasty – who would act as his dutiful subordinates, furnishing troops for his campaigns and guaranteeing the payment of tribute. The plunder and slaves from the cities sacked by Temür's troops flowed back to adorn and enrich his 'capital' at Samarqand. At the time of his death in February 1405, he was on the threshold of an ambitious campaign to reduce China, the only constituent part of the former Mongol empire that he had not so far attacked.

Temür's historians would embellish the role played by his thirteenth-century forebear, Qarachar of the Barlas tribe, one of Chaghadai's leading noyans, in the history of the Chaghadayid khanate. And twenty years or more after Temür's death, a bogus claim to common ancestry with Chinggis Khan himself would be advanced for him and his dynasty. His marriage to two Chaghadayid princesses entitled him to the style of *küregen* ('son-in-law') traditionally borne by those who married into Chinggis Khan's dynasty. Yet Temür was not of Chinggisid descent. He ruled, but did not reign. His title was simply 'Great Amir', and at no time did he assume the dignity of khan. Down until 1402, at least, he acted in the name of two successive shadow khans of Chaghadai's ulus, on whose behalf he asserted that Persia belonged to the Chaghadayids by virtue of Chinggis Khan's original distribution of territories.[8] Both these shadow khans were members, in fact, of Ögödei's line, and on occasions Temür claimed to be redressing the displacement of that branch of the Chinggisid dynasty by the Toluids in the 1250s (above, p. 115), a posture that may have been designed to enhance the universalist character of Temür's rule.[9]

However Turkicized his ancestry, Temür was – and acted like – a Mongol noble. Though not untouched by sedentary culture, he was the nomadic leader of an army of nomads.[10] A Muslim, he was accompanied on his campaigns by a portable mosque.[11] His forces were known as 'Chaghadais', both to their enemies in Asia and to the Latin observers who brought back reports about the conqueror; they also appear in Western sources under the time-honoured guise of 'Tartars'. The roots of Temürid military success which attracted the attention of these Europeans were those we have earlier met with in the campaigns of Chinggis Khan: tight discipline, skilful tactics, superb generalship, and techniques of terror designed to obtain rapid submission and to deter future *revanchisme*. In this last respect Temür may have consciously emulated Chinggis Khan. The question whether Temür's bad faith towards some of those who accepted his guarantee of safety and yielded to his forces, or the sadistic cruelty which made his name a byword, render him less worthy of admiration than his model is not one that can detain us here. What should be said is that he was undeniably inferior in administrative genius to his great precursor, so that when he died his empire splintered far more rapidly.

His operations in Mesopotamia and the Caucasus eventually brought Temür into conflict with the Ottoman Turks in Anatolia. Under Sultan Murād I (1359–89) and his son and successor, Bāyezīd I Yılderim ('the Thunderbolt'), the Ottomans had made spectacular territorial gains at the expense of the Byzantine empire and other Christian powers of the Balkans and had even begun to threaten Latin Europe. In 1396 Bāyezīd had scored a decisive victory at Nicopolis, on the Danube, over a crusading army led by King Sigismund of Hungary and including French and Burgundian contingents. By the turn of the century the Ottoman Sultan's meteoric advance was a matter of grave concern to all the Christian powers in the eastern Mediterranean and Black Sea regions, whether the Byzantine empire, the Latin kingdom of Cyprus, Venice and Genoa and their colonies, the autonomous Venetian and Genoese lords of the various Aegean islands, or the Knights Hospitallers at Rhodes.

Temür's first overtures towards the Ottomans were amicable in tone. As early as *c*.1395 he was endeavouring to draw Bāyezīd into his struggle with the recalcitrant Toqtamish by offering him all the Golden Horde's territory west of the Dnieper.[12] The Sultan, apprehensive regarding Temür's activities on his eastern flank, did not respond. Temür required no pretext to attack the Ottomans, since their core territories had once formed part of the Ilkhanate; but their readiness to shelter fugitive princes whom he had displaced, and Bāyezīd's attack on Temür's protégé, the ruler of Arzinjān, provided an additional incentive. Temür began in 1400 with the reduction of Sivas, which Bāyezīd had recently occupied, but then turned his attention to the Mamlūks, invading Syria and sacking Damascus in 1401. Only thereafter did he deal decisively with the Ottomans. On 28 July 1402 the Chaghadayid army crushed Bāyezīd's forces near Ankara, and the Sultan spent the last few months of his life as a captive accompanying Temür on his travels, while his sons fought over their inheritance. This did not amount to much, since one result of the Chaghadayid victory was that the Ottomans' Anatolian provinces largely passed back into the hands of the various Turkish dynasties which had ruled there prior to the conquests of Bāyezīd and his father; and Temür further fuelled the brothers' squabble by accepting pledges of allegiance from each of them in return for promises of his support.[13]

Temür's last operation in Anatolia was an attack in December 1402 on the Latin Christian fortress of Smyrna (now Izmir), which was held by the Knights Hospitallers. The castellan defiantly rejected his demand for surrender, and the place was taken by storm. The sources suggest that the knights themselves escaped by sea, though we do not have to believe the allegation that they had made a pact with the conqueror; in any event, the Greek refugees left behind were slaughtered.[14] Shortly afterwards an advance on Phocaea, where a great many 'Franks' had taken refuge, was bought off with the offer of tribute; representatives from one or two of the Latin-held islands in the Aegean also waited on the conqueror.[15] Then Temür, who lacked the naval power necessary to proceed beyond the Straits and may have anticipated a dearth of pasturage for his forces in the Balkans,[16] withdrew eastwards on the first stages of his long return march to Samarqand.

Temür and the Christian powers

The Byzantine capital of Constantinople had been under siege by Ottoman forces since 1394, and the Emperor Manuel II Palaeologus (1391–1425) had left in 1399 on a tour of western Europe with the aim of securing desperately-needed assistance. The Castilian envoy Clavijo subsequently heard that the emperor's nephew and regent, John VII, had reached an agreement with Bāyezīd, undertaking to surrender

Constantinople and become his subordinate if the Ottoman Sultan was victorious over Temür.[17] But John and the Genoese in Pera were simultaneously in diplomatic contact with the Central Asian conqueror.[18] In the summer of 1401 Temür had sent to Constantinople two envoys, the Dominican Francis and a Muslim, to discourage them from making peace with Bāyezīd, on the grounds that Temür himself was about to attack the Sultan.[19] John and the Genoese may have incited Temür against the Ottomans; they had certainly promised him the tribute hitherto yielded to the Sultan, and acquiesced in his demand to bar the Straits in order to prevent Turkish forces in Europe crossing to Bāyezīd's assistance.[20] In August 1402, after his victory over Bāyezīd, Temür again sent word to Constantinople and Pera, warning the authorities there to keep their galleys in readiness so that the remnants of the defeated Ottoman army could not flee across the Straits.[21] Further embassies from the conqueror were in Pera in January 1403 and in the late summer; we do not know whether they came with the same purpose.[22]

On two occasions – in May and in August 1402 – Venetian galleys complied by sailing to the Dardanelles.[23] A Genoese annalist reports that in the wake of Temür's first embassy the colonists at Pera hoisted his banner,[24] and Temür's court historians record the arrival of envoys from 'the king [*malik*] of Istanbūl' (presumably John VII) offering submission and tribute in October 1402.[25] Yet overall the response to the conqueror's overtures was ambivalent. Certain Genoese and Venetian sea-captains, alert to the possibilities of profit, disregarded all these undertakings, first allowing reinforcements to reach Bāyezīd and later shipping fugitives from his shattered army to safety.[26] The Venetians on the island of Samos, too, gave asylum to Turkish refugees.[27]

The Emperor Manuel had been cheered, it seems, by the news of Temür's capture of Sivas.[28] And he and his beleaguered subjects rejoiced when reports reached them of Bāyezīd's downfall at Ankara: for one Greek writer, Temür's victory signalled an intervention by the Virgin herself.[29] But the Byzantine rulers were under no illusions. Early in 1403 Manuel, who had not yet arrived back in his capital, was urging that the Straits be blocked against Temür.[30] Two years later, his ambassador assured the newly-elected Roman Pope, Innocent VII, that the purpose of the conqueror and his Tartars was not merely to overwhelm Constantinople and the neighbouring region but to attack all Christian territory and destroy Christians everywhere. The pope in response granted Manuel what was in fact a highly unusual privilege for a Byzantine Emperor, namely the right to select churchmen to preach the crusade against Temür and his armies in the Two Sicilies, Hungary, the Balkans and Romania.[31] Even allowing for hyperbole that was designed to elicit the fullest Western assistance, Byzantine anxiety about Chaghadayid operations, it seems, had not abated significantly.

Reports of Temür's advance had been reaching the West since his first campaigns of devastation in the Caucasus. As early as 1394 the Venetian Senate was urging Manuel II to stand firm against the Ottomans, on the grounds that Bāyezīd was distracted by Temür's activities.[32] Then in 1395 the Chaghadayid forces sacked Tana, on the Sea of Azov, and destroyed the Venetian outpost there; despite the friendly assurances given earlier to Tana's envoys, the representative of Temür who escorted them back to the town proved to have been spying with a view to the impending attack.[33] It has been suggested that the attack sprang simply from Temür's policy of wrecking the economy of the Golden Horde khanate, rather than out of any hostility specifically towards Europeans;[34] though this would hardly have softened the blow. Among the Venetian possessions lost in the flames were the privileges conferred on the community by successive khans of the Golden Horde.[35] In January 1401 the Venetian Senate, alarmed by fresh reports of Chaghadayid operations in the Near East, instructed its representatives in Crete to send up-to-date information on his movements, and authorized its consul in Alexandria to withdraw to Crete should Temür reach the city.[36]

Around this time the Mamlūk Sultan, who was at Damascus seeing to the city's defences, received an offer of naval assistance against Temür from the king of Cyprus and the Genoese at Famagusta; but such was the disarray within the Egyptian high command that the approach was ignored.[37] Both Venetian and Catalan merchants suffered losses when the Chaghadayid army sacked Damascus in the first months of that year.[38] And in a highly garbled account an English chronicler alleged that pilgrimage to the Holy Places had become more difficult as a result of the sack of Jerusalem.[39] The Roman Pope Boniface IX drew attention to the fact that 'the son of Perdition, Thamurlang, known as Themir Aksak, the oppressive conqueror of Asia', was persecuting Christians and threatening the very survival of the faith in those parts.[40] In 1403 Venetians in Syria reported fears of a fresh invasion by Temür.[41]

King Martin I of Aragon would have been kept abreast of events in the Near East by the Catalan mercantile communities in Damascus and Alexandria.[42] Writing to the Avignonese Pope Benedict XIII in March 1403 after learning of the sack of Smyrna from its castellan, Iñigo d'Alfaro (who may have been Aragonese), he described the perpetrator as 'the arrogant Belial called Tamerlan'.[43] At this stage it is possible that Martin, who for some years had been concerned to provide aid for the Byzantine empire, was told by Greek envoys of the presence of one of Bāyezīd's sons at Temür's headquarters and was misled into thinking that Temür had made common cause with the Ottomans.[44] When in June the king responded to a letter from the Emperor Manuel announcing the joyful news of Bāyezīd's overthrow, he expressed pleasure but referred, in measured tones, to the Sultan's capture by 'an infidel like himself'.[45] And although the letter which Martin wrote to Temür in April 1404 addressed him cordially, it pointedly attributed Bāyezīd's defeat to the hand of God, who 'does not permit unjust aggression long to flourish or ill-will against Christians who serve the Lord to be spread' – a thinly-veiled warning, perhaps, that Temür's own conduct risked bringing down on him the fate of his vanquished enemy.[46]

Whatever his usefulness in ridding Christendom of the Ottoman Sultan, Temür represented potentially an even greater menace, and his presence in Anatolia posed a serious dilemma for all the Christian powers.[47] According to Clavijo, he reacted angrily to the news that the Greeks and Genoese had helped the fleeing Ottomans and thereafter conceived a deep antipathy towards Christians;[48] a later writer blamed the sack of Smyrna on this assistance given to Temür's enemies.[49] The anonymous biographer of Jean Le Maingre, the celebrated Maréchal de Boucicaut and governor of Genoa for Charles VI of France, believed that Christendom had no reason to expect better treatment from Temür than it would have received from Bāyezīd, had he lived.[50] In January 1403 Boucicaut deputed a group of ambassadors to negotiate with various powers in the East, including the Turks and Temür; they were to make alliances and wage war as they saw fit.[51] As a result, within the next few months, John VII, Venice, Genoa and the Hospitallers of Rhodes entered into a treaty with Bāyezīd's son Süleymān Çelebī, who controlled the Ottoman possessions on the European side of the Straits: one object of the agreement was to secure his assistance against Temür with ships and men if need arose. According to a contemporary report by the Venetian lord of Andros, Pietro Zeno, the Christian powers decided to send galleys to rendezvous with Süleymān should Temür display any intention of crossing into Europe.[52]

The apprehensions roused among the Latins by Temür's operations, however, were by no means invariably mirrored in the rumours that circulated in Western circles or in the diplomatic activity which followed. We know nothing of the purpose of the embassy which Venice had sent to him late in 1399 or early in 1400; nor are we told the errand of the three emissaries from the Master of the Hospital who were with him by April 1403.[53] But the sack of Damascus in 1401, and the massacre there of a group of Muslim divines, which was rumoured to have shocked the Islamic world, may well have helped to nurture a more favourable impression of the conqueror in the West.[54] The chance fact, too, that some houses in the Christian quarter escaped the conflagration, as reported several years later by an Italian merchant who had been resident in Damascus, possibly reached Europe at an earlier date.[55] And as the news of the Ottoman *débâcle* at Ankara reverberated far and wide, some reacted more positively than the Aragonese king. Sigismund of Hungary wrote in 1404 that divine clemency had used the Tartars to eliminate the Turkish savagery. We might discount this on the grounds that the principal aim of his letter was to denounce the enmity of Pope Boniface IX, which prevented him moving against the Turks.[56] But already in the late summer of 1402 rumours were current that Temür was well disposed towards the Christian powers and sought perpetual peace with them; a report from Constantinople that Temür had offered to restore to Manuel II all the territories lost to Bāyezīd gave rise to considerable optimism in the West.[57]

Doubtless for this reason, other states, apart from those with vital interests in the Levant, were keen to make contact with the newcomer. At the very beginning of the century the Castilian king, Enrique III, had sent out two ambassadors to ascertain the relative strength of Temür and of Bāyezīd; and after his triumph at Ankara the victor sent them back to Castile with a Muslim envoy of his own, bearing gifts and a cordial letter. Enrique responded with a further embassy, which embarked near Cadiz in May 1403, was well received by the conqueror in Samarqand, and began its return journey in November 1404, though without having received from Temür any reply to the Castilian king's missive.[58] Temür, who was said to have fallen gravely ill, was probably no longer interested in campaigning against the Ottoman Sultanate and in any case may simply have turned his attention to the campaign against China.[59] One of the Castilian envoys, Ruy González de Clavijo, has left us an account of the mission, which is usually regarded as the most important single Western source on Temür and his empire.

Of greater significance in the contemporary diplomatic context than the Castilian embassy, however, were the peregrinations of the Dominican John, archbishop of Sulṭāniyya. In 1398/9 John, accompanied by his fellow Dominican, Francis, had headed an embassy from Temür to Charles VI of France, and had also visited Henry IV of England, taking letters from both monarchs back to the conqueror. In the wake of Ankara, he was despatched to France and Italy a second time, with letters from Temür and his son Mīrān Shāh (whose appanage included the archbishop's own seat, Sulṭāniyya), and spent several years travelling around Western capitals. During this time he wrote two works: a short account of Temür (1403), of which a partial Latin translation was later incorporated in the *Chronographia regum Francorum*, and a longer description of the world, entitled *Libellus de notitia orbis* (1404). He left the courts of France, England and Aragon (1404), as well as the head-quarters of the Teutonic Order in Prussia (1407), with letters for Temür; but in 1412 he had still not returned to the Near East.[60] By this juncture Temür had in any case been dead for seven years, and Mīrān Shāh had fallen in battle (1408) with the Qara Qoyunlu Türkmens, who were busy appropriating the westernmost regions of the Temürid empire.

The roots of misperception

The mission of John of Sulṭāniyya appears to have been designed to counter hostile perceptions of Temür in the West. Alongside the Persian original of Temür's letter to Charles VI there has survived a contemporary Latin translation drafted, in all probability, by John; it is followed by the Latin version of a letter to the Frankish kings and princes in general from Mīrān Shāh, of which the original is no longer extant. Significantly, whereas the Persian text of Temür's letter mentions only the desirability of commercial relations between Temür's dominions and the Franks (as does Mīrān Shāh's letter), the Latin rendering goes beyond this and speaks of a common hostility to Bāyezīd.[61] The reply of Henry IV of England suggests that the translation of Temür's letter to him (assuming it was identical with that to Charles VI) had been similarly doctored.[62] Like the Westerners who had accompanied Ilkhanid embassies in an earlier generation (above, pp. 174–5), John of Sulṭāniyya embellished the messages entrusted to him in order to elicit a warmer response.

In some degree, of course, John's *élan* fed on the elimination of Bāyezīd, which had brought a reprieve for the Byzantines and other Christians in the Balkans. He observed, for instance, that the Albanians hoped now to be delivered from the Ottoman yoke by the Serbian prince Stefan Lazarevich.[63] But when it came to Temür's more direct impact on Christians, John may have been somewhat disingenuous. He was perfectly well aware that Christians were to be numbered among the victims of Temür's cruelty alongside Muslims.[64] Yet he alleged that at Sivas the conqueror had spared the Greeks among the population when the rest were buried alive.[65] He claimed too that, as a result of conversations with himself and his fellow Dominican Francis, Temür's animosity towards Christians had been mitigated: now far more tolerant, he was especially well disposed towards Latins.[66] The archbishop further professed to believe that Temür had attacked Bāyezīd out of affection for the Christians who were allied with him.[67] But John was sufficiently realistic, of course, when taking charge of the English king's reply, to delete a sentence that warmly urged Temür to accept baptism.[68] He was keener, perhaps, to trumpet the virtues of the conqueror's son Mīrān Shāh. Mīrān Shāh is described as a wholehearted Christian and as much loved by Latin Christians in the east[69] – an assertion readily taken up by the Western rulers whose courts the archbishop visited.[70] Clavijo, who met the prince, says nothing whatever of any Christian leanings, merely describing the insane conduct for which Temür eventually removed him from the governorship of Tabrīz. Since this included the destruction of mosques,[71] it conceivably nurtured the idea that he was pro-Christian.

John's propaganda was ably seconded by others with whom he made contact during his tour of Western Europe or whom he may have influenced indirectly. The compiler of the *Chronographia regum Francorum*, in reproducing the archbishop's memoir on Temür, omits the statement that Christians too suffered from the conqueror's savagery.[72] And Dietrich von Nyem, who had become a close friend of John, claimed that Smyrna would have escaped destruction had the Hospitaller castellan only hoisted Temür's standard on the walls, as advised by 'a Christian bishop' (probably Francis, who had been briefly bishop of Nakhchivan).[73] Wild rumours that Temür's forces had taken Jerusalem, and that he and his troops had converted to Christianity, reached England and found their way into the historical works of Thomas Walsingham (d. *c.*1422).[74] For the Genoese annalist Giorgio Stella, writing around 1405, Temür was neither a Muslim nor a 'Tartar'.[75]

One piece of information which circulated as a result of John's journeyings in Latin Europe was that Temür and his son had released the Christian slaves they found in the defeated Ottoman army and had sent them in the direction of Constantinople.[76] In this context, at least, Dietrich von Nyem sounded a more sober note, giving the Chaghadayid forces no credit and instead ascribing the safe arrival of these Christian slaves solely to the intervention of Latin (i.e. probably Genoese) ships from Pera.[77] Some confusion may have arisen from the fact that Temür's embassy to the Castilian king was accompanied by two high-born Christian women who were believed to have been slaves in Bāyezīd's household at the time of his defeat.[78] Around this time, too, some of the Frankish soldiers taken at Nicopolis in 1396 made their way home to Europe. The chronicle of S. Denis, specifying 'the Great Count of Hungary' and an illegitimate son of the late count of Savoy, claims that Temür had released both of them from captivity at Bursa.[79] The second can be identified as Humbert, count of Romont (son of Amadeus VII), who arrived back in Chambéry in February 1404.[80] The first has been identified as the Palatine Eustache of Illsua, though the evidence suggests that he died in Ottoman captivity.[81] In any case, no other source confirms that the prisoners owed their deliverance to the Chaghadayid forces. It is more likely, on chronological grounds, that they were released, rather, by Süleymān when he occupied Bursa, as part of his attempt to reach an accommodation with the Christian powers; his treaty with them in 1403 certainly provided for the release of Greek and Italian prisoners.[82] Whatever the truth, and whoever the 'Great Count', the two prisoners were more fortunate than lower-ranking soldiers captured at Nicopolis. Far from gaining his freedom after Ankara, the Bavarian Johann Schildtberger, who later wrote an account of his adventures, simply exchanged one master for another.[83] A similar fate may have befallen the Hungarian knight Nicolaus Gerecz.[84]

We have encountered these themes – especial favour towards Christians, the release of Christian slaves found in the army of a defeated Muslim enemy – before, in various contexts: the first rumours of Mongol conquests that reached Damietta in 1221; the efforts of the Ilkhans Hülegü and Abaqa to secure Latin assistance against the Mamlūks; and especially the stories that rapidly grew up around Ghazan's spectacular Syrian campaign of 1299–1300, when Jerusalem had passed, if only for a few months, into Mongol hands. The enthusiastic reception which Temür's operations met with in the West should be viewed through a similar lens. No more than his Mongol precursors was he actuated by a sense of equal status in dealing with European powers. The nineteenth-century editor of his letter to Charles VI commented on the superior, even careless, tone in which the French king was addressed.[85] And in fact Clavijo several times heard Temür refer to Enrique III of Castile, whom he allegedly saw as the greatest of Western potentates, as his 'son' – just as his model Chinggis Khan had addressed the Khwārazmshāh on the eve of their conflict (above, p. 46).[86]

How should we assess Temür's approach to religious matters? A second-generation Muslim at the very least, he justified his conquests, in part, by the duty to safeguard and expand Islam. A Western author depicts him as taking pride in the capture of Smyrna, which had defied successive Muslim Ottoman Sultans; and there is nothing inherently implausible in this.[87] Temür relied in some degree on Muslim spiritual advisers, frequented the company of Muslim theologians, and enjoyed taking part in religious debate.[88] He also set great store, apparently, by the support and guidance of sufis and dervishes – Muslim holy men – and sought their support prior to particular campaigns.[89] The tale of his meeting with Khwāja 'Alī, head of the community at Ardabīl and a successor of Shaykh Ṣafī al-Dīn (the ancestor of the Safawid dynasty, which would rule over Persia from c.1500), is probably apocryphal; but Clavijo heard that the conqueror had lodged with the leading dervish of a village near Erzurum.[90] We might expect to find this preoccupation with religious guidance and legitimation in any ambitious Muslim prince. Yet conversely there was nothing intrinsically Islamic about such attachments. Pagan Mongol rulers had patronized saints from different religious communities, including Muslims. No doubt Temür's favour towards John of Sulṭāniyya and his fellow Dominican Francis sprang from the same roots. The sanction of holy men was an essential element in a steppe leader's claim to rule.[91] That Temür had by no means abandoned the more traditional beliefs of the steppe peoples is clear from his fascination with magic.[92] He claimed in addition to possess supernatural powers, to experience visions and to have mounted to Heaven on a ladder under the guidance of an angel.[93]

Temür's attitude towards Christianity is somewhat difficult to fathom. His early correspondence with Bāyezīd in 1395 had praised the Ottoman Sultan as a holy warrior against the infidel and had alluded to the presence of infidels (i.e. Christian Poles and Lithuanians) among the confederates of Temür's own enemy Toqtamish.[94] In a more recent letter, on the eve of his attack on Bāyezīd, he again mentioned with approval the Sultan's conflicts with the Franks and expressed reluctance to embark on a campaign in Anatolia which could only hearten Islam's enemies; and he subsequently issued a similar disclaimer when addressing Ottoman envoys.[95] All this, of course, could have amounted to little more than subterfuge. Temür's court histories and his own record alike suggest that he was content to leave Christian rulers in place, subject to the provision of tribute (generally interpreted as the Islamic poll-tax on unbelievers, the *jizya*) – rather as his Ottoman antagonist was accustomed to do. Thus Temür was perfectly willing to accept the submission and tribute of the Frankish island of Sāqiz (Chios) at the end of 1402.[96] It is true that after his defeat in 1394 the Georgian King Bagrat V had been obliged not only to pay an annual tribute but also to become a Muslim. But although the king subsequently apostatized and Georgia thereby incurred further attacks, this was probably an isolated case. The same stipulation to abjure the Christian faith does not appear to have been imposed on his son and successor, Giorgi VII.[97] Nor was the Emperor of Trebizond, in becoming tributary to Temür, additionally required to become a Muslim.[98] Given that the only Christian power on the Asiatic mainland which Temür eliminated was the tiny Hospitaller enclave at Smyrna, his hostility towards Christianity begins to seem less striking. But against this it could be argued that Smyrna was the sole Christian-ruled bastion which the conqueror's armies were really in a position to destroy prior to his withdrawal from Anatolia.

Where Christians were not the sovereign authority, moreover, they undoubtedly fared badly. This was not just an incidental result of the havoc wrought by Temür's troops, to which Armenian writers bear eloquent witness.[99] It was part of a deliberate policy. At Tana, Persian sources indicate that the Muslim population was separated from the infidels and was spared; the rest were massacred and their goods pillaged.[100] In the towns of Anatolia, similarly, the Christians were enslaved while the Muslims merely paid a ransom.[101] Clavijo heard that Temür had ordered the demolition of Christian churches in Greater Armenia.[102] The policy does not appear to have been implemented universally: the Armenian lord of Mākū and his subjects (including a Dominican convent) were left unharmed,[103] and Clavijo found 'a fine church' still standing at Erzurum.[104] Yet overall there can be little doubt that the Chaghadayid campaigns had gravely disrupted the fortunes of the eastern churches and hamstrung the endeavours of Latin missionaries (see chapter 10). As late as 1406 King Martin was responding to an appeal for financial assistance from the monastic community of St Catherine on Mount Sinai, who had been impoverished thanks to Chaghadayid depredations.[105] Apart from an extremely terse allusion in the *Libellus*,[106] however, John fails to notice the deleterious effects of Temür's campaigns on eastern Christians.

It is, in fact, difficult to resist the impression that this solitary – though extremely active and well-travelled – churchman was largely responsible for the persistent and widespread view of Temür not merely as a potential ally but also as a potential convert to Christianity. He may, of course, have genuinely believed this; but we should be prepared to identify other motives behind his propaganda. One motive is not far to seek. In the *Libellus* the archbishop outlines an Armenian prophecy that had come to his attention, concerning an oriental ruler who would attack the Muslims and join forces with the victorious Franks advancing from the west.[107] Suitably reworked to incorporate unmistakable allusions to Temür ('a man named Iron', from 'Media'), this was, it seems, an older prophecy, attributed to the fourth-century St Nerses, which Rubruck had heard as he passed through Armenia in 1255;[108] Armenian manuscript colophons testify to its resilience during the fourteenth and fifteenth centuries.[109] From the *Libellus* it is clear that John accepted the prophecy as genuine and as already in part fulfilled. He may have hoped to promote a crusade against Muslim princes whose strength had been profoundly sapped by Temür's campaigns. All this has to be seen in the light of his overriding concern, namely to revive the faltering Latin mission in the Near East, which he evidently felt had been neglected by the Roman popes.[110]

For all the sanguine expectations regarding Temür's motives and ambitions, diplomatic contact with him bore no fruit. He was the last 'Tartar' potentate whose operations fostered the illusion that he might become an ally against the major powers of the Islamic Near East or – better still – convert to the Christian faith. When such hopes recurred later in the fifteenth century, they focused on Muslim princes who were not Mongols, such as Uzun Ḥasan (d. 1478), the leader of the Aq Qoyunlu Türkmens and ruler of Mesopotamia and western Persia. Uzun Ḥasan's achievements included the destruction of the rival Türkmen confederation of the Qara Qoyunlu (1467) and – ironically – the overthrow of the Temürid sovereign of Khurāsān and Transoxiana (1469), who had briefly appeared to be on the point of recreating Temür's empire. But Uzun Ḥasan's humiliation by the Ottomans at Bashkent in 1473 put paid to any chance he had of providing effective assistance to the Western powers.[111] In the sixteenth century European publicists continued to flirt with the idea that particular Muslim rulers might act as a promising counterweight to Ottoman power, but with equally disappointing results.[112]

Clavijo and John of Sulṭāniyya both testify to their gracious treatment at Temür's hands. In the Near East, the blow he dealt the Ottoman Turks appeared to offer the ailing Byzantine empire a reprieve for a further fifty years;[113] in the Pontic steppe, his assault on Toqtamish effectively delivered the *coup de grâce* to the Golden Horde. Such exploits have helped to reinforce the notion that Temür was a potential ally of the Catholic world. It is true that this Muslim ruler does not, at first sight, appear an orthodox exponent of the Islamic *jihād*. His credentials as a holy warrior rested on nothing more than warfare with minor Hindu chieftains, with the Christians of Georgia, and with the Knights Hospitallers. The great majority of his campaigns were directed, in fact, against fellow Muslims, who were called upon, moreover, to endure his most appalling acts of barbarity, leading John of Sulṭāniyya to opine, in all seriousness, that Temür had destroyed three-quarters of the world's Muslim population.[114] All this served to obscure the fact that Temür's interest in correspondence with rulers in Latin Europe extended only as far as they might prove valuable trading-partners – and as their hostility towards the Ottomans and the Mamlūks made them useful adjuncts to his efforts to extend his dominions. In this latter respect, at least, he was a true successor of the Ilkhans.

Notes

1. I have transliterated the Turco-Mongol form of this name (Tu. *temür*, 'iron'), in preference to the Persian and Arabic form, Tīmūr, usually employed in secondary literature.

2. Beatrice Forbes Manz, 'Tamerlane and the symbolism of sovereignty', *Iranian Studies* 21:1–2 (1988), pp. 105–22 (here pp. 113–14, n.33).

3. Eadem, 'Mongol history rewritten and relived', *Revue des Mondes Musulmans et de la Méditerranée* 89–90 (1999), pp. 129–49 (esp. pp. 137–41).

4. David Morgan, 'The empire of Tamerlane: an unsuccessful re-run of the Mongol state?', in J.R. Maddicott and D.M. Palliser, eds, *The Medieval State. Essays Presented to James Campbell* (London, 2000), pp. 233–41.

5. See Peter Jackson, 'Chaghatayid dynasty', *Enc.Ir.*

6. The best survey of Temür's rise is Beatrice Forbes Manz, *The Rise and Rule of Tamerlane* (Cambridge, 1989). For brief accounts, see eadem, 'Tīmūr Lang', *Enc.Isl.*²; H.R. Roemer, 'Tīmūr in Iran', in *CHI*, VI, pp. 43–6.

7. Beatrice Forbes Manz, 'The ulus Chaghatay before and after Temür's rise to power: the transformation from tribal confederation to army of conquest', *CAJ* 27 (1983), pp. 79–100.

8. John E. Woods, 'Tīmūr's genealogy', in Michael M. Mazzaoui and Vera B. Moreen, eds, *Intellectual Studies on Islam: Essays Written in Honor of Martin B. Dickson* (Salt Lake City, UT, 1990), pp. 85–125.

9. Manz, 'Tamerlane and the symbolism', pp. 112–13. Morgan, 'Empire of Tamerlane', p. 237.

10. See, e.g., Manz, *Rise and Rule of Tamerlane*, pp. 37, 101–2; and for a different perspective, Roemer, 'Tīmūr in Iran', p. 90. Beatrice Forbes Manz, 'Tamerlane's career and its uses', *JWH* 13:1 (2002), pp. 1–25 (here pp. 2–5), discusses the contradictions in Temür's career.

11. Clavijo, p. 196 (tr. Le Strange, p. 272).

12. Zeki Velidi Togan, 'Timur's Osteuropapolitik', *ZDMG* 108 = n.F., 33 (1958), pp. 279–98. Roemer, 'Tīmūr in Iran', p. 72.

13. The standard work on the Anatolian expedition is M.M. Alexandrescu-Dersca, *La campagne de Timur en Anatolie (1402)* (Bucarest, 1942, repr. London, 1977). See further Donald M. Nicol, *The Last Centuries of Byzantium, 1261–1453*, 2nd edn (Cambridge, 1993), pp. 313–16.

14. Anthony Luttrell, 'The Hospitallers of Rhodes confront the Turks, 1306–1421', in Philip F. Gallagher, ed., *Christians, Jews and Other Worlds: Patterns of Conflict and Accommodation* (Lanham, MD, 1988), pp. 80–116 (here p. 100), and repr. in Luttrell, *The Hospitallers of Rhodes and Their Mediterranean World* (Aldershot, 1992). Jürgen Sarnowsky, 'Die Johanniter und Smyrna 1344–1402 (Teil 1)', *Römische Quartalschrift* 86 (1991), pp. 215–51 (here pp. 232–3).

15. On Phocaea, see Alexandrescu-Dersca, *La campagne*, p. 90.

16. Anthony Luttrell, 'The crisis in the Bosphorus following the battle near Ankara in 1402', in Rosario Villari, ed., *Controllo degli stretti e insediamenti militari nel Mediterraneo* (Rome and Bari, 2002), pp. 155–66 (here pp. 159–60).

17. Clavijo, pp. 27–8 (tr. Le Strange, p. 52).

18. For a brief discussion of Genoese attitudes, see Michel Balard, *La Romanie génoise*, 2 vols with continuous pagination (Genova, 1978 = *ASL*, n.s., 18:1–2), I, pp. 101–2.

19. Venetian report of 10 Sept. 1401, in Iorga, 'Notes', p. 245, and Dennis, 'Three reports', p. 245 (tr. p. 253). Byzantine relations with Temür are discussed in John W. Barker, *Manuel II Palaeologus 1391–1425. A Study in Late Byzantine Statesmanship* (New Brunswick, NJ, 1969), pp. 504–8 (appendix XVIII).

20. Temür to [John VII] the regent of Constantinople, 15 May 1402, in Alexandrescu-Dersca, *La campagne*, pp. 123–4. Letter of Gerardo Sagredo, 12 Oct. 1402, ibid., p. 131. Clavijo, p. 93 (tr. Le Strange, p. 135). Nicol, *Last Centuries of Byzantium*, pp. 314–15.

21. Letter of Marco Grimani, Aug. 1402, in Alexandrescu-Dersca, *La campagne*, p. 137.

22. Iorga, 'Notes', pp. 81, 83, 84.

23. Hippolyte Noiret, ed., *Documents inédits pour servir à l'histoire de la domination vénitienne en Crète de 1380 à 1485* (Paris, 1892), pp. 129–30. Letter of Giovanni Cornaro, 4 Sept. 1402, in Alexandrescu-Dersca, *La campagne*, pp. 125–6.

24. Giorgio Stella, 'Annales Genuenses' (*c*.1405), *RIS*², XVII:2, p. 260. Schmieder, *Europa*, p. 185, n.588, relegates this to the realm of fantasy.

25. Niẓām-i Shāmī, *Ẓafar-nāma* (1404), ed. Felix Tauer, *Histoire des conquêtes de Tamerlan*, 2 vols, Monografie Archivu Orientálního 5 (Prague, 1937–56), I, p. 264; fuller version, suggesting a date in or soon after Rabī' I 805 H./Oct. 1402, in Sharaf al-Dīn 'Alī Yazdī, *Ẓafar-nāma* (1424–5), ed. Muḥammad 'Abbāsī, 2 vols (Tehran, 1336 solar/1957), II, p. 331/ facsimile edn by A. Urunbaev (Tashkent, 1972), p. 858, and tr. F. Pétis de la Croix, *Histoire de Timur-Bec, connu sous le nom du Grand Tamerlan*, 4 vols (Paris, 1722), IV, pp. 37, 38–9.

26. Clavijo, p. 94 (tr. Le Strange, p. 136). Letter of Gerardo Sagredo, in Alexandrescu-Dersca, *La campagne*, pp. 131–2; some of the Turks were robbed and murdered by the Italians (ibid., pp. 83–4). Luttrell, 'Crisis', p. 158.

27. Freddy Thiriet, ed., *Duca di Candia. Ducali e lettere ricevute (1358–1360; 1401–1405)* (Venice, 1978), pp. 36–7 (no. 40). *DAV*, II, p. 95 (no. 1017, 25 March 1403). For Italian tergiversations, see Barker, *Manuel II*, pp. 217–18 and nn.24–25.

28. Donald M. Nicol, 'A Byzantine emperor in England: Manuel II's visit to London in 1400–1401', *University of Birmingham Historical Journal* 12 (1970), pp. 204–25 (here pp. 219–21).

29. P. Gautier, 'Un récit inédit du siège de Constantinople par les Turcs (1394–1402)', *REB* 23 (1965), pp. 100–17 (here pp. 108 ff., tr. pp. 109 ff.). For the complexity of the Byzantine reaction, see Klaus-Peter Matschke, *Die Schlacht bei Ankara und das Schicksal von Byzanz. Studien zur spätbyzantinischen Geschichte zwischen 1402 und 1422* (Weimar, 1981), pp. 9–14; N. Nicoloudis, 'Byzantine historians on the wars of Timur (Tamerlane) in Central Asia and the Middle East', *Journal of Oriental and African Studies* 8 (Athens, 1996), pp. 83–94 (here pp. 83–4).

30. Iorga, 'Notes', p. 264.
31. CICO, XIII:1, pp. 278–82 (no. 139).
32. *MHSM*, IV, p. 332; abstract in *RDSV*, I, p. 203 (no. 860).
33. Andrea de Redusiis de Quero, 'Chronicon Tarvisinum' (down to 1428), *RIS*, XIX, cols. 802–4. More generally, W. Heyd, *Histoire du commerce du Levant au moyen-âge*, tr. Furcy Raynaud, 2 vols (Leipzig, 1885–6), II, pp. 374–6.
34. See Benjamin Z. Kedar, *Merchants in Crisis. Genoese and Venetian Men of Affairs and the Fourteenth-Century Depression* (New Haven, CN, and London, 1976), p. 130, for references.
35. *RDSV*, I, p. 217 (no. 927, 20 Feb. 1397).
36. Noiret, p. 114. For Venetian reactions to rumours about Temür, see Eliyahu Ashtor, *Levant Trade in the Later Middle Ages* (Princeton, NJ, 1983), pp. 112–13.
37. Ibn Taghrībirdī (d. 1470), *al-Nujūm al-zāhira fī mulūk Miṣr wa l-Qāhira*, 16 vols so far (1348 H./1929–1392 H./1972), XII, p. 234; tr. William Popper, *History of Egypt 1382–1469 A.D.*, 8 vols, University of California Publications in Semitic Philology 13, 14, 17–19, 22–4 (Berkeley and Los Angeles, 1954–63), II, pp. 43–4. His source, al-Maqrīzī (d. 1442), *al-Sulūk li-ma'rifat duwal al-mulūk*, ed. Muṣṭafā al-Ziyāda and Sa'īd al-Fatḥ 'Āshūr, 4 vols in 10 (Cairo, 1934–72), III:3, p. 1039, omits to say that the offer was ignored.
38. Ashtor, *Levant Trade*, p. 113. Schmieder, *Europa*, pp. 182–3.
39. Adam of Usk, *Polychronicon*, ed. C. Given-Wilson, *The Chronicle of Adam Usk 1377–1421* (Oxford, 1997), p. 130 (tr. p. 131).
40. CICO, XIII:1, pp. 209–10 (no. 103, 7 Jan. 1401) = *BBTS*, V, pp. 331–3 = Sułkowska-Kuraś and Kuraś, *Bullarium Poloniae*, III, p. 121 (no. 724).
41. Ashtor, *Levant Trade*, p. 215.
42. Adam Knobler, 'The rise of Tīmūr and Western diplomatic response, 1390–1405', *JRAS*, 3rd series, 5 (1995), pp. 341–9 (here p. 345).
43. Antoni Rubió y Lluch, ed., *Diplomatari de l'Orient Català (1301–1409)* (Barcelona, 1947), p. 695 (no. 672, 5 March 1403). For d'Alfaro, see J. Delaville le Roulx, *Les Hospitaliers à Rhodes jusqu'à la mort de Philibert de Naillac (1310–1421)* (Paris, 1913, repr. London, 1974), pp. 284–5.
44. C. Marinesco, 'Du nouveau sur les relations de Manuel II Paléologue (1391–1425) avec l'Espagne', in *Atti dello VIII Congresso internazionale di studi Bizantini, Palermo 3–10 aprile 1951*, I (Rome, 1953), pp. 420–36 (here pp. 430–1).
45. Rubió y Lluch, *Diplomatari*, p. 699 (no. 677).
46. Ibid., pp. 700–1 (no. 679). Schmieder, *Europa*, p. 182.
47. Luttrell, 'Crisis', pp. 161–4: at pp. 162–3 he likens the choice to that facing the Franks of Syria in 1260.
48. Clavijo, p. 94 (tr. Le Strange, p. 136).
49. Andrea de Redusiis, 'Chronicon Tarvisinum', col. 801.
50. *Le livre des fais du bon messire Jehan le Maingre, dit Bouciquaut* (1405/9), i, 37, ed. Denis Lalande (Geneva, 1985), p. 159.
51. L. de Mas Latrie, ed., 'Commerce et expéditions militaires de la France et de Venise au moyen-âge', *Mélanges Historiques. Choix de documents*, III (Paris, 1880), pp. 172–7 (no. 21).

52. George T. Dennis, 'The Byzantine–Turkish treaty of 1403', *Orientalia Christiana Periodica* 33 (1967), pp. 72–88 (here pp. 78, §5, and 83, §3; abridged tr. pp. 81, 86), repr. in his *Byzantium and the Franks*. The treaty is also printed in Mas Latrie, 'Commerce', pp. 178–82 (no. 22), and Zeno's report in Iorga, 'Notes', p. 259. Luttrell, 'Crisis', p. 162. See generally Elizabeth A. Zachariadou, 'Süleyman Çelebi in Rumeli and the Ottoman chronicles', *Der Islam* 60 (1983), pp. 268–96.

53. Iorga, 'Notes', pp. 228, 239.

54. See Dietrich von Nyem, iii, 30, p. 173.

55. Beltramo da Mignanelli, 'Vita Tamerlani' (1416), in Ét. Baluze, ed., *Miscellanea novo ordine digesta et non paucis ineditis monumentis opportunisque animadversionibus aucta*, new edn by J.D. Mansi, IV (Lucca, 1764), p. 138; partial tr. Walter J. Fischel, 'A new Latin source on Tamerlane's conquest of Damascus (1400/1401)', *Oriens* 9 (1956), pp. 201–32 (here p. 229).

56. Bourgeois du Chastenet, *Nouvelle histoire du Concile de Constance* (Paris, 1718), p. 499: this is the only edition that supplies the full text and the date (12 June 1404).

57. Letter of Pasqualino Veniero, in Alexandrescu-Dersca, *La campagne*, p. 135. *Chronique du Religieux de Saint-Denys contenant le règne de Charles VI, de 1380 à 1422*, xxiii, 10, ed. Louis François Bellaguet, 6 vols (Paris, 1839–52), III, p. 50.

58. Clavijo, pp. 202–5 (tr. Le Strange, pp. 281–5); see ibid., pp. 4–6 (tr. Le Strange, pp. 24–6), for their departure from Spain.

59. Knobler, 'Rise of Tīmūr', p. 347.

60. For John's career, see Anthony Luttrell, 'Timur's Dominican envoy', in Colin Heywood and Colin Imber, eds, *Studies in Ottoman History in Honour of Professor V.L. Ménage* (Istanbul, 1994), pp. 209–29; ibid., pp. 213–15, for Francis. For John's propaganda on Temür's behalf, see also Schmieder, *Europa*, pp. 181–2. He was not, as formerly believed, the Englishman John Greenlaw or John 'de Galonifontibus' (i.e. Gaillefontaine in Normandy): Luttrell, 'Timur's Dominican envoy', p. 210, n.3; R. Loenertz, O.P., 'Evêques dominicains des Deux Arménies', *AFP* 10 (1940), pp. 258–81 (here pp. 258–68).

61. Texts in Baron Silvestre de Sacy, 'Mémoire sur une correspondance inédite de Tamerlan avec Charles VI', *MAIBL* 6 (1822), pp. 470–523 (pp. 473–4, Persian text; pp. 478–9, Latin trans.; pp. 479–80, Mīrān Shāh's letter; pp. 521–2, Charles VI's reply to Temür).

62. Sir Henry Ellis, ed., *Original Letters Illustrative of English History*, 3rd series, I (London, 1846), p. 57 (no. 25): *intelleximus etiam ex dictarum continentia litterarum qualiter ad partes Thurciae noviter accedentes. . . .*

63. John of Sulṭāniyya, *Libellus de notitia orbis*, extracts ed. Anton Kern, 'Der «Libellus de notitia orbis» Iohannes' III. (de Galonifontibus?) O.P. Erzbischofs von Sulthanyeh', *AFP* 8 (1938), pp. 82–123 (here p. 102). See also *Chronographia regum Francorum*, ed. H. Moranvillé, 3 vols (Paris, 1891–7), III, pp. 238–9.

64. H. Moranvillé, 'Mémoire sur Tamerlan et sa cour par un Dominicain, en 1403', *BEC* 55 (1894), pp. 441–64 (here p. 453).

65. Ibid., p. 454. *Chronographia regum Francorum*, III, p. 220.

66. Moranvillé, 'Mémoire', p. 462. *Chronographia regum Francorum*, III, p. 216.
67. John of Sulṭāniyya, *Libellus*, p. 104.
68. Henry IV to Temür, in Ellis, *Original Letters*, p. 57, note f.
69. Moranvillé, 'Mémoire', pp. 445–6: *comme tout christien*. Cf. *Chronographia regum Francorum*, III, p. 213: *totus Christianus*.
70. Henry IV to Mīrān Shāh, Feb. [1406], in F.C. Hingeston, ed., *Royal and Historical Letters During the Reign of Henry the Fourth*, RS, 2 vols (London, 1860–4), I, pp. 425–6 (no. 150). Martin I to Mīrān Shāh, 1 April 1404, in Rubió y Lluch, *Diplomatari*, p. 701 (no. 680). Conrad von Jungingen, Master of the Teutonic Knights, to Mīrān Shāh, 20 Jan. 1407, in Kurt Forstreuter, 'Der Deutsche Orden und Südosteuropa', *Kyrios. Vierteljahresschrift für Kirchen- und Geistesgeschichte Osteuropas* 1 (1936), pp. 245–72 (here p. 269).
71. Clavijo, pp. 114–15 (tr. Le Strange, pp. 162–3). For his conduct, see Beatrice Forbes Manz, 'Mīrānshāh b. Tīmūr', *Enc. Isl.*[2].
72. *Chronographia regum Francorum*, III, p. 219. Cf. John of Sulṭāniyya, as cited in n.64 above; for his other statements regarding Temür's cruelty (Moranvillé, 'Mémoire', pp. 451, 456), see *Chronographia*, III, pp. 217, 221–3.
73. Dietrich von Nyem, iii, 29, pp. 172–3; Luttrell, 'Timur's Dominican envoy', p. 215. See also Dietrich von Nyem, iii, 42, p. 306, for Tëmur's friendship with *quendam episcopum catholicum, qui secum per XII annos moram traxit*. This must be John of Sulṭāniyya: Loenertz, 'Evêques', p. 264; Schmieder, *Europa*, p. 187, n.598; Luttrell, 'Timur's Dominican envoy', p. 212.
74. Knobler, 'Rise of Tīmūr', p. 344; in addition to the works there cited, see Walsingham's *Ypodigma Neustriae*, ed. H.T. Riley, RS (London, 1876), p. 392. See also Knobler, 'Pseudo-conversions and patchwork pedigrees: the Christianization of Muslim princes and the diplomacy of Holy War', *JWH* 7:2 (1996), pp. 181–97 (here p. 191).
75. Giorgio Stella, 'Annales Genuenses', p. 260.
76. *Chronographia regum Francorum*, III, p. 205 (ascribing the information to John). *Chronique du Religieux de Saint-Denys*, xxiii, 10, ed. Bellaguet, III, p. 46. Conrad von Jungingen to Temür and to Mīrān Shāh, 20 Jan. 1407, in Forstreuter, p. 270. Alexandrescu-Dersca, *La campagne*, p. 82, seems to accept the release of the Christian captives as genuine, but cites no source. Schmieder, *Europa*, p. 186.
77. Dietrich von Nyem, iii, 29, pp. 171–2. Cf. also Iorga, 'Notes', p. 96.
78. Clavijo, p. 4 (tr. Le Strange, p. 25); our only source for the identity of the two women is the supplementary comments of the late 16th-century writer Gonzálo Argote de Molina, ibid., p. 255 (tr. Le Strange, p. 340, n.5).
79. *Chronique du Religieux de Saint-Denys*, xxiii, 10, ed. Bellaguet, III, p. 48.
80. Henri-Joseph Costa de Beauregard, *Souvenirs du règne d'Amédée VIII premier duc de Savoie* (Chambéry, 1859), pp. 24–6. Ferdinando Gabotto, *Gli ultimi principi d'Acaia e la politica subalpina dal 1383 al 1407* (Turin, 1898), pp. 350–1, 501. I owe these references to Dr Anthony Luttrell.
81. Elemér Mályusz, *Kaiser Sigismund in Ungarn 1387–1437*, tr. Anikó Szmodits (Budapest, 1990), p. 134. For Eustache as a captive at Bursa in 1397, see J. Delaville le Roulx, *La France en Orient au XIVe siècle. Expéditions du Maréchal Boucicaut*, 2 vols (Paris, 1886), II, pp. 47–8; the participation of 'the Great

Count of Hungary' at Nicopolis is mentioned in *Livre des fais*, i, 25, pp. 107, 110. Eustache called himself *magnus comes de* [*H*]*ungaria*: Elemér Mályusz and Iván Borsa, eds, *Zsigmondkori oklevéltár*, 7 vols so far (Budapest, 1951–), I, no. 5793, and II, no. 71. His death was known in Hungary by 18 July 1405: MOL, DL 101957 (abstract in Mályusz and Borsa, II, no. 4056).

82. Dennis, 'Byzantine–Turkish treaty', pp. 79–80 (tr. pp. 81–2).
83. *The Bondage and Travels of Johann Schiltberger, a Native of Bavaria, in Europe, Asia, and Africa, 1396–1427*, tr. J. Buchan Telfer, HS[1] 58 (London, 1879), p. 21.
84. Wolfgang Frhr. Stromer von Reichenbach, 'König Siegmunds Gesandte in den Orient', in *Festschrift für Hermann Heimpel zum 70. Geburtstag am 19. September 1971*, 3 vols (Göttingen, 1971–2), II, pp. 591–609 (here pp. 593–4).
85. De Sacy, 'Mémoire', pp. 471, 519, 521.
86. Clavijo, pp. 158, 159, 160 (tr. Le Strange, pp. 221, 222; at p. 223, *Su fijo, quera Su amigo* is rendered ambiguously as 'the good friend of Timur and his son'); cf. also p. 200 (tr. p. 277).
87. Andrea de Redusiis, 'Chronicon Tarvisinum', col. 801. Sarnowsky, 'Die Johanniter', pp. 215, 232.
88. Roemer, 'Tīmūr in Iran', pp. 87–90.
89. Manz, 'Tamerlane and the symbolism', pp. 112, 118. For a survey of those shaykhs whose names are linked with Temür, see Jürgen Paul, 'Scheiche und Herrscher im khanat Čaġatay', *Der Islam* 67 (1990), pp. 278–321 (here pp. 296–313).
90. Clavijo, p. 96 (tr. Le Strange, p. 139). For Temür and Khwāja 'Alī, see H.R. Roemer, 'The Safavid period', in *CHI*, VI, pp. 205–6.
91. Paul, 'Scheiche und Herrscher', pp. 313–18.
92. Mignanelli, p. 135 (tr. Fischel, p. 214). Jean Aubin, 'Comment Tamerlan prenait les villes', *SI* 19 (1963), pp. 83–122 (here pp. 85–8). See further pp. 276–8 below.
93. Moranvillé, 'Mémoire', pp. 462–3. *Chronographia regum Francorum*, III, pp. 216–17. See also Aubin, 'Comment Tamerlan', p. 88; Manz, 'Tamerlane and the symbolism', p. 118.
94. Sarı 'Abd-Allāh Efendi, *Munsha'āt*, text in Togan, 'Timur's Osteuropapolitik', p. 294; see also ibid., pp. 280–1, 284.
95. Niẓām-i Shāmī, I, pp. 218, 248; and see also the additions made to Shāmī's account in the *Zubdat al-tawārīkh* of Ḥāfiẓ-i Abrū (1433/4), ibid., II, p. 174. Sharaf al-Dīn 'Alī Yazdī, ed. 'Abbāsī, II, pp. 188, 280 (with 'WNJ in error for 'FRNJ)/ed. Urunbaev, pp. 747, 819 (tr. Pétis de la Croix, III, pp. 260, 396).
96. Niẓām-i Shāmī, I, p. 269. Sharaf al-Dīn 'Alī Yazdī, ed. 'Abbāsī, II, p. 344/ed. Urunbaev, pp. 869–70 (tr. Pétis de la Croix, IV, pp. 58–9). For 'Sāqiz' (described by Shāmī as a town and by Yazdī as an island) as Chios, see S. Soucek, 'Ṣaḳiz', *Enc.Isl.*[2]. Pétis de la Croix transliterated the name of its Latin lord (given as STH by Shāmī and as SBH or SYH by Yazdī) as 'Chibo', but the name garbled in Arabic–Persian script could conceivably be SNH = Zeno, i.e. Pietro Zeno, lord of Andros, who is known to have been in Chios in Sept. 1402 (letter of Gerardo Sagredo, in Alexandrescu-Dersca, *La campagne*, p. 133).

97. Allen, *History of the Georgian People*, pp. 123–5. Roemer, 'Tīmūr in Iran', pp. 59, 75, 79–80.

98. Clavijo, p. 75 (tr. Le Strange, p. 111).

99. Avedis K. Sanjian, *Colophons of Armenian Manuscripts, 1301–1480. A Source for Middle Eastern History* (Cambridge, MA, 1969), pp. 105–10, 113–15, 117–22, 124–5, 127–8.

100. Niẓām-i Shāmī, I, p. 162. Sharaf al-Dīn 'Alī Yazdī, ed. 'Abbāsī, I, p. 544/ed. Urunbaev, pp. 575–6 (tr. Pétis de la Croix, II, p. 365).

101. Aubin, 'Comment Tamerlan', p. 99.

102. Clavijo, pp. 89–90, 95 (tr. Le Strange, pp. 130, 138).

103. Ibid., pp. 101–3 (tr. Le Strange, pp. 144–7).

104. Ibid., p. 96 (tr. Le Strange, p. 139).

105. Rubió y Lluch, *Diplomatari*, pp. 713–14 (no. 691, 13 Jan. 1406).

106. John of Sulṭāniyya, *Libellus*, p. 118.

107. John of Sulṭāniyya, *Libellus*, Graz Universitätsbibliothek ms. 1221, fo. 57v; the passage is reproduced (with omissions) in Kern's edn, pp. 99–100. There is a vague echo of this prophecy – though attributed to St Gregory (the Illuminator) – in Dietrich von Nyem, iii, 30, p. 176.

108. WR, xxxviii, 3–3 *bis*, pp. 322–3 (tr. Jackson and Morgan, pp. 266–7). Von den Brincken, *Die „Nationes Christianorum Orientalium"*, p. 193, n.84, and Schmieder, *Europa*, p. 284, n.453, draw attention to the fact that the two travellers cite essentially the same prophecy, but this is contested by Möhring, *Der Weltkaiser*, p. 200, n.154.

109. Sanjian, *Colophons*, index *s.v.* 'Nerses' (esp. p. 94).

110. Luttrell, 'Timur's Dominican envoy', pp. 218–19, 227.

111. See H.R. Roemer, 'The Türkmen dynasties', in *CHI*, VI, pp. 175–80.

112. Knobler, 'Pseudo-conversions', pp. 191–6.

113. But see Nicol, *Last Centuries of Byzantium*, p. 316.

114. Moranvillé, 'Mémoire', p. 451. *Chronographia regum Francorum*, III, p. 217.

chapter 10

MISSION TO THE INFIDEL

The Mongols' emergence on the eastern borders of Latin Christendom might not have seemed to offer promising conditions for the spread of Christianity. But through their conquests vast tracts of Asia which hitherto had either lain beyond the West's horizons, or had been under Islamic rule and hence closed to Christian proselytism, were now subject to a regime which permitted the propagation of all faiths. From the late 1240s, moreover, word spread within Western Europe that the Mongols believed in one God; that individual Mongol princes were Christians or harboured Christian sympathies; and that large numbers of Christians (mostly adherents of the 'separated' churches – the Nestorians, or East Syrians, and the Jacobites – but also including Greek Orthodox and Armenians) lived under Mongol rule. These circumstances drew members of the newly-founded Mendicant Orders, the Franciscans and Dominicans, into Asia in the hope of converting the Mongols and their subjects. The dissolution of the Mongol empire into rival khanates after 1261–2 in no way curtailed the opportunities for Latin missionaries. Indeed, the Ilkhans' eagerness to obtain Western collaboration against the Mamlūk Sultanate seemed to heighten the possibility that they might embrace the Christian faith.

The growth of the Latin mission

We must discount, as evangelistic enterprises, the journeys of Carpini, Ascelin and Andrew of Longjumeau in 1245–51, which (even though the embassies of 1245 carried a letter inviting the Mongol ruler to embrace Christianity) were essentially diplomatic in character. The first missionaries, properly speaking, known to have visited the Mongol world were the Franciscans William of Rubruck and Bartholomew of Cremona, who set out in 1253 from Louis IX's crusade headquarters in Palestine for Sartaq's territory in the Pontic steppe. In part they were motivated by rumours that the prince was a Christian. But Rubruck's primary purpose, he tells us, was to bring spiritual comfort to a group of German slaves in Central Asia of whose existence Andrew had learned; though in the event he was unable to make contact with them.[1] During his return journey in 1255, Rubruck met a party of Dominicans, whose intention was to preach in Sartaq's domain; but the letter they carried from Pope Innocent IV referred *inter alia* to the Mongols' Christian captives.[2] The combination of aims recurs during these early years, when the plight of Latins whom the Mongols had enslaved may well have been paramount.[3]

We do not know what became of the Dominicans or of Bartholomew, who remained behind when Rubruck returned to the West. Nor is it clear when these first attempts were followed up. There may have been a Franciscan presence in the Golden Horde territories for several years by 1278, when the Hungarian provincial minister reported to the pope the large number of conversions the friars had achieved;[4] at some point prior to 1280 they secured a diploma from the khan Möngke Temür. A letter written by a Franciscan named László (Ladislaus) from Kaffa in 1287 reveals that his Order had convents there, in Soldaia (Sūdāq) and in Sarai, as well as a house in Qirq-yer.[5] The Dominicans reached the Golden Horde a little later, and were established at Kaffa in or soon after 1298.[6] In the Ilkhanate, the Franciscans had a convent at Sivas in the 1270s, and establishments in Salmās by 1284 and Tabrīz by 1287; there were Dominican houses in Sivas and Baghdad by the time Ricoldo of Montecroce arrived in the east in *c.*1288.[7]

On the other hand, it is unlikely that any Latin missionaries reached the qaghan's dominions in the Far East during the forty years following Rubruck's departure. The population of China was more diverse, perhaps, in religious terms than any other part of the Mongol empire. Here were to be found communities belonging to the different Christian sects, including Greek Orthodox, Jacobites and Armenians as well as Nestorians; Muslims; Manichaeans (whose survival, at one time subject to doubt, is now certain);[8] Buddhists, including representatives of the lamaistic Buddhism of Tibet; Taoists of various schools; and Confucians. If we can believe Marco Polo, Qubilai himself asked the two elder Polos (perhaps *c.*1267) to return to the pope and to bring back a hundred Christian priests to instruct his people.[9] There are doubts attached to the authenticity of this incident, and the story may be designed merely to boost the Polos' credit back in Europe. Reports that Qubilai was a Christian certainly reached the West in 1277, through the Ilkhanid ambassadors John and James Vassalli (above, pp. 168, 175). Yet the six Franciscans, headed by Gerard of Prato, whom Pope Nicholas III sent in response did not apparently remain in the Far East, but were already on their way back in 1279, when the Ilkhan Abaqa issued them with a safe-conduct.[10]

The election in 1288 of Jerome of Ascoli as Pope Nicholas IV seemed to inaugurate a new phase in the history of Latin missions.[11] Nicholas was the first Franciscan to occupy the Holy See, and the pontiff whose court Rabban Ṣawma had visited on behalf of the Ilkhan Arghun (above, p. 169). In 1289 he despatched eastwards as his legate, with letters for both Arghun and Qubilai, the Franciscan John of Montecorvino (d. c.1328), who had recently acted as the Curia's representative in Lesser Armenia. Leaving Tabrīz in 1291 and spending en route thirteen months among the St. Thomas Christians on the Coromandel coast (Ma'bar), Montecorvino must have reached Khanbaligh in 1294, following Qubilai's death and the accession of Temür Öljeitü.[12]

For many years Montecorvino worked alone; a Dominican companion had fallen ill and died in India. Apart from a few laymen – one of them the Italian merchant, Pietro da Lucalongo, who accompanied him out to China from Tabrīz and purchased the plot in Khanbaligh on which he built his first church; the other a visiting physician from Lombardy who spread disturbing rumours about the state of the Church and the Franciscan Order in Europe – the Franciscan seems to have had little personal contact with fellow Latins and none at all with other friars until the arrival of a German colleague named Arnold in c.1304.[13] Despite this handicap, Montecorvino initially achieved a considerable triumph by converting Körgüz ('King George'), the Nestorian ruler of the Önggüd to the north-east of the great bend in the Yellow River and a son-in-law of the late qaghan Qubilai. Körgüz built a church for the Franciscan in his capital, T'ien-te ('Tenduc'), and brought the majority of his people over to the Roman obedience. But his death in 1298–9 in the war against the Chaghadayids destroyed these promising shoots; his son, baptized John in honour of his Latin sponsor, was a minor, and Körgüz's brothers, committed Nestorians, took the new converts back into the Nestorian fold.[14]

When news of Montecorvino's solitary and herculean endeavours at length reached the West, Pope Clement V responded by making him archbishop of a new Latin see of Khanbaligh, with ecclesiastical jurisdiction over the entire Mongol world, and the bull *Rex regum* (23 July 1307) nominated seven Franciscans to act as his suffragans in China. A number of these appointees died in India en route, but three reached their destination, of whom only one, Andrew of Perugia (d. 1332), survived Montecorvino himself.[15] In this way the Order of St Francis for a short time enjoyed a monopoly of episcopal office in Asia; but on

1 April 1318 the bull *Redemptor noster* of Pope John XXII withdrew the Ilkhan's dominions and 'India' from the archdiocese of Khanbaligh, and subjected them to a second province staffed by Dominicans. The new archiepiscopal see was centred on Sulṭāniyya in Azerbaijan, one of the Ilkhan's chief halting-places: those of its suffragans who resided in Iran were based at Sivas, Tabrīz, Dih-i Khwāraqān and Marāgha.[16] Not only the Mongol empire but the whole of Asia (together with Ethiopia) was now divided between two vast Catholic provinces. Generally speaking, we have no reason to doubt that the Franciscans and Dominicans co-operated harmoniously where they came into contact; though just a hint of the competitive spirit in which some members of the two Orders back in Western Europe viewed the task surfaces in an account of a dispute at the papal Curia in 1322.[17]

The geographical expansion of Latin Christendom represented by these new sees was remarkable. In the Golden Horde lands, still part of the province of Khanbaligh, Kaffa was a bishopric by 1318; Tana, by 1343 at the very latest; Ürgench (in Khwārazm), by 1340. Within the Chaghadayid khanate (the so-called *Imperium Medium* or *Imperium Medorum*) – which belonged to Sulṭāniyya – Almaligh, the khans' principal residence, had a Latin bishop by 1328, and Samarqand, as a major centre in the western part of the khanate, received episcopal status in the following year.[18] From the Crimean peninsula to the major Chinese ports extended a network of Franciscan and Dominican houses, strung out along the trade routes followed by the Western merchants who were often the friars' travelling-companions and provided financial support for their activities.

Montecorvino died in 1328. His one long-term success, it appears, was among the Alans, Christians of the Greek Orthodox rite who had been transported across Asia from their homeland in the Caucasus to serve as part of the imperial guard.[19] It was the Alans who, with the backing of the qaghan and last Yüan Emperor of China, Toghan Temür (reigned as Shun-ti), wrote to the pope in 1336 asking for a new metropolitan to succeed their much-lamented pastor. The embassy which Pope Benedict XII sent back to Khanbaligh in 1338 was headed by the Franciscan John of Marignolli, who spent three years in China (1342–5). His mission has the distinction of being the only medieval papal embassy to have left an imprint in contemporary Chinese historiography, on account of the fine European horse included among the gifts it brought.[20] Thereafter the archdiocese of Khanbaligh slides into obscurity. Guillaume du Pré, appointed in 1370, may have been martyred during the journey out to China, though an entry in the Ming dynastic annals, mentioning the despatch in 1371 of a Frankish envoy 'P'u-la' (Pré?), could refer to him.[21] Charles of France, probably his successor, is mentioned as long dead by Archbishop John of Sulṭāniyya in 1404. In 1410 John himself was made administrator of the see, suggesting that the papacy did not consider it worthwhile to appoint a new incumbent.[22]

A number of circumstances were responsible for the disappearance of the far-flung Latin missionary communities.[23] One was the effects of the Black Death (1347–9) both in the mission field and on potential recruitment in Western Europe: all but three religious in the fifteen convents in Persia were wiped out, so that Pope Clement VI had to begin afresh in 1349.[24] Another important element was the onset of the Great Schism (1378–1417): the cleavage which split the allegiances of Latin Christian states between rival popes at Rome and at Avignon inevitably diluted papal attempts to sustain the Orders' activities. Christianity was also losing ground to its main competitors. In the qaghan's dominions, victory went to the Buddhists. The ruling strata in the three westernmost Mongol states, by contrast, adopted Islam: Ghazan in the Ilkhanate (1295), Uzbek in the Golden Horde (1313), and ʿAlī Sulṭān in the Chaghadayid dominions (c.1338) each inaugurated an uninterrupted sequence of Muslim khans. The phenomenal advance of the rival faith announced itself by a series of martyrdoms, notably in the Chaghadayid dominions, as friars who now lacked the protection of old-style Mongol pluralism were outspoken enough in their preaching publicly to denounce the Prophet Muḥammad. Temür's rise in Chaghadayid Transoxiana, and his brutal campaigns of conquest in Persia and the Near East during the period 1380–1405, further undermined the viability of the surviving missionary outposts. In the Far East, the Mongol dynasty, the Yüan, was expelled from China in 1368, and although the xenophobia of their Ming successors has been overstated,[25] it seems at least that the Latin missionaries ceased to benefit from the favourable patronage they had enjoyed under the qaghans. Whatever the reason, all traces of the Franciscan presence were eradicated so thoroughly that no memory of it lingered when the Jesuit Matteo Ricci arrived over two centuries later.

Missionary writings

Catholic proselytism in Mongol Asia has left behind rather less source material than we should wish. In contrast with precursors from a more heroic age in the history of Christian evangelism, only one of the missionaries, the Franciscan Odoric of Pordenone (d. 1331), has a *vita* dedicated to him; and even this is an exiguous piece, of which almost half is devoted to the miracles that followed Odoric's death and which claims that in the sixteen years he spent overseas he baptized 20,000 souls.[26] As a window onto the methods adopted by Latin missionaries and the problems they encountered, Rubruck's long *Itinerarium* stands alone. No subsequent document affords such rich insights, for instance, into the Mongols' attitudes to religious matters; indeed, Rubruck is our chief source for Mongol cultic practice in the era prior to its permeation by Buddhism in the sixteenth century.

The experiences of later missionaries are recounted in much briefer documents: three letters from Montecorvino (though the first, preserved only in a medieval Italian translation, is problematic); two which his suffragans at Zaitun (Ch'üan-chou), Peregrine of Castello and Andrew of Perugia, sent to their brethren in the West (in 1318/19 and 1326/7 respectively); a handful, belonging to the years 1314–23, from the Franciscans working in the Golden Horde territories; and a few from 1338–40, recounting the recent activities of Franciscans in the Chaghadayid khanate and their martyrdom. It is important to bear in mind that these documents are frequently designed to elicit the despatch of reinforcements for the missionaries, a purpose that may have coloured what the friars have to say. A more dispassionate observer, possibly, is John of Cori, archbishop of Sulṭāniyya and the author of a report on Asia (1330/4) for Pope John XXII which devoted some space to the state of the Mongol mission. In addition, various writings have come down to us from the Dominican Ricoldo of Montecroce (d. 1320), who preached the Gospel in the Ilkhanate in the last decade of the thirteenth century.[27] Benedict XII's ambassador, John of Marignolli, provides only meagre data in the account he wrote in 1353 after his return to Europe and which he embedded in a chronicle of Bohemia; and a little information can be gleaned from the *Relatio* of Odoric, who visited the bases of his fellow Franciscans in China during the 1320s. Both these last two authors display greater interest in recounting marvels than in the progress of the Christian mission.

Although it would be anachronistic to speak of 'missionary theory' in the context of Catholic proselytism in the Mongol dominions,[28] some writers – mainly back in Western Europe – did address theoretical matters. The English Franciscan Roger Bacon derived much of his information from Rubruck, whose *Itinerarium* he read and whom he met in person; and in his *Opus maius* of *c*.1267, which included a classification of the world's religions,[29] he put forward his ideas on how to convince pagans of the truth of the Christian faith.[30] More pragmatic, perhaps, was Ricoldo's so-called *Libellus ad nationes orientales* (*c*.1291) which, despite the title usually attributed to it, is in fact a guide for missionaries regarding the errors of eastern Christians, Jews, Muslims and Tartars and how to tackle them.[31] The voluminous works of the Franciscan

Ramón Lull (d. 1315) also contain scattered recommendations for the successful conduct of the mission. These writings can be supplemented by the letters sent by Innocent IV (1245), Nicholas III (1278), Nicholas IV (1288) and John XXII (1329) to Mongol rulers, which contain an exposition of the faith, and by the *Capitula fidei* produced between 1296 and 1299 by Giles of Rome at the behest of Pope Boniface VIII and allegedly sent to the qaghan in China.[32] To rely upon documents of this last type, of course, is to assume that the methods of proclaiming the Gospel in the field were determined by the perspectives of the Holy See or of 'high' theology. In practice, the popes tended expressly to leave it to the missionaries themselves to propagate the faith by whatever means they deemed appropriate;[33] and indeed, as Professor Ryan has recently pointed out, the papal role was limited to the issuance of privileges for the Mendicants and the establishment of new sees. The missionary journeys themselves – beginning with Rubruck's – sprang, for the most part, from the initiatives of individual friars rather than of the Curia.[34] On the other hand, the creation at Avignon in 1369 of a large dossier of documents pertaining to Catholic relations with schismatics and infidels testifies to an abiding papal concern for missionary matters.[35]

Methods and obstacles

It is perhaps advisable at this stage to establish what was meant by 'conversion', drawing, as far as possible, on what popes and Latin missionaries indicate as their goal. Here we need to bear in mind the warnings of Karl Morrison that the 'conversion experience' itself does not possess any kind of uniformity, that it is in any case beyond the historian's reach, and that we are dealing – and can only deal – instead with the metaphors for that experience found in our thirteenth- and fourteenth-century texts, which reflect a different range of premises and understandings from our own.[36] It is clear from the letters of Montecorvino and his suffragans that they regarded baptism as the essential first step. But this formal act of adhesion in itself, of course, was not enough; the process of conversion was an ongoing one, marked by the abandonment of idolatry and an exclusive and deepening commitment in proportion to the continuing operation of the Holy Spirit. When word reached Pope Innocent IV in 1254 that Sartaq had been baptized, he wrote expressing his delight but also urged the Mongol prince to keep in mind the commandments, to publicize his new-found faith, and to make his pious conduct an example to his subjects.[37] In practice, however, the number of friars in any particular field at one time meant that they were able to do little more than baptize; catechism was hardly feasible.[38]

Innocent IV's plea reminds us that the tactic historically adopted by Christian missionaries was to win peoples over through their rulers. Individual churchmen in the eleventh and twelfth centuries had successfully engineered the conversion of princes in the Slavic and Baltic worlds; the sources from a more remote age depict small groups of men, or even single missionaries, convincing pagan Germanic kings of the truth of Christianity and, with the support of these royal acolytes, baptizing thousands of their subjects in a single day. This policy of conversion from above – which Ricoldo was advocating *vis-à-vis* the Mongols in the 1290s, on the particular grounds that 'the common people are so doltish and bestial that they are in no way willing to be converted unless they are promised a monetary reward'[39] – seems to have been favoured initially by the Franciscans in Mongol Asia. We are told of the conversion of the subject ruler of Bashkiria, 'with his wife and children and many followers [*multa familia*]', in *c*.1321.[40] Körgüz, says Montecorvino, 'brought over the greater part of his people to the Catholic faith'; according to Peregrine, the prince had personally converted several thousands in one day. His death was a heavy blow to the Franciscan's hopes: had he only lived, asserts Peregrine, the whole of his people and kingdom would have been subjected to Christ and even the qaghan transformed.[41] But on his arrival in the Far East Montecorvino had found the qaghan already 'grown old in idolatry';[42] and his successors proved equally difficult. We know of no other prince in eastern Asia who followed Körgüz's example, and when Clement V set up a network of missionary sees in 1307 he did so regardless of the fact that none of the Chinggisid khans had been converted.[43]

Among the nomads in general, the missionaries' tactics enjoyed scant success. Ricoldo alleged, in vague terms, that certain 'kings and queens' and men and women of noble birth had been converted, but conceded that as yet the Tartars had not come over in great numbers.[44] Even without the qaghan's example, Montecorvino claimed in 1306 to have baptized approximately six thousand souls in Khanbaligh.[45] Yet just over twenty years later Andrew of Perugia admitted that the friars had converted none of the Jews or Muslims in China, and that though many of the 'idolators' (Buddhists) had been baptized they did not adhere strictly thereafter to Christian practice.[46] Possibly the surprising statement by John of Marignolli, that missionary efforts in China had reaped 'a great harvest of souls',[47] is based on baptisms rather than on longer-term criteria. It has frequently been observed that the friars' successes in China, such as they were, were confined to the schismatic Christian communities, like the Orthodox Alans, the Armenians and the Nestorians. Some, or most, of the last-named would have been Mongols. But Mendicant activity seems to have had no impact whatsoever on the Chinese majority of the population and in fact to have ignored them.[48]

On the face of it, there seemed no good reason why the Mongols should not embrace Christianity. Bacon thought that they were on the verge of accepting the faith.[49] A few years later the Dominican Master-General, Humbert of Romans, was equally sanguine.[50] For Ramón Lull, their lack of a religion in any proper sense meant that they would more easily be convinced by argument.[51] Ricoldo pointed to a paradox here. The Tartars appeared to be the most distant from the truth, since they had neither understanding nor religion other than the law of nature, no temples, no fasts, nor any external prop (*adminiculum*) to connect them to the spiritual life. And yet, as experience showed, they required less effort to be brought closer to the Christian faith and converted. In Ricoldo's hierarchical schema, they could be won over more readily than the Muslims; the Muslims more readily than the Jews; and the Jews more readily than eastern Christians.[52] By the time he wrote his *Epistolae ad ecclesiam triumphantem* (after 1298), however, he could observe gloomily that the Tartars had for the most part embraced Islam[53] – an allusion to the formal adoption of Islam by the Ilkhan Ghazan in 1295.

In the friars' own letters, two obstacles to their success surface frequently: language and numbers. Rubruck had complained repeatedly of the inadequacy of his interpreter – a man, he assures us, 'who was neither intelligent nor articulate' and whose preferred method of translation, the friar discovered, once he had himself acquired a little knowledge of the language, was 'to say something totally different, depending on what came into his head', with the result that Rubruck chose rather to remain silent.[54] In the conclusion to his report, he urged that any future representative from the West be accompanied by a good interpreter or, better, several.[55] Ramón Lull picked out the lack of linguistic expertise as the primary reason for the meagre harvest of the mission.[56] The problem continues to figure in the letters of the Franciscans in China: Peregrine described himself and his colleagues in 1318 as quite unskilled in the learning of languages.[57] But Montecorvino claims to have acquired an adequate knowledge of 'the Tartar language and script', enabling him to translate the New Testament and the Psalter.[58] Letters from Franciscans in the dominions of the Golden Horde, moreover, reveal that he was by no means alone in his achievement, commenting as they do on the alleged advantage that English, German and Hungarian friars enjoyed over their Romance-speaking brethren when it came to learning the languages.[59]

As far back as 1254 the Dominican Master-General, Humbert of Romans, had ordered brethren who travelled to the Mongol world to acquire the necessary languages beforehand;[60] and several voices were raised – including Bacon's – in favour of the establishment of schools of languages in the West.[61] The decree of the Council of Vienne (1312), authorizing the creation of chairs in eastern languages at Oxford, Paris and Bologna, was a belated response to the problem – and surely an inadequate one, since Turkish and Mongolian were not among those listed. Friars tended to acquire a knowledge of Turkish once they had arrived in the steppe (as Paschal da Vittoria, for instance, did at Sarai in the mid 1330s), and the production of that part of the Latin–Turkish vocabulary, the *Codex Cumanicus*, devoted to missionary purposes (and written in the middle decades of the fourteenth century) indicates the onset of a more methodical approach.[62] Yet learning the language, as has been pointed out, did not necessarily enable the missionary to express intricate theological concepts.[63]

As far as possible, the missionaries endeavoured to make good the deficiencies of the spoken word with the grandeur of the liturgy, the beauty of the chant and of bell-ringing, and the use of pictures.[64] In the first church he had built in Khanbaligh, just a stone's throw from the palace of Temür Öljeitü, Montecorvino tells us that he installed three bells and that the qaghan was delighted by the singing of his choirboys, which he could hear from his chamber.[65] In the Golden Horde lands the Franciscans' celebration of the liturgy allegedly made a profound impact on the pagans, who sought their permission to take part in it.[66] Skilful borrowing of ideas from the host culture also played a part: the cross Montecorvino set over his church in Khanbaligh was red, a colour associated with good luck by Buddhists and Taoists.[67]

The isolation of the missionaries was a formidable problem. 'The harvest is great, but the labourers are few' (Matthew, ix, 37) is a common refrain.[68] Montecorvino claimed that because he had no colleague in China and was unable to leave the qaghan's court he needed a few fellow workers in order to retrieve the ground lost among the Önggüd since Körgüz's death; and that if only he had possessed two or three helpers the qaghan himself might have been baptized.[69] There had never been such outstanding progress in the world at any time since Gregory the Great, the Franciscans of the Golden Horde territories assured the West in 1323 – if only enough helpers were available.[70] Jordanus of Séverac in 1328 offered a similar analysis of the situation in India: two or three hundred friars could bring more than 10,000 people annually to the Christian faith.[71] 'We lack nothing so much as the brothers we long for', wrote Peregrine in 1318.[72] Reading Montecorvino's thinly-veiled complaint that he had received no letters from his brethren in Persia,[73] or Ricoldo's lament that 'many tearful letters seeking reinforcements [succursu]' from the Dominican Master who had sent him had gone unanswered,[74] we might be forgiven for thinking that it was all a matter of manpower and mutual support. But even when new personnel were despatched eastwards, there was no guarantee of their safe arrival: the heats of southern India took a heavy toll of the Franciscans sent out to China by Clement V in 1307.[75]

It might have been expected that the friars would find ready allies among the Nestorian communities; but generally speaking this was not the case. We have seen already how sharply Nestorian attitudes towards the Mongols differed from those of the West (p. 102). Latin missionaries also misunderstood, for example, the Nestorian view of the crucifix, assuming that the Nestorians were ashamed of Christ's Passion, when in fact the cross venerated in the eastern church was that of the Second Coming (Parousia).[76] It may be that misapprehensions of this kind underlay the failure of the Latin Church to use the Nestorian wives of Mongol khans as intermediaries, a possibility grasped only fleetingly during the pontificate of Nicholas IV (1288–92).[77] Montecorvino's dealings with the Nestorians in China were far from harmonious. He complains of the hostility of the Nestorians at court, who traduced him to the qaghan and obstructed his efforts as best they could: otherwise, he might have baptized a further 30,000 souls.[78] John of Cori, writing a few years after Montecorvino's death, went further: had it not been for harassment by 'the false and faithless Nestorians', the archbishop 'would have converted the entire country to the Christian and Catholic faith'.[79] At stake here, perhaps, was the Nestorians' concern to safeguard their privileges, to which Peregrine draws attention,[80] against the newcomer. Rubruck, it is true, was on terms of friendship and mutual respect with one Nestorian priest, who acted as an archdeacon to the rest. Yet otherwise the Franciscan seems to have regarded many of the beliefs and practices of the local clergy with dismay and contempt. At one juncture he delivers himself of a ringing condemnation: the Nestorians were greedy and corrupt, drunkards, usurers and simoniacs. It should be said that Rubruck met no representative of the higher clergy and that he mentions only one Nestorian monk, with whom he did not apparently have personal contact. But his strictures failed to take into account the situation of a church that had no access to the landed endowments of its Western counterpart and had not, moreover, passed through the crucible of the Gregorian Reform.[81]

As a remedy for the problems of both language and numbers, it was vital to train up a priesthood from among the indigenous populations.

Over the years Montecorvino bought forty pagan boys, whom he instructed in Latin and the Divine Office: by 1305 eleven knew the office, and several were employed in copying psalters.[82] The Franciscans in the khanate of the Golden Horde, too, used the alms they were given in order to purchase native children, to whom they taught writing and the Christian faith; some of the boys had become clerics and are described as 'excellent proselytizers' (*optimi conversores*).[83] The difference, it seems, was that here the instruction given was less thoroughgoing than that envisaged by Montecorvino for the child oblates he trained. Yet from the absence of any reference to native-born Catholic priests by Peregrine and Andrew several years later, there is reason to doubt that even Montecorvino's efforts were crowned with any long-term success.[84]

In the Pontic steppe, at least, some of the friars adopted the nomadic way of life, in order to maximize the opportunities for conversion.[85] From their letters it is clear that the Franciscans in the east saw their own lifestyle, with its emphasis on poverty, hardship, and peaceful conduct, as the means whereby infidels and schismatic Christians were brought over to the Catholic faith. No doubt this emphasis had its disadvantages. Rubruck, who for some time was believed to be an official envoy, found that he received inferior lodgings, presumably because he had brought no costly gifts. The Mongols were astounded at this diplomatic *faux pas*.[86] Rubruck evidently deemed it important to assure the qaghan that he had not accepted any of the gifts of money that had been distributed among the Christians at court, and that the Franciscans were men of peace.[87] But whether the nomads really placed as great a value on these qualities as the friars supposed, we cannot say (see also p. 136 above). There seems little doubt, moreover, that some of the later Franciscan missionaries saw their own martyrdom as a desirable end in itself, rather than merely as the by-product of a fearless presentation of the Gospel. This stance may have owed something to contemporary apocalypticism;[88] though it is also possible, of course, that martyrdom was conceived of as positively influencing the would-be convert.

In 1255 Rubruck had warned the Dominicans he met in Greater Armenia that as mere preachers little heed would be paid to them,[89] and in his report to Louis IX he recommended that no more friars journey to the Mongols in a missionary capacity; rather, a bishop should be sent with the status of papal legate. For an envoy to the Mongols was permitted to say whatever he wished, was always asked if he wanted to say more, and was assured of a hearing, whereas a private individual could only reply to questions put to him.[90] This might purport to explain why in their final interview Rubruck was unable to expound the Christian faith to Möngke;[91] but it ignores the fact that, as we have seen, the despatch of an ambassador to the Mongols, whatever his privileges, was taken to indicate submission – the very reason why Louis had been unwilling to send any more envoys to the Mongols after Andrew of Longjumeau's return in 1251 and why Rubruck had been at pains from the outset to deny that his was a diplomatic mission.

Nevertheless, the observation points up one of the difficulties under which the missionary laboured: the absence of any association between the mission and political power. This is not to claim that nomadic rulers in Inner Asia had invariably opted for a faith that aligned them with a strong sedentary state: in the late eighth century the choices made by the Khazar and Uighur qaghans – of Judaism and Manichaeism respectively – seem to have represented a deliberate attempt to dissociate themselves from the religious affiliations of the Byzantine empire, the Islamic Caliphate and imperial China.[92] That said, from the missionary vantage-point there was an important difference between the efforts to evangelize the Turco-Mongolian nomads and the successful conversion of barbarian peoples in Europe in earlier centuries. Unlike the Roman monks and clerics who had baptized Frankish and Anglo-Saxon kings, for example, the Catholic missionaries of the thirteenth and fourteenth centuries did not represent, in Mongol eyes, a superior civilization. And in contrast with, say, the situation in the southern Baltic,[93] there was no question of the propagation of the Christian faith in the Mongol world being supported by the threat of military force.[94] In this respect the closing decades of the thirteenth century were an unpropitious time for the Christian cause, with the progressive dismemberment of the tiny Latin enclaves on the Syro-Palestinian coast; though Ricoldo's assertion that not merely the Saracens but the Tartars too asked Christians, jeeringly, 'Where is your God?', is probably just a rhetorical flourish.[95]

Mongol attitudes and Latin failure

The tendency in the secondary literature has been to seek to explain the demise of the Latin mission in Mongol Asia rather than the modesty of its achievements while it lasted. Some of the circumstances reviewed above may well have applied to both: the small number of friars; the terrible isolation so clearly in evidence in their letters to the West; the difficulty of working through unskilled interpreters or of learning, and translating into, unfamiliar languages like Mongolian and Turkish. It is also important to bear in mind that the susceptibility of the Mongol rulers to Christianity had been overstated. In the mid-thirteenth century, following the return of the papal envoys in 1247–8, dread of the

Mongols had been tempered in some small measure by the realization that they were not polytheistic barbarians but believed in one supreme God.[96] At one level, this optimism in Western ecclesiastical circles in the middle and later decades of the thirteenth century was part of the wider phenomenon of 'the dream of conversion', which also embraced the Islamic polities of Western Asia and North Africa.[97] In the Mongol case, of course, it was encouraged by eastern Christians, particularly the Nestorians (above, pp. 97–102), and by the promotion of Christians (among others) with administrative expertise to serve the new regimes within Muslim territories (pp. 102, 119–20). Mongol 'toleration', however, was two-edged; it was easy to ignore the fact that Muslims could profit from the situation in much the same way as Christians. Already in 1260 Juwaynī had been forcibly struck, not merely by the privileges the conquerors had bestowed on Muslim holy men (along with those of other faiths), but by the way in which the Mongol conquests had facilitated the spread of Islam into regions where it had not previously penetrated.[98] And twelve years previously Simon of Saint-Quentin had apparently been the first Western observer to comment that many within the Mongol armies were adopting Islam.[99] Berke was just the most eminent among a considerable number of Muslim converts.

Yet to notice Western over-optimism is ultimately to beg the question why Mongol sovereigns proved so much more resistant than pagan dynasts in Europe in an earlier generation. We should perhaps ask ourselves if cultural impediments prevented Chinggisid rulers and their Turco-Mongolian nomadic subjects from being attracted to the brand of religion that the friars offered. By this I am not referring so much to clashes between Christian norms and specific Inner Asian practices, like the consumption of *qumis* (fermented mare's milk),[100] or to divergent attitudes towards alcoholic consumption in general or towards death and burial.[101] Such discordances undoubtedly existed; and at one juncture there is even a hint that potential nomad converts objected to paying tithes.[102] But similar difficulties in other societies within Europe at an earlier date had not stopped 'barbarian' princes and their subjects from embracing Christianity; and we know that in the contexts of marriage and dress, for instance, the papacy was concerned not to make the transition for newly-converted Mongols too hard.[103] Nor does the progress of Islam in Mongol Asia in the thirteenth and fourteenth centuries seem seriously to have been impeded by comparable obstacles, like the Mongols' rejection of the Islamic slaughter-ritual. I have in mind, rather, some deeper antithesis between the Christian faith, as preached by the friars, and the cultural orientation of the nomads, specifically their attitude to the numinous.

Intent as the Mongols were on sharing the world only with subject peoples, they also had to share it with a plethora of spirits: those of their ancestors, which were well-disposed and were revered, particular individuals or groups being deputed to care for the ancestors' images (*ongghod*) and to supervise their cult;[104] and hostile spirits, which Western observers had no hesitation in describing as demons. It was the task of the shaman (Mo. *böge*; Tu. *qam*) to diagnose the activity of these latter powers and to guard against them by means of charms, incantations or some method of appeasement that might involve the exposure and punishment of some person who had offended them; he was also responsible for exorcisms, prophesies, the prescription and conduct of festivals, and ceremonies designed to influence the weather.[105] There is no dearth of testimony that by the mid-thirteenth century Mongol rulers manifested a heavy dependence upon shamans and fortune-tellers.[106]

And yet the nomads were ready – indeed, eager – to borrow from each and every religion whatever met their needs. Entering the Pontic steppe in 1253, Rubruck found himself in a world that would, on the surface, have been familiar to any Catholic cleric moving among the Franks in the sixth century or among the Anglo-Saxons in the seventh: a world of syncretistic belief and practice, where Christ had often simply been coopted into a pantheon of spirits. He saw the burial-mound of a recently-deceased nomad chief, in whose honour the remains of sixteen sacrificed horses were hung on high and for whom *qumis* and food had been left above the grave; 'and for all that', he tells us, 'they were claiming that he had been baptized'.[107] When his little party passed through an especially hazardous stretch of the Tarbaghatai range, their guide asked them to recite some auspicious *mantra* to keep at bay the demons which were known to haunt the region. The friars recited the *Credo* and the *Pater noster*, and in view of the inadequacy of his interpreter Rubruck also wrote them down for the Mongol attendants to use, presumably, as an amulet.[108]

A case in point is what the friars took to be reverence for the Cross. Rubruck repeatedly witnessed members of the qaghan's family – even princesses who were known to be adherents of 'the soothsayers and idolators' – kiss or revere the Cross.[109] Möngke's youngest brother, Arigh Böke, who allegedly acknowledged that Jesus was God, made the sign of the Cross like a bishop.[110] Odoric of Pordenone reported that the qaghan venerated the Cross seventy years later.[111] What these Western observers did not realize was that the use of the Cross, *inter alia*, as a magical device to secure protection against spirits in this life, even by the Nestorian communities, already had a long history in Central Asia.[112] In these circumstances, it was quite possible for an individual prince to

MISSION TO THE INFIDEL

make some gesture that implied the acceptance of, say, Christianity while continuing to sanction and observe the 'shamanistic' practices of his forebears or favouring another religious group altogether.[113]

In much the same way as the nomads relied upon their own religious specialists to foretell the future, to ward off the unwelcome attentions of hostile spirits, and the like, so they valued the skills and prayers of 'holy men' of all faiths and sects. Rubruck, who on his outward journey was taken to the encampments of 'wealthy Mongols' to give them his blessing, also observed that Möngke wanted all the different religious groups to pray for him; for, he says, 'they like one to pray for their lives'.[114] This requirement is included in the diplomas issued to religious groups, like those conferred, for instance, on the Rus' clergy by Möngke Temür of the Golden Horde in 1267 and on the Franciscans in China by the qaghan Buyantu (reigned as Jen-tsung) in 1314.[115] In the 1320s the friars were still expected to pray for the qaghan's life and to give him their blessing on ceremonial occasions.[116] Writing to Benedict XII in 1336, Toghan Temür asked for his blessing and to be remembered in the pope's prayers.[117]

We should notice that the focus of all this concern was the present life, not the next.[118] The Mongols were especially concerned about the means of gaining eternal life; but they understood this in a biological sense, to mean the prolongation of life, rather than in the sense of life everlasting in the world to come. When Chinggis Khan had summoned the Taoist patriarch Ch'ang-ch'un (Ch'iu Ch'u-chi), head of the Ch'üan-chen ('Complete Purity') Taoist sect, to his campaign headquarters in 1222, he had been under the impression that the old man had reached the age of 300 and had access to some elixir of longevity.[119] Rubruck testifies to the rumour among the nomads that the pope was 500 years old.[120] The rituals and prayers of other religious groups were valued not so much (if at all) for their efficacy in bringing rewards in an afterlife as for their influence over conditions in this life.[121] For this reason, incidentally, the suggestion that shamanistic activities were not in competition with the exercise of other faiths[122] is misleading.

Hence the favours and privileges which the Mongol rulers bestowed upon all holy men, a policy that, as we saw (p. 45), dated back to Chinggis Khan himself. Naturally, in exempting Christian priests and monks, Buddhist monks, and Muslim scholars ('ulamā) from taxation, forced labour and military service, the Mongol government also saw these people as useful agents in securing the submission of the local populations. 'Have you won over the common people for me?', Chinggis Khan wrote to Ch'ang-ch'un in 1223.[123] But the primary impulse behind the exemptions conferred on members of the 'religious classes' was that they were seen as allies in the day-to-day struggle with Nature and with hostile spirits.

While the Mongol imperial dynasty patronized religious specialists of many different kinds, it also presided even-handedly over all confessional groups. When the official cult of the imperial ancestors was adapted to the Chinese model, Qubilai refused to preside over it as required by Confucian tradition; so too did most of the Yüan Emperors.[124] Whatever his favour towards Buddhist scholars, moreover, it is clear that he and his immediate successors avoided constituting Buddhism as anything like a state religion.[125] Although the Taoists had been defeated in the great public debates organized by Möngke and himself in 1256–8, he nevertheless continued to show favour to the Ch'üan-chen sect; the persecution of the Taoists in 1281, which was probably sparked off by the failure of the Japanese campaign, was shortlived.[126] Even Körgüz, whose adhesion to the Roman Church proved to be the pinnacle of Montecorvino's achievement, is known from Chinese sources to have given hospitality to Confucian *literati* and provided them with funds for the construction of Confucian temples just as he did for Montecorvino's church.[127] The same reluctance to abandon the position of neutrality enjoined by Chinggis Khan seems to characterize the Ilkhans down to – and even following – Ghazan's conversion to Islam. After the initial persecution of the Christians and Jews, Ghazan reintroduced Chinggis Khan's prescription exempting the 'religious class' within both communities from payment of the Islamic poll-tax (*jizya*). It was in the reign of Öljeitu (described as having 'a kind of hatred of the Christians') that Christian clerics were again subject to the poll-tax and that Islam assumed the trappings of a cult that had the exclusive patronage and support of the administration.[128]

The Mongol rulers' pluralistic stance, defying neat boundaries, was liable first to fuel, and then to dash, hopes of conversion to Christianity – or indeed of conversion to any other faith. Qubilai, according to Marco Polo, acknowledged that there were four prophets – Jesus Christ, Muḥammad, Moses, and the Buddha – and claimed to honour and revere all four.[129] During his reign he manifested, in the words of his modern biographer, a series of 'chameleon-like transformations'.[130] The same might be said of Toqto'a, khan of the Golden Horde (d. 1312), who reputedly was baptized, died a Christian, and was buried in a grave belonging to the Franciscans.[131] A report reached Western Europe that Toqto'a was 'highly favourable to the Christians', while his antagonist Noghai was written off as 'the worst necromancer and a persecutor of everything good'.[132] According to Muslim observers, however, Toqto'a remained an 'idol-worshipper' and (in time-honoured Mongol fashion) showed favour to religious men of all faiths, though he preferred Muslims; one of his sons, who predeceased him, even became a Muslim.[133] The spiritual peregrinations of this ruler, who apparently convinced Christians and Muslims alike that they enjoyed his special favour, strikingly recall the contradictions surrounding the religious attachments of Möngke and his mother Sorqaqtani which we noticed earlier (p. 101). It would be unjust to blame all these sanguine reports on nothing more than the wishful thinking of the religious communities in question; their aspirations were nurtured by the attitudes and policies of the rulers themselves.

It is necessary to dispel certain misconceptions here. Religious pluralism is not to be equated with tolerance or indifference.[134] Admittedly, remarks by contemporary Western observers appear to furnish some warrant for such a view. For Jacopo d'Acqui (citing a version of Marco Polo), the Mongols did not care which God was worshipped in their dominions: 'if only all are faithful to the lord Kan, and quite obedient, and give therefore of the appointed tribute, and justice is well kept, thou mayest do what pleaseth thee with thy soul.'[135] 'Each and all are allowed to live according to their own sect', wrote Andrew of Perugia in 1326; 'for this is their opinion, or I should say their error, that every man is saved in his own sect'.[136] But though the Mongol government permitted the propagation of all faiths, it also demonstrated a considerable interest both in enforcing certain Inner Asian customs on its sedentary subjects and in forbidding actions that were taboo in steppe society. Thus in 1246 a Rus' prince was obliged to practise the levirate (marriage with a brother's widow), which was contrary to Christian teaching; for a time in the early 1270s the levirate was harshly enforced in Qubilai's China; and at different times Muslims in Mongol territory fell foul of prohibitions against washing in running water or slaughtering an animal by cutting its throat.[137] In certain respects, therefore, many of the qaghan's subjects experienced Mongol rule as decidedly intolerant.[138]

Nor were the Mongols practising what has been termed 'celestial insurance', as if actuated by a sense that any particular religion might be right.[139] Rather, in their eyes all faiths *were* right, i.e. they were equally valid ways of approaching the supreme God, Tenggeri (other than in those areas where they contravened nomadic practice). 'God has given mankind several paths', Möngke told Rubruck in their final interview.[140] And the Ilkhan Arghun, in a letter to Nicholas IV in 1290, was voicing the same opinion when he politely rejected the pope's recommendation that he be baptized: 'Now, saying that I have not accepted baptism [*silam*], you are offended and harbour sentiments [of discontent]. [Yet] if one prays to Eternal Heaven alone and thinks in the appropriate manner, is it not as if one had accepted baptism?'[141] This was more than a matter of *Realpolitik* (although it was that, certainly); it was also an expression of the deep-rooted cultural orientation of the steppe peoples.

The accent on inclusivism

If I have spent so long on the steppe-dwellers' approach to religious matters, it is because it helps us to see two possible reasons why the Christianity represented by the Mendicants was less attractive to the Mongols than were the teachings of its rivals. The first has to do with its relationship to these other faiths; the second, with its attitude towards the spirit-world of Inner Asia.

Since the Mongols' approach to religious matters was pluralist and syncretistic, they valued what might be termed inclusivism. Professor Richard Fox Young has examined Rubruck's account of the public debate between Buddhists, Christians and Muslims which was convened on Möngke's orders in 1254 and in which the Franciscan opened as the champion of the Christian viewpoint. If we can believe Rubruck himself, his performance was a *tour de force*; later it duly won the admiration of Bacon.[142] He showed himself superior in dialectic both to his Nestorian allies and to his Buddhist antagonist. When he had inquired of the Nestorians the previous evening how they intended to proceed, they proved incapable of doing anything but quoting scriptures which had no validity in the eyes of their opponents. Rubruck also had to dissuade them from commencing the debate by attacking the Muslims, with whom, as he pointed out, they shared a common monotheistic tradition, so that it was preferable to begin with the Buddhists. During the debate itself, the Buddhist, who wanted to discuss the creation of the world and the fate of souls after death, was manoeuvred onto the friar's chosen ground and vanquished by dint of Augustinian arguments about the essence of God and the nature of evil.[143] But it was not Western scholasticism that won souls in Inner Asia. Rubruck admits that at the conclusion of the debate nobody declared, 'I believe, and wish to become a Christian'.[144] The remark may be targeted at the ineffectual methods of the Nestorians, who had taken over from him in the debate, or at the proceedings as a whole; but it certainly applies in equal measure to the failure of Rubruck and his eastern *confrères*.

Young argues that the attraction of Buddhism to the qaghan lay in its inclusivism, i.e. that Buddhist teaching was inherently more capable of coexisting with, and even absorbing, Mongol folk religion.[145] This, it should be noted, is a far cry from the older notions that the Mongols perceived shamanistic practices as inferior to the foreign faiths they were encountering, and hence no longer 'adequate to the spiritual needs of world conquerors', or that Möngke was seeking 'more than a personal faith' and saw shamanism as 'no permanent basis of unity for the diverse peoples of the empire'.[146] Young's more nuanced and persuasive thesis is consonant with what is known of the tactics of Buddhist missionaries, who sought to bring local, indigenous deities and cults within the ambit of their own world-picture. For a time Taoism had won Chinggis Khan's favour because, by dint of Ch'ang-ch'un's tactics, it had been able to pose as embracing all ascetic groups in China.[147] The Taoists had advanced the claim that the Buddha was merely an incarnation of Lao-tzu and that Buddhism was consequently a vulgarized form of Taoism. But in the public debates of 1256–8 between adherents of the two faiths, when it emerged that Taoist philosophy, like that of the Confucians, 'posed a strict dichotomy between Chinese and barbarians',[148] and that the books on which they based their denigration of Buddhism were forgeries, the Taoists lost ground to the Buddhists.[149] Earlier (p. 101) we cited a statement imputed to Möngke – that Buddhism was like the palm and the other faiths like the fingers. This aphorism, of course (whether Möngke actually voiced it or not), may tell us more about the way in which the Buddhists wanted to portray their religion to the qaghan, i.e. as the *fons et origo* of all other teachings.

Now at this level Christianity could not compete with Buddhism. For all its universalist claims, it did not come across as an inclusive faith. It stood over against the rest, in opposition to them. This may well be the significance of the view attributed to the Tartars by Jacopo d'Acqui (probably on Marco Polo's authority), that Christ was a proud Lord who was unwilling to be associated with other gods.[150] And certainly the political pretensions encapsulated in papal letters were matched by an equally exclusive theological position on the part of the missionaries. John of Cori's phrasing suggests that one powerful reason for Nestorian opposition to Montecorvino was his relentless insistence that they acknowledge Roman primacy, without which, he told them, they could not be saved.[151] 'Be absolutely sure', Rubruck told Batu in 1253, 'that you will not possess the things of Heaven without having become a Christian. For God says, "He that believeth and is baptized, shall be saved; but he that believeth not shall be condemned"' (Mark, xvi, 16). At these words, he tells us, Batu gave a slight smile, and the other Mongols began to clap in derision; it was with difficulty that the friar and his interpreter were able to continue.[152] We learn more of this episode from a story found in a collection of Franciscan *exempla* and derived ultimately from King Het'um of Lesser Armenia, who passed through Batu's encampment in 1254, not long after Rubruck. 'The nurse', Batu had allegedly told Rubruck, 'begins first to let drops of milk fall into the child's mouth, so that the sweet taste may encourage the child to suck; only next does she offer him the nipple. Thus you should have first persuaded us in simple and reasonable fashion, as this teaching seems to us to be altogether alien. Yet you immediately threatened everlasting punishment.'[153] It looks as if the Christianity purveyed by the Franciscans in Eastern Asia may have had a relatively exclusive and uncompromising image.

In much the same way as Christianity appeared less inclusive than Buddhism, so it may have contrasted with Islam. Not that Islam, which sets its face resolutely against any hint of polytheism or idolatry, is obviously an 'inclusive' faith: Rubruck met Muslims who shunned the Buddhist monks and were unwilling even to talk about them.[154] But we cannot fail to be struck by an apparently bizarre incident during the public disputation of 1254. After the demolition of his Buddhist opponent, the Nestorians prevailed upon the Franciscan to stand down so that they could at last engage with the Muslims; but the latter refused to argue with them, conceding that everything in the Gospel was true.[155] This somewhat surprising admission raises the question whether the interpreters had misunderstood, since the Muslims presumably spoke in Persian, the *lingua franca* even in the eastern reaches of Mongol Asia.[156] But the statement could simply have reflected the fact that Muslims regard Christianity as an incomplete version of the revelation fulfilled in Islam[157] – as being in some measure, therefore, subsumed within Islam. This claim to inclusiveness contrasted sharply with the Christian view of Islam, which had sometimes been treated as a Christian heresy but was more often dismissed as arrant nonsense or a diabolical invention.[158]

The salience of magic

A second reason why the Christianity of the friars lost out to its non-Christian competitors has to do with its reaction particularly towards the spirit-world of the nomads. No less significant than the Mongols' religious pluralism was another element in their mindset, which has frequently been left out of the equation: their abiding interest in magic. The concern they displayed about techniques for the prolongation of life, which we noticed earlier, was just one aspect of it. True, for the steppe peoples, as for Western Christians, there was 'good' and 'bad' magic: they did indeed punish severely certain types of sorcery, aimed at harming or killing others.[159] But in general they were interested in ways of influencing or controlling Nature, in order to secure military victory for instance, and of predicting the future. To Qubilai, it has been said, 'the better religion was the one that could perform the more impressive feats of magic'.[160] One of the principal reasons he valued his Chinese adviser Liu Ping-chung so highly was Liu's command of the occult sciences, which had won the Mongols many victories.[161] Qubilai was not an isolated case, however. When Möngke asked the Confucians what use they were for magic or healing,[162] he was posing a question that might have been voiced by any other Chinggisid ruler.

This fascination with magic and healing accounts for the pronounced sympathy displayed by the Mongol qaghans in China not for Chinese Buddhism but for the Tibetan lamaistic variant, since as Marco Polo observed the Tibetans were renowned as the most skilled enchanters and astrologers in the world.[163] In this regard, incidentally, Buddhist lamas by no means monopolized the qaghan's favour: after the conquest of southern China in 1279, Qubilai patronized the Cheng-i ('True Unity') Taoists there, who (unlike the Ch'üan-chen sect) had never abandoned the quest for the prolongation of life and whose leaders enjoyed a reputation for magical skill, notably in the vanquishing of demons and in the use of charms to influence the weather.[164] Ricoldo describes the hold that Buddhist lamas (he uses the Persian term *bakhshīs*) enjoyed over the Ilkhans in Iran: they were honoured above all men; they were familiar with the magic arts, consulted demons, performed numerous miracles and foretold future events.[165] For him the lamas' influence constituted the greatest obstacle to the salvation of the Tartars.[166] Iron-ically, Ricoldo was writing when the lamas' influence was just about to give way to that of Muslim sufi dervishes. Although Professor Amitai has argued persuasively that the ascendancy of the sufis was not based on any resemblance to the shamans,[167] there are hints in the Islamic sources that the earliest Muslim Ilkhans – Aḥmad-Tegüder and Ghazan – valued them too for their mastery of magical techniques.[168]

Rubruck spoke truly, therefore, when he ended the account of his final interview with Möngke by saying, 'If I had possessed the power to work miracles, as Moses did, he might perhaps have humbled him-self'.[169] And he later told Bacon, it seems, that he would have enjoyed a warmer welcome had he known a little about the stars, but that the Mongols had despised him since he was ignorant of astronomy.[170] Mem-bers of the several religious groups who flocked to the qaghan's court knew that they would be required to demonstrate skill in magic. Rubruck mentions a Muslim soothsayer and a Rus' one in Möngke's encamp-ment.[171] The Muslims benefited from the fact that the Qur'ān accepted auguries and the use of charms and condemned only those magical devices which were designed to harm other human beings.[172] Nestorian priests in turn countenanced, and indeed shared in, sorcerous practices:

Marco Polo heard a story that they had predicted Chinggis Khan's victory over 'Prester John' by means of divination (though in this case the incantations were taken from a psalter).[173]

The only respect in which the Mendicants could compete was in healing. The Franciscan Francesco of Alessandria, who miraculously cured the Chaghadayid khan (? Yesün Temür, d. 1338/9) of a malignant tumour (*cancro et fistula*), gained his confidence to the extent that the khan called him his father and entrusted his son to be reared and baptized by the friar.[174] Similarly, the Franciscans both in Chaghadayid Central Asia and in China were believed to be winning souls by casting out demons.[175] But in other respects the Catholic Church had, by this stage, set its face against any attempt to influence Nature by the practice of magic.[176] This, for the friars, would have represented intercourse with the demonic, and was another source of friction between them and many of their eastern brethren. Rubruck criticized Nestorian priests for participating in such pagan rites, and upbraided the Armenian monk Sargis for consulting the Muslim soothsayer.[177]

One of the chapters of Marco Polo's book is entitled, 'Why the Great Khan does not become a Christian'. When Polo's father and uncle, in the course of their first visit to Qubilai, asked why he privately (so we are told) regarded Christianity as the superior faith and yet did not embrace it, he explained to them that he was in no position to do so. Were he to convert, the 'idolators' among his 'barons' would ask him what he was about, given the Christians' inability to perform the tricks and miracles at which the 'idolators' themselves excelled. It was to prepare for the defeat of idolatry and his own baptism that he supposedly urged the elder Polos to bring back a hundred learned Christians from Western Europe.[178] The story is doubtless garbled, the interview a fabrication; but I suggest that, if we discount the qaghan's secret preference for Christianity and the predictable snipe at the Nestorians, this passage does encapsulate a perceptive comment on the challenges confronting Catholic evangelism in Mongolia.

I have tried to suggest some reasons for the restricted appeal of Western Christianity to the Mongols and their nomadic subjects. Whatever the superficial resemblance between the pre-Christian cults of their European ancestors and the 'paganism' and 'idolatry' they encountered in Mongol Asia, Latin missionaries were confronted by a problem that they failed to grasp. It was of paramount importance for Mongol rulers to remain above all faiths and sects, utilizing for their own purposes, whether governmental or personal, the specialist resources found within each. They were ready to patronize, and even to participate in, cultic practices that contributed to those ends and that did not conflict with their ancestral customs. The 'religious classes' of all faiths and sects, like the nomads' own shamans, were valued for whatever power they might exercise over Nature, whether by prayer or by thaumaturgy. For the friars, conversely, such eclecticism meant no belief at all. In this milieu, the very rigour of the Mendicant Orders, their uncompromising hostility towards any accommodation with paganism, rendered the missionaries – for all their physical and spiritual resources – less well-equipped to thrive than either their competitors or their more supple and adaptable precursors who had worked among pagan peoples in Europe. Their efforts were accordingly doomed to failure. But we need to set that failure in context, by asking whether thirteenth- and fourteenth-century Mongol princes embraced, in a full sense, any of the universal religions. Our principal sources for the Yüan regime in China are Buddhist, as those for the Ilkhanate are Muslim: it is conceivable that when, like Latin writings, they describe preferences and conversions they merely mask attitudes that were in fact considerably more complex.

Notes

1. See the introduction to the Jackson and Morgan trans., p. 42; Richard, *La papauté*, pp. 78–9.
2. WR, xxxviii, 10, p. 326 (tr. Jackson and Morgan, pp. 270–1). For the background to this mission, see Pelliot, 'Les Mongols et la papauté', pp. 216–20; also ibid., pp. 71–3.
3. Richard, *La papauté*, p. 83.
4. CICO, V:2, p. 59 (no. 27).
5. Richard, *La papauté*, pp. 89–90. The letter is in Redlich, *Eine Wiener Briefsammlung*, pp. 248–50 (no. 250), and in BBTS, II, pp. 444–5. For Qirq-yer, mentioned by Rubruck as 'Forty Settlements' and probably denoting a stretch of the southern Crimean littoral, see Vasiliev, *Goths*, p. 166.
6. Richard, *La papauté*, pp. 95, 130.
7. Ibid., p. 115.
8. See Leonardo Olschki, 'Manichaeism, Buddhism and Christianity in Marco Polo's China', *AS* 5 (1951), pp. 1–21; L. Carrington Goodrich, 'Recent discoveries at Zayton', *JAOS* 77 (1957), pp. 161–5 (here pp. 163–4); Samuel N.C. Lieu, 'Nestorians and Manichaeans on the South China coast', in his *Manichaeism in Central Asia and China* (Leiden, 1998), pp. 177–95.
9. *DM*, p. 311/MP, I, pp. 78–9 (tr. Ricci, pp. 6–7).
10. Richard, *La papauté*, pp. 85–6. The mission is mentioned by Salimbene, *Cronica*, I, p. 317.
11. James Daniel Ryan, 'Nicholas IV and the evolution of the eastern missionary effort', *Archivum Historiae Pontificiae* 19 (1981), pp. 79–95.

12. At the time of writing (8 Jan. 1305/6) he was in his twelfth year in 'Cathay', and the reference to the current qaghan suggests he had been on the throne at the time of the Franciscan's arrival: Montecorvino, 'Epistolae II', §1, in *SF*, p. 346, and tr. in A.C. Moule, *Christians in China before the Year 1550* (Cambridge, 1930), p. 172, and in Dawson, *Mongol Mission*, p. 224. Richard, *La papauté*, p. 146, however, dates his arrival in 1293. See generally Regine Müller, 'Jean de Montecorvino (1247-1328) – premier archevêque de Chine. Action et contexte missionnaires', *NZM* 44 (1988), pp. 81-109, 197-217, 263-84 (pp. 92-8 for his earlier career).

13. Montecorvino, 'Epistolae II', §2, p. 347, for Arnold; §7, pp. 349-50, for the Lombard; and 'Epistolae III', §2, pp. 352-3, for Lucalongo (tr. in Moule, *Christians in China*, pp. 173, 175, 179; tr. Dawson, pp. 225, 226, 229).

14. Montecorvino, 'Epistolae II', §4, pp. 348-9 (tr. in Moule, *Christians in China*, pp. 173-4; tr. Dawson, pp. 225-6). For the Chinese evidence, see Moule, *Christians in China*, pp. 236-9; and for the church, N. Egami, 'Olonsume et la découverte de l'église catholique romaine de Jean de Montecorvino', *JA* 240 (1952), pp. 155-67.

15. The date of his death is inferred from the largely obscured funerary inscription in Ch'üan-chou: John Foster, 'Crosses from the walls of Zaitun', *JRAS* (1954), pp. 1-25 (here pp. 17-20). For a biographical sketch, see Giorgio Brugnoli, 'Andrea da Perugia', in Carlo Santini, ed., *Andrea da Perugia. Atti del convegno (Perugia, 19 settembre 1992)* (Rome, 1994), pp. 5-15.

16. Richard, *La papauté*, pp. 171-7.

17. 'Cronica della Quistione insorta nella Corte di Papa Giovanni XXII a Vignone, circa la povertà di Cristo', in Francesco Zambrini, ed., *Storia di Fra Michele minorita come fu arso in Firenze nel 1389, con documenti risguardanti i Fraticelli della povera vita*, Scelti di curiosità letterarie inedite o rare del secolo XIII al XIX 50 (Bologna, 1864), pp. 59-82 (here pp. 69-70); according to the editor (p. xxxiii), this source (the work of a Franciscan, 'N[icolaus]') dates from no earlier than 1377 (I owe this reference to Ann Fielding).

18. For these various creations, see Richard, *La papauté*, pp. 157-62, 180-9 *passim*. James D. Ryan, 'To baptize khans or to convert peoples? Missionary aims in Central Asia in the fourteenth century', in Guyda Armstrong and Ian N. Wood, eds, *Christianizing Peoples and Converting Individuals* (Turnhout, 2000), pp. 247-57 (here pp. 254-7), provides a good résumé of missionary activity in the Chaghadayid khanate.

19. Frank W. Iklé, 'The conversion of the Alani by the Franciscan missionaries in China in the fourteenth century', in James B. Parsons, ed., *Papers in Honor of Professor Woodbridge Bingham. A Festschrift for his Seventy-Fifth Birthday* (San Francisco, 1976), pp. 29-37.

20. Herbert Franke, 'Die Gesandtschaft des Johann von Marignola im Spiegel der chinesischen Literatur', in Lydia Brüll and Ulrich Kemper, eds, *Asien: Tradition und Fortschritt. Festschrift für Horst Hammitzsch zu seinem 60. Geburtstag* (Wiesbaden, 1971), pp. 117-34.

21. Luciano Petech, 'I francescani nell'Asia centrale e orientale nel XIII e XIV secolo', in *Espansione del francescanesimo*, pp. 213-40 (here p. 238).

22. Richard, *La papauté*, pp. 154-5.

23. For what follows, see ibid., pp. 282–96; Christian W. Troll, S.J., 'Die Chinamission im Mittelalter', *Franziskanische Studien* 48 (1966), pp. 109–50, and 49 (1967), pp. 22–79 (here pp. 68–9); Müller, 'Jean de Montecorvino', pp. 274–6.

24. Richard, *La papauté*, p. 181.

25. Jean Richard, 'Essor et déclin de l'Église catholique de Chine au XIVe siècle', *Bulletin de la Société des Missions Etrangères*, 2e série, 134 (1960), pp. 1–9 (here p. 5), repr. in his *Orient et Occident*. Idem, *La papauté*, pp. 154–5.

26. 'Chronica XXIV Generalium Ordinis Minorum' (mostly before 1369), in *Analecta Franciscana*, III (Quaracchi, 1897), pp. 499–504; extract tr. A.C. Moule, 'A life of Odoric of Pordenone', *TP* 20 (1921), pp. 275–90 (for the figure of 20,000, see p. 500, tr. Moule, p. 279).

27. Antoine Dondaine, O.P., 'Ricoldiana: notes sur les oeuvres de Ricoldo da Montecroce', *AFP* 37 (1967), pp. 119–79: see pp. 157–60 for the date of Ricoldo's death.

28. A point made by Troll, 'Die Chinamission', p. 55.

29. *OM*, II, pp. 370–1. See further Bezzola, pp. 203–4.

30. *OM*, II, pp. 372–6; on the religion of the Tartars, see also ibid., pp. 386–9.

31. The *Libellus* is printed in Dondaine, 'Ricoldiana', pp. 162–70: see ibid., pp. 139–41, on the purpose of the work.

32. Jean Richard, 'Le discours missionnaire: l'exposition de la foi chrétienne dans les lettres des papes aux Mongols', in *Prédication et propagande au Moyen-Age. Islam, Byzance, Occident*, Dumbarton Oaks Colloquia 3 (Paris, 1983), pp. 257–68 (here pp. 259–65), repr. in Richard, *Croisés*. Gerardo Bruni, 'Rari i inediti Egidiani: I. *Capitula fidei* inviati da Bonifazio VIII a Pechino', *Giornale Critico della Filosofia Italiana* 40 = terza serie, 15 (1961), pp. 310–23 (here pp. 313–18).

33. Müller, 'Jean de Montecorvino', p. 272 and n.167.

34. Ryan, 'To baptize khans', pp. 248–53.

35. See Muldoon, *Popes, Lawyers and Infidels*, pp. 74–85. The date has been established by Karl Borchardt, 'Reg. Vat. 62: ein päpstliches Dossier zur Politik gegenüber Ungläubigen und Schismatikern aus dem Jahre 1369', *QFIAB* 76 (1996), pp. 147–214 (here pp. 156–65).

36. Karl F. Morrison, *Understanding Conversion* (Charlottesville and London, 1992).

37. Lupprian, p. 211 (no. 39).

38. James D. Ryan, 'Conversion vs. baptism? European missionaries in Asia in the thirteenth and fourteenth centuries', in James Muldoon, ed., *Varieties of Religious Conversion in the Middle Ages* (Gainesville, FL, 1997), pp. 146–67.

39. Ricoldo of Montecroce, *Libellus*, in Dondaine, 'Ricoldiana', p. 167. Wolfgang Hage, 'Religiöse Toleranz in der nestorianischen Asienmission', in Trutz Rendtorff, ed., *Glaube und Toleranz. Das theologische Erbe der Aufklärung* (Gütersloh, 1982), pp. 99–112 (here p. 109).

40. *BBTS*, II, p. 73.

41. Montecorvino, 'Epistolae II', §4, p. 350 (tr. in Moule, *Christians in China*, p. 174; tr. Dawson, pp. 225–6). Peregrine, 'Epistola', §2, in *SF*, p. 365 (tr. Dawson, p. 232; cf. Moule trans., p. 208).

42. Montecorvino, 'Epistolae II', §1, p. 346 (tr. in Moule, *Christians in China*, p. 172; tr. Dawson, p. 224).
43. Richard, *La papauté*, pp. 123-4. Müller, 'Jean de Montecorvino', p. 213.
44. Ricoldo, *Libellus*, in Dondaine, 'Ricoldiana', p. 168.
45. Montecorvino, 'Epistolae II', §2, p. 347 (tr. in Moule, *Christians in China*, p. 173; tr. Dawson, p. 225).
46. Andrew of Perugia, 'Epistola', §5, in *SF*, p. 376 (tr. in Moule, *Christians in China*, p. 195; tr. Dawson, p. 237); a more critical edition in Brugnoli, pp. 10-13 (here p. 13).
47. John of Marignolli, 'Relatio', in *SF*, p. 529 = 'Kronika Jana z Marignoly', *FRB*, III, p. 496; Sir Henry Yule, *Cathay and the Way Thither*, new edn by Henri Cordier, 4 vols, HS² 33, 37, 38, 41 (London, 1913-16), III, p. 215, misconstrues the phrase to indicate that Marignolli's own party was responsible.
48. Iklé, p. 30. Petech, 'I francescani', pp. 230-1. John Larner, *Marco Polo and the Discovery of the World* (Newhaven, CN, 1999), pp. 120-1. A different view had been advanced by Anastase Van den Wyngaert, O.F.M., 'Méthode d'apostolat des missionnaires des XIIIᵉ et XIVᵉ siècles en Chine', *La France Franciscaine* 11 (1928), pp. 163-78 (here p. 173).
49. Bacon, *Opus tertium*, ed. Little, p. 70. See also 'Opus tertium', in *Fr. Rogeri Bacon opera quaedam hactenus inedita*, ed. J.S. Brewer, RS (London, 1859, vol. I only published), p. 86, where Bacon envisages that the Tartars might be converted *pro majori parte*.
50. Humbert of Romans, 'Opus tripartitum', i, 6 and 15, pp. 188, 195; second passage tr. in L. and J. Riley-Smith, eds, *The Crusades: Idea and Reality 1095-1274* (London, 1981), p. 112.
51. Ramón Lull, 'Petitio ad Coelestinum V' (1294), in *BBTS*, I, p. 374; cf. also his 'De fine', i, 5, p. 266.
52. Ricoldo, *Libellus*, in Dondaine, 'Ricoldiana', p. 163; cf. also p. 167. See generally Anna-Dorothee von den Brincken, 'Christen und Mongolen bei Ricold von Monte Croce (um 1300)', *Jahrbuch der Akademie der Wissenschaften in Göttingen* (1978), pp. 23-6.
53. Ricoldo, 'Lettres', ed. R. Röhricht, *AOL* 2 (1884), pp. 258-96 (here p. 285; cf. also pp. 276, 281).
54. WR, xiii, 6, p. 196 (tr. Jackson and Morgan, p. 108); see also xxv, 8, and xxvii, 4, pp. 232, 240 (tr. Jackson and Morgan, pp. 156, 167).
55. Ibid., epilogue, 5, p. 332 (tr. Jackson and Morgan, p. 278).
56. Schmieder, *Europa*, pp. 139-40.
57. Peregrine, 'Epistola', §4, pp. 366-7 (tr. in Moule, *Christians in China*, p. 209; tr. Dawson, p. 233).
58. Montecorvino, 'Epistolae II', §9, p. 350 (tr. in Moule, *Christians in China*, p. 176; tr. Dawson, p. 227).
59. Michael Bihl, O.F.M., and A.C. Moule, 'De duabus epistolis fratrum minorum Tartariae aquilonaris an. 1323', *AFH* 16 (1923), pp. 89-112 (here p. 109); tr. A.C. Moule, 'Fourteenth-century missionary letters', *The East and the West* 19 (1921), pp. 357-66 (here p. 363). Bihl and Moule, 'Tria nova documenta de missionibus fr. min. Tartariae aquilonaris annorum 1314-1322', *AFH* 17 (1924), pp. 55-71 (here p. 67).

60. Gerard of Frachet, *Vitae fratrum ordinis Praedicatorum*, ed. B.M. Reichert, Monumenta Ordinis Fratrum Praedicatorum Historica (Rome, 1897), pp. 151–2.

61. E. Randolph Daniel, *The Franciscan Concept of Mission in the High Middle Ages* (Lexington, KE, 1975), pp. 9–11, 57–64.

62. Louis Ligeti, 'Prolegomena to the Codex Cumanicus', *AOASH* 35 (1981), pp. 1–54. P.B. Golden, 'The Codex Cumanicus', in Hasan B. Paksoy, ed., *Central Asian Monuments* (Istanbul, 1992), pp. 33–63. For Paschal, see *BBTS*, IV, p. 246.

63. Schmieder, *Europa*, pp. 141–2.

64. For what follows, see Noè Simonut, *Il metodo d'evangelizzazione dei Francescani tra Musulmani e Mongoli nei secoli XIII–XIV* (Milan, 1947), pp. 138–9; Troll, 'Die Chinamission', pp. 63–5.

65. Montecorvino, 'Epistolae II', §§2–3, pp. 347–8, and 'Epistolae III', §3, p. 353 (tr. in Moule, *Christians in China*, pp. 173, 179–80; tr. Dawson, pp. 225, 229).

66. Bihl and Moule, 'De duabus epistolis', p. 109 (tr. Moule, 'Fourteenth-century missionary letters', p. 364).

67. Reichert, *Begegnungen*, p. 77.

68. Peregrine, 'Epistola', §4, p. 366 (tr. in Moule, *Christians in China*, p. 209; tr. Dawson, p. 233). MP, I, p. 60 (preface to Francesco Pipino's Latin translation, 1310/20).

69. Montecorvino, 'Epistolae II', §§4–5, pp. 348–9 (tr. in Moule, *Christians in China*, p. 174; tr. Dawson, p. 226).

70. Bihl and Moule, 'De duabus epistolis', p. 110 (tr. Moule, 'Fourteenth-century missionary letters', p. 364).

71. Jordanus, *Mirabilia descripta*, ed. and tr. Henri Cordier, *Les merveilles de l'Asie* (Paris, 1925), Latin text p. 123; tr. Henry Yule, *Wonders of the East*, HS[1] (London, 1863), p. 55.

72. Peregrine, 'Epistola', §6, p. 368 (tr. in Moule, *Christians in China*, p. 209; tr. Dawson, p. 234).

73. Montecorvino, 'Epistolae II', §6, p. 349, and '... III', §2, p. 353 (tr. in Moule, *Christians in China*, pp. 175, 177–8; tr. Dawson, pp. 226, 228).

74. Ricoldo, 'Lettres', p. 270.

75. Andrew, 'Epistola', §7, p. 377 (tr. in Moule, *Christians in China*, p. 195; tr. Dawson, p. 237) = Brugnoli, p. 13. Troll, 'Die Chinamission', p. 141.

76. Jean Dauvillier, 'Guillaume de Rubrouck et les communautés chaldéennes d'Asie centrale au moyen âge', *L'Orient Syrien* 2 (1957), pp. 223–42 (here pp. 237–8), repr. in his *Histoire et institutions des églises orientales au moyen âge* (London, 1983). Anna-Dorothee von den Brincken, 'Eine christliche Weltchronik von Qara Qorum: Wilhelm von Rubruck OFM und der Nestorianismus', *AK* 53 (1971), pp. 1–19 (here pp. 8–12).

77. James D. Ryan, 'Christian wives of Mongol khans: Tartar queens and missionary expectations in Asia', *JRAS*, 3rd series, 8 (1998), pp. 411–21 (here pp. 420–1).

78. Montecorvino, 'Epistolae II, §2, p. 347 (tr. in Moule, *Christians in China*, p. 173; slightly mistranslated in Dawson, p. 225).

79. John of Cori, *Livre de l'estat du Grant Caan*, ed. M. Jacquet, 'Le Livre du Grant Caan, extrait d'un manuscrit de la Bibliothèque du Roi', *JA* 6 (1830), pp. 57–72 (here pp. 68–9); tr. in Yule, *Cathay*, III, pp. 100–1.
80. Peregrine, 'Epistola', §2, pp. 365–6 (tr. in Moule, *Christians in China*, p. 208; tr. Dawson, p. 232).
81. WR, xxvi, 12–14, p. 238 (tr. Jackson and Morgan, pp. 163–4), for his criticisms; xxix, 56, and xxxi, 4–6, pp. 273, 283–4 (tr. pp. 206, 218–19), for his dealings with the Nestorian 'archdeacon'; cf. Von den Brincken, *Die „Nationes Christianorum Orientalium"*, pp. 304–6; Peter Jackson, 'William of Rubruck in the Mongol empire: perception and prejudices', in Zweder von Martels, ed., *Travel Fact and Travel Fiction. Studies on Fiction, Literary Tradition, Scholarly Discovery and Observation in Travel Writing* (Leiden, 1994), pp. 54–71 (here pp. 60–3).
82. Montecorvino, 'Epistolae II', §3, pp. 347–8 (tr. in Moule, *Christians in China*, p. 173; tr. Dawson, p. 225).
83. Bihl and Moule, 'De duabus epistolis', p. 109 (tr. Moule, 'Fourteenth-century missionary letters', p. 363).
84. Simonut, pp. 124–5.
85. Ibid., pp. 122–3.
86. WR, x, 2, and xv, 2, pp. 189–90, 200 (tr. Jackson and Morgan, pp. 100, 114–15).
87. Ibid., xxxiii, 7, and xxxiv, 2, pp. 292, 298 (tr. Jackson and Morgan, pp. 229, 236–7).
88. Ryan, 'To baptize khans', pp. 249–50, 255–6. For the desire for martyrdom, see Daniel, *Franciscan Concept*, pp. 40–54; Ryan, 'Conversion or the Crown', pp. 22–3, 33.
89. WR, xxxviii, 10, p. 326 (tr. Jackson and Morgan, p. 271).
90. Ibid., epilogue, 5, pp. 331–2 (tr. Jackson and Morgan, p. 278).
91. Ibid., xxxiv, 4, p. 299 (tr. Jackson and Morgan, p. 237).
92. Peter B. Golden, 'Khazaria and Judaism', *AEMA* 3 (1983), pp. 127–56 (here pp. 136–7), repr. in his *Nomads and Their Neighbours*; cf. also idem, 'Religion among the Qıpčaqs', pp. 230–1. Anatoly Khazanov, 'World religions in the Eurasian steppes: some regularities of dissemination', in Bethlenfalvy *et al.*, *Altaic Religious Beliefs*, pp. 197–201 (here p. 199). Idem, 'The spread of world religions in medieval nomadic societies of the Eurasian steppes', in Gervers and Schlepp, *Nomadic Diplomacy*, pp. 11–33 (here pp. 16–21).
93. Robert Bartlett, 'The conversion of a pagan society in the Middle Ages', *History* 70 (1985), pp. 185–201 (here pp. 194–6). Cf. also Thomas S. Noonan, 'Why Orthodoxy did not spread among the Bulgars of the Crimea during the early medieval era: an early Byzantine conversion model', in Armstrong and Wood, *Christianizing Peoples*, pp. 15–24; and, more generally, Fletcher, *Conversion of Europe*, pp. 487–8.
94. In practice, that is. Innocent IV had enunciated the principle that the papacy was entitled to intervene militarily against a pagan society which tolerated customs contrary to the natural law or which obstructed and persecuted Christian missionaries: Muldoon, *Popes, Lawyers and Infidels*, chaps. 1 and 2.
95. Ricoldo, 'Lettres', p. 266.

96. PC, iii, 2, p. 236 (tr. Dawson, p. 9); cf. also TR, §39, p. 25. WR, xxxiv, 2, p. 298 (tr. Jackson and Morgan, p. 236).

97. R.I. Burns, 'Christian–Islamic confrontation in the West: the thirteenth-century dream of conversion', *AHR* 76 (1971), pp. 1386–1412, repr. in his *Muslims, Christians and Jews in the Crusader Kingdom of Valencia: Societies in Symbiosis* (Cambridge, 1984), pp. 80–108.

98. Juwaynī, I, pp. 9–11 (tr. Boyle, I, pp. 13–16).

99. SSQ, p. 47 (= VB, xxx, 84).

100. WR, x, 5, xi, 2, and xii, 2, pp. 191, 192, 193 (tr. Jackson and Morgan, pp. 101, 102, 104). Dauvillier, 'Guillaume de Rubrouck', pp. 228–31.

101. Alcohol: Ruotsala, *Europeans and Mongols*, pp. 110–30. Death and burial: WR, xxx, 9, p. 279 (tr. Jackson and Morgan, p. 213); Ricoldo, *Liber peregrinationis*, p. 117; Wolfgang Hage, 'Christentum und Schamanismus: zur Krise des Nestorianertums in Zentralasien', in Bernd Jasper and Rudolf Mohr, eds, *Traditio-Krisis-Renovatio aus theologischer Sicht. Festschrift Winfried Zeller zum 65. Geburtstag* (Mainz, 1976), pp. 114–24 (here p. 120).

102. Marignolli, p. 550 = 'Kronika Jana z Marignoly', p. 515 (tr. in Yule, *Cathay*, III, pp. 265–6).

103. James Muldoon, 'Missionaries and the marriages of infidels: the case of the Mongol mission', *The Jurist* 35 (1975), pp. 125–41. Lupprian, p. 273 (no. 61: to Nicholas/Öljeitü).

104. K. Uray-Kőhalmi, '*Böge* und *beki*: Schamanentum und Ahnenkult bei den frühen Mongolen', in *Varia Eurasiatica. Festschrift für András Róna-Tas* (Szeged, 1991), pp. 229–38.

105. WR, xxxv, 2–13, pp. 301–5 (tr. Jackson and Morgan, pp. 240–5), gives examples.

106. Endicott-West, 'Notes on shamans', pp. 226–8.

107. WR, viii, 4, p. 187 (tr. Jackson and Morgan, pp. 95–6).

108. Ibid., xxvii, 4, p. 240 (tr. Jackson and Morgan, pp. 166–7). For other references to demons, see viii, 5, and xxxv, 12–13, pp. 187, 305 (tr. Jackson and Morgan, pp. 96, 245).

109. Ibid., xxix, 19, 30–33, 35, 40, pp. 258, 262–4, 266 (tr. Jackson and Morgan, pp. 189, 194–6, 198).

110. Ibid., xxxii, 7–8, p. 288 (tr. Jackson and Morgan, pp. 224–5).

111. Odoric, xxix, 6, and xxxviii, 4, in *SF*, pp. 481, 493–4 (omitted in Yule, *Cathay*, II). Müller, 'Jean de Montecorvino', p. 266.

112. Hans-Joachim Klimkeit, 'Das Kreuzessymbol in der zentralasiatischen Religionsbegegnung', in Gunther Stephenson, ed., *Leben und Tod in den Religionen: Symbol und Wirklichkeit* (Darmstadt, 1980), pp. 61–80 (here pp. 65–6). See also Klimkeit, 'Das Kreuzessymbol in der zentralasiatischen Religionsbegegnung. Zum Verhältnis von Christologie und Buddhologie in der zentralasiatischen Kunst', *ZRGG* 31 (1979), pp. 99–115; A.C. Moule, 'The use of the Cross among the Nestorians in China', *TP* 28 (1931), pp. 78–86.

113. Walther Heissig, *The Religions of Mongolia*, tr. Geoffrey Samuel (London, 1980), pp. 11, 16. Morgan, *Mongols*, p. 44. Sechin Jagchid, 'Why the Mongolian khans adopted Tibetan Buddhism as their faith', in *Proceedings of the 3rd East Asian Altaistic Conference* (Taipei, 1969), pp. 108–28 (here p. 109),

repr. in his *Essays*, pp. 83–93 (here pp. 83–4). Jagchid and Hyer, *Mongolia's Culture and Society*, pp. 172–3. Hage, 'Christentum', p. 121, and 'Religiöse Toleranz', pp. 101–2.

114. WR, xxviii, 16, and xxix, 15, pp. 250, 256 (tr. Jackson and Morgan, pp. 179, 187); see also xxii, 2, and xxvii, 6, pp. 221–2, 241 (tr. pp. 141, 167–8).

115. 1267: Fennell, *History of the Russian Church*, pp. 190–1; and see Bihl and Moule, 'Tria nova documenta', p. 65. 1314: Éd. Chavannes, 'Inscriptions et pièces de chancellerie chinoises de l'époque mongole', *TP* 9 (1908), pp. 297–428 (here p. 407).

116. John of Cori, p. 70 (cf. trans. in Yule, *Cathay*, III, p. 102). Odoric of Pordenone, xxvi, 8, and xxix, 6, pp. 474, 481 (tr. in Yule, *Cathay*, II, pp. 225, 239). Müller, 'Jean de Montecorvino', p. 266.

117. BBTS, IV, p. 250 (tr. in Moule, *Christians in China*, p. 252, and in Yule, *Cathay*, III, p. 181).

118. As Carpini had observed of the shamans' activities: PC, iii, 9, p. 240 (tr. Dawson, p. 12).

119. Li Chih-ch'ang, *Hsi-yu chi*, tr. Arthur Waley, *The Travels of an Alchemist. The Journey of the Taoist Ch'ang-ch'un from China to the Hindukush at the Summons of Chingiz Khan* (London, 1931), pp. 65, 101. See Yao, 'Ch'iu Ch'u-chi', pp. 205–7, 211–12.

120. WR, xxii, 2, p. 222 (tr. Jackson and Morgan, p. 142).

121. The point is well made by Roux, 'La tolérance', p. 164.

122. Heissig, *Religions of Mongolia*, pp. 11–12. Morgan, *Mongols*, p. 44. DeWeese, *Islamization*, pp. 58–9.

123. Paul Demiéville, 'La situation religieuse en Chine au temps de Marco Polo', in *Oriente Poliano. Studi e conferenze tenute all'Is.M.E.O. in occasione del VII. centenario della nascità di Marco Polo (1254–1954)* (Rome, 1957), pp. 193–236 (here p. 195). See more generally Paul Ratchnevsky, 'Die mongolischen Großkhane und die buddhistische Kirche', in J. Schubert and U. Schneider, eds, *Asiatica. Festschrift Friedrich Weller zum 65. Geburtstag gewidmet von seinen Freunden, Kollegen und Schülern* (Leipzig, 1954), pp. 489–504 (here pp. 489–90). I. de Rachewiltz and T. Russell, 'Ch'iu Ch'u-chi (1148–1227)', *PFEH* 29 (March 1984), pp. 1–26 (here p. 11); also in De Rachewiltz *et al.*, *In the Service of the Khan*, pp. 208–23 (here p. 214).

124. Paul Ratchnevsky, 'Über den mongolischen Kult am Hofe der Großkhane in China', in Louis Ligeti, ed., *Mongolian Studies*, Bibliotheca Orientalis Hungarica 14 (Budapest, 1970), pp. 417–43 (here p. 425).

125. Yüan evenhandedness is stressed by Sechin Jagchid, 'Chinese Buddhism and Taoism during the Mongolian rule of China', *MS* 6 (1980), pp. 61–98 (here pp. 90–1), repr. in his *Essays*, pp. 94–120 (here p. 113).

126. Joseph Thiel, S.V.D., 'Der Streit der Buddhisten und Taoisten zur Mongolenzeit', *Monumenta Serica* 20 (1961), pp. 1–81 (here pp. 48–58). Rossabi, *Khubilai Khan*, pp. 146–7.

127. Ch'en Yüan, *Western and Central Asians in China under the Mongols: Their Transformation into Chinese*, tr. Ch'ien Hsing-hai and L. Carrington-Goodrich, Monumenta Serica Monographs 16 (Los Angeles, 1966), pp. 53–7. Hage, 'Christentum', p. 123, and 'Religiöse Toleranz', p. 208.

128. Budge, *Monks of Kúblâi Khân*, pp. 255–6, 258–60. Bundy, 'Syriac and Armenian Christian responses', pp. 40–1. Spuler, *Die Mongolen in Iran*, p. 183.

129. MP, I, p. 201 (tr. Ricci, p. 110): a passage found only in Ramusio. Demiéville, 'La situation religieuse', p. 196.

130. Rossabi, *Khubilai Khan*, p. 141; for his patronage of different groups, see ibid., pp. 141–7.

131. DeWeese, *Islamization*, pp. 98–100.

132. Ptolomy of Lucca, *Annales*, p. 237.

133. DeWeese, *Islamization*, pp. 112–13: his earliest source is al-Birzālī (d. 1338/ 9), *al-Muqtafā*.

134. A notion first popularized, perhaps, by Gibbon: Morgan, *Mongols*, p. 41; idem, 'Edward Gibbon and the East', *Iran* 33 (1995), pp. 85–92 (here pp. 88–9). For objections to 'indifference', see Hage, 'Christentum', p. 121, and 'Religiöse Toleranz', pp. 110–12; DeWeese, *Islamization*, pp. 100–1, n.73.

135. MP, I, p. 96: for the original text, see Michieli, 'Il Milione', p. 162.

136. Andrew, 'Epistola', §5, p. 376 (tr. in Moule, *Christians in China*, p. 195; tr. Dawson, p. 237) = Brugnoli, pp. 12–13.

137. PC, iii, 6, p. 239 (tr. Dawson, p. 11). Bettine Birge, 'Levirate marriage and the revival of widow chastity in Yüan China', *Asia Major*, 3rd series, 8 (1995), pp. 107–46 (here pp. 120–4) (I owe this reference to Dr Michal Biran). Francis Woodman Cleaves, 'The rescript of Qubilai prohibiting the slaughter of animals by slitting the throat', in *Richard Nelson Frye Festschrift I. Essays Presented to Richard Nelson Frye on His Seventieth Birthday by His Colleagues and Students* (Cambridge, MA, 1992 = *JTS* 16), pp. 67–89. See more generally Paul Ratchnevsky, 'Die Rechtsverhältnisse bei den Mongolen im 12.–13. Jahrhundert', *CAJ* 31 (1987), pp. 64–110.

138. See Endicott-West, 'Notes on shamans', p. 236.

139. Morgan, *Mongols*, pp. 41, 44.

140. WR, xxxiv, 2, p. 298 (tr. Jackson and Morgan, p. 236).

141. Lupprian, p. 266 (no. 57). Richard, *La papauté*, pp. 103–4.

142. Bacon, *Opus tertium*, ed. Little, p. 70. OM, II, p. 376; also ibid., p. 388, where it is claimed that the Christians and Muslims rapidly vanquished the idolators, who then abandoned their religion.

143. WR, xxxiii, 13–20, pp. 294–7 (tr. Jackson and Morgan, pp. 232–4). See Samuel N.C. Lieu, 'Some themes in later Roman anti-Manichaean polemics: II', *BJRL* 69 (1986–7), pp. 235–75 (here pp. 248–50); Fried, 'Auf der Suche', pp. 310–11.

144. WR, xxxiii, 22, p. 297 (tr. Jackson and Morgan, p. 235).

145. Richard Fox Young, '*Deus unus* or *Dei plures sunt*? The function of inclusivism in the Buddhist defense of Mongol folk religion against William of Rubruck (1254)', in *Universality and Uniqueness in the Context of Religious Pluralism* (Philadelphia, 1989 = *Journal of Ecumenical Studies* 26:1), pp. 100–37 (here pp. 101–2, 117, 120–1, 124 ff., 129–30, 134).

146. The phrases used respectively by Jagchid, 'Why the Mongolian khans', p. 110 (repr. in his *Essays*, p. 84), and by Larry W. Moses, *The Political Role of Mongol Buddhism*, IUUAS 133 (Bloomington, IN, 1977), p. 60.

147. See Yao, 'Ch'iu Ch'u-chi'; Thiel, 'Der Streit', pp. 22–3; Roux, 'La tolérance', pp. 143–4.
148. Moses, p. 67. Cf. also Young, *Deus unus*, p. 122.
149. Thiel, 'Der Streit', pp. 33–46. Young, *Deus unus*, pp. 109–11.
150. MP, I, p. 96; original text in Michieli, 'Il Milione', p. 162.
151. John of Cori, p. 69 (tr. in Yule, *Cathay*, III, p. 101). Cf. Von den Brincken, 'Eine christliche Weltchronik', p. 16.
152. WR, xix, 7, p. 215 (tr. Jackson and Morgan, p. 133).
153. P. Livarius Oliger, O.F.M., 'Liber exemplorum fratrum minorum saeculi xiii (excerpta e Cod. Ottob. lat. 522)', *Antonianum* 2 (1927), pp. 203–76 (here p. 215); text also in *BBTS*, I, p. 233 (tr. in Jackson and Morgan, *Mission*, p. 282, appendix v). Although Rubruck is not named, the designation *lector flandricus* must surely apply to him. Oliger, pp. 209–10, dates the *exempla* to the period of the Minister-General Bonaventura (1256–1273).
154. WR, xxiv, 2, p. 228 (tr. Jackson and Morgan, p. 151).
155. Ibid., xxxiii, 20–1, p. 297 (tr. Jackson and Morgan, p. 234).
156. Huang Shijian, 'The Persian language in China during the Yüan dynasty', *PFEH* 34 (Sept. 1986), pp. 83–95.
157. Geoffrey Parrinder, *Jesus in the Qur'an* (London, 1965). Hamilton, 'Knowing the enemy', p. 378. Alternatively, the Muslims' capitulation may have been a tactic designed to throw into relief the more inclusive and accommodating nature of their religion and so to outflank the Christians.
158. Norman Daniel, *Islam and the West. The Making of an Image* (Edinburgh, 1960), pp. 67–73.
159. WR, viii, 2, and xxxv, 6–8, pp. 186, 302–4 (tr. Jackson and Morgan, pp. 94, 242–4). The cases mentioned seem always to centre around sorceresses. See Boyle, 'Kirakos of Ganjak', p. 208, n.34; and for more detail than is given here, Jackson, 'Mongols and the faith of the conquered'.
160. Young, *Deus unus*, p. 118.
161. Hok-lam Chan, 'Liu Ping-chung (1216–74): a Buddhist–Taoist statesman at the court of Khubilai Khan', *TP* 53 (1967), pp. 98–146 (here pp. 141–2; see also ibid., pp. 117, 137–8).
162. *Yüan shih*, chap. 125, cited in Demiéville, 'La situation religieuse', p. 217.
163. *DM*, pp. 402, 465/MP, I, pp. 188, 272 (tr. Ricci, pp. 100, 182). Cf. Young, *Deus unus*, p. 123; Jagchid, 'Why the Mongolian khans', pp. 123–4 (repr. in his *Essays*, p. 91), on the resemblance between the Tibetan *bon-po* and the Mongolian shaman; Sh. Bira, 'Qubilai Qa'an and 'Phags-pa bLa-ma', in Amitai-Preiss and Morgan, *Mongol Empire*, pp. 240–9 (here p. 242). Rossabi, *Khubilai Khan*, p. 143, while noticing the Tibetan lamas' magical skills, believes that Qubilai valued above all their tradition of involvement in secular politics.
164. Janet Rinaker Ten Broeck and Yiu Tung, 'A Taoist inscription of the Yüan dynasty: the Tao-chiao Pei', *TP* 40 (1951), pp. 60–122 (here pp. 63–72). Demiéville, 'La situation religieuse', pp. 209–10. K'o-k'uan Sun, 'Yü Chi and southern Taoism during the Yüan period', in John D. Langlois, Jr, ed., *China under Mongol Rule* (Princeton, NJ, 1981), pp. 212–53 (here pp. 215, 222–3, 247–8).

165. Ricoldo, *Liber peregrinationis*, p. 117.
166. Ricoldo, *Libellus*, in Dondaine, 'Ricoldiana', p. 167.
167. Reuven Amitai-Preiss, 'Sufis and shamans: some remarks on the Islamization of the Mongols in the Ilkhanate', *JESHO* 42 (1999), pp. 27–46.
168. Jackson, 'Mongols and the faith of the conquered', pp. 276–7.
169. WR, xxxiv, 7, p. 300 (tr. Jackson and Morgan, p. 239).
170. *OM*, I, p. 400. This statement, absent from the *Itinerarium*, must be based on Rubruck's oral testimony. Bezzola, pp. 202–5, ascribes it to Bacon himself, who was fascinated by magic and astronomy: see A.G. Molland, 'Roger Bacon as magician', *Traditio* 30 (1974), pp. 445–60.
171. WR, xxxi, 2 and 8, pp. 283, 285 (tr. Jackson and Morgan, pp. 217, 220).
172. T. Fahd, 'Ruḳya' and 'Siḥr', *Enc.Isl.*² D.B. MacDonald(-T. Fahd), 'Sīmiyā', ibid.
173. *DM*, p. 384/MP, I, pp. 165–6 (tr. Ricci, pp. 81–2).
174. 'Chronica XXIV Generalium', p. 531. Ryan, 'Conversion or the Crown', p. 33, assumes that the khan concerned is Yesün Temür's brother and predecessor, Changshi (d. *c*.1338).
175. Odoric, xxxvi, 1, pp. 490–1 (tr. in Yule, *Cathay*, II, pp. 260–2); Ryan, 'Conversion vs. baptism', pp. 157–8. 'Chronica XXIV Generalium', pp. 500–1 (tr. in Moule, 'A life of Odoric', p. 280). Bartholomew of Pisa, 'De conformitate vitae Beati Francisci ad vitam Domini Iesu' (1385/90), in *Analecta Franciscana*, IV (Quaracchi, 1906), p. 557.
176. Richard Kieckhefer, *Magic in the Middle Ages* (Cambridge, 1989), esp. pp. 12, 181.
177. WR, xxix, 42, and xxxi, 8, pp. 267, 285 (tr. Jackson and Morgan, pp. 199, 220).
178. MP, I, pp. 201–2 (tr. Ricci, p. 111): a section found only in Ramusio's text.

chapter 11
TRADERS AND ADVENTURERS

The Mongol regimes and the growth of Asian commerce

We noticed (p. 36) how the poverty and weakness of the twelfth-century Mongols was a byword among their descendants. One result of the conquests of Chinggis Khan was the emergence of a Mongol leadership whose purchasing power was considerably expanded and who, according to Carpini, owned great wealth in gold, silver, silk and precious stones.[1] This new élite, frequently willing to pay inflated prices for commodities that were not available within the steppe economy, constituted an attractive market for merchants, mainly Uighurs and Muslims travelling even from distant regions of Western Asia.[2] This is why traders within independent territories on occasions identified their own interests with a Mongol victory: Lahore fell in 1241, according to Jūzjānī, because merchants in the city, whom the Mongols had issued with permits to traffic beyond the Indus and the Hindu Kush, deliberately undermined the governor's efforts to defend it against the besieging Mongol army.[3]

The destructiveness of the initial conquests, which were often accompanied by considerable slaughter and displacement of populations, was partly offset by the attempts of Mongol regimes to revive agriculture and trade.[4] What success attended these efforts is a matter of debate. In Iran they are associated in particular with the reign of Ghazan, who stabilized the land-tax, reduced or abolished the imposts on trade and crafts, and reformed the currency; though it has to be borne in mind that our principal informant is Rashīd al-Dīn, who as that Ilkhan's chief minister is by no means a disinterested source in presenting these measures as highly effective.[5] Of the sincerity of the Ilkhan's intentions there can be little doubt: his wealth depended in part on the tax revenues from trade and agrarian production. Ghazan's concern was shared even by Mongol princes whose subjects were predominantly nomad pastoralists, like Qubilai's great rival Qaidu. Qaidu's chief minister, the Muslim Masʿūd Bek, reformed the coinage in the 1270s, and Qaidu and his ally, the Chaghadayid khan Duʾa, founded the town of Andijān (in Farghāna) in the 1280s, apparently with the aim of fostering commerce.[6]

As Professor Allsen has demonstrated, the Mongol ruling class did not act merely as the passive recipients of new merchandise or preside benignly over the growth of commercial traffic within their empire; they assiduously promoted the diffusion of goods and techniques.[7] Among the most striking symptoms of their new-found prosperity were luxury textiles – the gold brocades known in Western Europe as *panna tartarica*, 'Tartar cloth' – which were used for various purposes, notably for the robes donned by rulers and nobles on ceremonial occasions or bestowed as gifts, and to cover and line the tents of the imperial dynasty and the grandees.[8] Mongol regimes obtained these textiles in part as booty and tribute, but also through trade and officially-sponsored manufacture.[9] They served as one index of high status for a society in which, unlike feudal Western Europe, the horse performed no such function because the possession and use of horses were so widespread.[10]

The relationship between the Mongol leadership and foreign merchants was thus an intimate one. As early as *c*.1203 two Muslim traders are found among the few close adherents of the future Chinggis Khan.[11] For a time, until Möngke put a stop to the practice, merchants received from Mongol sovereigns the tablets of authority, known as *paizas*, which were bestowed on ambassadors and others engaged on imperial business, guaranteeing them safe-conduct within the empire, the use of the postal relays, and other privileges.[12] The reason was that many long-distance merchants entered into contracts with the Mongol government, which advanced them the capital to enable them to import the commodities the Mongols desired: traders who enjoyed this contractual relationship with the regime were known as *ortogh* (from Turkish *ortaq*, 'partner').[13] In Mongol China, at least until the reforms of Qubilai, a number of them proffered large cash advances to the rulers and acted as tax-farmers, a development heartily deplored, but unsuccessfully resisted, by Chinese and Khitan bureaucrats.[14]

Western mercantile enterprise

In these circumstances, it comes as no surprise to find Western European traders, too, active in the Mongol world from an early date. There had been a Latin mercantile presence in the Frankish-held coastal towns of Syria and Palestine since soon after 1100 and in Constantinople for longer still. During the twelfth century both Venetians and Genoese appeared in the Black Sea (the 'Greater Sea', as it was known in the Latin world). In the wake of the Fourth Crusade, the Venetians obtained a privileged position in the former Byzantine dominions, including three-eighths of the city of Constantinople, and of 'Romania' as a whole, in full sovereignty (1204). But despite this the evidence suggests that the scale of Venetian commercial activity in the Black Sea during the era of the Latin empire of Constantinople was modest.[15] In so far as the northern shores were concerned, it centred on the port of Soldaia (Sūdāq to the Muslims), in the Crimea; here Marco Polo's uncle and namesake owned a house, and from here too his two brothers set out on their first journey in c.1260.[16] The advent of the Mongols in the Pontic steppes greatly enhanced the commercial importance of the region. By the time Marco junior wrote, at the end of the thirteenth century, the Black Sea had become a major focus of Latin commercial activity. He – or perhaps, rather, the anonymous Tuscan writer who composed an epilogue to his book in the early fourteenth century – denied any necessity to describe the Black Sea region because so many Venetian, Pisan and Genoese traders plied its waters and were daily recounting their experiences back home; but this may have been no more than a literary device.[17]

Valid conclusions about Western commercial activity in Mongol Asia are not derived easily from the highly fragmentary source material, which emanates almost exclusively from the Latin side. Western merchants – though not always their names – surface in the letters of missionary friars and the martyrological accounts, which we noticed in the last chapter. These do not, of course, tell us anything about the nature of the merchants' business, the size of the investment, and the profit or loss made; and here we are dependent on documentation preserved in the state archives of the Italian mercantile cities. At this juncture a word is required concerning contracts. The form of contract traditionally employed by Italian merchants in recent decades to finance commercial voyages was called *commenda* by the Genoese and *colleganza* by the Venetians. The partner who remained at home (known as the *stans*) bore all the risks but stood to gain the lion's share (in Genoa, three-quarters) of the profits; the life of the contract was limited to the duration of the journey. This was especially appropriate for trading ventures to distant and barely-known regions of Asia. Around the turn of the thirteenth century, however, the *commenda*-type partnership would be superseded – at least within the relatively familiar territory of the Mediterranean and the Black Sea – by more permanent forms of association. Merchants tended, rather, to remain at home and deal with agents who resided permanently in the European trading-posts (*comptoirs*); or alternatively several members of the same family might pool their capital and operate from different centres.[18]

The contracts themselves have not survived. Instead, we have notarial instruments from certain brief periods, such as the *acta* of the Genoese notaries, Lamberto di Sambuceto, at Kaffa in the Crimea, and Antonio di Podenzolo, at Kilia, in the Danube estuary, from the years 1281–90 and 1360–1 respectively. The problem with this kind of material is that it is often highly reticent. The instrument concerned with the departure of Benedetto Vivaldi from Genoa in 1315 speaks only of a voyage to 'Romania', when we know from other sources that he in fact proceeded as far as India.[19] Such reticence was not necessarily due to a reluctance on the trader's part to spell out the nature of his business – still less his destination – for the benefit of would-be competitors; in a *colleganza* contract, the *stans* might well allow the geographical sphere of operations to remain vague simply from a desire to leave the travelling partner the maximum freedom of manoeuvre.[20] More informative, of course, are the surviving decisions made by the commercial magistracy of the mother city in cases of dispute, when the journey was already completed.

The texts of a number of treaties with the Ilkhans and the khans of the Golden Horde, relating to Western commercial activity in their dominions, have survived from the fourteenth century. Some useful details can also be gleaned from the *regesta* of the deliberations, for the period from 1329 onwards, of the Senate at Venice, where the government kept a stricter control over commerce than did its Genoese counterpart and despatched an official convoy (*muda*) to the east every few months. We possess, lastly, two fourteenth-century commercial manuals, both from Florence, which deal, *inter alia*, with the Asiatic trade and which utilize information from a common source. The first, by an anonymous author and relatively short, dates from *c.*1315;[21] the second is the celebrated work of Francesco Balducci Pegolotti, an employee of the Florentine banking-house of the Bardi, who wrote at some point in the 1330s. Naturally these handbooks do not constitute direct evidence, as would commercial documents; as has been pointed out, they tell us more about what merchants ideally expected to find in the East than what was actually accessible.[22] But the data they provide on such matters as commodities and routes are not altogether to be dismissed.

It was the Genoese who made the running in the Pontic region. Thanks to the Treaty of Nymphaeum, which they had sealed with the Nicaean Emperor Michael VIII in 1261, they replaced the Venetians in Constantinople following its recovery by Michael later that year, a development that compensated them for their expulsion from Acre in 1258 during the War of Saint-Sabas. In 1267 another agreement with Michael gave them their own quarter in Pera, to the east of the Golden Horn.[23] Only at this juncture, apparently, did they begin to make their presence felt in the Black Sea. Soldaia, which was flourishing at the time of Rubruck's visit in 1253, was rapidly supplanted by the base that the Genoese created at Kaffa (the ancient Theodosiopolis) in the Crimea ('Khazaria' or 'Gazaria', as the peninsula was known, after its one-time masters) from c.1275.[24]

By the opening years of the fourteenth century, the Genoese enjoyed the reputation of being in the lead over a much broader geographical area, whether for commercial operations in the Near East or for personal experience of China. Professor Balard has demonstrated how active Genoese traders were throughout the Mongol dominions during the first half of the fourteenth century.[25] Word had reached Polo that they had recently begun to sail in the Caspian.[26] Rashīd al-Dīn thought that all the Frankish merchants who visited North Africa, Egypt, Syria, Rūm or Tabrīz took ship from Genoa (though possibly his informant hailed from that city).[27] When Guillaume Adam recommended launching ships on the Red Sea in order to sabotage Egypt's commerce with the Indian Ocean, he proposed that the task be entrusted to the Genoese, as the people readiest to venture into distant parts.[28] It was the Genoese brothers Ugolino and Vadino Vivaldi who in 1291 disappeared after embarking on the first known attempt to reach India by way of the Straits of Gibraltar; though whether they planned to sail around Africa or west across the Atlantic – whether, in other words, their voyage should be seen as anticipating Da Gama or Columbus – we do not know.[29] Most suggestive of the city's preeminence, perhaps, is that Pegolotti's handbook cites Genoese equivalents for the weights and measures in use on the route to 'Cathay'.[30]

Goods of Chinese provenance had reached the West for some centuries, more recently through the agency of Muslim middlemen.[31] But the date at which Latin traders first made direct contact with China is uncertain. In 1247, to judge from Carpini's silence on the subject, there were no Western merchants to be found east of Kiev.[32] The men from 'Fu-lang' ('Franks'; one of the terms the Chinese used for Europe) who visited Qubilai's court at Shang-tu in 1261 are described as blonde and as originating from a land where the sun did not set; it has been suggested that they were from Novgorod.[33] The Polos were probably the first Latin Europeans to visit China; the next may well have been Pietro da Lucalongo, probably a Venetian, who accompanied Montecorvino on his outward journey in 1291–3.[34] And it was Venetian merchants who brought back Montecorvino's first letter in c.1305.[35] Possibly, therefore, the Venetians can claim to have reached the qaghan's dominions in advance of their rivals. Yet in China too the Genoese subsequently acquired a certain advantage. Documentary evidence indicates that

Genoese merchants were involved in direct trade with the Far East in greater numbers, and invested greater sums, than their Venetian counterparts. The two children of an Italian merchant who are commemorated on tombstones of 1342 and 1344 at Yang-chou belonged to the Genoese Ilioni family. A Latin bishop of Zaitun (Ch'üan-chou), reporting the value of the pension he received from the qaghan, quoted the estimate of Genoese merchants. When Boccaccio, writing in the 1350s, introduced into his *Decameron* a fictional story set in Cathay, he appealed to the authority of 'certain Genoese who have been there'.[36] All but one of the fifteen Europeans who participated in the embassy from Toghan Temür to Benedict XII in 1336–8 were Genoese.[37]

If the commercial activity surveyed in this chapter derived its momentum in part from the warm welcome merchants obtained from Mongol khans, it could not have occurred, equally, without the burgeoning prosperity of Western Europe by the thirteenth century. Symptomatic of this prosperity was the issue of a gold currency for the first time since the Carolingian era, with the minting of the Florentine florin and the Genoese *genovino* from 1252 and of the Venetian ducat from 1284; gold coinage did not emerge definitively in states outside Italy until well into the following century.[38] From the later decades of the thirteenth century, too, the use of water to power the throwing mills that produced silk in northern Italy greatly increased capacity and hence the demand for raw silk.[39] Although the Latin world undoubtedly lagged some considerable distance behind China in terms of both economic development and scientific achievement, its own technical expertise did nevertheless enable it to manufacture goods that would find a market in Asia. There had been a boom in cloth production, spearheaded by the Flemish towns, since the late twelfth century, and Western merchants carried with them finished woollen and linen cloths. The inventory of a Venetian merchant's effects, drawn up in Tabrīz in 1263, shows that he had set out with linens from Germany, Lombardy and Venice and with woollen cloth from Milan.[40]

Routes and commodities in the trans-Asiatic trade

Since the twelfth century, successive Egyptian sultans had deliberately prevented the Latin merchants who flocked to Alexandria from gaining access to the Red Sea and the Indian Ocean.[41] The victory at 'Ayn Jālūt in 1260, as we have seen, brought most of Syria, including the major centres of Aleppo and Damascus, under direct Mamlūk control. During the years 1268–91, moreover, the cities on, or close to, the Syrian coast that had served Latin merchants as a springboard for journeys into the hinterland – Antioch, Acre, Tyre and Beirut – also fell to the Mamlūks, and although Western merchants continued to trade with cities like Aleppo the routes inland were consequently barred to Europeans in much the same way as that through Egypt and the Red Sea. In any event, since 'Ayn Jālūt the territory along the Euphrates was a war-zone, disputed between the Mamlūks and the Ilkhans.[42] The overall effect of the Mongol advance into Persia and Iraq had been to deflect the trade-routes northwards and, to a lesser degree, eastwards. The coastal cities of Syria and Palestine and the Seljük port of Anṭālya alike lost out to ports situated within the territories that owed allegiance to the Mongols.[43]

The three principal western termini for trans-Asiatic trade during the Mongol era were Tana, near the Muslim settlement of Azāq, where the Don flows into the Sea of Azov; Laias (Laiazzo; Ayas), on the Gulf of Alexandretta; and Trebizond (now Trapezunt), on the southern shore of the Black Sea.[44] Tana, lying in the dominions of the Golden Horde, became the western terminus of the more northerly route to 'Cathay'. The anonymous Florentine author, closely followed by Pegolotti, lists the main halting-places along this, the so-called 'Tartar route': 25 days to Astrakhan ('Ghattarghati'/'Istarchati'; Pegolotti's 'Gittarcan' = Ḥājjī Tarkhān) with carts drawn by oxen (but only twelve days with horse-drawn carts); thence one day by water to Sarai, further up the Volga; eight days by water to Saraichik ('Little Sarai'; he calls it 'Saracingho', Pegolotti 'Saracanco') on the right bank of the Ural (Yayïq) River; thence 50 days to Uṭrār ('Oltarre', or 'Ioltrarre' as Pegolotti calls it), on the lower Sir-daryā.[45] At Saraichik a road branched off to Ürgench (in Khwārazm), described in the handbooks as 'a good place for merchan-dise', which gave its name to a highly-esteemed type of cloth ('organdi');[46] and from here it was possible to travel across the Hindu Kush to Ghazna (in present-day Afghanistan) and on to Delhi, the capital of an inde-pendent Muslim sultanate that dominated northern India.

From Uṭrār, following one of the two long-established 'silk routes', used by traders at least as far back as the era of the Roman empire and the Han dynasty, it was another 45 days' journey with asses to Almaligh ('Armalicchio' or 'Armalecco'), a principal residence of the Chaghadayid khans; and thence it took 70 days, again with asses, to reach Kan-chou ('Chamesu', Pegolotti's 'Camesu'). The Mamlūk encyclopaedist Ibn Faḍl-Allāh al-'Umarī, many of whose informants were merchants, says that the road passed through Qaraqocho, though he was told that the journey from Almaligh to Kan-chou lasted a mere 40 days. At this juncture the two Florentine writers appear confused, asserting that from Kan-chou it took 45 days on horseback to reach the river that flowed down through the great port of Hang-chou or Quinsai (Pegolotti's

'Cassai' is closer than the anonymous author's 'Chamesia'), and that from here Khanbaligh, the Yüan capital, was another 30 days distant. al-'Umarī furnishes a more plausible itinerary with the statement that it was a 40-day journey from Kan-chou to Khanbaligh, from where it took the same time to reach Hang-chou ('Khansā'), either overland or by water.[47]

The other two termini both belonged to client princes: Laias lay in the kingdom of Lesser Armenia, and Trebizond was the capital (since 1204) of the Greek empire of that name which paid tribute to the Mongols. Laias, assiduously built up by King Het'um I, who since 1246 had been attracting the Italians with privileges and exemptions, was a favourite haunt of merchants from Latin Cyprus; and from here the Polos twice set out on their eastward journey across Asia.[48] The roads from Laias and from Trebizond converged at Sivas (Pegolotti's 'Salvastro') to convey Western traders through Arzinjān and Erzurum to the important city of Tabrīz ('Tauris'); Edward I's envoy Geoffrey de Langley followed this route from Trebizond to Tabrīz in 1292. Since Abaqa's reign Tabrīz had been one of the Ilkhans' principal residences, which they had adorned with many fine buildings.[49] Marco Polo observed that goods arrived in the city from India, Baghdad, Mosul and Hurmuz ('Cormos'); and indeed Tabrīz served as the gateway to the Persian Gulf and the flourishing port of Hurmuz – in Polo's words, 'a town of very great trade', where valuable merchandise arrived from India in profusion, though the climate was insalubrious.[50] From Hurmuz the enterprising European merchant could take ship for India and the Far East.

Alternatively, one could travel due east from Tabrīz along the road that passed south of the Alburz mountains into Khurāsān. From Khurāsān the route to China[51] passed in a north-easterly direction across the River Oxus (Amū-daryā) into the territories of the Chaghadayid khanate and through the important cities of Bukhārā, Samarqand and Kāshghar; from Kāshghar, says Polo, numerous merchants travelled abroad to engage in commerce. Thereafter it led into the qaghan's dominions by the more southerly of the two silk routes, which crossed the desert through Cherchen and Lop (on the Lop Nor) to the Chinese cities of Sha-chou and Kan-chou. In this last-named place, Marco says, the three Polos stayed for a year on certain business of which, frustratingly, he tells us nothing.[52]

Tabrīz became the principal focus for the operations of Italian merchants in Persia, which have been so thoroughly examined by Professor Paviot.[53] Given the city's international trading connections, it was possible for merchants to obtain there the majority of the articles they sought from India or the Far East. As we have seen, at least one Venetian trader had visited Tabrīz by 1263; the Genoese first appear there in 1280, and a Genoese consul was in residence by 1304.[54] The Venetians obtained full trading rights in the Ilkhanate in successive treaties with the Ilkhans Öljeitü (1306) and Abū Saʿīd (1320).[55] By the 1320s there are indications of a sizeable Italian community in Tabrīz, and in 1341 the Genoese were numerous enough to warrant the creation of an *officium mercancie*.[56] Marco Polo tells us that Tabrīz specialized in the production of cloth of gold and of silk, and that European merchants purchased there precious stones in large quantities – testimony confirmed by the anonymous Florentine manual.[57] Pegolotti adds that one could buy incense, leather, coral, bits of amber, mercury, tin, vermilion, and furs such as ermine, leopard and marten.[58] Tabrīz also served as a distribution centre for the many different kinds of raw silk mentioned in our sources, since they all originated within the Ilkhan's territories: silk was produced in Merv (in Khurāsān), Lāhijān, Gīlān and Gurgān or Jurjān (regions lying just south of the Caspian), and Ganja and Tālish (both in Azerbaijan). Of these, the last-named type was the most highly-prized of all.[59] It should be stressed that silk from these regions had been reaching Italy for some time already – from Merv at least since 1191 and from the Caspian regions since the 1230s.[60]

By Pegolotti's era, the products of India and the Far East – spices such as pepper, ginger and saffron; silk, cotton, linen and pearls – were similarly available at Tana.[61] There were attractions, nevertheless, in proceeding further. The wares to be obtained from China that were especially valued were spices and silk; although porcelain was manufactured in the great port of Zaitun, only a few examples appear to have reached Europe prior to the fifteenth century.[62] The term 'spices' (*spezierie*) was frequently deployed in a wider sense to embrace all the products of the East.[63] Even in its narrower sense, it subsumed dyestuffs, drugs and aromatic gums in addition to culinary additives, and thus comprised pepper, ginger, cloves, cinnamon, nutmeg, sugar, indigo, brazil-wood, incense, aloes, shellac, galingale, mace and 'dragon's blood'.[64] Of these commodities, pepper was the most important. Marco Polo describes the enormous quantities of pepper that reached Zaitun and Quinsai, and cites a customs official for the latter city's daily consumption of 43 basket-loads of 223 lb each.[65] The chief sources of supply in the Yüan era were Java and the Malabar coast.[66] European merchants did not venture in person as far as Java, but they are known to have visited Malabar and very probably obtained pepper also in the ports of China, where imports from south-east Asia were available for a proverbially low price. The Franciscan Odoric of Pordenone, whose interests extended well beyond the harvesting of souls, was amazed at the cheapness of ginger in Canton ('Censcala', i.e. *Chīn-i kalān*, 'Great China') and of sugar at Zaitun.[67]

The volume of Chinese silk imported into the West is a matter of controversy. According to Pegolotti, it deteriorated considerably during the long overland journey, with the result that *seta catuia* (or *catuxia*), 'Cathay silk', became – by a pun that is lost in translation – *seta cattiva*, 'rogue silk', and sold for a lower price on the Genoese market than did silk from any other region of Asia.[68] Professor Bautier is convinced that this cheapness reflected its quality rather than plentiful supply, since for him documentary evidence indicates that Chinese silk imports were outstripped by other varieties in terms of volume also.[69] The counter-argument rests on a twofold basis. Firstly, the evidence Bautier adduces for the low price of Chinese silk in the West is taken exclusively from the years 1338–40; in 1333 the prices fetched at Genoa had been almost 25% higher.[70] And secondly, taking the period as a whole, in the great majority of cases our sources speak only of *seta* without mentioning its provenance: possibly, therefore, imported Chinese silk was so familiar that it was unnecessary to be more specific. It should also be noted that Odoric comments on the remarkable cheapness of silk in China.[71]

Linked with the price of silk is another controversial question, the number of Western merchants who participated actively in trade within Mongol China. Bautier's position is as follows. When Chinese silk first reached Italy, in 1257–61, it was clearly obtained in Tabrīz or Laias;[72] there could have been no question of Europeans accompanying it from its place of origin. Accordingly, we have no reason to believe that all the Chinese silk imported into Europe at a later date was necessarily fetched direct from the Far East by Latin traders. In any case, he argues, the low esteem enjoyed by *seta catuia* hardly rendered the long journey worth-while.[73] Against this, Lopez points to the satisfactory profit realized on purchases of Chinese silk at source (perhaps as high as 200%); while Balard cites unpublished documents that make no reference to silk but mention other, unspecified merchandise which may well have been more profitable and hence have justified the journey to the Far East. On balance, those who argue that by 1320 voyages to India and China were no longer an adventure, but were a routine experience for Genoese and Venetian businessmen, seem to have carried the day.[74] Yet one symptom, possibly, of the relatively small number of Europeans involved in trade beyond Persia and the Pontic steppes is the apparent lack of any official intervention on the part of the home governments (see below).

It was necessary that the commodities carried out east by European merchants should weigh no less than the anticipated purchases (and weight was a particularly important consideration on the long overland journey to China) and bring in a return that would more than suffice to pay for them. Pegolotti advised his readers to leave Venice or Genoa with cloth, to sell it in Ürgench for silver ingots, and to travel onward with no other medium of exchange except, at most, a few rolls of high-quality textiles which would be light to carry; at the frontier of the qaghan's dominions, the ingots would be changed for paper currency.[75] Among the commodities which were sold at Tana, he mentions wax, iron, tin, copper, pepper, ginger and all the 'great' spices, cotton, madder, tallow, cheeses, linen, oil, and honey. Some of these were imports from the West: we know of Italian traders who brought tin to Kaffa and Tana.[76]

The best opportunities, perhaps, came in the form of a business deal with a Mongol khan. Mongol rulers are known to have set especially high value on horses and jewellery, commodities which Toghan Temür's envoys requested on their master's behalf in 1338.[77] The list of objects that Temür particularly desired, as transmitted by John of Sulṭāniyya in 1403, is longer: luxury textiles of various kinds, coral, crystal and other goblets inlaid with gold and silver, silver vessels studded with polished emeralds 'as are found in France', fine camelets from Cyprus, exotic fish-teeth, 'banquiers', impressive tapestries, high-quality saffron, large and strong horses, large dogs and large mules from Spain.[78] Marco Polo tells us that his father and uncle, on their first journey eastwards in c.1261, sold their merchandise in Constantinople and used the profit to buy jewels – of amber or crystal – which they presented to Berke Khan of the Golden Horde. In return the khan bestowed upon them goods worth twice the value of the jewels, which he sent them off to sell.[79] Thus did the European merchant slip easily into the role of *ortogh*.

Many of those Europeans who ventured deep into Asia remain anonymous, particularly in the missionary accounts. Among those who made the journey to China and whose names have come down to us are Venetians – members of the widely-travelled Loredano family and the partners Andriolo Balanzano and Francesco Condulmer, who had a venture *insimul ad Cataiam* at some point prior to 1350.[80] But the Genoese loom larger, like Andalò di Savignone, who made at least two journeys to China, was in Khanbaligh in 1330, participated in an embassy from the qaghan to Pope Benedict XII in 1336 (below, p. 314) and travelled back east with John of Marignolli, the newly appointed archbishop of Khanbaligh.[81] The brothers Ansaldo and Jacopo Oliviero, setting out in 1333, were later joined in China by their nephew Franceschino.[82] A member of another group who made the journey to the Far East was Tommasino Gentile, left behind at Hurmuz owing to illness and obliged (not long before 1343) to return home via Tabrīz, thereby infringing the Genoese boycott of the city and provoking the lawsuit from which we learn all we know of this episode.[83] Turning to India, we know similarly of three Italian traders – two Genoese and a Pisan – encountered by Friar Jordanus in Gujarāt in c.1321, and two more Genoese, Benedetto Vivaldi and Percivalle Stancone, who were active in the subcontinent around the same date.[84] A Venetian *societas* headed by Giovanni Loredano made an unusual journey overland to northern India in the years 1338–43: lured, no doubt, by the fabled munificence of Sultan Muḥammad ibn Tughluq, they travelled from Ürgench to Ghazna (then a Chaghadayid possession) and on to Delhi.[85] The destination of the Genoese partners whose contract, dated 1343, envisages that they may end up *tam in partibus Catay et Indie quam in quibuscumque aliis partibus mondi* is regrettably unknown.[86] For the most part, these men belonged to a relatively restricted group. They tend to bear names that recur often in the affairs of the Commune of Genoa or in the list of doges of Venice. We might expect that in view of the magnitude of the required investment participation was confined to the well-to-do and that newcomers were debarred.[87] Even so, Lopez is able to adduce evidence involving figures who were definitely outside the patrician class, and concludes that society on this far-flung frontier of European endeavour was 'open', 'almost democratic'.[88]

The decline of trans-Asiatic ventures

It is clear that European trade directly with India and the Far East was shortlived. The years c.1320–c.1345 were its heyday – the era in which Western merchants, relatively few in number, travelled beyond Tana and Tabrīz, to participate personally in commercial ventures in the Indian subcontinent, in Central Asia, or in China. But this should not be overstated. Some Latins admittedly still visited China after this period, like the Genoese Gabriele Basso, who died not many years before 1363.[89] The Genoese merchant who, according to the *Songe du Vieil Pelerin* of Philippe de Mézières, had recently arrived in Cyprus after spending fifty years in China ('Inde le Major', as it sometimes appears in medieval Western sources)[90] may have left at the time of the final expulsion of the Yüan in 1368. Possibly the very last Latin to trade in China was the merchant 'Nieh-ku-lun' (Niccolò?) from 'Fu-lin' (i.e. the land of the Franks), who according to a Ming dynasty source had been stranded in the country at that point and was despatched by the new emperor with a letter for his 'king' in 1371.[91]

It is conventional to attribute the collapse of trans-Asiatic trade to a whole range of crises in the fourteenth century. In 1322 the Mamlūk

Sultan sacked Laias, which was, as we saw, a major terminus of one of the principal overland routes, and in 1337 the Egyptians finally occupied the city.[92] This latter blow coincided with the disintegration of the Ilkhanate: after 1340, the journey to China by way of Persia was abandoned in favour of the more northerly route from Tana.[93] Another contributory development was undoubtedly the Black Death, which was raging in the Chaghadayid dominions from c.1338 and may have been present in Muslim India as early as c.1335.[94] Indeed, a handful of deaths *in partibus Catagii*, concentrated in the early 1340s, has prompted the suggestion that Europeans abandoned China because of pestilence, rather than the political upheavals preceding the collapse of Mongol rule.[95] The recurrent struggle between Venice and Genoa – the 'War of the Straits' in 1350–5, followed by the 'War of Chioggia' in 1376–81 – may also have had a disruptive effect on trade in the Black Sea (though their thirteenth-century conflicts had not prevented the Italians from assiduously building up their respective positions in the East); the situation deteriorated still further, perhaps, with the collapse of the Golden Horde into internecine strife after 1360.

Possibly the single most important circumstance behind the eclipse of the transit traffic along the 'Tartar route' and through the Black Sea was the resumption of commerce between the Italian mercantile cities and the Mamlūk empire in 1345.[96] By 1395 the volume of spices that reached Venice via Alexandria and Beirut dwarfed the quantity that passed through Tana; and it has been argued that the fall in volume at Tana was purely relative.[97] What effect the sack of the town by Temür in 1395 had is uncertain. In 1436 the Venetian traveller Giosafa Barbaro wrote nostalgically of the flourishing condition of Astrakhan prior to Temür's campaigns in the Pontic steppe in the 1390s. But possibly the conqueror's activities had little impact on a trade that was already greatly diminished.[98] Writing in 1404, John of Sulṭāniyya mentions Moscow as the best point of departure for merchants travelling to China.[99] Temür's attack may therefore have deflected the trade route far to the north. Whatever the case, men did not cease to dream of the revival of the Tana route – the chief impulse behind King Sigismund's dealings with the Golden Horde khan Jalāl al-Dīn in 1412.[100]

One element in all this which has not received sufficient attention is the impact on the Western European and Iranian economies of bullion flows between Europe and the Ilkhan's dominions from the late thirteenth century to the 1320s. As we saw, gold currencies were slowly making their appearance in the West from the mid-thirteenth century onwards; but in the Islamic world, the currencies were in silver, which was relatively over-valued. To put it in simple terms, Latin merchants brought

TRADERS AND ADVENTURERS

silver to exchange for the gold (most of it arriving through the Gulf from southern India) that enjoyed greater prestige in Europe; the Ilkhans themselves manipulated the ratio of the two metals (usually 1:10) with a view to enhancing their revenues. By the mid-1320s a dramatic shift had occurred in the relative values of gold and silver; the ratios were equalized and the profitability of the bullion trade had greatly diminished. After 1340 the price of silver was rising once more, so that in 1352 the ratio was 1:5.[101] The collapse of the bullion trade surely underlies both the economic difficulties that afflicted the Ilkhanate and its neighbours and other trading-partners during the 1330s and 1340s and the bankruptcies of Italian banking firms like the Bardi and the Peruzzi in 1345.[102] But this is a subject that requires a good deal of further research.

In accounting for the demise of Italian participation in trans-Asiatic trade, it is important not to forget the domestic economic situation – the role of fourteenth-century economic stagnation in Western Europe in the process.[103] In Venice, for instance, the state authorities had taken steps to rein in the currently high level of investment in maritime commerce, by limiting, at intervals, the proportion of an individual's capital that could be invested: the *Capitulare navigantium*, promulgated in 1324, set the maximum at the amount of capital for which an individual was officially liable to make forced loans to the state. As the century progressed, these forced loans themselves acted as a further brake on the economic capacity of the wealthier citizens.[104] Economic restrictions at home made long-distance trade less alluring than other opportunities that were opening up closer at hand, like those that beckoned when the Genoese wrested the Aegean island of Chios from its Byzantine garrison in 1346.[105]

On occasions, the home governments were ready to intervene in order to secure an amelioration of conditions for their merchants. In this context, two recent papers by Professor Nicolà di Cosmo are of cardinal importance. In one he has pointed out that the turmoil in the Golden Horde from the 1360s onwards, far from administering the death-blow to Genoese interests in the region, coincided with the very period in which the Genoese intensified their control over Pontic trade (below).[106] In a second paper, he has distinguished two zones within the Asian trade networks: one, in which Italian traders were active as private individuals and owed nothing to any action on the part of their home governments; the other, in which these governments established direct relations with the Mongol khans in the interests of commerce. The former zone comprised China and Central Asia; the latter the Black Sea region and (to a lesser extent) Iran. There is no sign of Italian consuls in

· 303 ·

the ports of China, regulating the affairs of their co-nationals; nor are the Venetian Senate or the Genoese government known to have sent diplomatic missions to negotiate with the qaghan (or with the Mongol regimes in Central Asia), as they did to the Ilkhans and to the rulers of the Golden Horde. This readiness by the metropolis in Europe to influence foreign rulers on behalf of its nationals is yet another variable in the equation. Without it, Italian traders were dependent exclusively on the capacity, or the willingness, of Mongol sovereigns to guarantee a favourable environment for commercial activity; and when the Mongol regime failed them – as it did in China, Central Asia and Persia – there was nothing left to render their presence worthwhile.[107]

The Pontic zone

The depth of Italian involvement in Central Asia and the Far East at no time remotely approached the levels in the Black Sea region, where the relative proximity of the headquarters of the Golden Horde khans stimulated economic activity and the khans themselves fostered the growth of several new urban centres.[108] The terminology employed in discussing Western mercantile operations can be misleading, and we have to distinguish between the successive stages in which an Italian presence manifested itself: intermittent-to-regular visits by Genoese or Venetian ships; the construction of warehouses for the storage of goods; the growth of a settlement, centred on a church, a bakery and baths; the appointment by the mother city of a consul to preside over the affairs of its citizens; and the recognition of some degree of extraterritoriality through an official treaty with the Mongol khan.[109] A Genoese consul is first encountered at Kaffa in 1281, at Trebizond in 1290, at Vicina (in the Danube estuary) in 1298 and at Tana in 1304.[110] Despite the setback of 1261, the Venetians did not lag far behind. Michael VIII, reconciled with them, granted them in 1277 the right to pass the Straits, and in 1285 his son Andronicus II gave them a still more advantageous treaty. They had a consul in Soldaia by 1288.[111] In 1319 they secured their own quarter in Trebizond.[112] It is clear that the Venetians were already trading in Tana from the beginning of the century; a Venetian consul first appears there between 1317 and 1325. Yet it was not until 1333 that they obtained an agreement with the khan Uzbek permitting them to establish a base at Tana in return for the annual payment of a land-rent (*terraticum*) and a commercial tax (*commercium*) on all goods that passed through their hands.[113]

The growing commercial hegemony of the Genoese in the Pontic region constitutes the most impressive monument to their energies.

They had two aims: to assert their own sovereignty over Kaffa at the expense of the rulers of the Golden Horde, and to exclude their principal competitors from obtaining an autonomous base in the Black Sea that might rival Kaffa.[114] The former aspiration gave rise to tensions, and even full-blown hostilities, with the Golden Horde rulers. Noghai sacked Kaffa in 1298/9, after the Genoese killed the representative sent to collect tribute from them. In 1308 it was the turn of Toqto'a, on the grounds that the Genoese were kidnapping and enslaving his subjects; perhaps, too, he resented their close relations with his enemy the Ilkhan. In the wake of this latter attack, the town was abandoned for five years.[115] We are more fully informed about the prolonged conflict that broke out between the Italians and the khan Jānībek in 1343, entailing the massacre of Western merchants in the Horde's territory and a three-year siege of Kaffa.[116] The pretext was the death of a Mongol notable at the hands of a Venetian merchant in Tana; but a number of observers saw as the real cause of Jānībek's attack the above-mentioned ambitions of the Genoese (the khan's actions may also have been linked with the difficulties the Venetians were experiencing at both Trebizond and Tabrīz in the early 1340s).[117] The Venetian Senate, acting in concert with the Genoese, prohibited all journeys to Tana, while endeavouring unsuccessfully to reach an accommodation with the khan. In 1345 Pope Clement VI authorized a crusade against Jānībek in order to relieve Kaffa – the only known instance of a crusade in defence of a Latin population within Mongol territory.[118] The following year, in an incident immortalized by the contemporary writer Gabriel de Mussis, the khan's forces catapulted into the city the heads of comrades who had died of the plague, an act deemed to have accelerated the transmission of the Black Death to Western Europe.[119] In 1347 the two Italian powers made their peace with the khan separately, though the Venetians received less favourable terms than the Genoese.

Kaffa, described by a Venetian observer in 1404 as a huge city which could scarcely contain its populace,[120] was then only the foremost among Genoa's network of Black Sea ports. In the Crimean peninsula, the Genoese had occupied the fortress of Cembalo (Balaklava) at some point around 1350, as an additional bulwark for Kaffa;[121] and in 1365 Soldaia (which the Venetians had lost in 1343 and failed to retrieve), subsequently extending their authority over the eighteen settlements in its rural hinterland. Around the northern and western Black Sea littoral, they held Vicina (operational until c.1350); Licostomo, in the Danube estuary, seized in c.1350, during the War of the Straits[122] and the seat of a Genoese consul by 1372;[123] Maurocastro at the mouth of the Dniester; and Illice, in the Dnieper estuary, purchased from the Mongols at the beginning of the fifteenth century.[124] In the years 1380–7 the Genoese at Kaffa finally achieved sovereign status through a series of treaties with the khan Toqtamish, initially by dint of their support against Mamai, more latterly as the price of their neutrality during his campaigns into Temür's territory. These agreements gave Genoa full possession not only of Kaffa itself but also of a number of trading-posts around the north-western coast of the Black Sea.[125]

In their second aim, the Genoese were ultimately less successful. For well over half a century they made difficulties for their principal competitors. Returning to Kaffa in 1316, Genoese merchants were forbidden to trade with the Venetians at Soldaia.[126] In particular, as early as 1268 Genoa was striving to deny the Venetians the opportunity to ensconce themselves further east at Tana. After the Venetians' treaty with Uzbek, tensions with their Genoese neighbours in Tana ran high, so that in 1341 the Venetian Senate asked the khan to grant its nationals a different quarter of the town, at some distance from that of the Genoese.[127] Even during the conflict of 1343–7 with the Golden Horde, which had pushed the two Italian powers into a temporary alliance, the Genoese continued to work for the removal of their competitors from Tana. Their efforts were unavailing: in 1347 the Venetians returned to Tana by virtue of a new diploma from the khan, and remained there without further interruption until the town was sacked by Temür's forces in 1395. Reoccupying Tana in the early fifteenth century, they held on until it fell to the Ottomans, perhaps before Kaffa was taken in 1475.

If the Genoese efforts to limit and control Venetian activity in the Black Sea ultimately failed, we might note, nevertheless, that Tana was the only base which the Venetians successfully developed; they gained little from Jānībek's grant in 1355 of the insignificant port of Provato, between Kaffa and Soldaia.[128] Moreover, in contrast with the Genoese in their commercial outposts further west after the 1380s, or indeed with Crete and Venice's other island possessions in the Aegean, the Venetians never enjoyed sovereign rights over Tana. For this reason it is less appropriate to talk of a Venetian 'colony' here than of a 'concession'.[129]

The importance of the Pontic region is borne out by the behaviour of the Italians, which does not suggest that they viewed these outposts as dispensable or peripheral. After the Genoese returned to Kaffa in 1313, the home government thought it worthwhile to appoint a commission of eight of its citizens, the *Officium Gazarie*, to oversee Genoese interests in the Black Sea.[130] The Genoese entrenched themselves still more strongly in the city, embarking on an extensive fortification programme from 1316 onwards, to replace the earlier wooden palisade, and this work was still further extended following the siege by Jānībek, though the size of the garrison was never adequate.[131] So too the Venetians – though less successful than their rivals – took steps to fortify Tana in the early fifteenth century, after its sack by Temür. Evidently the Europeans were not unduly disheartened either by the periodic hostility of the Golden Horde or by the political vicissitudes of the region.

The fact is that Italian involvement in the Black Sea cannot be understood purely in the context of a transit trade in luxury products from the Far East. For only a few decades – perhaps for about thirty years after *c*.1315 – was this a major focus of Genoese and Venetian activities in Tana and Kaffa. Of the 900 or so documents drawn up at Kaffa by Lamberto di Sambuceto in 1289–90, only five mention silk (from Merv) and very few reveal a trace of spices; none is concerned with Tana. The Florentine manual of *c*.1315 says that *spezierie* were available at Tana in only limited quantities, except for sugar and saffron;[132] as we have seen, spices loomed larger here by Pegolotti's time.

The chief articles of trade were furs and slaves. In 1253 Rubruck had noticed the lively traffic at Soldaia, where merchants from Rus' met those from Anatolia and exchanged the furs of the northern forests for cotton cloth, silk and spices.[133] Since the advent of the Mongols, the northern Rus' principalities had been obliged to pay tribute mainly in pelts. Under pressure from the Golden Horde, luxury furs from the northern forests – sable, lynx and ermine – were channelled southwards through Bulghār to Sarai.[134] The Italians in the Tana–Kaffa region thus had access not only to the squirrel and beaver furs obtainable locally, for which in 1320 Genoese traders ventured as far as Sarai itself,[135] but mounting quantities of much more valuable pelts. These are mentioned by Pegolotti, but not by his anonymous precursor, suggesting that in the 1330s their arrival in the Pontic region was still recent. The flow of northern furs grew with the development of closer relations between the Golden Horde khans and the princes of Moscow, who in the late 1320s wrested control over the northern routes from their kinsmen, the princes of Rostov.

Italian merchants had been engaged in the Pontic slave traffic as early as 1246, when Innocent IV endeavoured to secure the release of Christian slaves – Greeks, Bulgarians, Vlachs and Rus' – whom they were selling to the Muslims.[136] Within a short time, however, these were probably greatly outnumbered by 'Tartars'. Marco Polo brought back with him a 'Tartar' slave, Peter, whom he freed in his will in 1324.[137] Tartar slaves were among the most frequent and most valuable exports to Western Europe from both Tana and Kaffa.[138] In this context the term 'Tartar' also denoted Cumans and peoples from the eastern coast of the Black Sea – Circassians, Abkhaz and Georgians.[139] Of those who were genuinely Mongols, many would have been prisoners of war enslaved in the numerous conflicts between the various khanates, even in regions as distant as eastern Asia. Muslim authors report a glut of slaves on the Egyptian market in 1288, following a victory by Qaidu over Qubilai's forces in present-day Mongolia;[140] there is no reason to doubt that a proportion of the captives would have found their way instead to the Crimea. Particularly in the wake of the depopulation caused by the Black Death in Europe, Tartar slaves were required for working the land in Venetian Crete;[141] a good many were employed in a domestic capacity in Italian households, where they appear right down into the fifteenth century;[142] and they turn up even as far west as the Iberian peninsula.[143] Towards the end of the fourteenth century the Venetian government attempted to limit the number of slaves carried by vessels from Tana, though to no avail. Another important, and still more lucrative, element in this commerce was the large number of adolescent Cuman/Qipchāq males shipped through the Straits to Egypt, to be bought by the Sultan and his amirs, reared as Muslims and trained as *mamlūk* troops. Such traffic in vital war material was roundly condemned by successive popes and crusade theorists – and continued, nevertheless, to be pursued by Italian merchants.[144] Professor Balard suggests that slave-dealing at Kaffa peaked around 1410–20 and declined steadily only thereafter.[145]

Among the principal attractions of the Pontic region, moreover, were its own products:[146] fish (particularly sturgeon), from the Danube delta, the Sea of Azov and also from the Caspian;[147] honey and wax from the lower Danube; wheat and millet from a vast hinterland extending to the west and north of the Black Sea; cattle- and horse-hides from the steppe nomads; salt from the lands east of the isthmus of Perekop (which according to Rubruck was in great demand in Rus' and was bringing Batu and Sartaq a considerable revenue) and from the lakes between the Danube and the Dniester;[148] copper from Kastamonu;[149] and alum, also from Anatolia and a mineral indispensable to the dyeing process. Two Italian businessmen, one of them Genoese, had secured a monopoly of the sale of alum from the Seljük Sultan as early as the mid-1240s; but by 1290 the Genoese enjoyed exclusive rights.[150]

These Black Sea ports served a market that was largely regional. Around 1290 some of the fish, and most of the salt, from the Don estuary were taken to Trebizond, and the vessels that carried these goods brought back alum.[151] Constantinople imported foodstuffs from the western littoral of the Black Sea.[152] The corn from the Russian plains exported through Kaffa, which Pegolotti thought was the best of the entire Pontic region,[153] was the chief source of supply for the cities on the southern coast of the Black Sea, not least Trebizond, and this trade too was in the hands of the Genoese and Venetians.[154] Yet the Pontic zone also served as a lifeline – an irregular and vulnerable lifeline, admittedly – for their mother cities. The years 1384 and 1406, when Kaffa alone furnished Genoa with 36% of its known imports of grain,[155] were doubtless exceptional; but in 1390–1 corn from Kaffa made up 10%–14% of Genoa's own supply, while 'Romania' provided a further 16%–18%.[156] The importance of Black Sea wheat to the Venetians (who were less dependent on it than were the Genoese) is clear from the fact that a dearth of grain in Venice pushed the Senate into seeking peace with Jānībek in 1347.[157] In times of crisis, of course, Kaffa itself was obliged to import grain – from Italy, 'Romania' or even from the southern Black Sea coast; and after 1420 the direction of the grain trade, which had run fairly consistently from north to south, would go into reverse.[158]

The salience of the Pontic zone was accentuated in the second half of the fourteenth century by the development of routes linking Genoa's *entrepôts* along the western littoral with Central Europe, where the Hungarian and Polish kings had pushed back the Mongol frontier and were keen to promote the prosperity of their newly-acquired dominions.[159] One of these routes began at Licostomo in the Danube estuary and passed through Wallachia to the Hungarian town of Brassó (Braşov), whose merchants received extensive privileges from King Louis I in 1358 and 1369. The other – of slightly later date, since it is first attested in 1386 – started from Maurocastro, traversed Moldavia to Lwów and thence passed through Poland to the Baltic.[160] Participation in this burgeoning trade compensated the Genoese for their failure to subordinate Venetian operations in the Black Sea to their own interests. Together with a flourishing network of local commerce, it guaranteed the florescence of Kaffa and other Genoese trading-posts well after the traffic in luxury items had dried up – and indeed right down to the Ottoman occupation in the late fifteenth century.

The Pax Mongolica: *hazards and profits*

There is little evidence to sustain the idea that the development of long-distance Eurasian trade was facilitated by a *Pax Mongolica*, stemming from the union of much of Asia under a single government. Pegolotti's pronouncement in the 1330s, that the northerly route from Tana to Cathay was safe for travelling merchants both by day and by night,[161] has attained a certain notoriety. Few historians now subscribe to the existence of a *Pax*, at least between the splintering of the empire in 1261–2 and the termination of a series of inter-Mongol conflicts in *c.*1315; and it may well be that the situation Pegolotti describes (if indeed it ever obtained) was true only for a decade or two around the time he wrote.[162] Instances abound of disruption caused by war. In the early 1260s Marco Polo's father and uncle were first obliged to prolong their journey instead of returning south through the Caucasus, on account of the outbreak of the titanic struggle between Hülegü and Berke; then, when they were on the point of setting out for the Far East, conflicts in Central Asia held them back in Bukhārā for three years.[163] During the 1280s the Uighur principality, lying athwart one of the silk routes, was fiercely disputed between the troops of Qubilai and those of Qaidu and his Chaghadayid subordinates.[164] Thereafter, the struggle continued on a broader front. In 1291, or thereabouts, the Polos and Montecorvino, setting out from opposite ends of Asia, took the decision to journey by sea, in order to avoid the hostilities between Qaidu and the qaghan's frontier forces; in a letter written in 1305 Montecorvino, while conceding that the northerly land route was in general shorter and safer, added that the fighting had now rendered it too hazardous for some time and indeed had prevented any news reaching him from Europe over the past twelve years.[165] Respite, when it came, might prove ephemeral. In 1344 it was reported at Kaffa that the road through the Chaghadayid dominions (*caminum inperii de medio*) was open once more, probably in the wake of a few years' hostilities with the Golden Horde.[166] Yet only a short time later, in *c.*1347, Marignolli would opt to leave China by sea because conflict (this time among the Chaghadayids themselves) had again rendered the land route impassable.[167]

Merchants figured among an enemy's assets, and just how much protection they could count on in time of war is grimly in evidence in 1263–4, when Hülegü and Berke each inaugurated a campaign in the Caucasus by deliberately slaughtering groups of *ortoghs* in the other's service.[168] Nor was it a matter only of discord between rival Mongol khanates. Pegolotti admitted that mercantile interests could suffer in the turbulence unleashed by the death of a ruler.[169] In 1341/2 the Venetians at Tana complained of difficulties after Uzbek's death;[170] and in *c.*1339 a Latin merchant, 'Gillottus', shared the fate of Franciscan friars in an anti-Christian pogrom which broke out in Almaligh following the death of the pagan Chaghadayid khan Yesün Temür and the enthronement of the Muslim 'Alī Sulṭān.[171] In Persia, chaos ensued on the demise of the Ilkhan Abū Saʿīd (1335) and especially after the collapse of Ilkhanid rule and the rise to power around *c.*1340 of non-Mongol dynasties. Of these, the Chobanid rulers in Azerbaijan, Ḥasan and his brother and successor Ashraf, seem to have been particularly prone to robbing and attacking foreign merchants. Exasperated by Ḥasan's murderous attacks on their nationals, the Venetians in 1338 issued a ban (*devetum*) on trade with Tabrīz, as did the Genoese in 1340/1. A later Genoese chronicler put the losses in 1344 – when Ashraf lured European merchants back only to despoil them – at over 200,000 Genoese pounds.[172] Italian traders may have suffered no greater harm than did their Muslim counterparts, who in 1352 were reported to have been emigrating from Persia to the Mamlūk sultanate for some years.[173] In the early 1360s the Jalayirid ruler Shaykh Uways, who had supplanted the Chobanids at Tabrīz, contrived to attract Venetian merchants back into his dominions; but the failure of the experiment led to a fresh ban.[174]

The journey by sea might well be thought to have sidestepped crises of this nature. But clashes, for instance, between petty rulers in the Persian Gulf, who financed their political ambitions through piracy against shipping, could disrupt traffic for years on end.[175] And the sea voyage carried other hazards of its own. Marco Polo commented dismissively on the Arab ships that sailed between the Persian Gulf and India, in which the planks were not nailed, but lashed together with twine made from coconut husks, with the result that the vessels often failed to withstand the rigours of the Indian Ocean.[176] The maritime voyage to China, moreover, could take twice as long as the overland journey, because of the monsoons. Montecorvino estimates that it could last up to two years;[177] and indeed Polo mentions having been stranded on Sumatra for five or six months by adverse weather.[178]

Latin merchants were accustomed to difficulties, of course, in more familiar territories such as Byzantium and Muslim Egypt and Syria – whether arrest and confiscation of property or even bloody pogroms. In 1296 the inhabitants of Constantinople, at Genoese instigation, massacred the Venetians in the city. Westerners experienced, too, the obstructions thrown up by contemporary non-Mongol princes like the Bulgarian king and the emperor of Trebizond; the latter, currently in dispute with Venice, misappropriated some of the Polos' goods as they made their way home in *c*.1294.[179] With one exception, the risks attending trade within Mongol Asia were perhaps no greater than in the eastern Mediterranean.

The exception involved the goods of a merchant who died in Asia. Some of the long-distance traders named earlier never saw their home city again: Jacopo Oliviero and his nephew died in China; Giovanni Loredano, in the region of Ghazna; Benedetto Vivaldi, in India. This might entail the forfeiture of a considerable investment. Since the twelfth century Muslim rulers like the Egyptian sultans had entered into commercial treaties with European city-states, whose merchants were thereby guaranteed the sort of rights that in the Islamic world had been traditionally enjoyed by *musta'minūn* – non-Muslim visitors in receipt of protection (*amān*).[180] One of these concessions was that the dead trader's property should be entrusted, in the absence of an accompanying relative, to any of his co-nationals (though Marco Polo indicates that this was not the custom in Hurmuz, where the ruler confiscated the goods of dead foreign merchants).[181] Since the late twelfth century, commercial agreements with Greek governments had begun to include similar guarantees.[182] In the Mongol dominions, by contrast, only a brother (or an associate who claimed to be a brother) could obtain the goods of the deceased.[183] Of all the agreements made by Mongol khans with the Venetians which have come down to us, only that issued by the Ilkhan Abū Saʿīd in 1320 stipulates that such goods be handed over to the Venetian consul.[184]

One may well ask what level of profit could be made on protracted journeys into Asia. In 1321 Marino Sanudo would state that the articles which reached the West through the Ilkhan's dominions, particularly ginger and cinnamon, were superior in quality to those which were channelled through Alexandria, because these latter were impaired in the course of the long sea journey.[185] He was, of course, advocating an economic blockade of Egypt, and the claim may have been disingenuous; but if it contained any truth it would help to explain the persistence of Westerners in seeking and using alternative routes. What ultimately decided whether Latin merchants made the journey across Asia or to the Far East, or instead refrained and fell back on Muslim intermediaries, was not so much considerations of security or danger as the cool calculation of profit and loss.[186]

Duties payable to Mongol rulers in Western Asia were relatively low, but could still be a subject for acrimonious dispute. By the terms of Uzbek's diploma of 1333, Venetian traders were liable to the payment of a commercial tax (*commercium*) of 3% on all transactions, except those involving pearls, precious stones, gold, silver and gold thread.[187] The treaty of 1347 raised the tax to 5%, so that in 1350 Venice was engaged in further negotiations with Jānībek, doubtless in order to secure a reduction.[188] In 1360 the Senate, having learned of the assassination of the khan Berdībek and resolved to send two ambassadors to his successor, was unable to find any willing candidates and was forced to entrust the task instead to Jacopo Cornaro, the newly appointed consul who was on his way to Tana. Despite the parlous situation in the Golden Horde, he appears to have enjoyed some success. By 1369 the *commercium* stood at 4%, though Venetian merchants were complaining that the Genoese paid only 3% and the Senate hoped to obtain a further reduction from Mamai.[189]

The documents examined by Lopez suggest that a return of 100% on the initial investment was not improbable and that the profit could rise to 500% on a long-distance venture; Tucci estimates the profits from the Delhi enterprise of 1338–9 at between 120% and 160%.[190] Such gains, of course, have to be set against the fact that the capital might be tied up for a few years. It is also true that according to Polo the costs of transport incurred in the great Chinese ports were markedly higher than those payable on the overland route – at Zaitun, 30% for small-bulk, high-value merchandise, 40% for aloe- and sandalwood and for heavier goods, and 44% for pepper – and that the duty payable to the qaghan stood at 10% (compared with the 3%–5% levied in the Golden Horde territories). When this outlay is taken into account, merchants were paying on average half of the value of the goods exported. Yet the cheapness of so many commodities in China seems amply to have compensated them: Polo adds that traders still made a weighty profit.[191]

The Polos and other Western adventurers in the Mongol dominions

The most celebrated Western visitor to the Mongol world[192] does not emerge from his book as primarily a merchant. True, some attention is given to the products of each city or region, but Marco Polo's book is no commercial manual of the sort produced by Pegolotti three decades or so later. It has been proposed that such was the original character of the work, obscured thanks to the intervention of Rustichello.[193] More recently, this view has been challenged, in part on the grounds that the book contains numerous observations that are of no commercial interest and that it antedates the commercial handbooks (with the exception of that produced by an anonymous Pisan in c.1278) by several years.[194] Rather, Polo comes across as a young man whose accomplishments rendered him in some measure valuable to the Mongol administration in China, even if he did not rise, as his book alleges, to the rank of provincial governor of Yang-chou (it has been suggested that he was merely in charge of the government salt monopoly in the city).[195] What he tells us might suggest that the skills for which the Polos were particularly valued were diplomatic and even nautical. The Yüan government, clearly concerned to revive China's maritime trade, despatched a series of missions to peninsular India and Ceylon from 1278 onwards, but some of these arose from the qaghan's own keenness to acquire exotica like the alms-bowl of the Buddha.[196] Marco himself clearly spent a significant proportion of his time in Qubilai's service at sea, on journeys designed to secure precious items for the imperial collection.[197]

The Polos, then, occupy the point on the spectrum where Western merchants blend with another group, those Latins (mainly Italians) who sought remunerative service with Mongol rulers. One possible means of self-enrichment was to be selected as an envoy; in Central Asia, the distinction between merchant and ambassador was traditionally blurred in any case.[198] We have seen how many expatriate Latins the Ilkhans employed in their negotiations with the West, notably the Genoese Buscarello de' Ghisolfi and the Pisan Isolo di Anastasio. Giovanni Villani tells of Guiscard Bustari, a fellow Florentine who had been at the Ilkhan's court since childhood, returning to the West in 1300 as part of Ghazan's embassy to Boniface VIII; he was the chronicler's informant concerning current events in Syria.[199] Relatively late examples are the two Genoese, Andrea di Nascio, who served the last Yüan emperor, Toghan Temür, as ambassador to Pope Benedict XII in 1336, and Andalò di Savignone, who accompanied the embassy (and was long believed to have been the ambassador).[200]

Another path to profit was simply to pass oneself off as an envoy. Rubruck was told of a cleric from Acre named Theodolus (alias Raymond), who had been at the qaghan's court a year or so before the Franciscan's own arrival. Having attached himself originally to the embassy of Andrew of Longjumeau (1249), he remained in Central Asia following Andrew's return and contrived to be sent on an embassy from Möngke to the pope; but en route, at the court of the Nicaean Emperor John III Vatatzes, his imposture was detected and he was thrown into prison. 'Hoaxers like this scurry about all over the world', explains Rubruck, 'and if the Mongols can catch them they put them to death.'[201] We encounter another example in 1276, when the Vassalli brothers warned Edward I of England that a certain Catalan was masquerading as the Ilkhan's ambassador, in order to acquire gerfalcons as gifts for his supposed master and to sell them later for a handsome profit.[202]

Other expatriate Westerners merely sought to sell their military, administrative or even medical talents to Mongol rulers. After an early encounter with Western valour which is described by Simon of Saint-Quentin – when they compelled two Latins captured at Arzinjān in 1242 to engage in a gladiatorial contest, only to suffer heavy casualties as the antagonists turned their swords on the audience[203] – the Mongols seem to have proved more accommodating towards European warriors. Bargadin, a soldier of fortune from Metz mentioned by Philippe de Mézières, would have fitted into this category – assuming, of course, that he genuinely existed. Philippe says that the man spent eight years at Khanbaligh in the qaghan's service, and claims to be indebted to him for certain details in the *Songe du Vieil Pelerin*.[204] Authentic or not, however, Bargadin represents a familiar type. A corps of Frankish mangonel experts accompanied an Ilkhanid army which took Herat in 1307, and Genoese mercenaries fought in Mamai's army against the prince of Moscow at Kulikovo Pole in 1380.[205] In 1301 Isolo di Anastasio, himself an expatriate who represented Ghazan on various diplomatic missions, interceded for a fellow Pisan, Strena di Bonfante, who had at one time served the Ilkhan against the Mamlūks, but had since been captured by the Neapolitans during a naval engagement with the Sicilian fleet.[206]

Military expertise was not, of course, the only kind the Mongols valued. The Lombard physician whose stories about the situation in Western Europe so disturbed Montecorvino had probably come out to China with the aim of capitalizing on his skills.[207] What we are told of other expatriates does not indicate the precise talents that might have rendered them useful. In 1328 recognition of his citizenship was granted to Isaccho Venerio, who as a child in 1291 had fled from Acre *ad partes ulteriores Tartarorum* and had now returned to Venice after 37 years' absence.[208] And as late as 1394 a Majorcan was reported to be freshly back in Aragon from the Great Khan's dominions after an absence of forty years.[209] If he had indeed been in China within the three decades or so preceding his homeward journey, he would have witnessed the fall of the Yüan and the establishment of the native Ming dynasty.

We have no way of ascertaining how many Latin Christians took up residence in the Mongol dominions in the later thirteenth and fourteenth centuries. And whether they played any part in the transmission of Chinese technical knowledge is uncertain – assuming that such transmission occurred. Just as Marco Polo's role in the introduction of spaghetti has been discredited as the product of late sixteenth-century English credulity, so the West's indebtedness to the Chinese for the development of, say, gunpowder, the compass or printing remains subject to serious doubt.[210] Nor do we know how many returning Westerners provided writers back in Europe with material on the East. Of the fact that there was a market for such material, in much the same way as for eastern products, there can be little doubt. One symptom of the 'vogue of the East', as it has been called,[211] is the frequency with which Genoese, Venetians and other Italians adopted Mongol names for their new-born children: Can Grande ('Great Khan'), Alaone (Hülegü), Argone (Arghun), Cassano (Ghazan), and so on[212] – though all these names, significantly, were borrowed from the friendly Ilkhans. What picture Western Europeans had of the East will be the subject of the final chapter.

Notes

1. PC, ii, 8, p. 235 (tr. Dawson, *Mongol Mission*, p. 8). Ratchnevsky, *Genghis Khan*, pp. 198-201.
2. Allsen, 'Mongolian princes', pp. 92-4.
3. Jūzjānī, II, pp. 163-4 (tr. Raverty, II, p. 1133). On merchants' interest in Mongol expansion, see also Allsen, 'Mongolian princes', pp. 124-5.
4. Iran: I.P. Petrushevsky, 'The socio-economic condition of Iran under the Īl-khāns', in *CHI*, V, pp. 491-537 *passim*. China: Morris Rossabi, 'The reign of Khubilai Khan', in *CHC*, VI, pp. 445-50, and his *Khubilai Khan*, pp. 116-24.
5. David O. Morgan, 'Rašīd al-Dīn and Ġazan Khan', in Aigle, *L'Iran*, pp. 179-88 (here pp. 184-6). For Ghazan's reforms, see Petrushevsky, pp. 494-500; and for a more positive view of the earlier Ilkhans, George Lane, *Early Mongol Rule in Thirteenth-Century Iran. A Persian Renaissance* (Richmond, Surrey, 2003).
6. See generally Biran, *Qaidu*, pp. 97-105.
7. Allsen, *Culture and Conquest, passim*.
8. Idem, *Commodity and Exchange*, esp. pp. 1-4, 11-26.
9. Ibid., pp. 27-45.
10. Ibid., p. 15.
11. Ratchnevsky, *Genghis Khan*, p. 72. Paul Pelliot, 'Une ville musulmane dans la Chine du Nord sous les Mongols', *JA* 211 (1927), pp. 261-79 (here pp. 264-8). Allsen, 'Mongolian princes', p. 87.
12. Juwaynī, III, pp. 87-8 (tr. Boyle, II, pp. 605-6).
13. Allsen, 'Mongolian princes', pp. 94-6. For the period after 1260, see Elizabeth Endicott-West, 'Merchant associations in Yüan China: the *ortoy*', *Asia Major*, 3rd series, 2:2 (1989), pp. 127-54.
14. Allsen, 'Mongolian princes', pp. 100-5. Idem, 'Rise of the Mongolian empire', pp. 377-88 *passim*.
15. M.E. Martin, 'The first Venetians in the Black Sea', *AP* 35 (1979), pp. 111-22. See also Marie Nystazopoulou Pélékedis, 'Venise et la mer Noire du XIe au XVe siècle', in Agostino Pertusi, ed., *Venezia e il Levante fino al secolo XV*, 2 vols in 3 (Firenze, 1973-4), I:2, pp. 541-82 (here pp. 549-50); Michel Balard, 'Byzance et les régions septentrionales de la mer Noire (XIIIe-XIVe siècles)', *RH* 288 (1992), pp. 19-38 (here pp. 28-9).
16. Rodolfo Gallo, 'Marco Polo, la sua famiglia e il suo libro', in *Nel VII centenario*, pp. 65-193 (here pp. 76-7).
17. *DM*, pp. 301-2/*MP*, I, pp. 489-90; and cf. Larner, *Marco Polo*, p. 95.
18. Kedar, *Merchants in Crisis*, pp. 24-8.
19. Robert Sabatino Lopez, 'European merchants in the medieval Indies: the evidence of commercial documents', *Journal of Economic History* 3 (1943), pp. 164-84 (here pp. 169, 171).
20. Ugo Tucci, 'Mercanti veneziani in Asia lungo l'itinerario poliano', in Lionello Lanciotti, ed., *Venezia e l'oriente* (Firenze, 1987), pp. 307-21 (here p. 307).
21. Robert-Henri Bautier, 'Les relations économiques des Occidentaux avec les pays d'Orient, au Moyen Âge: points de vue et documents', in Mollat du Jourdain, *Sociétés et compagnies*, pp. 263-331 (here pp. 311-20, appendix I),

and repr. in Bautier, *Commerce méditerranéan et banquiers italiens au Moyen Age* (London, 1992).

22. David Abulafia, 'Industrial products: the Middle Ages', in *Prodotti e tecniche d'Oltremare nelle economie europee, secc. XIII–XVIII. XXIX Settimana dell'Istituto Internazionale di Storia economica 'F. Datini'* (Firenze, 1998), pp. 333–58 (here pp. 335–6), and repr. in Abulafia, *Mediterranean Encounters, Economic, Religious, Political, 1100–1550* (Aldershot, 2000).
23. Balard, *La Romanie génoise*, I, pp. 113–18.
24. See generally G.I. Brătianu, *Recherches sur le commerce génois dans la mer Noire au XIIIᵉ siècle* (Paris, 1929), pp. 218 ff.; and for the date, M. Balard, 'Les Génois en Crimée aux XIIIᵉ–XIVᵉ siècles', *AP* 35 (1979), pp. 201–17 (here pp. 203–5).
25. Michel Balard, 'Les Gênois [*sic*] en Asie centrale et en extrême-orient au XIVᵉ siècle: un cas exceptionnel?', in *Economies et sociétés au moyen âge. Mélanges offerts à Edouard Perroy* (Paris, 1973), pp. 681–9. Balard, 'Precursori di Cristoforo Colombo: i Genovesi in estremo oriente nel XIV secolo', in *Atti del Convegno internazionale di Studi Colombiani (Genova, 13–14 ottobre 1973)* (Genova, 1974), pp. 149–64 (here pp. 154–9), and repr. in Balard, *La mer Noire*. For further evidence of Genoa's lead, see Kedar, *Merchants in Crisis*, p. 11; Petech, 'Les marchands italiens', p. 166.
26. *DM*, p. 328/*MP*, I, p. 99 (tr. Ricci, p. 23). Richard, 'Les navigations', p. 361.
27. Jahn, *Die Frankengeschichte*, Tafel 44, facsimile of Persian text, ms. Hazine 1653, fo. 415r (German trans., p. 51).
28. Guillaume Adam, 'De modo Sarracenos extirpandi', pp. 552–3.
29. Francis M. Rogers, 'The Vivaldi expedition', in *73rd Annual Report of the Dante Society* (1955), pp. 31–45. Gillian Moore, 'La spedizione dei fratelli Vivaldi e nuovi documenti d'archivio', *ASL*, n.s., 12 (1972), pp. 387–402. Lopez, 'Nuove luci', pp. 105–6.
30. Larner, *Marco Polo*, p. 118.
31. References in Reichert, *Begegnungen*, p. 81.
32. Guzman, 'European clerical envoys', pp. 59–60. Those at Kiev, listed by PC, ix, 51, p. 129 (tr. Dawson, p. 71), include a number of Italians.
33. Herbert Franke, 'Sino-Western contacts under the Mongol empire', *Journal of the Hong Kong Branch of the Royal Asiatic Society* 6 (1966), pp. 49–72 (here pp. 54–5), repr. in his *China under Mongol Rule*.
34. R. Morozzo della Rocca, 'Sulle orme di Polo', *L'Italia che Scrive* 37 (1954), pp. 120–2. Petech, 'Les marchands italiens', p. 165.
35. Giovanni Eleemosyna, 'Liber historiarum', in *BBTS*, II, p. 132, and III, p. 90. Regrettably, we do not know the origins of the merchants who, early in the 14th century, told the Master of the Temple in Cyprus that they had seen the great Chinese port of Quinsai (from *hing-tsai*, 'provisional capital', the name given to Hang-chou in the last days of the Sung): 'Gestes des Chiprois', p. 842, §584 (tr. Crawford, p. 147). See more generally, A.C. Moule, *Quinsai, with Other Notes on Marco Polo* (Cambridge, 1957).
36. Robert S. Lopez, 'Nouveaux documents sur les marchands italiens en Chine à l'époque mongole', *CRAIBL* (1977), pp. 445–57. Earlier scholarship had linked the first stone discovered at Yang-chou to the Venetian Vilioni family.

37. Geo Pistarino, 'Da Genova alla Cina nel secolo XIV', in Francesco Guida and Luisa Valmarin, eds, *Studi Balcanici pubblicati in occasione del VI Congresso internazionale dell'Association Internationale d'Études Sud-Est Européennes (AIESEE), Sofia 30 Agosto-5 Settembre 1989* (Rome, 1989), pp. 33-44 (here p. 38; and see pp. 39-43 on the Ilioni family).

38. Peter Spufford, 'Coinage and currency', in *CEHE*, II, pp. 828-36.

39. Robert S. Lopez, 'The trade of medieval Europe: the south', in *CEHE*, II, pp. 369-70.

40. Alfredo Stussi, 'Un testamento volgare scritto in Persia nel 1263', *L'Italia Dialettale* 25 = n.s., 2 (1962), pp. 23-37; previously ed. in [G. Cecchetti,] 'Testamento di Pietro Vioni veneziano fatto a Tauris (Persia), MCCLXIV, x dicembre', *Archivio Veneto* 26 (1883), pp. 161-5. Bautier, 'Les relations économiques', p. 282.

41. Subhi Labib, 'Egyptian commercial policy in the Middle Ages', in M.A. Cook, ed., *Studies in the Economic History of the Middle East from the Rise of Islam to the Present Day* (Oxford, 1970), pp. 63-77 (here p. 66).

42. But see the qualifying remarks of Reuven Amitai-Preiss, 'Northern Syria between the Mongols and Mamluks: political boundary, military frontier, and ethnic affinities', in Daniel Power and Naomi Standen, eds, *Frontiers in Question. Eurasian Borderlands, 700-1700* (Basingstoke, 1999), pp. 128-52 (here p. 143).

43. David Abulafia, 'Asia, Africa and the trade of medieval Europe', in *CEHE*, II, pp. 457-60. David Jacoby, 'Silk crosses the Mediterranean', in G. Airaldi, ed., *Le vie del Mediterraneo. Idee, uomini, oggetti (secoli XI-XVI), Genova, 19-20 aprile 1994* (Genova, 1997), pp. 55-79 (here p. 78), and repr. in Jacoby, *Byzantium, Latin Romania and the Mediterranean* (Aldershot, 2001).

44. For the most thoroughgoing information on routes across the western half of the Mongol empire, see W. Barthold, *An Historical Geography of Iran*, tr. Svat Soucek and ed. C.E. Bosworth (Princeton, NJ, 1984), and V.L. Egorov, *Istoricheskaia geografiia Zolotoi Ordy XIII-XIV vv.* (Moscow, 1985). Dorothea Krawulsky, *Iran - Das Reich der Ilḫāne*, Beihefte zum Tübinger Atlas des Vorderen Orients, Reihe B Geisteswissenschaften, 17 (Wiesbaden, 1978), provides a gazetteer.

45. For what follows, see Bautier, 'Les relations économiques', pp. 286-8, 315-16; Francesco Balducci Pegolotti, *La pratica della mercatura*, ed. Allan Evans (Cambridge, MA, 1936), p. 21. For Saraichik and Ürgench, see Egorov, pp. 124-5, 126, respectively.

46. Bautier, 'Les relations économiques', p. 315. Pegolotti, p. 21.

47. Ibn Faḍl-Allāh al-'Umarī, *Masālik*, ed. and tr. Lech, *Das mongolische Weltreich*, p. 30 (German tr. p. 111).

48. See Catherine Otten-Froux, 'L'Aïas dans le dernier tiers du XIIIe siècle d'après les notaires génois', in Kedar and Udovitch, *Medieval Levant*, pp. 147-71; and cf. also Michel Balard, 'L'activité commerciale en Chypre dans les années 1300', in Edbury, *Crusade and Settlement*, pp. 251-63 (here p. 257).

49. Karl Jahn, 'Täbris, ein mittelalterliches Kulturzentrum zwischen Ost und West', *Anzeiger der Österreichischen Akademie der Wissenschaften, phil.-hist. Klasse* (1968), pp. 201-12. The place-names along the Laias-Tabrīz route, which

appear in sometimes corrupt form in Pegolotti, pp. 28–9, are identified by Bautier, 'Les relations économiques', p. 281; see also Cornelio Desimoni, 'I conti dell'ambasciata al Chan di Persia nel MCCXCII', *ASL* 13 (1877–84), pp. 537–698; Jacques Paviot, 'Le séjour de l'ambassade de Geoffroy de Langley à Trébizonde et à Constantinople en 1292', *Médiévales* 12 (Printemps 1987), pp. 47–54.

50. Tabrīz: *DM*, p. 337/MP, I, p. 104 (tr. Ricci, p. 33). Hurmuz: *DM*, p. 347/ MP, I, p. 123 (tr. Ricci, p. 44). On this route, see Bautier, 'Les relations économiques', pp. 283–4.

51. Apparently described in *DM*, pp. 364–79/MP, I, pp. 141–60 (tr. Ricci, pp. 62–75), *passim*.

52. *DM*, p. 379/MP, I, p. 160 (tr. Ricci, p. 77).

53. Jacques Paviot, 'Les marchands italiens dans l'Iran mongol', in Aigle, *L'Iran*, pp. 71–86.

54. Balard, *La Romanie génoise*, I, pp. 138–40.

55. *DVL*, I, pp. 47–8 (no. 26). L. de Mas Latrie, 'Privilège commercial accordé en 1320 à la République de Venise par un roi de Perse, faussement attribué à un roi de Tunis', *BEC* 31 (1871), pp. 72–102 = *DVL*, I, pp. 173–6 (no. 85).

56. Bautier, 'Les relations économiques', pp. 284–5.

57. *DM*, p. 337/MP, I, p. 104 (tr. Ricci, pp. 32–3). Bautier, 'Les relations économiques', p. 318.

58. Pegolotti, pp. 26–7.

59. Bautier, 'Les relations économiques', p. 291 and n.1. Some are listed by Pegolotti, pp. 297–8.

60. Jacoby, 'Silk crosses the Mediterranean', pp. 74–6.

61. Pegolotti, p. 24.

62. Reichert, *Begegnungen*, p. 85 and n.124; but cf. Abulafia, 'Industrial products', p. 357. On porcelain, D. Howard Smith, 'Zaitún's five centuries of Sino-foreign trade', *JRAS* (1958), pp. 165–77 (here p. 169); for Zaitun itself, Pelliot, *Notes on Marco Polo*, I, pp. 583–97.

63. Balard, *La Romanie génoise*, II, p. 719.

64. Listed by Bautier, 'Les relations économiques', p. 293.

65. MP, II ('Z' text), p. xlviii (cf. trans., I, p. 340).

66. Ts'ao Yung-ho, 'Pepper trade in East Asia', *TP* 68 (1982), pp. 221–47 (here pp. 228–30).

67. Odoric, xx, 2, and xxi, 1, pp. 459, 460 (tr. Yule, *Cathay*, II, pp. 180–1, 184).

68. Pegolotti, pp. 300, 382. Robert Sabatino Lopez, 'China silk in Europe in the Yuan period', *JAOS* 72 (1952), pp. 72–6.

69. Bautier, 'Les relations économiques', pp. 288–9.

70. Balard, 'Precursori', pp. 159–60.

71. Odoric, xxv, 6, p. 471 (tr. Yule, *Cathay*, II, pp. 214–15): at 'Suçumato', i.e. the port of Hsin-chou, tentatively identified by Pelliot, *Notes on Marco Polo*, II, pp. 834–5, with Chi-ning.

72. Lopez, 'Nuove luci', pp. 100–1, and 'Nouveaux documents', pp. 446–7, pointing out that the family of one of the Genoese merchants named had been active in Laias for some decades; for the documents, see 'Nuove luci', pp. 129–31 (nos. 1–5).

73. Bautier, 'Les relations économiques', pp. 287, 289–91.
74. Balard, 'Precursori', p. 154, and 'Les Gênois', pp. 685, 687, n.47. Lopez, 'Nuove luci', pp. 103–4, and 'Nouveaux documents', pp. 451, 453–4; also idem, 'L'importance de la mer Noire dans l'histoire de Gênes', in Ştefan Pascu, ed., *Colloquio Romeno-Italiano, "I Genovesi nel Mar Nero durante i secoli XIII e XIV"*, Bucarest 27–28 marzo 1975 (Bucarest, 1977), pp. 13–33 (here pp. 27–8). Tucci, 'Mercanti veneziani', p. 319.
75. Pegolotti, pp. 22–3.
76. Ibid., p. 24. See Mihnea Berindei and Giustiniana Migliardi O'Riordan, 'Venise et la Horde d'Or, fin XIIIᵉ–début XIVᵉ siècle. A propos d'un document inédit de 1324', *CMRS* 29 (1988), pp. 243–56 (here pp. 248–9).
77. Lopez, 'Nuove luci', pp. 88–90. Franke, 'Das „himmlische Pferd"'.
78. Moranvillé, 'Mémoire', pp. 463–4.
79. *DM*, p. 307/MP, I, pp. 74–5 (Ricci trans., pp. 3–4, inaccurate).
80. Raimondo Morozzo della Rocca, 'Catay', in *Miscellanea in onore di Roberto Cessi*, I (Rome, 1958), pp. 299–303. Tucci, 'Mercanti veneziani', pp. 317–18.
81. Balard, 'Precursori', pp. 155–6, and 'Les Gênois', p. 685. There were actually, at this time, two Genoese named Andalò di Savignone: Benjamin Z. Kedar, 'Chi era Andrea Franco?', *ASL*, n.s., 17 (1977), pp. 369–77 (here pp. 375–6).
82. Roberto S. Lopez, '*Trafegando in partibus Catagii*: altri Genovesi in Cina nel Trecento', in his *Su e giù*, pp. 171–86.
83. Lopez, 'Nuove luci', pp. 124–5; text at pp. 134–5 (no. 13).
84. *Analecta Franciscana*, III, pp. 607, 609, 612; see also A.C. Moule, 'Brother Jordan of Sévérac', *JRAS* (1928), pp. 349–76 (here pp. 357–8, tr. pp. 371–2). Lopez, 'Nuove luci', pp. 86, 108–9.
85. Robert S. Lopez, 'Da Venezia a Delhi nel Trecento', in his *Su e giù*, pp. 137–59; also idem, 'European merchants', pp. 174–80. For Muḥammad's proverbial generosity, see Jackson, *Delhi Sultanate*, pp. 184–5, 255.
86. Roberto S. Lopez, '*In quibuscumque mondi partibus*', in *Miscellanea di storia italiana e mediterranea per Nino Lamboglia*, CSFS 23 (Genova, 1978), pp. 345–54.
87. Kedar, *Merchants in Crisis*, pp. 43–5.
88. Lopez, 'Nouveaux documents', p. 453.
89. Balard, 'Precursori', pp. 158–9, and 'Les Gênois', p. 687.
90. Philippe de Mézières, *Le songe du Vieil Pelerin*, i, 10, ed. G.W. Coopland, 2 vols (Cambridge, 1969), I, p. 223.
91. Lopez, 'Nouveaux documents', p. 455.
92. Boase, 'History of the kingdom', p. 31. The date is often given incorrectly as 1347.
93. Balard, 'Les Gênois', p. 688.
94. Wassilios Klein, *Das nestorianische Christentum an den Handelswegen durch Kyrgyzstan bis zum 14. Jh.*, Silk Road Studies 3 (Turnhout, 2000), pp. 287–9. See Jackson, *Delhi Sultanate*, p. 268, for a plague (*wubā*) which attacked the army of Sultan Muḥammad ibn Tughluq on its way to suppress an insurrection in Maʿbar in 1334–5. But cf. Ole J. Benedictow, *The Black Death 1346–1353. The Complete History* (Woodbridge, 2004), p. 48.
95. Lopez, 'Nouveaux documents', p. 457.

96. Ashtor, *Levant Trade*, pp. 65–70.
97. Mihnea Berindei and Gilles Veinstein, 'La Tana-Azaq de la présence italienne à l'emprise ottomane (fin XIIIe–milieu XVIe siècle)', *Turcica* 8:2 (1976), pp. 110–201 (here p. 125). M.E. Martin, 'Venetian Tana in the later fourteenth and early fifteenth centuries', *BF* 11 (1987), pp. 375–9 (here pp. 377–8).
98. Berindei and Veinstein, pp. 124–9. See Barbaro, in L. Lockhart, R. Morozzo della Rocca and M.F. Tiepolo, eds, *I viaggi in Persia degli ambasciatori veneti Barbaro e Contarini*, Il nuovo Ramusio 7 (Rome, 1973), p. 96; tr. Edward Thomas and ed. Lord Stanley of Alderley, *Travels to Tana and Persia by Giosafat Barbaro and Ambrogio Contarini*, HS¹ (London, 1873), p. 31.
99. John of Sulṭāniyya, *Libellus*, ed. Kern, pp. 104–5.
100. Heimpel, 'Zur Handelspolitik', pp. 148–52, 155.
101. Bautier, 'Les relations économiques', pp. 306–8.
102. A.P. Martinez, 'The wealth of Ormus and of Ind. The Levant trade in bullion, intergovernmental arbitrage, and currency manipulations in the Il-Xanate, 704–751/1304–1350', *AEMA* 9 (1995–7), pp. 123–251 (esp. pp. 134–7). Idem, 'Ducats and dinars. Currency manipulations, paper money, arbitrage, the India bullion trade, and monetary–commercial policy in the Il-Xanate, 654–694 H./1256–1295 A.D.', *AEMA* 10 (1998–9), pp. 118–206, and 11 (2000–1), pp. 65–139. The sequels to these articles have yet to appear.
103. For a good introduction, see Sergei Karpov, 'Black Sea and the crisis of the mid XIVth century: an underestimated turning point', *Thesaurismata* 27 (Venezia, 1997), pp. 65–77.
104. Kedar, *Merchants in Crisis*, pp. 27–8, 47–9. Nicola Di Cosmo, 'A note on the "Tana" route and 14th century international trade', in Denis Sinor, ed., *Aspects of Altaic Civilization III. Proceedings of the Thirtieth Meeting of the Permanent International Altaistic Conference, Indiana University, Bloomington, Indiana, June 19–25, 1987*, IUUAS 145 (Bloomington, IN, 1990), pp. 20–32.
105. On Chios, see Balard, *La Romanie génoise*, I, pp. 119–26.
106. Nicola Di Cosmo, 'Mongols and merchants on the Black Sea frontier in the thirteenth and fourteenth centuries: convergences and conflicts', in Amitai and Biran, eds, *Mongols, Turks and Others*, pp. 391–424.
107. Nicola Di Cosmo, 'Venice, Genoa, the Golden Horde, and the limits of European expansion in Asia': paper read at the international colloquium 'Il Codice Cumanico e il suo mondo', Venezia, 6–7 Dec. 2002.
108. See generally G.A. Fyodorov-Davydov, *The Culture of the Golden Horde Cities*, tr. H. Bartlett Wells, BAR International Series 198 (Oxford, 1984), esp. pp. 8–32; though the conceptual framework is unhelpful and the idea that the khans emancipated themselves from control by the qaghan's representatives only at the end of the 13th century must be discarded.
109. S.P. Karpov, 'On the origin of medieval Tana', in Στέφανος. *Studia byzantina ac slavica Vladimíro Vavřínek ad annum sexagesimum quintum dedicata* (Prague, 1995 = *Byzantinoslavica* 56), pp. 227–35 (here pp. 230–1).
110. Balard, *La Romanie génoise*, I, pp. 118, 134, 144, 151. For Tana, see also Roberto S. Lopez, 'Nelle terre dell'Orda d'oro: tre documenti genovesi inediti', in Michele Colucci, Giuseppe dell'Agata and Harvey Goldblatt, eds, *Studia*

Slavica medievalia et humanistica Riccardo Picchio dicata (Rome, 1986), II, pp. 463–74 (here p. 469).

111. Karpov, 'On the origin', p. 232.

112. Freddy Thiriet, La Romanie vénitienne au moyen âge. Le développement et l'exploitation du domaine colonial vénitien (XIIe–XVe siècles) (Paris, 1959), p. 162.

113. DVL, I, pp. 243–4 (no. 125). Karpov, 'On the origin', pp. 234–5. See also Berindei and O'Riordan, pp. 246–7.

114. On Genoese policy in the Black Sea, see Şerban Papacostea, '«Quod non iretur ad Tanam.» Un aspect fondamental de la politique génoise dans la Mer Noire au XIVe siècle', RESEE 17 (1979), pp. 201–17; more briefly, Michel Balard, 'Gênes et la mer Noire (XIIIe–XVe siècles)', RH 270 (1983), pp. 31–54 (here pp. 47–9), repr. in his La mer Noire.

115. Spuler, Die Goldene Horde, pp. 75, 84.

116. On this conflict, see Raimondo Morozzo della Rocca, 'Notizie da Caffa', in G. Barbieri, ed., Studi in onore di Amintore Fanfani (Milan, 1962), III, pp. 265–95 (here pp. 267–76); S.P. Karpov, 'Génois et Byzantins face à la crise de Tana de 1343 d'après les documents d'archives inédits', BF 22 (1996), pp. 33–51.

117. Berindei and Veinstein, pp. 122–3, n.42.

118. E. Déprez and G. Mollat, eds, Clément VI (1342–1352). Lettres closes, patentes et curiales intéressant les pays autres que la France, fasc. 1 (Paris, 1960), pp. 107–8 (no. 847); cf. also E. Déprez, J. Glénisson and G. Mollat, eds, Clément VI (1342–1352). Lettres closes, patentes et curiales se rapportant à la France, II (Paris, 1958), p. 94 (no. 2216), asking the Dauphin of Viennois (then planning an expedition against the Turks of Anatolia) to go to Kaffa's aid.

119. Gabriel de Mussis, De morbo, ed. A.G. Tononi, 'La Peste dell'anno 1348', Giornale Ligustico 11 (1884), pp. 139–52 (here p. 145). Schmieder, Europa, pp. 239–40. Cf. Benedictow, pp. 51–3.

120. Via sive iter a civitate Venetiarum usque ad Tanaim sive Tana, ed. N. Iorga, 'Un viaggio da Venezia alla Tana', Nuovo Archivio Veneto 11 (1896), pp. 5–13 (here p. 12: vix suum continet populum).

121. Giovanna Petti Balbi, 'Caffa e Pera a metà del Trecento', RESEE 16:2 (1978), pp. 217–28 (here pp. 218–23, 226–7).

122. Certainly by 1358/9, when they prevented Venetians from buying corn there: DVL, II, p. 58 (no. 31).

123. Octavian Iliescu, 'Contributions à l'histoire des colonies génoises en Romanie aux XIIIe–XVe siècles', RRH 28 (1989), pp. 25–52 (here pp. 27–8). For the argument that Kilia and Licostomo were identical, see Petre Diaconu, ' "Kilia et Licostomo", un faux problème de géographie historique', MN 2 (1995–6), pp. 235–63.

124. For these and other Genoese strongpoints, see generally Balard, La Romanie génoise, I, pp. 156–62.

125. Virgil Ciocîltan, 'Reichspolitik und Handel. Die tatarisch-genuesischen Verträge von 1380–1387', MN 1 (1994), pp. 261–78.

126. Balard, La Romanie génoise, I, p. 157.

127. *RDSV*, I, pp. 44, 46 (nos. 111, 120). Serghej Karpov, 'Venezia e Genova: rivalità e collaborazione a Trebisonda e Tana, secoli XIII–XV', in Gherardo Ortalli and Dino Puncuh, eds, *Genova, Venezia, il Levante nei secoli XII–XIV. Atti del Convegno internazionale di studi Genova–Venezia, 10–14 marzo 2000* (Genova, 2001 = *ASL*, n.s., 41:1), pp. 257–72 (here p. 263).

128. Elena Č. Skržinskaja, 'Storia della Tana', *SV* 10 (1968), pp. 3–45 (here pp. 12–13).

129. Nystazopoulou Pélékedis, 'Venise', pp. 565–6. B. Doumerc, 'La Tana au XVe siècle: comptoir ou colonie?', in Michel Balard, ed., *État et colonisation au Moyen Age* (Lyon, 1989), pp. 251–66.

130. Guido Astuti, 'Le colonie genovesi del Mar Nero e i loro ordinamenti giuridici', in Pascu, *Colloquio Romeno-Italiano*, pp. 87–129 (here pp. 102–7).

131. Michel Balard, '*Genuensis civitas in extremo Europae*: Caffa from the four-teenth to the fifteenth century', in Abulafia and Berend, *Medieval Frontiers*, pp. 143–51 (here pp. 144–6). For the fortification work, see Balard, *La Romanie génoise*, I, pp. 202–12.

132. Bautier, 'Les relations économiques', p. 314. Berindei and Veinstein, pp. 112–15.

133. WR, i, 2, p. 166 (tr. Jackson and Morgan, pp. 62, 64).

134. For what follows, see Janet Martin, 'The Land of Darkness and the Golden Horde. The fur trade under the Mongols, XIII–XIVth centuries', *CMRS* 19 (1978), pp. 401–21; eadem, *Treasure of the Land of Darkness. The Fur Trade and Its Significance for Medieval Russia* (Cambridge, 1986), pp. 88–90; Berindei and Veinstein, pp. 117–18. For the role of Orda's *ulus* in this traffic, see Allsen, 'Princes of the Left Hand', pp. 28–30.

135. Lopez, 'Nelle terre dell'Orda', pp. 473–4.

136. CICO, IV:1, p. 76 (no. 33), cited by Constantin C. Giurescu, 'The Genoese and the lower Danube in the XIIIth and XIVth centuries', *Journal of European Economic History* 5 (1976), pp. 587–600 (here p. 587, n.1).

137. Will of Marco Polo, 9 Jan. 1323/4, in MP, I, pp. 539–40.

138. Charles Verlinden, 'La colonie vénitienne de Tana, centre de la traite des esclaves au XIVe et au début du XVe siècle', in *Studi in onore di Gino Luzzatto*, 4 vols (Milan, 1949–50), II, pp. 1–25. Idem, 'Le recrutement des esclaves à Venise aux XIVe et XVe siècles', *Bulletin de l'Institut Historique Belge de Rome* 39 (1968), pp. 83–202. Robert Delort, 'Quelques précisions sur le commerce des esclaves à Gênes vers la fin du XIVe siècle', *MAH* 78 (1966), pp. 215–50. Michel Balard, 'Remarques sur les esclaves à Gênes dans la seconde moitié du XIIIe siècle', *MAH* 80 (1968), pp. 627–80. For slaves at Kaffa, see especially Balard, *La Romanie génoise*, II, pp. 790–6, and his 'Esclavage en Crimée et sources fiscales génoises au XVe siècle', in *6e Symposion Byzantinon, l'automne 1992: Byzance et l'Europe. Aufsätze* (Amsterdam, 1996 = *BF* 22), pp. 9–17; for Maurocastro, Victor Spinei, 'La génèse des villes du sud-est de la Moldavie et les rapports commerciaux des XIIIe–XIVe siècles', *Balkan Studies* 35 (1994), pp. 197–269 (here pp. 225–8). More generally, Balard, 'Gênes et la mer Noire', pp. 44–5.

139. For the Cumans, see Charles Verlinden, 'Esclavage et ethnographie sur les bords de la mer Noire (XIIIe et XIVe siècles)', in *Miscellanea historica in*

honorem Leonis van der Essen (Brussels and Paris, 1947), pp. 287–98 (here pp. 288–92, 297–8).

140. Baybars al-Manṣūrī, *Zubdat al-fikra*, p. 262, and al-Nuwayrī, *Nihāyat al-arab*, XXVII, pp. 354–5, both *ad annum* 687 H.: the details of the war in Mongolia are garbled. See Biran, *Qaidu*, p. 63 and n.219.

141. Freddy Thiriet, 'Les Vénitiens en mer Noire. Organisation et trafics (XIIIᵉ– XIVᵉ siècles)', *AP* 35 (1979), pp. 38–53 (here p. 48). See more generally Charles Verlinden, 'La Crète, débouché et plaque tournante de la traite des esclaves aux XIVᵉ et XVᵉ siècles', in Barbieri, *Studi*, III, pp. 591–669.

142. Iris Origo, 'The domestic enemy: the eastern slaves in Tuscany in the fourteenth and fifteenth centuries', *Speculum* 30 (1955), pp. 321–66. Laura Balletto, 'Stranieri e forestieri a Genova: schiavi e manomessi (secolo XV)', in *Forestieri e stranieri nelle città basso-medievali. Atti del Seminario Internazionale di Studio Bagno a Ripoli (Firenze), 4–8 giugno 1984* (Firenze, 1988), pp. 263–83.

143. Ch. Verlinden, 'Esclaves du Sud-Est et de l'Est européen en Espagne occidentale à la fin du moyen âge', *RHSEE* 19 (1942), pp. 371–406.

144. Andrew Ehrenkreutz, 'Strategic implications of the slave trade between Genoa and Mamluk Egypt in the second half of the thirteenth century', in Abraham L. Udovitch, ed., *The Islamic Middle East 700–1900* (Princeton, NJ, 1981), pp. 335–45. Sylvia Schein, 'From "milites Christi" to "mali Christiani". The Italian communes in Western historical literature', in Gabriella Airaldi and Benjamin Z. Kedar, eds, *I comuni italiani nel regno crociato di Gerusalemme*, CSFS 48 (Genova, 1986), pp. 679–89.

145. Balard, 'Esclavage en Crimée', pp. 16–17.

146. For what follows, see Balard, 'Gênes et la mer Noire', pp. 35, 39–44. The local products traded in 1289–90 are also examined by idem, 'Notes sur l'activité maritime des Génois de Caffa à la fin du XIIIᵉ siècle', in Mollat du Jourdain, *Sociétés et compagnies*, pp. 375–86 (here pp. 381–4), and repr. in Balard, *La mer Noire*; and by Vasil Gjuzelev, 'Du commerce génois dans les terres bulgares durant le XIVᵉ siècle', *BHR* 4 (1979), pp. 36–58; see also Giurescu, 'Genoese and the lower Danube', pp. 593–7. For exports from Kilia and Licostomo in 1360–1, see Octavian Iliescu, 'Nouvelles éditions d'actes notariés instrumentés au XIVᵉ siècle dans les colonies génoises des bouches du Danube', *RESEE* 15 (1977), pp. 113–29 (here pp. 118–19); and for the goods traded in the Pontic region generally, Balard, *La Romanie génoise*, II, pp. 719–868 *passim*.

147. Berindei and Veinstein, p. 133, n.80, citing Pegolotti, p. 380.

148. WR, i, 13, p. 171 (tr. Jackson and Morgan, p. 70). For salt from the Danube–Dniester region, see Spinei, 'La génèse', pp. 228–9.

149. Balard, *La Romanie génoise*, II, pp. 783–4.

150. WR, xxxviii, 15, p. 328 (tr. Jackson and Morgan, p. 273). Claude Cahen, 'L'alun avant Phocée: un chapitre d'histoire économique islamo-chrétienne au temps des croisades', *Revue d'Histoire Économique et Sociale* 41 (1963), pp. 433–47, and 'Le commerce anatolien au début du XIIIᵉ siècle', in *Mélanges d'histoire du moyen âge dédiés à la mémoire de Louis Halphen* (Paris, 1951), pp. 91–101, both repr. in Cahen, *Turcobyzantina et Oriens Christianus* (London, 1974).

151. Balard, 'Notes sur l'activité', pp. 382–3. Cf. also Berindei and Veinstein, pp. 131–2.

152. Octavian Iliescu, 'Notes sur l'apport roumain au ravitaillement de Byzance d'après une source inédite du XIVᵉ siècle', in *Nouvelles Études d'Histoire publiées à l'occasion du XIIe Congrès des Sciences Historiques, Vienne 1965,* III (Bucarest, 1965), pp. 105–16.

153. Pegolotti, p. 42.

154. S.P. Karpov, 'The grain trade in the southern Black Sea region: the thirteenth to the fifteenth century', *MHR* 8 (1993), pp. 55–73.

155. Michel Balard, 'Le commerce du blé en mer Noire (XIIIᵉ–XVᵉ siècles)', in *Aspetti della vita economica medievale: Atti del Convegno di studi nel Xᵒ anniversario della morte di Federigo Melis (Firenze–Pisa–Prato 10–14 marzo 1984)* (Firenze, 1985), pp. 64–80 (here pp. 74–5), and repr. in Balard, *La mer Noire.*

156. Balard, *La Romanie génoise,* II, p. 762; see generally ibid., I, p. 149, and II, pp. 758–68, for the export of Pontic grain to Genoa.

157. *RDSV,* I, p. 60 (no. 196). Balard, 'Le commerce du blé', p. 71. Berindei and Veinstein, pp. 135–7. More generally, see Papacostea, '«Quod non iretur»', pp. 201–7.

158. Karpov, 'Grain trade', pp. 65–6. Balard, 'Le commerce du blé', pp. 76–7.

159. For mid-14th-century efforts by the Bohemian and Hungarian kings to increase trade with Western Europe, see Balázs Nagy, 'Transcontinental trade from East-Central Europe to Western Europe (fourteenth and fifteenth centuries)', in Nagy and Sebők, *Man of Many Devices,* pp. 347–56 (here pp. 348–50).

160. Şerban Papacostea, 'Un tournant de la politique génoise en Mer Noire au XIVᵉ siècle: l'ouverture des routes continentales en direction de l'Europe centrale', in Laura Balletto, ed., *Oriente e Occidente tra medioevo ed età moderna. Studi in onore di Geo Pistarino* (Genova, 1997), II, pp. 939–47. Papacostea, 'La pénétration du commerce génois en Europe centrale: Maurocastrum (Moncastro) et la route moldave', *MN* 3 (1997–8), pp. 149–58.

161. Pegolotti, p. 22.

162. Balard, 'Gênes et la mer Noire', p. 36, and 'Les Génois en Crimée', pp. 212–13. Petech, 'I francescani', pp. 226–7, concedes that it may have been a reality in the era of Carpini and Rubruck. For more general doubts concerning the *Pax,* see, e.g., Morgan, *Mongols,* p. 83, Reichert, *Begegnungen,* pp. 83–4, and Larner, *Marco Polo,* p. 28.

163. *DM,* pp. 307–8/*MP,* I, pp. 75–6 (tr. Ricci, pp. 3–4). On the latter occasion, only Ramusio's text blames war for the delay (cf. Ricci trans., p. 4); in the former case, Pelliot, *Notes on Marco Polo,* I, pp. 94–5, thought Berke's attack on Byzantine Thrace (above, p. 202) a more likely explanation.

164. Thomas T. Allsen, 'The Yüan dynasty and the Uighurs of Turfan in the 13th century', in Morris Rossabi, ed., *China Among Equals. The Middle Kingdom and Its Neighbors, 10th–14th Centuries* (Berkeley and Los Angeles, 1983), pp. 243–80 (here pp. 254–8). Biran, *Qaidu,* pp. 43–4.

165. *MP,* I, p. 89 (tr. Ricci, p. 15): a section absent from the Tuscan or French–Italian texts. Montecorvino, 'Epistolae II', §6, p. 349 (tr. in Moule, *Christians in China,* p. 175; tr. Dawson, *Mongol Mission,* p. 226).

166. Morozzo della Rocca, 'Notizie da Caffa', p. 279 (no. 4). For these hostilities, which began in 742 H./1341–2, see above, p. 210.
167. Marignolli, p. 536 = 'Kronika Jana z Marignoly', p. 499 (tr. Yule, *Cathay*, III, p. 228). For unrest within Chaghadai's *ulus* at this time, see W. Barthold, *Zwölf Vorlesungen über die Geschichte der Türken Mittelasiens*, tr. Th. Menzel (Berlin, 1935; repr. Hildesheim, 1962), pp. 205–9; cf. also Paul, 'Scheiche und Herrscher', pp. 284–5.
168. Waṣṣāf, p. 50.
169. Pegolotti, p. 22.
170. *RDSV*, I, p. 49 (no. 138).
171. Marignolli, p. 528 = 'Kronika Jana z Marignoly', p. 495 (tr. Yule, *Cathay*, III, p. 212). Richard, *La papauté*, pp. 163–4.
172. Giorgio Stella, 'Annales', p. 139.
173. al-Maqrīzī, *al-Sulūk*, II:3, p. 863. On these princes, see Charles Melville and 'Abbās Zaryāb, 'Chobanids', *Enc.Ir.*
174. Ashtor, *Levant Trade*, pp. 64–5. Kedar, *Merchants in Crisis*, pp. 127–9. For this period, see generally Heyd, *Histoire du commerce*, II, pp. 128–31.
175. Ibn Baṭṭūṭa, *Tuḥfat al-nuẓẓār fī gharā'ib al-amṣār*, ed. Ch. Defrémery and B.S. Sanguinetti, 4 vols (Paris, 1853–8), II, p. 237, and III, p. 248; tr. H.A.R. Gibb, *The Travels of Ibn Baṭṭūṭa, A.D. 1325–1354*, 5 vols, HS², 110, 117, 141, 178, 190 (Cambridge and London, 1958–2000), II, pp. 403–4, and III, p. 674. Jean Aubin, 'Les princes d'Ormuz du XIIIᵉ au XVᵉ siècle', *JA* 241 (1953), pp. 77–138 (here p. 106).
176. *DM*, p. 348/MP, I, p. 124 (tr. Ricci, p. 45).
177. Montecorvino, 'Epistolae II', §6, p. 349 (tr. in Moule, *Christians in China*, p. 175; tr. Dawson, *Mongol Mission*, p. 226).
178. *DM*, p. 544/MP, I, p. 373 (tr. Ricci, p. 284).
179. 1296: Brătianu, *Recherches*, p. 270. Earlier Near Eastern examples: Charles M. Brand, *Byzantium Confronts the West 1180–1204* (Cambridge, MA, 1968), pp. 15–16 (arrest of all Venetian merchants in Constantinople, 1171), 41–2 (massacre of Latins there, 1182); Heyd, *Histoire du commerce*, I, pp. 404–5 (arrest of all Latin merchants in Alexandria, 1215/16). Bulgaria: Gjuzelev, 'Du commerce génois', pp. 38–9. Trebizond: Larner, *Marco Polo*, p. 43.
180. J. Schacht, 'Amān', *Enc.Isl.²*
181. For an example from 12th-century Egypt, see Karl-Heinz Allmendinger, *Die Beziehungen zwischen der Kommune Pisa und Ägypten im hohen Mittelalter*, VSWG Beiheft 54 (Wiesbaden, 1967), pp. 90–1. On Hurmuz, see *DM*, p. 347/MP, I, p. 123 (tr. Ricci, p. 44).
182. Angeliki E. Laiou, 'Byzantine trade with Christians and Muslims and the crusades', in Laiou and Mottahedeh, *Crusades from the Perspective of Byzantium*, pp. 157–96 (here pp. 180, 185–6).
183. Pegolotti, p. 22. Lopez, 'European merchants', p. 176, n.46.
184. Mas Latrie, 'Privilège commercial accordé en 1320', pp. 97–8 (§9) = *DVL*, I, p. 174.
185. Marino Sanudo, *Liber secretorum*, I:i, 1, p. 23.

186. See the comments of Roberto Sabatino Lopez, 'L'extrême frontière du commerce de l'Europe médiévale', *MA* 69 (1963), pp. 479–90 (here pp. 483, 486–7), repr. in his *Su e giù*, pp. 161–70 (here pp. 164, 166–7).
187. *DVL*, I, p. 243 (no. 125).
188. *RDSV*, I, p. 71 (no. 247). Schmieder, *Europa*, p. 168.
189. *RDSV*, I, pp. 95, 96, 121 (nos. 355, 363, 476). Elena Č. Skržinskaja, 'Un'ambasciatore veneziano all'Orda d'Oro (analisi dell'epitafio di Jacopo Cornaro – Tana, 1362)', *SV* 16 (1974), pp. 67–96 (here pp. 75–90).
190. Lopez, 'Nouveaux documents', pp. 449, 456. Tucci, 'Mercanti veneziani', p. 320.
191. *DM*, p. 528, gives the percentages, but only Ramusio's version contains the remark about profits: see MP, I, p. 351 (tr. Ricci, p. 264).
192. For the controversy over the authenticity of Marco Polo's travels, see Appendix I.
193. Franco Borlandi, 'Alle origini del libro di Marco Polo', in Barbieri, *Studi*, I, pp. 107–47.
194. Hyde, 'Ethnographers', pp. 188–9. Larner, *Marco Polo*, pp. 73–4, points out that, in any case, handbooks of the *La pratica della mercatura* type were designed to circulate only within the author's own immediate milieu and could not be allowed to fall into the hands of competitors. For the handbook of 1278, see Robert S. Lopez, 'Un texte inédit: le plus ancien manuel italien de technique commerciale', *RH* 243 (1970), pp. 67–76; Roberto Lopez and Gabriella Airaldi, eds, 'Il piu' antico manuale italiano di pratica della mercatura', in *Miscellanea di studi storici*, II, CSFS 38 (Genova, 1983), pp. 99–133. For a restatement of the case for Polo as a merchant, see Joan-Pau Rubiés, *Travel and Ethnology in the Renaissance. South India Through European Eyes, 1250–1625* (Cambridge, 2000), p. 81 and n.109.
195. As suggested by Pelliot, *Notes on Marco Polo*, II, p. 834. But cf. the objections of Critchley, pp. 78–9, and Larner, *Marco Polo*, p. 65.
196. W.W. Rockhill, 'Notes on the relations and trade of China with the eastern archipelago and the coast of the Indian Ocean during the fourteenth century: part I', *TP* 15 (1914), pp. 419–47 (here pp. 429–42). Peter Jackson, 'Marco Polo and his "Travels"', *BSOAS* 61 (1998), pp. 82–101 (here pp. 94–5).
197. Ibid., pp. 100–1.
198. Denis Sinor, 'Diplomatic practices in medieval Inner Asia', in C.E. Bosworth *et al.*, eds, *Essays in Honor of Bernard Lewis. The Islamic World from Classical to Modern Times* (Princeton, 1988), pp. 337–55 (here pp. 342–3), and repr. in Sinor, *Studies*.
199. Giovanni Villani, *Cronica*, viii, 35, ed. Dragomanni, II, p. 37. Schein, '*Gesta Dei*', p. 815.
200. See Kedar, 'Chi era Andrea Franco?'; on Andrea, also Pistarino, 'Da Genova', pp. 33–8.
201. WR, xxix, 7–13, pp. 253–6 (tr. Jackson and Morgan, pp. 184–7); on their fate, see also viii, 2, p. 186 (tr. p. 94).
202. Kohler and Langlois, 'Lettres inédites', p. 57. Jackson, 'Marco Polo', p. 100.
203. SSQ, pp. 73–4 (= VB, xxxi, 146).

204. Philippe de Mézières, *Le songe du Vieil Pelerin*, ii, 95, ed. Coopland, I, p. 485; cf. also i, 12, ed. Coopland, I, p. 228.

205. 1307: Sayf b. Muḥammad b. Yaʿqūb al-Harawī (commonly known as Sayfī), *Taʾrīkh-nāma-yi Harāt* (*c*.1322), ed. Muḥammad Zubayr aṣ-Ṣiddíqí (Calcutta, 1944; repr. Tehran, 1973), p. 504: *az farangistān chand ustād-i manjanīqī*. Allsen, 'Circulation', p. 271. Richard, 'An account', p. 174, wrongly calls them crossbowmen. 1380: Kedar, *Merchants in Crisis*, p. 69.

206. Ch. Kohler, 'Documents inédits concernant l'Orient Latin et les croisades (XIIᶜ–XIVᶜ siècle)', *ROL* 7 (1899), pp. 1–37 (here p. 37, no. 10); also in Valeria Polonio, ed., *Notai genovesi in Oltremare. Atti rogati a Cipro da Lamberto di Sambuceto (3 luglio 1300–3 agosto 1301)*, CSFS 31 (Genova, 1982), pp. 457–8 (no. 381).

207. Montecorvino, 'Epistolae II', §7, pp. 349–50 (tr. in Moule, *Christians in China*, p. 175; tr. Dawson, *Mongol Mission*, p. 226).

208. *DVL*, I, pp. 209–10 (no. 106). David Jacoby, 'L'expansion occidentale dans le Levant: les Vénitiens à Acre dans la seconde moitié du treizième siècle', *JMH* 3 (1977), pp. 225–64 (here p. 250), repr. in his *Recherches sur la Méditerranée orientale du XIIe au XVe siècle. Peuples, sociétés, économies* (London, 1979).

209. Antoni Rubió y Lluch, ed., *Documents per l'historia de la cultura catalana mig-eval*, 2 vols (Barcelona, 1908–21), I, p. 382 (no. 428) = Rubió y Lluch, *Diplomatari*, pp. 675–6 (no. 647).

210. Donald F. Lach, *Asia in the Making of Europe*, 3 vols in 9 (Chicago, IL, 1965–93), I:1, pp. 82–3. For Polo, see Larner, *Marco Polo*, pp. 163–4.

211. Jean Richard, 'La vogue de l'Orient dans la littérature occidentale du Moyen-Age', in *Mélanges René Crozet* (Poitiers, 1966), pp. 557–61, and repr. in Richard, *Les relations*.

212. Schmieder, *Europa*, p. 160.

chapter 12

A NEW WORLD DISCOVERED?

East and West

In the course of the last few chapters, reference has been made to all the accounts, written by Western Christians on the basis of their travels in the Mongol world between the 1240s and the early fifteenth century, that have come down to us: those of Carpini (1247), Simon of Saint-Quentin (via Vincent of Beauvais, 1253), Rubruck (1255), Marco Polo (1298), Jordanus (1328), Odoric (1330), Marignolli (*c.*1353), John of Sulṭāniyya (1404) and Clavijo (1404). We have also noticed the expatriate Armenian prince Hayton of Gorigos, who travelled in the opposite direction, to Western Europe, and whose *Flor des estoires* (1307) contained a description of the East, composed for a Latin Christian readership. This circumstance, even more than his status as a member of a church that was in union with Rome – an 'honorary Latin', as it were – and a Premonstratensian canon, requires him to be ranked together with the Western writers just listed.

What was known of Europe in the Mongol world is harder to tease out from comparatively meagre source material. Regrettably, apart from Hayton only one other easterner visited Europe and left a written account, namely Rabban Ṣawma, the Nestorian monk who served as ambassador for the Ilkhan Arghun in 1287–8. The Persian original of his narrative is now lost, and we have only the abridged Syriac translation that was incorporated in the biography of the Patriarch Mar Yahballaha III. This work would have been available only within a very restricted circle. The geopolitical survey in Rashīd al-Dīn's 'History of the Franks' (1305/6) – gleaned, perhaps, from Dominican friars or from Ghazan's Pisan agent Isolo – contains numerous interesting details. Rashīd al-Dīn is aware, for instance, of the composition of the electoral college that chose the Holy Roman Emperor, of the character of the regime of the Teutonic Knights in Prussia, of the current occupation of (part of)

Poland by the Bohemian King, and of the use of *mappae mundi* (presumably portolans) by Italian mariners; though he also believed, wrongly, that the Neapolitan King's recent destruction of the Muslim colony at Lucera was a reprisal for the fall of Acre and the demolition of churches in the Ilkhanate. His historical section, on the other hand, amounts to little more than a chronological list of popes and emperors, with exiguous detail on their reigns and derived ultimately from the chronicle of Martin of Troppau (d. 1278).[1]

That the Mongols' Chinese subjects held the peoples of the far west in relatively high esteem is clear from a saying attributed to them in a number of sources, namely that they themselves saw with two eyes, and the *Fu-lang* with one, while everybody else was blind. This adage clearly enjoyed a wide currency, since it is repeated by Hayton, by Clavijo, and even by the Muslim writers Zakariyā' al-Qazwīnī and Ibn Faḍl-Allāh al-'Umarī; but the fact that it is first encountered in a twelfth-century source suggests that it originally applied, not to the Franks but perhaps to the Byzantines.[2] More information may lie hidden in the largely untranslated Chinese material from the Yüan era. Minimal data about the West, obtained through an obscure embassy (quite unknown from European sources) in the period 1314–20, was deemed intriguing enough to be incorporated in a Chinese work dating from the middle of the century.[3] The maps produced in China in the late thirteenth and fourteenth centuries, which may themselves have been partly based on details supplied by Muslim cartographers, provide some information, notably Li Tsê-min's map of *c*.1330. This includes approximately a hundred European place-names, as well as about 35 for Africa: it is now lost, but the data it contained are reproduced in various later maps, notably the Korean world-map of *c*.1402.[4] Although this map is superior to anything produced in Europe prior to the end of the fifteenth century, the limited quantity of Far Eastern material in general that relates to the West contrasts sharply with the volume of European writing on Asia during the Mongol era. In the remainder of this chapter, we shall try to assess the impact of that writing on Western opinion.

Genuine and bogus travellers

Whereas Carpini and Rubruck had travelled only as far as present-day Mongolia, their successors who visited the qaghan's court after 1260 were obliged to go much further, to China. The earliest were the Polos, who stayed in China longer than any other medieval Western travellers known to us, for sixteen years or so (1275–91).[5] Of those Latin visitors who have left behind a written account, moreover, only the Polos entered China by the overland route through Central Asia, and Marco claims subsequently to have undertaken a mission on Qubilai's behalf that took him four months' journey to the west.[6] He accordingly furnishes information about the easternmost stages of the Silk Route that is lacking in other Western accounts: the desert of Lop, the towns of Kan-chou, Su-chou, and so on. Polo seems to have been based in the north, 'Catai' or 'Cathay' (named after the Khitai/Khitan); he was less familiar with the wealthier and more populous southern half of the country, known in European accounts as 'Manzi' or 'Mangi' (Chinese *man-tzŭ*, 'southern barbarians'). The book gives an account of only three of the nine provinces ('kingdoms') of Manzi, namely Yang-chou, Quinsai (Hang-chou) and Fu-chou, on the grounds that Marco passed through them; for the other six he was reliant on hearsay.[7] It should be remembered that at the time of the Polos' arrival parts of Manzi still held out under the Sung, who were not eliminated until 1279. Subsequent visitors from medieval Europe – notably Montecorvino, Odoric, Jordanus and Marignolli – were therefore able to reach the Yüan dominions by sea more easily; but for this reason they tend to describe only a number of coastal cities in the south of the country, together with the qaghan's capital, Khanbaligh.

We should notice that Latin travellers gained access not merely to territories under Mongol rule but also to those which maintained commercial and diplomatic relations with the Yüan court and sometimes paid the qaghan tribute – the coastal regions of peninsular India, for instance, and south-east Asia. Both missionaries and merchants from Europe, travelling by way of Hurmuz in the Persian Gulf, were to be found in India from the final decade of the thirteenth century.[8] But the world of the Indian Ocean also lay athwart the sea route to China, which was preferred when inter-Mongol warfare rendered the overland journey hazardous. The vagaries of the monsoon usually dictated a long delay in the subcontinent even for those proceeding further east. Thus on his way to the qaghan's dominions in *c*.1292–3 Montecorvino spent thirteen months in 'India and the Church of St Thomas' (probably in Ma'bar, as the Coromandel coast was called), while over fifty years later Marignolli was halted in Malabar (modern Kerala) for thirteen months.[9] These experiences gave Western travellers more than a nodding acquaintance with the 'real' India, rather than with the fantasy realm offered up by the writers of Antiquity. Marco Polo stayed so long in India that nobody was in a better position to describe its customs and its trade accurately – or so his book assures us.[10] Although the term 'India', as used here, embraces a much vaster area, extending as far as (and including) present-day Indonesia and even Japan, it is clear that

Marco did visit the subcontinent and on perhaps more than one occasion.

One of the difficulties attaching to the works of Polo and Odoric is that both of them, so to speak, dictated their accounts. Polo's book, it will be recalled, began life in a Genoese prison, as a text drafted by a fellow captive, the professional romance-writer Rustichello of Pisa. In its original form Odoric's work owed its composition to a fellow Franciscan, William of Solagna, to whom he dictated it in his final months. In neither case can we be sure how much of the material we have represents the original narrator and how much should be ascribed to the person who actually transmitted it. Rustichello was clearly responsible for the literary form of the Polo book, in which the first person plural, bewilderingly, does duty sometimes for all three Polos and at others for Marco and Rustichello himself as if he had been the Venetian's travelling-companion.[11] Did he restrict the content faithfully to what Polo told him, or did he embellish it with details of his own?[12] Odoric's book was composed when he was ill: did William of Solagna 'improve' upon what Odoric narrated?

A further, related problem is that in a pre-print culture it was not unknown for either the original author or copyists to add or delete material later. In the second decade of the fourteenth century the Dominican Francesco Pipino, translating the Polo text into Latin, made significant alterations in structure and tone. In addition, there are grounds for believing that at some point before 1307 Polo himself produced an amended version of his book, which included details omitted in the Rustichello text. From this revised draft, presumably, are descended both the Latin text found in the fifteenth-century 'Z' manuscript in Toledo Cathedral Library and certain material which the Venetian official Gian Battista Ramusio (d. 1557) extracted from an old Venetian manuscript of the Polo book and which in some degree overlaps with that in Z.[13] So too in 1340, less than ten years after Odoric's death, the Solagna version of his experiences was reworked by another Franciscan, Henry of Glatz; and further revised versions were produced later in the century. In this fashion, texts took on a life of their own, as different redactions evolved and were disseminated. The question 'What is the "authentic", "original" text?' may (as in the case of Polo's book) be impossible to answer; in the present context – the reception of the different texts and their contribution to knowledge of the East – it may be largely irrelevant.

Some of those who did not visit Asia nevertheless produced travel accounts or geographical surveys which purported to be based on their own experiences and which were regarded as genuine by their contemporaries and even until relatively recent times. One example of an author whose travels certainly took him no further than the nearest library is the anonymous Spanish Franciscan who soon after 1350 wrote the *Libro del conosçimiento de todos los reynos y tierras*: although presented as his itinerary, it amounts in fact to little more than a bald catalogue of often unidentifiable place-names. Another such bogus traveller is the mysterious writer who calls himself 'Sir John Mandeville', author of a much more skilful compilation, dating from *c*.1356, that drew on the account of an authentic voyager, Odoric, and the works of Hayton and Vincent of Beauvais, as well as on the 'Letter of Prester John' and the lore of Classical Antiquity.[14] As regards geographical content rather than authorship, accounts such as these were not necessarily designed to hoodwink their readers, and might do a good job of representing what was known on the basis of real journeys (even recent ones).[15] They need to be taken into consideration if we are to determine what impression more or less educated Western Europeans had of the wider world by 1400. This is not to say that 'ways of thinking' can be defined in uniform, monolithic terms, that there was general agreement on what elicited wonder, or indeed that scepticism was unknown; rather, that it is possible, by focusing on those works that appear to have been most popular, to delineate a corpus of information (and sometimes misinformation) that was available.

It should be noted that we are not necessarily dealing exclusively with the literate. At this date texts were very often designed to be read aloud to an audience.[16] That Rustichello's version of the Polo book was so intended emerges, perhaps, from the prologue: 'Take this book and cause it to be read . . .'.[17] Rustichello's opening is also aggressively unclerical, addressed as it is to 'Emperors, kings, dukes, marquesses, counts, knights and burgesses'. Pope and prelates are alike ignored; the choice of French itself indicates the desire to reach a secular, courtly milieu.[18] The author of Mandeville's 'travels' may well have been a cleric, but his work was cast, like Polo's, as that of a layman. Together the two books signal the arrival of a new genre of travel literature – written from a lay perspective for a lay readership.[19]

The best-known sources of information: Polo, Hayton and Odoric/'Mandeville'

The fourteenth century, then, witnessed an explosion – relatively speaking – in travel literature about Asia; it might appear that by the end of that century the frontiers of Western knowledge had been advanced hundreds of miles to the east. But the influence exerted by these various

Latin Christian writers varied considerably. All too often modern scholars have assumed that new knowledge was absorbed by the West simply because a European observer committed his experiences to writing: thus Montecorvino, for instance, is taken as a transmitter of information when in reality very few are likely to have read his letters.[20] This was similarly the fate of much more substantial documents. We have seen how Rubruck's report to Louis IX languished in comparative obscurity and that only scattered passages were used by Bacon. Marignolli inserted his description of the East in a Bohemian chronicle he was compiling at the behest of the Emperor Charles IV, in the years 1355–8, probably as a means of relieving the tedium; and there it remained buried for over four centuries. Like Jordanus's brief reminiscences, it has survived in only one manuscript – though it may nevertheless have been read by Columbus.[21]

By contrast, to judge from the number of surviving manuscripts, three of the works we have noticed – those of Marco Polo, Hayton and Odoric – enjoyed a wide circulation. It is noteworthy that none of these authors, ironically, was typical of the genre in which he might have been placed. Hayton was not a European, as were most of the authors of crusading treatises, but an expatriate Armenian, albeit one who had joined a Latin religious order. The account of the Franciscan Odoric betrays hardly any evidence of attempts to spread the Gospel. And although Marco Polo undoubtedly owed his lengthy employment in the qaghan's service to the entrepreneurial initiative of his father and uncle, the book associated with his name bears little imprint of a trading mentality.

Polo's book was translated into several vernacular languages, though Pipino's Latin rendering, made in the second decade of the fourteenth century and extant in over 50 manuscripts (not counting translations of Pipino's text into various vernaculars),[22] was the most widely read. Hayton's treatise was available from the outset both in the original French version by Nicolas Faucon and in a Latin translation which Faucon produced in the same year (1307). It has survived in over 50 fourteenth- or fifteenth-century copies (17 of the original French text, 28 of Faucon's Latin translation, and at least five representing retranslation from Latin into French, four of them in the version of Jean Le Long dated 1351).[23] As recast by Pipino, the Polo text soon inspired sufficient confidence among the friars for writers belonging to the Mendicant Orders to cite it for the recent history of the East.[24] Within half a century of their composition, both Polo's and Hayton's books were quoted by the Florentine chronicler Giovanni Villani.[25] Legends became attached to Hayton himself, notably in Tuscany.[26] His *Flor* was almost the only source utilized by Marino Sanudo for those sections of his *Secreta fidelium crucis* (1321) that dealt with the history of Lesser Armenia and of the Tartars;[27] it was also plundered by other authors, notably Paulinus Minorita and Pietro Vesconte in the 1320s, for their geographical surveys.[28]

Odoric's fame naturally spread rapidly among the Franciscans, one of whom, John of Winterthur, described it in *c*.1350 as 'highly comforting and enjoyable';[29] but his sanctity ensured that miracles were reported from his tomb within a few years of his death, and this may have guaranteed a wider circulation of his work.[30] More than 100 manuscripts have come down to us from the fourteenth and fifteenth centuries – the great majority in Latin, the rest mostly in Italian or French, but a few in German.[31] It was clearly popular reading, though less so than Polo. The accessibility of Odoric's experiences was greatly enhanced, however, when they became the principal source for Mandeville's description of Asia – the material coinciding to such an extent that Odoric was sometimes taken to be Mandeville's travelling-companion or to have lifted his own account from Mandeville's seemingly fuller work.[32] Mandeville's account is represented today by 234 fourteenth- or fifteenth-century manuscripts, as opposed to only 130 or so of Polo's book.[33]

Rustichello and Polo between them produced the broadest geographical description of Asia available to date (or for some considerable time to come), with part of East Africa thrown in – even though Polo had never been there. Pride of place goes, perhaps, to the qaghan's dominions and to Qubilai himself, his court, his harem, his great feasts, his hunting expeditions. The book also contains a good deal of information on certain Chinese cities, especially the major ports: Quinsai (Hang-chou), Zaitun (Ch'üan-chou), Fu-chou, and so on. Although no attempt is made to conceal the fact that devastation had accompanied the Mongol conquests,[34] the overall impression the book gives of China is one of unrivalled prosperity. Polo describes the huge Chinese ships, or junks, in which trade with India and other countries was carried on. He himself sailed from China to southern India at least twice, and he describes a number of the towns there, too, along the south-western littoral, Malabar, and on the Coromandel coast (Ma'bar).[35] He lists the products of the territories he is talking about, including fine porcelain from China, pepper and spices from India and the islands of south-east Asia. When it comes to religious differences, it cannot be said that he is especially profound: the inhabitants of this or that region are either Christians or 'idolators' or Muslims (termed, in a somewhat cavalier fashion, 'worshippers of Mahomet'), but in the section on China he does briefly distinguish between Buddhists and the other prominent religious group, the Taoists.[36]

Hayton's survey of the geography of Asia – apart from a fairly terse account of India – was largely confined to the lands under Mongol rule. He began with Cathay (even though he had never set foot there), describing it as 'the noblest and wealthiest of all the kingdoms in the world'. The book introduced Western readers properly to the idea that there now existed a number of rival Mongol states (a fact previously adumbrated, as far as I know, only by Bacon and Polo), naming the principal regions of each and even making some attempt to define their boundaries. By comparison with the other written accounts available, it was especially informative about conditions in Central Asia, the territories of the Chaghadayid khanate.[37] In view of his purpose – to bring about cooperation between the Ilkhans and the West (above, p. 120) – Hayton may have been especially responsible for popularizing the image of friendly Mongols, although the wide publicity given to Ghazan's recovery of the Holy Land in 1300 (pp. 172–3) must also have played a significant role.[38]

Unlike Polo's book, Odoric's is more an itinerary than a geography. It is laced with personal experiences, such as his eye-witness description of the way people in Szu-chiang fished using cormorants. He visited the cities of Canton, Zaitun, Fu-chou, Quinsai and Yang-chou in Manzi and the Great Khan's court at Khanbaligh. The details about China reinforce (and occasionally echo) Polo's, though seemingly independent of the earlier work. Odoric may have halted in Sumatra and Java, and furnishes us with a fuller description of those islands than Polo had done. On the other hand, his account of the regions that lay on his return route is hazy by comparison and markedly inferior to Polo's material. He was the last author to locate the kingdom of Prester John (presumably the Önggüd kingdom, with its centre at 'Tenduc') in the Far East (below, p. 347). The vague description of Tibet is tacked on at the end almost as an afterthought, though Odoric may actually have seen the fortified monastery of Sa-skya.[39] Yet his work is characterized by personal anecdotes that imbue it with greater vividness than is to be found in Polo's book.

In sum, a perusal of Polo, Hayton and Odoric would have imprinted on the mind a vision of Asia defined by certain characteristics. These authors provided the West with its first introduction to China – or, rather, to the two distinct regions of the country, Cathay and Manzi. They spoke of the wealth of China, with its paper currency backed up by vast reserves of gold; the huge, densely populated cities of Manzi, bursting with merchandise, and its broad, navigable rivers teeming with traffic; the formidable power of the Mongol qaghan, and the orderly and efficient administration over which he presided. Polo's claim that there is no kingdom on earth worth half as much as Manzi, frequently reinforced by descriptions of this or that great city, is expressed somewhat more succinctly by Hayton.[40] Polo and Odoric agree that Quinsai is the noblest and richest city in the world.[41] For every shipload of pepper that reaches Alexandria, a hundred are unloaded at Zaitun.[42] In addition a great deal of material was now made available about southern and south-east Asia. The Western reader learned of the existence of states like Ma'bar, ruled by five brothers; Malabar, rich in pepper; the island of Ceylon; Champa (corresponding roughly to the southern part of present-day Vietnam), whose king, says Polo, has 326 children, though according to Odoric he has fathered a mere 250;[43] Java (Polo's 'Greater Java', the empire of Majapahit); and the petty kingdoms of Sumatra (Polo's 'Java the Lesser').

The vast number of islands in the eastern seas clearly made a marked impression: 7,448 in the China Sea and 12,700 in the Indian Ocean, according to Polo, while Odoric spoke of 5,000 in the area of Manzi and another 24,000 within the limits of India, and for Hayton the islands off the coast of Cathay were simply beyond enumeration.[44] On certain of these islands cannibalism was practised; on some, the inhabitants went naked or almost naked. There was one island, in particular, on which Polo (and Polo alone) waxed eloquent. Lying allegedly fifteen hundred miles to the east of China, it was called 'Cipingu' (Chinese *Chi-pên kuo*, 'the kingdom of Japan'). Gold and pearls were in abundant supply there, and the walls and roofs of the ruler's palace were rumoured to be covered with gold.[45] The palace is a fiction presumably circulating in China (Odoric heard a very similar tale about a golden palace, but ascribed it to the ruler of Java instead).[46] Yet the importation of pearls and small quantities of low-price gold from Japan to China is confirmed by contemporary Chinese sources.[47] As we shall see, the chief attributes of Cipingu in Polo's account would be of prime importance in prompting both Columbus and Cabot to embark on their first journeys across the Atlantic.

The authors' perspectives

To any notion of an expansion in the West's horizons a number of qualifications must be made. The first has to do with the mental cargo that Western travellers carried. There has, I think, been some misunderstanding here. It has become fashionable to represent European observers as reporting what they saw in their own mind's eye as well as, or sometimes instead of, what confronted them, so that they looked for, and hence found, the fabulous elements that were the stock-in-trade of medieval Christian geography and ethnology. The distinguished French medievalist, Jacques Le Goff, has proposed that the Indian Ocean, for instance, represented for Latin Christians an 'oneiric horizon' – the frontiers of a world that was dreamed about, a world of fabulous riches (contrasting with the relative poverty and economic backwardness of Western Europe), of anti-nature (fabulous beasts and races, quite unlike the tedious normality of the West), of liberation from the shackles of civilization (as expressed in cannibalism, nudity and sexual licence; one might add, in the case of the king of Champa, unbridled conjugality).[48]

Whatever the virtues of this analysis, the pattern it evokes is incomplete. The Asia that confronted these visitors is simply too passive; no room is made for the perspectives of the people they met and spoke with.[49] The reports of Latin travellers did not just grow out of a projection of their own mental baggage. Their mental universe shows through, naturally; but it interacted with the information they acquired on the spot, in the form of other peoples' 'folk knowledge'. They often took on board, unconsciously no doubt, the mental frontiers of others, which played a crucial role in defining the regions Europeans did not penetrate. Some of the stories the Westerners heard evidently belonged to a common fund of tales that circulated in the Indian Ocean basin: the account of St Thomas's death which placed it in Ma'bar; or the association of the Biblical and Qur'ānic Adam with a mountain in Ceylon ('Adam's Peak'), which allegedly contained his giant footprint and which originally was linked with the Buddha;[50] the magnificent ruby in the king of Ceylon's possession, which the qaghan coveted but had never been able to persuade him to sell (one version of the Polo account claims that Marco, accompanying an embassy from Qubilai, actually saw the stone; but Odoric's account transposes the story of the ruby to 'Nicoveran', the Nicobar Islands).[51] Certain of these tales had been circulating for centuries and can without difficulty be married up with material found in Chinese sources: the Ceylon ruby, for instance, which had attracted the attention of Cosmas Indicopleustes in the sixth century, is referred to by Chao Ju-kua in 1225, just a few decades before Polo's travels.[52]

In other cases the local sources of information were often Muslims. When Polo speaks of 'Ferlec' (a kingdom in Sumatra), where he briefly stopped off during one of his trips on Qubilai's behalf, he unconsciously identifies his informants by saying that the people of the coastal towns have embraced Islam and are civilized; not so those in the interior ('they live like brute beasts').[53] When Odoric notices the cannibals of the

Kingdom of Lamori (north-west Sumatra), whom he never met, he has surely borrowed his categories from the Muslim traders he did encounter. Other stories are known both to have circulated in China and to have been transmitted by Muslim sailors to Arab and Persian geographers back in the tenth century: tales of the islands inhabited separately by men and women; or the 'ruc' or *rukh*, a gigantic bird capable of dropping elephants from a great height.[54] In describing a custom in Tibet, whereby people make goblets out of the skulls of their deceased fathers, Odoric transmits a folk-tale that had been current back in the eighth century (though applied to a people of eastern Asia) and that Rubruck had also heard recounted of Tibet eighty years before.[55] It follows from all this that the new frontiers of knowledge are not to be seen in linear terms. We might think of the world that these men discovered as a series of oases in a still imperfectly charted wilderness. Or, to put it another way, the vantage-point is still often the sea-coast; the overwhelming bulk of the land-mass, and the majority of the islands (especially the more remote ones), were alike known (if at all) only through hearsay.

The reception

The second qualification relates to the purpose with which these works were read. On this question a number of circumstances can throw some light: the additions made by copyists or translators, the other writings with which the texts were bound, and the marginal comments by owners and readers (though all too often anonymous and not datable with any marked precision). Pipino, for instance, turned the Polo text into a handbook for missionaries. The emendations in his Latin translation were evidently designed to impart a spiritual and moral gloss where Rustichello's version had been dangerously non-committal or had even registered approval. Thus the Tibetans' practice of lending their wives to passing foreign merchants ('into that country', wrote Rustichello slyly, 'the young gentlemen from sixteen years to twenty-four will do well to go') becomes for Pipino 'an absurd and deeply abominable custom arising from the blindness of idolatry'.[56] Conversely, a reworking of Odoric's 'Relatio' made in southern Germany in the latter half of the fourteenth century totally suppresses the missionary theme, to which William of Solagna had given some prominence, and accentuates the marvellous instead.[57]

The fact that the books of Polo and Odoric, as far as we can tell, are most often found bound together with the stuff of chivalric legend or works of an improving nature suggests that, for the first hundred years of their existence, they were read primarily for entertainment or edification: to dispel boredom, to feed a sense of wonder at the diversity of Creation, to amass knowledge of pagan customs with a view to future evangelization. Only in the second half of the fifteenth century did readers approach them in order to learn about the true layout of the land-mass and the oceans.[58] Hayton's *Flor des estoires* perhaps followed a different trajectory. Designed originally as a crusade treatise, it was on occasions bound together with other matter of relevance to crusading that dated from the early years of the fourteenth century: the geopolitical survey of Eastern Europe by an anonymous Dominican, to which we have already referred (p. 204), and the *Memoria Terrae Sanctae*. No less than five codices combining these three works have survived from the fourteenth and fifteenth centuries. This might lend support to the idea that they were first put together as early as 1308, when the French prince Charles of Valois (brother of Philip IV) planned a crusade against Byzantium, of which the anonymous Dominican, at least, was an enthusiastic advocate.[59]

Yet the distinctions are not as clear-cut as this. A copy of Polo's book was presented to the French king's ambassador when he visited Venice in 1307 in connection with the above-mentioned anti-Byzantine crusade.[60] And both Polo (particularly Pipino's Latin version) and Odoric are sometimes found bound together with Hayton in late medieval manuscripts that reflect unmistakeable crusading preoccupations.[61] A notable example is the assemblage of texts produced for Juan Fernández de Heredia (d. 1396), the Master of the Knights Hospitallers at Rhodes. At this time an interest in the East is to be found in the very westernmost reaches of Catholic Europe, the Iberian peninsula. As we saw, it was in the late fourteenth century that a Castilian Franciscan composed the *Libro del conosçimiento*. But Aragonese interest was more pronounced still. Between 1372 and 1374 King Pedro IV purchased no fewer than three copies of Polo's book. Roughly simultaneously, it is known to have been translated into Catalan, the language of part of Pedro's dominions, and this version underlay the Catalan Atlas of *c*.1380, containing, as we shall see, the earliest maps of the Far East to reflect a detailed knowledge of Polo's material. The codex produced for Heredia, a friend and one-time subject of King Pedro, represented an Aragonese translation, done in part, at least, at the Aragonese court. Not only did it comprise Polo's book and Hayton's *Flor des estoires* (possibly translated from the Catalan), but the Polo text itself included a few supplementary passages borrowed from Odoric, so that the manuscript represents a relatively full compendium of what was by now becoming common knowledge about the East.[62] Pedro's son, the future King Juan

I, exhibited a keen interest in fresh accounts of 'Tartaria' and the East, both before and after his succession to the throne.[63] An Aragonese translation of Mandeville's book (based on a copy of the work presented to Juan by Charles V of France in 1380) may have appeared not long after the Heredia codex.[64]

The fact that knowledge of these works was so widespread does not, of course, mean that all the detail they contained was necessarily accepted. The authors themselves clearly felt a need to guard against incredulity in advance. Generally speaking, primacy in these matters was ostensibly given to personal experience.[65] Marignolli was concerned to report what he had seen himself, even if the outcome was frequently to confirm the veracity of tradition.[66] Marco Polo's book guaranteed that what he himself had witnessed would be distinguished from hearsay (though this laudable principle is not always observed).[67] For Polo the wealth of Manzi was on such a stupendous scale that nobody could credit it who had not seen it.[68] In one version, he hesitated to give the number of boats that plied the Qara Mören (the Yellow River) for fear of being branded a liar.[69] Odoric, for his part, denied any desire to write about what was incredible unless witnessed.[70] How necessary these disclaimers actually were is not clear. Professor Larner argues persuasively that during the first few decades, when Latin merchants were free to travel within the Mongol realms, they provided corroboration of the written accounts. It was after these contacts with Central Asia and the Far East dried up, in the latter half of the fourteenth century, that scepticism began to be expressed more frequently; and not until Niccolò Conti reported back from his journeys in the Indian Ocean in the 1440s that Polo's truthfulness was again validated.[71] Nevertheless, Polo allegedly encountered disbelief in his lifetime – even, in one story, on his deathbed, when he was urged to excise from the book what was untrue and retorted that he had not described one half of what he had seen.[72]

This is not to claim that what prompted incredulity in fourteenth-century Europe was necessarily what would do so today. As we shall see (p. 345), the fabulous races still commanded a loyal following. That said, it is important to distinguish 'natural' marvels from the miraculous, a distinction that was just beginning to be drawn at the onset of the thirteenth century. The term 'marvels' was coming to embrace whatever *within* Nature inspired amazement and admiration, as opposed to that which lay outside it and often provoked scepticism.[73] With the occasional exception (like the 'ruc'), such 'natural' marvels were the kind that Polo purveyed; to a lesser extent, this is also true of Odoric. Breathless claims about this or that great city or the size of an eastern king's harem belong in a different class from traditional *mirabilia*. The reader is invited to share in the wonder conjured by superlatives rather than by the anthropologically or zoologically preposterous.

We are possibly approaching the reasons why Polo, in particular, was not believed. Not merely was he prepared to leave a void where no description of a region lay readily to hand, rather than to fill it with the fantastic;[74] but he seems further to take a positive pleasure (insofar as we can detect a personality at all behind Rustichello's deathless epic prose) in demolishing misconceptions that were prevalent back home. The salamander, for example, an animal that reputedly was capable of with-standing fire, was in fact not a beast but a mineral (asbestos). The corpses sold in India as dead pygmies were really those of dried monkeys. The unicorn is recognizable for the first time here as the rhinoceros: contrary to Western European tradition, says Marco, this is not at all the sort of creature that lets itself be ensnared by virgins.[75] Such iconoclastic disregard for cherished elements of traditional wisdom was objection-able enough; added to it was the manner in which Polo depicted the qaghan's empire. The stumbling-block here was not that the Western reader was predisposed to reject the notion of a highly organized and sophisticated polity in the East – witness the longevity of the Prester John legend. Rather, it was that Polo depicted such a polity as presided over by those from whom the West had grown accustomed to expect only coarse-grained barbarism.[76] As has been pointed out, the discovery of the 'simpler' society in the Canary Islands in the 1340s proved signi-ficantly easier to assimilate.[77]

Conflicts, contradictions and authority

The third thing that circumscribed Western perceptions of Asia has to do with discrepancies between new information and that found in tradi-tional authorities. Medieval Latin travellers themselves sometimes sought to correct what they viewed as misinformation by contemporaries who had trodden the same path not long before. Jordanus, assuring his readers that the Indian rhinoceros is not the unicorn (which he located instead in 'the Third India', i.e. Africa), may be consciously challenging Polo.[78] Marignolli, in turn, was almost certainly taking issue with Odoric in stating that the pepper in Malabar did not grow in forests and that its production was in the hands of the Christians there rather than of the Muslims; on the other hand, his denial that it was roasted cannot be aimed at Odoric, since Jordanus had earlier attacked the same 'lie'.[79]

More importantly, however, the new knowledge frequently clashed with that derived from venerable sources. Polo, of course, was not the only traveller who became aware of a conflict between his own experiences and traditional knowledge; he simply enjoyed a higher profile. By making a choice, Rubruck had impugned one of the highest authorities of all. It was untrue, he found, that the Caspian was a gulf linked to the Ocean, as Isidore had asserted; rather, it was entirely landlocked.[80] Yet such emphatic assertions were unusual. More often those who wrote about geography hedged their bets. The Spanish Franciscan who composed the *Libro del conosçimiento*, for instance, transmits the well-known fact that the Three Magi were buried in Cologne; but he then mentions the monument to them in the Chinese city of 'Solin' (which had been pointed out to him, he tells us, during his visit to the city), without committing himself to either location.[81]

The overall impact of the works of Polo, Hayton and Odoric was consequently patchy. Certain geographical treatises or encyclopaedias, and a minority of maps, reflect – in some measure – the journeys made and the new territories opened up to Europeans. But there are other contemporary prose works which parade none of this new knowledge whatsoever. Writers sometimes exhibit a bewilderingly 'compartmentalized' approach to learning. Vincent of Beauvais enriched the historical section of his encyclopaedia with detail on the Mongols borrowed from Carpini and Simon of Saint-Quentin; the geographical section, by contrast, makes no reference to the information furnished by these travellers and simply falls back on the writings of Antiquity. So too the geography inserted by Ranulf Higden in his *Polychronicon* (before 1350) is highly traditional; it makes no mention of the Mongols, in contrast with the historical part of his book.[82] And the material on the Far East purveyed by Polo took an especially long time to be incorporated into the work of the cartographers. Even the 'Catalan Atlas' of *c*.1380 – containing, as we noticed, the earliest maps to demonstrate a familiarity with Polo's book – is selective: it incorporates China, but no attempt is made to depict Cipingu. Thereafter we have to wait until the latter half of the fifteenth century before several maps, produced in relatively rapid succession and independently of one another, again bear the imprint of Polo's findings and – in the case of Fra Mauro (*c*.1459) – include the first Western representation of Japan.[83] It was incumbent on cartographers to tread more cautiously than the authors of prose accounts; easier to play safe and merely reproduce the geographical data inherited from Antiquity, or – at best – simply to graft the new material onto the existing corpus of sources that were deemed authoritative for the history and geography of the world.[84]

The problem of deference to authority is already illustrated by the example of Roger Bacon, writing back in *c*.1267 – no mere plodding compilator, but a scholar blest with an enquiring mind. Very commendably, Bacon insisted that he would give priority to those who wrote from personal experience rather than on the basis purely of report (*ex rumore*). Thus he used the writings of those who had travelled in Asia, such as Rubruck and others who had visited the Tartars; he knew of Carpini's *Ystoria Mongalorum*, though it is not certain whether he had read it completely.[85] And yet Bacon adds that he will rely also on the late eighth-century author known as Aethicus Ister – whose *Cosmographia* is a pastiche of nonsense and who was never east of Austria in his life – as if its account of 'Scythia' were likewise based on genuine travel experiences and equal in value to Rubruck's report.[86] In *c.*1400 the Florentine Domenico Silvestri was expressing an attitude rather akin to the policy Bacon had in practice followed, when he declared that he would include in his work on geography only what was supported by the authority of Antiquity, told by *viva voce* witnesses, or based on probable conjecture.[87] As these examples demonstrate, it was not enough to look for an empirical understanding in the works that one consulted; it was also necessary to know just where such an empirical understanding was truly to be found. Bad sources could so easily look like good ones.

It is sometimes said that the fifteenth-century Renaissance exacerbated the problem – that the rise of Humanism accentuated the reverence with which ancient writers were viewed and made scholars less likely to question or challenge them. This view, however, must be qualified. Classical sources themselves provided conflicting information: what eventually prompted a reassessment, and enhanced the priority of personal observation, was the rediscovery of Ptolemy's *Geographia* (translated into Latin in 1406/10) and of Strabo's *Geographia* a little later (the Latin translation dates from the mid-fifteenth century). The unearthing of these works led to the recognition that some of their material clashed with the geographical data inherited from other traditional sources.[88]

By way of illustration we may turn to the fabulous races. On this head, one or two of our travellers were sceptical. Rubruck voiced doubts regarding the existence of the monsters of which Solinus and Isidore had written.[89] Montecorvino felt bound to mention that he had found no monsters in southern India.[90] Marignolli went so far as to reject the notion of whole races who were deformed, proposing that it had arisen because the occasional individual 'monster' lurked in one locality or another, just as in Europe. And some of these peoples, he suggested, were completely fictitious: the Sciopods, for example, with the enormous foot they used for shading themselves, surely originated with the Indian practice of carrying a large parasol.[91]

Yet these were seemingly isolated voices. There was an internal rationality to the accounts of monsters, which reminds us that in the medieval context the distinction between 'factual' geography or 'rational' reporting, on the one hand, and the genre of marvels, on the other, can be misleading and anachronistic. Was not the authenticity of the marvels supported by a host of trustworthy writers in the ancient world? It was, moreover, licit for Christians – even obligatory – to stand in wonder before God's Creation; and not just a duty confined to the devout, either. It may be that the success of 'Mandeville' lay partly in his readiness to satisfy a profound need, by peopling Odoric's Indian islands with the whole gamut of monstrous races.[92] Locating the Cynocephali north of 'Tartaria', the author of the *Libro del conosçimiento* claimed to have met one of this race in Ürgench; though for some reason he dispatched the headless people, whose faces were on their chests, to the northern reaches of Norway and denied having sighted them.[93] Even genuine travellers felt compelled to mention the monstrous nations, while relegating them to the fringes of the world they described. Thus John of Sulṭāniyya, who passed to the south of the Caucasus ('Caspian') range in 1404, could cite rumours that its inhabitants included not only the peoples Gog and Magog, imprisoned by Alexander, but also the Monacli, who fed on human flesh, and a race who were half-canine, half-human.[94] His contemporary, Clavijo, whose mission to Temür took him as far as Samarqand, retails an account of the Amazons, in the assurance that they lived eleven days' march beyond that city.[95] Nor did the fact that Polo's book nowhere actually mentions the mythical monstrous races prevent some of those who copied the manuscripts of his work from including illustrations of them.[96] In some respects, therefore, and for many Western readers, the world went on much as before.

Within a relatively short time, moreover, all this new-found knowledge of Asia, such as it was, acquired a static, fossilized character, as the fourteenth century witnessed a progressive drying-up of journeys between Europe and Eastern Asia, the reasons for which we have already noticed (pp. 260, 301–4). There is no indication that anyone in Europe – with the possible exception of John of Sulṭāniyya[97] – ever learned that the Mongol rulers had been expelled from China and replaced by the native Ming dynasty in 1368. Having been made aware, therefore, of an impressive and powerful civilization in Cathay, Western Christians continued to imagine the 'Great Khan' presiding over it long after he had in fact withdrawn into the steppes of Mongolia.

Christians and pagans: a shifting balance in a larger world?

It has been suggested that, with the publicity given to the findings of Western travellers in Mongol Asia, the world appeared a much larger place. This impression, at any rate, would have been conveyed by the duration of journeys – three or three-and-a-half years – between China and the Near East given (though inaccurately) in Marco Polo's book.[98] And one consequence was that the territory in Christian hands accordingly came to seem a significantly smaller proportion of the earth's surface. Material to support this proposition can be gleaned from a variety of writers, beginning with the dejected comment of Roger Bacon in c.1267: 'There are few Christians. The whole breadth of the world is peopled by unbelievers, and there is no one to show them the truth.'[99] One circumstance that influenced his judgement, no doubt, was the discovery of Buddhism, a faith hitherto completely unknown to the West. Carpini, as we saw (p. 97), had heard of Buddhists while at the qaghan's encampment, but had mistaken them for Christians. It fell to Rubruck to identify such priests not merely as 'idolators' but as the representatives of an organized religion: he described their dress, the layout of their temples, and the beliefs of different sects (although he wrongly concluded that the Mongols represented a monotheistic tradition within Buddhism).[100] In China – outside the cities where Nestorianism was represented, that is – and beyond, only Buddhists ('idolators'), were allegedly to be found.[101] It was, of course, Marco Polo who first brought Buddhism to the attention of a Western readership; although his material on Buddhism was rather more superficial, he did (unlike Rubruck) devote some space to the life of the Buddha.[102]

The vast extent of the Mongol realms helped to reinforce the impression that Christians were a small minority. We find Robert Grosseteste expressing such a view as early as 1250, when visiting the papal Curia.[103] According to Ramón Lull the dominions of the qaghan, the Ilkhan and the khan of the Golden Horde were, in the aggregate, at least twice as large as those of the Christians and Muslims combined.[104] References to an apparently shrinking Christian world population could be multiplied;[105] and statements of this sort voiced after 1300, at least, must reflect in part an awareness of the successes achieved by Muslim arms (as in Syria and Palestine). Yet we need to approach such opinions with caution. Pessimism about the relative strength of Christians in the world was no new phenomenon. As early as the twelfth century, William of Malmesbury, in his account of the sermon that launched the First Crusade in 1095, makes Pope Urban II point to the fact that believers inhabited only a small fraction of the Earth's surface;[106] though of course it should be borne in mind that William wrote before Latin Christians became aware of the existence of the far-flung Nestorian communities, and that crusading successes, acts of union with separated churches and the spread of reports about Prester John all gave rise to more sanguine opinions (above, pp. 14–16, 20–1).

What had also changed in the intervening century and a half was the attitude towards Christians of other churches. It was no longer just a matter of the great number of pagans: the high proportion of schismatic Christians had also proved daunting. Rubruck had observed that Nestorians were established in fifteen Chinese cities.[107] Although he seems to have enjoyed a good working relationship with at least one Nestorian cleric (above, p. 266), his strictures on the Nestorians in general clearly influenced Bacon's judgement: they were 'bad Christians'.[108] Two generations later Marino Sanudo estimated that Christians (a term which for him excluded schismatics) held only a tenth of the world, and the author of the *Directorium ad passagium faciendum*, in what was perhaps an indirect allusion to Sanudo's verdict, was more pessimistic still: 'As for us, the true Christians, we number – let alone a tenth – not even a twentieth'.[109] Such sentiments were being expressed in the early fifteenth century: at the Council of Constance in 1417 it was noted that of the twelve regions of the world converted by the Apostles eleven were now heretical.[110]

In this context, it is worth noting the eclipse of the Asiatic Prester John. From being the mighty (and only incidentally heterodox) ally he had appeared to Otto of Freising, he had undergone a steady decline in status, until both Polo and Montecorvino identified him with a relatively minor prince, a former ruler of the Turkish Önggüd tribe, north-east of the great bend in the Yellow River.[111] The handling of the Prester John theme by different travellers reflects, in some measure, the immediate conditions, or the wider political circumstances, in which they operated. Thus Rubruck, frequently ill at ease in Nestorian circles, was content to dismiss the entire story as the product of Nestorian exaggeration;[112] and whereas previous writers had assumed that Chinggis Khan had killed the Christian Prester John, Polo transmitted a striking mutation of the legend. Flushed with the (doubtless overstated) patronage of a benevolent Mongol qaghan, he said nothing of Prester John's Christianity and made Christian astrologers in the victor's service foretell his downfall.[113] In any case, the arrival of an embassy from the Christian kingdom of Ethiopia (*c*.1310) dealt a new and fortuitous twist to the long career of Prester John. Jordanus of Séverac, who soon afterwards, in 1323, located him in Africa, was the first of many authors to do so; Odoric, conversely, was the last to associate him with Asia.[114] The Nestorians of the East no longer even had a useful king to offer.

It is true that some were still ready to count schismatics unequivocally within the ranks of the faithful, and that this bred a more positive outlook on the world. Burchard of Mount Sion, on pilgrimage in 1283, demonstrates a comparatively open attitude towards other sects, and clearly derived comfort from an overwhelming preponderance of eastern Christians in the territories 'beyond the sea, as far as India and Ethiopia', despite their unwarlike character.[115] In 1255 Rubruck, noticing that the (Greek) Christians in Seljük Anatolia outnumbered by ten to one the Muslims who ruled over them, seemed to be adducing this fact in support of a crusade.[116] But although the Rustichello version of Polo's book regularly mentions eastern Christians without pronouncing on their orthodoxy, such restraint does not characterize all those who subsequently copied and embellished the Polo account.[117] The majority of other texts were likely to dismiss Nestorians and other non-Latin Christians out of hand. For Odoric, they are 'schismatics and heretics' or 'the very worst heretics'; in Jordanus's eyes, similarly, the 'Thomas Christians' and the Nestorians of the Caucasus region are not Christians, although the Georgians qualify.[118] Some fourteenth-century writers went further, with the assertion that the Nestorians had fallen away from Christianity altogether.[119] Such dismissive judgements did not, even so, signal the end of illusions about high-ranking conversions in Asia: Clavijo in 1404 transmitted a false report that the new Ming Emperor (Yung-lo) had become a Christian.[120]

Prospect: the discovery of Asia in America

The discovery of Cathay, Java and Sumatra, and perhaps the vague consciousness also of the existence of Cipingu, did alter the lineaments of the world in one important respect. It was now clear that the Eurasian land-mass extended a considerable distance further to the east. Given the canonical statement in II Esdras, 6:42, that the land occupied six-sevenths of the earth, and that only one-seventh lay under water, this would be of prime importance. Roger Bacon was just one of several theorists grossly to underestimate the circumference of the globe, and hence the distance between Spain and the Far East for anyone travelling westwards across the Atlantic; and Bacon, through the medium of Pierre d'Ailly's *Imago Mundi* (*c*.1410), would have a profound impact on Columbus's determination to make the journey to Cipingu in 1492.[121]

The flurry of Spanish activity surrounding the Polo book and other texts in the late fourteenth century, which we noticed earlier, was perhaps unusual and shortlived; but it is important as evidence for a rise in interest in the East within this – one might think, perhaps, the most unlikely – part of Latin Europe. A hundred years later these texts took on a new significance when Europeans first conceived of reaching Asia by a westerly route. In his endeavour to reach Cipingu, Columbus was surely indebted to geographical notions that had been popularized by Polo.[122] Yet it is by no means certain that at the time of his first voyage he had read the book, of which he is known to have acquired a copy only in 1497/8. This was sent to him from England by the Bristol merchant John Day. Day was familiar with the recent expedition of the Venetian citizen John Cabot, whose own acquaintance with Marco Polo's information about Cipingu had inspired him to cross the Atlantic under the patronage of the English king.[123]

The great majority of the annotations (*postille*) that are to be found on the Pipino text Columbus owned (now in the Biblioteca Colombiana in Seville) cannot be dated – even where the hand can be reliably identified as the Admiral's own; those few that can, were made no earlier than the third voyage.[124] On the other hand, it is worth noting that Heredia's composite manuscript (including, as we saw, an Aragonese version of Polo's book) had been acquired by Columbus's patron, Queen Isabella of Castile (d. 1504).[125] Columbus may therefore have had access to a text at an early date. But this is purely conjectural. On balance, it seems safer to conclude that by 1492 he had imbibed only an outline familiarity with the world the Venetian had described (and for that matter, given the evidence, the same might be said of Cabot five years later). Even during his subsequent attempts Columbus may well have been guided more by a general awareness of what Polo and others had said. After his arrival in the Caribbean and the onset of doubts about the proximity of Cipingu, the presence of so many islands – surely that very plethora of islands referred to, but never visited, by Polo and by Odoric and Mandeville – must have helped to bolster his conviction that he was not far from the mainland of Cathay.[126] On the other hand, the dark skins of the islands' inhabitants – so difficult to reconcile with the received image of the Cathayans – would have been explicable only for someone who had read Polo, Odoric or Mandeville on the aboriginal inhabitants of the southern Chinese province of Fu-chou.[127]

The journeys of the thirteenth and fourteenth centuries that were both stimulated and facilitated by the rise of the Mongol world-empire did not, perhaps, have as profound and widespread an impact on contemporaries as did those of their successors from the last years of the fifteenth century onwards. Yet in the longer term their consequences were no less striking. Three of them, at least, were undoubtedly responsible for a pronounced growth in the availability of knowledge about the world beyond Islam after 1300, and through their agency 'Cathay' and its neighbours became part of an *idée fixe* within the West, which in turn prompted the voyages of discovery made by Columbus and others. How many persons read Marco Polo's book (in one form or another) during the two hundred years following his return to Italy, we have no sure way of knowing; how many more came to put their trust in Mandeville, it is impossible to surmise. Nor can we be certain how familiar Columbus was with the contents of either book prior to his departure in 1492 or even after his fourth and final voyage. What can be said with confidence is that in the broadest sense thirteenth- and fourteenth-century travellers (both real and imaginary), and Polo especially, exerted a decisive influence on the actions of their late-fifteenth-century successors.

Notes

1. On the view of the West found in both these works, see Morgan, *Mongols*, pp. 187–92. For the one known ms. (or possibly two mss.) of the life of Yahballaha III, see J.-B. Chabot, *Histoire de Mar Jabalaha III patriarche des Nestoriens (1281–1317) et du moine Rabban Çauma ambassadeur du roi Argoun en Occident (1287)* (Paris, 1895), pp. 1–2. Rashīd al-Dīn's debt to Martin is considered in Jahn's edn, *Die Frankengeschichte*, pp. 14–16; for the various details cited here, see ibid., Tafeln 35, 43–45, facsimiles of Persian text, mss. Hazine 1654, fo. 312v, and Hazine 1653, fos. 414v–415r, 415v (German trans., pp. 92, 46–9, 54; in that order).

2. Hayton, i, 1, Fr. text p. 121, Latin text p. 261. Clavijo, p. 208 (tr. Le Strange, p. 289). Cf. Ibn Faḍl-Allāh al-'Umarī, *Masālik*, ed. and tr. Lech, *Das mongolische Weltreich*, p. 33 (German tr. p. 113); and for earlier references, ibid., p. 260, n.56.

3. Walter Fuchs, 'Ein Gesandtschaftsbericht über Fu-lin in chinesischer Wiedergabe aus den Jahren 1314–1320', OE 6 (1959), pp. 123–30.

4. Joseph Needham, *Science and Civilisation in China* (Cambridge, 1954–), III, pp. 554–6. W. Fuchs, 'Drei neue Versionen der chinesisch-koreanischen Weltkarte von 1402', in Herbert Franke, ed., *Studia Sino-Altaica. Festschrift für Erich Haenisch zum 80. Geburtstag* (Wiesbaden, 1961), pp. 75–7. Allsen, *Culture and Conquest*, pp. 106–12. Lopez, 'Nuove luci', pp. 91–2, n.21, points out that the 1332 map nevertheless contains errors that hardly indicate a Muslim source.

5. Francis Woodman Cleaves, 'A Chinese source bearing on Marco Polo's departure from China and a Persian source on his arrival in Persia', HJAS 36 (1976), pp. 181–203.

6. DM, p. 450/MP, I, p. 255 (tr. Ricci, p. 167).

7. MP, II ('Z' text), p. 56; cf. I, p. 353 (tr. Ricci, p. 266).

8. James D. Ryan, 'European travelers before Columbus: the fourteenth century's discovery of India', CHR 79 (1993), pp. 648–70.

9. Montecorvino, 'Epistolae II', §1, p. 345 (tr. in Moule, *Christians in China*, p. 171, and Dawson, *Mongol Mission*, p. 224). Marignolli, p. 530 = 'Kronika

Jana z Marignoly', p. 496 (tr. Yule, *Cathay*, III, p. 217); slightly later he gives 1 year and 4 months.

10. *DM*, p. 529/MP, I, p. 354 (tr. Ricci, p. 267).

11. Dietmar Rieger, 'Marco Polo und Rustichello da Pisa: der Reisende und seiner Erzähler', in Xenja von Ertzdorff and Dieter Neukirch, eds, *Reisen und Reiseliteratur im Mittelalter und im frühen Neuzeit*, Chloe: Beihefte zum Daphnis 13 (Amsterdam and Atlanta, GA, 1992), pp. 289–312. But cf. Jennifer R. Goodman, *Chivalry and Exploration 1298–1600* (Woodbridge, 1998), pp. 89–90, for whom the voices of Polo and Rustichello 'are not separable'.

12. Campbell, *Witness and the Other World*, pp. 92–3, sees Rustichello as responsible only for the 'language of romance' and 'perhaps for the more thoroughly fictional of the stories . . . [about] cities that Marco did not visit'. Cf. Goodman, pp. 86–7.

13. See Larner, *Marco Polo*, pp. 46–58, 185. The arguments of Barbara Wehr, 'À propos de la génèse du «Devisement dou Monde» de Marco Polo', in Maria Selig, Barbara Frank and Jörg Hartmann, eds, *Le passage à l'écrit des langues romanes* (Tübingen, 1993), pp. 299–326, that Pipino's version represents the original Polo text and that Rustichello's is a subsequent reworking, have attracted little support.

14. There is no consensus as to the identity, or even the nationality, of 'Mandeville': see J.R.S. Phillips, 'The quest for Sir John Mandeville', in Marc Anthony Meyer, ed., *The Culture of Christendom. Essays in Medieval History in Commemoration of Denis L.T. Bethell* (London and Rio Grande, 1993), pp. 243–55; Mandeville, *Le livre des merveilles du monde*, ed. Christiane Deluz (Paris, 2000), introduction, pp. 7–14.

15. Jean Richard, 'Voyages réels et voyages imaginaires, instruments de la connaissance géographique au moyen âge', in G. Hasenohr and J. Longère, eds, *Culture et travail intellectuel dans l'Occident médiéval* (Paris, 1981), pp. 211–20, and repr. in Richard, *Croisés*. Phillips, *Medieval expansion*, pp. 197–9. On the *Libro*, see J.K. Hyde, 'Real and imaginary journeys in the later Middle Ages', *BJRL* 65 (1982–3), pp. 125–47 (here pp. 144–6).

16. M.T. Clanchy, *From Memory to Written Record: England 1066–1307*, 2nd edn (Oxford, 1993), esp. pp. 266–70. For the change that occurred in the significance of *literatus* (from 'one versed in letters' to 'one who is [minimally] literate'), see ibid., chap. 7.

17. *DM*, p. 305/MP, I, p. 73 (tr. Ricci, p. 1). Larner, *Marco Polo*, pp. 51–2, takes this as anachronistic and largely rhetorical; but cf. Rubiés, *Travel and Ethnology*, pp. 77–8.

18. See Goodman, p. 85.

19. Rubiés, *Travel and Ethnology*, pp. 77–83.

20. E.g. Gerd Tellenbach, 'Zur Frühgeschichte abendländischer Reisebeschreibungen', in Hans Fenske, Wolfgang Reinhard and Ernst Schulin, eds, *Historia integra. Festschrift für Erich Hassinger zum 70. Geburtstag* (Berlin, 1978), pp. 51–80 (here p. 60). Cf. *SF*, p. 335.

21. Valerie I.J. Flint, 'Christopher Columbus and the Friars', in Lesley Smith and Benedicta Ward, eds, *Intellectual Life in the Middle Ages. Essays Presented to*

Margaret Gibson (London, 1992), pp. 295–310. For Marignolli's work, see Anna-Dorothee von den Brincken, 'Die universalhistorischen Vorstellungen des Johann von Marignola OFM', *AK* 49 (1967), pp. 297–339 (here pp. 302–3).

22. Listed in MP, I, pp. 512–14; but cf. the figures quoted by Wehr, 'À propos de la génèse', p. 320.

23. See the list in *RHCDA*, II, pp. lxxxv–ccxxii.

24. Anna-Dorothee von den Brincken, 'Der „Oriens christianus" in der Chronik des Johannes Elemosyna OFM (1335–36)', in Wolfgang Voigt, ed., *XVIII. Deutscher Orientalistentag vom 1. bis 5. Oktober 1972 in Lübeck. Vorträge*, *ZDMG* Supplement 2 (Wiesbaden, 1974), pp. 63–75 (here pp. 71–2).

25. Giovanni Villani, *Cronica*, v, 29, and viii, 35, ed. Dragomanni, I, pp. 210–11, and II, p. 38, on each occasion citing both authors.

26. Gustave Soulier, 'Le moine arménien Hethoum et les apports d'Extrême-Orient à la fin du XIIIᵉ et au commencement du XIVᵉ siècle', *Revue des Études Arméniennes* 9 (1929), pp. 249–54.

27. Sanudo, *Liber secretorum*, III:xiii, 2–8, pp. 233–40, is largely an abridgement of Hayton, iii, 9–42, Fr. text pp. 155–203, Latin text pp. 290–324; the sections on the Mongols' homeland, origins and customs are taken from Carpini, probably via Vincent of Beauvais.

28. Schmieder, *Europa*, p. 300.

29. John of Winterthur, *Cronica*, p. 231: *opusculum valde solaciosum et delectabile*. See also John of Viktring, II, p. 113.

30. Reichert, *Begegnungen*, pp. 174, 212–16.

31. Giulio Cesare Testa, 'Bozza per un censimento dei manoscritti Odoriciani', in Melis, *Odorico da Pordenone e la Cina*, pp. 117–50 (here pp. 119–45), and Reichert, *Begegnungen*, pp. 172–3, supersede the data in Yule, *Cathay*, II, pp. 39–75. Printed texts: Alvise Andreose, ed., *Libro delle nuove e strane e meravigliose cose. Volgarizzamento italiano del secolo XIV dell'*Itinerarium *di Odorico da Pordenone* (Padova, 2000); D.A. Trotter, ed., *Jean de Vignay. Les merveilles de la Terre d'Outremer. Traduction du XIVe siècle du récit de voyage d'Odoric de Pordenone* (Exeter, 1990); Gilbert Strasmann, ed., *Konrad Steckels deutsche Übertragung der Reise nach China des Odorico de Pordenone*, Inaugural-Diss., Berlin, 1968.

32. Josephine Waters Bennett, *The Rediscovery of Sir John Mandeville* (New York, 1954), pp. 26–38, for Mandeville's adaptation of the Odoric material; cf. also Christiane Deluz, *Le Livre de Jehan de Mandeville: une «géographie» au XIVᵉ siècle* (Louvain-la-Neuve, 1988), pp. 249–52. For Odoric as Mandeville's companion, see Reichert, *Begegnungen*, p. 204 and n.40.

33. Calculation based on the most up-to-date list, given by Deluz, *Le Livre*, pp. 370–82; see also the list in her introduction to the edition, pp. 38–58. For Polo, see Reichert, *Begegnungen*, p. 172; and for comparisons of the two works, Malcolm Letts, *Sir John Mandeville: The Man and His Book* (London, 1949), p. 129, and Bennett, *Rediscovery*, p. 219. Cf. Larner, *Marco Polo*, p. 106, for still higher figures.

34. See, e.g., *DM*, p. 358/MP, I, p. 134 (tr. Ricci, p. 54), for the ruined condition in which they have left the city of Balkh.

35. For a convenient survey of Polo's information on India, see Franz Übleis, 'Marco Polo in Südasien (1293/94)', *AK* 60 (1978), pp. 268–304.
36. *DM*, pp. 404–5/*MP*, I, p. 191 (tr. Ricci, pp. 101–2).
37. F.E.A. Krause, 'Das Mongolenreich nach der Darstellung des Armeniers Haithon', in *Festschrift für Friedrich Hirth zu seinem 75. Geburtstag, 16. April 1920* (Berlin, 1920 = *Ostasiatische Zeitschrift* 8), pp. 238–67.
38. For the growth of the idea that the Mongols' attitude had changed, and that they were now more 'civilized', see Schmieder, *Europa*, pp. 9 (citing Jacopo d'Acqui), 132, 255.
39. Folker Reichert, 'Odorico da Pordenone über Tibet', *AFH* 82 (1989), pp. 183–93. Cf. the more negative verdict of Berthold Laufer, 'Was Odoric of Pordenone ever in Tibet?', *TP* 15 (1914), pp. 405–18.
40. *DM*, p. 499/*MP*, I, p. 312 (tr. Ricci, p. 221). Hayton, i, 1, and iii, 46, Fr. text pp. 121, 214, Latin text pp. 261, 334–5.
41. *MP*, II ('Z text'), p. 45 (cf. trans., I, p. 326). Odoric, xxiii, 1, p. 463 (tr. Yule, *Cathay*, II, pp. 192–3). Cf. 'Mandeville', BL, Egerton ms. 1982, fo. 85r ('the maste citee of the world'): 'maste' is misread as 'most' in Mandeville, *Le livre*, ed. Malcolm Letts, *Mandeville's Travels. Texts and Translations*, 2 vols, HS² 101–2 (London, 1953), I (the 'Egerton' text), p. 144; cf. Deluz edn, p. 361, 'la plus grande du mounde'.
42. *DM*, p. 527/*MP*, I, p. 351 (tr. Ricci, p. 264).
43. *DM*, p. 539/*MP*, I, pp. 367–8 (tr. Ricci, p. 279). Odoric, xv, 1, p. 450 (tr. Yule, *Cathay*, II, pp. 163–4); cf. Mandeville, ed. Letts, I, p. 135 ('a great number of sons and daughters'), and ed. Deluz, p. 347. The idea that the Japanese are the 'sun people' mentioned in TR, §13, p. 10, has been discredited by John Andrew Boyle, 'Narayrgen or the People of the Sun', in W. Heissig, ed., *Altaica Collecta. Berichte und Vorträge der XVII. Permanent International Altaistic Conference 3.–8. Juni 1974 in Bonn/Bad Honnef* (Wiesbaden, 1976), pp. 131–6.
44. *DM*, pp. 536–7, 598/*MP*, I, pp. 365, 434 (tr. Ricci, pp. 276, 346). Odoric, xviii, 6, and xxvi, 12, pp. 457, 476 (tr. Yule, *Cathay*, II, pp. 176, 231). Hayton, i, 1, Fr. text p. 121, Latin text p. 261; hence Mandeville, ed. Letts, I, p. 127, has simply 'many isles', though Deluz edn, p. 337, reads 'plus de Vᵐ isles'.
45. *DM*, pp. 531–2/*MP*, I, pp. 357–8 (tr. Ricci, pp. 270–1). For 'Cipingu', see Pelliot, *Notes on Marco Polo*, I, p. 608.
46. Odoric, xiii, 1, p. 447 (tr. Yule, *Cathay*, II, pp. 154–5); hence Mandeville, ed. Letts, I, p. 133/ed. Deluz, pp. 344–5.
47. K. Enoki, 'Marco Polo and Japan', in *Oriente Poliano*, pp. 23–44.
48. Jacques Le Goff, 'The medieval West and the Indian Ocean: an oneiric horizon', in his *Time, Work and Culture in the Middle Ages*, tr. Arthur Goldhammer (Chicago, 1980), pp. 189–200. See also Carole Bercovici, 'Prolégomènes à l'étude de l'Inde au XIIIème siècle', in *Voyage, quête, pèlerinage dans la littérature et la civilisation médiévales: senefiance nº 2* (Aix-en-Provence, 1976), pp. 223–36.
49. See Critchley, pp. 91–2; and Rubiés, *Travel and Ethnology*, p. xvi.
50. *DM*, pp. 564–6/*MP*, I, p. 400, on St Thomas; *DM*, pp. 572–6/*MP*, I, pp. 407–11, on Adam's Peak (tr. Ricci, pp. 309–12, 319–22). Odoric, x, 6,

p. 442 (tr. Yule, *Cathay*, II, p. 141). Marignolli, pp. 538 (Adam), 544–5 (St Thomas) = 'Kronika Jana z Marignoly', pp. 497–9, 508 (tr. Yule, *Cathay*, III, pp. 232–3, 250–1). On Adam's Peak, cf. Ma Huan, *Ying-yai sheng-lan chiao-chu* (1433), tr. J.V.G. Mills, *The Overall Survey of the Ocean's Shores*, IIS, extra series (Cambridge, 1970), p. 127.

51. Ceylon: *DM*, p. 551/*MP*, I, p. 380 (tr. Ricci, p. 291); the story of the king's ruby (but without the qaghan's covetousness) is found also in Hayton, i, 6, Fr. text p. 126, Latin text p. 265, and (with two rubies) in Jordanus, *Mirabilia descripta*, Latin text p. 116 (tr. Yule, *Wonders*, p. 30). Nicoveran: Odoric, xvi, 4, p. 453 (tr. Yule, *Cathay*, II, pp. 169–70); hence Mandeville, ed. Letts, I, pp. 138–9/ed. Deluz, p. 351.

52. Friedrich Hirth and W.W. Rockhill, *Chau Ju-kua: His Work on the Chinese and Arab Trade in the Twelfth and Thirteenth Centuries, Entitled Chu-fan chï* (St. Petersburg, 1911), p. 73; for Cosmas, see the editors' note at p. 74.

53. *DM*, p. 543/*MP*, I, p. 371 (tr. Ricci, p. 282).

54. Larner, *Marco Polo*, pp. 81–2 and n.35 at p. 204; Critchley, pp. 91–2. For the islands of men and of women in Islamic geography, see Miquel, *La géographie humaine*, II, pp. 487, 493–5; for the *rukh*, ibid., p. 91.

55. Lamori: Odoric, xii, 3, p. 446 (tr. Yule, *Cathay*, II, p. 148). Tibet: ibid., xxxiii, 5, p. 486 (tr. Yule, *Cathay*, II, p. 254); hence Mandeville, ed. Letts, I, pp. 218–19/ed. Deluz, p. 474. Cf. WR, xxvi, 3, p. 234 (tr. Jackson and Morgan, p. 158), Bacot, 'Reconnaissance', p. 145, and Clauson, 'A propos du manuscrit Pelliot', p. 19.

56. *DM*, p. 464/*MP*, I, p. 271 (tr. Ricci, p. 181). For Pipino's gloss, see Reichert, *Begegnungen*, p. 161; Jackson, 'Marco Polo', p. 88; and for other examples, relating to Islam and the Muslims or to the 'idolators', Critchley, pp. 144–6.

57. Folker Reichert, 'Eine unbekannte Version der Asienreise des Odorichs von Pordenone', *DA* 43 (1987), pp. 531–73 (here pp. 546–9).

58. See Reichert, *Begegnungen*, pp. 173–96. For examples of mss. containing both Pipino's text and Odoric, see Larner, *Marco Polo*, pp. 112, 114.

59. Górka, *Anonymi descriptio Europae Orientalis*, introduction, pp. xxix–xxxix; pp. xxxix–il [*sic*], for the mss. – Paris, BN, lat. 5515, 5515A and 14693; Poitiers, Bibliothèque municipale, 263; and Leiden, Rijksuniversiteit, B.P.L. 66. See further Josef Deér, 'Ungarn in der Descriptio Europae Orientalis', *MIOG* 45 (1931), pp. 1–22 (here pp. 2–4).

60. Joseph Petit, 'Un capitaine du règne de Philippe le Bel: Thibaut de Chepoy', *MA* 10 = 2e série, 1 (1897), pp. 224–39 (here pp. 231–4). Jackson, 'Marco Polo', p. 86 and n.25.

61. Larner, *Marco Polo*, p. 112.

62. John J. Nitti, ed., *Juan Fernández de Heredia's Aragonese Version of the Libro de Marco Polo* (Madison, WI, 1980), introduction, esp. pp. v–vi, x–xvi, xxiii–xxx. Wesley Robertson Long, ed., *La Flor de las Ystorias de Orient* (Chicago, IL, 1934), introduction, esp. pp. 3–17, 33–7.

63. Rubió y Lluch, *Documents*, I, pp. 257, 279–80 (a *mapamundi*, probably the Catalan Atlas), 365 (nos. 274, 303, 411); cf. also p. 382 (no. 428) = Rubió y Lluch, *Diplomatari*, pp. 675–6 (no. 647).

64. Pilar Liria Montañes, ed., *"Libro de la maravillas del mundo" de Juan de Man-devilla* (Zaragoza, 1979): for the date, see the editor's introduction, pp. 20–1.

65. This is of course a slight over-simplification: see Carl Watkins, 'Memories of the marvellous in the Anglo-Norman realm', in Elisabeth Van Houts, ed., *Medieval Memories. Men, Women and the Past, 700–1300* (Harlow, 2001), pp. 92–112.

66. Wolfgang Giese, 'Tradition und Empirie in den Reiseberichten der Kronika Marignolova', *AK* 56 (1974), pp. 447–56.

67. *DM*, p. 305/*MP*, I, p. 73 (tr. Ricci, p. 1). See further Jackson, 'Marco Polo', pp. 90–1.

68. *DM*, p. 517/*MP*, I, p. 336 (tr. Ricci, p. 246).

69. *MP*, II ('Z text'), p. 41 (cf. tr., I, p. 309, n.4).

70. Odoric, xv, 3, pp. 451–2 (tr. Yule, *Cathay*, II, p. 166).

71. Larner, *Marco Polo*, pp. 133–6, 138–9.

72. Ibid., p. 45, citing Jacopo d'Acqui: text in Michieli, 'Il Milione', p. 158.

73. Larner, *Marco Polo*, pp. 79, 82–3.

74. Campbell, *Witness and the Other World*, p. 90.

75. Salamander: *DM*, pp. 376–7/*MP*, I, pp. 156–7 (tr. Ricci, pp. 73–4); for Pipino's more non-committal phrasing, see Critchley, p. 146. Unicorn and pygmies: *DM*, pp. 543–4/*MP*, I, pp. 372–3 (tr. Ricci, pp. 283–4). Odoric, xxiv, 2, pp. 468–9 (tr. Yule, *Cathay*, II, pp. 207–9), took a more conventional line regarding the pygmies (cf. also Mandeville, ed. Letts, I, pp. 146–7/ed. Deluz, p. 358), as did Jordanus, p. 117 (tr. Yule, *Wonders*, pp. 30–1), who located them in 'Java' (Sumatra).

76. Martin Gosman, 'Marco Polo's voyages: the conflict between confirmation and observation', in Von Martels, *Travel Fact*, p. 83. Larner, *Marco Polo*, pp. 83, 107–8.

77. Hyde, 'Real and imaginary journeys', pp. 139–40.

78. Jordanus, p. 113 (tr. Yule, *Wonders*, p. 18); for the unicorn in Africa, see ibid., p. 119 (tr. Yule, pp. 42–3).

79. Marignolli, p. 530 = 'Kronika Jana z Marignoly', p. 496 (tr. Yule, *Cathay*, III, p. 217). Cf. Odoric, ix, 1, p. 439 (tr. Yule, *Cathay*, II, pp. 132–3, 136); Jordanus, p. 116 (tr. Yule, *Wonders*, p. 27).

80. *WR*, xviii, 5, p. 211 (tr. Jackson and Morgan, p. 129). Cf. also *OM*, I, pp. 365–6.

81. *Libro del conosçimiento de todos los rregnos et tierras et señorios que son por el mundo*, ed. (from the Bayerische Staatsbibliothek ms. hisp. 150) María Jésus Lacarra *et al.* (Zaragoza, 1999), p. 157; tr. Clements Markham, *The Book of the Knowledge of All the Kingdoms, Lands and Lordships of the World*, HS² 29 (London, 1912), pp. 5–6.

82. Reichert, *Begegnungen*, p. 229.

83. Lach, *Asia*, I:1, pp. 69–70. Larner, *Marco Polo*, p. 148.

84. Reichert, *Begegnungen*, pp. 234–6.

85. *OM*, I, pp. 304–5, 354, on those who have not written from their own experience. For Carpini, ibid., I, p. 371, and II, p. 368; at I, p. 322, Bacon refers to those who had visited the Mongols, such as Rubruck *et alii*, and at I,

p. 356, he speaks of *libr*[*i*] *de moribus Tartarorum*, of which Rubruck's is apparently just one.

86. Ibid., I, p. 356; for other citations of Aethicus, see I, pp. 268, 302–3, 361–2, 364–5, 375, and II, pp. 234, 368. Phillips, *Medieval Expansion*, pp. 189–90.
87. Cited by Larner, *Marco Polo*, p. 137.
88. Ingrid Baumgärtner, 'Weltbild und Empirie. Die Erweiterung des kartographischen Weltbilds durch die Asienreisen des späten Mittelalters', *JMH* 23 (1997), pp. 227–53 (here pp. 251–2). John Larner, 'The Church and the Quattrocento Renaissance in geography', *Renaissance Studies* 12 (1998), pp. 26–39. Idem, *Marco Polo*, pp. 134–5, 147–8.
89. WR, xxix, 46, p. 269 (tr. Jackson and Morgan, p. 201).
90. Montecorvino, 'Epistolae I', §8, p. 342.
91. Marignolli, pp. 545–6 = 'Kronika Jana z Marignoly', pp. 508–9 (tr. Yule, *Cathay*, III, pp. 254–6); cf. also pp. 548–9 = 'Kronika Jana z Marignoly', pp. 509–10 (tr. Yule, *Cathay*, III, pp. 258–60, 261).
92. Mandeville, ed. Letts, I, pp. 141–3/ed. Deluz, pp. 356–9. Iain Macleod Higgins, *Writing East. The "Travels" of Sir John Mandeville* (Phildadelphia, 1997), pp. 143–9.
93. Cynocephali: *Libro del conosçimiento*, p. 175: *et llaman synfalos* (sentence wrongly punctuated; cf. text in *SF*, p. 572, and Markham trans., p. 48); for the headless race, see p. 159 (tr. Markham, p. 11).
94. John of Sulṭāniyya, *Libellus*, pp. 108–9; for Gog and Magog, see also ibid., p. 113, and Moranvillé, 'Mémoire', p. 449.
95. Clavijo, p. 212 (Le Strange trans., pp. 293–4, has 'fifteen').
96. R. Wittkower, 'Marco Polo and the pictorial tradition of the marvels of the East', in *Oriente Poliano*, pp. 155–72, and repr. in Wittkower, *Allegory and the Migration of Symbols*, pp. 75–92.
97. Moranvillé, 'Mémoire', p. 460.
98. Larner, *Marco Polo*, p. 91.
99. *OM*, III, p. 122, cited by Southern, *Western Views of Islam*, p. 57. See also *Opus tertium*, ed. Little, p. 62.
100. Jackson, 'William of Rubruck', pp. 65–71.
101. WR, xxvi, 11, p. 237 (tr. Jackson and Morgan, p. 163).
102. DM, pp. 573–5/MP, I, pp. 407–11 (tr. Ricci, pp. 319–22).
103. Bigalli, 'Giudizio escatologico', pp. 153–4 and n.2.
104. Lull, *Disputatio Christiani et Hamar Saraceni*, cited in Reichert, *Begegnungen*, p. 226 and n.167.
105. For some early 15th-century examples, see Hay, *Europe*, pp. 74–81 *passim*.
106. William of Malmesbury, *Gesta regum Anglorum*, iv, 347, ed. and tr. R.A.B. Mynors, R.M. Thomson and M. Winterbottom (Oxford, 1998), p. 600 (tr. p. 601).
107. WR, xxvi, 11, p. 237 (tr. Jackson and Morgan, p. 163).
108. *OM*, I, pp. 373, 400; also Bacon, *Opus tertium*, ed. Little, p. 62.
109. Marino Sanudo to the bishop of Ostia (1330), in Kunstmann, 'Studien', pp. 781, 788. 'Directorium', p. 383.
110. Hay, *Europe*, p. 77; cf. also Petrarch's dismissive comment about once-Christian Asia, cited ibid., p. 60.

111. *DM*, pp. 397–8/*MP*, I, pp. 181–3 (tr. Ricci, pp. 94–5). This did not prevent Polo from calling him 'Uncan', i.e. Ong Khan of the Kereyid: *DM*, p. 380/ *MP*, I, p. 162 (tr. Ricci, p. 78); Morgan, 'Prester John and the Mongols', pp. 165–6. Montecorvino, 'Epistolae II', §4, p. 348 (tr. in Moule, *Christians in China*, p. 173; tr. Dawson, p. 225).

112. *WR*, xvii, 2, p. 206 (tr. Jackson and Morgan, p. 122); and see *OM*, I, p. 367.

113. *DM*, p. 384/*MP*, I, pp. 165–6 (tr. Ricci, pp. 81–2).

114. C.F. Beckingham, 'An Ethiopian embassy to Europe *c*.1310', *Journal of Semitic Studies* 34 (1989), pp. 337–46, repr. in Beckingham and Hamilton, *Prester John*, pp. 197–206. Hamilton, 'Continental drift', pp. 251–3.

115. Burchard, 'Descriptio Terrae Sanctae', xiii, 8, in Laurent, *Peregrinatores*, p. 90. Southern, *Western Views of Islam*, pp. 63–4. On Burchard's attitudes, see Aryeh Grabois, 'Christian pilgrims in the thirteenth century and the Latin Kingdom of Jerusalem: Burchard of Mount Sion', in B.Z. Kedar, H.E. Mayer and R.C. Smail, eds, *Outremer. Studies in the History of the Crusading Kingdom of Jerusalem Presented to Joshua Prawer* (Jerusalem, 1982), pp. 285–96 (here p. 295).

116. *WR*, epilogue, 2, p. 330 (tr. Jackson and Morgan, p. 276).

117. Odoric, viii, 1, and x, 6, pp. 424, 442 (cf. tr. Yule, *Cathay*, II, pp. 117, 142). For Polo, see Critchley, p. 154; and for the views of another transmitter of *Poliana*, cf. Michieli, 'Il Milione', pp. 163–4, 165, 166.

118. Jordanus, pp. 114, 122 (tr. Yule, *Wonders*, pp. 23, 51–2).

119. See Von den Brincken, *Die „Nationes Christianorum Orientalium"*, pp. 312–27 *passim*.

120. Clavijo, p. 211 (tr. Le Strange, p. 292).

121. *OM*, I, pp. 290–1 (citing Esdras). Jacques Heers, 'De Marco Polo à Christophe Colomb: comment lire le *Devisement du monde?*', *JMH* 10 (1984), pp. 125–43 (here pp. 140–2). Valerie I.J. Flint, *The Imaginative Landscape of Christopher Columbus* (Princeton, NJ, 1992), pp. 24–5, 52, 118–19.

122. Folker Reichert, 'Columbus und Marco Polo – Asien in Amerika', *Zeitschrift für Historische Forschung* 15 (1988), pp. 1–63. Flint, *Imaginative Landscape*, pp. 64–8.

123. J.A. Williamson, ed., *The Cabot Voyages and Bristol Discovery under Henry VII*, HS² 70 (Cambridge, 1962), esp. pp. 45–50, 55–6, 88–9; Day's letter is translated at pp. 211–14; other documents at pp. 207–11. Phillips, *Medieval Expansion*, pp. 228–9.

124. Larner, *Marco Polo*, pp. 153–60.

125. Nitti, *Juan Fernández de Heredia's Aragonese Version*, p. xvi.

126. Flint, *Imaginative Landscape*, p. 130 (citing Mandeville). See also Columbus's letter to the Catholic monarchs during the first voyage (1492), in Martin Davies, ed., *Columbus in Italy. An Italian Versification of the Letter on the Discovery of the New World* (London, 1991), facsimile text p. 41 (tr. p. 49).

127. Odoric, xxii, 2, pp. 461–2 (tr. Yule, *Cathay*, II, pp. 187–8). Cf. *MP*, I, pp. 345–6, who does not mention colour (apart from blue war-paint), but is clearly speaking of a cultural group quite distinct from the Chinese, usually identified with the 'Meau-tze'; this passage is not found in the Tuscan or French–Italian texts.

CONCLUSION

In the middle of the thirteenth century the rapidly growing Mongol world-empire and the expansionist Christian West were undoubtedly on a collision course. In a series of campaigns (1237–42) Mongol armies had devastated the eastern marches of Latin Christendom and destroyed the outcrops of recent Catholic evangelism in Cumania. Whether they could have advanced as far as the Atlantic coast of Europe must remain a matter for speculation. In 1241 they penetrated only to the eastern borders of Germany and Bohemia, perhaps because their principal objective on that occasion was to chastise the Hungarian king. There is no doubt that they envisaged further conquests; this was the mission entrusted to them by Heaven. Nor is it self-evident, given the qaghan's capacity to muster formidable resources over a vast area, that the Mongols lacked the strength to inflict a severe reverse upon Béla IV's western neighbours.

That this grim new power which had arisen on the borders of the Latin world did not follow up the assault of 1241–2 owed less to Western strength than to conditions within the Mongol empire. The idea that internal divisions rendered the West an easier target for Mongol attacks would remain alive well into the following century. Papal attempts to remonstrate with the Mongols, through the embassies of 1245–7, achieved little other than the accumulation of valuable information about the newcomers. The Mongols understood diplomatic overtures from independent rulers only as a preliminary to submission. Papal efforts, too, both to erect a *cordon sanitaire* of schismatic and pagan client princes in Eastern Europe under the umbrella of union with Rome, and to secure concessions from apprehensive Muslim rulers in Syria and Egypt, came to nothing.

The Mongol invasion of Poland in 1259 was probably meant to herald the next forward thrust into Europe; and similarly Hülegü's campaign of 1260 – had it not been aborted – could have brought about the elimination of the Latin states in Syria and Palestine as independent entities. As in 1241–2, the reaction of the papacy – the one element in Catholic Europe capable of coordinating the resistance of Western princes – proved inadequate; the Curia again had too many pressing concerns just in terms of crusade projects, amid which the Mongols simply had to take their place. It was fortunate for the West that the disintegration of the Mongol empire in 1260–1 put paid to any plans the invaders may have harboured. Henceforward, such military operations as occurred were no longer mounted with the support of the centre, but were the exclusive responsibility of the successor-states – the Golden Horde in the Pontic and Caspian steppes and the Ilkhanate in the Near East, each at least as embroiled in conflict with the other as with its non-Mongol enemies.

This is not to deny that the Golden Horde continued to menace Latin Christendom after 1260. Fear of further Mongol incursions surfaces at frequent intervals in our sources. But apart from a few major attacks – notably the devastation of Hungary in 1285 and of Poland in 1287 – Mongol military operations were confined to raids. More indirectly, the protectorates established by the Golden Horde over non-Latin states – the schismatic Rus', Bulgarians and Byzantines, and pagan Lithuania – had the effect of fortifying these polities against Latin pressure. The Mongols may have reacted particularly sharply to Western encroachments on 'Ruthenia', where the line of princes died out in 1340 and Polish intervention sparked off a series of conflicts that lasted into the 1350s. At various points the rulers of the 'front-line states' – Hungary and Poland – are found reaching an accommodation with the enemy in order to fend off an attack. When they did prove ready to stand against the Mongols, on the other hand, they found themselves relatively isolated. The papacy responded more readily to Polish appeals for help than to those of the Hungarians; but recruitment for the crusade among the nobility and knights of Germany and other regions further west seems to have been remarkably unimpressive.

After c.1360 the collapse of the Golden Horde into civil war greatly reduced the Mongols' striking power and, despite Toqtamish's achievement in restoring the Horde, the two campaigns by the Central Asian conqueror Temür (Tamerlane) in the Pontic steppe inflicted irretrievable damage upon the khanate. These upheavals enabled neighbouring states, particularly Christian Hungary and pagan Lithuania, to encroach upon the Horde's lands and those of its satellites, whether Wallachia and Moldavia or the Rus' principalities, and to extend their own spheres of influence as far as the Black Sea. By the time of the battle of Tannenberg (1410) the khans' forces, by contrast, were reduced to being just one among a number of evenly-matched elements vying for territory and tribute

Relations between the Latin West and the Ilkhans developed along different lines. In the Near East, the Mongols' principal antagonists were the Muslim Mamlūks of Egypt and Syria, who from 1262 were in friendly contact with the rival Mongol power on the Volga, and Hülegü and his successors turned to Christian European states as potential allies. Despite a series of diplomatic exchanges down into the early fourteenth century, no military collaboration materialized. By the late thirteenth century the logistics of a major crusade to the eastern Mediterranean were too complex, and Western public opinion was rather too wary. The apparent friendliness of the Ilkhans has served both to mask Mongol aims and to distort the nature of the choice confronting the Franks of Syria and Palestine in 1260, when Hülegü's forces first reached the Mediterranean. It used to be thought that by failing to cooperate with the Mongols against the Mamlūks, who would eventually eliminate the Latin presence in 1291, the Franks of the kingdom of Jerusalem sealed its death-warrant. In 1260, however, there had been no question of collaboration between allies on equal terms; the Mongols accepted only abject submission. Nor should the assiduousness with which the Ilkhans pursued their courtship of the West after 1262 blind us to its character. Ilkhanid overtures belonged squarely in a tradition that is in evidence as early as 1221: that of enlisting the aid, or at least the neutrality, of more distant powers as a purely temporary measure, in order to secure the overthrow of an antagonist closer at hand.

By the time Temür subjugated most of Persia in the late fourteenth century, the Ilkhans had long passed from the scene. But Temür – a non-Chinggisid who ruled in the name of Chinggisid puppet khans and who aspired to recreate Chinggis Khan's world-empire – appeared to offer the same potential as an ally as had the Ilkhans. He not only devastated Mamluk Syria in 1400–1; he also dealt a crushing blow to the rising Ottoman Turks at Ankara in 1402. His campaigns in the Near East, though mounted at least partly on behalf of Islam, secured a reprieve for Christian states like Byzantium and Serbia. Despite the reservations that many observers felt, he was courted by the envoys of Western European monarchs as well as by those of the Byzantine government, and his envoy, Archbishop John of Sulṭāniyya, promoted his claims as a worthy ally to several Western powers. Yet for all this diplomatic activity, what Temür offered essentially fell short of what had been offered by the Ilkhans. Insofar as we can discern his aims at all clearly, he merely sought to capitalize on Latin Christian good will in order to foster trade.

The great invasion of Eastern Europe in 1241–2 had dealt a profound shock to the West. In the eyes of many, the advent of the Mongols appeared to fulfil scriptural prophecy or, still more probably, the predictions of the seventh-century writer Pseudo-Methodius; such conclusions may have been encouraged by the similar rumours that circulated about the invaders in Orthodox Rus', by reports also from the Islamic world, and by what was to be gleaned of the Mongols' own origin-myths. But after the initial shock had subsided, the Latin world slowly became acclimatized to the presence of this new pagan power on its eastern frontiers, a process in which Ilkhanid overtures undoubtedly played a part.

The new opportunities provided by the advent of the Mongols lay in the mission field and in commerce. The elimination of Muslim sovereignty throughout a considerable proportion of Western and Central Asia meant that Christian proselytism was freed from the impediments it had hitherto encountered. Attempts by members of the newly-founded Mendicant Orders to convert the Mongols to Latin Christianity began within twelve years of the invasion of Eastern Europe and continued for over a century. The friars' achievements, however, were limited. They made the greatest headway with schismatic Christians, such as the Alans in Khanbaligh; but only a few Mongol grandees were apparently won over; and the subject Chinese population remained virtually untouched. The Mongols' approach to religious matters, like that of other steppe peoples, was pluralist and syncretistic. Their rulers patronized the 'religious' within every confessional group, with the aim of benefiting from their prayers and from any other techniques they might have for influencing Nature – a stance that itself contributed to Western misperceptions of Ilkhanid diplomacy. The comparatively rigorous and uncompromising position taken by the friars prevented them from competing with the representatives of the rival faiths of Buddhism and Islam.

The missionary friars followed the same routes as the Latin traders who were visiting the Mongol world from the middle of the thirteenth century. The ports of Kaffa and Trebizond, on the Black Sea, and Tana, on the Sea of Azov, and the Persian city of Tabrīz became the gateway to a vast world to which Western merchants had previously had no access and of whose very existence they had been unaware; it included not merely territories, like China, that owed obedience to the Mongols, but also both northern and peninsular India, which did not. Even if the *Pax Mongolica* ceased to be a reality following the dissolution of the empire in 1260–1, it was still much easier to travel in Asia than in the pre-Chinggisid era; the Mongol khans took an active interest in commerce within their dominions and beyond their borders; and Latin Christians could now deal directly with Central Asian or Far Eastern merchants instead of through Muslim middle-men. That said, the profits which accrued to Western traders from protracted ventures to 'Cathay' are a matter for debate; and such ventures, in any case, may well have flourished for only a few decades in the early fourteenth century. The real success-story of Western commercial expansionism, in fact, was not so much the penetration of Eastern Asia as the opening-up of the more localized trade of the Black Sea region, which became an Italian, and largely a Genoese, preserve right down until the Ottoman conquest of Kaffa in 1475.

The still-born attempt to launch Ilkhanid–Western collaboration, the relatively fruitless efforts of the friars, and the short-lived operations of Latin merchants in the Far East left, nevertheless, a more enduring legacy. All three phenomena indirectly gave rise to written accounts which circulated in Western Europe and thus introduced the Mongol territories and their neighbours to a Latin readership. The most widely circulated among these accounts were the book put together by Marco Polo and Rustichello, the crusade treatise of Hayton, and the account of the East dictated by the Franciscan Odoric of Pordenone. It was thanks above all to these three works, along with the book of the armchair traveller 'Sir John Mandeville' (drawing heavily on Odoric), that the wealth of Cathay and of neighbouring regions acquired a near-proverbial familiarity which long outlasted the European presence in the Mongol dominions.

The newly available material on Asia took a considerable time to become entrenched, not least in cartography. More often than not, it had to contend or coexist with older cosmological ideas derived from Scripture and from the works of late Antiquity; some of Polo's revelations, especially, proved hard to swallow, precisely because his brand of 'marvels' did not constitute the diet that Western taste demanded and to which it had grown accustomed. Nevertheless, in however dim and distorted a form, during the last years of the fifteenth century Polo would act as the principal stimulus to those who sought a westerly route to the qaghan's dominions. At whatever stage they read his book – and whether or not, indeed, they ever read it, as opposed to imbibing a general familiarity with its statements about Cathay and Cipingu – the enterprises of Columbus and of Cabot were in the tradition, not of contemporary Portuguese ventures into the African Atlantic, but of their Genoese and Venetian forebears who had made the daunting journey across Asia by land in the late thirteenth and fourteenth centuries.

APPENDIX I: THE AUTHENTICITY OF MARCO POLO'S TRAVELS

D id Marco Polo actually visit China or did he, as Dr Frances Wood claimed in a recent book, journey no further than the Crimea?[1] The book attracted a good deal of attention from the media. But reservations about the authenticity of the Venetian's travels had been expressed before: in 1978 Professor John Haeger had suggested that Polo's experience of the Far East was confined to Mongolia and the northernmost regions of China.[2] The grounds for doubting that Polo ever reached the Far East comprise: passages that inflate the Polos' importance by claiming, for instance, that they were instrumental in the capture of the city of Hsiang-yang (which transpired at least one year prior to their arrival in China) or that Marco governed the city of Yang-chou on Qubilai's behalf; the fact that so many Chinese proper names and terms appear in Persian garb; the omission of phenomena that would have made a strong impression on a genuine visitor from the West, such as the Great Wall, foot-binding, or tea-drinking; and the generally impersonal and formulaic tone in which the book describes numerous Chinese cities.

Most of these objections have been dealt with fairly rapidly in the articles and reviews provoked by Dr Wood's work.[3] That Polo's book exaggerates his standing, and that of his father and uncle, in the qaghan's empire is not in itself an argument that they were never there; and it is in any case noteworthy that the 'Z' text (which may well be descended from an early version) omits both participation in the siege of Hsiang-yang and the governorship of Yang-chou. In any case, authentic travellers have often yielded to the temptation to brag: Isolo ('Chol') – to take an exact contemporary of the Polos – convinced Rashīd al-Dīn that he was king (*pādishāh*) of his native city of Pisa.[4] As for Persian – during the Mongol era the *lingua franca* among the predominantly Muslim merchants engaged in trade in the Far East[5] – it was almost certainly one of the 'four languages and scripts' Marco allegedly acquired (which probably included Mongolian and the two scripts in which it was written during Qubilai's reign, Uighur and 'Phags-pa),[6] and it was surely the language of many of his informants. He is highly unlikely to have learned Chinese. The customary *riposte* to the arguments about his silences – that during his time in China, as an agent of the alien Mongol regime, he was insulated from the indigenous Han population and hence failed to notice much that we should like him to have seen – is not totally convincing; but the omissions themselves do not present insuperable obstacles. It is now known that the Great Wall as such did not exist in the thirteenth century: defensive walls there certainly were in the north, but not the continuous structure with which we are familiar today, which dates from the Ming era.[7] Apropos of foot-binding, it should be noted in Polo's defence that one version of the text does comment on the dainty steps taken by Chinese women, though explaining that this was to preserve their virginity.[8]

Nor is the impersonal way in which so many Chinese cities are described as damning as we might think. This was precisely the tone in which reports were traditionally drafted by Chinese emissaries – or, for that matter, by diplomats from the Polos' mother city.[9] Overall, however, I suggest that we need to focus on the book as a whole, rather than simply on the sections that deal with China. This is especially necessary in the context of omissions, where we have to bear in mind three circumstances: the way in which the book was written, the sort of book it is, and the framework within which Marco Polo experienced life in the Far East.

The book came into existence because in 1298 Marco, in a Genoese prison, recounted his experiences to a fellow captive, the Pisan romance-writer Rustichello. That he was able to supplement memory with material written during his time in the East is uncertain; but there is nothing inherently improbable in the statement (found only in Ramusio's sixteenth-century version) that he sent home to Venice for his notes to be forwarded.[10] We simply do not know what he told Rustichello – or what the latter determined to leave out because it struck him as lacking in interest. The book which the two men produced is in fact not Polo's memoirs or a travel itinerary, but a work of geography, only loosely based around the Polos' travels (the precise course of which is irretrievable).[11] In fact, the chapters on China, which actually present a remarkable amount of detail, are less problematic than the comparatively sketchy and superficial account of Western Asia. The reason for this is that the Polos' return journey did not take them overland. Arriving from China by sea at Hurmuz in 1295, Marco was in a position to describe only western Persia (like China itself) from recent experience, possibly relying on notes; the rest of Persia and Central Asia he had not seen since the age of seventeen, more than twenty years previously.

Marco Polo spent the whole of his career in the Far East as a servitor – a relatively minor servitor, perhaps – of the qaghan Qubilai; and as we saw (p. 313) he may have passed a significant proportion of this period at sea. He belonged to that class of foreigners whom the Mongols employed in administering China. They were drawn from a wide range of peoples: Uighurs, Tibetans, Muslims from Central and Western Asia: the imperial government and the subject Chinese characterized them all alike by the Chinese term *Sse-mu*, 'Westerners'. In other words, Marco was what might be called an 'honorary Mongol': it was through the eyes of the conquerors that he saw China, and the picture he paints of conditions in Qubilai's dominions is refracted through a Mongol prism.[12] This in itself is enough to account for those peculiarities of the sections on China which have attracted the most adverse comment: the tone that might suggest a vantage-point somewhere in the borderlands between Mongolia and China (Haeger); the omission of details of Chinese society that we might now regard as indispensable (Wood). The limitations of the experience of the Far East on which it was based, and the unusual circumstances in which it was first put together in Genoa, need to be borne in mind if we are to jettison expectations of its attitudes and contents that are quite unrealistic.

Notes

1. Frances Wood, *Did Marco Polo Go to China?* (London, 1995); see also her 'Did Marco Polo go to China?', *Asian Affairs* 27 (1996), pp. 296–304.
2. John W. Haeger, 'Marco Polo in China? Problems with internal evidence', *Bulletin of Sung-Yuan Studies* 14 (1978), pp. 22–30. For a more restrained expression of scepticism than Wood's, cf. Franke, 'Sino-Western contacts', pp. 53–4, where Polo is given 'the benefit of the doubt'.
3. See D.O. Morgan, 'Marco Polo in China – or not', *JRAS*, 3rd series, 6 (1996), pp. 221–5; Igor de Rachewiltz, 'Marco Polo went to China', *ZS* 27 (1997), pp. 34–92; Jean-Pierre Voiret, 'China, "objektiv" gesehen: Marco Polo als Berichterstatter', *AS* 51 (1997), pp. 805–21 (here pp. 815–19); Jackson, 'Marco Polo'; Ugo Tucci, 'Marco Polo andò veramente in Cina?', *SV*, n.s., 33 (1997), pp. 49–59; Larner, *Marco Polo*, pp. 58–67. Jørgen Jensen, 'The world's most diligent observer', *AS* 51 (1997), pp. 719–27, argues specifically that Marco visited Sumatra.
4. Jahn, *Die Frankengeschichte*, Tafel 45, facsimile of Persian text, ms. Hazine 1653, fo. 415v (German trans., p. 53). It is, of course, equally possible that Rashīd al-Dīn himself chose to inflate the status of Isolo, described as being on terms of 'friendship and concord [*dūstī wa-ittiḥād*] with the Mongol rulers and the house of Chinggis Khan', as a means of glorifying his own master, the Ilkhan.
5. Huang, 'Persian language', pp. 83–95.
6. *DM*, pp. 317–18/*MP*, I, pp. 85–6 (tr. Ricci, pp. 12–13). Reichert, *Begegnungen*, p. 115. The other language was doubtless Turkish. The older Polos likewise learned Mongolian: *DM*, p. 310/*MP*, I, p. 77 (cf. Ricci trans., p. 6). See more generally Igor de Rachewiltz, 'Some remarks on the language problem in Yüan China', *Journal of the Oriental Society of Australia* 5 (1967), pp. 65–80.

7. Arthur Waldron, 'The problem of the Great Wall of China', *HJAS* 42 (1983), pp. 643–63. Idem, *The Great Wall of China: From History to Myth* (Cambridge, 1990).
8. MP, II ('Z' text), p. 38; also I, p. 305 (tr. Ricci, p. 213). Voiret, 'China, "objektiv" gesehen', pp. 812, 816.
9. Critchley, pp. 78–80.
10. Ibid., p. 21. Larner, *Marco Polo*, pp. 52, 88–90.
11. Heers, 'De Marco Polo à Christophe Colomb', pp. 125–35.
12. See the comments of Larner, *Marco Polo*, pp. 101–2.

APPENDIX II: GLOSSARY

basqaq   (Turkish) 'Resident' appointed to supervise a subject ruler and muster resources on the Mongols' behalf; referred to by Arabic/Persian authors as *shiḥna*

il or *el*   (Turkish) Literally 'peace'; also 'submission'

jizya   (Arabic) The poll-tax levied by Islamic governments on the 'Peoples of the Book' (e.g. Christians and Jews)

noyan   (Mongolian) Military commander; the Muslim equivalent is amir

ongghon   (Mongolian; plural *ongghod*) Felt image of an ancestor

ortogh   (Mongolian) Merchant acting in partnership with a Mongol sovereign or prince

qaghan   (Turkish) Steppe emperor; 'Great Khan' of the Mongols

qumis   (Mongolian; from Turkish *qımız*) Fermented mare's milk, a beverage highly prized among the steppe peoples

quriltai   assembly of princes, princesses and commanders, called to choose a qaghan or to deliberate on other important matters such as forthcoming campaigns

shiḥna   (Arabic) See *basqaq* above

toyin   (Mongolian; from Chinese *tao-yen*, 'man of the path') Buddhist priest or lama

tümen   (Turkish) A Mongol military unit, notionally comprising 10,000 men

ulus   (Mongolian) Complex of herds, grazing-grounds and peoples granted to a Mongol prince; used especially of the larger territorial units held by Chinggis Khan's sons and their descendants

yasa   (Turkish; Mongolian *jasa*/*jasagh*) Regulation issued by a Mongol ruler

APPENDIX III: GENEALOGICAL TABLES AND LISTS OF RULERS

I   The Mongol Qaghans and their kinsmen in Central Asia
(showing persons mentioned in the text; qaghans in capitals)

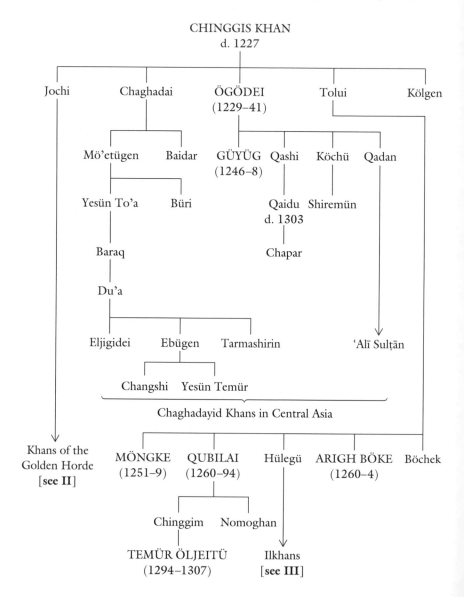

II Khans of the Golden Horde

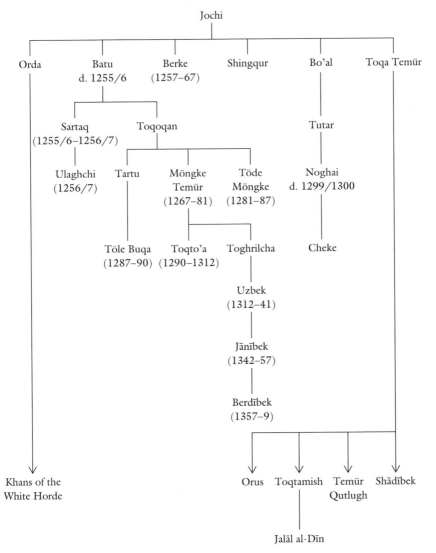

Jochi

Orda — Batu (d. 1255/6) — Berke (1257–67) — Shingqur — Bo'al — Toqa Temür

Sartaq (1255/6–1256/7) — Toqoqan — Tutar

Ulaghchi (1256/7) — Tartu — Möngke Temür (1267–81) — Töde Möngke (1281–87) — Noghai d. 1299/1300

Töle Buqa (1287–90) — Toqto'a (1290–1312) — Toghrilcha — Cheke

Uzbek (1312–41)

Jānībek (1342–57)

Berdībek (1357–9)

Khans of the White Horde

Orus — Toqtamish — Temür Qutlugh — Shādībek

Jalāl al-Dīn

III Ilkhans of Persia

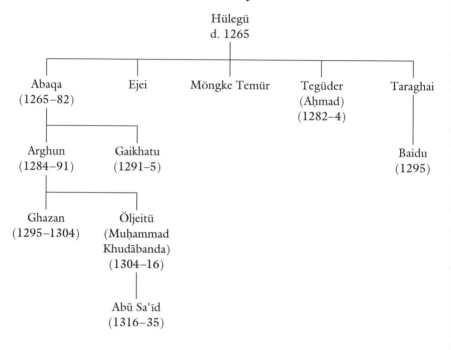

Hülegü
d. 1265

Abaqa (1265–82)	Ejei	Möngke Temür	Tegüder (Aḥmad) (1282–4)	Taraghai

Arghun (1284–91) Gaikhatu (1291–5)

Baidu (1295)

Ghazan (1295–1304) Öljeitü (Muḥammad Khudābanda) (1304–16)

Abū Saʿīd (1316–35)

IV Popes

Honorius III	1216–27
Gregory IX	1227–41
Celestine IV	1241
Innocent IV	1243–54
Alexander IV	1254–61
Urban IV	1261–4
Clement IV	1265–8
Gregory X	1271–6
Innocent V	1276
Adrian V	1276
John XXI	1276–7
Nicholas III	1277–80
Martin IV	1281–5
Honorius IV	1285–7
Nicholas IV	1288–92
Celestine V	1294
Boniface VIII	1294–1303
Benedict XI	1303–4
Clement V (at Avignon from 1309)	1305–14

John XXII	1316–34
Benedict XII	1334–42
Clement VI	1342–52
Innocent VI	1352–62
Urban V	1362–70
Gregory XI (returns to Rome 1377)	1371–8

(Rome)		(Avignon)	
Urban VI	(1378–89)	Clement VII	(1378–94)
Boniface IX	(1389–1404)	Benedict XIII	(1394–1417)
Innocent VII	(1404–6)		
Gregory XII	(1406–15)		

V Kings of Hungary

Béla IV	1235–70
István V	1270–2
László IV 'the Cuman'	1272–90
András III	1290–1301
Carobert (Charles Robert of Anjou)	1301–42
Lájos (Louis) I	1342–82
Maria	1382–7
Sigismund of Luxemburg	1387–1437

VI(a) Polish dukes at Cracow

Bolesław V 'the Chaste'	1241–79
Leszek 'the Black'	1279–88

VI(b) Kings of Poland

Władysław I Łokietek ('the Short')	1320–33
Casimir III	1333–70
Louis I (of Hungary)	1370–82
Jadwiga (Hedwig)	1382–6
Władysław II (Jogailo of Lithuania)	1386–1434

VII Kings of Bohemia

Václav I	1230–53
Ottokar II	1253–78
Václav II	1278–1305
Václav III	1305–6
John (of Luxemburg)	1310–46

BIBLIOGRAPHY

Manuscript sources

AN	J448, J451
BL	Cotton, Vespasian B XI (Hagnaby chronicle)
BN	lat. 3768, fos 76v–81r (letter of Eudes de Châteauroux, incorporating those of Smbat and Eljigidei, 1248–9)
Graz Universitätsbibliothek	1221 (John of Sulṭāniyya, *Libellus de notitia orbis*)
IUB	187 (Julian, *Epistula*; letters of 1241; prophetic discussion between Aristotle and Alexander)
MOL	DF 207181 (bull of Pope Clement VI, 1344)
	DF 290697, DF 290698 (letters of Uros, abbot of St. Martin in Pannonia [Pannonhalma], 1241)
	DL 40468
	DL 101957
OOLB	446 (report of Russian cleric Peter to First Council of Lyons, 1245)

From this point only works that appear in more than one footnote are listed.

Printed primary sources

Abū Shāma, Shihāb al-Dīn Abu l-Qāsim, *al-Dhayl 'alā l-Rawḍatayn*, ed. M.Z. al-Kawtharī as *Tarājim rijāl al-qarnayn al-sādis wa l-sābi'* (Cairo, 1366 H./ 1947).

Andrea Dandolo, 'Chronica per extensum descripta', *RIS²*, XII:1.

Andrea de Redusiis de Quero, 'Chronicon Tarvisinum', *RIS*, XIX.

Andrew of Perugia, 'Epistola', in *SF*, pp. 369–77; tr. in Dawson, *Mongol Mission*, pp. 235–7; a more critical edition in Brugnoli, pp. 10–13.

'Annales Admuntenses. Continuatio Garstensis', *MGHS*, IX.

'Annales capituli Cracoviensis', *MGHS*, XIX.

'Annales capituli Posnaniensis', *MGHS*, XXIX.

'Annales Colmarienses maiores', *MGHS*, XVII.

'Annales Erphordenses', *MGHS*, XVI.

'Annales Frisacenses', *MGHS*, XXIV.

'Annales Marbacenses', *MGHS*, XVII.

'Annales Mechovienses', *MGHS*, XIX.

'Annales Mellicenses. Continuatio Lambacensis', *MGHS*, IX.

'Annales monasterii de Burton', *AM*, I.

'Annales monasterii de Theokesberia', *AM*, I.

'Annales Polonorum', *MGHS*, XIX.

'Annales S. Justinae Patavini', *MGHS*, XIX.

'Annales S. Pantaleonis Coloniensis', *MGHS*, XXII.

'Annales Sancti Rudberti Salisburgenses', *MGHS*, IX.

'Annales Sandivogii', *MGHS*, XXIX.

'Annales Scheftlarienses maiores', *MGHS*, XVII.

'Annales Stadenses', *MGHS*, XVI.

'Annales Wormatienses', *MGHS*, XVII.

Annali Genovesi di Caffaro e de' suoi continuatori dal MXCIX al MCCXCII, ed. L.P. Belgrano *et al.*, Fonti per la Storia d'Italia, 5 vols (Rome, 1890–1929).

Aubry of Trois-Fontaines, 'Cronica', *MGHS*, XXIII.

Bacon, Roger, *Opus maius*, ed. John Henry Bridges, 3 vols (London and Oxford, 1897–1900).

Bacon, Roger, *Opus tertium*, partial ed. A.G. Little (Aberdeen, 1912, repr. Farnborough, 1966); 'Opus tertium', in *Fr. Rogeri Bacon opera quaedam hactenus inedita*, ed. J.S. Brewer, RS (London, 1859, vol. I only published).

'Balduini Ninovensis chronicon', *MGHS*, XXV.

Bar Hebraeus, Gregorius Abu l-Faraj, *Chronicon ecclesiasticum*, ed. and tr. J.B. Abbeloos and T.J. Lamy, 3 vols (Louvain, 1872–7).

Bar Hebraeus, Gregorius Abu l-Faraj, *Makhtebhânúth zabhnê*, tr. E.A. Wallis Budge, *The Chronography of Gregory Abu'l-Faraj . . . Commonly Known as Bar Hebraeus*, 2 vols (Oxford and London, 1932), I (trans.).

Bar Hebraeus (Ibn al-'Ibrī), Gregorius Abu l-Faraj, *Mukhtaṣar ta'rīkh al-duwal*, ed. Anṭūn Ṣāliḥānī (Beirut, 1890; repr. 1403 H./1983).

Bartholomew Cotton, *Historia Anglicana*, ed. H.R. Luard, RS (London, 1859).

Baybars al-Manṣūrī al-Dawādār, Rukn al-Dīn, *Zubdat al-fikra fī ta'rīkh al-hijra*, ed. D.S. Richards, Bibliotheca Islamica 42 (Beirut, 1419 H./1998).

Benedict Polonus, 'Relatio', in *SF*, pp. 131–44; tr. in Dawson, *Mongol Mission*, pp. 77–84.

Bielowski, August, *et al.*, eds, *Monumenta Poloniae Historica (Pomniki dziejowe polski)*, 6 vols (Lwów, 1864–93).

Bihl, Michael, O.F.M., and Moule, A.C., 'De duabus epistolis fratrum minorum Tartariae aquilonaris an. 1323', *AFH* 16 (1923), pp. 89–112; partial trans. by A.C. Moule, 'Fourteenth-century missionary letters', *The East and the West* 19 (1921), pp. 357–66.

Bihl, Michael, and Moule, A.C., 'Tria nova documenta de missionibus fr. min. Tartariae aquilonaris annorum 1314–1322', *AFH* 17 (1924), pp. 55–71.

Böhmer, J.F., 'Briefe über den Anmarsch der Mongolen gegen Deutschland im Jahr 1241', in K.Ed. Förstemann, ed., *Neue Mittheilungen aus dem Gebiet historisch-antiquarischer Forschungen*, IV:2 (Halle, 1839), pp. 105–17.

Brewer, J.S., ed., *Monumenta Franciscana*, RS (London, 1858).

Brosset, M.F., *Histoire de la Siounie*, 2 vols (St Petersburg, 1864–6).

Bruno of Olmütz, 'Relatio de statu ecclesiae in regno Alemanniae (1273. Dec. 16.)', *MGHLeg.*, III, pp. 589–94 (no. 620).

Budge, E.A. Wallis, tr., *The monks of Kûblâi Khân emperor of China* (London, 1928).

Busson, G., and Ledru, A., eds, 'Actus pontificum Cenomannis in urbe degentium', *Archives Historiques du Maine* 2 (1901), pp. 1–336.

'Carmina de regno Ungariae destructo per Tartaros', *MGHS*, XXIX.

Chaplais, Pierre, ed., *Diplomatic Documents Preserved in the Public Record Office*, I. *1101–1272* (London, 1964).

Chronica Johannis de Oxenedes, ed. H. Ellis, RS (London, 1859).

'Chronica minor auctore Minorita Erphordiensi', *MGHS*, XXIV.

'Chronica XXIV Generalium Ordinis Minorum', *Analecta Franciscana*, III (Quaracchi, 1897).

'Chronici Hungarici compositio saeculi XIV', ed. Alexander Domanovszky, *SRH*, I, pp. 217–505.

The Chronicle of Bury St. Edmunds (1212–1301), ed. and tr. Antonia Gransden, Nelson's Medieval Texts (London, 1964).

The Chronicle of Melrose, from the Cottonian Manuscript, Faustina B.IX in the British Museum, facsimile edn by Alan Orr Anderson and Marjorie Ogilvie Anderson (London, 1936).

The Chronicle of Novgorod 1016–1471, tr. Robert Michell and Nevill Forbes, CS, 3rd series, 25 (London, 1914).

Chronicon Budense, ed. J. Podhradczky (Buda, 1838).

'Chronicon Dubnicense', in Flórián Mátyás, ed., *Historiae Hungaricae fontes domestici*, 4 vols (Leipzig, 1881–5), III, pp. 1–207.

'Chronicon Hanoniense quod dicitur Balduini Avennensis', *MGHS*, XXV.

'Chronicon S. Medardi Suessionensis', in D'Achéry, ed., *Spicilegium*, II, pp. 486–92.

Chronique d'Amadi, ed. René de Mas Latrie (Paris, 1891).

'Chronique de Primat, traduite par Jean de Vignay', *RHGF*, XXIII.

Chronique du Religieux de Saint-Denys contenant le règne de Charles VI, de 1380 à 1422, ed. Louis François Bellaguet, 6 vols (Paris, 1839–52).

Chronographia regum Francorum, ed. H. Moranvillé, 3 vols (Paris, 1891–7).

Clavijo, Ruy González de, *Embajada a Tamorlán*, ed. Francisco López Estrada (Madrid, 1943); tr. G. Le Strange, *Embassy to Tamerlane 1403–1406* (London, 1928).

'Continuatio Altahensis', *MGHS*, XVII.

'Continuatio Sancrucensis secunda', *MGHS*, IX.

'Cronica Reinhardsbrunnensis', *MGHS*, XXX.

'Cronica S. Petri Erfordensis moderna', *MGHS*, XXX.

D'Achéry, Luc, ed., *Spicilegium sive collectio veterum aliquot scriptorum qui in Galliae bibliothecis delituerant*, new edn by Étienne Baluze and L.F.J. de la Barre, 3 vols (Paris, 1723).

Dawson, Christopher, ed., *The Mongol Mission. Narratives and Letters of the Franciscan Missionaries in Mongolia and China in the Thirteenth and Fourteenth Centuries* (London and New York, 1955).

'De invasione Tartartorum fragmentum', *MGHS*, XXIX.

Delaville le Roulx, J., ed., *Cartulaire général de l'Ordre des Hospitaliers de S. Jean de Jérusalem (1100–1310)*, 4 vols (Paris, 1894–1906).

al-Dhahabī, Shams al-Dīn Abū 'Abd-Allāh Muḥammad ibn 'Uthmān, *Taʾrīkh al-Islām 611–620*, ed. 'Umar 'Abd al-Salām Tadmurī (Beirut, 1417 H./1997); *651–660*, ed. 'Umar 'Abd al-Salām Tadmurī (Beirut, 1419 H./1999).

Dietrich von Nyem, *De scismate libri tres*, ed. G. Erler (Leipzig, 1890).

'Directorium ad passagium faciendum', *RHCDA*, II, pp. 365–517.

Dörrie, Heinrich, 'Drei Texte zur Geschichte der Ungarn und Mongolen. Die Missionsreisen des fr. Iulianus O.P. ins Ural-Gebiet (1234/5) und nach Rußland (1237) und der Bericht des Erzbischofs Peter über die Tartaren', *Nachrichten der Akademie der Wissenschaften in Göttingen, phil.-hist. Klasse* (1956), no. 6, pp. 125–202.

Ellis, Sir Henry, ed., *Original Letters Illustrative of English History*, 11 vols (London, 1824–46).

Emler, Josef, ed., *Fontes rerum Bohemicarum. Prameny dějin českých*, 7 vols published of 8 (Prague, 1873–1922).

'Ex Historiae regum Franciae continuatione Parisiensi', *MGHS*, XXVI.

Fejér, György, ed., *Codex diplomaticus Hungariae ecclesiasticus ac civilis*, 11 vols in 40 (Buda, 1829–44).

Fidenzio of Padua, 'Liber recuperationis Terrae Sanctae', in *BBTS*, II, pp. 1–60.

Finke, Heinrich, ed., *Papsttum und Untergang des Templerordens*, 3 vols (Münster, 1907).

Flores historiarum, ed. H.R. Luard, RS, 3 vols (London, 1890).

František of Prague, 'Chronica Pragensis', *FRB*, IV, pp. 347–456; also ed. as 'Continuatio Francisci Pragensis', in Johann Loserth, ed., *Die Königsaaler Geschichts-Quellen mit den Zusätzen und der Fortsetzung des Domherrn Franz von Prag*, FRAS[1] 8 (Vienna, 1875), pp. 535–606.

Frenz, Thomas, and Herde, Peter, eds, *Das Brief- und Memorialbuch des Albert Behaim*, MGH Briefe des späten Mittelalters 1 (Munich, 2000).

Friedrich, Gustav, *et al.*, eds, *Codex diplomaticus et epistolaris regni Bohemiae*, 5 vols in 8 parts so far (Prague, 1907–93).

Galician-Volynian Chronicle, in *PSRL*, II. *Ipatievskaia letopis'*, 2nd edn (St Petersburg, 1908); tr. George A. Perfecky, *The Hypatian Codex, Part II: The Galician-Volynian Chronicle*, Harvard Series in Ukrainian Studies 16:2 (Munich, 1974).

Galstian, A.G., *Armianskie istochniki o mongolakh* (Moscow, 1962).

Galvano Fiamma, 'Opusculum de rebus gestis ab Azone, Luchino, et Johanne Vicecomitibus', *RIS*[2], XII.

'Gesta Boemundi archiepiscopi Treverensis', *MGHS*, XXIV.

'Gestes des Chiprois', *RHCDA*, II, pp. 651–872; tr. Paul Crawford, *The 'Templar of Tyre'. Part III of the 'Deeds of the Cypriots'*, CTT 6 (Aldershot, 2003).

'Gestorum Treverorum continuatio quarta', *MGHS*, XXIV.

Giorgio Stella, 'Annales Genuenses', *RIS*[2], XVII:2.

Giovanni Villani, *Cronica*, ed. Francesco Gherardi Dragomanni, 4 vols, Collezione di storici e cronisti italiani editi ed inediti 1–4 (Firenze, 1844).

Göckenjan, Hansgerd, and Sweeney, James Ross, eds, *Der Mongolensturm. Berichte von Augenzeugen und Zeitgenossen 1235–1250*, Ungarns Geschichtsschreiber 3 (Graz, Köln etc., 1985).

Golubovich, Girolamo, ed., *Biblioteca bio-bibliografica della Terra Santa e dell'Oriente francescano*, 5 vols (Quaracchi-Firenze, 1906–27).

Górka, Olgierd, ed., *Anonymi descriptio Europae orientalis »imperium Constantinopolitanum, Albania, Serbia, Bulgaria, Ruthenia, Ungaria, Polonia, Bohemia« anno MCCCVIII exarata* (Cracow, 1916).

Guillaume Adam, 'De modo Sarracenos extirpandi', *RHCDA*, II, pp. 519–55.

Guillaume de Nangis, 'Chronicon', *RHGF*, XX.

Guillaume de Nangis, 'Gesta Ludovici sanctae memoriae vegis Franciae', *RHGF*, XX.

Guillaume de Nangis, 'Gesta Philippi tertii Francorum regis'/'Vie de Philippe III', *RHGF*, XX.

Györffy, György, 'Adatok a románok XIII. századi történetéhez és a román allam kezdeteihez (I. rész.)', *Történelmi Szemle* 7 (1964), pp. 1–25.

Hagnaby chronicle, BL Cotton ms. Vespasian B XI.

Hayton of Gorigos, 'La flor des estoires de la terre d'Orient', *RHCDA*, II, French text pp. 111–253, Latin text pp. 255–363.

Henry of Livonia, *Chronicon*, ed. Leonid Arbusow and Albert Bauer, *Heinrichs Livländische Chronik*, SRG (Hannover, 1955); tr. James A. Brundage, *The Chronicle of Henry of Livonia* (Madison, WI, 1961).

'Hermanni Altahensis annales', *MGHS*, XVII.

Hirsch, Theodor, *et al.*, eds, *Scriptores rerum Prussicarum. Die Geschichtsquellen der preussischen Vorzeit bis zum Untergange der Ordensherrschaft*, 5 vols (Leipzig, 1861–74).

Höfler, Constantin, ed., *Albert von Beham und Regesten Pabst Innocenz IV.* (Stuttgart, 1847).

Huillard-Bréholles, J.L.A., ed., *Historia diplomatica Friderici Secundi*, 6 vols in 11 (Paris, 1852–61).

Humbert of Romans, 'Opusculum tripartitum', in Orthuinus Gratius, *Fasciculum rerum expetendarum et fugiendarum*, new edn by Edward Brown, 2 vols (London, 1690), II, pp. 185–229.

Hurmuzaki, Eudoxiu de, Densusianu, Nic., *et al.*, eds, *Documente privitóre la istoria Românilor*, 19 vols in 36 (Bucarest and Cernăuţi, 1887–1938).

Ibn 'Abd al-Ẓāhir, Muḥyī al-Dīn Abu l-Faḍl 'Abd-Allāh, *al-Rawḍ al-zāhir fī sīrat al-malik al-Ẓāhir*, ed. 'Abd al-'Azīz al-Khuwayṭir (Riyāḍ, 1396 H./1976).

Ibn Abi l-Ḥadīd, 'Izz al-Dīn Abū Ḥāmid, *Sharḥ Nahj al-balāgha*, partial ed. and tr. Mukhtār Jabalī, *Les invasions mongoles en Orient vécues par un savant arabe* (Paris, 1995).

Ibn al-ʿAmīd, al-Makīn ibn Jirjīs, *Kitāb al-majmūʿ al-mubārak*, ed. Claude Cahen, 'La «Chronique des Ayyoubides» d'al-Makīn b. al-ʿAmīd', *BEO* 15 (1955–7), pp. 108–84; tr. Anne-Marie Eddé and Françoise Micheau, *Al-Makīn ibn al-ʿAmīd. Chronique des Ayyoubides (602–658/1205–6–1259–60)*, DRHC 16 (Paris, 1994).

Ibn al-Athīr, ʿIzz al-Dīn Abu l-Ḥasan ʿAlī, *al-Kāmil fi l-taʾrīkh*, 12 vols (Beirut, 1385–6 H./1965–6).

Ibn Faḍl-Allāh al-ʿUmarī: see al-ʿUmarī.

Ibn al-Labbād (ʿAbd al-Laṭīf al-Baghdādī): see Cahen (below).

Ibn Wāṣil, Abū ʿAbd-Allāh Jamāl al-Dīn Muḥammad ibn Sālim, *Mufarrij al-kurūb fi akhbār banī Ayyūb*, ed. Jamāl al-Dīn al-Shayyāl *et al.*, 5 vols (Cairo, 1953–77); also BN ms. arabe 1703.

'Iohannis Longi Chronica S. Bertini', *MGHS*, XXV.

Iorga, N., 'Notes et extraits pour servir à l'histoire des croisades au XVᵉ siècle', *ROL* 4 (1896), pp. 25–118, 226–320, 503–622.

Irgang, Winfried, ed., *Schlesisches Urkundenbuch*, II. *1231–1250* (Vienna etc., 1978).

Jacques de Vitry, *Epistolae*, ed. R.B.C. Huygens, *Lettres de Jacques de Vitry (1160/70–1240) évêque de Saint-Jean-d'Acre* (Leiden, 1960).

Jahn, Karl, ed., *Die Frankengeschichte des Rašīd ad-Dīn*, 2nd edn (Vienna, 1977).

Jaime I, king of Aragon, *Llibre dels fets*, tr. Damian Smith and Helena Buffery, *The Book of Deeds of James I of Aragon*, CTT 10 (Aldershot, 2003).

Jakó, Zsigmond, ed., *Erdélyi okmánytár (Codex diplomaticus Transsyylvaniae)*. *Oklevelek, levelek, és más írásos emlékek Erdély történetéhez*, I. *1023–1300* (Budapest, 1997).

Jan of Czarnków, 'Kronika', *MPH*, II.

John of Cori, *Livre de l'estat du Grant Caan*, ed. M. Jacquet, 'Le Livre du Grant Caan, extrait d'un manuscrit de la Bibliothèque du Roi', *JA* 6 (1830), pp. 57–72; tr. in Yule, *Cathay*, III, pp. 89–103.

John of Garlande, *De triumphis ecclesiae libri octo*, ed. Thomas Wright (London, 1856).

John of Marignolli, 'Relatio', in *SF*, pp. 513–60; also ed. as 'Kronika Jana z Marignoly', *FRB*, III, pp. 485–604.

John of Montecorvino, 'Epistolae', in *SF*, pp. 333–55; nos 2 and 3 tr. in Dawson, *Mongol Mission*, pp. 224–31.

John of Plano Carpini, *Ystoria Mongalorum*, ed. Enrico Menestò *et al.*, *Giovanni di Pian di Carpine. Storia dei Mongoli* (Spoleto, 1989); tr. in Dawson, *Mongol Mission*, pp. 1–72.

John of Sulṭāniyya, *Libellus de notitia orbis*, partial edn by Anton Kern, 'Der «Libellus de notitia orbis» Iohannes' III. (de Galonifontibus?) O.P. Erzbischofs von Sulthanyeh', *AFP* 8 (1938), pp. 82–123; also Graz Universitätsbibliothek ms. 1221. See also Moranvillé.

John of Viktring, *Liber certarum historiarum*, ed. Fedor Schneider, SRG, 2 vols (Hannover and Leipzig, 1909–10).

John of Winterthur, *Cronica*, ed. Friedrich Baethgen, SRG² 3 (Berlin, 1924).

Jordanus of Séverac, *Mirabilia descripta*, ed. and tr. Henri Cordier, *Les merveilles de l'Asie* (Paris, 1925); tr. Henry Yule, *Wonders of the East*, HS¹ (London, 1863).

Julian, 'Epistula de vita Tartarorum', in Dörrie, 'Drei Texte', pp. 161–82; tr. in Göckenjan and Sweeney, *Mongolensturm*, pp. 93–125.

Juwaynī, 'Alā' al-Dīn Aṭā Malik, *Ta'rīkh-i jahān-gushā*, ed. Mīrzā Muḥammad Qazwīnī, 3 vols, GMS 16 (Leiden and London, 1912–37); tr. John Andrew Boyle, *The History of the World-Conqueror*, 2 vols with continuous pagination (Manchester, 1958; repr. in 1 vol., 1997).

Jūzjānī, Minhāj al-Dīn Abū 'Umar ibn Sirāj al-Dīn 'Uthmān, *Ṭabaqāt-i Nāṣirī*, ed. 'Abd al-Ḥaiy Ḥabībī, 2nd edn, 2 vols (Kabul, 1342–3 H. solar/1963–4); tr. H.G. Raverty, *Ṭabakāt-i-Nāṣirī. A General History of the Muhammadan Dynasties of Asia*, Bibliotheca Indica, 2 vols with continuous pagination (London, 1873–81).

Kirakos Ganjakec'i, *Patmut'iwn Hayoc'*, tr. Robert Bedrosian, *Kirakos Ganjakets'i's History of the Armenians* (New York, 1986); and see also Boyle, 'Kirakos of Ganjak'.

Knauz, Ferdinandus, and Dedek, Ludovicus Crescens, eds, *Monumenta ecclesiae Strigoniensis*, I–III (Esztergom, 1874–1924); Gabriel Dreska *et al.*, eds, *Monumenta ecclesiae Strigoniensis*, IV (Esztergom and Budapest, 1999).

Kohler, Ch., 'Deux projets de croisade en Terre-Sainte composés à la fin du XIIIᵉ siècle et au début du XIVᵉ siècle', *ROL* 10 (1903–4), pp. 406–57.

Kohler, Ch., and Langlois, C.-V., 'Lettres inédites concernant les croisades (1275–1307)', *BEC* 52 (1891), pp. 46–63.

'Kronika Wielkopolska', *MPH²*, VIII.

Kunstmann, Friedrich, 'Studien über Marino Sanudo den Aelteren, mit einem Abhange seiner ungedruckten Briefe', *Abhandlungen der historischen Klasse der königlich bayerischen Akademie der Wissenschaften* 7 (1853–5), pp. 695–819.

Lange, Chr. C.A., and Unger, Carl R., eds, *Diplomatarium Norvegicum*, I (Christiania, 1849).

L[anglois], C.V., 'Lettre à Charles d'Anjou sur les affaires de Terre Sainte (Acre, 22 avril 1260)', *BEC* 78 (1917), pp. 487–90.

Libro del conosçimiento de todos los rregnos et tierras et señorios que son por el mundo, ed. María Jésus Lacarra, María del Carmen Lacarra Ducay and Alberto Montaner (Zaragoza, 1999); tr. Clements Markham, *The Book of the Knowledge of All the Kingdoms, Lands and Lordships of the World*, HS² 29 (London, 1912).

Le livre des fais du bon messire Jehan le Maingre, dit Bouciquaut, ed. Denis Lalande (Geneva, 1985).

Luard, Henry Richards, ed., *Annales monastici*, RS, 5 vols (London, 1864–9).

Lupprian, Karl-Ernst, ed., *Die Beziehungen der Päpste zu islamischen und mongolischen Herrschern im 13. Jahrhundert anhand ihres Briefwechsels*, Studi e Testi 291 (Vatican City, 1981).

Mandeville, Jehan de, *Le livre des merveilles du monde*, ed. Malcolm Letts, *Mandeville's Travels. Texts and Translations*, 2 vols, HS² 101–2 (London, 1953); ed. Christiane Deluz, *Le livre des merveilles du monde* (Paris, 2000).

al-Maqrīzī, Taqī al-Dīn Abu l-'Abbās Aḥmad ibn 'Alī, *al-Sulūk li-maʿrifat duwal al-mulūk*, ed. Muṣṭafā al-Ziyāda and Saʿīd al-Fatḥ ʿĀshūr, 4 vols in 10 (Cairo, 1934–72).

Marco Polo, *Le divisament dou monde*, ed. Gabriella Ronchi, *Milione. Le divisament dou monde* (Milan, 1982) [Tuscan text pp. 1–302; French–Italian text pp. 303–662]; tr. Aldo Ricci, *The Travels of Marco Polo* (London, 1931); composite trans. by A.C. Moule and Paul Pelliot, *Marco Polo. The Description of the World*, 2 vols (London, 1938), I; edn of 'Z' text, ibid., II. See also Nitti.

Marignolli: see John of Marignolli.

'Martini continuationes Anglicae Fratrum Minorum', *MGHS*, XXIV.

Mas Latrie, L. de, 'Privilège commercial accordé en 1320 à la République de Venise par un roi de Perse, faussement attribué à un roi de Tunis', *BEC* 31 (1871), pp. 72–102.

Mas Latrie, L. de, 'Commerce et expéditions militaires de la France et de Venise au moyen-âge', *Mélanges Historiques. Choix de documents*, III (Paris, 1880).

Matthew Paris, *Chronica majora*, ed. H.R. Luard, RS, 7 vols (London, 1872–83).

'Menkonis chronicon', *MGHS*, XXIII.

Meyvaert, Paul, 'An unknown letter of Hulagu, Il-khan of Persia, to King Louis IX of France', *Viator* 11 (1980), pp. 245–59.

Mignanelli, Beltramo da, 'Vita Tamerlani', in Ét. Baluze, ed., *Miscellanea novo ordine digesta et non paucis ineditis monumentis opportunisque animadversionibus aucta*, new edn by J.D. Mansi, IV (Lucca, 1764), pp. 131–41; partial tr. Walter J. Fischel, 'A new Latin source on Tamerlane's conquest of Damascus (1400/1401)', *Oriens* 9 (1956), pp. 201–32.

Moranvillé, H., ed., 'Mémoire sur Tamerlan et sa cour par un Dominicain, en 1403', *BEC* 55 (1894), pp. 441–64.

Mostaert, Antoine, and Cleaves, Francis Woodman, 'Trois documents mongols des archives secrètes vaticanes', *HJAS* 15 (1952), pp. 419–506.

Mostaert, Antoine, C.I.C.M., and Cleaves, Francis Woodman, eds, *Les lettres de 1289 et 1305 des ilkhan Aryun et Öljeitü à Philippe le Bel*, Harvard–Yenching Institute, Scripta Mongolica Monograph Series 1 (Cambridge, MA, 1962).

Muʿizz al-ansāb, BN ms. Ancien fonds persan 67.

Nagy, Imre, Ipolyi, Arnold, and Vághely, Dezsö, eds, *Hazai okmánytár. Codex diplomaticus patrius Hungaricus*, 8 vols (Győr and Budapest, 1865–91).

Nagy, Imre, and Nagy, Gyula Tasnadi, eds, *Anjoukori okmánytár. Codex diplomaticus Hungaricus Andegavensis*, 6 vols (Budapest, 1878–1920).

Niccolò di Calvi, 'Vita Innocentii IV', in Alberto Melloni, *Innocenzo IV. La concezione e l'esperienza della cristianità come regimen unius personae* (Genova, 1990), appendice, pp. 257–93.

Nitti, John J., ed., *Juan Fernández de Heredia's Aragonese version of the* Libro de Marco Polo (Madison, WI, 1980).

Nizām-i Shāmī, *Zafar-nāma*, ed. Felix Tauer, *Histoire des conquêtes de Tamerlan*, 2 vols, Monografie Archivu Orientálního 5 (Prague, 1937–56).

Noiret, Hippolyte, ed., *Documents inédits pour servir à l'histoire de la domination vénitienne en Crète de 1380 à 1485* (Paris, 1892).

Novgorodskaia pervaia letopis' starshego i mladshego izvodov, ed. A.N. Nasonov (Moscow and Leningrad, 1950); tr. Michell and Forbes: see *Chronicle of Novgorod* (above).

al-Nuwayrī, Shihāb al-Dīn Ahmad ibn 'Abd al-Wahhāb, *Nihāyat al-arab fī funūn al-adab*, 33 vols (Cairo, 1923–98).

Odoric of Pordenone, 'Relatio', in *SF*, pp. 379–495; tr. in Yule, *Cathay*, II, pp. 1–277.

Olbricht, Peter, and Pinks, Elisabeth, eds, *Meng-Ta pei-lu und Hei-Ta shih-lüeh. Chinesische Gesandtenberichte über die frühen Mongolen 1221 und 1237*, AF 56 (Wiesbaden, 1980).

Ottokar of Styria, *Reimchronik*, ed. Joseph Seemüller, *Ottokars Österreichische Reimchronik*, 2 vols, MGH Deutsche Chroniken 5 (Hannover, 1890–3).

Pachymeres, Georgios, *De Michaele et Andronico Palaeologo*, ed. Albert Failler and tr. Vitalien Laurent, *Georges Pachymérès. Relations historiques*, 5 vols (Paris, 1984–2000).

Pegolotti, Francesco Balducci, *La pratica della mercatura*, ed. Allan Evans (Cambridge, MA, 1936).

Peregrine di Castello, 'Epistola', in *SF*, pp. 357–68; tr. in Dawson, *Mongol Mission*, pp. 232–4.

Peter (Russian cleric), 'Relatio', in Dörrie, 'Drei Texte', pp. 187–94; also OOLB ms. 446.

Philippe de Mézières, *Le songe du Vieil Pelerin*, ed. G.W. Coopland, 2 vols (Cambridge, 1969).

Philippe Mouskès, *Chronique rimée*, ed. Baron F.A.F.T. de Reiffenberg, 2 vols (Brussels, 1836–8).

Philippi, R., *et al.*, eds, *Preußisches Urkundenbuch*, 6 vols so far (Königsberg and Marburg, 1882–1986).

Piekosiński, Franciszek, ed., *Kodeks dyplomatyczny małopolski*, I. *1178–1386*, MMAH 3 (Cracow, 1876).

Pseudo-Methodius, *Sermo* or *Revelationes*: see Sackur.

Ptaśnik, Jan, ed., *Monumenta Poloniae Vaticana*, I. *Acta Camerae Apostolicae*, I. *1207–1344* (Cracow, 1913); II. *Acta Camerae Apostolicae*, II. *1344–1374* (Cracow, 1913); III. *Analecta Vaticana 1202–1366* (Cracow, 1914).

Ptolomy of Lucca, *Annales*, ed. Bernhard Schmeidler, *Die Annalen des Tholomeus von Lucca in doppelter Fassung*, SRG² 8 (Berlin, 1930).

al-Qazwīnī, Zakariyyā' ibn Muhammad, *Āthār al-bilād*, ed. F. Wüstenfeld, *Zakarija ben Muhammed bin Mahmud el-Cazwini's Cosmographie, zweiter Teil: Die Denkmäler der Länder* (Göttingen, 1848).

Ralph of Coggeshall, *Chronicon Anglicanum*, ed. Joseph Stevenson, RS (London, 1875).

Ramón Lull, 'De fine', in A. Madre, ed., *Raimundi Lulli opera Latina*, IX, CCCM 35 (Turnhout, 1981), pp. 233–91.

Rashīd al-Dīn Faḍl-Allāh al-Hamadānī, *Jāmiʿ al-tawārīkh*, ed. Muḥammad Rawshan and Muṣṭafā Mūsawī, 4 vols with continuous pagination (Tehran, 1373 H. solar/1994); tr. Wheeler M. Thackston, *Jamiʿuʾt-tawarikh. Compendium of Chronicles*, 3 vols with continuous pagination (Cambridge, MA, 1998–9); partial tr. J.A. Boyle, *The Successors of Genghis Khan* (London and New York, 1971). See also Jahn, *Die Frankengeschichte*.

Raynaldus, Odoricus, *et al.*, eds, *Annales ecclesiastici*, 34 vols (Lucca, 1738–59).

Redlich, Oswald, ed., *Eine Wiener Briefsammlung zur Geschichte des deutschen Reiches und der österreichischen Länder in der zweiten Hälfte des XIII. Jahrhunderts* (Vienna, 1894).

Richard of San Germano, 'Chronica', *RIS²*, VII:2.

Richardus, 'De facto Ungarie Magne', in Dörrie, 'Drei Texte', pp. 147–61.

'Richeri Gesta Senoniensis ecclesiae', *MGHS*, XXV.

Ricoldo of Montecroce, 'Lettres', ed. R. Röhricht, *AOL* 2 (1884), pp. 258–96.

Ricoldo of Montecroce, *Libellus*: see Dondaine (below).

Ricoldo of Montecroce, *Liber peregrinationis*, in J.C.M. Laurent, ed., *Peregrinatores medii aevi quatuor*, 2nd edn (Leipzig, 1873), pp. 105–41.

Rishanger, William, 'Chronica', in Henry Thomas Riley, ed., *Willelmi Rishanger, quondam monachi S. Albani, et quorundam anonymorum Chronica et Annales*, RS (London, 1865).

'Rocznik kapituły krakowskiej', *MPH²*, V.

'Rocznik małopolski', *MPH*, III.

'Rocznik miechowski', *MPH*, II.

'Rocznik Traski', *MPH*, II.

Rodenberg, C., ed., *MGH Epistolae saeculi XIII e regestis pontificum Romanorum selectae*, 3 vols (Berlin, 1883–94).

Roger of Várad, 'Epistola', ed. L. Juhász as 'Carmen miserabile', *SRH*, II, pp. 543–88; tr. in Göckenjan and Sweeney, *Mongolensturm*, pp. 127–223.

Rubió y Lluch, Antoni, ed., *Documents per l'historia de la cultura catalana mig-eval*, 2 vols (Barcelona, 1908–21).

Rubió y Lluch, Antoni, ed., *Diplomatari de l'Orient Català (1301–1409)* (Barcelona, 1947).

Rymer, Thomas, ed., *Foedera, conventiones, litterae et cuiuscumque generis acta publica inter reges Angliae et alios quosvis imperatores, reges, pontifices, principes vel communitates ab ineunte saeculo duodecimo, viz. ab anno 1101 ad nostra usque tempora habita aut tractata*, 3rd edn, 10 vols in 20 parts (Amsterdam, 1739–45; repr. Farnborough, 1967).

Sackur, E., ed., *Sibyllinische Texte und Forschungen. Pseudomethodius, Adso und die Tiburtinische Sibylle* (Halle, 1898), new edn by Raoul Manselli (Turin, 1976).

Salimbene de Adam, *Cronica*, ed. Giuseppe Scalia, 2 vols, CCCM 125–125A (Turnhout, 1998–9).

Sanjian, Avedis K., *Colophons of Armenian Manuscripts, 1301–1480. A Source for Middle Eastern History* (Cambridge, MA, 1969).

Sanudo, Marino, *Liber secretorum fidelium crucis*, in J. Bongars, ed., *Gesta Dei per Francos*, I (Hannover, 1611, repr. Toronto, 1972).

Sanudo, Marino, *Epistolae*: see Kunstmann (above).

Schneider, Fedor, 'Ein Schreiben der Ungarn an die Kurie aus der letzten Zeit des Tatareneinfalles (2. Februar 1242)', *MIOG* 36 (1915), pp. 661–70.

'Secret History of the Mongols', tr. Igor de Rachewiltz, *The Secret History of the Mongols: A Mongolian Epic Chronicle of the Thirteenth Century*, 2 vols with continuous pagination (Leiden, 2004).

Sharaf al-Dīn 'Alī Yazdī, *Ẓafar-nāma*, ed. Muḥammad 'Abbāsī, 2 vols (Tehran, 1336 solar/1957); facsimile edn by A. Urunbaev (Tashkent, 1972); tr. F. Pétis de la Croix, *Histoire de Timur-Bec, connu sous le nom du Grand Tamerlan*, 4 vols (Paris, 1722).

Sibṭ Ibn al-Jawzī (Shams al-Dīn Abu l-Muẓaffar Yūsuf ibn Qizūghlī), *Mir'āt al-zamān fī ta'rīkh al-a'yān*, VIII, 2 parts (Hyderabad, A.P., 1371 H./ 1952).

Simon of Saint-Quentin, *Historia Tartarorum*, ed. Jean Richard, *Simon de Saint-Quentin. Histoire des Tartares*, DRHC 8 (Paris, 1965).

Siyar al-abā' al-baṭārika, ed. and tr. O.H.E. Khs-Burmester and A. Khater, *History of the Patriarchs of the Egyptian Church*, IV, 2 parts (Paris, 1974).

Societas literaria Poznaniensis, eds., *Kodeks dyplomatyczny wielkopolski*, 2 vols (Poznań, 1877–8).

Spuler, Bertold, ed., *History of the Mongols*, tr. Helga and Stuart Drummond (London, 1972).

Stubbs, William, ed., *The Historical Works of Gervase of Canterbury*, RS, 2 vols (London, 1879–80).

Sułkowska-Kuraś, Irena, and Kuraś, Stanisław, eds, *Bullarium Poloniae*, 6 vols so far (Rome and Lublin, 1982–98).

Szabó, Károly, ed., *Székely oklevéltár*, 8 vols (Kolozsvár, 1872–98).

Szentpétery, Imre, ed., *Scriptores rerum Hungaricarum tempore ducum regumque stirpis Arpadianae gestarum*, 2 vols (Budapest, 1937–8; repr. 1999).

Szentpétery, Imre, and Borsa, Iván, eds, *Az Árpád-házi királyok okleveleinek kritikai jegyzéke. Regesta regum stirpis Arpadianae critico-diplomatica*, 2 vols in 5 parts (Budapest, 1923–87).

Tanner, Norman P., ed., *Decrees of the Ecumenical Councils*, I. *Nicaea I to Lateran V* (London and Georgetown, 1990).

'Tartar Relation', ed. Alf Önnerfors, *Hystoria Tartarorum C. de Bridia monachi*, Kleine Texte für Vorlesungen und Übungen 186 (Berlin, 1967).

Teulet, Alexandre, *et al.*, eds, *Layettes du Trésor des Chartes*, 5 vols (Paris, 1863–1909).

Teutsch, G.D., and Firnhaber, Fr., eds, *Urkundenbuch zur Geschichte Siebenbürgens* (vol. I only published), FRAS² 15 (Vienna, 1857).

Theiner, Augustin, ed., *Vetera monumenta historica Hungariam sacram illustrantia*, 2 vols (Rome, 1859–61).

Theiner, Augustin, ed., *Vetera monumenta Poloniae et Lithuaniae gentiumque finitimarum historiam illustrantia*, 4 vols (Rome, 1860–4).

Thiriet, F., ed., *Régestes des délibérations du Sénat de Venise concernant la Romanie*, 3 vols, DREP 1, 2 and 4 (Paris and The Hague, 1958–61).

Thiriet, F., ed., *Délibérations des assemblées vénitiennes concernant la Romanie*, I. *1160–1363*, DREP 8 (Paris and The Hague, 1966); II. *1364–1463*, DREP 11 (Paris and The Hague, 1971).

Thomas, Georg Martin, ed., *Diplomatarium Veneto-Levantinum sive acta et diplomata res Venetas Graecas atque Levantis illustrantia*, I. *a.1300–1350* (Venice, 1880); II. *a.1351–1454*, ed. Riccardo Predelli (Venice, 1899).

Thomas of Spalato, *Historia Salonitanorum pontificum atque Spalatensium*, ed. Fr. Rački (Zagreb, 1894 = *MHSM* 26); partial tr. in Göckenjan and Sweeney, *Mongolensturm*, pp. 225–70.

Tisserant, Eugène Card., 'Une lettre de l'Ilkhan de Perse Abaga adressée au Pape Clément IV', *Le Muséon* 59 (1946), pp. 547–56.

Tizengauzen, V.G. Frhr. von, ed., *Sbornik materialov otnosiashchikhsia k istorii Zolotoi Ordy*, I (St Petersburg, 1884); II, ed. A.A. Romaskevich and S.L. Volin (Moscow and Leningrad, 1941).

al-ʿUmarī, Shihāb al-Dīn Aḥmad ibn Faḍl-Allāh, *Masālik al-abṣār fī mamālik al-amṣār*, ed. and tr. Klaus Lech, *Das mongolische Weltreich: Al-ʿUmarī's Darstellung der mongolischen Reiche in seinem Werk . . .* , AF 22 (Wiesbaden, 1968).

Van den Wyngaert, Anastasius, ed., *Sinica Franciscana*, I. *Itinera et relationes Fratrum Minorum saeculi XIII et XIV* (Quaracchi-Firenze, 1929).

Vardan Arewelcʿi, *Hawakʿumn patmutʿean*, tr. Robert W. Thomson, 'The historical compilation of Vardan Arewelcʿi', *Dumbarton Oaks Papers* 34 (1989), pp. 125–226.

Vincent of Beauvais, *Speculum historiale*, ed. Johann Mentelin (Straßburg, 1473).

Wagner, Hans, and Lindeck-Pozza, Irmtraut, eds, *Urkundenbuch des Burgenlandes und der angrenzenden Gebiete der Komitate Wieselburg, Ödenburg und Eisenburg*, 4 vols (Graz, Köln and Vienna, 1955–85).

Waṣṣāf (Shihāb al-Dīn ʿAbd-Allāh ibn Faḍl-Allāh Shīrāzī), *Tajziyat al-amṣār wa-tazjiyat al-aʿṣār*, lithograph edn (Bombay, 1269 H./1853; repr. Tehran, 1338 H. solar/1959–60).

Weiland, L., ed., *MGH Legum sectio IV. Constitutiones et acta publica imperatorum et regum*, 11 vols so far (Hannover, 1893–1992).

Wenzel, Gusztáv, ed., *Árpádkori új okmánytár. Codex diplomaticus Arpadianus continuatus*, 12 vols (Pest, 1860–74).

William of Rubruck, 'Itinerarium', in *SF*, pp. 145–332; tr. in Peter Jackson and David Morgan, eds, *The Mission of Friar William of Rubruck: His Journey to the Court of the Great Khan Möngke 1253–1255*, HS² 173 (London, 1990).

Yule, Sir Henry, *Cathay and the Way Thither*, new edn by Henri Cordier, 4 vols, HS² 33, 37, 38, 41 (London, 1913–16).

al-Yūnīnī, Quṭb al-Dīn Abu l-Fatḥ Mūsā ibn Muḥammad, *al-Dhayl 'alā' Mir'āt al-zamān*, 4 vols (Hyderabad, A.P., 1374–80 H./1954–61).

Zimmermann, Franz, and Werner, Karl, eds, *Urkundenbuch zur Geschichte der Deutschen in Siebenbürgen*, 4 vols (Hermannstadt/Sibiu, 1892–1937).

Secondary material

Aalto, Pentti, 'Swells of the Mongol-storm around the Baltic', *AOASH* 36 (1982), pp. 5–15.

Abel-Rémusat, 'Mémoires sur les relations politiques des princes chrétiens, et particulièrement des rois de France, avec les empereurs mongols', *MAIBL* 6 (1822), pp. 396–469, and 7 (1824), pp. 335–438.

Abulafia, David, *Frederick II. A Medieval Emperor* (London, 1988).

Abulafia, David, 'Industrial products: the Middle Ages', in *Prodotti e tecniche d'Oltremare nelle economie europee, secc. XIII–XVIII. XXIX Settimana dell'Istituto Internazionale di Storia economica 'F. Datini'* (Firenze, 1998), pp. 333–58; repr. in Abulafia, *Mediterranean Encounters, Economic, Religious, Political, 1100–1550* (Aldershot, 2000).

Abulafia, David, and Berend, Nora, eds, *Medieval Frontiers: Concepts and Practices* (Aldershot, 2002).

Aigle, Denise, ed., *L'Iran face à la domination mongole*, Bibliothèque Iranienne 45 (Tehran, 1997).

Alexandrescu-Dersca, M.M., *La campagne de Timur en Anatolie (1402)* (Bucarest, 1942, repr. London, 1977).

Alexandrescu-Dersca, M., 'L'expédition d'Umur Beg d'Aydin aux bouches du Danube (1337 ou 1338)', *Studia et Acta Orientalia* 2 (1959 [Bucarest, 1960]), pp. 3–23.

Allen, W.E.D., *A History of the Georgian People* (London, 1932).

Allouche, Adel, 'Tegüder's ultimatum to Qalawun', *IJMES* 22 (1990), pp. 437–46.

Allsen, Thomas T., 'Prelude to the western campaigns: Mongol military operations in the Volga-Ural region, 1217–1237', *AEMA* 3 (1983), pp. 5–24.

Allsen, Thomas T., 'The Princes of the Left Hand: an introduction to the history of the *ulus* of Orda in the thirteenth and early fourteenth centuries', *AEMA* 5 (1985 [1987]), pp. 5–40.

Allsen, Thomas T., *Mongol Imperialism. The Policies of the Grand Qan Möngke in China, Russia, and the Islamic Lands, 1251–1259* (Berkeley and Los Angeles, 1987).

Allsen, Thomas T., 'Mongolian princes and their merchant partners, 1200–1260', *Asia Major*, 3rd series, 2:2 (1989), pp. 83–126.

Allsen, Thomas T., 'Mongols and North Caucasia', *AEMA* 7 (1987–91), pp. 5–40.

Allsen, Thomas, 'The rise of the Mongolian empire and the Mongol conquest of North China', in *CHC*, VI, pp. 321–413.

Allsen, Thomas T., 'Spiritual geography and political legitimacy in the eastern steppe', in Henri J.M. Claessen and Jarich G. Oosten, eds, *Ideology and the Formation of Early States* (Leiden, 1996), pp. 116–35.

Allsen, Thomas T., *Commodity and Exchange in the Mongol Empire. A Cultural History of Islamic Textiles* (Cambridge, 1997).

Allsen, Thomas T., *Culture and Conquest in Mongol Eurasia* (Cambridge, 2001).

Allsen, Thomas T., 'The circulation of military technology in the Mongolian empire', in Di Cosmo, *Warfare in Inner Asian History*, pp. 265–93.

Amitai-Preiss, Reuven, 'Mamluk perceptions of the Mongol–Frankish rapprochement', *MHR* 7 (1992), pp. 50–65.

Amitai-Preiss, Reuven, *Mongols and Mamluks. The Mamluk–Īlkhānid War, 1260–1281* (Cambridge, 1995).

Amitai-Preiss, Reuven, 'Mongol imperial ideology and the Ilkhanid war against the Mamluks', in Amitai-Preiss and Morgan, *Mongol Empire*, pp. 57–72.

Amitai, Reuven, 'Whither the Ilkhanid army? Ghazan's first campaign into Syria (1299–1300)', in Di Cosmo, *Warfare in Inner Asian History*, pp. 221–64.

Amitai, Reuven, and Biran, Michal, eds, *Mongols, Turks and Others. Eurasian Nomads and the Sedentary World* (Leiden, 2005).

Amitai-Preiss, Reuven, and Morgan, David O., eds, *The Mongol Empire and Its Legacy*, Islamic History and Civilization: Studies and Texts 24 (Leiden, 1999).

Anderson, Andrew Runni, *Alexander's Gate, Gog and Magog, and the Inclosed Nations* (Cambridge, MA, 1932).

Armstrong, Guyda, and Wood, Ian N., eds, *Christianizing Peoples and Converting Individuals* (Turnhout, 2000).

Ashtor, Eliyahu, *Levant Trade in the Later Middle Ages* (Princeton, NJ, 1983).

Aubin, Jean, 'Comment Tamerlan prenait les villes', *SI* 19 (1963), pp. 83–122.

Ayalon, David, 'The Great *Yāsa* of Chingiz Khān: a reexamination. Part B', *SI* 34 (1971), pp. 151–80; repr. in Ayalon, *Outsiders in the Lands of Islam: Mamlūks, Mongols and Eunuchs* (London, 1988).

Bacot, Jacques, 'Reconnaissance en Haute Asie septentrionale par cinq envoyés ouigours au VIII° siècle', *JA* 244 (1956), pp. 137–53.

Balard, Michel, 'Notes sur l'activité maritime des Génois de Caffa à la fin du XIII° siècle', in Mollat du Jourdain, *Sociétés et compagnies*, pp. 375–86; repr. in Balard, *La mer Noire*.

Balard, Michel, 'Les Gênois [*sic*] en Asie centrale et en extrême-orient au XIV° siècle: un cas exceptionnel?', in *Economies et sociétés au moyen âge. Mélanges offerts à Edouard Perroy* (Paris, 1973), pp. 681–9.

Balard, Michel, 'Precursori di Cristoforo Colombo: i Genovesi in estremo oriente nel XIV secolo', in *Atti del Convegno internazionale di Studi Colombiani (Genova, 13–14 ottobre 1973)* (Genova, 1974), pp. 149–64; repr. in Balard, *La mer Noire*.

Balard, Michel, *La Romanie génoise*, 2 vols with continuous pagination (Genova, 1978 = *ASL*, n.s., 18:1–2).

Balard, M., 'Les Génois en Crimée aux XIIIe–XIVe siècles', *AP* 35 (1979), pp. 201–17.

Balard, Michel, 'Gênes et la mer Noire (XIIIe–XVe siècles)', *RH* 270 (1983), pp. 31–54; repr. in Balard, *La mer Noire*.

Balard, Michel, 'Le commerce du blé en mer Noire (XIIIe–XVe siècles)', in *Aspetti della vita economica medievale: Atti del Convegno di studi nel X° anniversario della morte di Federigo Melis (Firenze–Pisa–Prato 10–14 marzo 1984)* (Firenze, 1985), pp. 64–80; repr. in Balard, *La mer Noire*.

Balard, Michel, *La mer Noire et la Romanie génoise (XIIIe–XVe siècles)* (London, 1989).

Balard, Michel, 'Esclavage en Crimée et sources fiscales génoises au XVe siècle', in *6e Symposion Byzantinon, l'automne 1992: Byzance et l'Europe. Aufsätze* (Amsterdam, 1996 = *BF* 22), pp. 9–17.

Balard, Michel, Kedar, B.Z., and Riley-Smith, J.S.C., eds, *Dei gesta per Francos. Études sur les croisades dédiées à Jean Richard* (Aldershot, 2001).

Barbieri, G., ed., *Studi in onore di Amintore Fanfani*, 6 vols (Milan, 1962).

Barfield, Thomas J., *The Perilous Frontier. Nomadic Empires and China* (Oxford, 1989).

Barker, John W., *Manuel II Palaeologus 1391–1425. A Study in Late Byzantine Statesmanship* (New Brunswick, NJ, 1969).

Barthold, W., *Turkestan Down to the Mongol Invasion*, 3rd edn, ed. C.E. Bosworth with additional chapter tr. T. Minorsky, GMS, new series, 5 (London, 1968).

Bartlett, Robert, *The Making of Europe. Conquest, Colonization and Cultural Change 950–1350* (Harmondsworth, 1993).

Bautier, Robert-Henri, 'Les relations économiques des Occidentaux avec les pays d'Orient, au Moyen Âge: points de vue et documents', in Mollat du Jourdain, *Sociétés et compagnies*, pp. 263–331; repr. in Bautier, *Commerce méditerranéen et banquiers italiens au Moyen Age* (London, 1992).

Becker, Joseph, 'Zum Mongoleneinfall von 1241', *Zeitschrift des Vereins für Geschichte Schlesiens* 66 (1932), pp. 34–57.

Beckingham, Charles F. and Hamilton, Bernard, eds, *Prester John, the Mongols and the Ten Lost Tribes* (Aldershot, 1996).

Beffa, Marie-Lise, 'Le concept de *tänggäri*, «ciel», dans l'*Histoire secrète des Mongols*', *EMS* 24 (1993), pp. 215–36.

Benedictow, Ole J., *The Black Death 1346–1353. The Complete History* (Woodbridge, 2004).

Bennett, Josephine Waters, *The Rediscovery of Sir John Mandeville* (New York, 1954).

Berend, Nora, *At the Gate of Christendom: Jews, Muslims and 'Pagans' in Medieval Hungary, c.1000–c.1300* (Cambridge, 2001).

Berindei, Mihnea, and O'Riordan, Giustiniana Migliardi, 'Venise et la Horde d'Or, fin XIIIe–début XIVe siècle. A propos d'un document inédit de 1324', *CMRS* 29 (1988), pp. 243–56.

Berindei, Mihnea, and Veinstein, Gilles, 'La Tana-Azaq de la présence italienne à l'emprise ottomane (fin XIIIe–milieu XVIe siècle)', *Turcica* 8:2 (1976), pp. 110–201.

Bethlenfalvy, Géza, Birtalan, Ágnes, Sárközi, Alice, and Vinkovics, J., eds, *Altaic Religious Beliefs and Practices. Proceedings of the 33rd Meeting of the Permanent International Altaistic Conference, Budapest June 24–29, 1990* (Budapest, 1992).

Bezzola, Gian Andri, *Die Mongolen in abendländischer Sicht (1220–1270). Ein Beitrag zur Frage der Völkerbegegnungen* (Berne and Munich, 1974).

Bigalli, Davide, *I Tartari e l'Apocalisse. Ricerche sull'escatologia in Adamo Marsh e Ruggero Bacone* (Firenze, 1971).

Bigalli, Davide, 'Giudizio escatologico e tecnica di missione nei pensatori francescani: Ruggero Bacone', in *Espansione del francescanesimo*, pp. 151–86.

Biran, Michal, *Qaidu and the Rise of the Independent Mongol State in Central Asia* (Richmond, Surrey, 1997).

Biran, Michal, '"Like a mighty wall": the armies of the Qara Khitai', *JSAI* 25 (2001), pp. 44–91.

Boase, T.S.R., ed., *The Cilician Kingdom of Armenia* (Edinburgh, 1978).

Boase, T.S.R., 'The history of the kingdom', in Boase, *Cilician Kingdom*, pp. 1–33.

Boyle, J.A., 'Kirakos of Ganjak on the Mongols', *CAJ* 8 (1963), pp. 199–214; repr. in Boyle, *Mongol World-Empire*.

Boyle, J.A., 'Dynastic and political history of the Īlkhāns', in *CHI*, V, pp. 303–421.

Boyle, J.A., 'The Ilkhans of Persia and the princes of Europe', *CAJ* 20 (1976), pp. 25–40.

Boyle, J.A., *The Mongol World-Empire 1206–1370* (London, 1977).

Brătianu, G.I., *Recherches sur le commerce génois dans la mer Noire au XIIIe siècle* (Paris, 1929).

Brugnoli, Giorgio, 'Andrea da Perugia', in Carlo Santini, ed., *Andrea da Perugia. Atti del convegno (Perugia, 19 settembre 1992)* (Rome, 1994), pp. 5–15.

Brunel, Clovis, 'David d'Ashby auteur méconnu des *Faits des Tartares*', *Romania* 79 (1958), pp. 39–46.

Buell, Paul D., 'Kalmyk Tanggaci people: thoughts on the mechanics and impact of Mongol expansion', *MS* 6 (1979), pp. 41–59.

Buell, Paul D., 'Sino-Khitan administration in Mongol Bukhara', *JAH* 13 (1979), pp. 121–51.

Bundy, David, 'The Syriac and Armenian Christian responses to the Islamification of the Mongols', in John Victor Tolan, ed., *Medieval Christian Perceptions of Islam: A Book of Essays* (New York and London, 1996), pp. 33–53.

Cahen, Claude, ''Abdallaṭīf al-Baghdādī, portraitiste et historien de son temps: extraits inédits de ses mémoires', *BEO* 23 (1970), pp. 101–28.

Cahen, Claude, ''Abdallaṭīf al-Baghdādī et les Khwārizmiens', in C.E. Bosworth, ed., *Iran and Islam: In Memory of the Late Vladimir Minorsky* (Edinburgh, 1971), pp. 149–66.

Cahen, Claude, *The Formation of Turkey. The Seljukid Sultanate of Rūm: Eleventh to Fourteenth Century*, tr. P.M. Holt (London, 2001).

Campbell, Mary B., *The Witness and the Other World. Exotic European Travel Writing, 400–1600* (Ithaca, NY, and London, 1988).

Cazacu, Matei, 'A propos de l'expansion polono-lituanienne au nord de la mer Noire aux XIVᶜ–XVᶜ siècles: Czarnigrad, la "Cité Noire" de l'embouchure du Dniestr', in Ch. Lemercier-Quelquejay, G. Veinstein and S.E. Wimbush, eds, *Passé turco-tatar, présent soviétique. Études offertes à Alexandre Bennigsen* (Paris and Louvain, 1986), pp. 99–122.

Chabot, J.-B., 'Notes sur les relations du roi Argoun avec l'Occident', *ROL* 2 (1894), pp. 566–629.

Chekin, Leonid S., 'The Godless Ishmaelites: the image of the steppe in eleventh–thirteenth-century Rus'', *Russian History* 19 (1992), pp. 9–28.

Christiansen, Eric, *The Northern Crusades*, 2nd edn (Harmondsworth, 1997).

Clark, Larry V., and Draghi, Paul Alexander, eds, *Aspects of Altaic Civilization II. Proceedings of the XVIII PIAC, Bloomington, June 29–July 5, 1975*, IUUAS 134 (Bloomington, IN, 1978).

Clauson, Gerard, 'À propos du manuscrit Pelliot tibétain 1283', *JA* 245 (1957), pp. 11–24.

Claverie, Pierre-Vincent, 'L'apparition des Mongols sur la scène politique occidentale (1220–1223)', *MA* 105 (1999), pp. 601–13.

Connell, C.W., 'Western views of the origin of the "Tartars": an example of the influence of myth in the second half of the thirteenth century', *Journal of Medieval and Renaissance Studies* 3 (1973), pp. 115–37.

Critchley, John, *Marco Polo's Book* (Aldershot, 1992).

Daniel, E. Randolph, *The Franciscan Concept of Mission in the High Middle Ages* (Lexington, KE, 1975).

Dauvillier, Jean, 'Guillaume de Rubrouck et les communautés chaldéennes d'Asie centrale au moyen âge', *L'Orient Syrien* 2 (1957), pp. 223–42; repr. in his *Histoire et institutions*.

Dauvillier, Jean, *Histoire et institutions des Églises orientales au Moyen Age* (London, 1983).

De Rachewiltz, Igor, 'Personnel and personalities in North China in the early Mongol period', *JESHO* 9 (1966), pp. 86–144.

De Rachewiltz, Igor, *Papal Envoys to the Great Khans* (London and Stanford, CA, 1971).

De Rachewiltz, Igor, 'Some remarks on the ideological foundations of Chingis Khan's empire', *PFEH* 7 (1973), pp. 21–36.

De Rachewiltz, Igor, Chan, Hok-lam, Hsiao Ch'i-ch'ing and Geier, Peter W., eds, *In the Service of the Khan. Eminent Personalities of the Early Mongol-Yüan Period*, AF 121 (Wiesbaden, 1993).

De Sacy, Silvestre, Baron, 'Mémoire sur une correspondance inédite de Tamerlan avec Charles VI', *MAIBL* 6 (1822), pp. 470–523.

Deletant, Dennis, 'Genoese, Tatars and Rumanians at the mouth of the Danube in the fourteenth century', *SEER* 62 (1984), pp. 511–30.

Deluz, Christiane, *Le Livre de Jehan de Mandeville: une «géographie» au XIVᵉ siècle* (Louvain-la-Neuve, 1988).

Demiéville, Paul, 'La situation religieuse en Chine au temps de Marco Polo', in *Oriente Poliano*, pp. 193–236.

Dennis, George T., 'The Byzantine–Turkish treaty of 1403', *Orientalia Christiana Periodica* 33 (1967), pp. 72–88; repr. in Dennis, *Byzantium and the Franks.*

Dennis, George T., 'Three reports from Crete on the situation in Romania, 1401–1402', *SV* 12 (1970), pp. 243–65; repr. in Dennis, *Byzantium and the Franks.*

Dennis, George T., *Byzantium and the Franks 1350–1420* (London, 1982).

Devéria, G., 'Notes d'épigraphie mongole-chinoise', *JA*, 9e série, 8:2 (1896), pp. 94–128, 395–443.

DeWeese, D.A., 'The influence of the Mongols on the religious consciousness of thirteenth century Europe', *MS* 5 (1978–9), pp. 41–78.

DeWeese, Devin, *Islamization and Native Religion in the Golden Horde. Baba Tükles and Conversion to Islam in Historical and Epic Tradition* (University Park, PA, 1994).

DeWeese, Devin, 'Toḵtami<u>sh</u>', *Enc.Isl.²*

Di Cosmo, Nicola, ed., *Warfare in Inner Asian History (500–1800)* (Leiden, 2002).

Dimitrov, Hristo, 'Über die bulgarisch-ungarischen Beziehungen (1218–1255)', *BHR* 25:2–3 (1997), pp. 3–27.

Dimnik, Martin, *The Dynasty of Chernigov, 1146–1246* (Cambridge, 2003).

Dondaine, Antoine, O.P., 'Ricoldiana: notes sur les oeuvres de Ricoldo da Montecroce', *AFP* 37 (1967), pp. 119–79.

Edbury, Peter W., ed., *Crusade and Settlement. Papers Read to the First Conference of the Society for the Study of the Crusades and the Latin East and Presented to R.C. Smail* (Cardiff, 1985).

Egorov, V.L., *Istoricheskaia geografiia Zolotoi Ordy XIII–XIV vv.* (Moscow, 1985).

Endicott-West, Elizabeth, 'Notes on shamans, fortune-tellers and *yin-yang* practitioners and civil administration in Yüan China', in Amitai-Preiss and Morgan, *Mongol Empire*, pp. 224–39.

Engel, Pál, *The Realm of Saint Stephen. A History of Medieval Hungary, 895–1526*, tr. Tamás Pálosfalvi (London, 2001).

Espansione del francescanesimo tra Occidente e Oriente nel secolo XIII. Atti del VI Convegno internazionale, Assisi, 12–14 ottobre 1978 (Assisi, 1979).

Fennell, John, *The Crisis of Medieval Russia 1200–1304* (London, 1983).

Fennell, John, *A History of the Russian Church to 1448* (Harlow, 1995).

Fine, John V.A., Jr, *The Late Medieval Balkans. A Critical Survey from the Late Twelfth Century to the Ottoman Conquest* (Ann Arbor, MC, 1987).

Fletcher, Richard, *The Conversion of Europe from Paganism to Christianity 371–1386 AD* (London, 1997).

Flint, Valerie I.J., *The Imaginative Landscape of Christopher Columbus* (Princeton, NJ, 1992).

Forstreuter, Kurt, 'Der Deutsche Orden und Südosteuropa', *Kyrios. Vierteljahresschrift für Kirchen- und Geistesgeschichte Osteuropas* 1 (1936), pp. 245–72.

Franke, Herbert, 'Sino-Western contacts under the Mongol empire', *Journal of the Hong Kong Branch of the Royal Asiatic Society* 6 (1966), pp. 49–72; repr. in Franke, *China under Mongol Rule*.

Franke, Herbert, 'Das „himmlische Pferd" des Johann von Marignola', *AK* 50 (1968), pp. 33–40.

Franke, Herbert, *China under Mongol Rule* (Aldershot, 1994).

Franke, Herbert, and Twitchett, Denis, eds, *The Cambridge History of China*, VI. *Alien Regimes and Border States, 907–1368* (Cambridge, 1994).

Franklin, Simon, and Shepard, Jonathan, *The Emergence of Rus 750–1200* (Harlow, 1996).

Freibergs, Gunar, 'The *Descripciones Terrarum*: its date, sources, author and purpose', in Jerzy Kłoczowski, ed., *Christianity in East Central Europe: Late Middle Ages*, Proceedings of the Commission internationale d'histoire ecclésiastique comparée, Lublin 1996, part 2 (Lublin, 1999), pp. 180–201.

Fried, Johannes, 'Auf der Suche nach der Wirklichkeit: die Mongolen und die europäische Erfahrungswissenschaft im 13. Jahrhundert', *HZ* 243 (1986), pp. 287–332.

Fügedi, Erik, *Castle and Society in Medieval Hungary (1000–1437)*, Studia Historica Academiae Scientiarum Hungaricae 187 (Budapest, 1986).

Gervers, Michael, and Schlepp, Wayne, eds, *Nomadic Diplomacy, Destruction and Religion from the Pacific to the Adriatic*, TSCIA 1 (Toronto, 1994).

Giurescu, Constantin C., 'The Genoese and the Lower Danube in the XIIIth and XIVth centuries', *Journal of European Economic History* 5 (1976), pp. 587–600.

Gjuzelev, Vasil, 'Du commerce génois dans les terres bulgares durant le XIVe siècle', *BHR* 4 (1979), pp. 36–58.

Göckenjan, Hansgerd, 'Der Westfeldzug (1236–1242) aus mongolischer Sicht', in Schmilewski, *Wahlstatt 1241*, pp. 35–75.

Golden, P.B., 'Imperial ideology and the sources of political unity amongst the pre-Činggisid nomads of western Eurasia', *AEMA* 2 (1982), pp. 37–76, repr. in Golden, *Nomads and Their Neighbours*.

Golden, P.B., 'Religion among the Qıpčaqs of medieval Eurasia', *CAJ* 42 (1998), pp. 180–237; repr. in Golden, *Nomads and Their Neighbours*.

Golden, P.B., '"I will give the people unto thee": the Činggisid conquests and their aftermath in the Turkic world', *JRAS*, 3rd series, 10 (2000), pp. 21–41.

Golden, Peter B., *Nomads and Their Neighbours in the Russian Steppe. Turks, Khazars and Qipchaqs* (Aldershot, 2003).

Goodman, Jennifer R., *Chivalry and Exploration 1298–1600* (Woodbridge, 1998).

Guzman, Gregory G., 'European clerical envoys to the Mongols: reports of Western merchants in Eastern Europe and Central Asia, 1231–1255', *JMH* 22 (1996), pp. 53–67.

Haeusler, Martin, *Das Ende der Geschichte in der mittelalterlichen Weltchronistik* (Köln and Vienna, 1980).

Hage, Wolfgang, 'Christentum und Schamanismus: zur Krise des Nestorianertums in Zentralasien', in Bernd Jasper and Rudolf Mohr, eds, *Traditio-Krisis-Renovatio aus theologischer Sicht. Festschrift Winfried Zeller zum 65. Geburtstag* (Mainz, 1976), pp. 114-24.

Hage, Wolfgang, 'Religiöse Toleranz in der nestorianischen Asienmission', in Trutz Rendtorff, ed., *Glaube und Toleranz. Das theologische Erbe der Aufklärung* (Gütersloh, 1982), pp. 99-112.

Hamilton, Bernard, 'Continental drift: Prester John's progress through the Indies', in Beckingham and Hamilton, *Prester John*, pp. 237-69.

Hamilton, Bernard, 'Knowing the enemy: Western understanding of Islam at the time of the crusades', *JRAS*, 3rd series, 7 (1997), pp. 373-87.

Hay, Denys, *Europe: The Emergence of an Idea* (Edinburgh, 1957).

Heers, Jacques, 'De Marco Polo à Christophe Colomb: comment lire le *Devisement du monde?*', *JMH* 10 (1984), pp. 125-43.

Heimpel, Hermann, 'Zur Handelspolitik Kaiser Sigismunds', *VSWG* 23 (1930), pp. 145-56.

Heissig, Walther, *The Religions of Mongolia*, tr. Geoffrey Samuel (London, 1980).

Heyd, W., *Histoire du commerce du Levant au moyen-âge*, tr. Furcy Raynaud, 2 vols (Leipzig, 1885-6).

Hilpert, Hans-Eberhard, *Kaiser- und Papstbriefe in den Chronica Majora des Matthaeus Paris*, Veröffentlichungen des Deutschen Historischen Instituts London 9 (Stuttgart, 1981).

Housley, Norman, *The Avignon Papacy and the Crusades, 1305-1378* (Oxford, 1986).

Housley, Norman, *The Later Crusades, 1274-1580. From Lyons to Alcazar* (Oxford, 1992).

Huang, Shijian, 'The Persian language in China during the Yüan dynasty', *PFEH* 34 (Sept. 1986), pp. 83-95.

Humphreys, R. Stephen, *From Saladin to the Mongols: The Ayyubids of Damascus, 1193-1260* (Albany, NY, 1977).

Hunter, Erica C.D., 'The conversion of the Kerait to Christianity in A.D. 1007', *ZS* 22 (1989), pp. 142-63.

Hyde, J.K., 'Real and imaginary journeys in the later Middle Ages', *BJRL* 65 (1982-3), pp. 125-47.

Hyde, J.K., 'Ethnographers in search of an audience', in his *Literacy and Its Uses. Studies on Late Medieval Italy*, ed. Daniel Waley (Manchester, 1993), pp. 162-216.

Iklé, Frank W., 'The conversion of the Alani by the Franciscan missionaries in China in the fourteenth century', in James B. Parsons, ed., *Papers in Honor of Professor Woodbridge Bingham. A Festschrift for his Seventy-Fifth Birthday* (San Francisco, 1976), pp. 29-37.

Irwin, Robert, *The Middle East in the Middle Ages. The Early Mamluk Sultanate 1250-1382* (London, 1986).

Jackson, Peter, 'The dissolution of the Mongol empire', *CAJ* 22 (1978), pp. 186–244.

Jackson, Peter, 'The crisis in the Holy Land in 1260', *EHR* 95 (1980), pp. 481–513.

Jackson, Peter, 'The crusades of 1239–1241 and their aftermath', *BSOAS* 50 (1987), pp. 32–60.

Jackson, Peter, 'The crusade against the Mongols (1241)', *JEH* 42 (1991), pp. 1–18; Hungarian trans. as 'Keresztes hadjárat a Mongolok ellen (1241)', in Balázs Nagy, ed., *Tatárjárás* (Budapest, 2003), pp. 348–61.

Jackson, Peter, 'William of Rubruck in the Mongol empire: perception and prejudices', in Von Martels, *Travel Fact and Travel Fiction*, pp. 54–71.

Jackson, Peter, 'Marco Polo and his "Travels"', *BSOAS* 61 (1998), pp. 82–101.

Jackson, Peter, *The Delhi Sultanate: A Political and Military History* (Cambridge, 1999).

Jackson, Peter, 'The Mongols and Europe', in *NCMH*, V, pp. 703–19.

Jackson, Peter, 'From *ulus* to khanate: the making of the Mongol states, *c.*1220–*c.*1290', in Amitai-Preiss and Morgan, *Mongol Empire*, pp. 12–38.

Jackson, Peter, 'Medieval Christendom's encounter with the alien', *Historical Research* 74 (2001), pp. 347–69.

Jackson, Peter, 'The Mongols and the faith of the conquered', in Amitai and Biran, *Mongols, Turks and Others*, pp. 245–90.

Jacoby, David, 'Silk crosses the Mediterranean', in G. Airaldi, ed., *Le vie del Mediterraneo. Idee, uomini, oggetti (secoli XI–XVI), Genova, 19–20 aprile 1994* (Genova, 1997), pp. 55–79; repr. in Jacoby, *Byzantium, Latin Romania and the Mediterranean* (Aldershot, 2001).

Jagchid, Sechin, 'Why the Mongolian khans adopted Tibetan Buddhism as their faith', in *Proceedings of the 3rd East Asian Altaistic Conference* (Taipei, 1969), pp. 108–28; repr. in Jagchid, *Essays*, pp. 83–93.

Jagchid, Sechin, *Essays in Mongolian Studies* (Provo, UT, 1988).

Jagchid, Sechin, and Hyer, Paul, *Mongolia's Culture and Society* (Boulder, CO, 1979).

Karpov, S.P., 'The grain trade in the southern Black Sea region: the thirteenth to the fifteenth century', *MHR* 8 (1993), pp. 55–73.

Karpov, S.P., 'On the origin of medieval Tana', in Στεφανoς. *Studia byzantina ac slavica Vladimíro Vavřínek ad annum sexagesimum quintum dedicata* (Prague, 1995 = *Byzantinoslavica* 56), pp. 227–35.

Kedar, Benjamin Z., *Merchants in Crisis. Genoese and Venetian Men of Affairs and the Fourteenth-Century Depression* (New Haven, CN, and London, 1976).

Kedar, Benjamin Z., 'Chi era Andrea Franco?', *ASL*, n.s., 17 (1977), pp. 369–77.

Kedar, Benjamin Z., *Crusade and Mission. European Approaches Towards the Muslims* (Princeton, NJ, 1984).

Kedar, B.Z., and Udovich, A.L., eds, *The Medieval Levant. Studies in Memory of Eliyahu Ashtor (1914–1984)* (Haifa, 1988 = *AAS* 22).

Khazanov, Anatoly M., 'Muhammad and Jenghiz Khan compared: the religious factor in world empire building', *CSSH* 35 (1993), pp. 461–79.

Khazanov, A.M., *Nomads and the Outside World*, tr. Julia Crookenden, 2nd edn (Madison, WI, 1994).

Klopprogge, Axel, *Ursprung und Ausprägung des abendländischen Mongolenbildes im 13. Jahrhundert: ein Versuch zur Ideengeschichte des Mittelalters*, AF 122 (Wiesbaden, 1993).

Klopprogge, Axel, 'Das Mongolenbild im Abendland', in Stephan Conermann and Jan Kusber, eds, *Die Mongolen in Asien und Europa* (Frankfurt-am-Main, 1997), pp. 81–101.

Knobler, Adam, 'The rise of Tīmūr and Western diplomatic response, 1390–1405', *JRAS*, 3rd series, 5 (1995), pp. 341–9.

Knobler, Adam, 'Pseudo-conversions and patchwork pedigrees: the Christianization of Muslim princes and the diplomacy of Holy War', *JWH* 7:2 (1996), pp. 181–97.

Knoll, Paul W., *The Rise of the Polish Monarchy: Piast Poland in East Central Europe, 1320–1370* (Chicago, IL, 1972).

Kosztolnyik, Z.J., *Hungary in the Thirteenth Century* (New York, 1996).

Krawulsky, Dorothea, 'Die Dynastie der Ilkhâne: Eine Untersuchung zu Regierungsbeginn, Dynastie- und Reichsname', in her *Mongolen und Ilkhâne*, pp. 87–112.

Krawulsky, Dorothea, *Mongolen und Ilkhâne – Ideologie und Geschichte. 5 Studien* (Beirut, 1989).

Lach, Donald F., *Asia in the Making of Europe*, 3 vols in 9 (Chicago, IL, 1965–93).

Laiou, Angeliki E., and Mottahedeh, Roy Parviz, eds, *The Crusades from the Perspective of Byzantium and the Muslim World* (Washington, 2001).

Larner, John, *Marco Polo and the Discovery of the World* (Newhaven, CN, 1999).

Leopold, Antony, *How to Recover the Holy Land. The Crusade Proposals of the Late Thirteenth and Early Fourteenth Centuries* (Aldershot, 2000).

Lerner, Robert E., *The Powers of Prophecy: The Cedar of Lebanon Vision from the Mongol Onslaught to the Dawn of the Enlightenment* (Berkeley and Los Angeles, 1983).

Lloyd, Simon, *English Society and the Crusade 1216–1307* (Oxford, 1988).

Lockhart, L., 'The relations between Edward I and Edward II of England and the Mongol Īl-khāns of Persia', *Iran* 6 (1968), pp. 23–31.

Loenertz, R., O.P., 'Evêques dominicains des Deux Arménies', *AFP* 10 (1940), pp. 258–81.

Lopez, Robert Sabatino, 'European merchants in the medieval Indies: the evidence of commercial documents', *Journal of Economic History* 3 (1943), pp. 164–84.

Lopez, Robert Sabatino, *Su e giù per la storia di Genova* (Genova, 1975).

Lopez, Robert Sabatino, 'Nuove luci sugli Italiani in estremo oriente prima di Colombo', in Lopez, *Su e giù*, pp. 81–135.

Lopez, Robert S., 'Nouveaux documents sur les marchands italiens en Chine à l'époque mongole', *CRAIBL* (1977), pp. 445–57.

Lopez, Roberto S., 'Nelle terre dell'Orda d'oro: tre documenti genovesi inediti', in Michele Colucci, Giuseppe dell'Agata and Harvey Goldblatt, eds, *Studia Slavica medievalia et humanistica Riccardo Picchio dicata* (Rome, 1986), II, pp. 463–74.

Luttrell, Anthony, 'Timur's Dominican envoy', in Colin Heywood and Colin Imber, eds, *Studies in Ottoman History in Honour of Professor V.L. Ménage* (Istanbul, 1994), pp. 209–29.

Luttrell, Anthony, 'The crisis in the Bosphorus following the battle near Ankara in 1402', in Rosario Villari, ed., *Controllo degli stretti e insediamenti militari nel Mediterraneo* (Rome and Bari, 2002), pp. 155–66.

Maier, Christoph T., *Preaching the Crusades. Mendicant Friars and the Cross in the Thirteenth Century* (Cambridge, 1994).

Manz, Beatrice Forbes, 'Tamerlane and the symbolism of sovereignty', *Iranian Studies* 21:1–2 (1988), pp. 105–22.

Manz, Beatrice Forbes, *The Rise and Rule of Tamerlane* (Cambridge, 1989).

Menache, Sophia, 'Tartars, Jews, Saracens and the Jewish-Mongol "plot" of 1241', *History* 81 (1996), pp. 319–42.

Michieli, A.A., 'Il Milione di Marco Polo e un cronista del 1300', *La Geografia* 12 (1924), pp. 153–66.

Miquel, André, *La géographie humaine du monde musulman jusqu'au milieu du 11ᵉ siècle*, II. *Géographie arabe et représentation du monde: la terre et l'étranger*, Civilisations et Sociétés 37 (Paris, 1975).

Möhring, Hannes, *Der Weltkaiser der Endzeit. Entstehung, Wandel und Wirkung einer tausendjährigen Weissagung*, Mittelalter-Forschungen 3 (Stuttgart, 2000).

Mollat du Jourdain, M., ed., *Sociétés et compagnies de commerce en Orient et dans l'Océan Indien. Actes du VIIIe colloque international d'histoire maritime, Beyrouth 5–10 septembre 1966* (Paris, 1970).

Monti, G.M., 'I tre primi sovrani angioini e i Tartari', in his *Da Carlo I a Roberto di Angiò. Ricerche e documenti* (Trani, 1936), pp. 17–36.

Morgan, David O., 'The Mongols in Syria, 1260–1300', in Edbury, *Crusade and Settlement*, pp. 231–5.

Morgan, David, *The Mongols* (Oxford, 1986).

Morgan, David, 'Prester John and the Mongols', in Beckingham and Hamilton, *Prester John*, pp. 159–70.

Morgan, David, 'The empire of Tamerlane: an unsuccessful re-run of the Mongol state?', in J.R. Maddicott and D.M. Palliser, eds, *The Medieval State. Essays Presented to James Campbell* (London, 2000), pp. 233–41.

Morozzo della Rocca, Raimondo, 'Notizie da Caffa', in Barbieri, *Studi*, III, pp. 265–95.

Moses, Larry W., *The Political Role of Mongol Buddhism*, IUUAS 133 (Bloomington, IN, 1977).

Moule, A.C., 'A life of Odoric of Pordenone', *TP* 20 (1921), pp. 275–90.

Moule, A.C., *Christians in China Before the Year 1550* (Cambridge, 1930).

Muldoon, James, *Popes, Lawyers and Infidels. The Church and the Non-Christian World, 1250–1550* (Liverpool, 1979).

Müller, Regine, 'Jean de Montecorvino (1247–1328) – premier archevêque de Chine. Action et contexte missionnaires', *NZM* 44 (1988), pp. 81–109, 197–217, 263–84.

Murray, Alan V., ed., *Crusade and Conversion on the Baltic Frontier 1150–1500* (Aldershot, 2001).

Nagy, Balázs, and Sebők, Marcell, eds, . . . *The Man of Many Devices Who Wandered Full Many Ways . . . Festschrift in Honor of János M. Bak* (Budapest, 1999).

Nazarova, Evgeniya L., 'The crusades against Votians and Izhorians in the thirteenth century', in Murray, *Crusade and Conversion*, pp. 177–95.

Nel VII centenario della nascita di Marco Polo (Venezia, 1955).

Nicol, Donald M., *The Last Centuries of Byzantium, 1261–1453*, 2nd edn (Cambridge, 1993).

Nystazopoulou Pélékidis, Marie, 'Venise et la mer Noire du XIe au XVe siècle', in Agostino Pertusi, ed., *Venezia e il Levante fino al secolo XV* (Firenze, 1973–4), I:2, pp. 541–82.

Oberländer-Târnoveanu, Ernest, 'Numismatical contributions to the history of south-eastern Europe at the end of the 13th century', *RRH* 26 (1987), pp. 245–58.

Oberländer-Târnoveanu, Ernest, 'Byzantino-Tartarica – le monnayage dans la zone des bouches du Danube à la fin du XIIIe et au commencement du XIVe siècle', *MN* 2 (1995–6), pp. 191–214.

Oriente Poliano. Studi e conferenze tenute all'Is.M.E.O. in occasione del VII. centenario della nascità di Marco Polo (1254–1954) (Rome, 1957).

Ostrowski, Donald, 'Second-redaction additions in Carpini's *Ystoria Mongalorum*', in *Adelphotes: A Tribute to Omeljan Pritsak by His Students* (Cambridge, MA, 1990 = *HUS* 14:3–4), pp. 522–50.

Panaitescu, P.P., 'Mircea l'Ancien et les Tatares', *RHSEE* 19 (1942), pp. 438–48.

Papacostea, Şerban, 'De Vicina à Kilia. Byzantins et Génois aux bouches du Danube au XIVe siècle', *RESEE* 16 (1978), pp. 65–79.

Papacostea, Şerban, '«Quod non iretur ad Tanam.» Un aspect fondamental de la politique génoise dans la Mer Noire au XIVe siècle', *RESEE* 17 (1979), pp. 201–17.

Papacostea, Şerban, 'Gênes, Venise et la mer Noire à la fin du XIIIe siècle', *RRH* 29 (1990), pp. 211–36.

Pascu, Ştefan, ed., *Colloquio Romeno-Italiano. 'I Genovesi nel Mar Nero durante i secoli XIII e XIV'*, *Bucarest 27–28 marzo 1975* (Bucarest, 1977).

Pashuto, V.T., 'Mongol'skii pokhod v glub' Evropy', in Tikhvinskii, *Tataro-Mongoly*, pp. 210–27.

Paul, Jürgen, 'Scheiche und Herrscher im khanat Čaġatay', *Der Islam* 67 (1990), pp. 278–321.

Paul, Jürgen, 'L'invasion mongole comme "révélateur" de la société iranienne', in Aigle, *L'Iran*, pp. 37–53.

Pauler, Gyula, *A magyar nemzet története az Árpádházi királyok alatt*, 2 vols (Budapest, 1899).

Pelenski, Jaroslav, 'The contest between Lithuania-Rus' and the Golden Horde in the fourteenth century for supremacy over eastern Europe', *AEMA* 2 (1982), pp. 303–20; repr. in Pelenski, *The Contest for the Legacy of Kievan Rus'* (Boulder, CO, 1998), pp. 131–50.

Pelliot, Paul, 'Les Mongols et la papauté', *ROC* 23, 24, 28 (1922–3, 1924, 1931–2) [references are to the pagination of the separatum].

Pelliot, Paul, *Notes sur l'histoire de la Horde d'Or* (Paris, 1950).

Pelliot, Paul, *Notes on Marco Polo*, 3 vols with continuous pagination (Paris, 1959–73).

Pelliot, Paul, *Recherches sur les Chrétiens d'Asie centrale et d'Extrême-Orient*, ed. with additional notes by Jean Dauvillier (Paris, 1973).

Petech, Luciano, 'I francescani nell'Asia centrale e orientale nel XIII e XIV secolo', in *Espansione del francescanesimo*, pp. 213–40.

Petech, Luciano, 'Les marchands italiens dans l'empire mongol', in his *Selected Papers on Asian History*, Serie Orientale Roma 60 (Rome, 1988), pp. 161–86.

Petrushevsky, I.P., 'The socio-economic condition of Iran under the Īl-khāns', in *CHI*, V, pp. 483–537.

Phillips, J.R.S., *The Medieval Expansion of Europe*, 2nd edn (Oxford, 1998).

Pistarino, Geo, 'Da Genova alla Cina nel secolo XIV', in Francesco Guida and Luisa Valmarin, eds, *Studi Balcanici pubblicati in occasione del VI Congresso internazionale dell'Association Internationale d'Études Sud-Est Européennes (AIESEE), Sofia 30 Agosto–5 Settembre 1989* (Rome, 1989), pp. 33–44.

Postan, M.M., and Miller, Edward, eds, *The Cambridge Economic History of Europe*, II. *Trade and Industry in the Middle Ages*, 2nd edn (Cambridge, 1987).

Raby, Julian, and Fitzherbert, Teresa, eds, *The Court of the Il-khans 1290–1340*, Oxford Studies in Islamic Art 12 (Oxford, 1996).

Ratchnevsky, Paul, *Genghis Khan. His Life and Legacy*, tr. Thomas N. Haining (Oxford, 1991).

Reeves, Marjorie, *The Influence of Prophecy in the Later Middle Ages. A Study in Joachimism* (Oxford, 1969).

Reichert, Folker E., *Begegnungen mit China. Die Entdeckung Ostasiens im Mittelalter*, BGQM 15 (Sigmaringen, 1992).

Reichert, Folker, 'Geographie und Weltbild am Hofe Friedrichs II.', *DA* 51 (1995), pp. 433–91.

Rhode, Gotthold, *Die Ostgrenze Polens. Politische Entwicklung, kulturelle Bedeutung und geistige Auswirkung*, I. *Im Mittelalter bis zum Jahre 1401* (Köln and Graz, 1955).

Richard, Jean, 'An account of the battle of Hattin referring to the Frankish mercenaries in Oriental Moslem states', *Speculum* 27 (1952), pp. 168–77; repr. in Richard, *Orient et Occident*.

Richard, Jean, 'The Mongols and the Franks', *JAH* 3 (1969), pp. 45–57; repr. in Richard, *Orient et Occident*.

Richard, Jean, 'Les navigations des Occidentaux sur l'Océan Indien et la mer Caspienne (XIIᵉ–XVᵉ siècles)', in Mollat du Jourdain, *Sociétés et compagnies*, pp. 353–63; repr. in Richard, *Orient et Occident*.

Richard, Jean, 'Ultimatums mongols et lettres apocryphes: l'Occident et les motifs de guerre des Tartares', *CAJ* 17 (1973), pp. 212–22; repr. in Richard, *Orient et Occident*.

Richard, Jean, *Orient et Occident au moyen âge: contacts et relations (XIIe–XVe s.)* (London, 1976).

Richard, Jean, *La papauté et les missions d'Orient au moyen âge (XIIIᵉ–XVᵉ siècles)*, Collection de l'École Française de Rome 33 (Rome, 1977).

Richard, Jean, *Les relations entre l'Orient et l'Occident au Moyen Age. Études et documents* (London, 1977).

Richard, Jean, 'Sur les pas de Plancarpin et de Rubrouck: la lettre de saint Louis à Sartaq', *JS* (1977), pp. 49–61; repr. in Richard, *Croisés*.

Richard, Jean, 'Chrétiens et Mongols au Concile: la Papauté et les Mongols de Perse dans la seconde moitié du XIIIᵉ siècle', in *1274 année charnière*, pp. 31–44; repr. in Richard, *Croisés*.

Richard, Jean, 'Les causes des victoires mongoles d'après les historiens occidentaux du XIIIe siècle', *CAJ* 23 (1979), pp. 104–17; repr. in Richard, *Croisés*.

Richard, Jean, 'Une ambassade mongole à Paris en 1262', *JS* (1979), pp. 295–303; repr. in Richard, *Croisés*.

Richard, Jean, *Croisés, missionnaires et voyageurs. Les perspectives orientales du monde latin médiéval* (London, 1983).

Richard, Jean, 'La croisade de 1270, premier «passage général»?', *CRAIBL* (1989), pp. 510–23; repr. in Richard, *Croisades et états latins*.

Richard, Jean, *Croisades et états latins d'Orient* (Aldershot, 1992).

Richard, Jean, 'À propos de la mission de Baudouin de Hainaut: l'empire latin de Constantinople et les Mongols', *JS* (1992), pp. 115–21; repr. in Richard, *Francs et Orientaux*.

Richard, Jean, 'D'Älğigidäi à Ġazan: la continuité d'une politique franque chez les Mongols d'Iran', in Aigle, *L'Iran*, pp. 57–69; repr. in Richard, *Francs et Orientaux*.

Richard, Jean, *The Crusades c.1071–c.1291*, tr. Jean Birrell (Cambridge, 1999).

Richard, Jean, *Francs et Orientaux dans le monde des croisades* (Aldershot, 2003).

Roberg, Burkhard, 'Die Tartaren auf dem 2. Konzil von Lyon 1274', *Annuarium Historiae Conciliorum* 5 (1973), pp. 241–302.

Roemer, H.R., 'Tīmūr in Iran', in *CHI*, VI, pp. 42–97.

Rossabi, Morris, *Khubilai Khan. His Life and Times* (Berkeley and Los Angeles, 1988).

Roux, Jean-Paul, 'La tolérance religieuse dans les empires turco-mongols', *RHR* 203 (1986), pp. 131–68.

Rowell, S.C., *Lithuania Ascending: A Pagan Empire Within East-Central Europe, 1295–1345* (Cambridge, 1994).

Rubiés, Joan-Pau, *Travel and Ethnology in the Renaissance. South India through European Eyes, 1250–1625* (Cambridge, 2000).

Rudolf, Karl, 'Die Tartaren 1241/1242. Nachrichten und Wiedergabe: Korrespondenz und Historiographie', *Römische Historische Mitteilungen* 19 (1977), pp. 79–107.

Ruotsala, Antti, *Europeans and Mongols in the Middle of the Thirteenth Century: Encountering the Other* (Helsinki, 2001).

Rutkowska-Plachcinska, Anna, 'L'image du danger tatar dans les sources polonaises', in *Histoire et société. Mélanges offerts à Georges Duby*, Textes réunis par les médiévistes de l'Université de Provence 4 (Aix-en-Provence, 1992), pp. 87–95.

Ryan, James D., 'Conversion vs. baptism? European missionaries in Asia in the thirteenth and fourteenth centuries', in James Muldoon, ed., *Varieties of Religious Conversion in the Middle Ages* (Gainesville, FL, 1997), pp. 146–67.

Ryan, James D., 'To baptize khans or to convert peoples? Missionary aims in Central Asia in the fourteenth century', in Armstrong and Wood, *Christianizing Peoples*, pp. 247–57.

Ryan, James D., 'Conversion or the Crown of martyrdom: conflicting goals for fourteenth-century missionaries in Central Asia?', in Richard F. Gyug, ed., *Medieval Cultures in Contact* (Fordham, NY, 2003), pp. 19–38.

Sarnowsky, Jürgen, 'Die Johanniter und Smyrna 1344–1402 (Teil 1)', *Römische Quartalschrift* 86 (1991), pp. 215–51.

Sarnowsky, Jürgen, 'The Teutonic Order confronts Mongols and Turks', in Malcolm Barber, ed., *The Military Orders. Fighting for the Faith and Caring for the Sick* (Aldershot, 1994), pp. 253–62.

Schaller, Hans Martin, *Stauferzeit. Ausgewählte Aufsätze* (Hannover, 1993).

Schein, Sylvia, '*Gesta Dei per Mongolos* 1300: the genesis of a non-event', *EHR* 94 (1979), pp. 805–19.

Schmieder, Felicitas, *Europa und die Fremden. Die Mongolen im Urteil des Abendlandes vom 13. bis in das 15. Jahrhundert*, BGQM 16 (Sigmaringen, 1994).

Schmilewski, Ulrich, ed., *Wahlstatt 1241: Beiträge zur Mongolenschlacht bei Liegnitz und zu ihre Nachwirkungen* (Würzburg, 1991).

Seaman, Gary, and Marks, Daniel, eds, *Rulers from the Steppe. State Formation on the Eurasian Periphery* (Los Angeles, 1991).

Senga, Toru, 'IV Béla külpolitikája és IV Ince pápához intézett "tátár" levele', *Századok* 121 (1987), pp. 583–612.

Senga, Toru, 'Ungarisch-bulgarische Beziehungen nach dem Mongolensturm', *Slavica* 24 (1990), pp. 77–90.

Simonut, Noè, *Il metodo d'evangelizzazione dei Francescani tra Musulmani e Mongoli nei secoli XIII–XIV* (Milan, 1947).

Sinor, Denis, 'Un voyageur du treizième siècle: le Dominicain Julien de Hongrie', *BSOAS* 14 (1952), pp. 589–602; repr. in Sinor, *Inner Asia*.

Sinor, Denis, 'Les relations entre les Mongols et l'Europe jusqu'à la mort d'Arghoun et de Béla IV', *Journal of World History* 3:1 (Neuchâtel, 1956), pp. 39–62; repr. in Sinor, *Inner Asia*.

Sinor, Denis, 'John of Plano Carpini's return from the Mongols: new light from a Luxemburg manuscript', *JRAS* (1957), pp. 193–206; repr. in Sinor, *Inner Asia*.

Sinor, Denis, 'Horse and pasture in Inner Asian history', *OE* 19 (1972), pp. 171–84; repr. in Sinor, *Inner Asia*.

Sinor, Denis, *Inner Asia and its Contacts with Medieval Europe* (London, 1977).

Sinor, Denis, 'Le Mongol vu par l'Occident', in *1274 année charnière*, pp. 55–72; repr. in Sinor, *Studies*.

Sinor, Denis, *Studies in Medieval Inner Asia* (Aldershot, 1997).

Smith, John Masson, Jr, "Ayn Jālūt: Mamlūk success or Mongol failure?', *HJAS* 44 (1984), pp. 307–45.

Soranzo, Giovanni, *Il papato, l'Europa cristiana e i Tartari. Un secolo di penetrazione occidentale in Asia* (Milan, 1930).

Sourdel, Dominique, 'Bohémond et les chrétiens à Damas sous l'occupation mongole', in Balard *et al.*, *Dei gesta*, pp. 295–9.

Southern, R.W., *Western Views of Islam in the Middle Ages* (Cambridge, MA, 1962).

Spinei, Victor, *Moldavia in the 11th–14th Centuries*, tr. Liliana Teodoreanu and Ioana Sturza ([Bucarest], 1986).

Spinei, Victor, 'La génèse des villes du sud-est de la Moldavie et les rapports commerciaux des XIIIe–XIVe siècles', *Balkan Studies* 35 (1994), pp. 197–269.

Spuler, Bertold, *Die Goldene Horde: die Mongolen in Rußland 1223–1502*, 2nd edn (Wiesbaden, 1965).

Spuler, Bertold, *Die Mongolen in Iran. Politik, Verwaltung und Kultur der Ilchanzeit 1220–1350*, 4th edn (Leiden, 1985).

Strakosch-Grassmann, Gustav, *Der Einfall der Mongolen in Mitteleuropa in den Jahren 1241 und 1242* (Innsbruck, 1893).

Świętosławski, Witold, *Arms and Armour of the Nomads of the Great Steppe in the Times of the Mongol Expansion (12th–14th Centuries)* (Łódź, 1999).

Thiel, Joseph, S.V.D., 'Der Streit der Buddhisten und Taoisten zur Mongolenzeit', *Monumenta Serica* 20 (1961), pp. 1–81.

Tikhvinskii, S.L., ed., *Tataro-Mongoly v Azii i Evrope. Sbornik statei*, 2nd edn (Moscow, 1977).

Togan, İsenbike, *Flexibility and Limitation in Steppe Formations. The Kereit Khanate and Chinggis Khan* (Leiden, 1998).

Togan, Zeki Velidi, 'Timur's Osteuropapolitik', *ZDMG* 108 = n.F., 33 (1958), pp. 279–98.

Troll, Christian W., S.J., 'Die Chinamission im Mittelalter', *Franziskanische Studien* 48 (1966), pp. 109–50; 49 (1967), pp. 22–79.

Tucci, Ugo, 'Mercanti veneziani in Asia lungo l'itinerario poliano', in Lionello Lanciotti, ed., *Venezia e l'oriente* (Firenze, 1987), pp. 307–21.

Vasiliev, Alexander A., *The Goths in the Crimea* (Cambridge, MA, 1936).

Voiret, Jean-Pierre, 'China, "objektiv" gesehen: Marco Polo als Berichterstatter', *AS* 51 (1997), pp. 805–21.

Von den Brincken, Anna-Dorothee, 'Eine christliche Weltchronik von Qara Qorum: Wilhelm von Rubruck OFM und der Nestorianismus', *AK* 53 (1971), pp. 1–19.

Von den Brincken, Anna-Dorothee, *Die „Nationes Christianorum Orientalium" im Verständnis der lateinischen Historiographie von der Mitte des 12. bis in die zweite Hälfte des 14. Jahrhunderts*, Kölner Historische Abhandlungen 22 (Köln, 1973).

Von den Brincken, Anna-Dorothee, 'Die Mongolen im Weltbild der Lateiner um die Mitte des 13. Jahrhunderts unter besonderer Berücksichtigung des „Speculum Historiale" des Vincenz von Beauvais OP', *AK* 57 (1975), pp. 117–40.

Von Martels, Zweder, ed., *Travel Fact and Travel Fiction. Studies on Fiction, Literary Tradition, Scholarly Discovery and Observation in Travel Writing* (Leiden, 1994).

Wehr, Barbara, 'À propos de la génèse du «Devisement dou Monde» de Marco Polo', in Maria Selig, Barbara Frank and Jörg Hartmann, eds, *Le passage à l'écrit des langues romanes* (Tübingen, 1993), pp. 299–326.

Weiers, Michael, ed., *Die Mongolen. Beiträge zu ihrer Geschichte und Kultur* (Darmstadt, 1986).

Weiers, Michael, 'Von Ögödei bis Möngke – Das mongolische Großreich', in Weiers, *Die Mongolen*, pp. 192–216.

Weiler, Björn, 'The *Negotium Terrae Sanctae* in the political discourse of Latin Christendom, 1215–1311', *International History Review* 25 (2003), pp. 1–36.

Wittkower, Rudolf, *Allegory and the Migration of Symbols* (London, 1977).

Yao, Tao-chung, 'Ch'iu Ch'u-chi and Chinggis Khan', *HJAS* 46 (1986), pp. 201–19.

Young, Richard Fox, '*Deus unus* or *Dei plures sunt*? The function of inclusivism in the Buddhist defense of Mongol folk religion against William of Rubruck (1254)', in *Universality and Uniqueness in the Context of Religious Pluralism* (Philadelphia, 1989 = *Journal of Ecumenical Studies* 26:1), pp. 100–37.

Zarncke, Friedrich, 'Zur Sage vom Priester Johannes', *NA* 2 (1877), pp. 611–15.

Zarncke, Friedrich, 'Der Priester Johannes' [part 1], *Abhandlungen der phil.-hist. Klasse der königlich sächsischen Gesellschaft der Wissenschaften* 7 (1879), pp. 827–1030; [part 2] 8 (1883), pp. 1–186.

Zatko, James J., 'The Union of Suzdal, 1222–1252', *JEH* 8 (1957), pp. 33–52.

Zdan, Michael B., 'The dependence of Halych-Volyn' Rus' on the Golden Horde', *SEER* 35 (1956–7), pp. 505–22.

1274 année charnière: mutations et continuités (Lyon–Paris 1974), Colloques internationaux du C.N.R.S. 558 (Paris, 1977).

INDEX

INDEX

Khanbaligh (Chung-tu, Ta-tu), 127, 258–60, 263,
265, 297, 300, 314, 331, 336, 361
archdiocese of, 258–60
see also Charles of France, Guillaume du Pré,
Montecorvino
'Khazaria'/'Gazaria' *see* Crimea
Khazars, 33, 268
Khitan, tribe, 12, 33–4, 38, 42–4, 46, 149,
331
see also Qara-Khitan
Khurāsān, 41, 125, 162n, 248, 297
Khwāja 'Alī, 245
Khwārazm, 11, 114, 177, 216
Khwarazmians, 39, 74–5, 92–3, 139, 148
Khwārazmshāhs, 11, 46, 48, 162n, 178, 245
Jalāl al-Dīn, 39, 149
Muḥammad ibn Tekish, 'Alā' al-Dīn, 11, 38–9,
43, 148
Tekish, 148
Kiestutis, Lithuanian prince, 217–18
Kiev, 40, 96, 107n, 202, 219, 232n, 294
Kilia, 293, 322n
Kirakos Ganjakec'i, 49, 100, 176
Kitbuqa, Mongol general, 116–20, 122, 124, 166,
174
Knut, Norwegian duke, 104
Kököchü *see* Teb-Tenggeri
Kölgen, Mongol prince, 85n
Korea, Koreans, 91, 164n, 330
Körgüz ('George'), prince of the Önggüd, 258,
263, 265, 272
Koriatas, Lithuanian prince, 217
Korneuburg, 63
Kösedagh, battle of, 74
Köten, Cuman khan, 61–3, 69
Kozel'sk, 43
Küchlüg, Naiman prince and Gür-khan of the
Qara-Khitan, 37–8, 43, 46, 48, 120
Kujavia, 196
Kulikovo Pole, battle of, 216, 315
Kynga (Kunigunde), St, 205

La Forbie (al-Ḥarbiyya), battle of, 75, 121
Lāhijān, 298
Lahore, 290
Laias, 296–7, 299, 302
Laodicea, 122
'Last Things', 13, 19, 147–8
László IV ('the Cuman'), king of Hungary, 197,
201, 203–5, 208–9, 213
László, Franciscan, 257
Laurence, Franciscan, 88
Lausitz, 63
Leszek the Black, duke of Cracow and Sandomir,
202, 205, 209
levirate, 273
Li Tsè-min, 330
Liao dynasty *see* Khitan
Libellus de notitia orbis, 243, 247
see also John, archbishop of Sulṭāniyya

Libro del conosçimiento de todos los reynos y tierras,
333, 340, 343, 345
Licostomo, 305, 309, 322n
Liegnitz (Wahlstatt), battle of, 63, 73
Lithuania, Lithuanians, 96, 123, 196, 200–2, 207,
209–12, 214, 216–20, 246, 359
Algirdas, grand duke of, 210, 217–18
Gediminas, grand duke of, 202, 217
Mindaugas, king of, 96
Vytautas (Witołd), grand duke of, 217–19
see also Władysław II (Jogailo)
Liu Ping-chung, 277
Liubartis, Lithuanian prince, 210–11
Livonia, Livonians, 10, 61, 91, 95, 104, 153n, 215
Lombardy, 143, 258, 295
Lop, 297, 331
Loredano, Giovanni, 301, 311
Louis IV, Emperor, 209, 215
Louis IX (St Louis), king of France, 16, 24, 98,
101–4, 108n, 116–17, 119–20, 126, 135,
138, 143, 167, 173–4, 178, 180, 185,
200, 267–8, 334
and the Mongols, 98–100, 123, 166–7, 181
Louis (Lájos) I, king of Hungary and Poland, 207,
209–15, 217–18, 309
Lublin, 202, 210
Lucalongo, Pietro da, 258, 294
Lwów, 210, 212, 309
Lyons, 87, 97, 137
First Council of (1245), 23, 87, 104, 140, 142,
147
Second Council of (1274), 138, 166–8, 172–3,
175, 180, 186, 196

Ma'bar (Coromandel coast), 258, 320n, 331, 335,
337–8
Mačva, 206
Maeotis, marshes of (the Sea of Azov), 18
Magi *see* Three Kings
Majapahit, 337
Mākū, 247
Malabar, 298, 331, 335, 337, 342
Mamai, Mongol amir, 216, 306, 312, 315
mamlūks, 24, 74–5, 124, 126, 165, 308
Mamlūk Sultans, Sultanate, 3, 24, 116, 118–19,
121, 123–4, 126, 165–75, 177–8, 180,
185, 198, 220, 236, 238, 240, 245, 248,
256, 296, 301–2, 311, 315, 359–60
see also Baybars, al-Nāṣir Muḥammad, Qalāwūn,
Quṭuz
Mandeville, Sir John, 333, 335, 341, 345,
349–50, 362
Manichaeans, Manichaeism, 45, 257, 268
Manzi (southern China), 331, 336–7, 341
Maraclea, 171
Marāgha, 125, 259
Margaret, St, Hungarian princess, 207
Margat (Marqab), 168
Marignolli, John of, 259, 261, 263, 300, 310,
329, 331, 334, 341–2, 344

INDEX

Podolia, 217, 232n
Poland, Poles, 10, 40, 49, 58, 63, 66, 72–3, 75,
  91, 94, 104–5, 123, 126, 128, 138, 142,
  183, 196, 199–202, 204, 207, 209–11,
  213–20, 246, 309, 330, 359
  Mongol invasions of: (1241), 1, 63–4, 68;
  (1259), 96, 123, 358; (later), 205–6, 210
Polo, Marco, 2, 127, 137, 184, 257, 272–3, 275,
  277–8, 292, 294, 297–8, 300, 307,
  310–13, 315, 329–32, 334, 336–8,
  341–3, 346–50, 362–5
  his book (Le divisament dou monde), 313,
  332–6, 339–41, 345, 348–50, 364–5
  his father and uncle, 257, 278, 292, 294, 297,
  300, 310–11, 313, 330, 332, 334, 363–4
Polotsk, 202
Pomerania, 104
Premonstratensians, 9, 329
Prester John, 20–1, 48, 60, 97–9, 101, 138, 172,
  175, 278, 336, 342, 347
  'Letter' of, 21, 59, 333
printing, 315
Provato, 306
Prussia, Prussians, 10, 78n, 91, 95–6, 104, 123,
  153n, 199, 201, 206, 212, 215, 243, 329
Przemysław II, duke of Great Poland, 196–7
Pseudo-Methodius, 21–2, 144–8, 150–2, 164n,
  360
Pskov, 95
Ptolemy, 19, 344
pygmies, 342

Qadan, Mongol prince, 40, 63–5, 69, 72
Qadaq, Mongol minister, 100
Qaghans (Great Khans, in China and Mongolia),
  126, 257, 260, 262–3, 294, 304, 313,
  321n, 330, 335–7, 342, 345–6, 367
  see also Yüan dynasty, Buyantu, Güyüg, Möngke,
  Ögödei, Qubilai, Temür Öljeitü, Toghan
  Temür
Qaidu, Mongol khan, 127, 179, 198–9, 291, 308,
  310
Qal'at al-Rūm, 172
Qalāwūn, Mamlūk Sultan, 165, 168–70
Qangli, Turkish people, 39–40
Qāqūn (Caco), 167
Qara Qoyunlu, 243, 248
Qara-Khitan (Western Liao), 12, 20–1, 33, 36,
  38, 44–5, 47–8, 120, 148–9
  see also, Gür-khan
Qaraqocho, 296
Qaraqorum, 37, 124, 126–7, 139
Qayaligh, 114
Qazaghan, Mongol amir, 236
al-Qazwīnī, Zakariyā', 330
Qinnasrīn, 170
Qipchāq, 17, 40, 124, 126, 165, 178
  see also Cumans
Qirghiz, 33
Qirim (Krim), 216

Qirq-yer, 257
Qubilai, Mongol qaghan, 34–5, 38, 115, 124,
  126–7, 169, 175, 188n, 198, 257–8,
  272–3, 276–8, 291, 294, 308, 310, 313,
  331, 335, 338, 363–5
Quilichinus of Spoleto, 59
Quinsai (Hang-chou), 296–8, 317n, 331, 335–7
qumis, 31, 41, 140, 269–70, 367
Qur'ān, 19, 277
Qutlugh Shāh, Mongol general, 170–1, 185
Qutuz, Sayf al-Dīn, Mamlūk Sultan, 117–18,
  121–2
*Quyaq ('Coiac'), Mongol official, 100

Raab (Győr), 64
Rabban Ṣawma, 169, 173, 175, 179, 258, 329
al-Raḥba, 172
Rákos, 64
Ramón Lull, 176, 262, 264, 346
Ramusio, Gian Battista, 332, 364
Rashīd al-Dīn Faḍl-Allāh al-Hamadānī, 34–5, 42,
  58, 65, 72, 102, 115, 118, 125, 135, 149,
  176, 180–1, 204, 290, 294, 329, 363
  his history of the Franks, 135, 180, 329–30
  letters of, 193–4n
Red Sea, 169, 294–6
Relatio de Davide rege, 48, 143–4
Revelations, see Pseudo-Methodius
Rhodes, 237, 241, 340
Riazan', 40
Richard, earl of Cornwall, 24, 198
Richard of San Germano, 137
Richardus, Dominican, 137
Richardus, Latin secretary to the Ilkhan, 168,
  173
Ricoldo of Montecroce, 176, 184, 257, 261,
  263–4, 266, 268, 277
  his Libellus ad nationes orientales, 261
'Riphaean mountains', 18
Riurikid dynasty, 43, 209
Rodana (Ó-Radna), 69
Roger of Várad, 58, 62, 64, 69–70, 87, 136, 142
'Romania' (Latin Greece), 14, 104, 239, 292–3,
  309
  see also Constantinople, Latin Empire of
Rome, 9, 13, 21, 23, 66, 87, 95, 172, 197, 201,
  260, 358
  as the Mongols' objective, 73, 144
Rosetta, 171
Rostov, 307
Ruad, 171, 185
Rubruck, William of, 2, 35, 37, 41, 45, 70, 73,
  90, 92, 101, 103, 105, 115, 117, 135,
  138–41, 148, 150–2, 247, 261–2, 264,
  266–8, 270–1, 273–8, 294, 307–8, 314,
  329–30, 339, 343–4, 346–8
  his mission to the Mongols, 99–100, 136,
  256–7
  his report (Itinerarium), 138, 334
rukh ('ruc'), 339, 341

INDEX

Strabo, 344
Straits, 238–9, 241, 308
  War of the, 302, 305
Stuhlweissenburg (Alba Regia), 64, 69
Styria, 213
Su-chou, 331
al-Ṣubayba, 116
Sübe'etei, Mongol general, 39–40, 47, 49, 58, 63, 73, 125
Sübe'etei, Mongol prince, 112n
Süleymān Çelebī, Ottoman prince, 241, 245
Sulṭāniyya, 242, 259
  archbishops of see John, John of Cori
Sumatra, 311, 336–9, 348
Sung dynasty, 33, 36–8, 40, 47, 115, 124, 127, 331
Suzdal', 60
Svać (Suagium), 65
Sweden, Swedes, 15, 24, 96
Syria, 9, 12, 20, 22, 24, 74–5, 88, 92, 94, 103–4, 116, 118, 121–2, 126, 136, 139, 142, 149, 165, 168, 170–1, 178–9, 184–5, 236, 238, 240, 291, 295–6, 311, 314, 346, 358–60
  unsuitability for nomadic cavalry, 74, 178
  see also Franks
Szatmár (Satu Mare), 207
Székely, 205, 213
Szepes (Zips), 205, 225n

Tabrīz, 88, 125, 244, 257–9, 294–5, 297–301, 305, 311, 361
Tālish, 298
tama (or tamma) system, 113
Tana, 240, 247, 259, 296, 298, 300–2, 304–10, 312, 361
Tanggud (Hsi-Hsia), 37–9, 42
Tannenberg, battle of, 3, 219, 359
Taoism, Taoists, 45, 257, 265, 271–2, 275, 277, 336
  see also Cheng-i, Ch'üan-chen
Tarachonta, 139
Ta'rīkh-i Jahān-gushā, see Juwaynī
'Tarse', 138, 145
'Tartar Relation', 58, 71, 73, 88, 114, 135, 145, 151
'Tartars', as a term for the Mongols, 59
  etymologies of, 139
Tartarus, 59
Tatars, tribe, 36–7, 41–2, 45
  as a general designation, 36, 41
Ta-tu, 127
  see also Khanbaligh
Tayichi'ud, Mongol clan, 37
Teb-Tenggeri (Kököchü), shaman, 46, 101–2, 182
Templar, Knights, 9, 63, 105, 122, 171, 317n
  Bérard, Thomas, Master of, 121
  Molay, Jacques de, Master of, 171, 185
'Templar of Tyre', 178

Temüjin see Chinggis Khan
Temür (Tamerlane), 3, 126, 216–19, 233n, 235–48, 260, 300, 302, 306–7, 345, 359–60
  his name, 249n
  his sobriquet, 236
  and Christians/Christianity, 239–47
  and Islam/Muslims, 237, 241, 243, 245–7
  and the Latin West, 239–48
Temür Öljeitü, Mongol qaghan, 127, 171, 181, 258, 265
Temür Qutlugh, khan of the Golden Horde, 217–19
Temürid dynasty, 248
  see also Mīrān Shāh
Ten Lost Tribes see Israel
'Tenduc' (T'ien-te), 258, 336
Tenggeri (Heaven), 32, 44–5, 273
terraticum, 304
Teutonic Knights, 10, 17, 24, 78n, 95–6, 123, 196–7, 201, 206, 209–11, 215, 219–20, 243, 329
  Anno von Sangerhausen, Master of, 118
  Poppo of Osternau, Master of, 78n
Theodolus, 314
Thomas of Cantimpré, 101
Thomas of Spalato, 58–9, 62, 65, 68–9, 71–2, 136, 139–40, 143, 145–6
Thomas Agni di Lentino, 117, 122, 167
Thrace, 202–3, 325n
Three Kings (Magi), 18, 98, 138, 343
Thuringia, 68
Tibet, Tibetans, 152, 257, 277, 336, 339, 365
Töde Möngke, khan of the Golden Horde, 198
Toghan Temür, Mongol qaghan, 259, 271, 295, 300, 314
Toghril (Ong Khan), khan of the Kereyid, 37, 45, 356n
Töle Buqa, khan of the Golden Horde, 199, 205, 207
Tolui, Mongol prince, 39, 40, 114
Toluids, 114, 127–8, 237
  see also Ilkhans, Qaghans
Tommaso de' Anfossi, 173
Tommaso Ugi, 173, 178
Toqa Temür, Mongol prince, 216–17
Toqtamish, khan of the Golden Horde, 216–19, 236, 238, 246, 248, 306, 359
Toqto'a, khan of the Golden Horde, 171, 199, 203–5, 272–3, 305
Töregene, Mongol regent, 95
Tortosa, 171, 185
toyins (Buddhist priests), 176, 367
trade, 290–304, 307–13
  trans-Asiatic, 296–304, 307, 309–13, 361
  see also cloth, furs, grain trade, silk, slave trade, spices
  commercial manuals, 293, 313
  routes, 295–7, 309
  see also silk routes

· 413 ·